T0189964

Lecture Notes in Computer Science   12067

More information about this series at http://www.springer.com/series/7409

Marié Hattingh · Machdel Matthee ·
Hanlie Smuts · Ilias Pappas ·
Yogesh K. Dwivedi · Matti Mäntymäki (Eds.)

Responsible Design, Implementation and Use of Information and Communication Technology

19th IFIP WG 6.11 Conference on
e-Business, e-Services, and e-Society, I3E 2020
Skukuza, South Africa, April 6–8, 2020
Proceedings, Part II

 Springer

Editors
Marié Hattingh (ID)
University of Pretoria
Pretoria, South Africa

Machdel Matthee (ID)
University of Pretoria
Pretoria, South Africa

Hanlie Smuts (ID)
University of Pretoria
Pretoria, South Africa

Ilias Pappas (ID)
University of Agder
Kristiansand, Norway

Yogesh K. Dwivedi (ID)
Swansea University
Swansea, UK

Matti Mäntymäki (ID)
University of Turku
Turku, Finland

ISSN 0302-9743 ISSN 1611-3349 (electronic)
Lecture Notes in Computer Science
ISBN 978-3-030-45001-4 ISBN 978-3-030-45002-1 (eBook)
https://doi.org/10.1007/978-3-030-45002-1

LNCS Sublibrary: SL3 – Information Systems and Applications, incl. Internet/Web, and HCI

This Springer imprint is published by the registered company Springer Nature Switzerland AG
The registered company address is: Gewerbestrasse 11, 6330 Cham, Switzerland

Preface

This book presents the proceedings of the 19th International Federation of Information Processing (IFIP) Conference on e-Business, e-Services, and e-Society (I3E 2020), which was held in Skukuza, Kruger National Park, South Africa, during April 6–8, 2020. The annual I3E conference is a core part of Working Group 6.11, which aims to organize and promote the exchange of information and co-operation related to all aspects of e-Business, e-Services, and e-Society (the three Es). The I3E conference series is truly interdisciplinary and welcomed contributions from both academics and practitioners alike.

The main theme of the 2020 conference was "Responsible design, implementation and use of information and communication technology." In line with the inclusive nature of the I3E series, all papers related to e-Business, e-Services, and e-Society were welcomed.

The age of digital transformation opens up exciting new avenues for design and application of ICTs. Yet, with the ubiquitous connectedness of a digitally transformed world, come unintended, unpredictable, and often adverse consequences for individuals, societies, and organizations – in developed and developing contexts. Security, privacy, trustworthiness, exploitation, and well-being are some of the pressing concerns resulting from new digital realities.

There is need for responsible design, implementation, and use of information systems (IS) based on critical awareness and ethical practices. As rightly put by Schultze (2017:65): "As IS researchers we need to examine our own practices – including the questions we ask, the methods we deploy and theories we adopt – to understand and critically review our world-making."

The IFIP I3E 2020 was held during April 6–8, 2020, and brought together contributions from a variety of perspectives, disciplines, and communities for the advancement of knowledge regarding responsible design, implementation, and use of information and communications technology. This was evident by our variety of keynote speakers and topics for the panel discussions. We were delighted to welcome three distinguished keynote speakers:

– Mr. James van der Westhuizen who is the founder and managing partner of KnowHouse, founded 20 years ago out of a passion to work differently with the challenge of learning and change in organizations. He is a global consultant and facilitator working across the African continent, the Middle East, Europe, and Asia.
– Prof. Irwin Brown is a full Professor and Head of the Department of Information Systems (IS) at the University of Cape Town. His research interests relate to theorizing about IS phenomena in developing countries.
– Prof. Dr. Shirish C. Srivastava is a tenured full Professor and holds the GS1 Chair on 'Digital Content for Omni Channel' at HEC Paris. His rich experience includes coaching senior executives on issues related to managing technology emerging technologies (such as big data, blockchains, and artificial intelligence), technology

enabled innovation, entrepreneurship, and managing cross-border business relationships.

The conference held two panels to facilitate discussions on important topics. The first panel on "Blockchain – hope or hype? Blockchain as a disruptive force" was chaired by Dr. Matti Mäntymäki. Blockchain is surrounded by considerable optimism and enthusiasm among businesses and academia. This enthusiasm is evidenced by the numerous calls for papers in journals and dedicated blockchain tracks in conferences. The purpose of the panel was to make sense of the actual significance of the blockchain phenomenon and provoke discussion and exchange of ideas among the I3E community. To this end, the panel paid homage to the heterogenous nature of the I3E community and invited a diverse of group of expert panellists to share their distinctive perspectives on blockchain.

The second panel, made up of a panel of editors, was chaired by Dr. Shirish C. Srivastava. The panel consisted of six journal editors from international and local (South African) publications. Each editor gave an explanation on the requirements for authors when submitting to their journal.

The Call for Papers solicited submissions in two main categories: full research papers and short research-in-progress papers. Each submission was reviewed by at least two knowledgeable academics in the field, in a double-blind process. The 2020 conference received 191 submissions. Out of the 191 papers, 91 papers were selected to be presented at the conference. Four of the accepted papers were not included in the final proceedings because the authors decided to withdraw it. Thus, the acceptance rate was 45.5%.

Following the conference, two special issues were organized for selected best papers of the I3E 2020. The two special issues are in the *International Journal of Information Management* (IJIM) and the *International Journal of Electronic Government Research* (IJEGR).

The final set of 87 full and short papers submitted to I3E 2020 that appear in these proceedings were clustered into 14 groups, each of which are outlined below.

Part I: addressing the area of Blockchain. Three papers were grouped under this theme. One of the papers proposed a framework for the adoption of blockchain whilst another reported on the application of blockchain technology in Healthcare. The third paper examined the potential disruptive impact of cryptocurrencies.

Part II of the book addressed papers on the Fourth Industrial Revolution. Nine papers were grouped under this theme. Paper details range from a systematic literature review on the incompatibility of Smart manufacturing for SMMEs to the development of models and frameworks through the application of Smart technologies. One paper included a bibliographic coupling and co-occurrence on the topic of Smart City and Economy, whilst another reported on robotic automation and the consequences for knowledge workers. The final paper reported on the co-creation for digitalization in Norwegian business clusters.

Part III of the book addressed e-Business. 12 papers were grouped under this theme. The papers presented works on online banking quality, a conceptual framework for digital entrepreneurship, mobile applications, online switching behavior, and how games are used in business. Three papers reported on systematic review of literature on eWOM, mobile shopping acceptance predictors and social commerce adoption predictors. The final paper presented a review of papers published from 2001 to 2019 by I3E.

Part IV of the book addressed Business Processes. 10 papers were grouped under this theme. The papers presented works on governance achieved through business process management, how IT is being used in Fintech Innovation, a meta model for maturity models, and a strategic model for the safeguarding the preservation of business value. In addition to these themes, papers were presented on using the story-card method for business process re-engineering, using Zachman's framework as an IS theory and a review of the Task-Technology Fit Theory.

Part V of the book addressed Big Data and Machine Learning. Seven papers were grouped under this theme. The papers presented work on using machine learning in the field of healthcare, data governance, using a deep learning neural network model to predict information diffusion on Twitter, and big data visualization tools.

Part VI of the book addresses ICT and Education. Seven papers were grouped under this theme. The papers presented work on mobile learning, new considerations for flipped classroom approach, and eModeration system considerations.

Part VII of the book addressed eGovernment. Six papers were grouped under this theme. The papers presented work on the use of social media in eParticipation, enterprise architectures in eGovernments, and eGovernment implementation framework. Other themes included were digital innovation in public organizations, implementation challenges in eProcurement, and a case from Ghana on the effects on National Health Insurance digital platform development and use.

Part VIII of the book addressed eHealth. Six papers were grouped under this theme. Papers presented work on the use of technology for diabetic patients, factors influencing community health workers, wearable devices, and a Twitter social network analysis of the South African Health Insurance Bill.

Part IX of the book addressed Security. Four papers were grouped under this theme. Papers presented work on cyber-harassment among LGBTQIA+ youth, online identity theft, cybersecurity readiness of e-tail organizations, and the ethics of using publicly available data.

Part X of the book addressed Social Media. Six papers were grouped under this theme. Papers presented works on a conceptual framework for media use behavior, metaphors of social media, credibility of online information (fake news), and problematic media and technology use.

Part XI of the book addressed Knowledge and Knowledge Management. Three papers were grouped under this theme. Papers presented work on knowledge transfer science education, a knowledge asset management implementation framework, and a conceptual knowledge visualization framework for knowledge transfer.

Part XII of the book addressed ICT for Gender Equality and Development. Nine papers were grouped under this theme. Papers presented work on the rural vs urban digital divide, socio-economic factors in Internet usage in Nigeria, and enablers and barriers of mobile commerce and banking services among elderly individuals. A methodology for addressing the second-level digital divide, gender equality in the ICT context, digital competence requirements, and the influence of culture on women's IT career choices were also presented.

Part XIII of the book addressed Information Systems for Governance. Four papers were grouped under this theme. Papers presented work on the use of machine learning on financial inclusion data for governance in Eswatini, ordinance-tweet mining to disseminate urban policy knowledge for smart governance, open technology innovation in healthcare services, and multi-stakeholder-centric data analytics governance framework.

Part XIV of the book addressed User Experience and Usability. Three papers were grouped under this theme. Papers presented work on the use of machine learning and eye tracking to predict users' ratings on the aesthetics of websites, a systematic review on designing for positive emotional responses in users of interactive digital technologies, and a methodology to compare the usability of information systems.

The success of the 19th IFIP I3E Conference (I3E 2020) was a result of the enormous efforts of numerous people and organizations. Firstly, this conference was only made possible by the continued support of WG 6.11 for this conference series and for selecting South Africa to host it in 2020, for which we are extremely grateful. We received many good-quality submissions from authors across the globe and we would like to thank them for choosing I3E 2020 as the outlet to present and publish their current research. We are indebted to the Program Committee, who generously gave up their time to provide constructive reviews and facilitate the improvement of the submitted manuscripts. We would like to thank the Department of Informatics of the University of Pretoria for their support in enabling us to host this conference. Thank you to AfricaMassive that assisted us with all the logistical arrangements with hosting the conference in Skukuza located in the Kruger National Park. Finally, we extend our sincere gratitude to everyone involved in organizing the conference, to our esteemed keynote speakers, and to Springer LNCS as the publisher of these proceedings, which we hope will be of use for the continued development of research related to the three Es[1].

February 2020

Marié Hattingh
Machdel Matthee
Hanlie Smuts
Ilias Pappas
Yogesh K. Dwivedi
Matti Mäntymäki

---

[1] Due to the global COVID-19 pandemic and the consequential worldwide imposed travel restrictions and lock down, the I3E 2020 conference event scheduled to take place in Skukuza, South Africa, was unfortunately cancelled.

Organization

Conference Chairs

Marié (M. J.) Hattingh	University of Pretoria, South Africa
Machdel Matthee	University of Pretoria, South Africa
Hanlie Smuts	University of Pretoria, South Africa
Ilias Pappas	University of Adger and Norwegian University of Science and Technology (NTNU), Norway
Yogesh K. Dwivedi	Swansea University, UK
Matti Mäntymäki	University of Turku, Finland

Program Committee Chairs

Marié (M. J.) Hattingh	University of Pretoria, South Africa
Machdel Matthee	University of Pretoria, South Africa
Hanlie Smuts	University of Pretoria, South Africa
Ilias Pappas	University of Adger and Norwegian University of Science and Technology, Norway
Yogesh K. Dwivedi	Swansea University, UK
Matti Mäntymäki	University of Turku, Finland

Keynote Speakers

Irwin Brown	University of Cape Town, South Africa
James van der Westhuizen	KnowHouse, South Africa
Shirish C. Srivastava	HEC Paris, France

Program Committee

Rami Abu Wadi	Ahlia University, Bahrain
Funmi Adebesin	University of Pretoria, South Africa
Kayode Ibrahim Adenuga	Universiti Tecknologi, Malaysia
Michael Adu Kwarteng	Tomas Bata University, Czech Republic
Augustus Barnnet Anderson	University of Ghana, Ghana
Bokolo Anthony Jnr.	Norwegian University of Science and Technology, Norway
Oluwasefunmi Arogundade	Chinese Academy of Science, China
Lynette Barnard	Nelson Mandela University, South Africa
Clara Benac Earle	Polytechnic University of Madrid, Spain
Khalid Benali	University of Lorraine, France
Djamal Benslimane	Claude Bernard University Lyon 1, France
Edward Bernroider	Vienna University of Economic and Business, Austria

Elmi Bester	UNISA, South Africa
Dzifa Bibi	University of Ghana, Ghana
Katja Bley	Dresden University of Technology, Germany
Deonie Botha	Deloitte, South Africa
Jacques Brosens	University of Pretoria, South Africa
Paul Brous	Delft University of Technology, The Netherlands
Peter André Busch	University of Agder, Norway
Andre Calitz	Nelson Mandela University, South Africa
Sunil Choenni	Research and Documentation Centre (WODC), Ministry of Justice, The Netherlands
Mahdieh Darvish	ESCP Business School, Germany
Dinara Davlembayeva	Newcastle University, UK
Carina De Villiers	University of Pretoria, South Africa
Marne de Vries	University of Pretoria, South Africa
Jules Degila	Institute of Mathematics and Physics, Benin
Denis Dennehy	National University of Ireland, Ireland
Vipin Deval	Tallinn University of Technology, Estonia
Christos Douligeris	University of Piraeus, Greece
Dirk Draheim	Software Competence Center Hagenberg, Austria
Alena Droit	Osnabrueck University, Germany
Jacobus Du Preez	University of Pretoria, South Africa
Edward Entee	University of Ghana, Ghana
Sunet Eybers	University of Pretoria, South Africa
Olakumbi Fadiran	UNISA, South Africa
Sam February	Accenture, South Africa
Jennifer Ferreira	Victoria University of Wellington, New Zealand
Blanka Frydrychova Klimova	University of Hradec Kralove, Czech Republic
Shang Gao	Örebro University, Sweden
Ping Gao	The University of Manchester, UK
Aurona Gerber	University of Pretoria, South Africa
Claude Godart	University of Lorraine, France
Javier Gomez	Autonomous University of Madrid, Spain
Anastasia Griva	Athens University of Economics and Business, Greece
Sara Grobbelaar	Stellenbosch University, South Africa
Lucas Gumbi	UNISA, South Africa
Hong Guo	Anhui University, China
Remko Helms	The Open University, The Netherlands
Raoul Hentschel	Dresden University of Technology, Germany
Grant Royd Howard	UNISA, South Africa
Vigneswara Ilavarasan	Indian Institute of Technology, India
Marijn Janssen	Delft University of Technology, The Netherlands
Debora Jeske	University College Cork, Ireland
Arpan Kar	Indian Institute of Technology, India
Caroline Khene	Rhodes University, South Africa
Eija Koskivaara	University of Turku, Finland

Paula Kotzé	University of Pretoria, South Africa
Jan H. Kroeze	UNISA, South Africa
Rendani Kruger	University of Pretoria, South Africa
Abhinav Kumar	The National Institute of Technology Patna, India
Amit Kumar	Kushwaha GAP, India
Andreas D. Landmark	SINTEF, Norway
Sven Laumer	Friedrich-Alexander-Universität Erlangen-Nürnberg, Germany
Daniel Le Roux	Stellenbosch University, South Africa
Hongxiu Li	Turku School of Economics, Finland
Lieb Liebenberg	University of Pretoria, South Africa
Marianne Loock	UNISA, South Africa
Hugo Lotriet	UNISA, South Africa
Mario Marais	CSIR Meraka Institute, South Africa
Emanuele Gabriel Margherita	Tuscia University, Italy
Davit Marikyan	Newcastle University, UK
Linda Marshall	University of Pretoria, South Africa
Tendani Mawela	University of Pretoria, South Africa
Nita Mennega	University of Pretoria, South Africa
Jan Mentz	UNISA, South Africa
Patrick Mikalef	Norwegian University of Science and Technology, Norway
Tshepiso Mokoena	CSIR, South Africa
Mathias Mujinga	UNISA, South Africa
Matthias Murawski	ESCP Europe Business School, Germany
Mohammed Khaled Mustafa	Bangladesh University of Professionals, Bangladesh
Mpho Mzingelwa	University of KwaZulu Natal, South Africa
Rennie Naidoo	University of Pretoria, South Africa
Alex Norta	Tallinn University of Technology, Estonia
Kayode Odusanya	Loughborough University, UK
Kwame Simpe Ofori	University of Electronic Science and Technology of China, China
Kingsley Ofosu-Ampong	University of Ghana, Ghana
Olabode Ogunbodede	Newcastle University, UK
Leif Erik Opland	Norwegian University of Science and Technology, Norway
Makoto Oya	Computer Institute of Japan, Japan
Niki Panteli	Royal Holloway University of London, UK
Savvas Papagiannidis	Newcastle University, UK
Zacharoula Papamitsiou	Norwegian University of Science and Technology, Norway
Sofia Papavlasopoulou	Norwegian University of Science and Technology, Norway

Elena Parmiggiani	Norwegian University of Science and Technology, Norway
Douglas Parry	Stellenbosch University, South Africa
Marcel Pikhart	University of Hradec Kralove, Czech Republic
Colin Pilkington	UNISA, South Africa
Komla Pillay	University of Pretoria, South Africa
Henk Pretorius	University of Pretoria, South Africa
Tania Prinsloo	University of Pretoria, South Africa
Maciel Queiroz	Paulista University, Brazil
Van Raj	UNISA, South Africa
Nripendra Rana	Swansea University, UK
Anthony Renner-Micah	University of Ghana, Ghana
Suzanne Sackstein	WITS University, South Africa
Brenda Scholtz	Nelson Mandela University, South Africa
Lisa Seymour	University of Cape Town, South Africa
Anuragini Shirish	University of Paris-Saclay, France
Djofack Sidonie	University of Yaounde II, Cameroon
Ivana Simonova	University of Jan Evangelista Purkyne, Czech Republic
Konstantina Spanaki	Loughborough University, UK
Ruan Spies	Stellenbosch University, South Africa
Riana Steyn	University of Pretoria, South Africa
Ilse Struweg	University of Johannesburg, South Africa
Zhaohao Sun	Federation University Australia, Australia
Reima Vesa Suomi	University of Turku, Finland
Libuse Svobodova	University of Hradec Kralove, Czechia
Kuttimani Tamilmani	Swansea University, UK
Maureen Tanner	University of Cape Town, South Africa
Ali Tarhini	Sultan Qaboos University, Oman
Temitope Oluwaseyi Tokosi	Nelson Mandela University, South Africa
Cathrine Tømte	University of Adger, Noway
Juan Carlos Torrado Vidal	Autonomous University of Madrid, Spain
Pieter Toussaint	Norwegian University of Science and Technology, Norway
Rakhi Tripathi	FORE School of Management, India
Valentyna Tsap	Tallinn University of Technology, Estonia
Pitso Tsibolane	Stellenbosch University, South Africa
Marita Turpin	University of Pretoria, South Africa
Parijat Upadhyay	IMT Nagpur, India
Jean-Paul Van Belle	University of Cape Town, South Africa
Judy van Biljon	UNISA, South Africa
Rogier Van de Wetering	Open University, The Netherlands
Thomas van der Merwe	UNISA, South Africa
Alta Van der Merwe	University of Pretoria, South Africa
J. P. van Deventer	University of Pretoria, South Africa

Corné Van Staden   UNISA, South Africa
Izak Van Zyl   Cape Peninsula University of Technology,
                          South Africa
Polyxeni Vassilakopoulou University of Agder, Norway
Jari Veijalainen   University of Jyvaskyla, Finland
Hans Weigand   Tilburg University, The Netherlands
Lizette Weilbach   University of Pretoria, South Africa
Ted White   UNISA, South Africa
Michael Williams   Swansea University, UK
Milla Wiren   University of Turku, Finland
Khulekani Yakobi   Nelson Mandela University, South Africa
Hiroshi Yoshiura   The University of Electro-Communications, Japan
Hans-Dieter Zimmermann   FHS St. Gallen University of Applied Sciences,
                          Switzerland

Contents – Part II

Knowledge and Knowledge Management

ICT and Gender Equality and Development

Information Systems for Governance

User Experience and Usability

Contents – Part I

eBusiness

Business Processes

Big Data and Machine Learning

ICT and Education

eGovernment

Enterprise Architectures in E-Governments Studies: Why, What and How?

Hong Guo[1,2(✉)] ⑩ and Shang Gao[3] ⑩

[1] Anhui University, No. 111 Jiulong Road, Hefei, People's Republic of China
`homekuo@gmail.com`
[2] Norwegian University of Science and Technology, Sem Saelands vei 7-9, Trondheim, Norway
[3] Örebro University, Fakultetsgatan 1, Örebro, Sweden
`shang.gao@oru.se`

Abstract. Enterprise Architecture (EA) is an important tool when developing e-governments and smart cities as it can help improve the alignment between business goals and Information and Communication Technologies (ICT) implementations. Although some studies have been performed to study the applications of EA in public sectors, governments, and cities, most of such studies are scattered and there is no strong research stream. As a result, it is difficult to effectively accumulate relevant knowledge and experiences. In this research, we attempt to explore research streams and trends by analyzing why existing studies were conducted, what outcomes were produced, and what methods were used in these studies. Starting from these three questions, a thematic framework was developed, and a literature synthesis was presented. The result shows the complexity of this area, the importance of balancing technical factors and non-technical factors, the challenges brought by non-functional requirements. Despite the importance of EA frameworks, few studies have been found in which government or city relevant requirements were addressed in a general way. Such findings are expected to provide useful insights for possible future research in this area.

Keywords: Enterprise architecture · E-government · Public sector · Smart cities

1 Introduction

More than half of the world's population lives in cities [1]. And it was predicted that by 2050, the world population will reach nearly 10 billion [2]. By leveraging the power of Information and Communication Technologies (ICT) in public sectors or governments and making a city "smart", e-governments and smart cities are emerging as a strategy to mitigate problems generated by the urban population growth and rapid urbanization, improve the efficiency of urban management and bring better life to residents. However, as a giant system which involves various kinds of stakeholders, new technologies and complicated ICT subsystems, challenges such as complexity, interoperability and alignment between business goals and ICT implementations have been met [3, 4].

© IFIP International Federation for Information Processing 2020
Published by Springer Nature Switzerland AG 2020
M. Hattingh et al. (Eds.): I3E 2020, LNCS 12067, pp. 3–14, 2020.
https://doi.org/10.1007/978-3-030-45002-1_1

Especially, with the ever-expanding scale of cities, the continuous updating of ICT, and the higher expectations of people for a better life, how to make the advantages of ICT more effective and efficient becomes a problem. Enterprise Architecture (EA) has been adopted as an important tool to tackle such challenges [5] as they can help integrate ICT to achieve urban management, business operations and personal life goals.

Although some earlier studies on applying EA in public sectors, e-governments and smart cities have been performed, existing studies in this area are scattered and no strong research stream has been formulated [6]. As a result, general knowledge regarding EA in e-governments is difficult to be accumulated and be reused elsewhere. And in return, practices cannot be improved efficiently accordingly. To address this problem, we propose to characterize existing studies in this field by answering three important questions: why one research on applying EA in e-government or smart cities was required (motivation), what kind of outcome was contributed (contribution), and how the research was performed (method). These three questions have been thought fundamental and used widely to get an overview of studies in specific fields [7–9]. Starting on this characterization theme, we developed a framework and performed initial explorations by analyzing and grouping a set of studies in this area based on the framework. The result was presented as a literature synthesis. Findings from this synthesis are expected to bring some insights for possible future research directions.

The rest of this article is organized as below. In Sect. 2, we introduce how we developed the thematic framework and selected scientific articles to perform the literature synthesis. In Sect. 3, we present the literature synthesis. We then discuss the synthesis result and present some findings accordingly in Sect. 4. Later, Sect. 5 introduces some related works. Lastly in Sect. 6, we talk about limitations of this study, point out some possible future research directions, and conclude this paper.

2 Methods

We aim to disclose fundamental knowledge about main research streams, critical issues, and possible future trends in the area of applying EA when developing ICT systems for public sectors, governments, and cities. To address this, widely used three questions, namely Why, What, and How were employed in this study. These three questions have been used in various domains such as [8, 10, 11] to help organize and analyze existing studies. Starting from them, we extracted four or five answers to each question through a simplified research synthesis [12] based on a sample of ten highly relevant studies. Because we have read these papers previously, we are familiar with the depth and breadth of the evidences in these studies. Further, with the three questions as the structure, we then identify specific segments of text for each question, label, reduce overlap, and translate them into enumerated answers. The three questions together with the enumerated answers constitute a framework for further literature synthesis.

Later, we applied this framework to a larger set of studies and performed grouping and analysis. We searched keywords in titles of scientific articles to find relevant studies in Google Scholar. The keywords include combination of "Enterprise Architecture" and "cities", "government", or "public sector". Although our original interest domain is smart city, papers regarding applying EA in smart cities are rare. We expand the domains to e-government and public sectors as they are highly relevant, and the concepts started to be used interchangeably during recent years [13]. Due to time and resources constraints, we put our focus on more recently published and highly qualified papers by restricting publication years and checking the relevance with this study. We searched papers that have been published between 2009 to 2019. After excluding duplicated papers and papers that were not written in English or full texts are not available, we collected 35 scientific papers. The overview of the synthesis framework is presented in Table 1. And the detailed meaning for each category (answer) in the framework will be introduced together with the literature synthesis in Sect. 3.

Table 1. A framework for a literature synthesis

Why (Motivation)	What (Contribution)	How (How)
• Gaining general knowledge	• Perspectives	• Literature analysis
• Technical motivation	• Review	• Case studies
• Non-technical motivation	• Design artifacts	• Survey & interview
• Improving performance	• Frameworks	• Others
• Studies analysis		

3 Literature Synthesis

The studies on the application of EA in public sectors, e-governments, and smart cities were examined based the following themes: RQ1: *Why* a study was performed (motivation); RQ2: *What* was produced from the study (contribution); and RQ3: *How* the study was conducted (methods) (see Table 1). The following subsections provide an overview of each theme.

3.1 Why (Motivations)

Research motivation describes why a study has been initiated. In addition, it provides information regarding which problems were expected to be solved by conducting the research. Five types of motivations were identified as summarized in Table 2.

- Gaining general knowledge: This is to gain some general knowledge (definition, scope, challenges, and etc.) in the area;
- Technical motivation: This is to solve some technical problems;
- Non-technical motivation: The research was performed to solve some non-technical (managerial, social, or economic, and etc.) problems;
- Improving performance: The motivation was to improve some aspects (e.g., interoperability) of the performance;
- Gaining insights to studies: This is to analyze studies in the area (e.g., by performing a literature review).

Gaining General Knowledge

Some studies were performed to obtain general knowledge of applying EA in governments. Such knowledge includes what has driven the adoption and use of EA in the Danish government [14], how EA was understood by public sector organizations in Finland [15], prominent reasons for investment failure in Nigerian government [16], challenges faced by the Malaysian public sector agencies [17], root causes of challenges faced by the organizations and important requirements for smart cities [18, 19], and if EA was useful as a reference for smart city development [20].

Table 2. Motivation of the researches

	General knowledge	Technical	Non-technical	Improving performance	Gaining insights to studies
Literature	[14, 15, 16, 19, 17, 18, 20]	[21, 22, 23, 24, 25, 26]	[27, 28, 29, 30, 31, 32]	[33, 34, 35, 36, 37, 38, 39, 40, 41, 42, 43]	[44, 45, 46, 47, 6]

Technical Motivation

Some studies have been motivated to satisfy technical requirements. Such efforts are like an agile EA framework proposed to support government transformation with cloud technology enabled [21], an EA based approach to manage state-level data in real time in the Indian public sector of healthcare [22], a method to find patterns for enterprise information architecture in governments [23], a proposal for a framework for ICT governance [25], and a government EA framework to support big and open linked data and cloud computing [24, 26].

Non-technical Motivation

On the other side, some studies emphasized the importance of non-technical aspects when applying EA in governments. It was underscored that simply taking an IT perspective is a serious mistake [27], EAs were primarily product oriented while sociopolitical aspects were often neglected [29]. Non-technical factors were ignored or considered less significant than technical ones [30]. To address such non-technical issues, institutional aspects of applying EA in governments were investigated [28, 31, 32]. EA did not create administrative or political transformation by itself. Instead, fundamental transformation can only be achieved when the institutional force at the micro and macro level promotes transformation [28]. How institutional change helped practitioners legitimize EA practices [32] and how EA programs have been institutionalized in Vietnam [31] were investigated. Inductive communication and the deployment of experts to local contexts could be introduced to overcome struggles when applying EA to US governments.

Improving Performance

More studies looked at both technical aspects and non-technical aspects and focused on how to improve the overall performance. Ways of improving e-government performance in developing countries [39], lessons learned from the case of Finnish and Colombia government EA [37, 38] were investigated. Further, key factors for raising the maturity of government EA practices, such as management commitment and participation of business units, which were influenced by the perceived usefulness of the government EA efforts [35] were explored.

In particular, some studies focused on improving the interoperability. This could be achieved by means of a procedure to provide guidance on how to rationally specify scope dimensions for a complex enterprise such as a government [42] and a meta-model approach to design government EA database and communication with agencies [36]. EA was also introduced as an information systems architecture approach to solve interoperability challenges at different levels of government [33].

In addition to interoperability, architectural design principles to better support the decentralization/centralization relationships among central and local governments in the Netherlands (1980s–2004) [34], nation-wide strategy and holistic guiding plans to better support broad government integration and alignment between business processes and IT implementations [43], an EA framework to better align IT needs and organization business [40] and to enhance the support of transparency of processes, information and applications in public organizations were investigated [41].

Gaining Insights to Studies
Several articles were motivated to gain insights of existing studies themselves. Thus efforts have been done to review government EA papers published in China [44] and 71 articles about applying EA in public sectors published during the past 15 years [6]. More specifically, smart city frameworks were reviewed [46, 47] from an EA perspective or based on EA requirements, several EA frameworks were compared and mapped to provide guidance on how to choose EA frameworks [45].

3.2   What (Contributions)

In the information system field, there are primarily two main research genres, namely behavior science and design science [48]. For behavior science, people are trying to better understand the world and usually contribute with some perspectives. For design science, people usually construct complicated artifacts such as a model, a method or an application to extend the ability to manage the world. Specifically, the literature review can be thought as one specific way to understand the world. And EA frameworks can be thought as specific artifacts. More information is presented in Table 3.

- Perspectives: The research was performed by providing some perspectives to understand the world;
- Review: Some literature analyses was provided;
- Design artifacts: Artifacts were proposed to extend the ability to manage the world;
- Frameworks: Some EA frameworks used in governments were proposed.

Table 3. Contribution of the studies

	Perspectives	Review	Artifacts	EA frameworks
Literature	[33, 27, 28, 14, 29, 35, 15, 16, 19, 30, 17, 18, 32]	[45, 44, 46, 6, 47]	[34, 36, 39, 23, 31, 43, 42]	[38, 37, 21, 22, 41, 40, 24, 25, 20, 26]

Perspectives

Some studies contributed by presenting understandings on the problem of interests, such as the role of EA in aligning business and IT in Nigerian government [16] or the statement that EA in government was to a large extend driven by fashion while compliance and imitation primarily drove the EA adoption [14, 28]. Therefore, fundamental transformation to organizational tasks can only be achieved when transformation is promoted by institutional forces. Similarly, it was reported that current EAs were primarily product oriented, with their sociopolitical aspects neglected often [29], and simply taking an IT perspective on EA as a prerequisite to e-government implementation was a serious mistake [27]. Both technical and nontechnical factors should be considered [30], and two key institutionalization techniques, inductive communication and deployment of experts to local contexts, might help overcome the struggles of translating new practices [32].

More concrete contributions were produced in some studies such as how EA was understood by public sector authorities [15], twenty challenges faced by the public sector agencies [17], sixteen problems and eight root causes in the context of public sectors [18] when developing and implementing EA. Such contributions also include important quality and functional requirements and a conceptual architecture framework to address requirements [19], key factors for raising the maturity of the government EA practice [35] and a conceptual framework addressing different interoperability types in institutional level, sector level, and national level [33].

Review

Some studies review scientific articles on the area of applying EA in governments or public sectors [6, 44], published in China in particular [44]. Some studies classified or compared artifacts such as four EA frameworks [45] and smart city frameworks [46, 47].

Design Artifacts

For design science studies, principles, guidelines, models or methods have usually been produced as the contributions. For instance, architectural design *principles* were identified [34], m*eta-models* to design government EA database were presented [36]. Further, an EA development life cycle [43], a *procedure* to specify critical aspects in scoping government EA efforts [42], and a *method* to find enterprise information architecture patterns [23] were introduced. More such artifacts include a benefit model to measure government performance [39] and how rules, norms, and values influenced EA programs in different phases institutionally [31].

EA Frameworks

In several papers, government EA frameworks have been presented as the main contribution of the studies. For instance, government EA frameworks that have been used in Colombia [38], Finland [37], Indonesia [20], Brazil [41] were presented. More specifically, the EA framework including the architecture and methodology to support using big data and cloud computing was described [24, 26]. Similarly, the use of an agile EA framework to develop and implement the cloud-enabled government was proposed [21]. An government EA framework developed based on TOGAF and SONA that have been used in Indonesia was presented [40]. The modified EA of the health management information system at India was studied [22]. What is more, an ICT governance framework [25] and a theoretical framework to manage information systems at different levels in government were introduced.

3.3 How (Methods)

Methods to perform a research or evaluate contributions were identified in Table 4.

- Literature analysis: The research was performed by comparatively in-depth literature analysis (classification, comparison etc.) and usually resulted in a table for better visualization;
- Case study: Case studies were performed, or examples were provided, usually in labs, and in a qualitative way;
- Survey and interview: Surveys, questionnaires, interviews, focus group, and etc. were utilized, usually outside labs, and in a quantitative way;
- Others: Research methods other than above were used.

Table 4. Methods of the studies

	Literature analysis	Case study	Survey & Interview	Others
Literature	[44, 45, 46, 6, 47]	[15, 16, 36, 21, 38, 37, 30, 41, 23, 40, 24, 20, 43, 26]	[34, 28, 14, 35, 29, 19, 22, 39, 18, 31, 17, 32, 25, 42]	[27, 33]

Literature Analysis
In addition to typical literature review studies [6, 44], some other studies performed comparatively in-depth literature analysis for smart cities frameworks [46, 47] and EA frameworks [45]. For some studies such as [32], although literature analysis was also performed, we do not include it in this group as its primary method was interview.

Case Studies
Performing case studies is a frequently used method in this area. Examples, demos or case have been presented regarding the practices of applying EA in governments of different countries such as Indonesia [20, 43], Korea [36], Australia [21], Colombia [38], Finland [37], Brazil [41], and Portugal [23].

Some studies employed theories to improve the rigorous of research methods. For instance, activity theory was used to help revealing the importance of non-technical factors in the deployment of EA [30]. Action design was used when performing the longitudinal case study of government EA adoption in Finnish public sector [24]. TOGAF and SONA were used to develop EAs in the case of the volcanoes monitoring system [40] and EA score card was used for validation and assessment. In some studies, Design Science Research (DSR) approach was adopted as the overall method while validation and verification of the proposed framework was performed with more specific methods [26].

Most studies in this group have been performed in a qualitative way except for [16] and [15]. In [16], IT investments by Nigerian government was studied and according to the quantitative result, the reasons of investment failure were identified. While in [15], a content analysis was conducted (both qualitatively and quantitatively) on the statements of public sector organizations about the proposed EA in Finland.

Survey & Interview

A survey or a questionnaire is widely used to quickly and efficiently gather as well as analyze data from a population. More quantitative studies were performed in this group than in the Case Studies group. In these studies, a survey to identify smart city important requirements [19], a questionnaire to identify the maturity level in city councils for visualizing the governance maturity model [25], a survey to disclose the fact that current EAs were primarily product oriented [29] and a survey involving 33 agencies to figure out maturity factors of the government EA practice were conducted.

Interviews were also employed to obtain open and unstructured opinions from a population [18, 22, 28, 31, 32]. In some studies, interviews were utilized in addition to case studies. In [17], a multiple case study was utilized in addition to data collected through interviews. One instance is the comparative case studies together with semi-structured interviews used to gather data [34]. In addition, interviews have been used together with other methods such as surveys [39] and focus groups [14]. A field demo was another way to help gather on-spot data [42].

Others

In some studies, no specific research method has been explicitly specified such as [27, 33]. In the studies, some discussion and arguments were presented.

4   Discussion

By identifying and grouping motivations, contributions, and methods of existing studies, some research streams and trends can be found below.

Basing on the synthesis of motivations of existing studies, we found that, despite of the fact that applying EA in e-governments is not a new tradition, there have been continuously studies aiming to achieve *understandings about some general knowledge*, such as challenges, problems, and root causes. This might indicate the potential complexity of EA and EA application. As a result, more studies have been done in a quantitative way in order to gain more objective, generic, and precise insights. In addition to *technical factors*, *non-technical factors* also play important roles when applying EA in e-government development. However, along with the development of new technologies such as big data and cloud computing during recent years, how to apply them in this area has also become a rising hot spot. Another stream of research is about achieving non-functional requirements. Around one third of selected studies have described their efforts to improve specific aspect of the overall *performance* of e-governments, which involves both technical factors and/ or non-technical factors generally.

Concerning research contributions, we found many studies were performed and some *perspectives* were produced as the results. This was partly caused by the motivation of gaining general knowledge of such studies. On the other hand, compared to proposing general design artifacts, proposing *EA Frameworks* has been a continuous research stream for the past five years. For this part, most studies focused on how to improve the practice of using EA, while few studies addressed how to improve EA according to the practices.

Further, the synthesis on research methods disclosed that, *case studies, surveys& interviews* have been the dominant methods that have been adopted. This might be due to the fact that non-functional factors, including human factors, play important roles in this area. Due to limited and unmatured benchmark and evaluation methods that are available, achieving satisfaction of stakeholders are important. Particularly, we found that in many studies, EA frameworks were proposed in local contexts. However, it was not intensively clarified that what unique characteristics such a framework had compared with other widely used ones, and what was the use of such a framework in a general scenario. Despite that new requirements of e-government development have arises when cities are expected to be smarter and more sustainable, few studies were found which addressed such government or city specific requirements.

5 Related Work

There are some related works. For example, [44] reviewed literature that have been published in Chinese journals about EA in government departments during past six years until 2013. In [16], the authors focused on investments of information technologies. And in [6], the authors collected and analyzed articles regarding applying EA in public sectors that have been published until 2017. Compared with them, present research collected more recently published articles. In [6], it was mentioned that studies in the area of interests have been quite scattered and there was no main stream of research. As a result, knowledge and experiences cannot be accumulated in an efficient way. In present research, we selected articles and analyzed motivations, contributions and methods, and provided insights on the streams and trends based on the review results.

6 Conclusions

In this article, we propose to answer three fundamental questions (why, what, and how) on studies regarding applying EA in public sectors, e-governments and smart cities to gain fundamental knowledge for future research. By analyzing and grouping motivations, contributions, and methods of researches presented in 35 selected articles, some findings are disclosed based on a literature synthesis. The result shows the complexity of this area, the importance of balancing technical & non-technical factors, the importance and challenges brought by non-functional requirements. Despite the importance of EA framework, few studies have been found in which government or city specific requirements have be addressed in a general way. Such findings are expected to provide useful insights for future possible research in this area.

There are limitations for present research. We provided a literature analysis and synthesis on 35 articles that were selected from a literature search. It is possible that some research streams and trends could not be disclosed due to the restricted scope. Therefore, we plan to expand the scope and validate our results by performing a systematic review. In addition, based on the results of this article, we have scoped and defined several more specific and concrete research projects in this area.

Acknowledgement. This research is financially supported by The European Research Consortium for Informatics and Mathematics (ERCIM).

References

1. UN: World Urbanization Prospects 2018 (2018)
2. UN: World population projected to reach 9.8 billion in 2050, and 11.2 billion in 2100 – says UN (2019)
3. Höjer, M., Wangel, J.: Smart sustainable cities: definition and challenges. In: Hilty, L.M., Aebischer, B. (eds.) ICT Innovations for Sustainability. AISC, vol. 310, pp. 333–349. Springer, Cham (2015). https://doi.org/10.1007/978-3-319-09228-7_20
4. Santana, E.F.Z., Chaves, A.P., Gerosa, M.A., et al.: Software platforms for smart cities: concepts, requirements, challenges, and a unified reference architecture. ACM Comput. Surv. (CSUR) **50**(6), 78 (2018)
5. Saha, P.: Advances in Government Enterprise Architecture. IGI Global, Pennsylvania (2008)
6. Dang, D.D., Pekkola, S.: Systematic literature review on enterprise architecture in the public sector. Electron. J. E-Govern. **15**(2), 57–154 (2017)
7. Kellner, M.I., Madachy, R.J., Raffo, D.M.: Software process simulation modeling: why? what? how? J. Syst. Softw. **46**(2–3), 91–105 (1999)
8. Pauwels, K., Ambler, T., Clark, B.H., et al.: Dashboards as a service: why, what, how, and what research is needed? J. Serv. Res. **12**(2), 175–189 (2009)
9. Van't Wout, J., Waage, M., Hartman, H., et al.: The Integrated Architecture Framework Explained: Why What How. Springer, Heidelberg (2010). https://doi.org/10.1007/978-3-642-11518-9
10. Hamel, G.: The why, what, and how of management innovation. Harvard Bus. Rev. **84**(2), 72 (2006)
11. Kiesler, S., Kraut, R.E., Koedinger, K.R., et al.: Gamification in education: what, how, why bother? Acad. Exch. Q. **15**(2), 1–5 (2011)
12. Cruzes, D.S., Dyba, T.: Recommended steps for thematic synthesis in software engineering. In: 2011 International Symposium on Empirical Software Engineering and Measurement, pp. 275–284. IEEE (2011)
13. Mechant, P., Walravens, N.: E-government and smart cities: theoretical reflections and case studies. Media Commun. **6**(4), 119–122 (2018)
14. Hjort-Madsen, K., Pries-Heje, J.: Enterprise architecture in government: fad or future? In: 2009 42nd Hawaii International Conference on System Sciences, pp. 1–10. IEEE (2009)
15. Lemmetti, J., Pekkola, S.: Understanding enterprise architecture: perceptions by the finnish public sector. In: Scholl, H.J., Janssen, M., Wimmer, M.A., Moe, C.E., Flak, L.S. (eds.) EGOV 2012. LNCS, vol. 7443, pp. 162–173. Springer, Heidelberg (2012). https://doi.org/10.1007/978-3-642-33489-4_14

16. Enagi, M.A., Ochoche, A.: The role of enterprise architecture in aligning business and information technology in organisations: Nigerian government investment on information technology. Int. J. Eng. Technol. **3**(1), 59–65 (2013)
17. Bakar, N.A.A., Kama, N., Harihodin, S.: Enterprise architecture development and implementation in public sector: the Malaysian perspective. J. Theor. Appl. Inf. Technol. **88**(1), 176–188 (2016)
18. Dang, D.D., Pekkola, S.: Root causes of enterprise architecture problems in the public sector. In: PACIS, p. 287 (2016)
19. Kakarontzas, G., Anthopoulos, L., Chatzakou, D., et al.: A conceptual enterprise architecture framework for smart cities: a survey based approach. In: 2014 11th International Conference on e-Business (ICE-B), pp. 47–54. IEEE (2014)
20. Saluky, S.: Development of enterprise architecture model for smart city. ITEJ (Inf. Technol. Eng. J.), **2**(2) (2018)
21. Gill, A.Q., Smith, S., Beydoun, G., et al.: Agile enterprise architecture: a case of a cloud technology-enabled government enterprise transformation (2014)
22. Kaushik, A., Raman, A.: The new data-driven enterprise architecture for e-healthcare: lessons from the Indian public sector. Govern. Inf. Q. **32**(1), 63–74 (2015)
23. Lemos, R.S.C.: Enterprise Information Architecture Patterns for Government (2016)
24. Valtonen, M.K.: Management structure based government enterprise architecture framework adaption in Situ. In: Poels, G., Gailly, F., Serral Asensio, E., Snoeck, M. (eds.) PoEM 2017. LNBIP, vol. 305, pp. 267–282. Springer, Cham (2017). https://doi.org/10.1007/978-3-319-70241-4_18
25. Tanaka, S.A., de Barros, R.M., de Souza Mendes, L.: A proposal to a framework for governance of ICT aiming at smart cities with a focus on enterprise architecture. In: Proceedings of the XIV Brazilian Symposium on Information Systems, p. 52. ACM (2018)
26. Lnenicka, M., Komarkova, J.: Developing a government enterprise architecture framework to support the requirements of big and open linked data with the use of cloud computing. Int. J. Inf. Manage. **46**, 124–141 (2019)
27. Bellman, B., Rausch, F.: Enterprise architecture for e-Government. In: Traunmüller, R. (ed.) EGOV 2004. LNCS, vol. 3183, pp. 48–56. Springer, Heidelberg (2004). https://doi.org/10.1007/978-3-540-30078-6_9
28. Hjort-Madsen, K.: Institutional patterns of enterprise architecture adoption in government. Transform. Govern. People Process Policy **1**(4), 333–349 (2007)
29. Janssen, M.: Sociopolitical aspects of interoperability and enterprise architecture in e-government. Soc. Sci. Comput. Rev. **30**(1), 24–36 (2012)
30. Shaanika, I., Iyamu, T.: Deployment of enterprise architecture in the Namibian government: the use of activity theory to examine the influencing factors. Electron. J. Inf. Syst. Dev. Countries **71**(1), 1–21 (2015)
31. Dang, D.D., Pekkola, S.: Institutionalising enterprise architecture in the public sector in Vietnam. In: ECIS, p. 139 (2016)
32. Bui, Q., Levy, M.: Institutionalization of Contested Practices: A Case of Enterprise Architecture Implementation in a US State Government (2017)
33. Hjort-Madsen, K., Gøtze, J.: Enterprise architecture in government-Towards a multi-level framework for managing IT in government. In: 4th European Conference on e-Government, Dublin Castle, Ireland, pp. 365–374. Citeseer (2004)
34. Janssen, M., Kuk, G.: A complex adaptive system perspective of enterprise architecture in electronic government. In: Proceedings of the 39th Annual Hawaii International Conference on System Sciences (HICSS 2006), p. 71b. IEEE (2006)

35. Ojo, A., Janowski, T., Estevez, E.: Improving government enterprise architecture practice–maturity factor analysis. In: 2012 45th Hawaii International Conference on System Sciences, pp. 4260–4269. IEEE (2012)
36. Lee, Y.-J., Kwon, Y.-I., Shin, S., et al.: Advancing government-wide Enterprise Architecture-A meta-model approach. In: 2013 15th International Conference on Advanced Communications Technology (ICACT), pp. 886–892. IEEE (2013)
37. Lahtela, A., Kortelainen, P.: Government enterprise architecture in practice. In: Proceedings of the 14th European Conference on e-Government: ECEG, pp. 414–423 (2014)
38. Moreno, L.M.M., Páez, J.O.T., Parra, A., et al.: The Colombian government enterprise architecture framework. In: Proceedings of the 2014 Conference on Electronic Governance and Open Society: Challenges in Eurasia, pp. 38–41. ACM (2014)
39. Hanafiah, M.A.: Improving E-Government Performance Through Enterprise Architecture In Developing Countries: The Case Of The Indonesian Treasury. Flinders University of South Australia (2015)
40. Firmansyah, C.M., Bandung, Y.: Designing an enterprise architecture government organization based on TOGAF ADM and SONA. In: 2016 International Conference on Information Technology Systems and Innovation (ICITSI), pp. 1–6. IEEE (2016)
41. Nunes, V., Cappelli, C., Costa, M.: Promoting transparency in government through FACIN: the Brazilian government enterprise architecture framework. In: Workshop de Transparência em Sistemas, Rio de Janeiro (2016)
42. Nakakawa, A., Namagembe, F., Proper, E.H.A.: Dimensions for scoping e-government enterprise architecture development efforts. In: Panetto, H., Debruyne, C., Proper, H.A., Ardagna, C.A., Roman, D., Meersman, R. (eds.) OTM 2018. LNCS, vol. 11229, pp. 661–679. Springer, Cham (2018). https://doi.org/10.1007/978-3-030-02610-3_37
43. Saiya, A.A., Arman, A.A.: Indonesian enterprise architecture framework: a platform for integrated and connected government. In: 2018 International Conference on ICT for Smart Society (ICISS), pp. 1–6. IEEE (2018)
44. Zheng, T., Zheng, L.: Examining e-government enterprise architecture research in China: a systematic approach and research agenda. Govern. Inf. Q. **30**, S59–S67 (2013)
45. Al-Nasrawi, S., Ibrahim, M.: An enterprise architecture mapping approach for realizing e-government. In: 2013 Third International Conference on Communications and Information Technology (ICCIT), pp. 17–21. IEEE (2013)
46. Mamkaitis, A., Bezbradica, M., Helfert, M.: Urban enterprise: a review of Smart City frameworks from an Enterprise Architecture perspective. In: 2016 IEEE International Smart Cities Conference (ISC2), pp. 1–5. IEEE (2016)
47. Bastidas, V., Bezbradica, M., Helfert, M.: Cities as enterprises: a comparison of smart city frameworks based on enterprise architecture requirements. In: Alba, E., Chicano, F., Luque, G. (eds.) International Conference on Smart Cities, pp. 20–28. Springer, Cham (2017). https://doi.org/10.1007/978-3-319-59513-9_3
48. Hevner, A.R., March, S.T., Park, J., et al.: Design science in information systems research. MIS Q. **28**, 75–105 (2004)

An e-Government Implementation Framework: A Developing Country Case Study

Anele Apleni[1] and Hanlie Smuts[2]([⊠]) [iD]

[1] Milpark Business School, Johannesburg, South Africa
aneleapleni@gmail.com
[2] Department of Informatics, University of Pretoria, Pretoria, South Africa
hanlie.smuts@up.ac.za

Abstract. The implementation of Information and Communication Technology (ICT) is seen globally as a means to efficient and effective delivery of business and organisational mandates. Governments, in their quest to serve citizens, harness ICT to streamline their service delivery processes. e-Government transforms administrations into "smart governments" enhancing the social, political and economic inclusion and the quality of life of its citizens. However, the governments of developing countries are still facing challenges regarding transformation due to a myriad of obstacles, which include the lack of interoperability of e-government, lack of resources and lack of management commitment. Therefore, the aim of this study is to define an e-government implementation framework for developing countries. The 12 critical success factors identified for developing countries were mapped to the variables of Diffusion of Innovation (DOI) Theory in order to create the proposed implementation framework. The framework was then applied in a single case study at a government department in South Africa (SA) where the opinions of 110 managers were collected through an on-line questionnaire. By considering the e-government implementation framework, government departments are guided and enabled to prioritise specific elements in their implementation plan focusing on improved e-government delivery.

Keywords: e-Government implementation framework · Diffusion of Innovation

1 Introduction

e-Government is one of the key priorities of governments worldwide to increase efficacy in service delivery and to advance interaction and collaboration across government departments [1]. e-Government refers to the process that governments utilise to achieve efficiency and effectiveness in government, allowing citizens greater access to services, while bringing more government accountability to the public [2, 3]. e-Government has therefore developed beyond just electronic service delivery and introduction to web-based technologies in government [2]. e-Government implementation is also considered to be a complicated societal system which includes organizational, social and economic issues [4].

© IFIP International Federation for Information Processing 2020
Published by Springer Nature Switzerland AG 2020
M. Hattingh et al. (Eds.): I3E 2020, LNCS 12067, pp. 15–27, 2020.
https://doi.org/10.1007/978-3-030-45002-1_2

There are several constraints that must be addressed for the successful implementation of electronic public services [5]. The failure rate of e-government projects, especially in developing countries, are significant and the gap between developed, and developing countries, is vast [6, 7]. Slow adoption to ICT has been the result of limited resources, such as poor ICT infrastructure, and insufficient Information Technology (IT) human capital to spearhead ICT advancement and improvement [6, 8]. Other factors cited that impact the adoption of e-government in developing countries include top management support, organisational size, ease of use, competitive pressure, compatibility, competitive pressure, strategic relevance and IT support infrastructure [2, 3, 8, 9]. Furthermore, slow adoption of an e-government approach is impacted by the fact that it is a long term project that requires an integrative implementation framework approach, more so in developing countries [10].

In an attempt to address the slow rate of e-government adoption, scholars considered critical success factors (CSFs) specifically pertaining to developing countries [6, 11]. The concept of CSFs point to the limited number of key areas where the implementation of e-government must be accomplished in order to achieve improved service delivery, making the difference between success and failure for the government department or team [2]. Therefore, in order to guide the implementation of e-government in developing countries, this research study considers the following research question: *what are the components of an e-government implementation framework for developing countries?* We reflect on this research question by considering the CSFs for developing countries and by mapping the CSFs to the DOI theory for guiding the e-government implementation programme. Thereafter, we evaluated the proposed framework in a single case study of a government department in SA.

The remainder of the paper is structured as follows: in Sect. 2 we provide the background to the study presenting an overview of e-government, as well as the DOI theory. The approach to this study is discussed in Sect. 3 where after we provide an overview of the findings in Sect. 4. In Sect. 4 we present the CSFs for improved service delivery mapping and conclude in Sect. 5.

2   Background

e-Government is influenced by a combination of factors, such as; political conditions, cultural dimensions, technological advances, and organizational changes all designed to support and drive transformation in government departments [5]. It involves providing transparency, simplified processes and efficiency by rethinking government through the introduction of models for business management, increased public involvement in decision-making processes and by using ICT for the successful adoption of administration- and government services [12]. Furthermore, e-government depends on the effective directing of e-government stakeholders, the coordination of many government department activities, close cooperation among employees, managers, IT specialists, citizens and industry, as well as ICT application [8, 13].

ICT is an enabler from 2 perspectives: firstly, ICT facilitates government efficiency, provides infrastructure for better decision-making, improves service offers and enhance communication. Secondly, ICT improves access and utility for citizens [8]. It is more difficult to realise government growth, economic growth, poverty reduction, the prosperity of citizens as well as a nation's sustainability, without e-government operating effectively [14]. Public sector restructuring, and its transformation into a digital public sector, is a necessity to achieving both of these perspectives [15, 16]. Furthermore, public sector digital transformation is context specific [16–18] and to identify factors influencing the success of e-government, this study suggests the use of CSFs [19].

In the next sections we present a high-level synopsis of e-government with specific focus on developing countries, an overview of the DOI theory in the context of e-government service delivery, and an overview of CSFs in the context of e-government in developing countries.

2.1 e-Government and ICT Implementation in Developing Countries

In the context of global economic integration and competition, ICT implementation is increasingly important to sustainable economic growth of developing countries in particular [20]. Diffusion of e-government innovation in developing countries was observed during the last two decades benefitting citizens and governments [20, 21]. For *citizens*, ICT implementation managed data, enhanced public service delivery and expanded communication channels. For *governments*, ICT implementation increased productivity, grew the business economy, shared global knowledge and automated business processes and communications [21].

Improved delivery of government services and products is the ultimate goal for e-government adoption and the role of ICT in providing these public activities of government improves efficiency and effectiveness, consequently reducing bureaucracy [22]. e-Government allows accessibility of up to date services bringing access and convenience to the citizens, thereby empowering them [16]. Furthermore, the transparency of government activities is enhanced through e-government actions, as well as through digital literacy development and the fostering of citizen appreciation of information technology [7, 23].

Readiness for e-government in developing countries is dependent on a number of favourable political, cultural, social, economic and technological conditions that need to exist for the e-government paradigm shift to take hold [7]. In countries where e-government is competing with other significant factors such as housing, health services, and a high unemployment rate, these conditions are difficult to establish in the short term [7]. In this context, at the turn of the century, SA started out as an e-government leader among developing countries. However, a decade later, states that were much less developed have surpassed SA [7].

The proponents of e-government have promised many benefits to those who adopt and implement e-government systems and standards [23]. Such standards, consisting of technical specification sets, constitute a common foundation of advanced technological knowledge, presented in an easily transferrable form for extensive acceptance [20]. These standards and standardisations facilitate the diffusion of innovation and describes the rate at which a new product or service is accepted. The DOI theory assist with a better understanding of how trends emerge, and may serve as early indication of success or failure of the new introduction [16, 20]. Therefore, we discuss DOI theory in the next section.

2.2 Diffusion of Innovation (DOI) Theory

The DOI Theory is a well-known framework where new technologies are being investigated for adoption [24, 25] and DOI Theory can be applied in terms of guiding e-government implementation [26]. In the context of this paper, innovation refers to the e-government implementation which in most cases, also include an aspect of ICT.

For the diffusion of a new idea, the DOI framework consists of 4 main elements: the innovation itself, communication channels, time and social systems. Diffusion, in the context of the DOI theory, is the process whereby an innovation is communicated over a period of time. Rogers [25: 172] described the innovation-decision process as "an information-seeking and information-processing activity, where an individual is motivated to reduce uncertainty about the advantages and disadvantages of an innovation". This innovation-decision process involves five steps in a time-ordered manner: knowledge, persuasion, decision, implementation, and confirmation [27]. Firstly, citizens form an opinion of an innovation based on knowledge they have about the innovation. Secondly, citizens decide if they want to adopt or reject the implementation of the innovation. The final stage of communication is the confirmation stage where citizens evaluate the outcomes of the innovation-decision that is considered [27]. Communication during the innovation implementation takes place within a social system through multiple channels, where stakeholders create and share the information with one another in order to reach a mutual understanding of the adoption of the innovation. The adoption process is the stages through which citizens decide on the acceptance or rejection of an innovation [25].

The adoption rate of an idea is determined by five characteristics, namely: the *relative advantage* of the innovation compared to the advances it supersedes; *compatibility* to existing needs and past experiences, *complexity* in relation to the difficulty and use; *trialability* with respect to the limited experimentation; and the *observability* of results of the innovation to the citizens within the social system [25, 27]. *Prior conditions* focus on the conditions that increase or decrease the likelihood that an innovation or new idea will be adopted by citizens and include previous practices, norms of the social system and needs or problems experienced [25, 27].

In order to apply CSFs as a means to improve e-government service delivery, we consider CSF categories in the next section.

2.3 e-Government Critical Success Factors

In order for nations to remain competitive in a globalised world, it is required to fully utilize e-government, and factors influencing e-government adoption are relevant in both the government internal and external environment [15]. Incompatible systems, complex organizational systems, initial cost increase associated with non-conformities, lack of integration guidance, lack of resources, lack of management commitment, the demand for training and cultural change compromises e-government initiatives [28].

A mechanism utilised to consider this government internal and external environment, is CSFs referring to a limited number of conditions, variables or characteristics that have a direct and significant impact on objectives such as effectiveness, efficiency, and viability of a government [29]. To achieve the intended overall objectives, activities related to the CSFs must be performed at the highest possible level of excellence [30]. As a result, we extracted CSFs relevant to developing countries as shown in Table 1.

Any e-government initiatives require *funding* to initiate and maintain e-government projects. e-Government services are provided through *ICT infrastructure* that is able to automate and digitise e-government services. The e-government ICT infrastructure may consist of a number of components forming the backbone of e-government implementation, namely infrastructure application server environment, infrastructure security, operating systems, application development tools, data and content management tools, and hardware.

New *legal issues* arise through e-government implementation processes as e-government implementation often requires the development and implementation of new legislation and policies, through a series of legislative updates. Accountability and transparency mechanisms are attributes of good governance-focussed regimes, and includes elements like best practice standards, quality controls, administrative law, and regulatory bodies as watchdogs such as auditors and ombudsmen. Therefore, good governance practice for e-government implementation requires all stakeholders to implement their programs in such a way that accountability and transparency is included, that it complies with all relevant laws, standards and best practice, and that it accommodates audit, quality assurance and recordkeeping programs that support sound administration and responsibility.

Table 1. Critical success factors for e-government service delivery in developing countries

Critical success factor	References
Funding	[5, 6, 13, 19, 31, 32]
ICT infrastructure	[2, 4–6, 18, 31]
Adequate legal and policy formulation	[2, 19, 31]
Awareness	[3, 4, 9, 32]
Top management and government support	[2, 3, 6, 32]
User computer efficacy	[4, 5, 32]
Stakeholder involvement	[2, 5, 9, 32]
Communication and change management	[3, 4, 32]
Clear vision and strategy	[2–4, 6, 9, 31]
Training	[2, 19, 32]
Government departmental goals	[2, 4, 9, 32]
Citizen empowerment (as opposed to marginalising groups)	[2, 4, 5, 9, 33]

Awareness in e-government refers to the process of pro-actively and earnestly marketing the benefits of e-government services to citizens in both rural and urban areas. Raising awareness of e-government early on in the programme and at the initial stage of the e-government implementation, resistance may be avoided and growth and adoption may be fostered. In addition, senior management *support and commitment* is a priority and is required throughout the entire e-services implementation life cycle in order to provide and allocate sufficient resources.

The ability of users – both citizens and civil servants - to *use and cope with new technology,* must be attended to for e-government implementation. Such skills typically include digital literacy skills such as information literacy, identity management, learning skills and ICT literacy skills normally associated with access to the Internet. These citizen skills are commonly classified into abilities needed in order to acquire and understand e-government services information, and the ability required to make decisions, solve problems, and collect and disseminate information. In addition, as e-government may be a new concept for citizens and civil servants in developing countries, e-government should provide incentives for stakeholders to support these new systems. Therefore, *stakeholder involvement* should focus on and encourage participation at a significant level of work.

Potential resistance to change by citizens is a concern and attention should be given during the e-government implementation to ensure that citizens understand the benefits of the new e-services. Some reasons for resistance that must be addressed may be fear of new technology, lack of understanding of the e-process and trouble-shooting (understanding outcomes and the course of action should processes go awry). The outcomes of e-government implementation transform traditional establishments and inevitably include changes to patterns of communication, work practices, organisational structures, procedures and processes enabled by the ICT implementation. In order to ensure the success of e-government initiatives, potential changes that may transpire must be anticipated and addressed. For this purpose, a well-designed *communication and change management strategy* needs to be developed and implemented. Components of this communication and change management strategy includes ICT education and ICT impact, as well as a clear *vision and strategy* for the e-government implementation. Successful e-government considerations entail a clear vision and strategy that leads and supports the entire e-government implementation process and focuses on the realisation of specific and well-articulated e-government goals.

Training is an important element to improve the overall success of e-government and goes hand in hand with communication and change management, as well as coping with new technology. Training is associated with endowing citizens with the hard, technical skills required to use technology and leads to the increased diffusion of e-government services into societies. Training and confidence in using technology, also impact the rate at which citizens adopt e-government. For democratic and participative decision-making, e-government facilitates *citizen empowerment* by providing information, as well as opportunities, to take part and contribute to public policy-making. Different forms of online forums enhance citizen participation and involvement. Such public discussions and the aggregation of differing citizens' interests, is an important requirement that is emphasized by democracy models.

In the next section we consider the research approach before we present the data analysis and findings.

3   Research Approach

Our overall objective of this paper was to define an implementation framework for e-government in developing countries. A means to identify and achieve this enabling environment, is to consider CSFs focussing on the underlying enabling and inhibiting conditions. In order to achieve this outcome, we conducted quantitative research and employed a case study research strategy [34]. The case study environment consisted of a government department in SA (GDSA). Within the SA context, e-government is sectorial according to government functionalities such as health, education, home affairs, etc. This is based on the political will of the SA Government with regards to enhancing its processes and systems through ICT implementation and adoption. A large sample of participants from a predetermined population of interest was selected [35, 36]. The rationale used in identifying the research participants, was the management level of the GDSA as this organisational level is accountable for decisions regarding ICT implementation.

An online questionnaire was used for data collection as it enabled us to obtain the similar data from a large group of people, in a homogenous format [37]. In order to structure the online questionnaire, we proceeded to map the CSFs (Table 1) to the DOI theory (Sect. 2) as shown in Fig. 1. The mapping was done based on the specific definitions of the CSFs and how it relates to the DOI theory definitions.

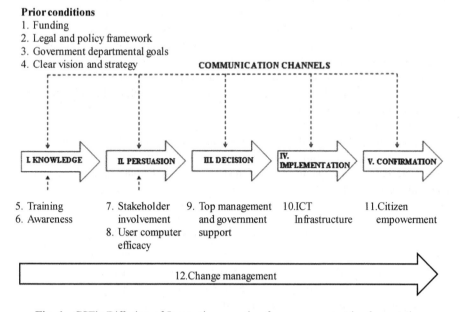

Fig. 1. CSF's-Diffusion of Innovation mapping for e-government implementation

Prior conditions that need to be met before embarking on the programme, includes 4 CSFs namely, funding, legal and policies, departmental goals and a clear vision and strategy. These CSFs were identified as they would increase or decrease the likelihood that the e-government implementation will materialise or not. The innovation-decision process starts with the *knowledge* stage where the citizen attempts to deduce what the innovation is and how it works. In order to create new knowledge during this stage, technology education and practice should provide both how-to and know-why experiences. Therefore, two CSFs, namely training and awareness, are relevant to both civil servants and citizens at this stage. The next step, a feeling-centred stage, is *persuasion* and during this stage an individual has a negative or positive attitude toward the innovation. Two CSFs are important at this point – one civil servant related and one citizen related. The *stakeholder involvement* CSF applies to civil servants acknowledging the IT skill that they require and bring to the innovation, and *user computer efficacy* points to citizens where efficient execution plays a major role. The third stage is the *decision* phase where an individual chooses to adopt or reject the innovation. The CSF focus for this stage is *top management and government support* that is mainly focused on civil servants and visible government support, calling on citizens to embrace the e-government service delivery innovation. The *implementation* stage is the fourth stage and the innovation is put into practice in this stage. An innovation may be modified by a user during the process of its adoption and implementation, and this usually takes place during the implementation stage. Based on the degree to which an innovation is changed, the implementation stakeholders may need technical assistance to reduce the degree of uncertainty about the consequences and subsequently placing emphasis on the *ICT infrastructure* CSF. The last step is the *confirmation* stage where the individual looks for support for his or her decision by seeking reassuring messages that confirm his or her decision. The CSF significant here is citizen empowerment enticing citizens to stay involved, to apply the innovation and assist with enhancing and improving it. The final CSF is change management which is relevant across all 5 stages of the innovation-decision process where change agents may increase the predictability of the rate of adoption of innovations.

Respondents had to provide demographic data and rate the CSF statements (Fig. 1) using a 5-point Likert rating scale. Based on the specific criteria used to identify potential research participants, 46% of respondents were male and 54% female as shown in the respondent profile in Table 2.

Table 2. Profile of questionnaire respondents (N = 110)

Gender		Age		Tenure		Education	
Male	51 (46%)	<25 yrs	0 (0%)	<5 yrs	9 (8%)	High School	0 (0%)
		25–35 yrs	14 (12%)	5–10 yrs	34 (31%)	Diploma	9 (8%)
Female	59 (54%)	36–45 yrs	42 (38%)	11–15 yrs	38 (35%)	Degree	75 (68%)
		46–55 yrs	38 (35%)	>15 yrs	29 (26%)	Post-Graduate	26 (24%)
		>55 yrs	16 (15%)				

Most respondents (42%) were in the age group 36–45, followed by 35% in the 46–55 age group. None of the respondents were younger than 25 years which is expected as only managers were included in the sample of 140. Of the respondents, 35% had a tenure of 11–15 years, while 31% indicated a tenure of 5–10 years. Only 8% had a tenure of less than 5 years. All respondents reported tertiary qualifications as 68% indicated that they hold a degree, followed by 24% that indicated post-graduate qualifications.

In the next section, we discuss the analysis of the data collected in order to derive a prioritised e-government implementation plan for the GDSA.

4 Case Study Data Analysis and Findings

The main aim of this paper was to define an implementation framework for e-government in developing countries by using CSFs mapped to the DOI theory as a framework. Data was analysed quantitatively and Table 3 depicts the opinion of the 110 respondents based on the questions related to the CSFs.

The respondents confirmed that *funding* and *ICT infrastructure* are the priority factors for successful e-government adoption in the GDSA with ratings of 93% and 84%, respectively. Adequate *legal and policies formulation* for e-government service delivery in the public sector provides a healthy platform for successful implementation highlighted by 58% of respondents. 53% of respondents stressed that in order to achieve successful adoption of e-government, civil servants ought to be *aware* of ICT capabilities to improve service delivery to citizens, as well as optimisation of their processes. 62% of respondents emphasised that *top management and government support* are essential for successful adoption of e-government service delivery, while 30% emphasised the importance of *user computer efficacy*. In order to curb the skills flight of GDSA IT staff to better paying private sector jobs, which is an existing public service problem that hampers e-government service delivery implementation, IT personnel at GDSA should have an attractive *stakeholder involvement plan* to retain them. Hence, 40% of the respondents prioritised this CSF. *Communication and change management* focuses on addressing resistance to change – from both civil servant and citizen perspectives - and 56% of the respondents agreed this CSF is essential for the successful adoption of e-government in the GDSA. A *clear vision and strategy* attracted a rating of 74% while *training* was prioritised by 40% of respondents. 68% of respondents highlighted the importance of *department goals* and 75% of respondents emphasised the significance of *empowering citizens*.

In order to visualise the priorities identified by the GDSA respondents for their particular implementation plan, a diagram was utilised shown in Fig. 2. As all CSFs are important as a means to guiding implementation of the GDSA e-government service delivery programme, the rating shared by 110 GDSA managers may now guide implementation focus and priority. By tallying the *somewhat important* and *very important categories*, an importance rating per CSF pertinent to the GDSA is shown in

Table 3. GDSA critical success factors importance rating

Critical success factor	Very unimportant		Somewhat unimportant		Neutral		Somewhat important		Very important	
Funding	2	2%	2	2%	3	3%	45	41%	57	52%
ICT infrastructure	6	5%	7	6%	6	5%	54	49%	39	35%
Adequate legal and policy formulation	6	5%	6	5%	35	32%	43	39%	21	19%
Awareness	8	7%	11	10%	43	39%	31	28%	18	16%
Top management and government support	6	5%	12	11%	24	22%	41	37%	28	25%
User computer efficacy	15	14%	17	15%	45	41%	23	21%	10	9%
Stakeholder involvement	13	12%	15	14%	37	34%	28	25%	17	15%
Communication and change management	10	9%	6	5%	33	30%	48	44%	13	12%
Clear vision and strategy	4	4%	8	7%	17	15%	37	34%	44	40%
Training	28	25%	14	13%	24	22%	26	24%	18	16%
Government departmental goals	14	13%	9	8%	12	11%	57	52%	18	16%
Citizen empowerment	7	6%	13	12%	8	7%	47	43%	35	32%
N = 110										

Fig. 2. Respondents identified the top 6 prioritise for the particular GDSA with a rating of more than 60% as top management and government support (62%), clear departmental goals (68%), clear vision and strategy (74%), empowerment of citizens (75%), ICT infrastructure (84%) and funding (93%).

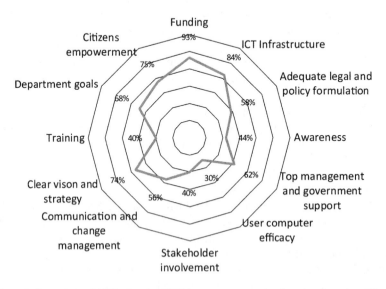

Fig. 2. Priority rating of CSFs for the GDSA e-government implementation plan (N = 110)

In order to achieve e-government service delivery improvement at the GDSA, an enabling environment is necessary. When considering the proposed framework in Fig. 1 and the prioritisation in Fig. 2, a clear implementation plan may be designed for the GDSA. There is a priority requirement for government to provide adequate funding that will ensure that IT skills are retained, ICT infrastructure is put in place, and clear goals are set on how e-government will roll out across interactive stages. Furthermore, better government support will ensure that priority is given to ICT implementation initiatives. It is important that SA citizens are aware of, and understand, the e-government products that the GDSA offers so they can benefit from utilizing them. A large number of citizens in developing countries live in rural areas, often away from technology and infrastructure. The GDSA implementation project needs to be executed in such a way that it does not marginalise any group of SA citizens as these implementation plans should empower citizens and civil servants with the necessary knowledge and skills for the implementation and usage of e-government systems. Initiatives for road shows in rural areas on how citizens can register online should be done for the benefit of ordinary citizens. IT education to citizens is another way of dealing with the digital divide to ensure digital literate citizens. For the implementation of the GDSA project, high priority must be allocated to the approval of adequate budgets and funding from national government.

5   Conclusion

In order to address the requirement of e-government implementation in developing countries, this research proposed an implementation framework derived from CSFs for e-government implementation in developing countries mapped to DOI theory for the adoption of new ideas. Twelve relevant CSFs were identified and mapped across the DOI innovation-decision process. These CSFs give a comprehensive view of what a government department specifically needs to address when implementing an e-government programme.

The proposed e-government implementation framework was applied in a government department in SA where 110 managers utilised the framework to prioritise the focus areas of their e-government implementation. In addition, by considering specific CSF priorities within the government department as illustrated by the case study example, precedence can be given to the real enablers and a fit-for-purpose e-government implementation plan can be designed.

Although our starting point with identifying CSFs was related to e-government implementation in developing countries and evaluated in one government department in SA, further research is required on how the proposed implementation framework can be extended at a government level across multiple departments.

References

1. Pardo, T.A., Nam, T., Burke, G.B.: E-government interoperability interaction of policy, management, and technology dimensions. Soc. Sci. Comput. Rev. **30**(1), 7–23 (2012)
2. Napitupulu, D., Sensuse, D.I.: The critical success factors study for e-government implementation. Int. J. Comput. Appl. **89**(16), 23–32 (2014)
3. Siddique, W.: Critical success factors affecting e-government policy implementation in Pakistan. E-J. E-Democr. Open Gov. **8**(1), 102–126 (2016)
4. Meiyanti, R., et al.: Systematic review of critical success factors of e-government: definition and realization. In: 2017 International Conference on Sustainable Information Engineering and Technology (SIET), Malang, Indonesia. IEEE (2018)
5. Ziemba, E., et al.: Factors influencing the success of e-government. J. Comput. Inf. Syst. **56**(2), 156–167 (2016)
6. Napitupulu, D., et al.: Content validity of critical success factors for e-Government implementation in Indonesia. In: Materials Science and Engineering. IOP Publishing Ltd. (2018)
7. Cloete, F.: E-government lessons from South Africa 2001–2011. Afr. J. Inf. Commun. **12**, 128–142 (2012)
8. Michael, P., et al.: e-Government implementation challenges in developing countries: the project manager's perspective. Int. J. Public Adm. Manag. Res. (IJPAMR) **4**(3), 1–17 (2018)
9. Othman, M.H., Razali, R.: Whole of government critical success factors towards integrated e-government services: a preliminary review. J. Pengur. **2018**(53), 73–82 (2018)
10. Ebrahim, Z., Irani, Z.: e-Government adoption: architecture and barriers. Bus. Process Manag. J. **11**(5), 589–611 (2005)
11. Ntaliani, M., et al.: Agricultural e-government services: an implementation framework and case study. Comput. Electron. Agric. **2010**(70), 337–347 (2010)
12. Yadav, J., Saini, A.K., Yadav, A.K.: Measuring citizens engagement in e-Government projects – Indian perspective. J. Stat. Manag. Syst. **22**(2), 327–346 (2019)
13. Ziemba, E., Papaj, T., Żelazny, R.: A model of success factors for e-government adoption – the case of Poland. Issues Inf. Syst. **14**, 87–100 (2013)
14. Hanna, N.K.: Transforming Government and Building the Information Society: Challenges and Opportunities for the Developing World. Springer, New York (2010). https://doi.org/10.1007/978-1-4419-1506-1
15. Savoldelli, A., Codagnone, C., Misuraca, G.: Understanding the e-government paradox: learning from literature and practice on barriers to adoption. Gov. Inf. Q. **31**, 63–71 (2014)
16. Shareef, M.A., Yogesh, N.A., Dwivedi, K.: Examining adoption behavior of mobile government. J. Comput. Inf. Syst. **53**, 39–49 (2012)
17. Fonseca-Lind, S., Ramaswamy, M.: E-governance in Puerto Rico: perspectives for the next decade. Issues Inf. Syst. **14**, 207–214 (2013)
18. Xu, X., Zhang, W., Barkhi, R.: IT infrastructure capabilities and IT project success: a development team perspective. Inf. Technol. Manag. **11**, 123–142 (2010)
19. Adendorff, R., Smuts, H.: Critical success factors for cloud computing adoption in South Africa. In: The Americas Conference on Information Systems 2019 (AMCIS 2019), Cancun, Mexico. Association for Information Systems (2019)
20. Zoo, H., de Vries, H.J., Lee, H.: Interplay of innovation and standardization: exploring the relevance in developing countries. Technol. Forecast. Soc. Chang. **118**, 334–348 (2017)
21. Ali, K.E., Mazen, S.A., Hassanein, E.E.: A proposed framework for the organization readiness assessment of IT innovation adoption in e-government environment. Int. J. Intell. Comput. Inf. Sci. **17**(2), 33–50 (2017)

22. Olaniyi, E.: Digital government: ICT and public sector management in Africa. In: New Trends in Management: Regional and Cross-Border Perspectives, pp. 269–286. London Scientific Publishing, London (2018)
23. Ahn, M.J., Bretschneider, S.: Politics of e-government: e-government and the political control of bureaucracy. Public Adm. Rev. **71**(3), 414–424 (2011)
24. Botha, A., Smuts, H., de Villiers, C.: Applying diffusion of innovation theory to learning management system feature implementation in higher education: lessons learned. In: Hao, T., Chen, W., Xie, H., Nadee, W., Lau, R. (eds.) SETE 2018. LNCS, vol. 11284, pp. 56–65. Springer, Cham (2018). https://doi.org/10.1007/978-3-030-03580-8_7
25. Rogers, E.M.: Diffusion of Innovations. The Free Press, New York (2003)
26. Akça, Y., Özer, G.: Diffusion of innovation theory and an implementation on enterprise resource planning systems. Int. J. Bus. Manag. **9**(4), 92–114 (2014)
27. Sahin, I.: Detailed review of Rogers' diffusion of innovations theory and educational technology-related studies based on Rogers' theory. Turk. Online J. Educ. Technol. **5**(2), 14–23 (2006)
28. Lam, W.: Integration challenges towards increasing e-government maturity. J. E-Gov. **1**(2), 45–58 (2008)
29. Aziz, N.A.A., Manab, N.A., Othman, S.N.: Critical success factors of sustainability risk management (SRM) practices in Malaysian environmentally sensitive industries. Soc. Behav. Sci. **2016**(219), 4–11 (2016)
30. Critical Success Factor. The Business Dictionary (2019)
31. Nkohkwo, Q.N., Islam, M.S.: Challenges to the successful implementation of e-government initiatives in Sub-Saharan Africa: a literature review. Electron. J. E-Gov. **11**, 253–267 (2013)
32. Ramadhan, A., Sensuse, D.I., Arymurthy, A.M.: Synthesizing success factors for e-government initiative. Res. J. Appl. Sci. Eng. Technol. **6**(9), 1685–1702 (2013)
33. Alathur, S., Vigneswara Ilavarasan, I., Gupta, M.P.: Citizen empowerment and participation in e-democracy: Indian context. In: Proceedings of the 5th International Conference on Theory and Practice of Electronic Governance, Tallinn, Estonia. ACM (2011)
34. Yin, R.K.: Case Study Research: Design and Methods, 5th edn. Sage Publications Inc., Thousand Oaks (2014)
35. Oates, B.J.: Researching Information Systems and Computing. SAGE Publications, London (2008)
36. Leedy, P.D., Ormrod, J.E.: Practical Research: Planning and Design, 10th edn. Pearson Education Limited, New Jersey (2014)
37. De Villiers, M.R.: Models for interpretive information systems research, part 2: design research, development research, design-science research, and design-based research - a meta-study and examples. In: Research Methodologies, Innovations and Philosophies in Software Systems Engineering and Information Systems, pp. 238–255 (2012)

Institutional Effects on National Health Insurance Digital Platform Development and Use: The Case of Ghana

Anthony Renner-Micah, John Effah[✉], and Richard Boateng

Department of Operations and Management Information Systems,
University of Ghana Business School, Accra, Ghana
jeffah@ug.edu.gh

Abstract. The purpose of this study is to understand institutional effects on digital platform development and use for national health insurance in a developing country. Information systems research on digital platforms for the health sector has focused more on healthcare. Less research exists on health insurance. This study, therefore, addresses the research gap by focusing on digital platform for national health insurance service in a developing country. The study employs qualitative, interpretive case study as methodology and institutional theory as analytical lens to investigate regulative, normative, and cultural-cognitive institutional effects on digital platform development and use for national health insurance in Ghana. The findings show the institutional enablers as: (1) health-seeking culture; (2) mobile network penetration and use; and (3) appropriate laws and regulations. Conversely, the constraints are (1) Unstructured supplementary service data (USSD) functionality; and (2) extended family system.

Keywords: Digital platform · Mobile platform · Institutional theory · Health insurance · Interpretive case study · Developing country · Ghana

1 Introduction

The purpose of this study is to understand institutional effects on digital platform development and use for national health insurance in a developing country. Digital platforms are characterised as having layered modular architecture with a core module and loosely-coupled components [1]. By their nature, digital platforms facilitate change and evolution of their use through re-configuration of their architecture and components. There is widespread use of digital platforms in various organisations and sectors [2, 3]. Within the developing country health sector, some health insurance organisations have implemented digital platforms while others are in the process of doing so amidst some challenges.

Digital platform development for health insurance is underpinned by the need for efficient operational processes and effective service delivery [4]. Unlike traditional information systems (IS), which limit access to internal users for specified times, digital platform extends access to external users [5, 6] such as subscribers anytime anywhere.

© IFIP International Federation for Information Processing 2020
Published by Springer Nature Switzerland AG 2020
M. Hattingh et al. (Eds.): I3E 2020, LNCS 12067, pp. 28–38, 2020.
https://doi.org/10.1007/978-3-030-45002-1_3

Generally, literature on digital platforms for the health sector has focused more on health care [7, 8]. Less research, therefore, exists on health insurance as an important sector for providing health care financing, especially in relation to national health insurance in developing country context. Following this research gap, the research question for this study concerns how regulative, normative and cultural-cognitive institutions affect digital platform development and use for national health insurance in a developing country.

To address the research question, the study employs institutional theory [9] as analytical lens and qualitative, interpretive case study [10] as methodology to gain insight into digital platform development and use for national health insurance system in Ghana, as a developing country. Ghana was chosen because it has recently migrated its national health insurance from traditional information system environment onto a digital platform to improve its operational processes and service delivery.

The rest of the paper is structured as follows. The following section reviews relevant literature on digital platforms and the health sector. The next section presents institutional theory as the analytical lens for data analysis. The section after describes the research setting and the methodology. The subsequent section reports on the case description. The section after focuses on analysis and discussion, while the final section presents the conclusion.

2 Digital Platform and Health Care

Digital platform is a facilitator of multi-sided activities. IS research views digital platform as an organisational and technological innovation for product development and transactions [1]. Several digital platforms have emerged over the last several years in different sectors [8]. These platforms are underpinned by computing and network infrastructure that allow distributed actors to interact and transact [11]. The architecture builds on components that have well-defined application programming interfaces (APIs). The APIs allow interconnection and uses in new ways than initially intended [12], which make them engine for innovation in service delivery.

Vassilakopoulou et al. [7] examine the introduction of e-health platform to understand how inclusiveness was pursued in relation to the political orientation of platform development, coordination of work among multiple contributors, and handling of technical heterogeneity. Furstenau and Auschra [8] also investigate strategies to implement and scale digital platforms in highly-regulated settings such as health care. The authors observed that openness on code and content layers fuel platform growth and contribution. However, financial risks and uncertainties in health care regulations can result in platform failure and avoid opportunities to achieve potential benefits. Implementing and scaling digital platform – especially in health care-based organisations – is a difficult task and requires the resolution of tensions around autonomy-related benefits and control [8, 13].

Digital platforms exhibit four dimensions: infrastructure, core module, ecosystem, and service dimensions [14]. This research focuses on the service dimension. The service dimension is the application of specialised competences (knowledge and skills) through deeds, processes, and performances for the benefit of another entity or the entity itself [15]. Because an organisation can always do better at serving clients, the service dimension views digital platform development and use as a continuous process directed at improving service delivery.

Despite the benefits offered by digital platforms, we are still less informed about how they support health insurance, as the focus has so far been on the health care sector. In the words of Rye and Kimberly, "We still do not know as much as we would like, and what we do know, we may not know for sure" [16, p. 254].

3   Theoretical Foundation: Institutional Theory

The theoretical foundation for this study is institutional theory of organisations [9, 17]. The fundamental concept of the theory is institution, which refers to established social structures such as laws, norms, culture and practices that influence people's thinking and behaviour in societal and organisational contexts [9]. Moreover, institutions are classified into three pillars, namely regulative, normative, and cultural-cognitive.

First, the regulative pillar explains how laws, rules and regulations enable or constrain behaviour of actors [18]. It explains how people need to conform to rules or attract punishments if they break the rules [9]. As this study concerns health insurance, regulative institutions are the acts of parliament and laws that regulate behaviour in the sector.

Second, the normative pillar is based on agents' social obligations, which are observable through values and norms [18] with the aim of guiding and promoting certain preferred behaviours [19]. They specify how things should be done, how goals should be set and legitimate means to pursue them [9]. In this study, normative institutions refer to established norms, traditions and practices in national health insurance services.

Finally, cultural-cognitive institutions are the taken-for-granted customs, traditions, and assumptions that control the thinking process and actions of social actors [20]. In this study, cognitive institutions refer to the thinking and decision-making patterns of actors in the national health insurance sector.

In theory, the three pillars are only separated for analytical purpose [9]. In practice, they work in combination. Within a given context, one pillar may dominate the others. In IS research, institutional theory has been recognised as useful for analysing change and stability related to information technology and organisational elements [21]. The motivation for choosing it as the theoretical foundation in this study is based on its useful concepts to understand the effects of normative, regulative and cultural-cognitive factors on digital platform development and use for national health insurance in a developing country.

4   Research Setting and Methodology

This study forms part of a larger research project into health insurance platformisation in a developing country. The current study focuses on a digital platform initiative and the regulative, normative and cognitive institutional effects on the process and the outcome. This research is based on a single case study method of the national health insurance in Ghana.

4.1 Methodology

Following the interpretive paradigm [10, 22], this study seeks to understand the interaction between digital platform development and use in health insurance and the effects of the institutional environment. Interpretivists argue that organisations are not static and that the relationship between people, organisations, and technology evolve. The motivation for choosing qualitative, interpretive case study approach is based on the understanding that the research phenomenon and its context can be understood through the meanings that participants assign to them within and their institutional environment [23, 24].

4.2 Data Collection

Data collection occurred from June 2018 to September 2019. In line with the interpretive case study tradition [10], this study obtained data from multiple sources, including interviews, documents, observations, and websites. The multiple data sources included semi-structured interviews with key informants who had knowledge and experience with the digital platform initiative, its implementation, and outcomes. The key informants were selected through purposive and snowball sampling [25] based on the relevance of their role in understanding the phenomenon.

A total of thirty-two (32) interview participants were selected for this study. The participants included one director of MIS, two deputy directors for business systems and claims management, respectively. Other participants were ten regional ICT coordinators, two data center administrators, one database administrator and one senior manager ICT for business systems. Additional data came from discussion with ten district MIS officers and five health insurance subscribers. Interviews lasted between 45 min and two hours, were tape-recorded, transcribed and verified by participants.

The researchers also obtained further data from observing the digital platform modules through demonstrations and walkthroughs organised by the national health insurance IT staff. In addition, documentary data were gathered from project documentation and reports as well as from websites.

4.3 Data Analysis

Based on the interpretive tradition, data analysis occurred alongside data gathering [10]. The analysis occurred at two stages. The first stage was based on inductive thematic analysis. The process involved inductively deriving concepts from the collected data to identify themes related to the development, use and outcome of the digital platform and the roles of stakeholders to inform the case description.

The second stage was theory-based analysis. Under this approach, concepts from institutional theory were used as sensitising devices to identify regulative, normative and cultural-cognitive institutions as enablers and constraints of the development and use of national health insurance digital platform. From the interpretive analysis perspective, the goal of the analysis was not to test the theory, but use it as a sensitising device to guide the analysis [26]. Where necessary, follow up with the interview participants were undertaken to verify emerging findings or seek additional data in line with the hermeneutic circle.

5   Case Description

Ghana, with an estimated population of 29 million as of 2018 and classified as a middle-income country, is a developing country in Africa. Health care financing has gone through a chequered history in Ghana since independence in 1957 where all governments have pursued, with varying degrees of success, several policies, and programmes to accelerate economic growth and raise the living standards. The national health insurance scheme (NHIS) was established under Act 650 of 2003 by the Government of Ghana to provide essential health care services to persons' resident in the country through district mutual health insurance scheme (DMHIS) and private health insurance schemes. The mission of the scheme has been towards securing the implementation of the national health insurance policy that ensures access to essential health care services for all residents of Ghana and drive universal health coverage [27].

5.1   Pre-digital Platform

In order to qualify as a member with the national health insurance, residents need to register first with the scheme and be given some form of identification to visit the health provider and receive health care for free. At the onset of the scheme in 2003, DMHIS used manual means to register and identify members or subscribers as they are known. From 2005 to 2008, DMHIS attempted some level of automation with mix results. The software installed at the DMHIS were on standalone computers with no network connectivity to undertake data entry.

With the exponential growth in membership of the scheme from 2008 came problems with accessing health services. From 2008, the NHIS introduced several digital interventions including a centralised database and a biometric system (BMS) to address operational challenges which included dwindling or stagnated growth. Moreover, the systems introduced produced unintended consequences of long queues and citizens waiting several hours and sometimes days in rural areas at the DMHIS to register to access health care. Essentially the systems introduced up to 2016 were not client-side friendly (for health insurance subscribers to access services) resulting in long queues and waiting times at DMHIS offices.

The members of the NHIS have been mostly at the receiving end of unintended consequences resulting from digital technology led attempts at digital service innovation. First, the non-portability of the scheme and silos of client-facing systems rendered accessing health care problematic for NHIS members. As a result, the scheme recorded stagnated or dwindling growth. There were also the intermittent shortages of consumables needed to ensure a very smooth registration process as well as the constant breakdown of biometric equipment. A senior management official with the scheme recounts:

"We are at the crossroads if you ask me as a scheme where technology is driving the way things ought to be done; so, services, services, services is something that we want to take to the very next level."

5.2 Digital Platform Development (Mobile Renewals and Digital Authentication)

Conceptualised in 2017, the digital platform development received funding from the international labour organisation (ILO) to boost membership registration in order to meet the united nations universal health coverage goals. A prototype version of the platform was initially developed from which it was scaled to pilot and production. Modules of the platform include a payment system linked to a mobile service aggregator. The payment module channels payments between NHIS members using the mobile renewal application on their mobile devices and NHIS digital platform over the mobile telecommunications network of the participating telecoms companies Vodafone, MTN and AirtelTigo. It also includes an application programming interface (APIs) to integrate with health provider platforms for authentications. The mobile renewal application was piloted successfully in two districts in Ghana and eventually rolled out nationwide from December 2018. The mobile renewal part of the solution uses unstructured supplementary service data (USSD) to provide messaging service to health insurance members, including the renewal of their membership and payment of premium.

The mobile application sends SMS reminder before the expiration of the subscribers' eligibility. The reminder offers the option to complete payment of the insurance premium immediately after the SMS. Insurance subscribers can check when their policy is due to expire. Other features available within the application is the ability to view the benefits packages as well as a comprehensive list of medicines. Service benefits to members expected from the platform include improved member renewal and registration, and reduced waiting times at DMHIS offices. In driving the schemes overall policy goal of attaining universal health coverage, the digital platform is also expected to eliminate process bottlenecks to increase NHIS penetration in Ghana by allowing members to renew their policies at the comfort of their homes without having to queue at district offices.

5.3 Post-digital Platform Development

The NHIS continued to implement the mobile membership renewal and digital authentication system across all its district offices nationwide since the national roll-out in December 2018. The response from the NHIS membership and providers on the use of these initiatives have been very positive. Membership and claims check code authentication are helping to improve upon the validity of membership numbers and cost containment in claims payment. Through this process, a comprehensive analysis of membership and claims validity checks can be undertaken from which appropriate punitive measures for invalid claims submission can be taken. There is now the possibility to link legacy data to new data generated from the project's implementation to drive more timely and actionable insights, significantly improving efficiency of NHIS operations and service accessibility. Importantly, more wide-reaching policy reforms to bring the scheme back to full sustainability can be attempted.

A number of key challenges have, however, been observed. First is differences in how mobile telecommunications companies present their USSD menu following the shortcode issued by the health insurance member to access the service. For example, whiles MTN has been adjudged simpler in terms of plugging in by the mobile platform aggregator and presenting a much simpler interface for approving payment out of health insurance members mobile wallet without leaving the screen, Vodafone and AirtelTigo are said to have a complicated menu system. This process involves the health insurance member first generating a code called a voucher number. After the code is received, the health insurance member will have to dial another shortcode to complete the health insurance renewal process, resulting in two separate steps for the subscriber. Even though the mobile telecommunications companies such as AirtelTigo claim the voucher system is more secure and clients more protected, this presents challenges for easy adoption by health insurance members.

Secondly, resulting from degraded network connectivity from the mobile telecommunications network, health insurance members have had to contend with trying multiple times before the transactions eventually get completed to renew their memberships. At other times, health insurance members have money deducted from their mobile wallet without a corresponding renewal of their membership. This has been attributed to integration challenges between the other platform partners such as the mobile aggregator, the mobile telecommunications provider, including the NHIS where system handshakes are not completed. Lastly, digital illiteracy, the inability to use and access digital information and tools have resulted in the situation where some health insurance members are unable to use the service and rely on third parties, including mobile money vendors with the unintended consequence of giving out their personal information.

6   Analysis and Discussion

The findings of the case study present us with a number of interesting issues for analysis and discussion. Based on the research question and institutional theory as a lens, this section discusses the regulative, normative and cultural-cognitive institutional enablers and constraints. Enablers generally mediate the successful achievement of organisational goals whiles constraints makes an action difficult or impossible to act upon [28].

6.1   Institutional Enablers

The findings show that the initial objective of the national health insurance was to provide a digital platform to address service accessibility problems leading to increased enrolment towards meeting universal health coverage targets. International non-governmental normative institution funded and drove the digital platform initiative. First, the normative health-seeking culture in the country supported the need for a digital platform that could facilitate expanded coverage and access to health service.

This normative health-seeking behaviour is manifested in the increased utilisation of health services under national health insurance.

For example, active membership has risen from 10 million as at the end of 2016 to 11.7 million in 2019. Mobile renewals under the platform continue to account for about 65–70% of total renewals recorded. As at the end of September 2019, the cumulative (January to September) mobile renewals was 3,970,408. The total revenue generated from these renewals is GHS 52, 463, 584 or approximately $9.5 million accounting for 53.58% of total transactions (mobile & BMS renewals and new registrations) and 68.78% of all renewals (mobile and BMS). Again, as at the end of September 2019, a total of 4,553 health providers are using the authentication module regularly. Within the same period, a total of 23,975,774 health care attendances have been validated digitally. As noted in the literature, despite the relatively high percentage of its gross domestic product (GDP) on health [29], universal health coverage remains a long way from being attained as a result of service accessibility problems [30]. Nevertheless, digital platforms offer several advantages for health seekers, health provider and payer [31].

Another normative institution that enabled the digital platform initiative was the penetration and use of mobile technology. Mobile network penetration continues to surge in the country at 75%, as at 2016 [32] meaning an estimated 75 out of every 100 Ghanaian adults own a mobile phone. These include some of the over 11 million currently active members of national health insurance. These normative factors encouraged the NHIS to seek the development of digital platform capabilities that apart from facilitating access to health care also provides online payment services. Normative use and growth of mobile banking and payment systems for economic transactions and exchange [33] further ensured the integration of the payment system into the NHIS digital platform. The outcome is a more efficient and transparent means of accounting for cash inflows to the scheme from premium payments.

A regulative institution would ascertain whether the organisation is legally established and whether it is acting in accord with relevant laws and regulations. The research findings suggest that the principal regulative institution establishing the NHIS is Act 852 that replaced Act 650 in October 2012 to consolidate the NHIS. The objective of the revised law is to remove operational bottlenecks and drive transparency towards the attainment of universal health insurance coverage. The regulative pillar's legitimising influence supports and authorises individuals within the NHIS to take specific actions, in this case, the development and implementation of a digital platform to boost membership registration in order to meet the united nations universal health coverage goals. The design and construction of digital artefacts and technologies are mandated by regulative authorities often in the interests of the larger society [9].

6.2 Institutional Constraints

Digital platform has the potential for increased levels of health insurance member engagement, a model of participatory health care that could improve service outcomes while also lowering cost. However, normative constraints embedded in USSD interface across mobile telecommunications provider platforms poses challenges to continued adoption and use of the service platform. Health insurance members experiencing challenges will revert to travelling to DMHIS offices to renew their health insurance memberships defeating the goal of improving service experience using the platform.

The extended family system, which is deeply embedded in the Ghanaian culture is a group consisting of close kin organised around either patrilineal or matrilineal relatives or lines. The extended family system results from the communal rather than individualistic social network based on a fundamental need to care for other members of the extended family [34]. This system typically includes a man, his wife, children or offspring in addition to other kin. By extension of this system, reverence is accorded family heads and community leaders. In practice, family heads can register for national health insurance membership on behalf of an entire household while community leaders do same for community members. In secondary schools, mass registration of students unto the national health insurance can be linked to a single phone number of a school head. Within the NHIS mobile authentication platform, when a member visits the health provider to access health care, the member after consultation receives a notification on their mobile device asking them to confirm whether they were at the health provider on a given day and time to access health care. This verification system is for purposes of enabling the NHIS to link attendance to claims received from the health provider, many of which are fraudulently sent for payment.

In most cases, these notifications are not responded to because the receiver has no knowledge of a visit to the health provider by an individual family member on whose behalf, he/she undertook the NHIS member registration. This cultural-cognitive institution is a major constraint on the NHIS ability to obtain proper feedback to validate claims received from health providers. This constraint goes to the heart of the schemes cost containment and financial sustainability drive.

7   Conclusion

The purpose of this study was to understand how institutional effects enable or constrain digital platform development and use in national health insurance from a developing country context. By applying institutional theory to analyse digital platform in national health insurance, our work contributes to digital platform research in the health sector in general and health insurance in particular. The findings show that digital platform is a promising means to help health insurance organisations in developing countries to achieve national coverage. However, to derive the benefits, health insurance managers should pay attention to institutional enablers and constraints that affect digital platform development and use.

The study contributes to research, practice and policy. For research, the study reveals regulative, normative, and cultural-cognitive enablers and constraints and how they can shape the development and use of digital platform for health insurance in a developing country context. By identifying these institutions, this study extends existing knowledge on digital platform development and access in developing countries.

For practice, the study shows that health insurance managers should not only address technical issues related to digital platforms but also focus on social issues such as institutional enablers and constraints that affect digital platform development, use and outcomes. The findings offer practical lessons on how institutions can facilitate or promote successful deployment and use of digital platforms for national health insurance. For policy, the study calls on developing country governments to create the appropriate institutional environment and frameworks to support digital platform development and use for health insurance and the public sector in general.

For future research, there is the possibility of uncovering other institutional enablers and constraints to enhance our understanding of digital platforms and their institutional environments. We encourage future research to explore how private health insurance develop and use digital platforms and the institutional factors that affect them.

References

1. Yoo, Y., Henfridsson, O., Lyytinen, K.: Research commentary—the new organizing logic of digital innovation: an agenda for information systems research. Inf. Syst. Res. **21**(4), 724–735 (2010)
2. Ashrafi, R., Murtaza, M.: Use and impact of ICT on SMEs in Oman. Electron. J. Inf. Syst. Eval. **11**(3), 125–138 (2008)
3. Sedera, D., Lokuge, S., Grover, V., Sarker, S., Sarker, S.: Innovating with enterprise systems and digital platforms: a contingent resource-based theory view. Inf. Manag. **53**(3), 366–379 (2016)
4. Williams, I.: Organizational readiness for innovation in health care: some lessons from the recent literature. Health Serv. Manag. Res. **24**(4), 213–218 (2011)
5. Petter, S., Delone, W., Mclean, E.R.: The past, present, and future of 'IS Success'. J. Assoc. Inf. Syst. **13**, 341–362 (2012). Special Issue
6. Nikayin, F., De Reuver, M., Itälä, T.: Collective action for a common service platform for independent living services. Int. J. Med. Inform. **82**(10), 922–939 (2013)
7. Vassilakopoulou, P., et al.: Building national ehealth platforms: the challenge of inclusiveness. In: ICIS 2017 Proceedings (2017)
8. Furstenau, D., Auschra, C.: Open digital platforms in health care: implementation and scaling strategies. In: Proceedings of the International Conference on Information Systems, Google 2011, pp. 1–12 (2016)
9. Scott, W.R.: Institutions and Organizations: Ideas Interests and Identities, 4th edn. SAGE, Los Angeles (2014)
10. Walsham, G.: Doing interpretive research. Eur. J. Inf. Syst. **15**(3), 320–330 (2006)
11. Constantinides, P., Henfridsson, O., Parker, G.G.: Platforms and infrastructures in the digital age. Inf. Syst. Res. **29**(2), 381–400 (2018)
12. Estrin, D., Sim, I.: Open mHealth architecture: an engine for health care innovation. Science **330**(6005), 759–760 (2010)
13. Eaton, B., Elaluf-Calderwood, S., Sørensen, C., Yoo, Y.: Distributed tuning of boundary resources: the case of Apple's iOS service system. MIS Q. **39**(1), 217–243 (2015)
14. Blaschke, M., Haki, K., Aier, S., Winter, R.: Taxonomy of digital platforms: a platform architecture perspective. In: 14th International Conference on Wirtschaftsinformatik, pp. 572–586 (2019)
15. Vargo, S., Lusch, R.: Evolving to a new dominant logic for marketing. J. Mark. **68**(1), 1–17 (2004)
16. Rye, C.B., Kimberly, J.R.: Review: the adoption of innovations by provider organizations in health care. Med. Care Res. Rev. **64**(3), 235–278 (2007)

17. Scott, R.: Institutional theory: contributing to a theoretical research program. In: Smith, K., Hitt, M. (eds.) Great Minds in Management: The Process of Theory Development. Oxford University Press, Oxford (2005)
18. Mignerat, M., Rivard, S.: Positioning the institutional perspective in information systems research. J. Inf. Technol. 24(4), 369–391 (2009)
19. Connolly, R., Gauzente, C., Dumoulin, R.: IT adoption in the public healthcare sector: an institutional research agenda. IADIS Int. J. Comput. Sci. Inf. Syst. 7(2), 101–116 (2012)
20. Effah, J.: Institutional effects on e-payment entrepreneurship in a developing country: enablers and constraints. Inf. Technol. Dev. 22(2), 205–219 (2016)
21. Orlikowski, W.J., Barley, S.: Technology and institutions: what can research on information technology and research on organizations learn from each other? MIS Q. 25(2), 145–165 (2001)
22. Walsham, G.: Interpretive case studies in IS research: nature and method. Eur. J. Inf. Syst. 4(2), 74–81 (1995)
23. Bygstad, B., Munkvold, B.E.: Exploring the role of informants in interpretive case study research in IS. J. Inf. Technol. 26, 32–45 (2011)
24. Schwartz-Shea, P., Yanow, D.: Interpretive Research Design-Concepts and Processes. Routledge, Abingdon (2014)
25. Miles, M.B., Huberman, A.M., Saldaña, J.: Qualitative Data Analysis: A Methods Sourcebook, 3rd edn. SAGE Publications Inc., Thousand Oaks (2014)
26. Klein, H.K., Myers, M.D.: A set of principles for conducting and evaluating interpretive field studies in information systems. MIS Q. 23(1), 67–93 (1999)
27. NHIA: Benefits Package (2018). http://www.nhis.gov.gh/benefits.aspx. Accessed 23 Dec 2018
28. Hurtta, K., Elie-Dit-Cosaque, C.: Digital innovation in public service ecosystem: enacting the generative affordance. In: 25th European Conference on Information Systems (ECIS 2017), vol. 2017, pp. 2744–2754 (2017)
29. Alhassan, R.K., Nketiah-Amponsah, E., Arhinful, D.K.: A review of the national health insurance scheme in Ghana: what are the sustainability threats and prospects? PLoS ONE 11(11), e0165151 (2016)
30. Duku, S.K.O., Nketiah-Amponsah, E., Janssens, W., Pradhan, M.: Perceptions of healthcare quality in Ghana: does health insurance status matter? PLoS ONE 13(1), 1–17 (2018)
31. Summers, M.J., et al.: The My Active and Healthy Aging (My-AHA) ICT platform to detect and prevent frailty in older adults: randomized control trial design and protocol. Alzheimer's Dement. Transl. Res. Clin. Interv. 4, 252–262 (2018)
32. Apau, R., Obeng, E., Darko, A.N.: An empirical evaluation of cashless systems implementation in Ghana. Int. J. Bus. Econ. Manag. 6(3), 159–173 (2019)
33. Karakara, A.A., Osabuohien, E.S.: Households' ICT access and bank patronage in West Africa: empirical insights from Burkina Faso and Ghana. Technol. Soc. 56, 116–125 (2019)
34. Effah, J.: Tracing the emergence and formation of small dot-corns in an emerging digital economy: an actor-network theory approach. University of Salford (2011)

Toward Employee-Driven Digital Innovation in Public Organizations Through the Use of Action Design Research

Leif Erik Opland[1(✉)], Letizia Jaccheri[1], Jostein Engesmo[1], and Ilias O. Pappas[1,2]

[1] Norwegian University of Science and Technology (NTNU), Trondheim, Norway
leif.e.opland@ntnu.no
[2] University of Agder, Kristiansand, Norway

Abstract. Innovation is important for development in the private sector, but inevitably public sector also needs innovation to enhance services and processes, with research on employee-driven digital innovation in public organizations being limited. We propose a study in a public organization based on action design research (ADR) methodology to enhance theoretical knowledge and develop practice in relation to employee-driven digital innovation. This research-in-progress study follows the divided stages of ADR, where the stage of problem formulation is to be conducted through semi-structured interviews. Findings from stage 1 will provide knowledge about the phenomenon with a public organization as a context and make up the problem definition within ADR. The stage of building, interventions and evaluation is to be conducted with interventions in focus groups where we will investigate how to increase adoption of employee-driven digital innovation and how introducing digital tools can support employee-driven digital innovation as an innovation practice. The study aims to contribute by creating general solution concepts about employee-driven digital innovation.

Keywords: Employee-driven innovation · Digital innovation · Employee-driven digital innovation · Public organization · Action design research

1 Introduction

To enhance innovation organizations have increasingly started to recognize the innovation potential their employees represent [1]. Employee-driven innovation is founded upon the argument that organizations cannot ignore the innovative resources and potential of ordinary employees [2]. This new approach to innovation, although the underlying elements are not new, has been attracting more interest in recent years [3]. Looking into the subject shows that most of the research in the quest to understand employee-driven digital innovation has been done towards private organizations. But there exist knowledge gaps to the understanding of the phenomenon with regard to public organizations, not at least in relation to digital innovation. This brings us to our research questions for our study:

The original version of this chapter was revised: the missing acknowledgements section has been added. The correction to this chapter is available at https://doi.org/10.1007/978-3-030-45002-1_40

R.Q.1: How do employee-driven digital innovation work in a public organization?
R.Q.2: How to increase employee-driven digital innovation in a public organization?
R.Q.3: How to introduce digital tools to support employee-driven digital innovation?

To address these research questions, we intend to use the ADR methodology [4]. One of the strengths of this research method is that it contributes both to building theoretical knowledge in the field being investigated as well as solving practical problems. In Sect. 2 we present a background on employee-driven digital innovation, in Sect. 3 we present details about the methodological approach, before presenting the expected contribution and potential further research in Sect. 4.

2   Background

Organizations, private as public, are increasingly facing global competition, ever-changing environments, new technology and more informed and demanding customers and users. Some researchers claim that organizations that are not interested in innovation to face the dynamic environments will apparently disappear [5]. Organizations seek to exploit the opportunities to innovate in pursuit of competitive advantages. Innovation is more than just a creation of an idea, it is also about idea-creation and idea-development (exploring), and how these can be utilized (exploited) through new product and service offerings [6]. Innovation in the public sector however is an area that has not been extensively studied before, and there is no common understanding of what innovation in public organizations is or developed a framework for understanding innovation within [7]. One reason for this might be the fundamental differences between public and private organizations that might affect their interest and ability to innovate, such as purpose and innovation focus. In recent years, several new approaches to innovation have emerged, including user-driven innovation and open innovation [8]. Lately we have also seen the emergence of employee-driven innovation [9]. The understanding of innovation, and how innovation develops in the organizations, is no longer limited to R&D units or experts. Innovation processes initiated by employees, and often in collaboration with the external ecosystem, are recognized. Because of these new approaches improved explanatory models are required to innovation.

Employee-driven innovation research concentrates on how organizations can create innovative practices among ordinary employees [10]. In employee-driven innovation, the focus is on utilizing the innovation potential that the organization has overall and, not least, the knowledge, skills and experience that the ordinary employees possess. Organizations increasingly recognize that innovation does not just happen exclusively through top-down decisions, internally by investing in R&D units or externally by pursuing open innovation or creating innovation hubs [11]. The core idea of employee-driven innovation is that by inciting cooperation between employees and managers, companies' innovation performance will improve greatly [1]. A bottom-up approach, like employee-driven innovation, might produce value to the organization by utilizing employee's knowledge, experience and ideas to provide continuous innovation. Changing environment and conditions in work life also underpin employee-driven innovation, as a growing number of innovations will be intangible and service oriented [12]. These changes, together with increasing focus on digital innovation, has created what we have chosen to call employee-driven digital innovation. Digital innovation can be understood as using digital technology during the process of innovation or that the outcome of the innovation is fully or partly digital [13]. When ordinary employees, through involvement in the innovation process, creating ideas and contributing to the realization of these, with elements of digital innovation, one can talk about employee-driven digital innovation. Despite the emerging interest in digital innovation, it emerges as a research area to the extent that it is not fully developed [14]. Digital innovation initiatives still need further theorization [14].

The need for more theorizing and understanding of employee-driven digital innovation also applies to the context of public organizations. Increasing focus on digital transformation has seen the rise of a new type of innovation which influences not only private but also public organizations [15]. Many have the misperception that the public sector does not engage in innovation practices, and at least not through the involvement of ordinary employees. However, the fact that public organizations do not have traditional R&D units, can emphasize the advantages employee-driven digital innovation can create [16]. Therefore, there seems to be a greater need to include these activities into the daily activities of these organizations. Knowledge is needed both in relation to the phenomenon in public organizations, and not at least how to make use of this way of practicing innovation throughout organizations.

3 Research Methodology

Within Information Systems research there is a consensus for the need to both make theoretical contributions and solve the current and anticipated problems addressed by practitioners [17, 18]. The field of Information Systems earlier relied on design research [19] and action research [20] to address these challenges. The emergence of ADR [4], as a variant of design science research [19], privileges organizational influences on the design and evolution of the design artifact, emphasizing concurrent building, intervention and evaluation [21]. In our study the aim is to both contribute to theory and practice, and to elucidate our research questions, we have chosen to use the methodology of ADR. ADR is a research method for generating prescriptive design knowledge through building and evaluating ensemble IT artifacts in an organizational setting [4]. This methodological approach deals with two seemingly disparate challenges: (1) addressing a problem situation encountered in a specific organizational setting by intervening and evaluating; and (2) constructing and evaluating an IT artifact that addresses the class of problems typified by the encountered situation [4]. Employee-driven digital innovation has knowledge gaps when it comes to application in public organizations. Our aim is to study employee-driven digital innovation through the use the ADR method in the context of a public organization (theoretical contribution) and increase the use of employee-driven digital innovation and implement digital tools to support the innovation practice (practical contribution).

We are studying employee-driven digital innovation in a large public organization with about 13000 employees. In this organization, there are several digital innovation projects that are already employee-driven, and they have an ambition to increase the impact of digital innovation through new and better services for their inhabitants. The management has expressed a desire to increase adoption of employee-driven digital innovation, as an innovation practice, to the whole organization. We therefore think that using ADR is an appropriate approach to the problem. Our research approach can be attributed to the four stages in the ADR methodology (Fig. 1). Through this approach we will be both gaining an understanding of the problem as well as generating interventions in the innovation practice and adoption and support of employee-driven digital innovation. According to [4] the ADR research method can be broken down into four different stages:

Problem formulation (problem perceived in practice or anticipated by researchers).
Building, Intervention, and Evaluation (building of artifact shaped by organizational use).
Reflection and Learning (continuous stage that parallels all stages).
Formalization of Learning (development of general solution concepts).

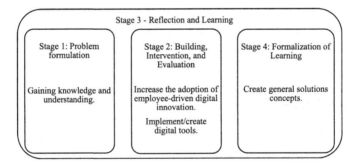

Fig. 1. Intended contribution of our research in relation to the stages in the ADR method.

Design science addresses research through the building and evaluation of artifacts designed to meet the identified business needs [20]. In our research design this is precisely what we are trying to do in stage one, before we in stage two try to solve the problem by increasing the prevalence of employee-driven digital innovation and the introduction of one or more digital artifacts to support innovation in the public organization. There are still uncertainties about how the ADR method is being used in practice [21]. This relates to two conflicts: (a) how to balance the competing interests of the organizational stakeholders and the research team, and (b) how to balance the situated implementation of the design artifact against the need to produce generalized knowledge outcomes.

3.1 Problem Formulation

At stage one in ADR our aim is to build knowledge about employee-driven digital innovation in the context of a public organization (Fig. 1). This is a diagnostic phase and contribute to the problem definition of employee-driven digital innovation. The problem formulation stage in ADR identifies and conceptualizes a research opportunity based on existing theories and technologies [4, 20]. Here we do that through the use of existing theory of employee-driven digital innovation. The data collection is done through the use of semi-structured interviews with respondents, including project leaders and project members, from three different ongoing employee-driven digital innovation projects. There will also be conducted semi-structured interviews with people holding other positions across the organization close to the different projects (support positions). These respondents both include the strategic level in the organization, as well as at the IT-department (programmers) who interact across the various digital innovation projects. This also gives us opportunities to compare between the different projects and increases the validity of the potential findings. This acquisition of knowledge will also be important when we face the stage of intervention later in the research design. These innovation projects are at different stages in the innovation process, which gives us different perspectives on the innovation process.

3.2   Building, Intervention and Evaluation

After building knowledge and framing the problem in relation to employee-driven digital innovation in this specific context, we will move on to stage two in the ADR methodology (Fig. 1). This stage consists of building, intervening and evaluating [4] around the construct of employee-driven digital innovation, and will be a therapeutic phase. This stage heavily rests upon the framing and theoretical premises adopted at stage one [4]. Through this stage we will build further knowledge about the phenomenon of employee-driven digital innovation and do interventions through the use of focus groups to increase adoption in parts of the organization that have not yet adopted and implemented the innovation practice. This stage will create knowledge about best practices of employee-driven digital innovation in public organizations that also can be used in stage four to create general solution concepts. The design of the model/construct/approach for how to increase the adoption of employee-driven digital innovation in the organization must be done in close collaboration with the employees and management of the organization. This also applies for introduction of digital tools to support this innovation practice. The outcome of stage two of the ADR is the realized design of the artifact [4]. This type of research is aimed at changing the organization's practice, and not just studying the phenomenon from an outside perspective [19]. There is also conceivable to apply iterations to the ADR method at stage one and two. This will give the possibilities of further developing knowledge and practices about adoption of employee-driven digital innovation in the organization and how introduction of digital tools to support it can be done [22]. This building of knowledge and practices will also contribute to the reflection and learning in stage three in the ADR method.

The ambition is to use the acquired knowledge through stage one and two to implement digital tools that can support the innovation process associated with employee-driven digital innovation in the public organization (Fig. 1), e.g. to gather innovative ideas, collaborating with development of ideas, seeing ideas through towards realization and so on. This may include utilizing existing artifacts in the organization, implementing new artifacts or developing customized artifacts for the organization. This also contributes to the building, intervention and evaluation in stage two in the ADR methodology [4]. This will be based on knowledge in relation to how employee-driven digital innovation takes place in this organization (stage one and two) and general theory of how organizations can be supported through the use of digital tools.

3.3 Formalization of Learning

At stage four the ambition is through knowledge and practical experience from all stages to formalize learning through the development of general solutions concepts [4] for employee-driven digital innovation that can be used across public organizations. This is based on the initial problem definition in stage one, the interventions in stage two and the continuous reflection and learning in stage three of ADR. Reflection and learning recognize that the research process involves more than just solving a problem [4]. Conscious reflection on the problem framing, the theories chosen, and the emerging ensemble is critical to ensure that contributions to knowledge are identified [4].

4 Expected Results, Conclusion and Further Research

This research-in-progress paper describes the intended research design for our study of employee-driven digital innovation in a public organization. Our main goal of the study is to increase the knowledge and understanding of employee-driven digital innovation in a public organization. There is reason to believe that employee-driven digital innovation in private and public organizations might have differences in terms of factors (e.g. innovation focus and tasks) affecting employees' willingness to participate in the innovation process. One of the reasons for this may be that innovation in public organizations is based on providing the best and most effective services to the citizens, while in private organizations it is based on innovating with a view to products and services that will maximize profits. These differences in basic assumptions in the organizations can influence how innovation processes are adopted, implemented and practiced, and not least the outcomes. It may also be that factors known as basis for creating employee-driven innovation in private organizations; as autonomy, organizations innovation focus, willingness to collaborate, etc., may appear different in the context of public organizations. We believe that using ADR, with the possibilities of numerous iterations at stage two, will give a better understanding of employee-driven digital innovation in a public organization, and provide the ability to create general solution concepts of how to increase adoption and digital supporting tools that are more applicable then the use of any other research methods.

Acknowledgements. This work has received funding from the European Union's Horizon 2020 research and innovation programme, under the Marie Sklodowska-Curie Grant Agreements No. 751510.

References

1. Hansen, K., Amundsen, O., Aasen, T.M.B., Gressgård, L.J.: Management practices for promoting employee-driven innovation. In: Oeij, P.R.A., Rus, D., Pot, F.D. (eds.) Workplace Innovation. APHSW, pp. 321–338. Springer, Cham (2017). https://doi.org/10. 1007/978-3-319-56333-6_19
2. Haapasaari, A., Engeström, Y., Kerosuo, H.: From initiatives to employee-driven innovations. Eur. J. Innov. Manag. 21(2), 206–226 (2018)
3. Høyrup, S.: Employee-driven innovation: a new phenomenon, concept and mode of innovation. In: Høyrup, S., Bonnafous-Boucher, M., Hasse, C., Lotz, M., Moller, K. (eds.) Employee-Driven Innovation. A New Approach, pp. 3–13. Palgrave Macmillan, New York (2012)
4. Sein, M.K., Henfridsson, O., Purao, S., Rossi, M., Lindgren, R.: Action design research. MIS Q. 35(1), 37–56 (2011)
5. Chesbrough, H.W.: Open Innovation: The New Imperative for Creating and Profiting from Technology. Harvard Business Press, Cambridge (2003)
6. Whittington, D.: Digital Innovation and Entrepreneurship. Cambridge University Press, Cambridge (2018)
7. Moussa, M., McMurray, A., Muenjohn, N.: A conceptual framework of the factors influencing innovation in public sector organizations. J. Dev. Areas 52(3), 231–240 (2018)
8. Gambardella, A., Raasch, C., von Hippel, E.: The user innovation paradigm: impacts on markets and welfare. Manag. Sci. 63(5), 1450–1468 (2017)
9. Kesting, P., Ulhøi, J.P.: Employee-driven innovation: extending the license to foster innovation. Manag. Decis. 48(1), 65–84 (2010)
10. Høyrup, S.: Employee-driven innovation and workplace learning: basic concepts, approaches and themes. Transfer 16(2), 143–154 (2010)
11. Birkinshaw, J., Duke, L.: Employee-led innovation. Bus. Strat. Rev. 24(2), 46–51 (2013)
12. Alasoini, T.: A new model for workplace development in Finland. Rethinking employee participation and the quality of working life in the context of broad-based innovation policy. Int. J. Action Res. 8(3), 245–265 (2012)
13. Nambisan, S., Lyytinen, K., Majchrzak, A., Song, M.: Digital innovation management: reinventing innovation management research in a digital world. MIS Q. 41(1), 223–228 (2017)
14. Holmstrøm, J.: Recombination in digital innovation: challenges, opportunities, and the importance of a theoretical framework. Inf. Organ. 28, 107–110 (2018)
15. Janowski, T.: Digital government evolution: from transformation to contextualization. Gov. Inf. Q. 32(3), 221–236 (2015)
16. Bäckström, I., Bengtsson, L.: A mapping study of employee innovation: proposing a research agenda. Eur. J. Innov. Manag. 22(3), 468–492 (2019)
17. Rosemann, M., Vessey, I.: Toward Improving the relevance of information systems research to practice: the role of applicability checks. MIS Q. 32(1), 1–22 (2008)
18. Cole, R., Purao, S., Rossi, M., Sein, M.: Being proactive: where action research meets design research. In: Proceedings International Conference on Information Systems (ICIS) (2005)
19. Baskerville, R., Myers, M.D.: Making IS research relevant to practice-foreword. MIS Q. 28 (3), 329–335 (2004)
20. Hevner, A.R., March, S.T., Park, J., Ram, S.: Design science in information systems research. MIS Q. 28(1), 75–105 (2004)
21. Haj-Bolouri, A., Purao, S., Rossi, M., Bernhardsson, L.: Action design research in practice: lessons and concerns. In: Proceedings European Conference on Information Systems (ECIS) (2018)
22. Mullarkey, M.T., Hevner, A.R.: An elaborated action design research process model. Eur. J. Inf. Syst. 28(1), 6–20 (2018)

A Systematic Review of Implementation Challenges in Public E-Procurement

Idah Mohungoo, Irwin Brown(⊠), and Salah Kabanda(⊠)

Department of Information System, University of Cape Town,
Private Bag X3, Rondebosch 7701, South Africa
imohungoo@hotmail.co.uk,
{irwin.brown, salah.kabanda}@uct.ac.za

Abstract. Challenges faced in public e-procurement implementation are not well understood despite past studies focusing on the phenomenon. This paper, which is based on a systematic literature review of academic papers, seeks to synthesize and examine the key challenges impeding public e-procurement implementation. These challenges are categorized using the Technology-Organization-Environment (TOE) framework as follows (1) Technological challenges: e-procurement acceptance and usage, disruptive innovation characteristic of e-procurement, use of digital signatures, security and privacy of technology and technical aspects of e-procurement (2) Organizational challenges: stakeholders' behavior, leaders' behavior, shortcomings in leadership, lack of training and skilled personnel, resistance to change, organizational power and politics and the creation of public value underlying e-procurement (3) Environmental/Contextual challenges: regulatory framework for public procurement, Small-and-Medium-Size Enterprise issues, and context of the country. Key e-procurement implementation challenges are grounded in human and contextual issues. So we recommend more case studies on public e-procurement implementation in the future.

Keywords: Public e-procurement · Implementation challenges · TOE

1 Introduction

Public e-procurement, commonly referred to as e-GP, is an inter-organizational system (IOS) that is intended to facilitate Government-to-Business (G2B) and Government-Government (G2G) electronic communication, information exchange, and transaction support [53]. E-procurement, which is part of public procurement reform, is a powerful tool to reduce corruption in public procurement as it reinforces transparency, accountability, and integrity in procurement functions [38]. Several developed countries such as Singapore, Australia, the UK, the USA, and Japan have successfully implemented public e-procurement systems and are reaping its benefits [37]. However, in many countries, the implementation of public e-procurement systems is perceived as daunting [9, 16, 18, 34, 37, 52] and it is not used to its full potential.

Sub-Saharan African countries, which on average have low scores on the corruption perception index [51], have expressed enthusiasm and interest in adopting

M. Hattingh et al. (Eds.): I3E 2020, LNCS 12067, pp. 46–58, 2020.
https://doi.org/10.1007/978-3-030-45002-1_5

e-procurement to help to curb corruption and make significant economic impacts. However, these countries face several e-procurement implementation challenges, which if not addressed, can firstly, delay the implementation process which has cost implications and; secondly, motivated leaders can lose interest and enthusiasm in driving implementation if there are too many challenges to be addressed.

Given that public e-procurement implementation is still problematic implies that implementation challenges of public e-procurement have not been well understood to date. To this end, this paper aims to provide an in-depth examination and synthesis from an information system (IS) perspective of the challenges to public e-procurement implementation using a sequentially-phased qualitative systematic literature review approach as informed by Okoli [39]. The research question, *"What are the imple-mentation challenges to public e-procurement?"* will thus be addressed.

2 Conceptual Background

Public e-procurement implementation is a complex endeavour characterized by multiple Government-to-Business organizations (G2B), and private sector companies. These stakeholders have interests and power that can influence the outcome of the Inter-Organizational Information System (IOIS) implementation [9]. Under the assumption of information system (IS) as a socio-technical endeavour, the interplay between the implementation of e-procurement and the public-private sector context is deemed to be challenging [55]. These implementation challenges should be understood in order to formulate effective strategies to contain them. Furthermore, unlike e-procurement in the private sector context, public e-procurement is expected to reflect public values such as accountability and transparency.

Public e-procurement can be understood as a hybrid of e-government, information systems, and public administration. Thus, it is highly likely that e-procurement chal-lenges are documented in papers published in these different domains. So far, there is a lack of an integrated approach to the synthesis of e-procurement implementation challenges; and when there is an attempt to do so, it is carried out in a rather fragmented manner. Researchers have seldom stepped outside a specific discipline in e-procurement literature reviews. For example, Patrucco [43] undertook a systematic literature review on public e-procurement, focusing only on papers published in the Journal of Public Procurement. While this provides an initial view of e-procurement, such studies fail to provide a holistic view of the phenomenon given that e-procurement spans works in e-government, information systems, and public administration. To address this short-coming, this paper offers a systematic approach to synthesizing e-procurement imple-mentation challenges by including publications from the three domains mentioned above. The Technology-Organizational-Environment (TOE) framework [50] which is popular in studies of adoption and implementation of innovations, will be used to present the e-procurement implementation challenges. The TOE framework [50] allows the identification of the main factors influencing the adoption and implementation of innovations within different organizational contexts and therefore serves a good starting point for structuring the study – specifically the identification of technological, orga-nizational and environmental challenges constraining e-procurement implementation.

3 Research Methodology

3.1 Research Approach

A sequentially-phased, qualitative systematic literature review approach informed by Okoli [39] is used in this paper. It is characterized by a sequence of activities starting with article search, followed by practical screening, a full reading of papers, synthesis, and analysis.

3.2 Data Collection

A Desktop search of relevant articles was systematically done using a timeline from 2001 to date. Based on Google Scholar, the earliest case studies on public e-procurement were published around the year 2001. Data collection was focused consistently around the aim of the research, and the keywords used were specific to the goal of the study, as shown in Fig. 1, which depicts the different systematic passes used in the search and selection of relevant articles:

1. *The first pass*: articles were searched and selected from top-rated journals in the streams of information systems, e-government, and public administration, e.g.:
   - Basket of eight leading Information Systems (IS) journals: European Journal of Information Systems, Information Systems Journal, Information Systems Research, Journal of Association of Information Systems, Journal of Management Information System, MIS Quarterly, Journal of Strategic Information Systems and Journal of Information Technology.
   - Given that in several developing countries including those in Africa, e-procurement implementation is an important issue, the top 3 IT4D journals, i.e., Electronic Journal of Information System in Developing Countries (EJISDC), IT for Development and IT for International Development were also searched.
   - IS conference proceedings focusing on emerging e-procurement implementation challenges that are found in research-in-progress in the respective afore-mentioned streams. The AIS top 4 conferences (ICIS, ECIS, PACIS, and AMCIS) were searched as well as IFIP conferences.
   - Leading top-rated e-government journals consulted were: International Journal of E-Government Research (IJEGR), Journal of E-Government, Journal of e-Governance, Government Information Quarterly
   - In public administration stream: the Journal of Public Administration and Public Administration Review were searched.
2. *The second pass* was a backward search after the initial search yielded few papers. The purpose of the second pass was to look for additional relevant conference papers and journal articles in other domains.
3. *The third pass* involved searching for adoption-focused e-procurement papers that were previously eliminated in the first-pass. This pass increased the likelihood of gathering additional secondary data on implementation challenges of e-procurement because some adoption-focused papers were case studies of post-acquisition of

e-procurement software and thus were likely to contain facts on e-procurement implementation challenges.

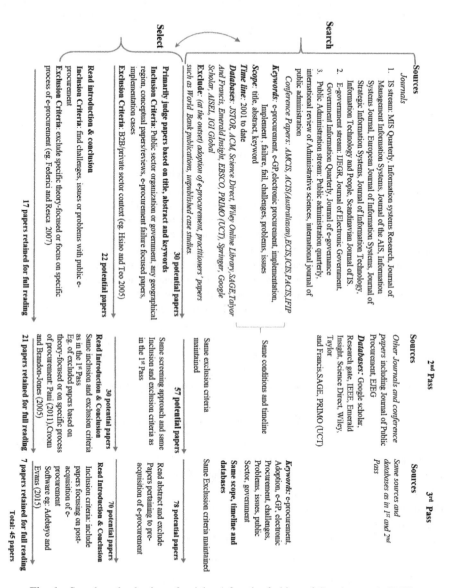

Fig. 1. Search and selection of articles (after the fashion of Gunther et al. 2017)

3.3   Analysis

The data corpus, which now stood at 165 articles after the previous process, was subjected to a 'Practical Screening' phase to remove irrelevant articles [39] using a process of inclusion and exclusion criteria. This process required the principal researcher reading the article's Title, Abstract, Introduction, and Conclusion, as explained in Table 1. Following the screening, 45 papers were retained for full reading and 34 for the final analysis as shown in Table 2. After this analysis process, relevant arguments that explain the implementation challenges faced in e-procurement implementation were extracted from the 34 papers. The key arguments were then subjected to thematic analysis in NVIVO. Emergent themes generated from common patterns in the data corpus are shown in Table 3. These themes were then structured as per the TOE framework [50] for easier conceptualization.

Table 1. Screening of papers – exclusion criteria

Exclusion criteria	Rationale underlying exclusion	Exclusion[a]
B2B/private sector	The study focused only on public e-procurement	[31]
E-procurement adoption focused research	All e-procurement adoption papers focusing on pre-acquisition of the software were excluded because, in this study, implementation is understood as a stage of post-acquisition of the software	[8]
E-procurement research papers with theory-focused or with focus on a specific process of e-procurement	(1) Articles that focus on a specific theory were discarded, for example, the economic aspects of e-procurement, use of knowledge management approach to understand e-procurement implementation and issues, evidence of good governance in public e-procurement (2) Articles focusing in detail on a specific process or aspect of e-procurement such as reverse auctions were also excluded	[14, 22], [42, 48] [12]

[a]Examples of papers that are excluded as part of the screening process

Table 2. Breakdown of selected articles by publication outlet

Journals	Read[a]	Retained
AIS basket of eight leading IS journals (MISQ, ISR, JMIS, JAIS, ISJ, JSIS, EJIS JIT); ICT4D Top 3 (EJISDC, IT4D and ITID)	4	2
Information Technology & People	1	1
Electronic Commerce Research	1	0
Scandinavian Journal of Information Systems	2	2
Journal of Information Technology Teaching Cases	1	1
IFIP Advances in IS Research, Education and Practice Proceedings	1	1
Information Systems Frontiers	1	1
Management and Labour Studies	1	0
Electronic Journal of Electronic Government	2	1
Journal of Public Procurement	5	4
Public Administration Quarterly	1	1
Emerging Markets Finance and Trade	1	1

(continued)

Table 2. (*continued*)

Journals	Read[a]	Retained
International Review of Administrative Sciences	1	1
International Journal of Public Administration	2	2
Journal of Purchasing and Supply and Management	1	1
International Journal of Production and Operations Management	1	1
Journal of Enterprise Information Management	1	0
Strategic Change	1	1
AIS Conference Proceedings (ICIS, ECIS, PACIS, AMCIS)	5	4
Other Conference proceedings and papers	8	6
Vikalpa: Journal for Decision Makers	1	1
Advances in e-Government, Digital Divide & Regional Development	3	2
	45	34

[a]Full length paper read

Table 3. Empirical findings of public e-procurement implementation challenges

	Implementation challenges	Authors
Technological	Acceptance and usage issues	[3, 5, 7, 9, 16, 20, 24, 33, 37, 55]
	Disruptive nature of e-procurement	[4, 35]
	Digital/Electronic signature	[17, 40]
	IT security issues	[23, 37, 46, 52]
	Complicated system	[34]
	Multi-platform	[5, 17]
	Lack of system integration	[2, 16, 17, 23, 34, 36, 46, 47]
	Shortcomings in online product catalogue	[16, 34]
	Challenges for software specifications	[46]
	Inadequate IT & networking infrastructure	[2, 46]
Organizational	Stakeholders' issues	[15, 33, 36]
	Leaders' behavior	[56]
	Shortcomings in leadership	[24, 34, 36]
	Change management problems	[1, 24]
	Lack of a project champion	[56]
	Lack of training and skilled personnel	[17, 24, 30, 34, 46, 52]
	Resistance to change	[2, 5, 16, 28, 53, 56]
	Slow-to-change culture	[6, 36]
	Departmentalism	[6]
	Major reforms through ICT	[36, 45]
	Value-driven outcome	[6, 37, 53]
Environmental	Regulatory frameworks	[21, 29, 57]
	SME issues	[3, 17, 24, 36, 41, 54, 55]
	Country context	[46, 54, 56]

4 Findings and Discussion

4.1 Technological Challenges

Key technological challenges that deserve due attention given that they are tied with human and contextual issues are acceptance and usage issues, disruptive innovation, digital signature, and IT security issues. The remaining ones pertain to the technical aspects of e-procurement, and they are grouped as 'other technological challenges' in the discussion below.

Acceptance and Usage Issues. The findings indicate that acceptance and usage is an important challenge for e-procurement. The reasons were vast, ranging from techno-centric issues to broader dimensions such as dissatisfaction with e-procurement systems that do not meet the needs of users with the consequence of emergence of multiple workarounds [37]; Lack of user-friendliness of e-procurement [5, 34]; Complicated systems [5, 20]; Inability to enlist sufficient suppliers in a timely manner to encourage IS use [53]; The use of technology which is in tension with cultural histories of IT usage, bureaucratic processes and business practices [55].

Disruptive Innovation. E-procurement is viewed as a disruptive innovation [4, 35] that can drive a radical transformation, thereby uprooting some institutionalized work practices. It may conflict with the slow-to-change culture of G2G stakeholders of e-procurement [36].

Digital Signature/Electronic Signature. Costa, Arantes, and Tavarez [17] found that digital signature, which is mandatory for e-procurement, is complex to use and is costly, whereas Ojha and Pandey [40] found that the digital signature is a means of excessive security on e-procurement causing exclusion of some suppliers. Beyond these techno-centric aspects, the use of digital or electronic signatures can directly clash with the stakeholders' values, beliefs, and customs associated with manuscript signatures [49].

IT Security issues. Mc cue Roman [37] found that IT security and authenticity was the major challenge in e-procurement as stakeholders had concerns and demanded more re-assurance with regards to the robustness of the security aspect of the e-procurement platform in terms of IT security measures implemented for access control, backup and recovery [22].

Other Technological Challenges. Other technological challenges include amongst others, system integration problems with legacy and suppliers' systems, which is an important technical issue and is underpinned by the use of different enterprise software systems to handle each stage of the procurement cycle [2, 34]; the presence of multi-platforms for tendering which confuse bidders [5]; excessively complicated systems and; different data formats [5, 17].

4.2   Organizational Challenges

Organizational issues in e-procurement implementation are interlinked. Lack of a project champion and problems of change management are associated with short-comings in leadership. Resistance to change is explained alongside other challenges, including departmentalism, major reform through ICT and organizational power and politics.

Stakeholders' Issues. Drawing from e-government studies, scholars advocated the importance of sustained engagement of stakeholders in e-government implementation to enhance IS acceptance [13]. The review findings indicate a lack of stakeholder engagement in e-procurement implementation [15, 33, 36]. Scholars advised imple-menters to convince stakeholders to get their buy-in to improve IS usage [15, 34, 52].

Leaders' Behavior. Williams-Elegbe [56] argues that public sector leaders often exhibit unethical behaviours which can hamper the implementation of e-procurement. Leaders' behavior was associated with the failure of past e-government projects [25, 28]. Some leaders played overt rationality whilst having buried agendas [18], and obfuscated the objectives behind e-government to achieve their interests [44].

Shortcomings in Leadership. In some cases, public sector leaders are genuinely committed to achieving success in e-procurement implementation, but they may lack leadership skills [24, 34] to address change management problems [1, 24], and become good project champions which is a critical success factor in any e-government implementation [56].

Lack of Training and Skilled Personnel. Inadequate staff training on e-procurement results in low e-procurement usage ([17, 24, 34]). Furthermore, lack of skilled ICT personnel on-site to deal with technical e-procurement issues, service-level agreements, and operationalization of the private-public partnership model of e-procurement imple-mentation are serious impediments to e-procurement implementation ([30, 40, 46]).

Resistance to Change. Resistance to change is a significant e-procurement imple-mentation challenge with multiple underlying causes. Small and Medium Enterprises (SMEs) resist to e-procurement because they require equitable access to government business [55]. Besides, the reforms driven through e-government projects often conflict with reforms prescribed in public policies which follow the New Public Management (NPM): Somasundaram [46] found that centralization ideas underlying e-procurement, conflicted with the decentralization ideology [46] which challenged the norms of Danish local authorities; while Barca and Cordella [6] found that e-procurement faces departmentalism challenges which are perceived as a strong cultural and organizational barrier [6]. Resistance to change is also grounded in organizational power and politics [2] that shadowed the benefits of e-procurement: purchase managers were unwilling to use e-procurement despite agreeing with the economic arguments of cost-saving, and reduction of direct procurement costs related to the new e-procurement platform [29].

Value-Driven Outcome. Unlike the private sector, implementation of public e-procurement is expected to reflect public values of transparency, integrity, and accountability [6, 37, 53]. If the government expects e-procurement to enforce accountability and transparency for good governance, implementation will be called a success when stakeholders make sense of these public values and embrace them, which is indeed challenging to achieve.

4.3   Environmental Challenges

E-procurement implementation yielded different outcomes in different countries, with varying success in Italy, Australia and, Scotland [55] but failure in Turkey whereby expected results of increased competition and lower procurement prices were not achieved [27]. Regulatory frameworks, SME issues, and the country context are among the key environmental challenges that have been found as relevant in this review.

Regulatory Framework. Public procurement regulatory frameworks may present significant challenges in e-procurement implementation [21, 29, 57], the most pertinent ones being the mandated use of e-procurement; and the laws governing the use of digital signatures which limits the participation of SMEs in government bids.

SME Issues. The difficulties that SMEs face with respect to e-procurement and public procurement process are amongst others: exclusion of SMEs [17, 54]; SME lack of investment in ICT infrastructure [3, 27]; lack of financial capabilities and contract guarantees as needed by government procurement; insufficient competence in terms of standards and technical qualifications set by the market [41]. The business context of a country, therefore, poses a challenge to the success of e-procurement implementation especially if SMEs make a substantial contribution to the GDP. In Turkey, exclusion of SMEs negatively affected competition in the market and caused a rise in prices which ran contrary to the proclaimed expectations from public e-procurement implementation [27].

Country Context. The federal-state dynamic, especially in big countries has been found to be a key challenge for e-procurement [46], whereby the best practices underlying the success of e-procurement in a specific state were not replicated to other states as it could compromise the degree of autonomy of the other states. Considering cultural challenges, some developing countries continue with corrupt practices despite e-procurement because corruption has become entrenched in the culture. Overt and covert corruption has become the norm in these countries [56]. It is challenging to achieve the expected objectives of e-procurement, i.e., transparency, accountability and curbing corruption.

Other Country-Related Challenges. E-procurement which is a G2B e-government project and is based on e-commerce technology, faces similar country-context challenges of e-government implementation in developing countries such as poor ICT infrastructure, language barriers, impact of local customs, norms and national culture, lack of financial instruments such as debit/credit card to facilitate e-commerce [11, 32]. These contextual challenges are beyond the scope of this review but are directly relevant to e-procurement.

The key e-procurement implementation challenges are interlinked, as presented under the TOE typology [50] in Fig. 2. The arrows indicate the relationship between the key challenges identified and discussed in this study.

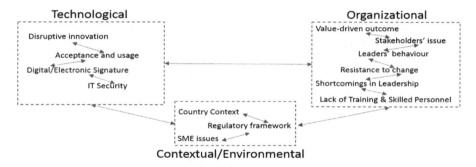

Fig. 2. Inter-relationship of key e-procurement implementation challenges

5 Conclusion

This study aimed to synthesize and examine the implementation challenges to public e-procurement. A multi-disciplinary qualitative systematic literature review was done based on papers published in the e-government, information systems and public administration domains. The study identified (1) technological challenges of acceptance and usage, e-procurement as a disruptive innovation and technical issues with e-procurement; (2) organizational challenges of stakeholders' issues, leadership, inadequate training, and skilled personnel, resistance to change and value-driven outcome and (3) key environmental factors of procurement regulatory framework, the country context and, the problems faced by SMEs. These findings enlighten practitioners and policy implementors with information on the possible hindrances to successful e-procurement implementation. Building upon this awareness, future studies can embark on explaining the causal mechanism of these challenges and how best to address them in a context-specific manner. This research work focused on e-procurement implementation challenges as a whole and excluded challenges pertaining to specific e-procurement processes such as e-tendering and e-reverse auction. The proposed framework in this paper can be used in future case studies to examine e-procurement implementation challenges under each focus area of the TOE [50] and their relationship.

References

1. Al-Moalla, A., Li, D.: Organisational issues with electronic government procurement - a case study of the UAE. EJISDC **41**(3), 1–18 (2010)
2. Adebayo, V.O., Evans, R.D.: Adoption of E-procurement systems in developing countries: a Nigerian public sector perspective. In: 2nd International Conference on Knowledge-Based Engineering and Innovation. IEEE, Tehran, pp. 356–376 (2015)
3. Alomar, M.A., Visscher, C.: E-public procurement: which factors determine its acceptance by small to medium-sized enterprises and large companies in Belgium? Int. Rev. Adm. Sci. **85**(2), 356–376 (2017)
4. Barahona, J.C., Elizondo, A.M.: The Disruptive innovation theory applied to national implementations of E-procurement. EJEG **10**(2), 107–119 (2012)

5. Barahona, J.C., Elizondo, A., Santos, M.: The dilemma of public E-procurement in Costa Rica: case on the duality of technological platforms and implementation models. J. Inf. Technol. Teach. Cases **5**(2), 57–64 (2015)

6. Barca, C., Cordella, A.: Seconds out, round two: contextualising e-government projects within their institutional Milieu—a London local authority case study. Scand. J. Inf. Syst. **18**(2), 5 (2004)

7. Brandon-Jones, A., Kauppi, K.: Examining the antecedents of the technology acceptance model within E-procurement. Int. J. Oper. Prod. Manag. **38**(1), 22–42 (2018)

8. Bof, F., Previtali, P.: Organisational pre-conditions for E-procurement in governments: the Italian experience in the public health care sector. EJEG **5**(1), 1–10 (2007)

9. Bromberg, D., Manoharan, A.: E-procurement implementation in the US – Understanding progress in Local Government. Public administration Quarterly **39**(3), 360–392 (2015)

10. Boonstra, A., Vires, J.D.: Managing stakeholders around inter-organizational systems: a diagnostic approach. J. Strat. Inf. Syst. **17**, 190–201 (2008)

11. Bwalya, K.J., Mutula, S.: A conceptual framework for e-government development in resource-constrained countries: the case of Zambia. Inf. Dev. **32**(4), 1183–1198 (2016)

12. Cabral, L., Ferreira, L., Dias, G.P.: Adoption of reverse auctions in public E-procurement: the case of Portugal. In: 11th Iberian Conference (CISTI), pp. 1–5. IEEE, Las Palmas (2016)

13. Chan, C.M.L., Pan, S.L.: User engagement in e-government systems implementation: a comparative case study of two Singaporean e-government initiatives. J. Strat. Inf. Syst. **17**, 124–139 (2008)

14. Croom, S.R., Brandon-Jones, A.: Key issues in E-procurement: procurement implementation and operation in the public sector. J. Public Procure. **5**(3), 367–387 (2005)

15. Chomchaiya, S., Esichaikul, S.: Consolidated performance measurement framework for government E-procurement focusing on internal stakeholders. Inf. Technol. People **29**(2), 354–380 (2016)

16. Croom, S., Brandon-Jones, A.: Impact of eprocurement: experiences from implementation in the UK public sector. J. Purch. Supply Manag. **13**(4), 294–303 (2007)

17. Costa, A., Arantes, A., Tavares, L.: Evidence of the impacts of public E-procurement: the Portuguese experience. J. Purch. Supply Manag. **19**, 238–246 (2018)

18. De', R., Sarkar, S.: Rituals in E-Government implementation: an analysis of failure. In: Wimmer, M.A., Chappelet, J.-L., Janssen, M., Scholl, Hans J. (eds.) EGOV 2010. LNCS, vol. 6228, pp. 226–237. Springer, Heidelberg (2010). https://doi.org/10.1007/978-3-642-14799-9_20

19. Elbanna, A.: From intention to use to actual rejection: the journey of an E-procurement system. J. Enterp. Inf. Manag. **23**(1), 81–99 (2010)

20. Engstrom, A., Wallstrom, A., Sangari, E.: Implementation of public E-procurement in Swedish government entities. In: Proceedings of the IMCSIT, pp 315–319 (2009)

21. Faridian, P.: Innovation in public management: is public eprocurement a wave of the future? A theoretical and exploratory analysis. Int. J. Public Adm. **38**(9), 654–662 (2015)

22. Federici, T.R., Resca, A.: Managing a widespread E-procurement implementation in public healthcare. In: MCIS 2007 Proceedings, vol. 5. MCIS, Italy (2007)

23. Fedorowicz, J., Gelinas, U., Gogan, J., Williams, C.: E-Government, E-Procurement, and E-Payments: data sharing issues associated with an appreciating database. In: AMCIS 2004 Proceedings, vol. 137. AMCIS, New York (2004)

24. Gasco, M., Cucciniello, M., Nasi, G.: Determinants and barriers of E-procurement: a European comparison of public sector experiences. In: Proceedings of the 51st Hawaii International Conference on System Sciences (2018)

25. Goldfinch, S.: Pessimism, computer failure, and information systems development in the public sector. Public Adm. Rev. **67**, 917–929 (2007)

26. Günther, W.A., Mehrizi, M.H.R., Huysman, M., Feldberg, F.: Debating big data: a literature review on realizing value from big data. J. Strat. Inf. Syst. **26**(3), 191–209 (2017)
27. Gurakar, E.C., Tas, B.D.: Does public E-procurement deliver what it promises? Empirical evidence from Turkey. Emerg. Mark. Finance Trade **52**(11), 2669–2684 (2016)
28. Heeks, R.: Information systems and developing countries: failure, success and local improvisations. Inf. Soc. **18**(2), 101–112 (2002)
29. Henriksen, H.Z., Mahnke, V.: E-procurement adoption in the Danish public sector: the influence of economic and political rationality. Scand. J. Inf. Syst. **17**(2), 85–106 (2005)
30. Hashim, R., Mazuki, M.A.: Electronic procurement (E-procurement) implementation in municipalities: lessons learned. In: E-procurement Management for Successful Electronic Government System, pp. 220–238. IGI-Global (2013)
31. Hsiao, R.L., Teo, T.: Delivering on the promise of E-procurement. MIS Q. Exec. **4**(3), 4 (2005)
32. Kabanda, S., Brown, I.: E-commerce enablers and barriers in Tanzanian small and medium enterprises. EJISDC **67**(7), 1024 (2015)
33. Kaliannan, M., Raman, M., Dorasamy, M.: E-procurement adoption in the Malaysian public sector: organizational perspectives. In: 13th Enterprise Distributed Object Computing Conference Workshops, Auckland, pp. 189–194 (2009)
34. Krogstie, J.: Introduction of a public sector E-procurement solution: lessons learned from disappointing adoption. In: Avison, D., Kasper, G.M., Pernici, B., Ramos, I., Roode, D. (eds.) Advances in Information Systems Research, Education and Practice. ITIFIP, vol. 274, pp. 203–214. Springer, Boston, MA (2008). https://doi.org/10.1007/978-0-387-09682-7-9_17
35. Lyytinen, K., Rose, G.: The disruptive nature of information technology innovations: the case of Internet computing in systems development organizations. MIS Q. **27**(4) (2003)
36. MacManus, S.A.: Understanding the incremental nature of E-procurement implementation at the state and local levels. J. Public Procure. **2**(1), 5–28 (2003)
37. McCue, C., Roman, V.: E-procurement: myth or reality? J. Public Procure. **12**(2), 221–248 (2012)
38. Neupane, A., Soar, J., Vaidya, K.: An empirical evaluation of the potential of public E-procurement to reduce corruption. AJIS **18**, 21–44 (2014)
39. Okoli, C.: A guide to conducting a standalone systematic literature review. Commun. Assoc. Inf. Syst. **37** (2015)
40. Ojha, S., Pandey, I.M.: E-procurement project in Karnataka: a case of public private partnership. Vikalpa **39**, 113–118 (2014)
41. Ortuzar, G.B., Sevillano, E., Castro, C., Uribe, C.: Challenges in Chilean E-procurement system: a critical review. In: Digital Governance and E-Government Principles Applied to Public Procurement, pp. 170–190. IGI Global (2017)
42. Pani, M.R., Agrahari, A., De, S.K.: Literature review and research issues in E-procurement. Manag. Labour Stud. **36**(3), 225–246 (2011)
43. Patrucco, A.S., Luzzini, D., Ronchi, S., Essig, M., Amman, M., Glas, A.: Research perspectives on public procurement: content analysis of 14 years of publications in the journal of public procurement. J. Public Procure. **17**(2), 229–269 (2017)
44. Quinta, N.N., Islam, S.: Challenges to the successful implementation of e-government initiatives in sub-Saharan Africa: a literature review. EJEG **11**(2), 253 (2013)
45. Somasundaram, R.: Diffusion of eprocurement in the public sector - revisiting centralization versus decentralisation, debates as a twist in the tale. In: ECIS Proceedings, Turku, Finland, pp. 1546–1556. ECIS (2004)
46. Somasundaram, R.: Challenges in implementation of E-procurement in the indian government. In: Ari-Veikko, A. (eds.) Electronic Government: Concepts, Methodologies, Tools, and Applications, pp. 2106–2121. IGI Global (2008)

47. Scriven, G.: Interoperability in Australian government E-procurement - strategy versus reality. In: 7th PACIS 2003 Proceedings, pp. 1436–1454. PACIS, Adelaide (2003)

48. Siriluck, R.: Critical governance concerns of Thailand e-government procurement. In: CONF-IRM 2012 Proceedings, vol. 52 (2012)

49. Srivastava, A.: Resistance to change: six reasons why businesses don't use e-signatures. J. Electron. Commer. Res. 11(4), 357–382 (2011)

50. Tornatzky, L.G., Fleischer, M., Chakrabarti, A.K.: The process of Technological Innovation. Lexington Books (1990)

51. Transparency International (2018). https://www.transparency.org/news/feature/cpi2018-sub saharan-africa-regional-analysis. Accessed 10 Mar 2019

52. Vaidya, K., Sajeev, A., Callender, G.: Critical factors that influence E-procurement implementation success in the public sector. J. Public Procure. 6(1), 70–99 (2006)

53. Vaidya, K., Campbell, J.: Multidisciplinary approach to defining public E-procurement and evaluating its impact on procurement efficiency. Inf. Syst. Front. 18, 333–348 (2016)

54. Walker, H., Brammer, S.: The relationship between sustainable procurement and E-procurement in the public sector. Int. J. Prod. Econ. 140, 256–268 (2012)

55. Williams, S., Hardy, C.: Public E-procurement as socio-technical change. Strat. Change 14, 273–281 (2005)

56. Williams-Elegbe, S.: Beyond uncitral: the challenges of procurement reform implementation in africa. Stellenbosch Law Rev. 25(1), 209–224 (2014)

57. Wirtz, B., Lütje, S., Schierz, P.G.: An empirical analysis of the acceptance of E-procurement in the german public sector. Int. J. Public Adm. 33(1), 26–42 (2009)

eHealth

Barriers for User Acceptance of Mobile Health Applications for Diabetic Patients: Applying the UTAUT Model

Fazlyn Petersen$^{(\boxtimes)}$ ⓘ, Mariam Jacobs ⓘ, and Shaun Pather ⓘ

University of the Western Cape, Bellville, South Africa
{fapetersen, spather}@uwc.ac.za, 3462668@myuwc.ac.za

Abstract. The literature illustrates that technology will widen health disparity if its use is restricted to patients who are already motivated and demonstrate good self-management behaviours. Additionally, despite the availability of free mobile health (m-health) applications for diabetes self-management, usage is low. There are also limited studies of m-health acceptance in South Africa. This research is delineated to the Western Cape, South Africa. The populace suffers from increasing numbers of diabetic patients. Segments of the population also suffer from technological forms of exclusion, such as limited internet access. Therefore, the objective of this study was to identify challenges for user acceptance that discourages the use of m-health applications. This study analysed 130 semi-structured interviews, using thematic content analysis. Respondents were predominantly female with type 2 diabetes, older than 50, residing in the Western Cape. It used key constructs from the Unified Theory of Acceptance and Use of Technology (UTAUT) model. The results confirmed that all four UTAUT constructs; performance expectancy ("the degree to which an individual believes that using the system will help him or her to attain gains in performance"), effort expectancy ("the degree of ease associated with the use of the system", social influence ("the degree to which an individual perceives that important others believe he or she should use the new system") and facilitating conditions ("the degree to which an individual believes that an organisational and technical infrastructure exists to support the use of the system"), explains the challenges for m-health acceptance in low socio-economic areas. Factors such as technology anxiety, resistance to change and a lack of trust in the use of devices for self-management need to be considered when implementing future interventions.

Keywords: Unified Theory of Acceptance and Use of Technology (UTAUT) · Challenges for user acceptance · Mobile health (m-health) · Diabetes self-management · Low socio-economic areas · South Africa

1 Introduction

The use of technology is warranted due to the increasing number of patients with diabetes, especially in Low- and Middle-Income Countries (LMIC). Diabetes is the leading cause of mortality, of which 80% of deaths occur in LMIC [1]. Many of the

© IFIP International Federation for Information Processing 2020
Published by Springer Nature Switzerland AG 2020
M. Hattingh et al. (Eds.): I3E 2020, LNCS 12067, pp. 61–72, 2020.
https://doi.org/10.1007/978-3-030-45002-1_6

deaths directly attributable to diabetes occur before the age of 70 [2]. Low socioeconomic status has been associated with the prevalence of type 2 diabetes [3, 4]. Research indicates that there are inequalities in diabetes control amongst "racial/ethnic minorities and those with low socioeconomic status" [4].

Therefore, the Western Cape (WC), a province in South Africa, provides the geographical area where challenges for use can be studied. This is due to the fact that 10.4% of the WC population has succumbed to diabetes [5]. Type 2 diabetes mellitus (T2DM) is the leading underlying cause of death in women (7.2%) and second amongst both genders and people of all ages [5]. It is forecasted that by the year 2040, one in every ten adults residing in LMICs will be living with diabetes [6]. Therefore, self-management is an important part of the treatment in Non-Communicable Diseases (NCD) [7] such as diabetes. Diabetes self-management is crucial to ensure that long-term complications are decreased. Diabetes self-management is based on seven self-care behaviours [8]. These include; healthy eating, being active, monitoring, taking medication, problem-solving, healthy coping, and reducing risks [8].

It is estimated that 49.2% of the South African adult population lives below the upper-body poverty line [9] with less than R 1 183 (nearly $79) per person per month [10]. Additionally, the digital divide remains evident as parts of this populace experience technology inequalities [11].

Research indicates that the use of smartphone technologies and mobile phone applications, such as mobile health (m-health), may facilitate diabetes self-management [12]. This is due to m-health being an interactive, inexpensive and dynamic means of supporting diabetes patients with self-care behaviours [13]. Thereby reducing mortality rates by delivering effective interventions to patients [14]. However, despite the availability of m-health for diabetes self-management, the overall uptake of m-health diabetes management was low [12] and continued use is low [15].

2 Challenges for User Acceptance

Models for user acceptance demonstrates that individuals' reaction to information technology drives their intention to use information technology, such as m-health. This then ultimately determines their actual use. Research indicates that an individuals' intention to use a system such as m-health may explain the actual use of information of a system [16] or alternatively can be used to explain the challenges when use behavior is low. For example, if using the information technology is slow and difficult to use, this may influence individuals to use it less frequently or abandoning the technology [16].

The UTAUT model is an established user acceptance model with eight models used to develop it, including the Theory of Reasoned Action, the Technology Acceptance Model and the Theory of Planned Behaviour, explained between 17% and 53% variance in user intentions to use technology [16]. The UTAUT model explained 77% of the variance in behavioural intention to use technology and 52% of the variance in technology use.

The UTAUT (Fig. 1) includes four core constructs (performance expectancy, effort expectancy, social influence and facilitating conditions) that are direct determinants of

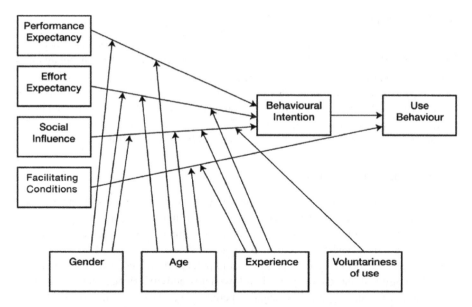

Fig. 1. Unified theory of acceptance and use of technology (Source: [16], p. 447)

behavioural intention and use. These constructs are moderated by gender, age, experience, and voluntariness of use [16].

This paper's authors have conducted a study on user acceptance of Information Communication and Technology (ICT) for diabetes self-management in the Western Cape, South Africa. This study also used the UTAUT model [16]. The research found that behavioural intention did not translate into usage [17]. This was due to the fact that almost 70% of respondents did not use forms of ICT, such as m-health applications, for their diabetes self-management. Disparities in use have been identified in the literature for older adults, low income and racial/ethnic minorities [18, 19]. Therefore, this paradox serves as the problem in this study, which focuses on analysing challenges to the acceptance and usage of mobile health applications.

Based on the areas identified by the study above [17], the objective of this study is to determine barriers for the acceptance of diabetes m-health applications, given the currently low levels of m-health use for diabetes self-management in the Western Cape.

The literature indicates that context may impede the acceptance and use of m-health applications [20]. Research already indicates mixed findings on reaching at-risk populations as most apps focus on high-cost populations [21], leaving unexplored the reach to the most at-risk population groups in South Africa, who will then remain disadvantaged because the actualisation of mobile phones for aiding service access will remain confined [22]. It is imperative to address the cost-effectiveness challenges inherent in implementation [22, 23]. Designers of interventions must recognise the constraints of the South African health system and consider appropriate options for this context.

2.1 Effort Expectancy

For patients aged 50 years or older, effort expectancy was identified as a key factor for diabetes applications [24]. The positive impact of effort expectancy on behavioural intention is supported by other studies that analysed consumer usage of health informatics [25]. However, the impact of effort expectancy on behavioural intention is more prominent for older users as a study with younger and well-educated users found that this relationship was not significant [25]. Therefore, diabetes applications should be designed so that they are easy to use and understand, especially for older users.

2.2 Performance Expectancy

Research indicates that performance expectancy is an important determinant of the intention to use diabetes management apps [25]. The finding is supported by a study that indicates performance expectancy's significant impact on the users' behavioural intention to adopt mHealth services in Bangladesh [19].

Performance expectancy may be low as the perception of medical professionals is that technology use and data capture is a low-status activity. Hence, the task is delegated to junior personnel [26]. The negative perception and delegation may lead to user resistance [26].

2.3 Social Influence

Social influence is found to be a significant determinant of the intention to use diabetes management apps [25]. This finding is supported by the fact that supportive health care professionals and family members are core to m-health acceptance [27].

M-health data on applications, such as Glucose buddy, can be shared with health care providers. However, this may leave patients to feel vulnerable when their health care providers do not provide empathy or solutions when they are sharing their high glucose readings [28]. A lack of empathy and concern by the people who patients deem as important may lead to the discontinued use of m-health applications.

2.4 Facilitating Conditions

Only 25.8% of Western Cape residents have access to the internet at home [29]. Additionally, 61.7% of people in the Western Cape have access to the internet using their mobile devices of which 26.8% of people in the rural have access to the internet [29]. With the increasing inequalities amongst different ethnicities, there are disparities between income, access, education and health literacy amongst LMICs. Subsequently, it may impact diabetes self-management as access to information is essential for successful self-management [30].

Additionally, South African m-health services are based on unsustainable business models due to the dependence on donor funding [22, 23]. There is a high risk for discontinuation of services. Therefore, there is a need for innovative business models that are based on best practice [31, 32].

There are limited information technology (IT) skills and training especially among older users [33]. Health apps are downloaded and used without guidance [34]. Therefore, to raise the level of acceptance among older users, allow for personal contact persons during the initial phase of use [24] and training.

3   Methodology

This research used an interpretivist paradigm [35]. Interpretivism highlights the view that reality is socially constructed and subjective [36]. Therefore, it is a suitable paradigm for this research seeks to interpret the perception of individuals' acceptance and use of m-health to identify barriers.

3.1   Data Collection and Analysis

This research used qualitative data collected from 26% of respondents used in the initial study, User acceptance of ICT for diabetes self-management in the Western Cape, South Africa [17]. The initial study analysed quantitative data from 498 respondents using an online survey. Respondents resided in predominantly low socio-economic areas, such as Mitchell's Plain, Belhar, Khayelitsha, Athlone, Delft as well as Gugulethu, in the Western Cape. For this study, 130 diabetic respondents who participated in the initial study were selected using random sampling and semi-structured interviews [37]. Interviews were conducted by third-year Information Systems students working as field workers, using an interview guide.

Interview questions included the following to gain insight into the broader use of Information Communication and Technology (ICT), including m-health applications, as it could not be assumed that the lack of m-health application usage meant that no alternative ICT options were being used:

"Which technology (ICT) do you use to help manage your diabetes?
Prompt if required: Do you use a glucose testing machine? Do you search for diabetes-related information on the internet? Do you use an application on your mobile phone?
What prevents you from using ICT, including mobile applications, for managing your diabetes?
Prompt if required: If they don't use ICT such as mobile applications, ask them if it's related to cost or whether it's too difficult to use. Is it anything else?
Do you find ICT, including mobile applications, useful for managing your diabetes?
Prompt if required: Does it help you achieve better results when you go to the doctor?
What do you like or dislike about the current technology for managing your diabetes?
Prompt if required: Is it easy to use and understand? Is it easy to incorporate into your life?"
[30].

The study used thematic content analysis, using Atlas.ti software. The data analysis was based on the key thematic areas identified in the theoretical framework (Fig. 1). The steps for thematic content analysis included the preparation, organisation and reporting of the transcribed interviews [38].

3.2   Ethical Considerations

The study was subjected to the protocols for ethical clearance by the Human and Social Sciences Research Ethics Committee at the University of the Western Cape. In this regard, a high level of attention was paid to observing the strictest levels of confidence during the data collection exercise. All respondents were advised of their rights and had to consent to participate in the research. It should be noted though, that the nature of the questions was restricted to issues of m-health acceptance and use, rather than on specifics of an individuals' personal and private health situation.

4   Results

The results commence with demographics and conclude with thematic content analysis findings.

4.1   Demographics

The demographics below indicate that the majority of the respondents are females (52%). The predominant respondent age group is older than 50 (36%) (Table 1). A limited number of respondents (17.69%) used mobile health applications while the highest percentage (30.76%) preferred to use glucose testing machines.

Table 1. Demographics

		Frequency	Percentage
Gender	Male	55	42.31
	Female	67	51.54
	Unknown	8	6.15
	Total	130	100
Age	Between 16 & 24	10	7.69
	Between 25 & 34	17	13.08
	Between 35 & 49	43	33.08
	Older than 50	47	36.15
	Unknown	13	10
	Total	130	100

4.2   Themes Identified from the UTAUT Model

To reach the objective, themes were coded according to UTAUT constructs. It was found that all four constructs explain the challenges experienced for acceptance in low socio-economic areas.

4.2.1 Performance Expectancy

Respondents indicated that they did not believe that using m-health applications would assist them to attain better health. This was highlighted by the following quotation:

> *"I don't see the purpose. I receive everything from my testing machine"* and *"I don't want to play with my health and get things wrong and end up making myself sick. I'm comfortable with the doctors handling the heavy work."*

Older respondents use their mobile phones to make phone calls and thus their willingness to use m-health is lower. Respondents also mentioned that there is no need for m-health apps because their condition is manageable. This was summarised by the following quote *"I don't use anything else because I don't see the need to. I have my family to help me, and if I need more info I will ask one of them to find out for me, or I will get the information when I go to the doctor again".*

4.2.2 Effort Expectancy

Respondents indicated that they dislike using technology as it is too complex for older people as well as being too difficult for them to use. One respondent mentioned, *"For the older generation, technology can be a bit complex to use".*

Evidence shows that respondents that they are unable to complete self-management activities, using m-health. Respondents mentioned that using m-health is intimidating to them. The intimidation is due to respondents having limited ICT experience and skills to use m-health. This was prevalent for older respondents and resulted in lower usage. Therefore, the design of the m-health application is seen as a challenge as patients do not have the ability to use the m-health on their own.

Furthermore, respondents identified that using m-health will be easier than using the traditional approach to seek medical consultation. Attending health care facilities is inconvenient for elderly patients as they will have to wait for hours or even a full day to be examined by a professional. Therefore, using m-health will allow more time for other activities.

A respondent stated, *"I really do not know, I take it from myself, it's difficult for me because my eyes are blurry".* Thus, the interface should be user-friendly for older patients to incorporate into their daily lifestyles. Moreover, respondents use other tools such as glucose meters rather than m-health as it is easy to use and understand. Furthermore, individuals mentioned that operating m-health was not easy at first and after many attempts, it became easier. This is summarised by the following comments, *"Found it challenging in the beginning"* and *"I struggled at first but I think I'm getting better now".*

4.2.3 Social Influence

Respondents stated that family and friends encouraged m-health usage to manage their diabetes. However, the results also indicated that respondents preferred the assistance and social support of family and friends as opposed to using a device for self-management activities.

Respondents also indicated that having in-person consultations with healthcare professionals provides a more accurate representation of their illness than managing it using m-health. This is summarised by the following statements: *"Feel like the doctor is more accurate at giving results"* and *"the doctor learns [teaches] you more"*.

4.2.4   Facilitating Conditions

Cost was identified as a determining factor for m-health acceptance across all the respondents in all age groups. This is due to data being too expensive for people residing in low resource areas to afford. This is a salient factor as many people prefer spending their funds on supporting their families with their basic needs as to spending on m-health. This was summarised by one respondent who stated that *"They [m-health] are quite costly & being a family man, it can be hard to afford"*.

Respondents stated that they have access to technology. Yet, it is mainly used for social media such as WhatsApp, Facebook and phone calls as opposed to diabetes self-management. Despite having access to a cell phone, respondents do not have the necessary resources to download m-health applications as it requires certain software and data/WIFI to download, update and track the results on an application.

Interoperability was identified as a challenge for the acceptance of m-health. Respondents mentioned that m-health is not compatible with other systems, such as glucose testing machines. Therefore, in order for patients to monitor their self-management activities, they have to use more than one ICT tool. Respondents mentioned that privacy and security is a concern. They fear that others can potentially obtain their personal information.

Lack of training is identified as a reason for the lack of use or the discontinuation of use. This further illustrates that respondents will accept and use m-health provided that a specific person is available for assistance with m-health difficulties. Respondents indicated that they are unable to afford to pay for training. Respondents further indicated that when training is provided, they are not aware of it. Respondents mentioned that they *"Don't have the right training for it"*, *"People can't afford to learn"* and *"do not know when it [training] is available"*.

5   Implications for the Design of M-Health Interventions

Practical approaches to privacy and security need to be implemented as patients are entering personal health information [39]. Personal contact persons, especially during the initial phase of use, are essential to reduce the fear of data loss or erroneous data input. This may raise acceptance among older patients [43]. Additionally, elderly patients should be included as part of the stakeholder group to design health applications so that the needs and limitations of the target user group into consideration [57]. This will result in m-health applications designed in a way that is easy to use and understand by older patients.

Results show that patients prefer social support from family and friends as opposed to seeking information from a mobile application. This may be linked to factors such as technology anxiety, resistance to change and a lack of trust in the use of devices for self-management. Therefore, interventions such as personal contact during the initial phase of use should be leveraged as this will allow the acceptance of use amongst patients, especially older adults [24]. Respondents stated that face-to-face consultations provide more accurate information than a self-management tool such as m-health applications. To overcome the challenge of inaccurate information provided by health applications, a single framework should be developed to evaluate the role of m-health and e-health tools in strengthening the health system.

Affordability and access to ICT are identified by authors as an important factor for acceptance and use for m-health [39–41]. Access as a barrier may be difficult to overcome as many of the WC population are living below the poverty line with limited device and internet access, failing to consider these factors may result in a limited reach of at-risk patients. Literature supports the view that training is necessary to improve usage for patients as well as health care staff [42, 43]. However, funding will be required to implement training initiatives and health care in the Western Cape has experienced significant downsizing of personnel as well as population growth exceeding funding growth [44]. Essentially, training among older users is required as participants mentioned that they would accept m-health application given that assistance is available for any m-health difficulties. To raise the level of acceptance among older users, personal contact persons should be available during the initial phase of use. Despite having access to technology, patients are unable to complete self-management activities on their own due to lack of resources to download m-health applications. Interventions should take into account the constraints of South African's health system and consider the use of open-source options [24, 45].

6   Conclusion

This study set out to investigate the barriers to user acceptance of m-health applications. Drawing on the literature, the UTAUT model was used as a basis to inform this study. In particular, the four key constructs of the UTAUT model, performance expectancy, effort expectancy, social influence and facilitating conditions were used to determine the barriers for user acceptance of mobile applications discourage use and prevent behavioural intention to be converted into use. The results indicate that all four constructs of the UTAUT model can explain the barriers for user acceptance of m-health applications for diabetic patients in the Western Cape.

Despite the many barriers, the study has found that diabetic patients stated that using m-health will be easier than using the traditional approach to seek medical consultation. This is due to m-health applications being more convenient. Furthermore, diabetic patients mentioned that operating m-health became easier after many attempts. Therefore, interventions such as training should be implemented.

The barriers identified in this study is limited to diabetic patients residing in the Western Cape and may not be generalised to the entire South African population. Further research into the reasons for the lack of trust and not identifying a need to use m-health, by patients in the low socio-economic areas in the Western Cape, is required. There may also be other challenges identified by using the themes from another acceptance model, such as the Innovation Diffusion Model [46].

References

1. World Health Organization: Noncommunicable disease. WHO (2015)
2. World Health Organisation: Diabetes (2018). http://www.who.int/news-room/fact-sheets/detail/diabetes. Accessed 25 Nov 2018
3. Berkowitz, S., et al.: Low socioeconomic status is associated with increased risk for hypoglycemia in diabetes patients: the Diabetes Study of Northern California (DISTANCE). J. Health Care Poor Underserv. 25(2), 478–490 (2014)
4. Ruddock, J.S., Poindexter, M., Gary-Webb, T.L., Walker, E.A., Davis, N.J.: Innovative strategies to improve diabetes outcomes in disadvantaged populations. Diabet. Med. 33, 723–733 (2016)
5. Statistics South Africa: Mortality and causes of death in South Africa. Pretoria (2016)
6. Reid, M., et al.: Development of a health dialogue model for patients with diabetes: a complex intervention in a low-/middle income country. Int. J. Africa Nurs. Sci. 8(July), 122–131 (2018)
7. Lunde, P., Nilaaon, B., Bergland, A., Kvaerner, K., Bye, A.: The effectiveness of smartphone apps for lifestyle improvement in noncommunicable diseases: systematic review and meta-analyses. J. Med. Internet Res. 20(5), e162 (2018)
8. American Association of Diabetes Educators: Self care behaviors. Diabetes Self Manag. 1–11 (1997)
9. Statistics South Africa: Living conditions of households in South Africa: an analysis of household expenditure and income data using the LCS 2014/2015. Statistical release P0310 (2017)
10. Statistics South Africa: National Poverty Lines 2018. Statistical release P0310, no. July, pp. 1–10 (2018)
11. Gillwald, A., Mothobi, O., Rademan, B.: After access paper series: the state of ICT in South Africa (2017)
12. Garabedian, L.F., Ross-Degnan, D., LeCates, R.F., Wharam, J.F.: Uptake and use of a diabetes management program with a mobile glucometer. Prim. Care Diabetes 13, 549–555 (2019)
13. Hou, C., Xu, Q., Diao, S., Hewitt, J., Li, J., Carter, B.: Mobile phone applications and self-management of diabetes: a systematic review with meta-analysis, meta-regression of 21 randomized trials and GRADE. Diabetes Obes. Metab. 20(8), 2009–2013 (2018)
14. Zhao, J., Freeman, B., Li, M.: Can mobile phone apps influence people's health behavior change? An evidence review. J. Med. Internet Res. 18(11), 1–15 (2016)
15. Deacon, A.J., Chee, J.J., Chang, W.J.R., Harbourne, B.A.: Mobile applications for diabetes mellitus self-management: a systematic narrative analysis. In: Successes and Failures in Telehealth Conference, SFT-2017, pp. 17–30 (2017)
16. Venkatesh, V., Morris, M.G., Davis, G.B., Davis, F.D.: User acceptance of information technology: toward a unified view. MIS Q. 27(3), 425–478 (2003)
17. Petersen, F., Pather, S., Tucker, W.D.: User acceptance of ICT for diabetes self-management in the Western Cape, South Africa. In: African Conference of Information Systems and Technology (ACIST), pp. 1–11 (2018)
18. Nelson, L.A., Mulvaney, S.A., Gebretsadik, T., Ho, Y.X., Johnson, K.B., Osborn, C.Y.: Disparities in the use of a mHealth medication adherence promotion intervention for low-income adults with type 2 diabetes. J. Am. Med. Inform. Assoc. 23(1), 12–18 (2016)
19. Hoque, R., Sorwar, G.: Understanding factors influencing the adoption of mHealth by the elderly: an extension of the UTAUT model. Int. J. Med. Inform. 101, 75–84 (2017)

20. Müller, A.M.: Behavioural mHealth in developing countries: what about culture? Eur. Health Psychol. **18**(6), 294–296 (2016)
21. Singh, K., et al.: Many mobile health apps target high-need, high-cost populations, but gaps remain. Health Aff. **35**(12), 2310–2318 (2016)
22. GSMA: South Africa mHealth Landscape (2013). http://www.gsma.com/mobilefordevelo pment/wp-content/uploads/2013/08/South-Africa-mHealth-Landscape_June-2013.pdf. Accessed 15 Sept 2015
23. Aranda-Jan, C.B., Mohutsiwa-Dibe, N., Loukanova, S.: Systematic review on what works, what does not work and why of implementation of mobile health (mHealth) projects in Africa. BMC Public Health **14**(1), 188 (2014)
24. Scheibe, M., Reichelt, J., Bellmann, M., Kirch, W.: Acceptance factors of mobile apps for diabetes by patients aged 50 or older: a qualitative study. Med. 2.0 **4**(1), e1 (2015)
25. Zhang, Y., et al.: Factors influencing patients' intentions to use diabetes management apps based on an extended unified theory of acceptance and use of technology model: web-based survey. J. Med. Internet Res. **21**(8), e15023 (2019)
26. Wolff-Piggott, B., Coleman, J., Rivett, U.: The clinic-level perspective on mHealth implementation: a South African case study. Inf. Technol. Dev. **24**(3), 532–553 (2018)
27. Macdonald, E.M., Perrin, B.M., Kingsley, M.I.: Enablers and barriers to using two-way information technology in the management of adults with diabetes: a descriptive systematic review. J. Telemed. Telecare **24**, 319–340 (2018)
28. Dadgar, M., Joshi, K.D.: The role of information and communication technology in self-management of chronic diseases: an empirical investigation through value sensitive design. J. Assoc. Inf. Syst. **19**(2), 86–112 (2018)
29. Statistics South Africa: General Household Survey. Statistical release P0318, May 2018
30. Petersen, F., Brown, A., Pather, S., Tucker, W.D.: Challenges for the adoption of ICT for diabetes self-management in South Africa. Electron. J. Inf. Syst. Dev. Ctries. 1–14 (2019). https://doi.org/10.1002/isd2.12113
31. GSMA: The Mobile Economy: Africa 2016 (2016)
32. Department of Health: mHealth Strategy 2015–2019. South Africa (2015)
33. Coetzer, J.: Application of HCI design principles in overcoming information illiteracy: case of a m-health application for a rural community in South Africa. In: 2018 International Conference on Intelligent and Innovative Computing Applications, ICONIC 2018, pp. 1–7 (2018)
34. Huang, Z., Soljak, M., Boehm, B.O., Car, J.: Clinical relevance of smartphone apps for diabetes management: a global overview. Diabetes Metab. Res. Rev. **34**(4), e2990 (2018)
35. Myers, M.D.: Qualitative research in information systems. MIS Q. **21**(2), 241 (1997)
36. Saunders, M., Lewis, P., Thornhill, A.: Understanding research philosophies and approaches. Res. Methods Bus. Stud. **2009**, 106–136 (2009)
37. Marshall, M.N.: Sampling for qualitative research. Family Pract. **13**(6), 522–525 (1996)
38. Cresswell, J.W.: Research Design: Qualitative, Quantitative, and Mixed Methods Approaches, 3rd edn. SAGE Publications, Thousand Oaks (2014)
39. Kleine, D.: ICT4WHAT?—Using the choice framework to operationalise the capability approach to development. J. Int. Dev. **22**(5), 674–692 (2010)
40. Quaglio, G.L., et al.: Information and communications technologies in low and middle-income countries: survey results on economic development and health. Health Policy Technol. **5**(4), 318–329 (2016)
41. Ahmed, T., Lucas, H., Khan, A.S., Islam, R., Bhuiya, A., Iqbal, M.: eHealth and mHealth initiatives in Bangladesh: a scoping study. BMC Health Serv. Res. **14**(1), 260 (2014)

42. Akhlaq, A., McKinstry, B., Bin Muhammad, K., Sheikh, A.: Barriers and facilitators to health information exchange in low- and middle-income country settings: a systematic review. Health Policy Plan. **31**(9), 1310–1325 (2016)
43. Kenny, G., O'Connor, Y., Eze, E., Ndibuagu, E., Heavin, C.: A ground-up approach to mHealth in Nigeria: a study of primary healthcare workers' attitude to mHealth adoption. Procedia Comput. Sci. **121**, 809–816 (2017)
44. Health Systems Trust: South African Health Review 2013/2014 (2014)
45. Department of Health: mHealth Strategy. South Africa (2015)
46. Rogers, E.M.: Diffusion of Innovations. Free Press, New York (2003)

Impact of Socio-Demographic Factors on the Acceptance of Information Communication and Technology (ICT) for Diabetes Self-care

Fazlyn Petersen[(⊠)] ⓘ, Adiel Baker ⓘ, Shaun Pather ⓘ,
and William D. Tucker ⓘ

University of the Western Cape, Bellville, South Africa
{fapetersen, spather, btucker}@uwc.ac.za,
adiel.baker@gmail.com

Abstract. This research investigates the impact of socio-demographic factors such as age, gender, income and location on ICT acceptance for diabetes self-care. The investigation is due to the increasing number of diabetic patients in South Africa, where large segments of the population experience technological forms of exclusions. The context warrants research in geographical areas where ICT use is not pervasive yet. This research, used the UTAUT model with purposive sampling for 497 diabetic respondents, residing in low socio-economic communities. It analysed survey data using linear regression. It found that age had a strong moderating effect on all four UTAUT constructs. Gender only had a moderating effect on performance expectancy and social influence. In contrast to findings in the extant literature, income and location had no significant moderating effect in this context.

Keywords: Socio-demographic factors · ICT acceptance · Diabetes self-care · UTAUT · Western Cape · South Africa

1 Introduction

The Western Cape, one of the nine provinces in South Africa, [1] has a history of racial segregation, officially implemented by the Group Areas Act in 1950 [2]. The Act issued identity cards, which indicated has five racial groups; Black, Coloured, Indian, Malay and White [2]. Coloured people are typically mixed race, descendants of Malaysian slaves or Khoisan descendants [3]. 'Non-white' groups were forcibly removed from areas in the City, such as District Six, and placed in township areas such as Khayelitsha and Mitchells Plain [4]. These areas are regarded as the Cape Flats [4]. Approximately 63% of households in the Khayelitsha and Mitchells Plain have incomes of less than R4166 per month (approximately $296), of which 16.5% have no income [5].

The Western Cape reports a decline in the number of households connected to the mains electricity supply, from 93.5% in 2008 to 87.9% in 2018 [6]. Also, 19% of the Western Cape population live in informal dwellings [6]. Informal dwellings may not have access to water and electricity. However, it was found that "having adequate

© IFIP International Federation for Information Processing 2020
Published by Springer Nature Switzerland AG 2020
M. Hattingh et al. (Eds.): I3E 2020, LNCS 12067, pp. 73–83, 2020.
https://doi.org/10.1007/978-3-030-45002-1_7

access to appropriate forms of energy is critical for improving living standards, health and reducing poverty" [7]. Therefore, the demographics of the province reflect that the socio-economic plight of a substantive population is bleak.

The Western Cape includes large segments of the South African population who experience "technological forms of exclusion" as well as educational and income inequalities [8]. Despite the penetration of mobile phones (95.5%) in the Western Cape, 25.8% had internet access at home [6]. Therefore, the resulting digital divide between rich and poor is substantial [8]. This may impact the achievement of diabetes self-management as access to information is a key component in managing chronic conditions [9].

The Western Cape Government has recognised that broadband costs are still unaffordable to many citizens, so the Broadband Game Changer aims to provide all residents with access to affordable high-speed broadband infrastructure [10]. Also, the City of Cape Town is providing public Wi-Fi zones in more than 100 public buildings such as clinics, administration buildings and traffic departments, across Cape Town. Also, Wi-Fi is available in several public spaces, such as the Company Gardens. Wi-Fi services are also being implemented at public transport interchanges such as Athlone, Atlantis, City Centre, Langa, Nyanga, Uitsig and Valhalla Park. Users are allowed 50 MB per day and may purchase more data after that [11]. This improvement in the access layer provides a fertile ground for citizens, even from low socio-economic demographics, to harness m-health apps for various personal uses, including that of diabetes self- management.

According to the annual trends for diabetes incidence by province, 2013/14–2016/17, the Western Cape is indicating a rapid increase [12]. The Overberg West has the highest average (1.4) of diabetes incidence per 1000 total population, followed by Cape Town (1.2) [12]. It is also the leading cause of mortality in this province [13].

Therefore, there is a significant disease burden that requires comprehensive health care to manage these conditions [14]. However, health care in South Africa experiences severe staff shortages in the public health sector [15]. These shortages are particularly prevalent in rural and underserved areas [15]. Therefore, there is an increased need for patients to practice self-care.

Self-care involves "the ability to make decisions and perform actions directly under the control of the individual, and is influenced by a variety of individual characteristics" [9 p. 1734]. Diabetes self-care is multidimensional and includes a range of activities such as self-monitoring of blood glucose, diet and foot care [16]. It is found that self-care is situationally influenced [9].

The use of Information, Communication and Technology (ICT) as an enabler for self-care activities, performed by the patient, includes the use of the Internet (47%), cellular phones (32%), telemedicine (12%), and decision support techniques (9%) [17]. Also, ICT interventions can also be used to reduce diabetes risk factors by improving physical inactivity and smoking [18].

However, despite increased access to ICT in developing countries like South Africa, the promise of ICT to deliver diabetes self-care improvements will be limited by uptake and high attrition rates [19]. The use of ICT, such as mobile health (m-health) applications for diabetes, is low [20]. The low usage is prevalent, especially amongst older patients [20]. A population study in Germany supports this finding. It revealed that age and socio-economic status led to disparities in m-health usage [21]. However, the most prominent type of diabetes (90%) is type 2 diabetes [22]. Type 2 diabetes is most often diagnosed in older patients [22]. Therefore, the introduction of ICT, will not lead to the improvement of self-care unless it is accepted and used by the intended user population, i.e. older patients with diabetes [23].

In order to assess the acceptance and use of technology, the literature points to a number of models such as the Theory of Reasoned Action (TRA) [24], Theory of Planned Behaviour (TPB) [25], Technology Acceptance Model (TAM) [26] and the Unified Theory of Acceptance and Use of Technology (UTAUT) [27]. It was found that the eight models used to develop UTAUT, including TRA, TPB and TAM, explained between 17% and 53% variance in user intentions to use technology [27]. However, the UTAUT model explained 77% of the variance in behavioural intention to use technology and 52% of the variance in technology use [28]. The UTAUT model was therefore applied in this study, given that it outperforms other models of acceptance.

More recent research provide evidence of 1,267 UTAUT citations including new exogenous, endogenous or moderation variables [28]. This research provides new moderation variables in the South African context. Additionally, it was used in a study conducted in the Western Cape on the usage of ICT for diabetes self-management [29]. In that study, it was found that despite a high behavioural intention, there is low usage to almost 70% of the target population not using forms of ICT, such as mobile health. However, the Petersen et al. [29] study did account for how socio-demographic factors (e.g. age, gender, income or location), could explain the lack of use. Consequently, the main research question that forms the basis of this paper is *'what is the impact of socio-demographic factors on the acceptance of ICT for diabetes self-care?'*

2 Objectives

Behavioural intention has a direct influence on the usage of technology [27]. The extant literature indicates that low levels of ICT for DM self-management amongst the elderly. Therefore, for succinctness, only behavioural intention was examined. This is due to the main objective is to understand the impact of socio-demographic factors on technology acceptance for diabetes self-care. This study, therefore, expands on the original study [29], and seeks to determine if the following factors affect the acceptance of ICT for diabetes self-care in the Western Cape, South Africa using constructs identified by Venkatesh et al. [28]:

- Age,
- Gender,
- Income and
- Patient's location, i.e. rural/urban [28].

3   Methodology

This research was framed within a positivist paradigm which posits that at an onto-logical level, knowledge is quantifiable and objective [30]. Positivist methodology uses quantitative methods and quantitative analysis [31]. Purposive sampling [32] was used in this research to select patients with diabetes (n = 497) living predominantly within low socio-economic communities in Western Cape.

Quantitative data from online surveys were analysed via descriptive statistics and linear regression, using SPSS software [33]. A 6 point Likert scale (strongly disagree to strongly agree) was used. The survey questions were based on the core constructs inherent in the UTAUT model [27] and adapted for this research. The survey questions are provided in Table 1.

Table 1. Survey questions

Construct	Survey question
Performance expectancy	I find that using Information, Communication and Technology (ICT), such as glucose machines and mobile applications, useful tools in managing my diabetes
	Using ICT enables me to accomplish tasks, such as insulin administration, carb counting and glucose testing, more quickly
	Using ICT increases my productivity as I spend less time on diabetes activities
	Using ICT increases my chances of getting a good HBA1c reading
Effort expectancy	My interaction with ICT, for my diabetes, is clear and understandable
	It is easy for me to become skilful at using ICT for my diabetes.
	I find ICT easy to use for my diabetes
	Learning to operate ICT for my diabetes is easy for me
Social influence	People who influence my behaviour (e.g. family, friends, doctor, etc.) think that I should use ICT to manage my diabetes
	People who are important to me think that I should use ICT to manage my diabetes
	My health care team, e.g. doctors, nurses, have been helpful in the use of ICT to manage my diabetes
	In general, my peer support group/community has supported the use of ICT to manage my diabetes
Facilitating conditions	I have the resources necessary to use ICT to manage my diabetes
	I have the knowledge necessary to use ICT to manage my diabetes
	Using ICT is compatible with other systems I use, such as my mobile phone
	A specific person (or group) is available for assistance with ICT difficulties

Based on [34], no clinical data or unique identifiers (such as names or ID numbers) were collected to ensure anonymity and the protection of the identities and interests of those involved. The researchers respected the confidentiality of the data supplied by all parties involved by storing data in a restricted access folder on Google drive.

4 Research Model

The UTAUT model includes four independent variables [27]:

1. Performance expectancy (PE): "is the degree to which an individual believes that using the system will help him or her to attain gains in job performance" (p. 447).
2. Effort expectancy (EE): "is the degree of ease associated with the use of the system" (p. 450).
3. Social influence (SI): "is the degree to which an individual perceives that important others believe he or she should use the new system" (p. 451).
4. Facilitating conditions (FC): "is the degree to which an individual believes that an organisational and technical infrastructure exists to support the use of the system" (p. 453).

The relationships between the key constructs and moderators were hypothesised as follows (Table 2):

Table 2. Research hypotheses

No.	Hypothesis
H1	Performance expectancy will have a positive influence on behavioural intention to use ICT for diabetes self-care
H2	Effort expectancy will have a positive influence on behavioural intention to use ICT for diabetes self-care
H3	Social influence will have a positive influence on behavioural intention to use ICT for diabetes self-care
H4	Facilitating conditions will have a positive influence on behavioural intention to use ICT for diabetes self-care
H5A	Age will positively moderate the influence of performance expectancy on behavioural intention to use ICT for diabetes self-care
	Age will positively moderate the influence of effort expectancy on behavioural intention to use ICT for diabetes self-care
	Age will positively moderate the influence of social influence on behavioural intention to use ICT for diabetes self-care
	Age will positively moderate the influence of facilitating conditions on behavioural intention to use ICT for diabetes self-care
H5B	Gender will positively moderate the influence of performance expectancy on behavioural intention to use ICT for diabetes self-care
	Gender will positively moderate the influence of effort expectancy on behavioural intention to use ICT for diabetes self-care
	Gender will positively moderate the influence of social influence on behavioural intention to use ICT for diabetes self-care
	Gender will positively moderate the influence of facilitating conditions on behavioural intention to use ICT for diabetes self-care

(continued)

Table 2. (*continued*)

No.	Hypothesis
H5C	Income will positively moderate the influence of performance expectancy on behavioural intention to use ICT for diabetes self-care
	Income will positively moderate the influence of effort expectancy on behavioural intention to use ICT for diabetes self-care
	Income will positively moderate the influence of social influence on behavioural intention to use ICT for diabetes self-care
	Income will positively moderate the influence of facilitating conditions on behavioural intention to use ICT for diabetes self-care
H5D	Location will positively moderate the influence of performance expectancy on behavioural intention to use ICT for diabetes self-care
	Location will positively moderate the influence of effort expectancy on behavioural intention to use ICT for diabetes self-care
	Location will positively moderate the influence of social influence on behavioural intention to use ICT for diabetes self-care
	Location will positively moderate the influence of facilitating conditions on behavioural intention to use ICT for diabetes self-care

The conceptual model, based on the UTAUT model [27], was developed to achieve the stated research objectives (Fig. 1).

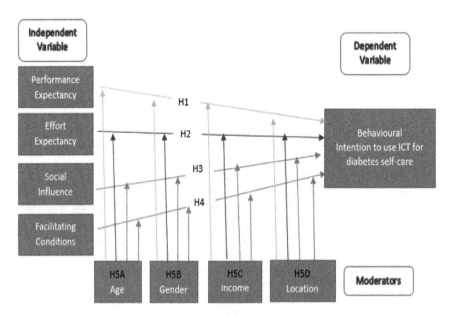

Fig. 1. Conceptual framework to identify moderators affecting the acceptance of ICT for self-management, using the UTAUT model

5   Results

The 497 Western Cape respondents, who participated in this research, were predominantly females (55.9%) older than 50 years (40.6%) who had type 2 diabetes (89.1%). They resided in low socio-economic areas on the Cape Flats such as Mitchell's Plain (11.4%), Belhar (10.8%), Khayelitsha (9.4%), Athlone (6.0%), Delft as well as Gugulethu (4.6%).

A series of regression analyses were run to examine the relationships between effort expectancy, performance expectancy, social influence and facilitating conditions. Table 3 shows the univariate statistics, correlations of each variable with behavioural intention, and the regression weights for the socio-demographic moderators added.

The strength of the linear fit is explained by R-squared (R^2). This explains the amount of variation of the independent variables on the dependent variable, behavioural intention [33]. The full model had an $R^2 = 0.534$ and $p < .0001$.

Table 3. Research hypotheses

Hypotheses	R^2	P – value	Changes when moderator added		Result
			R^2	P	
H1 PE → BI	0.363	0.000	–	–	Accept
H2 EE → BI	0.414	0.000	–	–	Accept
H3 SI → BI	0.343	0.000	–	–	Accept
H4 FC → BI	0.406	0.000	–	–	Accept
H5A					
PE*Age → BI	0.384	0.000	0.021	None	Accept
EE*Age → BI	0.426	0.004	0.012	0.004	Accept
SI*Age → BI	0.363	0.000	0.022	None	Accept
FC*Age → BI	0.414	0.021	0.008	0.021	Accept
H5B					
PE*Gender → BI	0.364	0.040	0.007	0.040	Accept
EE*Gender → BI	0.413	0.424	0.001	0.424	Reject
SI*Gender → BI	0.348	0.021	0.009	0.021	Accept
FC*Gender → BI	0.411	0.110	0.004	0.110	Reject
H5C					
PE*Income → BI	0.348	0.982	No change	0.982	Reject
EE*Income → BI	0.405	0.072	0.005	0.072	Reject
SI*Income → BI	0.343	0.857	No change	0.857	Reject
FC*Income → BI	0.405	0.334	0.001	0.334	Reject
H5D					
PE* Location → BI	0.363	0.803	No change	0.803	Reject
EE* Location → BI	0.416	0.261	0.002	0.261	Reject
SI*Location → BI	0.345	0.312	0.002	0.312	Reject
FC* Location → BI	0.407	0.532	0.001	0.532	Reject

Despite high behavioural intention and the socio-demographic factors investigated, 67.4% of respondents indicated that they did not use ICT such as diabetes applications on their smartphone, insulin pump, continuous glucose monitoring (CGM).

6 Discussion

This discussion will address the significant and non-significant factors affecting the acceptance of ICT for diabetes self-care.

6.1 Significant Factors

The summarised table of findings indicates that the strongest moderating factor was age (Table 3). Age had a significant effect on all four of the constructs but reduced the p-values. However, the relationships were still significant at a 95% confidence interval. Gender affected PE and SI but also reduced the original model p-values. However, it was still significant at a 95% confidence interval. Age and gender have been identified in previous studies as a critical factor for the acceptance and use of ICT, such as m-health applications in developed [21] and developing countries [35].

Literature also indicates that the digital divide is more prevalent for people older than 65 years [36], an age group that is linked to patients with Type 2 (non-insulin-dependent) diabetes [37]. The needs of diabetic patients may be varied due to varying previous knowledge, education, age, income, type of diabetes and therapy [38, 39]. Interventions should include the elderly as part of the stakeholder group, or critical factors that are necessary to address the real problem may be overlooked. This may result in poor adoption and inefficient use of technology [40]. Interventions should include new perspectives and use patients' tactic knowledge [40].

6.2 Non-significant Factors

Diabetes is a non-communicable disease that affects disadvantaged populations more than in higher-income countries [41]. This constitutes a challenge to the achievement of the third SDG, focusing on the health and wellbeing of all [42]. Literature indicates that people of low socioeconomic status may not have the capability to achieve optimal health functioning [43]. Low income is identified as a barrier to achieving diabetes treatment goals [44]. This is prevalent for medication non-adherence being higher among minorities groups and those with low socio-economic status [45].

However, in this research, income and locations proved not to be significant for any constructs. This finding is contrary to research conducted in urban China, that indicates that age and location have strong moderating effects on acceptance [46]. This suggests that findings in respect of technology acceptance are not necessarily transferable between different geographical locations.

7   Conclusion

The research aimed to expand on an exploratory study [29] by investigating additional socio-demographic factors which affect the acceptance of ICTs for diabetes self-care. Despite findings that indicate age is a significant moderating variable, income and location were not. Intervention design, including co-design strategies, should consider highlighting the additional benefits of using ICT interventions. This could result in making m-health applications easier to use, especially for older users.

It is possible that acceptance may be influenced by other factors. For instance, in lower-income groups where medication non-adherence is common, patient engagement is crucial for an intervention's success [45]. Research suggests, for patients 50 years or older, the lack of additional benefits and ease of use are significant factors for the acceptance of diabetes m-health applications. Therefore, intervention design in the case of ICT applications for diabetes self-management should take into consideration these factors.

Further research should use qualitative methods to examine why location and income are not moderating factors, despite research indicating this in other contexts.

References

1. The Local Government Handbook: City of Cape Town Metropolitan Municipality. The Local Government Handbook: A Complete guide to municipalities in South Africa (2017). https://municipalities.co.za/map/6/city-of-cape-town-metropolitan-municipality. Accessed 18 Jan 2018
2. South African History Online. Cape Town the Segregated city (2011)
3. Mthembu, J.: What it means to be a coloured man on the Cape Flats. UCT News (2015). https://www.news.uct.ac.za/article/-2015-07-30-what-it-means-to-be-a-coloured-man-on-the-cape-flats. Accessed 24 Oct 2018
4. Bähre, E.: Housing for the urban poor: a post-apartheid dream or nightmare? South African History Online (2014)
5. Western Cape Government: Socio-economic Profile (2017)
6. Statistics South Africa: P0318 - General Household Survey (GHS), 2018 (2018)
7. Statistics South Africa: Mbalo Brief - the missing piece of the puzzle, Pretoria (2015)
8. Gillwald, A., Mothobi, O., Rademan, B.: After access paper series: the state of ICT in South Africa (2017)
9. Omisakin, F.D., Ncama, B.P.: Self, self-care and self-management concepts: implications for self-management education. Educ. Res. 2(12), 2141–5161 (2011)
10. Western Cape Government: Switching on public Wi-Fi hotspots across the Western Cape (2017). https://www.westerncape.gov.za/general-publication/switching-public-wi-fi-hotspots-across-western-cape. Accessed 24 Aug 2018
11. City of Cape Town: Wi-Fi zones across Cape Town (2018). http://www.capetown.gov.za/Localandcommunities/Get-online/Public-WiFi-Zones/Public-WiFi-across-the-City. Accessed 23 Aug 2018
12. Kengne, A.P., Sayed, B.: Non-communicable diseases, vol. 56, no. July, pp. 83–95 (2017)
13. Statistics South Africa: Mortality and causes of death in South Africa, Pretoria (2016)
14. International Diabetes Federation (IDF): IDF Diabetes Atlas Eighth edition, pp. 8–30 (2017)
15. Health Systems Trust: South African Health Review 2018 (2018)

16. Toobert, D.J., Hampson, S.E., Glasgow, R.E.: The summary of diabetes self-care activities measure: results from 7 studies and a revised scale. Diabet. Care **23**(7), 943–950 (2000)
17. El-Gayar, O., Timsina, P., Nawar, N., Eid, W.: A systematic review of IT for diabetes self-management: Are we there yet? Int. J. Med. Inform. **82**(8), 637–652 (2013)
18. Rehman, H., Kamal, A.K., Sayani, S., Morris, P.B., Merchant, A.T., Virani, S.S.: Using mobile health (mHealth) technology in the management of diabetes mellitus, physical inactivity, and smoking. Curr. Atheroscler. Rep. **19**(4), 16 (2017)
19. Yu, C.H., et al.: A web-based intervention to support self-management of patients with type 2 diabetes mellitus: effect on self-efficacy, self-care and diabetes distress. BMC Med. Inform. Decis. Mak. **14**(1), 117 (2014)
20. Li, M., et al.: Analysis of obstacles and motivations found utilizing a diabetes health app for older patients. Innov. Aging **1**(suppl_1), 642 (2017)
21. Ernsting, C., et al.: Using smartphones and health apps to change and manage health behaviors: a population-based survey. J. Med. Internet Res. **19**(4), e101 (2017)
22. IDF: IDF Africa Members (2018). https://www.idf.org/our-network/regions-members/africa/members/25-south-africa. Accessed 22 Oct 2018
23. Heffernan, C., Lin, Y., Thomson, K.: Drawing from development: towards unifying theory and practice of ICT4D. J. Int. Dev. **28**(6), 902–918 (2016)
24. Fishbein, M., Ajzen, I.: Belief, Attitude, Intention, and Behavior: An Introduction to Theory and Research. Addison-Wesley, Boston (1975)
25. Ajzen, I.: The theory of planned behavior. Organ. Behav. Hum. Decis. Process. **50**, 179–211 (1991)
26. Davis, F.D.: Perceived ease of use, and user acceptance of information technology. MIS Q. **13**(3), 319–340 (1989)
27. Venkatesh, V., Morris, M.G., Davis, G.B., Davis, F.D.: User acceptance of information technology: toward a unified view. MIS Q. **27**(3), 425–478 (2003)
28. Venkatesh, V., Thong, J., Xu, X.: Unified theory of acceptance and use of technology: a synthesis and the road ahead. J. Assoc. Inf. Syst. **17**(5), 328–376 (2016)
29. Petersen, F., Pather, S., Tucker, W.D.: User acceptance of ICT for diabetes self-management in the Western Cape, South Africa. In: African Conference of Information Systems and Technology (ACIST), pp. 1–11 (2018)
30. Mingers, J.: Philosophical foundations: critical realism. In: Mingers, J. (ed.) Realising Systems Thinking: Knowledge and Action in Management Science, pp. 11–31. Springer, Boston (2006). https://doi.org/10.1007/0-387-29841-X_2
31. Thomas, P.Y.: Research methodology and design. In: Research Methodology and Design, pp. 291–334. Unisa, South Africa (2010)
32. Marshall, M.N.: Sampling for qualitative research. Family Pract. **13**(6), 522–525 (1996)
33. Diez, D.M., Barr, C.D., Centinkaya, M.: OpenIntro: Statistics Preliminary Edition, vol. 1, CreateSpace Independent Publishing Platform (2012)
34. Dearden, A., Kleine, D.: A proposal for minimum ethical standards in ICTD/ICT4D research (2018)
35. Jennings, L., Omoni, A., Akerele, A., Ibrahim, Y., Ekanem, E.: Disparities in mobile phone access and maternal health service utilization in Nigeria: a population-based survey. Int. J. Med. Inform. **84**(5), 341–348 (2015)
36. Friemel, T.N.: The digital divide has grown old: determinants of a digital divide among seniors. New Media Soc. **18**(2), 313–331 (2016)
37. American Diabetes Association: Improving care and promoting health in populations: standards of medical care in diabetes (2019)
38. Scheibe, M., Reichelt, J., Bellmann, M., Kirch, W.: Acceptance factors of mobile apps for diabetes by patients aged 50 or older: a qualitative study. Medicine 2.0 **4**(1), e1 (2015)

39. Coetzer, J.: Application of HCI design principles in overcoming information illiteracy: case of a M-health application for a rural community in South Africa. In: 2018 International Conference on Intelligent and Innovative Computing Applications, ICONIC 2018, pp. 1–7 (2018)
40. Isaković, M., Sedlar, U., Volk, M., Bešter, J.: Usability pitfalls of diabetes mHealth apps for the elderly. J. Diabetes Res. **2016**, 9 p (2016)
41. World Health Organisation: Diabetes (2018). http://www.who.int/news-room/fact-sheets/detail/diabetes. Accessed 25 Nov 2018
42. United Nations: Transforming our world: the 2030 Agenda for Sustainable Development, vol. 16301, no. October, pp. 1–35 (2015)
43. Weaver, R.R., Lemonde, M., Payman, N., Goodman, W.M.: Health capabilities and diabetes self-management: the impact of economic, social, and cultural resources. Soc. Sci. Med. **102**, 58–68 (2014)
44. American Diabetes Association: Standards of medical care in diabetes - 2015. J. Clin. Appl. Res. Educ. **38**(January), 1–94 (2015)
45. Nelson, L.A., Mulvaney, S.A., Gebretsadik, T., Ho, Y.X., Johnson, K.B., Osborn, C.Y.: Disparities in the use of a mHealth medication adherence promotion intervention for low-income adults with type 2 diabetes. J. Am. Med. Inform. Assoc. **23**(1), 12–18 (2016)
46. Lu, J., Yu, C.-S., Liu, C.: Mobile data service demographics in urban china. J. Comput. Inf. Syst. **50**(2), 117–126 (2009)

Categorization of Factors Influencing Community Health Workers from a Socio-Technical Systems Perspective

Lilies Ratshidi[1] , Sara Grobbelaar[1,2(✉)] , and Adele Botha[1,3]

[1] Department of Industrial Engineering, Stellenbosch University,
Stellenbosch, South Africa
ssgrobbelaar@sun.ac.za
[2] DST-NRF Centre of Excellence in Scientometrics and Science,
Technology and Innovation Policy (SciSTIP), Stellenbosch University,
Stellenbosch, South Africa
[3] CSIR, Pretoria, South Africa

Abstract. In low-and-middle-income countries (LMICs), community health workers (CHWs) are often seen as a connecting bridge between two dynamic and overlapping systems- the community and formal health systems. Although the importance of CHWs is acknowledged, there is minimal aggregated evidence contributing towards understanding their position, technological capabilities, barriers and facilitators of their effectiveness in the South African context. Despite the widespread enthusiasm around the potential that mobile health (mHealth) technology holds in extending healthcare through CHW to under-served communities, an understanding of mHealth's various implications in a developing world context is imperative to appreciate both the community and health systems context. The CHWs within this context need to assume multiple roles as they work and live amongst and in the community. The study argues that by examining their multiple roles as part of the healthcare continuum and from within the community setting, appropriating technological solutions can be conceptualized to facilitate and enhance their impact and visibility. This research article then aims to articulate the key conceptual factors which should be considered when implementing technological solutions for CHWs within the South African context. The aim is operationalized by means of the best-fit framework synthesis method to explore the body of knowledge towards presenting a conceptual understanding through a categorization of Factors Influencing Community Health Workers from a Socio-Technical Systems Perspective.

Keywords: Community health worker · Social system · Technical system · Technological solutions · Concepts · Factors

1 Introduction

The constitution of South Africa enshrines the provision of healthcare access as a basic human right for all its citizens. However, the South African healthcare system is fraught with challenges, some of the major ones include the inadequacy of human and

M. Hattingh et al. (Eds.): I3E 2020, LNCS 12067, pp. 84–95, 2020.
https://doi.org/10.1007/978-3-030-45002-1_8

equipment resources [1], difficulties in synergizing and collaborating policies and lack of legislative commitment to improving the public health sector [2]. According to the World Health Organization, the shortage of healthcare workers is a major challenge in a country's ability to overhaul its healthcare system and ultimately, achieve universal healthcare coverage [2]. Given South Africa's limited resources, the need for cost-effective strategies is paramount. Recent studies [3, 4] identify an adequately competent workforce with multi-faceted roles as having the potential to relieve some of the healthcare system burdens by bridging the healthcare equity gap.

Several authors [1, 2, 4] have suggested that CHWs as a workforce could be beneficial in the South African context. In addition, it is noted that CHWs are considered a dependable vehicle to provide quality contextual health services both in urban and rural settings within the South African context [5]. The South African government has introduced various initiatives to address the historic disparate healthcare system [1]. One such initiative is the National Development Plan for 2030 that involves building human resources to ensure shared competencies for the health system as part of its plan of action. Part of this plan includes a goal of employing and training between 700 000 and 1.3 million CHWs to implement community-based primary healthcare [5]. Regardless of the effort needed to reach this goal quantitively, it can be argued that the potential benefits of CHWs have not to be realized. This can be attributed to a misalignment in national policies and standards to their work practices, and the significant barriers in training CHWs to function at the expected level of competence [2, 6].

With the widespread use of mobile technology in Sub Saharan Africa over the past years, there is an estimated increase to 40% of mobile internet penetration [7]. There is mounting evidence that suggests the use of mobile health has the potential to enable CHWs to mitigate some of the challenges faced [7]. Consequently, the utilization of technology as a viable solution for CHWs has steadily gained significant popularity. Despite this, various authors' calls for research specifically focused on investigating mHealth implementation for CHWS in low-and-medium-income countries (LMICs). The definition of LMICs adopted was according to the World Bank classification with the study focusing more on the Sub-Saharan region [8]. Winters *et al.* [9] articulate this as a call for more robust evidence on mobile technology implementation strategies as a means of supporting CHW practices [9]. Granja *et al.* [10] suggest the successful implementation of technological solutions interventions can be improved through the identification of factors that influences the intervention's outcomes.

From these insights, it can be inferred that an in-depth understanding of the healthcare domain and the processes of technology adoption and use by CHW are a needed step towards achieving the full potential of mHealth. In this regard, various studies have identified factors influencing CHWs. These factors include their perceived performance, motivation and job satisfaction [6, 10]. However, verification of how these factors affect the implementation and evaluation of technological solutions for LMICs has not sufficiently been documented. This study aims to articulate the key conceptual factors which should be considered when implementing technological solutions for CHWs within the South African context. The paper outline is as follows: method, descriptive statistics of the results, discussion and construction of the framework, and the conclusion.

2   Method

2.1   Methodological Approach

The study is grounded in social and technical perspectives as it facilitates the duality of the CHWs' work and community role, further adopts the technique of the "best-fit" framework synthesis method in the exploration. The best-fit framework synthesis is defined in [12] as "a means to test, reinforce and build on an existing model, conceived for a potentially different but relevant population". This method involves creating or employing a framework with priori themes and using it to code the data obtained from the relevant studies as a means to produce a rapid and pragmatic form of synthesis [12]. It advises the use of criteria; one for identifying the models and theories to generate a priori framework, and one for populating the scoping review of primary qualitative research studies. In this study, only one set of the literature search and a study selection was considered for the scoping review as the socio-technical system (STS) framework was used as a *priori* framework. Figure 1 illustrates the methodology approach applied.

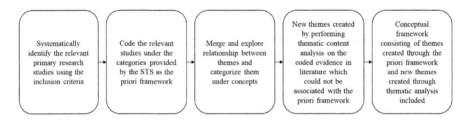

Fig. 1.   Methodology approach

2.2   The Case for STS as a Priori Framework

Davis *et al.* [13] describes the STS framework as a system which considers the people involved with distinct social behaviors and skills, working within a physical infrastructure, using a range of technologies and tools to achieve a set of goals and metrics by following sets of processes and practices under a set of cultural assumptions and norms [12, 13]. STS is defined as an approach to complex work design consisting of technical systems; social systems with an interplay of human agents employing social dependencies that either hold or emerge between them; and finally, organizations that are heterogeneous within unpredictable operational environments, which are autonomous and poorly controllable [14].

The STS theory premises on the combination of social and technical aspects to design a functional work system that can cope with the complexities of the environment within which the system operates in, as well as the dynamics introduced by new technological interventions [15]. Hence, to account for the delicate dynamic relationships within the CHWs' work system, the STS framework was used to diagnose, identify and categorize the literature into the factors and interactions between the social and technical elements, and a summary of the study characteristics was transferred to Excel for further synthesis, where they were categorized as either technical or social to generate key inferences regarding the factors which should be considered. The six interrelated elements used are people, infrastructures, goals, technologies, culture, and processes embedded within an external environment [13]. Having overviewed the methodology approach the following section outlines the search strategy employed. In [13], six interrelated elements were presented in the conceptualization of an STS and were used to evaluate the initiatives documented in the literature, from which relevant factors related to each element were identified.

2.3   Search Strategy and Inclusion Criteria

A broad literature search was conducted on Scopus, Google, Research Gate, and Google Scholar to identify studies related to CHW initiatives and technology implementation previously conducted in LMICs. The keywords used for the search were: *CHWs, framework, technology, healthcare innovation ecosystem, social factors, technical factors, socio-technical systems approach in healthcare,* and *LMICs.* Figure 2 illustrates how the selected inclusion criteria were applied to identify the relevant articles. An iterative process facilitated the addition and removal of studies that were not explicitly addressed by the inclusion criteria. The data extraction process involved recording the full-text articles into publication year, region setting, study type, methodology and key findings after which the six elements were used to identify the relevant factors from the selected literature and categorize them under social or technical perspective [13].

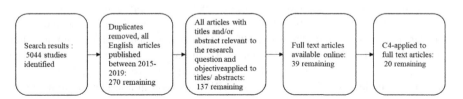

Fig. 2. Flow diagram of the applied inclusion criteria

3   Descriptive Statistics Findings

Of the 20 articles included for full-text analysis, most of them used qualitative and mixed methods inquiries involving interviews, focus group discussions with CHWs, healthcare systems stakeholders from government and non-governmental initiatives. The studies were conducted in LMICs including South Africa, Uganda, Ethiopia, Kenya, Mozambique, India, and Zimbabwe. The type of publications resulted in 10 articles on reviews, 6 articles on empirical and 4 on analysis studies.

4 Discussion: Synthesis and Categorization of Factors

The conceptualization of an STS presented in [13] was adapted and applied to the categorization in this study. The following discussion reflects on the analysis and synthesis deduced from the identified literature studies and used to categorize the relevant factors.

4.1 Social Aspect

A study by Naimoli *et al.* [16] posit that the health outcomes achieved through CHWs programs are a function of a robust, high performing health and community sectoral systems. The study further postulates that the programming activities categorized under social, technical and incentives support functions are influenced by a range of contextual factors in both community and health sectoral systems [16]. However, the narrative presented in the previous studies alludes there is unbalanced attention on the impact of the complex and diverse context-specific nature within which CHWs work and live in [17]. As a result, De Neve *et al.* [17] propose the need for countries to develop coherent and context-specific approaches to ensure optimal performance by CHWs through the consideration of the broader context, including demographic, socioeconomic, political, legislative, ecological, sociocultural, and technological factors contributing towards facilitating or inhibiting the success of many CHWs initiatives [18, 19]. Some of the solutions to achieve what is postulated in the studies include coordinating the health system and community system to prioritize factors that inhibit or facilitate the understanding of CHWs programs' compatibility with community structures, cultural values, and perception, socio-economic context and support system [20].

In addition, integrating and adopting interventions supported by technological solutions, and the sustainability of these interventions should be considered when exploring efforts until the desired health outcomes are achieved to gain a better understanding of CHWs programs and their roles in LMICs [17]. Previous research that was focused on CHWs and their performance placed emphasis on developing frameworks that provide a broad context of the CHW's position in a larger environment by describing the interrelations of intrapersonal, family, community, and organizational settings as health professionals [6, 10]. This perspective to a larger extent provides a limited understanding of the impact of the ecological environment on CHWs [20]. Most programs have not been able to effectively address the gap between research evidence and the routine practicality of CHWs as health professions, hence the poor integration of CHWs within the healthcare system and an even poorer understanding of their roles within their communities. Subsequently, the implication of this postulates the need for a comprehensive approach to plan and design programs that can be integrated with the formal healthcare system's approach to healthcare service delivery through CHWs roles and organizations [17].

Moreover, the CHW system requires an interface with the formal healthcare and the community systems involving the political structures, civic groups, faith-based organizations. Schneider and Lehmann [21] argue that integrating CHWs into the primary healthcare systems while embedding and supporting them through the community is vital to realize their potential. Contrarily, most studies emphasize the need for CHWs to be integrated within the formal healthcare system whilst placing minimal emphasis on understanding how they are embedded within the community system [21]. Moreover, minimal work has been done locally in terms of implementing universal guidelines to guide the integration strategies required to resolve the above-stated implications. Previous research has proved that the effectiveness of CHWs holds the potential to increase access to equitable health in LMICs [20]. As a result, CHWs' understanding of the socio-cultural norms of their communities, their unique intermediary position between communities and the health system places them in a central setting in delivering key health interventions. On an individual level, their effectiveness is influenced by contextual factors, such as socio-cultural factors, gender, traditions and norms, training and supervision, health policies combined with intervention-related factors [22].

Furthermore, it is postulated in [16] that support for CHWs has to be strategic, collaborative and well-coordinated to enhance CHWs performance between the two overlapping dynamic systems they are expected to function within. Among the key challenges presented in the study, the definition and optimization of the impact of the CHWs' roles are highlighted as an influence on CHW performance. Also, [3] argues that government and non-governmental institutions are continuously adding functions and tasks to CHWs, which buttresses the need to inform the type of tasks and position they hold within the healthcare system through competency-based or educational qualification rather than on functionalities. In most LMICs such as South Africa, the roles and responsibilities of CHWs with regards to technical and social capital is limited and yet to be understood [11]. Khalala *et al.* [23] state that understanding the nature of the work CHWs do, enables researchers to explore the relevant technologies that can be exploited to facilitate and support their daily work. This understanding potentially provides information with regards to the choice of technology and how it can be implemented to support the roles of CHWs. Regardless of the evidence on the social factors influencing CHWs, the exact mechanisms on how to assess the interdependencies of social and technical dynamics' influence on CHWs outcomes remains understudied.

4.2 Technical Aspect

Technologies are not neutral or passive objects but rather shape the environment and provoke social dynamics as a result of their existence and necessity for human survival. Previous studies reveal that technologies have the potential to influence social, cultural and economic contexts and improve healthcare quality for communities when employed in the healthcare domain [24]. Expectedly, the use of mobile technology in South Africa in the healthcare system has also increased, particularly among CHWs [25]. Despite CHWs having limited formal education and training, with poorly defined roles in using technologies within their line of work, it has been emphasized in [4] that most research has focused on the usability and reliability of technologies with minimal emphasis on the users and the important aspect that they are social beings who interact with their immediate and remote communities. Iluyemi *et al.* [26] state that to conceptualize technological solutions and their policy interventions, it is important to start by gaining an understanding of the context of use and needs for the technology from the CHWs' perspective. In addition, the challenges of technology's usability and supportive structures. Existing literature have focused on the reliability, functionality and infrastructure of the technology while paying minimal attention to the end-users perception on the usability and intentions to use the technology, as a result most of the research focus on the technical characteristics whilst neglecting the impact of the social characteristics of both the individual and community setting where the technology is utilized [27].

Nonetheless, this implies there is a need to conceptualize the appropriate technologies which can both fit the task they are used to as well as have the capabilities to perform the task. Moreover, technology and policy interventions are deemed as necessary developments to enhance technological effectiveness and efficiency, and to ensure sustainability and scalability through the initiatives whilst amplifying their impact [28]. Thus, the technology acceptance dimensions are considered in describing the understanding of the technological capabilities of CHWs, their ability to access and utilize the appropriate technologies applicable to their social backgrounds. There is undeniable evidence from previous studies about the importance of considering the sociotechnical determinants in developing implementation and evaluation conceptual models for technological solutions. Determinants including technological appropriateness and socio-cultural sensitivity, political infrastructures, the technology end-users' attributes and variables of ecological settings [29]. In a formative study about the adoption and usage of mHealth by CHWs in India, Kaphle *et al.* [20] hypothesized that individual characteristics of end-users such as education, experience of care, and demographics hold the potential to influence the uptake of technological adoptions and quality of care. In addition, Kim *et al.* [30] reinforces that the attitude of health professions to use technology influences the behavioral intention to use it.

As a result, the relationship between technology and CHWs' performance is associated with their readiness to align their behavioral intention to use the technology. Important to note, technological solutions and processes are not autonomous vehicles, but rather are embedded within systems in a social world where they are used to perform activities which have consequences and influences changes on human behavior, social constructs, and cultural meanings. Thus, the effect of this is that not only does the interaction between the technical and social systems exhibit complexity and unpredictable behavior; it inevitably increases the complexities of dynamic and autonomous relationships, which can be detrimental to the system in place. From the above sections, the following is presented in summary to illustrate the factors identified in the discussion using the STS hexagon for illustration as provided in [13]. Figure 3 illustrates the social and technical perspectives identified from previous literature according to [13].

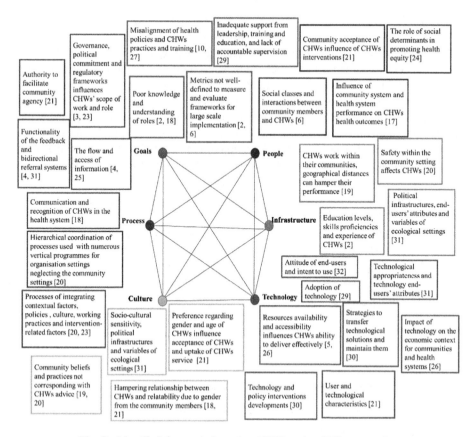

Fig. 3. Identified factors influencing CHWs using STS perspective

4.3   Integrating Factors into Concepts

From the discussion above, the factors (see Fig. 3) were categorized into concepts according to their similarities to allow for a reasonable number of concepts to be considered. The approach followed in this study desired that the design activities involve gaining understanding and specification of the context in which the system will be used by referring to the social factors, cultural factors, working practices factors, and the structure of the organization [31]. Thus, the terminologies for the concepts were adapted from this standpoint and were cautiously selected by the author through interpretation about the relevant literature as a means to preserve the relevance of the factors. The concepts were grouped under technical and social context depending on the interpretation of the author, from there, they were categorized under the two social dimensions: health and community systems context depending on whether the influence of the factor on the CHWs was related and reflective of the context in question. This study considers the following fundamental areas under the social system: the individual's needs, humans' social behaviors in work systems, internal and external environmental factors and support systems of the work system under investigation [15].

Whilst the technical system focuses on the processes, tasks, infrastructures, and technologies required and used in the work system to achieve the set goals [14]. Additionally, the technical dimensions included technology readiness which was concerned with categorizing the factors related to the technological solutions characteristics and compatibility to be used. The second dimension was technology acceptance and utilization which was concerned with factors concerning the CHWs perspectives and readiness to use and accept the technological solution within the environment they work. Finally, the compatibility/fit element was considered as a means to provide the measures required to ensure a balanced joint optimization of both the technical and social aspects [31]. Figure 4 illustrates the concepts classed under social and technical context.

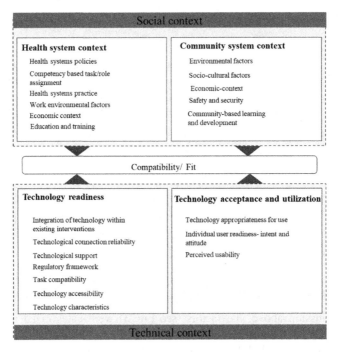

Fig. 4. Overview of the factors categorized as concepts

5   Conclusion

This research article aimed to articulate the key conceptual factors which should be considered when implementing technological solutions for CHWs within the South African context. The STS framework was used for the categorization of the factors which were integrated into concepts. For future work, each of these concepts will be evaluated and the categorization refined to present a broader conceptual framework. This study forms part of a dissertation project and the findings in this study form part of the first high-level conceptual framework which will be used in conducting scoping literature review to identify additional components for the secondary-level conceptual framework. In addition, future plans involve exploring the task-technology fit model to identify the relevant technological solutions fit for peri-urban and rural contexts in South Africa.

References

1. Maphumulo, W.T., Bhengu, B.R.: Challenges of quality improvement in the healthcare of South Africa post-apartheid: a critical review. Curationis **42**(1), 1–9 (2019)
2. White, M.S., Govender, P., Lister, H.E.: Community health workers lensed through a South African backdrop of two peri-urban communities in KwaZulu-Natal. African J. Disabil. **6**, 1–8 (2017). https://doi.org/10.4102/ajod.v6i0.294
3. Olaniran, A., Smith, H., Unkels, R., Bar-Zeev, S., van den Broek, N.: Who is a community health worker? - A systematic review of definitions. Glob. Health Action **10**(1), 1272223 (2017). https://doi.org/10.1080/16549716.2017.1272223
4. Early, J., Gonzalez, C., Gordon-Dseagu, V., Robles-Calderon, L.: Use of mobile health (mHealth) technologies and interventions among community health workers globally: a scoping review. Health Promot. Pract. **20**, 1–13 (2019). https://doi.org/10.1177/152483 9919855391
5. van Heerden, A., et al.: Perceived mHealth barriers and benefits for home-based HIV testing and counseling and other care: qualitative findings from health officials, community health workers, and persons living with HIV in South Africa. Soc. Sci. Med. **183**, 97–105 (2017). https://doi.org/10.1016/j.socscimed.2017.04.046
6. Zalani, G.S., et al.: Affecting factors on the performance of community health workers in Iran's rural areas: a review article. Iran J. Public Health **45**(11), 1399–1410 (2016)
7. Aranda-Jan, C.B., Mohutsiwa-Dibe, N., Loukanova, S.: Systematic review on what works, what does not work and why of implementation of mobile health (mHealth) projects in Africa. BMC Public Health **14**(188), 1–15 (2014)
8. World Bank Country and Lending Groups – World Bank Data Help Desk. https://datahelpdesk.worldbank.org/knowledgebase/articles/906519. Accessed 06 Jan 2020
9. Winters, N., et al.: Using mobile technologies to support the training of community health workers in low-income and middle-income countries: mapping the evidence. BMJ Glob. Heal. **4**, 1–10 (2019). https://doi.org/10.1136/bmjgh-2019-001421
10. Granja, C., Janssen, W., Johansen, M.A.: Factors determining the success and failure of ehealth interventions: systematic review of the literature. J. Med. Internet Res. **20**(5), 1–21 (2018). https://doi.org/10.2196/10235
11. Buehler, B., Ruggiero, R., Mehta, K.: Empowering community health workers with technology solutions. IEEE Technol. Soc. Mag. **32**(1), 44–52 (2013). https://doi.org/10.1109/mts.2013.2241831
12. Carroll, C., Booth, A., Leaviss, J., Rick, J.: "Best fit" framework synthesis: refining the method. BMC Med. Res. Methodol. **13**(1), 13–37 (2013). https://doi.org/10.1186/1471-2288-13-37
13. Davis, M.C., Challenger, R., Jayewardene, D.N.W.W., Clegg, C.W.: Advancing socio-technical systems thinking: a call for bravery. Appl. Ergon. **45**(2), 171–180 (2014). https://doi.org/10.1016/j.apergo.2013.02.009
14. Dalpiaz, F., Giorgini, P., Mylopoulos, J.: Adaptive socio-technical systems: a requirements-based approach, **18**, 1–24 (2013). https://doi.org/10.1007/s00766-011-0132-1

15. Mwendwa, P.: What encourages community health workers to use mobile technologies for health interventions? Emerging lessons from rural Rwanda. Dev. Policy Rev. **36**, 111–129 (2018). https://doi.org/10.1111/dpr.12275

16. Naimoli, J.F., Perry, H.B., Townsend, J.W., Frymus, D.E., McCaffery, J.A.: Strategic partnering to improve community health worker programming and performance: features of a community-health system integrated approach. Hum. Resour. Health **13**(46), 1–13 (2015). https://doi.org/10.1186/s12960-015-0041-3

17. De Neve, J.W., et al.: Harmonizing community-based health worker programs for HIV: a narrative review and analytic framework. Hum. Resour. Health **15**(1), 1–10 (2017). https://doi.org/10.1186/s12960-017-0219-y

18. Kambarami, R.A., Mbuya, N.N., Pelletier, D., Fundira, D., Tavengwa, N.V., Stoltzfus, R.J.: Factors associated with community health worker performance differ by task in a multi-tasked setting in rural Zimbabwe. Glob. Health Sci. Pract. **4**(2), 238–250 (2016)

19. Kok, M.C., et al.: Which intervention design factors influence performance of community health workers in low- and middle-income countries? A systematic review. Health Policy Plan. **30**(9), 1207–1227 (2015). https://doi.org/10.1093/heapol/czu126

20. Kaphle, S., Chaturvedi, S., Chaudhuri, I., Krishnan, R., Lesh, N.: Adoption and usage of mHealth technology on quality and experience of care provided by frontline workers: observations from rural India. JMIR mHealth uHealth **3**(2), e61 (2015). https://doi.org/10.2196/mhealth.4047

21. Schneider, H., Lehmann, U.: From community health workers to community health systems: time to widen the horizon? Health Syst. Reform **2**(2), 112–118 (2016). https://doi.org/10.1080/23288604.2016.1166307

22. Saprii, L., Richards, E., Kokho, P., Theobald, S.: Community health workers in rural India: analysing the opportunities and challenges Accredited Social Health Activists (ASHAs) face in realising their multiple roles. Hum. Resour. Health **13**(95), 1–13 (2015). https://doi.org/10.1186/s12960-015-0094-3

23. Khalala, G., Makitla, I., Botha, A., Alberts, R.: The roles and needs of community health workers in developing countries: an exploratory case study in South Africa. In: IEEE International Conference on Adaptation Science Technology ICAST, pp. 1–5 (2013). https://doi.org/10.1109/icastech.2013.6707498

24. Grover, P., Kar, A.K., Davies, G.: "Technology enabled health" – Insights from twitter analytics with a socio-technical perspective. Int. J. Inf. Manag. **43**, 85–97 (2018). https://doi.org/10.1016/j.ijinfomgt.2018.07.003

25. Lindberg, M., Rosborg, S., Ramukumba, M.M., Hägglund, M.: Adapting mHealth to workflow - a case study in South Africa. Stud. Health Technol. Inform. **265**, 48–53 (2019). https://doi.org/10.3233/SHTI190136

26. Iluyemi, A., Briggs, J., Adams, C.: Mobile information system, health work and community health workers in less developed countries. In: Proceedings of Workshops on Enabling Technologies: Infrastructure for Collaborative Enterprises, WETICE, pp. 208–209 (2007). https://doi.org/10.1109/wetice.2007.4407155

27. Winters, N., Langer, L., Geniets, A.: Scoping review assessing the evidence used to support the adoption of mobile health (mHealth) technologies for the education and training of community health workers (CHWs) in low-income and middle-income countries. BMJ Open **8**(7), 1–10 (2018). https://doi.org/10.1136/bmjopen-2017-019827

28. Gagnon, M.P., Ngangue, P., Payne-Gagnon, J., Desmartis, M.: M-Health adoption by healthcare professionals: a systematic review. J. Am. Med. Inform. Assoc. **23**(1), 212–220 (2016). https://doi.org/10.1093/jamia/ocv052

29. Aamir, J., Ali, S.M., Kamel Boulos, M.N., Anjum, N., Ishaq, M.: Enablers and inhibitors: a review of the situation regarding mHealth adoption in low- and middle-income countries. Health Policy Technol. **7**, 88–97 (2018). https://doi.org/10.1016/j.hlpt.2017.11.005
30. Kim, S., Lee, K., Hwang, H., Yoo, S.: Analysis of the factors influencing healthcare professionals' adoption of mobile electronic medical record (EMR) using the unified theory of acceptance and use of technology (UTAUT) in a tertiary hospital. BMC Med. Inform. Decis. Mak. **16**, 1–12 (2016). https://doi.org/10.1186/s12911-016-0249-8
31. Baxter, G., Sommerville, I.: Socio-technical systems: from design methods to systems engineering. Interact. Comput. **23**(1), 4–17 (2011). https://doi.org/10.1016/j.intcom.2010.07.003

A Systematic Literature Review of the Factors that Influence the Accuracy of Consumer Wearable Health Device Data

Lerato Mahloko and Funmi Adebesin$^{(\boxtimes)}$ (iD)

Department of Informatics, University of Pretoria,
Hatfield 0083, Pretoria, South Africa
Lwanyane@gmail.com, funmi.adebesin@up.ac.za

Abstract. The use of consumer wearable health device (CWHD) for fitness tracing has seen an upward trend worldwide. CWHDs support individuals in taking ownership of their personal well-being and keeping track of their fitness goals. However, there are genuine concerns over the accuracy of the data collected by these devices. In this study, we investigated the factors that influence the accuracy of the data collected by CWHDs for heart rate measurement, physical activity (PA), and sleep monitoring using a systematic literature review. Forty-seven papers were analyzed from five electronic databases based on specific inclusion and exclusion criteria. All 47 papers that we analyzed were published by authors from developed countries. Using thematic analysis, we classified the factors that influence the accuracy of the data collected by CWHDs into three main groups, namely (i) the tracker and sensor type, (ii) the algorithm used in the device, and (iii) the limitation in the design, energy consumption, and processing capability of the device. The research results point to a dearth of studies that focus on the accuracy of the data collected by CWHDs by researchers from developing countries.

Keywords: Consumer wearable health device · CWHD · Wearable health device · Wearable health device data accuracy · Systematic literature review

1 Introduction and Background

Physical inactivity is listed as one of the major contributors to mortality, resulting in an estimated 3.2 million deaths worldwide [1]. Adults are advised to engage in a minimum of 150 min of moderate-to-vigorous-intensity physical activity (PA) per week to reduce the risk of chronic diseases like hypertension, diabetes, and obesity [2, 3]. Physical inactivity can be reduced by walking, which is an inexpensive form of exercise for many adults and requires no special equipment [2, 4]. The adoption and use of consumer wearable health device (CWHD) for PA tracking is increasing. This increase is evident in wearable health technologies retaining the top-three global fitness trends since 2016, taking the first spot in 2016, 2017, and 2019 [5].

CWHDs support individuals to take ownership of their personal well-being and keep track of their fitness goals. To do this, CWHDs have features that support continuous monitoring and recording of physiological (e.g. heart rate, sleep pattern, blood

© IFIP International Federation for Information Processing 2020
Published by Springer Nature Switzerland AG 2020
M. Hattingh et al. (Eds.): I3E 2020, LNCS 12067, pp. 96–107, 2020.
https://doi.org/10.1007/978-3-030-45002-1_9

sugar levels, and so on) and PA data (e.g. duration of PA, distance covered, energy expended, and so forth) [6, 7]. To promote healthy habits, CWHDs incorporate behavioural change techniques like goal setting, self-monitoring, feedback, social influence, and reward [8]. In South Africa, the uptake of CWHDs are on the rise, especially among health-conscious individuals in the urban areas. This increase can partly be attributed to new practice by health insurers who use incentives to motivate their members to use wearable health device to track their PA [9].

In addition to the increase in the adoption of CWHDs by health-conscious individuals to track PA, wearable health devices are also used for remote monitoring of people with chronic disease conditions [6, 10, 11]. In both of these usage conditions, it is important that the data collected by the device is accurate. Inaccurate data from wearable health devices could lead to dire consequences, especially when the device is integrated with healthcare applications [12]. Manufacturers of CWDHs often make strong claims about the accuracy and reliability of their devices [13]. However, there are genuine concerns over the accuracy of the data collected by CWHDs [14]. For example accelerometer and pedometer-based CWHDs are known to be inaccurate in their estimation of energy expended (EE), and are unable to accurately track the number of steps in PA like cycling [6, 7]. Users of CWHDs expect, and are increasingly demanding that manufacturers deliver on their promises. The two class action lawsuits filed by users against one of the major manufacturers of CWHD in 2016 underscore the importance of accurate and reliable data collected by CWHDs [15]. Hence, it is no surprise that many researchers from developed countries [16–18] are focusing on the accuracy of the data collected by CWHDs. As discussed later in Sect. 3, all the papers analyzed in this systematic literature review (SLR) were published by authors from developed countries. This points to an apparent dearth of studies that focus on the accuracy of the data collected by CWHDs by researchers from developed countries, including Africa. To address this gap, this research investigates the factors that influence the accuracy of the data collected by CWHDs. More specifically the research focuses on the accuracy of the data generated from heart rate measurement, PA, and sleep monitoring. The research question that we address in the paper is: *"What are the factors that influence the accuracy of the data collected by consumer health wearable devices?"*.

The remaining sections of the paper are structured as follow: In Sect. 2 we present the process that was followed in the SLR. This is followed by detailed discussions of our analysis of the papers included in the SLR in Sect. 3. In Sect. 4, we discuss the study contribution, limitations, and the implications for the manufacturers of CWHDs.

2 Systematic Literature Review Process

In order to scope the SLR process, research articles were retrieved from the following scientific databases, based on their publication of quality and high impact research journals and conference papers: IEEE, PUBMED-NCBI, ScienceDirect, MDPI, and Springer. To ensure that we retrieve relevant papers, we used the following search phrases: "Consumer wearable health device" OR "wearable health device" OR "wearable health technology" OR "Personal health device" AND "Data Accuracy" OR "Reliability".

Inclusion and Exclusion Criteria. Only candidate papers that met the inclusion criteria, specified in Fig. 1, were screened for possible inclusion in the SLR. Papers were excluded based on the criteria specified in Fig. 1.

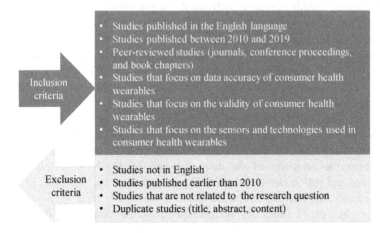

Fig. 1. Inclusion and exclusion criteria.

Source Selection. The search period for the SLR was between April and October 2019. An initial search on Google Scholar returned more than 22 000 results. To ensure a more realistic number of potential papers to screen for eligibility, we focused specifically on five databases, namely IEEE, PUBMED-NCBI, ScienceDirect, MDPI, and Springer. A total of 1393 papers were retrieved from the five databases. An additional 20 papers were retrieved from other sources (see Sect. 3 for the list of other sources), thus yielding a total of 1413 candidate papers for screening. Details of all 1413 papers were extracted and copied into an Excel worksheet with the following columns: Title, Author, Publication type, DOI, Abstract, Relevance, Included/Excluded 1st Screening, and Included/Excluded 2nd Screening.

In Excel, a Vertical Lookup (VLOOKUP) was performed on the papers' Title and DOI to check for duplicates. This process resulted in 1214 unique sources. Thereafter, the 1214 sources were reviewed against the inclusion and exclusion criteria specified in Fig. 1, resulting in 465 papers. We then screened the 465 papers for relevance based on their title, keywords, and abstract. Of the 465 papers, 311 were excluded based on their title and 70 were excluded based on their abstracts. Thus, the remaining 84 papers were marked as relevant and eligible for further screening.

We carried out a first level screening on the remaining 84 papers by reading the abstracts, findings, and conclusion sections of the papers. After reading the three sections, we assigned a priority level of 'high' (focus is on accuracy of CWHDs with comparisons/validation between various devices), 'medium' (focus is on accuracy of CWHDs but no comparisons/validation between various devices) or 'low' (focus is on CWHDs but with emphasis on big data, mobile health apps, smart cloth technologies, etc.) to the relevance column of each paper. Following the first level screening, a total of 36 papers were assigned 'low' priority and thus excluded from the study. The second level of screening involved full text reading of the remaining 47 papers. Figure 2 illustrates the source selection process.

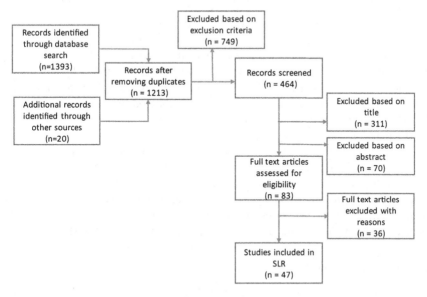

Fig. 2. Source selection process.

3   Results

In this section, we present the results obtained from the analysis of the 47 papers included in the SLR.

Quantitative analysis of the 47 papers using descriptive statistics showed that 17 were published in IEEE, 16 in PUBMED-NCBI database, five were published in ScienceDirect, and two were published in MDPI and Springer databases respectively. The remaining six were papers from BMC Public Health, PLOS Medicine, Routledge, Albany Law Journal of Science & Technology, and USENIX. Table 1 shows the distribution of the papers across the databases.

Table 1. Distribution of research papers per database.

Database	No of papers	% of papers
IEEE	17	36%
PUBMED-NCBI	16	34%
ScienceDirect	4	9%
MDPI	2	4%
Springer	2	4%
Others	6	13%
Total	47	100%

Our analysis of the papers according to year of publication shows that the majority of papers were published between 2016 (13) and 2017 (12). The number of publications tapered down to eight in 2018, with only one of the papers analyzed being published in 2019. These statistics show increasing interest of researchers in the accuracy of the data collected by CWHDs. The limited number of papers in 2019 should not be construed as waning interest in the topic. Rather, it can be attributed to the search period for sources that were included in the SLR.

Our analysis of the papers included in the SLR shows that all authors are from developed countries. The majority of the papers (13) were published by authors from the United States of America (USA). There were six papers from Australia, five from China, and four from Korea. Three papers were published by authors from Italy and Japan respectively. There were two papers published by authors from Denmark, the United Kingdom, and Germany respectively. Authors from Argentina, Canada, India, Malaysia, Netherlands, Portugal, and Spain published one paper each. Based on our analysis, authors from African countries are conspicuously absent in the publication of papers that focus on the accuracy of the data collected by CWHDs.

Following the quantitative analysis, we identified common themes in the papers and grouped them into three categories. In the following sub-sections, we discuss the three main factors that influence the accuracy of the data collected by CWHDs.

3.1 The Tracker and Sensor Types

The type of sensor technology fitted into CWHD and the body part where the device is attached can influence the accuracy of the data collected by the device. [10, 11, 19]. Our analysis of the papers included in the SLR showed that the sensor type that typically comes with CWHDs include one or a combination of the following:

- Photoplethysmography (PPG) sensors: PPG sensors are used in CWHD to monitor heart rate. Using optical sensors, changes in the blood volume of body tissues can be detected by shining light on the surface of the skin to detect discoloration when oxygen-rich blood is 'flushed' underneath the skin [12, 20].
- Pedometer and accelerometer: Pedometer is a lightweight device with sensor that measures the number of steps taken or the distance covered. Accelerometer measures PA by detecting movements across three planes (side-to-side, up-and-down, or forward-and-backward) [21].
- Actigraphy: This is a non-invasive, wrist-worn device that comes with accelerometer to measure sleep pattern by distinguishing between the states of wakefulness and sleep unobtrusively. This is based on the premise that limited movement is associated with sleep while increased movement is linked with wakefulness [22, 23].

PPG sensors can be attached to various body parts, including the upper arm, the earlobe, the forehead, the wrist, or the finger. The part of the body where a PPG sensor is attached can influence its level of accuracy. Signals from finger-based PPG sensors have higher wavelengths compared to other sites. This makes finger-based PPG sensors more accurate. However, wearing a finger-based PPG sensor can interfere with daily routines, which makes their use less practical compared to other PPG sensors [19].

Another factor that could influence the accuracy of PPG sensors is the colour of the light emitting diode (LED) light that comes with the sensor. The majority of CWHDs that utilize PPG sensors for monitoring heart rate come with green light PPG (gPPG) [12, 24, 25]. However, red light PPG (rPPG) sensors (i.e. pulse oximeters) are commonly used in clinical environments [12, 25–27]. rPPG sensors have a number of advantages over gPPG sensors. The green light in gPPG sensors emits shorter wavelengths and does not penetrate deeper into the innermost layer of the skin. In contrast, rPPG sensors can penetrate deeper into the skin because the human body does not absorb the red light [25, 26]. This property enables rPPG sensors to detect other biological signals like the arterial oxygen saturation, respiration, and blood pressure [24, 26, 27]. In addition, rPPG light is not absorbed by melanin (the pigmentation that is responsible for the colour of the human skin) but gPPG light absorbs melanin. Therefore, the skin colour does not influence the accuracy of heart rate measurements when using rPPG sensors. In contrast, darker skin colours influence the accuracy of gPPG sensors [19, 26, 28].

A drawback of rPPG sensors is that they are more susceptible to background noise generated from the body part that the device is attached (for example, hand waving or rubbing), often referred to as 'motion artefact'. Motion artefacts are known to have negative influence on the accuracy of rPPG sensors. This is not the case for gPPG sensors, which are less vulnerable to the effects of motion artifacts [19, 25, 29].

Sleep, increased PA, and good nutrition are integral parts of maintaining personal well-being. Prior to the pervasive adoption and use of CWHDs, monitoring and tracking of sleep can only be carried out in specialized sleep laboratories using polysomnography (PSG). PSG measures sleep quality by collecting data on eye movements, heart rates, muscle tones, brain activities, and physical movements [13, 22]. The unnatural setting and the need for a sleep technologist to set up PSG equipment make its use impractical in a home setting. Consumer wearable sleep monitoring sensors, called actigraphy, is a non-invasive wrist-worn device that comes with accelerometer, heart rate, and respiratory monitor to detect and record the movements of the wearer at regular intervals in order to estimate sleep and wakefulness [13, 22, 23, 30, 31].

Actigraphy has been shown to be accurate in detecting the state of sleep, but less so in sensing wakefulness. For example, lying down could be misinterpreted as sleep due to the absence of movements, thereby leading to overestimation [13, 23, 32]. This deficiency is primarily due to the fact that actigraphy associates reduced movements with sleep. As such, actigraphy is not very effective in monitoring the different stages of sleep.

CWHDs are equipped with sensors to track PA in the form of pedometer or accelerometer. Previous studies show that while CWHDs with pedometer sensors are effective in estimating step counts, they typically underestimate energy expenditure (EE). Accelerometers on the other hand are deficient in their accurate measurement of steps taken in PA like cycling [3, 6, 7, 33]. The placement of a PA sensor and the speed of walking are some of the factors that could influence its accuracy. Pedometers are less accurate when the sensor is attached to the wrist or hip, compared to ankle-based pedometers. Similarly, slower walking speed, unsteady and uneven gaits influence accuracy [33–36]. In the case of accelerometers, Nelson et al. [6] found that wrist-worn accelerometers are more accurate than hip-worn sensors. However, Simpson et al. [36]

suggest that better accuracy could be achieved when an accelerator sensor is place around the ankle, especially for individuals that walk at slower speeds.

3.2 The Algorithm Used in Consumer Wearable Health Devices

The algorithm used to monitor health parameters by CWHDs is another factor that influence the accuracy of the data collected by the devices [37]. The built-in algorithms in CWHDs support the measurement of bio-sensory and PA data, their processing, and the communication of the outcome of the measurements to the user. Manufacturers of CWHDs do not disclose the algorithms that are used to track and measure bio-sensory and PA for proprietary reasons [17, 33, 38, 39]. This makes it difficult for users to objectively make comparison between devices. In this section, we summarize the algorithms that could be used to monitor heart rate and PA. The discussion of algorithms is limited to the ones reported in the papers that were included in the SLR.

Algorithms for detecting and monitoring motion and PA, developed or proposed by researchers, include pedestrian dead reckoning (PDR) and zero velocity update (ZUPT) algorithms [38, 40, 41]. PDR algorithm estimates walking distance by sensing the number of steps taken and the length of each step. PDR algorithms are more accurate in their estimation of distance covered when the tracking device is attached to the foot [40]. ZUPT algorithm is used to detect and bound static position errors that are accumulated when calculating distance covered using a PDR algorithm. The ZUPT algorithm then detects the periodic static states when the foot returns flat to the ground during walking [40, 41].

Researchers like [27, 41–44] have proposed algorithms that could improve signals from PPG sensors, thereby improving their accuracy. As discussed in Sect. 3.1, the PPG sensors used to monitor heart rates are susceptible to background noise from 'motion artefacts', which could affect the accuracy of heart rate measurements. In their study, Yang et al. [27] develop an Adaptive Spectrum Noise Cancellation (ASNC) algorithm that significantly improve accuracy when 'motion artefact' increases. Yousefi et al. [41] also propose a motion-tolerant algorithm to improve signals from PPG sensors by removing 'motion artefacts'. Similarly, Tang et al. [44] use the Empirical Mode Decomposition (EMD) and Discrete Wavelet Transform (DWT) algorithms to enhance and reduce noise from PPG signals. These authors provide evidence that demonstrate the ability of the algorithms to improve the accuracy of heart rates captured by PPG sensors.

Another element that is closely linked to the algorithms used to measure bio-sensory and PA data is the firmware installed on CWHDs. Firmware updates are necessary to ensure optimal performance and the security the data collected by the device. However, CWHDs can become vulnerable to privacy and security threats during firmware updates. The authors, Fereidooni et al. [45] and, Lin and Sun [46] provide evidence that it is possible for people with the technical wherewithal to inject arbitrary or malicious codes into CWHDs' firmware during updates. The ability to modify firmware by unauthorized persons can affect the integrity of the data collected by CWHDs. Another concern about firmware updates is that the same CWHD could provide different measurements, depending on the firmware applied. Thus distorting the measurements even if other variables remain unchanged [39].

3.3   Limitations in the Design, Energy Consumption, and Processing Capabilities

Based on our analysis of the papers included in this SLR, the third main factor that could influence the accuracy of the data collected by CWHDs relates to inherent limitations in the design, energy consumption, and the processing capability of a device.

CWHDs are increasingly becoming part of the evolving Internet of Things (IoT) ecosystem. IoT-enabled wearable health devices provide opportunity for continuous monitoring of patients from the comfort of their homes and the transfer of health data to healthcare providers. However, the performance, energy consumption, and the form factor could influence the success of IoT-enabled CWHDs [47]. The convenience and usefulness of a CWHD is dependent on the balance between the device's size and its battery life. Smaller devices are easier to carry, but do not always have longer battery life. Conversely, longer battery life is commonly associated with bigger size devices [47, 48]. Additional strain is placed on the energy requirements of CWHDs due to continuous collection and exchange of physiological data between a CWHD, other connected IoT devices and applications (apps) [49].

The quality of the components (battery, storage capacity, Bluetooth module, etc.) fitted unto CWHDs can influence the accuracy of the data collected by the device. In a study by Haghi et al. [50], the authors confirm the influence of high-quality components on the performance of CWHDs. Components such as high storage capacity, long wearing battery, Bluetooth, and Wi-Fi compatibility performed better and were more accurate than devices with low quality components.

4   Conclusion

This paper presents a SLR of 47 papers that focus on the accuracy of the data collected by CWHDs. The results of our analysis showed that the highest number of papers were published in two high-quality databases, namely IEEE (36%) and PUBMED-NCBI (33%). 10% of the papers were published in ScienceDirect, while MDPI and Springer were at 2% respectively. The remaining 13% papers were published in journals such as BMC Public Health and PLOS Medicine. All 47 papers analyzed in the SLR were published by authors from developed countries, with the majority from the USA, followed by Australia and China. None of the authors are from developing countries, including Africa. This points to a gap in studies that focus on the accuracy of the data collected by CWHDs by authors are from developing countries. Based on our analysis, there are three main factors that influence the accuracy of the data collected by CWHDs. These are (i) the tracker and sensor type, (ii) the algorithm used in the CWHD, and (iii) the limitation in the design, energy consumption, and the processing capability of the device.

The study has a number of limitations. Firstly, the search and extraction of sources were based on specific key phrases that include consumer wearable health device and data accuracy. This meant that papers that could potentially have been relevant were excluded from the study because they did not use our search phrases in their keywords.

Secondly, the study focused specifically on the accuracy of the data generated from heart rate measurement, PA, and sleep monitoring data. Research papers that focused on the accuracy of CWHDs in general were excluded from the study. The inclusion of such papers could have increased the number of factors beyond the three identified in this study. Finally, the proprietary nature of algorithms used to track and measure bio-sensory and PA data meant that the algorithms reported on in the study were those developed or proposed by researchers.

This study contributes to the number research that focus on the accuracy of the data collected by CWHDs. Given the increasing trend in the use of CWHDs across the globe, and the limited number of studies from developing countries that focus on the topic of accuracy of the data collected by CWHDs, it is imperative that more research is done to better understand the factors that influence their accuracy. The study also has implications for the manufacturers of CWHDs. It is important that the manufacturers of CWHDs take into account the factors that influence data accuracy in the design and development of their devices. This will enable users and healthcare professionals to make meaningful use of the data generated by these device, thus contributing to improved personal well-being and the quality of healthcare service delivery.

References

1. WHO: Fiscal policies for diet and the prevention of noncommunicable diseases. https://www.who.int/dietphysicalactivity/publications/fiscal-policies-diet-prevention/en/. Accessed 06 May 2019
2. Faghri, P.D., Omokaro, C., Parker, C., Nichols, E., Gustavesen, S., Blozie, E.: E-technology and pedometer walking program to increase physical activity at work. J. Prim. Prevent. **29**, 73–91 (2008). https://doi.org/10.1007/s10935-007-0121-9
3. Wise, J., Hongu, N.: Pedometer, accelerometer, and mobile technology for promoting physical activity. https://extension.arizona.edu/sites/extension.arizona.edu/files/pubs/az1491-2014.pdf. Accessed 17 Aug 2019
4. Dunton, G.F., Schneider, M.: Perceived barriers to walking for physical activity. Prevent. Chronic Dis. **3**, A116 (2006)
5. Thompson, W.R.: Worldwide survey of fitness trends for 2019. ACSM's Health Fitness J. **22**, 10–17 (2018). https://doi.org/10.1249/FIT.0000000000000438
6. Nelson, M.B., Kaminsky, L.A., Dickin, D.C., Montoye, A.H.: Validity of consumer-based physical activity monitors for specific activity types. Med. Sci. Sports Exerc. **48**, 1619–1628 (2016). https://doi.org/10.1249/MSS.0000000000000933
7. Butte, N.F., Ekelund, U., Westerterp, K.R.: Assessing physical activity using wearable monitors: measures of physical activity. Med. Sci. Sports Exerc. **44**, S5–S12 (2012). https://doi.org/10.1249/MSS.0b013e3182399c0e
8. Mercer, K., Li, M., Giangregorio, L., Burns, C., Grindrod, K.: Behavior change techniques present in wearable activity trackers: a critical analysis. JMIR mHealth uHealth **4**, e40 (2016). https://doi.org/10.2196/mhealth.4461
9. Bond-Myatt, C.: Health wearables, apps & information protection. https://home.kpmg.com/za/en/home/insights/2016/06/health-wearables–apps—information-protection.html. Accessed 22 Oct 2019

10. Kakria, P., Tripathi, N., Kitipawang, P.: A real-time health monitoring system for remote cardiac patients using smartphone and wearable sensors. Int. J. Telemed. Appl. **2015**, 8 (2015). https://doi.org/10.1155/2015/373474

11. Kalantarian, H., Lee, S.I., Mishra, A., Ghasemzadeh, H., Liu, J., Sarrafzadeh, M.: Multimodal energy expenditure calculation for pervasive health: a data fusion model using wearable sensors. In: 2013 IEEE International Conference on Pervasive Computing and Communications Workshops (PERCOM Workshops), pp. 676–681. IEEE (2013)

12. Naeinia, E.K., Azimib, I., Rahmania, A.M., Liljebergb, P., Dutta, N.: A real-time PPG quality assessment approach for healthcare Internet-of-Things. Procedia Comput. Sci. **151**, 551–558 (2019). https://doi.org/10.1016/j.procs.2019.04.074

13. Roomkham, S., Lovell, D., Cheung, J., Perrin, D.: Promises and challenges in the use of consumer-grade devices for sleep monitoring. IEEE Rev. Biomed. Eng. **11**, 53–67 (2018). https://doi.org/10.1109/RBME.2018.2811735

14. Xie, J., Wen, D., Liang, L., Jia, Y., Gao, L., Lei, J.: Evaluating the validity of current mainstream wearable devices in fitness tracking under various physical activities: comparative study. JMIR mHealth uHealth **6**, e94 (2018). https://doi.org/10.2196/mhealth.9754

15. Lang, M.: Beyond fitbit: a critical appraisal of optical heart rate monitoring wearables and apps, their current limitations and legal implications. Albany Law J. Sci. Technol. **28**, 39–72 (2017)

16. Shcherbina, A., et al.: Accuracy in wrist-worn, sensor-based measurements of heart rate and energy expenditure in a diverse cohort. J. Personal. Med. **7**, 3 (2017). https://doi.org/10.3390/jpm7020003

17. Thiebaud, R.S., et al.: Validity of wrist-worn consumer products to measure heart rate and energy expenditure. Digit. Health **4**, 1–7 (2018). https://doi.org/10.1177/2055207618770322

18. Wallen, M.P., Gomersall, S.R., Keating, S.E., Wisløff, U., Coombes, J.S.: Accuracy of heart rate watches: implications for weight management. PLoS ONE **11**, e0154420 (2016). https://doi.org/10.1371/journal.pone.0154420

19. Tamura, T., Maeda, Y., Sekine, M., Yoshida, M.: Wearable photoplethysmographic sensors-past and present. Electronics **3**, 282–302 (2014). https://doi.org/10.3390/electronics3020282

20. Holtermann, A., et al.: A practical guidance for assessments of sedentary behavior at work: a PEROSH initiative. Appl. Ergon. **63**, 41–52 (2017). https://doi.org/10.1016/j.apergo.2017.03.012

21. Wise, J., Hongu, N.: Pedometer, accelerometer, and mobile technology for promoting physical activity. https://extension.arizona.edu/sites/extension.arizona.edu/files/pubs/az1491-2014.pdf. Accessed 8 Nov 2019

22. Kosmadopoulos, A., Sargent, C., Darwent, D., Zhou, X., Roach, G.D.: Alternatives to polysomnography (PSG): a validation of wrist actigraphy and a partial-PSG system. Behav. Res. Methods **46**, 1032–1041 (2014). https://doi.org/10.3758/s13428-013-0438-7

23. Park, K.S., Choi, S.H.: Smart technologies toward sleep monitoring at home. Biomed. Eng. Lett. **9**, 73–85 (2019). https://doi.org/10.1007/s13534-018-0091-2

24. Lee, S., Shin, H., Hahm, C.: Effective PPG sensor placement for reflected red and green light, and infrared wristband-type photoplethysmography. In: 18th International Conference on Advanced Communication Technology (ICACT), pp. 556–558. IEEE (2016)

25. Sviridova, N., Zhao, T., Aihara, K., Nakamura, K., Nakano, A.: Photoplethysmogram at green light: Where does chaos arise from? Chaos, Solitons Fractals **116**, 157–165 (2018). https://doi.org/10.1016/j.chaos.2018.09.016

26. Allen, J.: Photoplethysmography and its application in clinical physiological measurement. Physiol. Meas. **28**, R1 (2007). https://doi.org/10.1088/0967-3334/28/3/R01

27. Yang, D., et al.: A novel adaptive spectrum noise cancellation approach for enhancing heartbeat rate monitoring in a wearable device. IEEE Access **6**, 8364–8375 (2018). https://doi.org/10.1109/ACCESS.2018.2805223

28. Fallow, B.A., Tarumi, T., Tanaka, H.: Influence of skin type and wavelength on light wave reflectance. J. Clin. Monit. Comput. **27**, 313–317 (2013). https://doi.org/10.1007/s10877-013-9436-7

29. Matsumura, K., Rolfe, P., Lee, J., Yamakoshi, T.: iPhone 4 s photoplethysmography: which light color yields the most accurate heart rate and normalized pulse volume using the iPhysioMeter application in the presence of motion artifact? PLoS ONE **9**, e91205 (2014). https://doi.org/10.1371/journal.pone.0091205

30. Bellone, G.J., Plano, S.A., Cardinali, D.P., Chada, D.P., Vigo, D.E., Golombek, D.A.: Comparative analysis of actigraphy performance in healthy young subjects. Sleep Sci. **9**, 272–279 (2016). https://doi.org/10.1016/j.slsci.2016.05.004

31. Russo, K., Goparaju, B., Bianchi, M.T.: Consumer sleep monitors: is there a baby in the bathwater? Nat. Sci. Sleep **7**, 147 (2015). https://doi.org/10.2147/NSS.S94182

32. Rosenberger, M.E., Buman, M.P., Haskell, W.L., McConnell, M.V., Carstensen, L.L.: 24 hours of sleep, sedentary behavior, and physical activity with nine wearable devices. Med. Sci. Sports Exerc. **48**, 457 (2016). https://doi.org/10.1249/MSS.0000000000000778

33. Ainsworth, B., Cahalin, L., Buman, M., Ross, R.: The current state of physical activity assessment tools. Prog. Cardiovasc. Dis. **57**, 387–395 (2015). https://doi.org/10.1016/j.pcad.2014.10.005

34. Straiton, N., et al.: The validity and reliability of consumer-grade activity trackers in older, community-dwelling adults: a systematic review. Maturitas **112**, 85–93 (2018). https://doi.org/10.1016/j.maturitas.2018.03.016

35. Thorup, C.B., Andreasen, J.J., Sørensen, E.E., Grønkjær, M., Dinesen, B.I., Hansen, J.: Accuracy of a step counter during treadmill and daily life walking by healthy adults and patients with cardiac disease. BMJ Open **7**, e011742 (2017). https://doi.org/10.1136/bmjopen-2016-011742

36. Simpson, L.A., et al.: Capturing step counts at slow walking speeds in older adults: comparison of ankle and waist placement of measuring device. J. Rehabil. Med. **47**, 830–835 (2015). https://doi.org/10.2340/16501977-1993

37. Buke, A., Gaoli, F., Yongcai, W., Lei, S., Zhiqi, Y.: Healthcare algorithms by wearable inertial sensors: a survey. China Commun. **12**, 1–12 (2015). https://doi.org/10.1109/CC.2015.7114054

38. Migueles, J.H., et al.: Accelerometer data collection and processing criteria to assess physical activity and other outcomes: a systematic review and practical considerations. Sports Med. **47**, 1821–1845 (2017). https://doi.org/10.1007/s40279-017-0716-0

39. Nelson, B.W., Allen, N.B.: Accuracy of consumer wearable heart rate measurement during an ecologically valid 24-hour period: intraindividual validation study. JMIR mHealth uHealth **7**, e10828 (2019). https://doi.org/10.2196/10828

40. Skog, I., Handel, P., Nilsson, J.-O., Rantakokko, J.: Zero-velocity detection—an algorithm evaluation. IEEE Trans. Biomed. Eng. **57**, 2657–2666 (2010). https://doi.org/10.1109/TBME.2010.2060723

41. Yousefi, R., Nourani, M., Ostadabbas, S., Panahi, I.: A motion-tolerant adaptive algorithm for wearable photoplethysmographic biosensors. IEEE J. Biomed. Health Inform. **18**, 670–681 (2014). https://doi.org/10.1109/JBHI.2013.2264358

42. Chowdhury, S.S., Hyder, R., Hafiz, M.S.B., Haque, M.A.: Real-time robust heart rate estimation from wrist-type PPG signals using multiple reference adaptive noise cancellation. IEEE J. Biomed. Health Inform. **22**, 450–459 (2018). https://doi.org/10.1109/JBHI.2016.2632201

43. Ban, D., Kwon, S.: Movement noise cancellation in PPG signals. In: IEEE International Conference on Consumer Electronics (ICCE), pp. 47–48. IEEE (2016)

44. Tang, S.D., Goh, Y.S., Wong, M.D., Lew, Y.E.: PPG signal reconstruction using a combination of discrete wavelet transform and empirical mode decomposition. In: 6th International Conference on Intelligent and Advanced Systems (ICIAS), pp. 1–4. IEEE (2016)

45. Fereidooni, H., Frassetto, T., Miettinen, M., Sadeghi, A.-R., Conti, M.: Fitness trackers: fit for health but unfit for security and privacy. In: IEEE/ACM International Conference on Connected Health: Applications, Systems and Engineering Technologies (CHASE), pp. 19–24. IEEE (2017)

46. Liu, J., Sun, W.: Smart attacks against intelligent wearables in people-centric internet of things. IEEE Commun. Mag. **54**, 44–49 (2016). https://doi.org/10.1109/MCOM.2016.1600553CM

47. Sharma, A., Pande, T., Aroul, P., Soundarapandian, K., Lee, W.: Circuits and systems for energy efficient smart wearables. In: IEEE International Electron Devices Meeting (IEDM), pp. 6.2. 1–6.2. 4. IEEE (2016)

48. Huang, J., Badam, A., Chandra, R., Nightingale, E.B.: Weardrive: fast and energy-efficient storage for wearables. In: Annual Technical Conference (USENIX ATC 2015), pp. 613–625 (2015)

49. Krachunov, S., et al.: Energy efficient heart rate sensing using a painted electrode ECG wearable. In: Global Internet of Things Summit (GIoTS), pp. 1–6. IEEE (2017)

50. Haghi, M., Thurow, K., Stoll, R.: Wearable devices in medical internet of things: scientific research and commercially available devices. Healthc. Inform. Res. **23**, 4–15 (2017). https://doi.org/10.4258/hir.2017.23.1.4

Gamification in Healthcare: Motivating South Africans to Exercise

Thaverson Devar$^{(\boxtimes)}$ ⓘ and Marie Hattingh ⓘ

Department of Informatics, University of Pretoria, Pretoria, South Africa
thaverson.devar@gmail.com, marie.hattingh@up.ac.za

Abstract. Studies have shown that daily exercise has a positive effect on the prevention of heart disease. However, many South Africans do not have a healthy lifestyle. Some forms of gamification have been applied in health-related programmes in South Africa such as Multiply's Active Dayz™ and Discovery's Active rewards. This study looks at the motivational aspects of gamification in healthcare. It investigates the impact of gamification on clients' use of activity rewards programmes, and aims to identify the core motivational factors that would drive people in South Africa to improve their health through exercise. We use Yu-Kai Chou's Octalysis framework of motivation in gamification as guide. The results show that time is a barrier for engaging in exercise, rewards programmes lead to more health check-ups, knowing the benefits of exercise not enough motivation to engage in exercise, and members of rewards programmes have different motivational factors for their behaviour than non-members.

Keywords: Gamification · Motivation · Healthcare · Hear disease · Exercise · Rewards

1 Introduction

Sustainable healthcare is attained when people are motivated to proactively take care of their health before it deteriorates [1]. In a survey of over 2000 South Africans conducted by Pharma Dynamics in 2017 [2], more than 46% of respondents acknowledged that they indulge in activities that put their health at risk. Some important results of this study were that 21% of young adults do not take any interest in improving their health, whereas 88% of older adults have actively sought a change in lifestyle to improve their health. Of these older people, 69% make an effort to exercise regularly. This study also claims that 215 South Africans die every day from heart disease and even though genetic factors are at play, living a healthier lifestyle can avoid about 80% of these deaths.

Exercise can help prevent heart disease by: decreasing blood pressure; increasing good high-density lipoprotein cholesterol that transports fat away from arteries; reducing low density lipoprotein cholesterol that can form fatty deposits in arteries; improving blood circulation; increasing fat loss; and building muscle mass [3]. One

© IFIP International Federation for Information Processing 2020
Published by Springer Nature Switzerland AG 2020
M. Hattingh et al. (Eds.): I3E 2020, LNCS 12067, pp. 108–119, 2020.
https://doi.org/10.1007/978-3-030-45002-1_10

aim of our study was to determine if South Africans are aware of the positive effects of exercise on heart disease.

Gamification has the potential to motivate a more active lifestyle. Gamification has also been successfully used in marketing [4], e-learning [5] and business [6] to motivate individuals to accomplish a goal. Pokémon Go, for example, is an augmented reality game that positions virtual Pokémon characters at different places where gamers have to move around, locate and capture them. Pokémon Go users are twice as likely to achieve the recommended goal of 10000 steps a day, with some achieving 7600 more steps on average [7]. Pokémon Go is not a health-related app, it is merely a game that increases physical activity, thereby improving players' health.

The second part of our study focused on understanding what factors used in gamification would motivate South Africans to exercise. The motivational factors that emerged were analysed with reference to Yu-Kai Chou's Octalysis Framework [8] to gain an understanding of the ways in which people can be motivated to improve their health.

The results of this research will be of value to designers of gamified health applications by showing which motivational factors to address in their designs. It will also be of particular value to organisations such as health insurance companies who want people to sign up for rewards programs aimed at motivating customers to pursue a healthy lifestyle.

2 Related Work

2.1 What Is Gamification?

According to Chou [9], gamification is "the craft of deriving all the fun and addicting elements found in games and applying them to real-world or productive activities". Gamification applies game-like elements and mechanics, but is a serious business. Companies in the healthcare and banking industries, amongst others, are increasingly adopting gamification in their operations.

The concept of gamification emerged in the 1800 s when S&H Green Stamps started selling stamps to retailers to reward loyal customers [10]. Nelson [11] argues that gamification originated in the early to mid-20th century in Soviet Union to motivate workers without capitalist-style financial incentives. Modern gamification was driven by airline loyalty programmes that reward customers with free "air miles" [12].

Different theories of gamification provide different views on gamification based on the industry where it is applied. One theory is that gamification is more effective than branding because of the emotional effect it has on the audience that leads to a longer relationship [13]. Another theory is that games create a natural reward compulsion loop driven by its effect on dopamine levels in the brain [14]. The origins and mechanics may differ, but the concept is simple: users are rewarded for certain behaviour based on their performance.

2.2 The Octalysis Framework

Chou [9] views gamification as a part of human-focused design. He acknowledges that

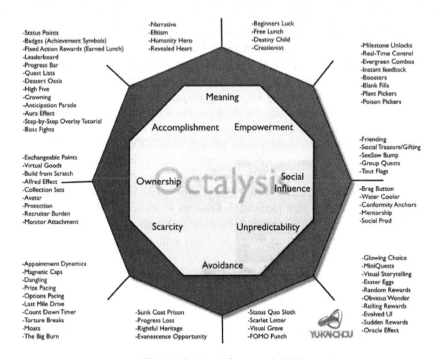

Fig. 1. Octalysis framework [15]

users of a system have feelings, insecurities, and reasons why they do certain things or not. His Octalysis Framework (Fig. 1) represents eight core drivers that inspire, empower, manipulate or make us obsess, but ultimately drive us toward a particular action. The eight drivers are:

1. Epic Meaning and Calling: People feel they have a purpose that is greater than themselves, or they feel unique and that they can achieve a certain task.
2. Development and Accomplishment: A person feels challenged and is constantly developing. Points and badges validates that they have overcome the challenge, and feel rewarded for it.
3. Empowerment of Creativity and Feedback: A person is able to try different things and given the opportunity to explore. They receive feedback and are able to use this feedback positively.
4. Ownership and Possession: When people can own something, they will be keener to grow or improve it. This is often seen when people customise their personal space or their avatars.

5. Social Influence and Relatedness: A person feels accepted, part of a group, or in esteemed company. Competitiveness is at play here. Relatedness applies to objects, places, activities, as well as people.
6. Scarcity and Impatience: A person has a limited time period in which to achieve goals. When they cannot, they constantly yearn for it.
7. Unpredictability and Curiosity: A person wants to find out what happens next, at the next level or what challenge they might face.
8. Loss and Avoidance: A person feels like they will lose out or fail. The fact that something negative might happen keeps them going.

A person becomes motivated and the gamified concept becomes more effective when one or more of these drivers have been triggered [15].

2.3   Examples of Gamification in E-Health

The World Health Organization (WHO) defines health as "a state of physical, mental and social well-being" [16]. Although we focused on heart disease, exercise or physical activity has an overall positive impact on health. WHO claims that the leading causes of global mortality are blood pressure (13%), tobacco use (9%), high blood glucose (6%) physical inactivity (6%) and obesity (5%). They say that physical activity has a positive effect on blood pressure, blood sugar levels and weight loss, which help prevent cardiovascular disease, diabetes and cancer [16]. Physical activity can also help with mental disorders, such as depression, anxiety and low self-esteem [17, 18].

The following are international examples of successful use of gamification in healthcare [9]: The *Mango Health* app encourages patients to take their medication because busy lifestyles make people forget to take their medication. They are motivated by earning monetary rewards such as gift cards at Target and GAP or a donation to the SPCA. The app includes Core Drivers 2 and 4 listed in Sect. 2.2. *Respond Well's* platform uses a virtual animated trainer. Patients can choose a trainer, music and a 3D environment and can even get their friends and family involved. It uses Microsoft Kinect, a motion-sensor technology that analyses the movement of patients and reports back to the patient and their doctors on their progress. This app includes Core Drivers 4 and 5. Pact users are paid by making a pact to exercise and eat healthier, and they lose money if they fail to do so. Users decide how much money to put into the pool with their friends and the person who reaches their goals receives the pay-out. This app reflects Core Drivers 2, 5 and 8.

A number of insurance companies in South Africa uses gamified rewards programmes to motivate health insurance policyholders to be more active. Momentum's *Multiply Active Dayz™* (MAD) tracks physical activity using wearable devices, phone apps and gym visits. If members achieve certain daily milestones, they are awarded with "active days". Active days earn a discount on their medical aid premium and a cash back in medical savings (up to R1 000 a month) [19]. Since the launch of MAD in 2016, clients covered a distance of 98 million kilometres through their steps until October 2017 [19]. Seventy-four percent of clients have improved their cholesterol levels and 54% reported weight loss. Multiply also claims to have a lower claims rate for chronic illnesses as a result of Active Dayz™ [20]. Discovery's *Vitality Active*

Rewards allows members to set personalised fitness goals and tracks them against the goals on a weekly basis. Members are rewarded with discounts on partner products, free rewards such as coffee or smoothies and fitness points to enhance their Vitality Status. Old Mutual's *Greenlight Gym Benefit* is available to all Greenlight policy-holders and their family members. Members receive discounts on gym membership fees for certain gyms.

Our research aimed to uncover which factors motivate or will motivate South Africans to join such gamified systems.

3   Research Question and Objectives

Our main research objective was to determine which motivational factors in gamification would encourage South Africans to exercise and thereby reduce their risk of developing heart disease. We investigated the following questions:

1. How active are people on gamified health programmes compared with people who are not?
2. Do people on gamified health programs care more about their health than those who are not?
3. Do people on gamified health programs know more about their health than those who are not?
4. What factors derived from the Octalysis Framework will motivate people to start exercising and to take care of their health?

4   Research Methodology

4.1   Research Strategy and Data Collection

We used an online survey to study the phenomenon of interest – gamification in eHealth systems that promotes a healthy lifestyle, with specific focus on factors that motivate adoption. We targeted two groups in the survey, namely current members and non-members of activity rewards programmes.

Two separate, but similar, questionnaires were used – one for members and one for non-members of some rewards programme. Both groups answered questions about their frequency of exercise and knowledge of their health. Members were asked about factors that motivated them to join their activity rewards programme, and non-members about factors that would motivate them to join such a programme. We based the questions relating to motivational factors on the Octalysis Framework. The questionnaires included multiple choice, yes/no, open ended and ranking questions. We compiled them using Google FormsTM. We recruited participants through our own social media networks. In particular, we posted a link to the questionnaire on Slack and Facebook, and sent out an e-mail (with permission) to employees at a large company where one of the authors is employed. There were 100 responses – 50 members and 50 non-members.

4.2 Data Analysis

An advantage of Google Forms is that we could easily export data in graph format or as an Excel spreadsheet. The data analysis involved reading the responses to each questionnaire individually, collating the results per question of members and non-members respectively in graph format, and comparing the results of the two groups.

Two open-ended questions in each of the questionnaires required manual analysis of the data. For the questions, "If you exercise, why do you exercise? If not, why don't you exercise?" and "What health conditions do you think can be positively affected by exercise? If possible, list 5." each response was transferred into a Word document. We analysed these through simple descriptive statistics (e.g. counting the number of times a specific answer appeared).

5 Results

There were two data collection instruments used, Multiply Active Dayz and the questionnaire results. The results of each of these instruments will be discussed in turn.

5.1 Multiply Active Dayz™ Results

Since the launch of Active Dayz™, Multiply clients would have covered a distance of 98 million kilometres through their steps taken. This is equivalent to approximately 70 000 trips from Johannesburg to Cape Town. The calories burned by Multiply clients through Active Dayz™ would be enough to power 100 households for a year. According to Multiply, 74% of clients have improved their cholesterol levels since joining, with a further 54% reporting weight loss. Multiply also claims to have a lower chronic claims rate as a result of Active Dayz™ [20]. Active Dayz™ is linked to Core Driver 2 – Development and Accomplishment, and Core Driver 8 – Loss and Avoidance.

5.2 Questionnaire Results

This section gives the results of both sets of participants. The age distribution of the two groups of respondents appear in Table 1. The biggest difference between the two groups is that the members are older. Of the 50 non-members, 21 fall in the 18 to 25 range while only four members fall in that range.

Table 1. Age distribution of questionnaire respondents

Age range (years)	18–25	26–35	36–45	46–45	55+
Non members	21 (42%)	22 (44%)	5 (10%)	2 (4%)	0
Members	4 (8%)	26 (52%)	18 (36%)	2 (4%)	0

The members had to indicate to which activity rewards programme they belong. The results are as follows: Discovery Active Rewards – 53%, MAD – 43%, Old Mutual Greenlight – 2%. Three respondents had both MAD and Active Rewards, and one answered the question incorrectly.

The remainder of the discussion is organised according the questionnaire questions.

How Aware Are You About the State of Your Health? The answers to this question are summarised in Figs. 2 and 3. An equal number of members either go for a check-up when something is wrong or they go once a year – together 80% of the group. Most non-members (64%) only go when they think something is wrong. Only 16% of members and 14% of non-members have regular check-ups and are well-informed about their health. Twelve percent of non-members blame time constraints. Overall the activity rewards group members are more proactive when it comes to monitoring their health than the non-members.

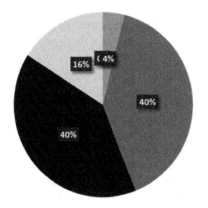

Fig. 2. Members' awareness of their health status

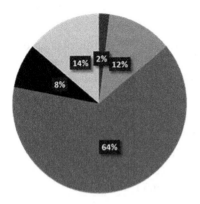

Fig. 3. Non-members' awareness of their health status

Which of These Best Describes Your Exercise Routine? More than half (52%) of members of an activity rewards programme visit a gym or exercise four or more times a week, while only 12.2% of the non-members fell into this category. The most popular response among non-members was that they do not gym but try to take the stairs (44.9%). Seventy-eight percent of members exercise at least once a week. Of the non-members, 18.4% do no exercise at all. None of the members chose this option. Figures 4 and 5 summarise the results for this question. Belonging to a gamified programme doubles the likelihood that a person will exercise.

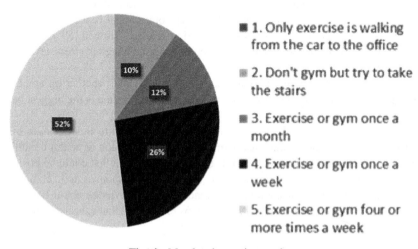

Fig. 4. Members' exercise routine

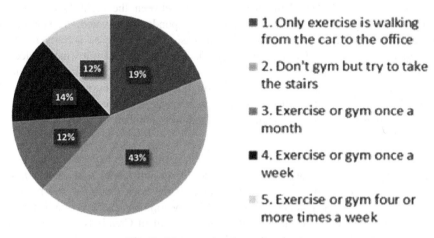

Fig. 5. Non-members' exercise routine

If You Exercise, Why Do You Exercise? If Not, Why Don't You Exercise?
Respondents could provide multiple answers to this question. We received 74 responses
from members. All but one gave reasons for doing exercise. Forty-five percent (45%) of
responses were members. All but one gave reasons for doing exercise. Forty-five percent
(45%) of responses were "to keep fit and healthy". The next most popular reasons were
"weight loss" and "to look good" (12% each). In the "Other" category reasons such as
"to test myself" and "it was recommended by my doctor" were mentioned. The one
member who does not exercise said the reason was lack of time.

Fifty non-members responded to the question – 29 said they do not exercise.
Twenty-three of these (79.3%) claimed that they had no time, while 13.8% admitted
laziness. The remaining participants said they have commitment issues or that they are
already fit. Twenty-one non-members said they do exercise. Thirteen (59.1%) do it "to
stay healthy". Two responses each were recorded for "managing stress levels" and
"because I play sport".

This question has uncovered two key outcomes: (1) people, whether on an activity
rewards programme or not, want to be fit and healthy; and (2) time is the biggest barrier
to exercising.

Forty-one participants in the non-member group responded to this question giving
134 responses. These participants also named 18 different groups of health conditions.
Of the responses, 14.5% included "heart disease" as a condition that could be positively
affected by exercise. "Diabetes" appeared in 13.7% of the responses and "cholesterol"
in 12.1%. There is not a considerable difference in the knowledge about health conditions that can benefit from exercise. Both groups recognised that exercise is important
and plays a positive role in their health.

**Choose ALL of the factors listed that motivated you to join your active rewards
programme.**

Member Responses. Respondents had to choose between the eight factors of the
Octalysis Framework listed in Sect. 2.3. All fifty respondents answered. "Development
and Accomplishment" was the most selected reason for joining an activity rewards
programme, selected by 70% (35 participants). The second and third most selected
options were "Social Influence and Relatedness" (30%) and "Loss and Avoidance"
(24%). This could be related to peers comparing steps, calories burned, etc. in social
situations, as well as to the fact that on activity rewards programmes, one could miss
out on discounts, points and status if the required number of activities are not
completed.

Non-member Responses. We first asked the non-members if they had heard about
rewards programmes such as Active Dayz. More than half (56%) said they had. We
asked all of the non-member respondents which of the eight factors would motivate
them to join. Fifty-nine percent (59%) chose "Development and Accomplishment",
while "Epic Meaning and Calling" and "Empowerment of Creativity and Feedback"
were each selected by 34%. We can link this to the earlier outcome that non-members
do not exercise as much as members, and they may want to be empowered or require
feedback on whether their exercise is done correctly and is not a waste of their time.
Ten percent said outright that they would not join an activity rewards programme.

6 Discussion and Conclusions

This paper aimed to understand which motivational factors in gamification will encourage people to exercise. We investigated four sub-questions. We next provide the answers to each, highlighting the lessons learnt. Firstly, we asked *how active people on gamified health programmes are versus people who are not.* The findings show that those on activity rewards programmes are more than twice as active as those who are not. We can conclude that these programmes are beneficial in improving healthcare. These findings are in line with previous studies who found that gamification of health programmes positively influenced users' emotional experiences and as a consequence improves their self-esteem [21, 22]. Furthermore, it supports Marshedi's [22] finding of gamification motivating users to adapt their health habits for the better. However, it has been shown that users might lose interest in the gamification aspects over time [23]. A key outcome from non-members are that time is a significant barrier to exercising.

Secondly, *do people who are on gamified health programmes care more about their health than those who are not?* The answer is yes, they are more proactive in checking up on their health. Because they will be more likely to identify issues related to their health sooner, they will be more likely to take preventative measures. Members are incentivised with rewards for completing tests, which could be the reason they have more check-ups with a doctor than the non-members. This result could mean that health conscious people are more likely to sign up for these programmes, but the answer to the next question contests this.

Thirdly, do people who are on gamified health programmes know more about health issues than those who are not? This answer is no. The respondents in the non-members group could name nearly as many health conditions as the members. The percentage of each condition listed was very similar between the two groups. The key outcome of this question is that even though people know how beneficial exercise is, it is not enough of a motivation to ensure that they exercise. Added benefits are required to ensure that they do. Some people openly claimed they were lazy and that they are okay with that, despite knowing the health risks.

Finally, what factors derived from the Octalysis Framework will motivate people to exercise and take care of their health? "Development and Accomplishment" was the most chosen option for both groups. This finding is in line with the findings of a systematic review of gamification in e-Health [24] who found that the gamification elements that were most often used were "feedback, rewards, progression and social features". Another key outcome was that members and non-members need to be motivated differently. The members want to ensure they do not lose their points and statuses – an element of fear might drive them. The social aspect is also important to them, and it will be beneficial to add concepts that encourage competition or challenges between friends. This outcome supports the research of Roa and Pandas (cited in [24]) who reported that "developing positive social relationships and promoting a feeling of integration are the key social benefits noted for gamification". For the non-members, it is more important to receive feedback and be empowered. Another important factor for this group was "Epic Meaning and Calling", which could be attributed to the fact that they want to know these goals are achievable. It should not waste their time, and the rewards should be immediate and notable. They have to be convinced that the value justifies the effort or money invested.

Health insurance providers and games designers can use the above results when designing programmes or apps that are aimed at making people more active. As a starting point, they should acknowledge that different kinds of users will be motivated by different factors and their products should cater for all.

This study was conducted in one African country among people who are customers of health insurance organisations. The results thus apply to countries where people use such health assurance. The adoption of health insurance programmes is influenced by the socio-economic context and often poor people working in the informal sector do not subscribe to health insurance at organisations with rewards programmes such as those investigated here [25]. Research therefore needs to be done to determine how, for example, community health insurance programmes that are aimed at low income workers can incorporate gamification to attract users.

References

1. Lee, C., Lee, K., Lee, D.: Mobile healthcare applications and gamification for sustained health maintenance. Sustainability 9, 772 (2017)
2. Krishna, C.: Relationship with hearts, 'on the rocks' (2017). https://www.news24.com/SouthAfrica/Local/South-Coast-Fever/relationship-with-hearts-on-the-rocks-20170208. Accessed 17 Aug 2017
3. Henderson, D.: Exercise, heart disease and high blood pressure (2015). http://www.netdoctor.co.uk/healthy-living/a1168/exercise-heart-disease-and-high-blood-pressure/. Accessed 10 Sept 2017
4. Zichermann, G., Linder, J.: Game-Based Marketing: Inspire Customer Loyalty Through Rewards, Challenges, and Contests. Wiley, Hoboken (2010)
5. Abu-Dawood, S.: The cognitive and social motivational affordances of gamification in E-learning environment. In: The 16th IEEE International Conference on Advanced Learning Technologies, pp. 373–375 (2016)
6. Herzig, P., Ameling, M., Schill, A.: A generic platform for enterprise gamification. In: Proceedings of the 2012 Joint Working Conference on Software Architecture (WICSA) and European Conference on Software Architecture (ECSA), pp. 219–223. IEEE (2012)
7. Time.com.: Pokémon Go makes people walk 2,000 more steps (2017). http://time.com/4695726/pokemon-go-walking-steps/. Accessed 25 May 2017
8. Chou, Y.K.: Actionable Gamification: Beyond Points, Badges, and Leaderboards. Octalysis Group, Fremont (2016)
9. Chou, Y.K.: Top ten gamified healthcare games that will extend your life. Gamification & Behavioral Design (2017). http://yukaichou.com/gamification-examples/top-ten-gamification-healthcare-games/. Accessed 10 Sept 2017
10. Goodhue, E.: What is Gamification? (And How Does It Differ From Gaming?) (2016). https://elearningindustry.com/what-is-gamification-differs-gaming. Accessed 25 May 2017
11. Nelson, M.J.: Soviet and American precursors to the gamification of work. In: Proceedings of the 16th International Academic MindTrek Conference, Tampere, Finland, pp. 23–26 (2012)

12. McEachern, A.: A loyalty program becomes a retention hub (2017). https://blog.hubspot.com/marketing/loyalty-program-retention-hub#sm.000002ffzijwp8d1ipz3uejnvqcuw. Accessed 25 May 2017
13. Matthews, K.: Why gamification works: how brands are marketing with fun (2017). http://www.convinceandconvert.com/social-media-case-studies/why-gamification-works-how-brands-are-marketing-with-fun. Accessed 10 Sept 2017
14. Eisenhauer, T.: The psychology of gamification in the workplace. Axero Solutions (2016). https://axerosolutions.com/blogs/timeisenhauer/pulse/390/the-psychology-of-gamification-in-the-workplace. Accessed 20 Apr 2017
15. Chou, Y.K.: Octalysis: complete gamification framework. Gamification & Behavioral Design (2017). http://yukaichou.com/gamification-examples/octalysis-complete-gamification-framework/. Accessed 25 May 2017
16. World Health Organization: Global recommendations on physical activity for health (2010). http://www.who.int/dietphysicalactivity/factsheet_recommendations/en/. Accessed 17 Aug 2017
17. Fontaine, K.R.: Physical activity improves mental health. Phys. Sports Med. **28**(10), 83–84 (2000)
18. Neff, K.D.: Self-compassion, self-esteem, and well-being. Soc. Pers. Psychol. Compass **5**(1), 1–12 (2011)
19. Multiply: What is active dayz? (2017). https://www.multiply.co.za/engaged/get-well/get-active/active-dayz/. Accessed 1 Nov 2017
20. Minnie, N.L.: Everything is connected. Presentation Delivered in Centurion, RSA, October 2017
21. Lentelink, S.J., Spil, A.A.M., Broens, T., Hermens, H.J., Jones, V.M.: Healthy weight game: lose weight together. In: Proceedings of the 2nd International Conference on Serious Games and Applications for Health, pp. 1–8. IEEE (2013)
22. AlMarshedi, A., Wills, G.B., Ranchhod, A.: The wheel of Sukr: a framework for gamifying diabetes self-management in Saudi Arabia. Proc. Comput. Sci. **63**, 475–480 (2015)
23. Munson, S.A., Consolvo, S.: Exploring goal-setting, rewards, self-monitoring, and sharing to motivate physical activity. In: Proceedings of the 6th International Conference on Pervasive Computing Technologies for Healthcare, pp. 25–32. IEEE (2012)
24. Sardi, L., Idri, A., Fernandez-Aleman, J.: A systematic review of gamification in e-Health. J. Biomed. Inform. **71**(July), 31–48 (2017)
25. De Allegri, M., Sauerborn, R., Kouyaté, B., Flessa, S.: Community health insurance in sub-Saharan Africa: what operational difficulties hamper its successful development? Trop. Med. Int. Health **14**(5), 586–596 (2009)

A Twitter Social Network Analysis:
The South African Health Insurance Bill Case

Ilse Struweg[✉] iD

Department of Marketing Management, School of Consumer Intelligence
and Information Systems, University of Johannesburg, Johannesburg,
South Africa
istruweg@uj.ac.za

Abstract. The process of extricating relationships and interchanges via visual mapping refers to Social Network Analysis (SNA). Through social network and graph theory lenses, this study explore Twitter data shortly after the announcement of the National Health Insurance (NHI) Bill to the South African parliament. An instrumental, single case study design and SNA secured contextual and timely Twitter interchanges of 4 112 tweets of the hashtag "NHI". Given the growing call for the comprehension of social media network interactions in different contexts, this paper use the underutilized tool for social media analytics, 'Network Overview, Discovery and Exploration for Excel Pro' (NodeXL Pro) to extract and visually present knowledge from pairwise relations between actors in the #NHI social media network. The findings explain the data dispersion and network structure of the #NHI case. The results clearly identifies the influencers – mostly the South African government, specific Twitter users and gatekeepers in the announcement of a highly controversial healthcare bill that will affect all South African citizens. The paper contributes theoretically by adding graph theory to the social media research field and to a less studied social media research cluster, namely social media during critical events. The practical contribution of the study is the use of NodeXL Pro, a unique SNA tool for advanced social media crawling, SNA and advanced network metric analysis.

Keywords: Social network analysis · Twitter · NodeXL Pro

1 Introduction

Innovations in information and communication technologies, more specifically the extensive proliferation of social media tools, has proofed to have the possibility of greatly contributing to "open government" by providing not only public information disseminating forums, but also stakeholder participation avenues [1]. Considering that the consequences of social media as a major source of influence grows, extant inquiry to explore who takes the lead in information sharing, and more importantly the patterns of information exchange among these users become more prevalent. Therefore, the data from online social networks affords fresh opportunities and views regarding the creation and influence of large-scale social networks and communities and the evaluation of these networks. In recent times, social networks have evolved into influential

© IFIP International Federation for Information Processing 2020
Published by Springer Nature Switzerland AG 2020
M. Hattingh et al. (Eds.): I3E 2020, LNCS 12067, pp. 120–132, 2020.
https://doi.org/10.1007/978-3-030-45002-1_11

platforms of human communication, conducting business, information sharing and various countenances of normal facets of life [33].

Social media in general has received substantial attention from researchers across information systems and marketing disciplines, as social media affects a range of stakeholders. In a study of 132 social media research papers between 1997 and 2017, the literature landscape ranges mostly from the examination of social media behaviour to its marketing possibilities and resultant organisational impact [37]. Also, social media's information sharing and exchange capabilities are shared unanimously. However, there is a particular cluster of studies, which distinguish its efficiency during important events [37]. This paper falls into this cluster, and follows the use of Twitter analysis from other available social media information sources [37–40].

In particular, this study makes the following practical and theoretical contributions: Most studies utilize social exchange theory, network theory and organisation theory [37]. Firstly, this study use social network theory, but adds a graph theoretical lens, a lesser used theory to enrich the existing body of knowledge. Secondly, it adds to the existing group of studies which focuses on social media research during an important event – in this case, the emergence of a new idea (the South African National Health Insurance Bill hand-over to parliament - #NHI). The third contribution, is that it considers both the network topology and the behavior of network actors in the comprehensive #NHI networked system. This study therefore not only considers the predominant behavioural examination of social data, but it enables the use of the combined knowledge of network structure and behaviour which is substantially distinct from the "straight-forward analysis" of single limited graphs [11, 12]. The fundamental research objectives in this study can be listed as:

1. To model the emergence of a new idea (i.e. the South African National Health Insurance Bill announcement in parliament - #NHI), based on Twitter users and their interactions on Twitter.
2. To determine the key influential actors in Twitter as social network in the #NHI conversation.
3. To describe the degree distributions of the relationships between Twitter users in the #NHI Twitter conversation.

Among the sections to follow, the next section briefly reviews the broader social media literature and how this study is positioned therein, followed by the methodological framework of this inquiry, with a brief discussion of the #NHI case. The next section describes the data collection and analysis of this inquiry. This is followed by the results section of the SNA of the #NHI case. The paper concludes with a discussion of the findings and their implications for using social media to offer not only public information dissemination platforms, but also stakeholder participation and interaction opportunities.

2   Literature Review

Social media has developed beyond mere platforms for socialisation or virtual congregation, to being acknowledged for its abilities to encourage aggregation. Similarly, information systems are developing beyond organisational boundaries, to come to be a part of the larger societal context, necessitating strategic information system research to explore the competitive setting of dynamic social systems. Literature on social media over the past years abounds, whereas an agreed definition of the concept, is less clarified [37]. In this study, social media is defined as a collection of user-defined platforms which allows for information interactivity and diffusion between users of open platforms which enables them to expand social relationships with their social networks [2, 9, 10, 34, 37]. Social media literature is synthesised into twelve clusters. These clusters are as follows [37]: (1) Social media usage, behaviours and consequences; (2) Reviews and recommendations on social media platforms; (3) Organisational impact of social media; (4) Social media for marketing; (5) Participation in social media communities; (6) Social media risks; (7) Stigmatisation of social media usage behaviour; (8) Value creation through social media; (9) Social media during an important event; (10) Support-seeking through social media; (11) Social media in the public sector; and (12) Traditional/social media divide.

From these clusters, it is evident that clusters one to eight have received considerable attention in information systems research. Cluster nine is where this paper is situated, as indicated in the introduction. However, it could also be argued that there is an overlap with cluster 11, as the event studied for the purpose of this paper is within the realm of the public sector. Little research has been carried out lately in cluster 12, which could be as a result of the widespread acceptance of social media beyond the traditional media age.

Consequently, it comprises the field of social network analysis (SNA), where this inquiry focuses on the connections and exposure of the relations between the networks and actors. SNA models "relations and associations, developments and associations and dynamic forces in networks and activities on social media platforms" [2]. Although SNA has been used more so in social and behavioural sciences [3, 4], more recently it has also been applied to "more complex areas" including economics, business and medicine [5]. SNA is also observed as a group of theories, practices and instruments [6]. This phenomenon is well summarized as being typically rooted in three main beliefs [7]: (1) Networks' structure and characteristics influence system performance; (2) Actors' position in a network impacts their behaviour; and (3) Actors' behaviour is in conformity with their network environment.

Moreover, in this study, the use of SNA is proposed to facilitate (based on graph theory) the identification of social networks consisting of nodes with which actors are linked to each other through their shared ideas, values, visions, social contacts and disagreement. This study argues that when social networks are successful, it has wider societal impact, which can affect programs, projects, policies, strategies, and partnerships (including its designs, implementations and results) [8] through access to human, social and financial information [5]. Therefore, social media grew central to civil society discourse – a platform where public debate and disputes, as well as knowledge exchange occur. As the public pulpit, social media exchanges are as important to note as any other large public gathering. Network maps of public social media discussions in services like Twitter can provide insights into the role social media plays in our society. These features and the size of online social networks puts SNA central to address many problems globally. This prevalence of increased user activities among social media users allow people to be more connected than ever before across the globe [13].

3   Methodology

3.1   Methodological Framework

This quantitative inquiry follows an instrumental, single case study design. In an instrumental case study, the case (#NHI) is selected as it represents some other issue under investigation (i.e. social network analysis) which can provide insights in that issue [14]. However, as a case study design could be regarded as a rather loose design, and as such, the methodological choices are addressed in a principled manner [15]. Therefore, these choices are outlined in Table 1:

Table 1. Methodological considerations and choices for this inquiry

Methodological consideration	Methodological choice
Research paradigm	Quantitative research
Research design	Instrumental, single case study design
Sampling strategy	Case selection
The case	#NHI: The South African National Health Insurance Bill hand-over to parliament for debate
Sampling units	4 112 tweets: #NHI
Data collection	Social media mining through NodeXL Pro API
Data analysis	NodeXL Pro social network analysis and NodeXL Pro advanced network metrics

The following section offers a brief overview of the South African National Health Insurance case, followed by an overview of NodeXL Pro as SNA tool applied for sampling, data collection and data analysis in this inquiry.

3.2   The Case: Announcement of the South African NHI Bill in Parliament

The functioning of the South African bicameral health system (public and private) has long been deteriorating. Politicians directed the decline in specifically the public health sector, to countless problems (claiming no responsibility). "However, the real reasons place the blame firmly at their door" [17]. In December 2015 the South African Government's White Paper of the NHI was announced which proposed a single, compulsory medical aid scheme which would cover all South African citizens and permanent residents, with private medical schemes being reduced to "complimentary services" [16]. On 8 August 2019, the highly anticipated and controversial South African National Health Insurance Bill was unveiled by the Health Minister Zweli Mkhize in parliament. The Bill proposes that the government will provide a package of comprehensive health services for free at both private and public health facilities in their bid to more equitable quality healthcare access [17]. But, since the introduction of the NHI Bill in the South African parliament, an "enormous amount" [18] of commentary, analysis, interpretation and trepidation has played out across media platforms and society. Within hours of the unveiling of the NHI Bill, Twitter users were actively tweeting – the most popular hashtag, #NHI.

3.3   NodeXL Pro for SNA

To address the research questions, this inquiry conducted a SNA, using NodeXL Pro, the licence-based software developed by the Social Media Research foundation. NodeXL (Network Overview for Discovery and Exploration in Excel) includes two versions: NodeXL Basic, and NodeXL Pro, which enable social network and content analysis [19]. It is a well-structured workbook template in Word Excel consisting of multiple worksheets required to denote a network graph. An 'edge list' denotes the network relationships (named 'graph edges') and contains all the pairs of entities which are linked in the network. It also includes matching worksheets with information about each cluster and vertex [2]. The visualisation features of the NodeXL software can illustrate various network graph representations, as well as chart data features to visualise aspects such as shape, size, colour and location [20].

NodeXL Pro, offers more advanced features, building on those in NodeXL Basic. These features include, inter alia [19], advanced network metrics, content analysis, sentiment analysis, time series analysis, text analysis, top items, and most importantly access to the application programming interfaces of various social networks. For this study, only network visualisation, social network APIs, the data import and export functions and SNA were used.

3.4   Data Collection and Analysis

Data Description and Dispersion. For the purpose of this inquiry, the Twitter data was imported on 20 August 2019 through NodeXL Pro's Twitter Importer, which passes a query (in this case #NHI) to the Twitter API focusing on relevance, not completeness [21].

The mined #NHI data is then routinely entered in the NodeXL Pro Excel template in keeping with edges and vertices. The edges and vertices are central concepts in network theory [22], one of the theories grounding this inquiry. Firstly, 'edges' (similarly termed 'links', 'ties', 'connections', or 'relationships'), involve social interactions, organisational structures, physical immediacies or abstract connections (for example hyperlinks). Secondly, vertices (similarly termed 'agents', 'nodes', 'items' or 'entities') can include individuals, locations, events, social structures, and content (for example keyword tags, videos or web pages) [23]. From a network theory perspective, an edge therefore links two vertices in the social network [24].

Network Structure Analysis. After the dispersion of the #NHI was created, the next step was to analyse the network structure quantitatively and represent it visually. The network was presented visually using Clauset-Newman-Moore cluster layout algorithm and Harel-Koren Fast Multi-scale layout algorithm to reduce the number of visible elements, so as to lessen the visual complexity of the graph [26, 27]. This allowed for improved intelligibility and concurrently it increased the execution of layout and interpretation [25]. The next step in the social network analysis involved the calculation of each of the vertices' relevant network metrics. For the purpose of this inquiry, the following metrices were calculated, to describe the network structure of the gathered #NHI data.

One of the key characteristics of SNA is finding prominent, influential "players" in these social media networks. This concept of identifying the important vertices in a graph based on the ranking, which in turn produced by the values is called centrality [28]. As the #NHI network is directed, it calls for the calculation of both *in-degree* and *out-degree centrality*. Similarly, the number of other accounts that have arrows pointing towards each Twitter account, is known as in-degree centrality. In this context, *in-degree* is regarded as a measure of popularity [29]. *Out-degree centrality* then refers to the number of arrows directed away from the Tweeter. The Tweeter with the highest out-degree calculation is then referred to as the main influencers in the network.

From a social network theory perspective, another centrality metric that should be considered, is *betweenness centrality*. Betweenness Centrality is a measure of how often a given vertex lies on the shortest path between two other vertices [20]. The Tweeter with the highest betweenness centrality is referred to as the bridges in the network. *Closeness centrality* describes the mean distance between a vertex and every second vertex in the social network [2]. Presuming vertices can only deliver messages to or effect its existing linkages (vertices), low closeness centrality requires the Tweeter to be directly linked to, or "just a hop away" [20] from, the majority other vertices in the social network. *Eigenvector centrality* (contrary to degree centrality), explicitly supports vertices that are connected to other similar vertices. Eigenvector centrality network metric considers, not only the number of vertex connections (its degree), but moreover the vertices' degree to which it is connected [30]. Lastly, with NodeXL Pro, the clustering coefficient is calculated and analyzed using a community detection algorithm [31], which resulted in visible clusters. Based on the data analysis, the results and the discussion thereof, follows below.

4 Results and Discussion

4.1 Prevalence and Patterns of #NHI Twitter Users

NodeXL Pro's sophisticated 'crawling' (extraction of data) of the '#NHI' resulted in the mining of 4 112 tweets. The resultant data set of 4 112 tweets were "cleaned" through eliminating tweets which are not applicable to tweet relationships vital to the study. The mined #NHI network contained 1902 distinctive vertices and 4110 edges among them. The mined edges in this inquiry included original tweets, comments and mentions and were all directed. Figure 1 illustrates the 'overall graph', showing the #NHI social network according to the Harel-Koren multiscale layout algorithm [32]. Therefore, Fig. 1 is a visual representation of the overall networked data from by the #NHI Twitter users and Table 2, provides a summary of the overall graph metrics of the case.

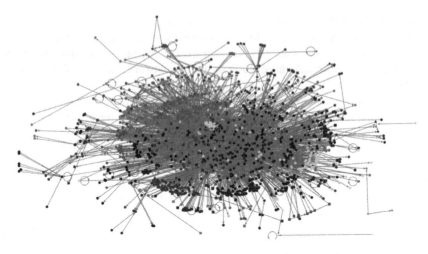

Fig. 1. Overall social media network structure of #NHI Twitter users

Table 2. Overall graph metrics of #NHI Twitter case (Source: NodeXL Pro version 1.0.1.419)

Graph type	Directed
Total edges	4110
Unique edges	4110
Reciprocated edge ratio	0,026842105
Self-loops	310
Connected components	155
maximum edges in a connected component	3888
Vertices	1902
Single-vertex connected components	106
Maximum vertices in a connected component	1672
Reciprocated vertex pair ratio	0,013603628
Average geodesic distance	4,01792
Maximum geodesic distance (diameter)	10
Modularity	0,605805
Graph density	0,001050972

4.2   Influence and Network Analysis Results

This section reports on the internal connectivity and the size of the #NHI social network. It further reports on the characteristics of every vertex, based upon in-degree and out-degree, closeness, betweenness, and eigenvector centrality.

In-Degree and Out-Degree Centrality Results. Tables 3 and 4 represents the in-degree and out- degree centrality of #NHI.

Table 3. #NHI: In-degree centrality

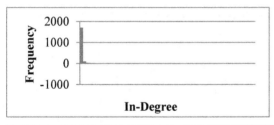

Minimum in-degree	0
Maximum in-degree	215
Average in-degree	2,161
Median in-degree	0,000

Table 4. #NHI: out-degree centrality

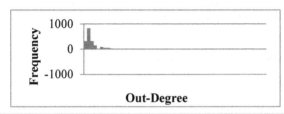

Minimum out-degree	0
Maximum out-degree	44
Average out-degree	2,161
Median out-degree	1,000

The in-degree value is the number of Twitter users that replied to or mentioned #NHI. Based on the in-degree values generated by NodeXL Pro, the top 3 vertices had over 100 arrows pointing towards them. The top 3 most popular accounts included from highest to lowest in this inquiry, were (1) The Minister of Health – an in-degree of 215; (2) What appears to be a general citizen "Leon" – an indegree of 164; and (3) A highly regarded South African investigative journalist with an indegree of 160. Therefore, the Minister of Health, Dr Zweli Mkhize appears to be the most popular account in this inquiry. The remaining members in this social network occupy various "in-between" position.

Popularity is not the single suggestion of impact in a social media network. For the purpose of this inquiry, the influential accounts (out-degree centrality) were considered. Firstly, there were only 10 accounts that interacted directly with the Minister of Health on Twitter. However, when the out-degree Twitter accounts were ranked, the top Twitter account was "Velloccerosso" – appearing from the Twitter account data to be a citizen. However, what this also say, is that this is an influential account, which is quite vocal and mentions many others in the account's discussion on #NHI. Therefore, by referring to others, the authoring account is extracting them into the linkage or engaging with them for a second time, if they were previously in the network. The out-degree of a Twitter account refers to mentions in the network, i.e. the number of arrows pointing away from it or the number of accounts it replies to. It is thus an indication of attention which an account points to others [30].

Closeness Centrality Results. As indicated earlier in this paper, closeness centrality measures calculate the shortest paths between all nodes, then assigns each node a score based on its sum of shortest paths. This type of centrality is used for finding the individuals who are best placed to influence the entire network most quickly. Therefore, closeness centrality can help find good 'broadcasters' in a social network. Of the 1 902 #NHI Twitter users, only 3.6% of users had a similar score of 1, whereas 93.3% of the total of #NHI Twitter users have a closeness centrality score of 0. In this inquiry of #NHI, it can therefore be deduced that the connectedness of the network is complex but not significantly connected.

Betweenness Centrality Results. Table 5 represents the betweenness centrality results of the #NHI inquiry. This measure shows which #NHI Twitter users act as 'bridges' between vertices in the social media network, by identifying all the shortest paths and then counting how many times each vertex falls on one.

Table 5. Betweenness centrality

Minimum Betweenness Centrality	0
Maximum Betweenness Centrality	613179,948
Average Betweenness Centrality	4437,562
Median Betweenness Centrality	0,000

In Twitter, information spreads through relatively short paths. Consequently, those Twitter accounts on short paths, control the information dissemination through that social media network. Thus, Twitter accounts with many short paths have high betweenness centrality, are considered as influential information gatekeepers. In the #NHI case, the Twitter account with the highest betweenness centrality was that of the Minister of Health, followed by the journalist and thirdly 'Leon' the Twitter users identified in the in-degree centrality discussion above. Therefore, these three Twitter users can not only be regarded as most popular, but also as most influential in the #NHI social network.

Eigenvector Centrality Results. Eigenvector centrality is regarded as a "higher-level" type of centrality. With Eigenvector centrality, a Twitter user with fewer connections could hold a very high eigenvector centrality. However, those few connections need to be very well linked to permit connections high variable value. This implies that connecting to certain vertices is more beneficial than a connection to others. In the #NHI inquiry, the eigenvector centrality scores were notably low, implying insufficient evidence that connecting to some #NHI Twitter users are more beneficial to other users in the social network.

4.3   Analytics and Visualisation

The layout of the sociogram in Fig. 2 is presented as groups. The groups cluster vertices through a decided cluster algorithm. These groups are clustered according to its relative network density. These clusters assist in combining groups of vertices (network users) displaying high network density. This therefor refers to network users who exhibit high in-degree and/or out-degree centrality. It is also these network users who are considered as network influencers. The groups further assist in clustering the network users with a lesser degree of network density and disregard them as isolated cases which are not significant in the visualization of the clusters. This is mainly because they do not communicate with others in the network. For the purpose of this analysis and visualisation, the Clauset-Newman-Moore algorithm [35] was applied to display these vertices' connections to each other. Modularity as network property is used in this algorithm to form a network distributed into communities.

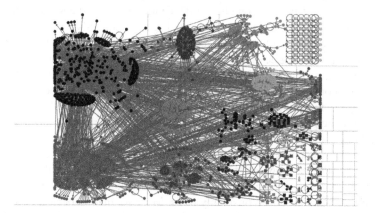

Fig. 2. Groups of clusters and the direction of cluster communication of #NHI Twitter users

The groups were arranged in separate boxes, in order to present the isolates in a separate group. NodeXL Pro then computes the clusters based on the parameters used in choosing the groups [36]. In the #NHI case NodeXL pro generated 78 groups. The resulting sociogram (Fig. 2) displays the clusters through a variety of colours in different boxes with links to different clusters. The isolates are positioned in separate boxes at the top and bottom righthand corner of Fig. 2. These isolates fail to impact the overall visualization, based on its non-communication in the network. That is also the reason why the connections are demonstrated in a circular form in the figure. The communication between the groups should also be noted. From Fig. 2, the largest clusters are focused to the left-hand side with references to many other nodes in the social network.

It could be argued that the primary limitation of this study is that it falls short in terms of some degree of restricted impact. More specifically, this refers to the seemingly lack of public interaction on social media regarding the #NHI case. This seemingly lack of social media traction, more specifically on twitter, might have been influenced by the many other big news events both globally and locally at the time. Although information overload, specifically via social media is a reality that is not going to change in the near future. This could therefore present an opportunity for further research to explore the despondence of social media users during critical events, especially those which directly affect the individual.

5   Conclusions

Social media networks' big data are among the most influential, yet it remains an under researched phenomena. In this inquiry, Twitter, a very widely used social media platform was used to gather big data, using the hashtag #NHI. The choice of this hashtag was a result of the controversies and uncertainties created among South Africans with the unveiling of the National Health Insurance Bill for discussion in parliament. This inquiry was grounded in graph and network theory in order to conduct a social network analysis of the national conversation of #NHI. This resulted in a visual graph model based on 4112 #NHI tweets, done by 1 902 Twitter users (vertices) indicating 4 110 Twitter interactions (edges). The key influential actors in this SNA was the Minister of Health, the media and to a limited degree, citizens of South Africa who will be influenced by the bill. The degree distributions revealed that relationships between the major #NHI Twitter users were limited, as the majority of closeness and eigenvector centrality indicated low connectivity. This could indicate the lack of involvement of the South African citizens in public discourse around the NHI bill which will affect all South African. From the preceding discussions, it is clear that social media is inevitably central to modern day society, with widespread influence that cannot be refuted or disregarded. In this paper, it was demonstrated how big, real-time data from Twitter can be employed using NodeXL Pro, to draw insights through social media metrics with visualizations. The paper further demonstrated NodeXL Pro as an enabler to harness big unstructured data which are mass-produced on a daily basis. More so, that it enables, through using appropriate analytic techniques, inference from seemingly uncoordinated microblogs that may assist businesses and governments alike in decision-making. The #NHI case study further reinforces that emerging economics are part of the social media race.

References

1. Gao, X.: Networked co-production of 311 services: investigating the use of Twitter in five US cities. Int. J. Public Adm. **41**(9), 712–724 (2018)
2. Struweg, I.: # Liberty breach: an exploratory usage case of NodeXL Pro as a social media analytics tool for Twitter. In: ICMBD Conference Proceedings, pp. 153–163 (2018)

3. Otte, E., Rousseau, R.: Social network analysis: a powerful strategy, also for the information sciences. J. Inform. Sci. **28**(6), 441–453 (2002)
4. Wasserman, S., Faust, K.: Social network analysis in the social and behavioral sciences. Soc. Netw. Anal.: Methods Appl. **1994**, 1–27 (1994)
5. Can, U., Alatas, B.: A new direction in social network analysis: online social network analysis problems and applications. Phys. A: Stat. Mech. Appl. **535**, 122372 (2019)
6. Valente, T.W., Dyal, S.R., Chu, K.H., Wipfli, H., Fujimoto, K.: Diffusion of innovations theory applied to global tobacco control treaty ratification. Soc. Sci. Med. **145**, 89–97 (2015)
7. Valente, T.W.: Social networks and health behavior. In: Glanz, K., Rimer, B., Viswanath, K. (eds.) Health Behavior: Theory, Research and Practice, 5th edn, pp. 205–222. JosseyBass, San Francisco (2015)
8. Serrat, O.: Knowledge solutions: tools, methods, and approaches to drive development forward and enhance its effects, vol. 382. Asian Development Bank (2010)
9. Lee, Y.J., O'Donnell, N.H., Hust, S.J.: Interaction effects of system generated information and consumer scepticism: an evaluation of issue support behaviour in CSR Twitter campaigns. J. Interact. Advert. **19**(2), 1–37 (2018)
10. Statista: Number of monthly active users worldwide from first quarter 2010 to first quarter 2018 (2018). https://www.statista.com/statistics/282087/number-of-monthly-active-twitter-users/. Accessed 25 June 2018
11. Albert, R., Barabási, A.L.: Statistical mechanics of complex networks. Rev. Mod. Phys. **74**(1), 47 (2002)
12. Newman, M.E.: The structure and function of complex networks. SIAM Rev. **45**(2), 167–256 (2003)
13. Zhang, Y., Chang, H.C.: Selfies of Twitter data stream through the lens of information theory: a comparative case study of tweet-trails with healthcare hashtags. In: Proceedings of the 51st Hawaii International Conference on System Sciences (2018)
14. Ary, D., Jacobs, L.C., Irvine, C.K.S., Walker, D.: Introduction to Research in Education. Cengage Learning, Boston (2018)
15. Meyer, C.B.: A case in case study methodology. Field Methods **13**(4), 329–352 (2001)
16. Anon: How South Africa's NHI will work. News24, 11 December 2015 (2015). https://www.health24.com/News/Public-Health/how-south-africas-nhi-will-work-20151211. Accessed 25 Aug 2019
17. Van den Heever, A.: Only a failing government could have come up with the NHI. The Citizen, 24 August 2019 (2019). https://citizen.co.za/news/south-africa/health/2170905/only-a-failing-government-could-have-come-up-with-the-nhi/. Accessed 24 Aug 2019
18. Louw, M.: NHI: in search of common ground. Daily Maverick, 26 August 219 (2019). Available at: https://www.dailymaverick.co.za/article/2019-08-26-nhi-in-search-of-common-ground/. Accessed 26 Aug 2019
19. Social Media Research Foundation: What is NodeXL? (2018). https://www.smrfoundation.org/nodexl/. Accessed 27 June 2018
20. Hansen, D.L., et al.: Do you know the way to SNA? A process model for analyzing and visualizing social media network data. In: 2012 International Conference on Social Informatics, pp. 304–313. IEEE (2012)
21. Zhang, L., Luo, M., Boncella, R.J.: Product information diffusion in a social network. Electron. Commer. Res. **20**, 1–17 (2018)
22. Banica, L., Brinzea, V.M., Radulescu, M.: Analyzing social networks from the perspective of marketing decisions. Sci. Bull. Econ. Sci. **14**, 1437–1450 (2015)
23. Chae, B.: Insights from hashtag #supplychain and Twitter analytics: considering Twitter and Twitter data for supply chain practice and research. Int. J. Prod. Econ. **165**, 247–259 (2015)

24. Alhajj, R., Rokne, J. (eds.): Encyclopaedia of Social Network Analysis and Mining. Springer, New York (2014)
25. Agapito, G., Guzzi, P.H., Cannataro, M.: Visualization of protein interaction networks: problems and solutions. BMC Bioinform. **14**(1), S1 (2013)
26. Smith, M.A., Rainie, L., Shneiderman, B., Himelboim, I.: Mapping Twitter topic networks: from polarized crowds to community clusters. Pew Research Center **20**, 1–56 (2014)
27. Lipschultz, J.H.: Social media communication in the classroom: a pedagogical case study of social network analysis. In: Conway, D.F., et al. (eds.) Digital Media in Teaching and Its Added Value, pp. 191–207. Waxmann Verlag, New York (2015)
28. Wang, Z., Tan, Y., Zhang, M.: Graph-based recommendation on social networks. In: 2010 12th International Asia-Pacific Web Conference, pp. 116–122. IEEE, April 2010
29. Miller, P.R., Bobkowski, P.S., Maliniak, D., Rapoport, R.B.: Talking politics on Facebook: network centrality and political discussion practices in social media. Polit. Res. Q. **68**(2), 377–391 (2015)
30. Lohmann, G., et al.: Eigenvector centrality mapping for analyzing connectivity patterns in fMRI data of the human brain. PLoS One **5**(4), e10232 (2010)
31. Clauset, A., Newman, M.E., Moore, C.: Finding community structure in very large networks. Phys. Rev. E **70**(6), 066111 (2004)
32. Harel, D., Koren, Y.: A fast multi-scale method for drawing large graphs. In: Marks, J. (ed.) GD 2000. LNCS, vol. 1984, pp. 183–196. Springer, Heidelberg (2001). https://doi.org/10.1007/3-540-44541-2_18
33. Desai, T., et al.: Tweeting the meeting: an in-depth analysis of Twitter activity at Kidney Week 2011. PLoS One **7**(7), e40253 (2012)
34. Kandadai, V., Yang, H., Jiang, L., Yang, C.C., Fleisher, L., Winston, F.K.: Measuring health information dissemination and identifying target interest communities on Twitter: methods development and case study of the@ SafetyMD network. JMIR Res. Protocols **5**(2), e50 (2016)
35. Clauset, A., Newman, M.E.J., Moore, C.: Finding community structure in very large networks. http://ece-research.unm.edu/ifis/papers/community-moore.pdf. Accessed 7 Oct 2019
36. Udanor, C., Aneke, S., Ogbuokiri, B.O.: Determining social media impact on the politics of developing countries using social network analytics. Program **50**(4), 481–507 (2016)
37. Kapoor, K.K., Tamilmani, K., Rana, N.P., Patil, P., Dwivedi, Y.K., Nerur, S.: Advances in social media research: past, present and future. Inform. Syst. Front. **20**(3), 531–558 (2018)
38. Oh, O., Agrawal, M., Rao, H.R.: Community intelligence and social media services: a rumour theoretic analysis of tweets during social crises. MIS Q. 407–426 (2013)
39. Miranda, S.M., Young, A., Yetgin, E.: Are social media emancipatory or hegemonic? Societal effects of mass media digitization. MIS Q. **40**(2), 303–329 (2016)
40. Shi, Z., Rui, H., Whinston, A.B.: Content sharing in a social broadcasting environment: evidence from twitter. MIS Q. **38**(1), 123–142 (2013)

Security

Cyber-Harassment Victimization Among South African LGBTQIA+ Youth

Kayla Hendricks (ID), Pitso Tsibolane (ID), and Jean-Paul van Belle$^{(\boxtimes)}$ (ID)

University of Cape Town, Cape Town, South Africa
hndkay004@myuct.ac.za, {pitso.tsibolane,
jean-paul.vanbelle}@uct.ac.za

Abstract. Cyber-harassment victimization is one of today's major problems affecting the wellbeing of youth, particularly those that identify as lesbian, gay, bisexual, transgender, queer/questioning, intersex, asexual and gender non-conforming (LGBTQIA+). This exploratory study aims to determine the nature of cyber-harassment victimization, its enablers, and the coping mechanisms that online platforms provide to prevent or stop cyber-harassment. An online survey of ninety (n = 90) LGBTQIA+ young adults of ages between 18 and 34 from South Africa reveals a high incidence of exclusion, outing and harassment, covering a wide variety of types, duration and experienced severity, taking place through text messaging and social media sites such as Facebook, Instagram and Twitter. Most LGBTQIA+ youth resort to measures such as blocking, deleting offensive content and adjusting privacy settings to cope with cyber-victimization. Worryingly, the most severe effects of harassment such as depression, drug abuse, self-harm and suicide contemplation, have significant correlations with the harassment type used, harassment duration and harassment frequency. The paper discusses the implications for educational and social practice and future studies.

Keywords: Cyber-harassment · Cyber victimization · LGBTQIA+ · Negative impact of social media

1 Introduction

One of the negative impacts due to the rapid growth in social media access and connectivity is online harassment [21]. Studies show that LGBTQIA+ youth experience higher levels of cyber-harassment victimization than their non-LGBTQIA+ peers [14]. Despite intense social, cultural and political challenges, academic research into harassment and victimization amongst LGBTQIA+ individuals in Africa is growing [14] but gaps exist, particularly in the area of online harassment victimization. Research into the rate of victimization among LGBTQIA+ individuals in South Africa shows that prejudice based on sexual orientation ranks as the second highest form of discrimination, with prejudice based on nationality rank as the most prevalent form [14] but it is not clear what the levels and the nature of online based harassment victimization looks like.

This study, therefore, aims to address this research gap regarding the online harassment of LGBTQIA+ youth in South Africa. The study uses exploratory quantitative

M. Hattingh et al. (Eds.): I3E 2020, LNCS 12067, pp. 135–146, 2020.
https://doi.org/10.1007/978-3-030-45002-1_12

research to gain a better understanding of this problem. The overall goal of this study is to determine the nature of cyber-harassment victimization, its enablers, and the coping mechanisms that online platforms provide to prevent or stop cyber-harassment. The three questions explored are:

- What is the current nature and level of cyber-harassment victimization among LGBTQIA+ youth in South Africa?
- Which aspects of online platforms enable cyber-harassment victimization of South African LGBTQIA+ youth?
- Which aspects of online platforms afford LGBTQIA+ youths coping mechanisms against cyber-harassment victimization?

2   Literature Review

Online social networking has seen a vast period of growth in the past two decades globally [9, 13, 19]. The wide range of communication channels including emails, instant messengers, text messages, social networking sites, blogs, wikis and chat rooms continues to fuel this growth [9, 13]. The use of social networking technologies is a convenient way for the youth to explore their identity, better social skills and to improve media literacy [8]. Despite the many benefits attributed to the rapid growth of social networking technologies, it has also been associated with serious undesirable social implications, such as cyber-harassment victimization [21].

2.1   Cyber-Harassment

Cyber harassment affects individuals of different age groups and is a prevalent cause for concern linked to negative social effects such as depression and suicide [16, 21]. While cyber-harassment is an extension of traditional harassment, various definitions of cyber-harassment exist. There are two forms of cyber-harassment, direct/physical and direct [16]. Direct cyber harassment consists of physical methods such as the sending of viruses, threatening verbal messages and nonverbal methods, which could include the sending of offensive or explicit images, as well as social methods, which include censoring or kicking an individual out of an online group. Indirect cyber-harassment comprises of online gossip around the subject of the individual and taking part in activities such as commenting or voting on insulting websites.

More formally, cyber harassment refers to "any behavior performed through electronic or digital media by individuals or groups that repeatedly communicates hostile or aggressive messages intended to inflict harm or discomfort on others" [21]. Victims of cyber harassment are often victims of traditional harassment [20]. However, cyber harassment has emerged as a significant issue because of its rapidly evolving digital nature. Cyber-harassment differs from traditional harassment in many respects such its potential anonymity, being unconstrained by time, larger audience size, lack of physical interaction, high frequency of violation, the variety of media that can be used and the reduced threat of intervention [16]. Some of the common forms of cyber-harassment include the use of swear words, various insults, unwelcome jokes, fake names, teasing, spreading rumors, humiliating and making physical threats, with female students specifically using methods such as gossiping and using attacks that are personal to the individual [19]. A categorization of cyber-harassment outlines eight different types of victimization [22].

Table 1. Types of cyber-harassment victimization

Cyber-harassment	Description
Flaming	Engaging online arguments usually involving unfounded personal attacks
Impersonation	Pretending to be another in order to inflict harm
Denigration	The spreading of offensive information about a person
Exclusion	Deliberately removing or leaving out an individual in an online group setting
Outing	Sharing of an individual's confidential information with outside parties
Trickery	Deceiving an individual into sharing confidential information
Cyberstalking	Threating or harassing an individual
Sexting	Sending sexually inappropriate and offensive images to an individual

New descriptors that form part of the cyber-harassment victimization types are "trolling" and "griefing" [19]. Trolling is the act of making random unsolicited and/or controversial comments on various online social networking internet forums with the intent to provoke an emotional knee jerk reaction from unsuspecting readers to engage in a fight or argument. Griefing is performing actions in an online game for instance, to prevent another individual from enjoying the game i.e. causing them 'grief' [19].

Factors Linked to Victimization. Victims, in the context of this study are those who report they are the target of cyberbullying. This study makes a link between these victims and several characteristics that are common amongst them and could have an impact on the likelihood of victimization. Studies have shown factors such as comparative physical weakness, fear of aggressive behavior, more trusting and open behavior, and poor social skills and low popularity [5]. In addition, in comparison to traditional harassment, the cyber-harassment victimization rates are higher for females than they are for males [9, 13]. However, in contrast to these findings, other studies show that demographic factors such as age and gender do not seem to provide a clear link to victimization prevalence [21]. Shyness is a potential contributory factor to cyber-victimization but there is still clear evidence to isolate shyness as a victimization characteristic specifically as it could be the consequence of cyber harassment [1]. Similarly, forming relationships with strangers is a factor that is more prevalent amongst victimized youth [13]. Following on from that notion, much of the studies developed around the topic of cyber-harassment victimization, as well as their instruments of measurement, consist of inadequate, empirically limited findings, which further extensive research can illuminate [14].

Enabling Factors. Anonymity or the ability to hide or falsify an individual's real identity, a capability that comes with various online platforms, enables cyber-harassment. Most cyber-harassment victimization is largely anonymous, and this factor enables hostile and thoughtless behavior intended to instill fear and feelings of distress into victims [2]. The lack of physical interaction may lead to individuals acting in ways that they would not if they were in the public eye, and this relates to the extent to which an individual is at ease behind the relative safety of their communicative technologies [13]. The larger audience that is accessible through the click of a button in comparison to traditional harassment methods also enables cyber-harassment victimization.

The lack of interference by authority figures such as parents and teachers is often much more pronounced in cyber harassment victimization incidents than in comparison to traditional harassment [2]. The notion of free speech also increases the likelihood of individuals feeling like they are able to communicate any content that they feel is necessary online, which has been associated with increases in online harassment [9].

Impact on Victims. There have been numerous negative impacts linked to the after-math of cyber harassment victimization namely social, psychological, emotional and academic [21]. These effects could differ in severity ranging from "trivial levels of distress and frustration" to more serious mental or life problems such as deteriorating grades to difficulties concerning home life [21]. Absence from school is more prevalent amongst youth who are cyber-victimized as well as depression is also common among youth who are victims of cyber-harassment [2, 5]. Anxiety, low empathy, declining confidence levels, rejection by peers, substance abuse and aggression are additional factors positively associated with victimization effects [5, 16]. Cyber-harassment worsens the intensity pre-existing negative emotions such as hopelessness and low self-esteem particularly among young people [5, 16]. Other studies show a rise of the incidence in self-harm and suicidal ideation due to cyber-victimization among youth that struggle with hopelessness and self-esteem [19].

Mitigation Plans and Safeguards. Research show several technological coping mechanisms that serve as means to mitigate the negative effects of concerning cyber-harassment [21]. The nature or type of these mechanisms differs from case to case depending on the severity of harassment experienced by a victim [21]. These coping mechanisms include blocking and deletion of offender/offensive messages; adjusting to more strict privacy settings; removing offensive content; changing of username; changing of email address; avoidance of technology; changing of number; changing of passwords; tracking of IP addresses; contacting of site administrators; responding to the offender online and bystanders defending victims [2, 16, 19].

2.2   Context: The LGBTQIA+ Community in South Africa

The LGBTQIA+ community is a collective term referring to lesbian, gay, bisexual, transgender, queer, questioning, asexual, and other identities that are not heterosexual and/or cisgender [11]. Research concerning the LGBTQIA+ community in Africa is still developing. This is not due to the lack of prevalence but rather attributable to the lack of social and legislative acceptance that surrounds the topic [7]. This is borne by the fact that several African countries have some law criminalizing either homosexuality or an aspect of it.

While several African countries do not recognize the LGBTQIA+ community, South Africa seems to be the relative exception [17]. South Africa's post-apartheid constitution prohibits discrimination on the grounds of sexual orientation and legalizes same sex marriage [4]. However, while the state is fully accepting of non-heterosexual sexuality, the attitude of some members of the population are still discriminatory of homosexuality. Surveys show that the populace still highly values heteronormativity and remains deeply conservative, only marginally accepting of homosexuality. Many South Africans still harbor a judgmental outlook towards the LGBTQIA+ community [4]. The negative attitudes and discrimination surrounding the LGBTQIA+ community were central to the study conducted by the Hate Crimes Working Group [15]. This study also observed that most of the community rhetoric, harassment or hate crime incidents take place through social media platforms or electronic communication [14, 15]. There is therefore a need for a greater number of studies investigating different aspects of online discrimination concerning LGBTQIA+ individuals.

2.3 Theoretical Framework

The theoretical framework chosen for this study combined aspects of two behavioral theories: The Lifestyle Exposure Theory and The Social Presence Theory. The theoretical constructs enabled insights into aspects of victimization, behavior and the detrimental factors of cyber harassment concerning individuals in the LGBTQIA+ community.

The Lifestyle Exposure Theory aims to understand if specific lifestyles are associable with different probabilities of victimization [3]. It suggests that due to certain demographic profiles, certain people are more at risk of victimization due to the perceived lifestyles risks [12]. It posits a link between both the lifestyle and demographics of individuals and the types of victimization potential. The Lifestyle Exposure Theory lends itself particularly to why the LGBTQIA+ community is at risk for cyber harassment victimization. The role played by the peer pressure in the victimization of LGBTQIA+ is also considered [10].

The Social Presence Theory posits that the extent to which a person perceives another as a real person (presence) in mediated communication (such as online communication) varies according to the quality of the medium used [6]. This quality of the medium includes the extent to which the medium conveys information about facial expression, direction of looking, posture, dress and nonverbal cues [6]. The Social Presence Theory helps in the identification of factors that could be more detrimental in cyber harassment rather than traditional face-to-face harassment.

3   Research Methodology

The study aims to determine the nature of cyber-harassment victimization, its enablers, and the coping mechanisms that online platforms provide to prevent or stop cyber-harassment. The study is both descriptive and exploratory [18]. The research used a quantitative survey approach to obtain the empirical data. The target population of this study are young individuals (18 to 35 years) in the LGBTQIA+ community. The survey instrument was developed based on the pre-validated questions from the Lifestyle Exposure Theory study [12] as well The Social Presence Theory study [6]. Face validity was conducted with 3 experts who are also gender activists on the resulting survey. We distributed a mass email, requesting participants for the study to the members of a large academic university in South Africa. Requests to participate in the study were distributed through social media sites such as Facebook and Twitter to the public. The study employed the three theories to enable the testing of certain statements contained in the literature as well as to develop the survey instrument. The University's ethics committee approved the research and the survey instrument. Respondents are anonymous and were able to opt out at any time during the online survey. A number of direct 24/7 help line numbers, email addresses and details of the University's student help as well as relevant NGOs dedicated to the LGBTQIA+ community were listed in case respondents wanted psychological or any other assistance during or after the survey.

4   Research Findings and Discussion

4.1   Demographics

The sample consisted of 90 valid responses of which 2% (n = 2) of respondents identified as asexual, 29% (n = 26) as bisexual, 36% as homosexual (gay or lesbian), 19% (n = 17) as pansexual, 2% (n = 2) as plus (+) and 12% (n = 11) as queer. The age distribution was positively skewed with the largest response from the 18–25 years age group representing 94% (n = 85) of the respondents and only 2% (n = 2) between the ages of 25 and 30 and 3% (n = 3) being between the age of 30 and 35.

Of the valid responses, 82% (n = 74) of LGBTQIA+ individuals reported to have been harassed due to their orientation while 18% (n = 16) reported to have never been harassed online due to their sexual orientation. We note that there may be a response bias i.e. those that were harassed may have a higher inclination to complete the survey.

4.2   Research Question 1: "What Is the Current Nature and Level of Cyber-Harassment?"

The types of harassment experienced by members of the LGBTQIA+ community are depicted in Fig. 1 (left). Being outed is the highest ranked type of cyber-harassment experienced by most respondents, followed by harassment, exclusion, flaming and denigration. Figure 1 (right) shows the online mediums on which LGBTQIA+ individuals most commonly experience cyber-harassment. Text-based harassment seems to be the most prevalent, followed by Facebook, Instagram and Twitter. Text-based services include SMS (Short Message Service) and WhatsApp are the most affordable and commonly used services in South Africa.

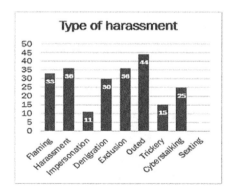
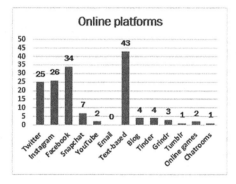

Fig. 1. The occurrence of types of cyber-harassment and the associated online platforms

4.3 Research Question 2: "Which Aspects of Online Platforms Enable Cyber-Harassment?"

The severity of the harassment experienced by individuals in the LGBTQIA+ community in Fig. 2 follows a normal distribution, with the majority of respondents experiencing a medium severity level (3) and fewer respondents on the outer more extreme ends of the rankings (the ranking system ranges from 1 being 'not severe at all' to 5 being 'very severe').

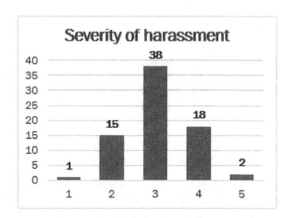

Fig. 2. Severity of harassment

The duration of harassment in the research instrument ranged from 1 being brief to 5 being years. The results indicate that there is an even spread amongst duration ranks, with the "brief" ranking being most prevalent amongst respondents (Fig. 3).

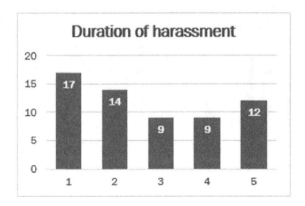

Fig. 3. Duration of harassment

The majority of the cyber-victimization incidents (66%) that members of the LGBTQIA+ community experienced were perpetrated by people that were identifiable i.e. not anonymous. Only 9% of the perpetrators were anonymous and 25% were sometimes anonymous. This contradicts research that anonymity is as an enabler of cyber harassment [2, 13]. Most cyber-harassment incidents involved an online audience (44 out of 72). This seems to support the finding that ease of spread is an enabling factor for cyber harassment [16].

Most incidents, 57 out of 74 (77%), were not reported with the authorities for further action. The fact that victims do not seem to report incidents could potentially lead to the reason why offenders show a lack of fear of being caught. This could contribute to the high rates of harassment in the LGBTQIA+ community [2, 13]. Most incidents were experienced in the evening (55%), with afternoon the second-most (34%). Only 3% of the incidents were in the morning, 9% occurring at any time of the day. This result aligns with prior research findings that the incidence of cyber-harassment increases in the evenings [16, 21].

4.4   Research Question 3: "Which Aspects of Online Platforms Are Considered as Coping Mechanisms Against Harassment?"

Figure 4 depicts the types of safeguards used by members of the LGBTQIA+ community to prevent/stop cyber-harassment. Blocking (where the victim stops the abuser from accessing their profile) ranks as the most prevalent type of safeguard utilized by cyber-victims. The deletion of the offensive content (the victim removing abusive messages) follows. The adjustments of settings (e.g. making the victim's account private or inaccessible by the abusers) follows closely. Other coping mechanisms such as responding back, deleting own content and withdrawal from technology are also common. Our research does not give conclusive evidence on how effective the following coping mechanisms/safeguards are in the prevention or remedy of cyber harassment [21].

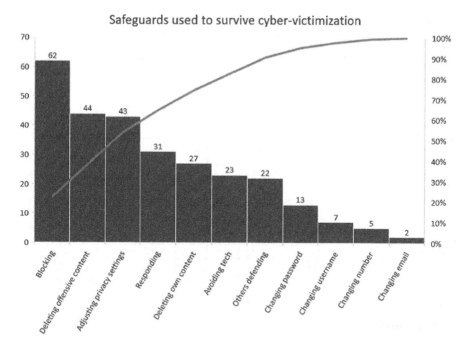

Fig. 4. Safeguards used to prevent/stop harassment

4.5 Inferential Statistics: Harassment Effects by Harassment Type and Attribute

To test the differences in harassment effects based on harassment type, each harassment effect and harassment type were grouped into two categories (Yes, No) and tested against one another. We used a Chi-Squared test to examine any relationships. The p-value associated with each Chi-Square statistics is listed in Table 1, with the significant values ($p < 0.05$) highlighted. For the harassment attributes duration, severity and frequency (bottom three rows in Table 2) the Pearson correlation coefficient was used as the relevant test statistic.

The test revealed a number of significant associations, although some of these may be an artefact of the data. However, the harassment types (reading by row) of denigration, exclusion and cyber-stalking seem to have the biggest impacts, as do the harassment duration, as well as frequency. Extremely worrying is the fact that the most significant impacts (reading by column) seem to be quite severe: depression, substance abuse, self-harm and suicide contemplation all have at least three significant correlations.

Table 2. Harassment type/attributed and their impact (p-value based on test-statistic)

Effect experienced as a consequence from: Harassment type	Anxiety	Depression	Low confidence	Low self-esteem	Low empathy	Rejection by peers	Substance abuse	Aggression	Hopelessness	Self-harm	Suicide contemplation
Flaming	.897	.730	.363	.776	.473	.211	.624	.175	.251	.430	.850
Harassment	.271	.253	.247	.345	.146	.506	.843	.306	.511	.339	.151
Impersonation	.088	.618	.377	.601	.333	.331	.423	.076	.763	.713	.524
Denigration	.089	.004	.848	.299	.359	.171	.020	.650	.891	.004	.018
Exclusion	.271	.107	.011	.159	.599	.000	.025	.843	.032	.039	.000
Outed	.391	.056	.219	.183	.980	.938	.429	.650	.891	.028	.787
Trickery	.112	.406	.132	.204	.975	.538	.611	.611	.202	.840	.281
Cyber-stalking	.683	.555	.936	.369	.199	.665	.092	.092	.041	.002	.001
Harassment *attribute*											
Duration	.387	.180	.220	.025	.637	.024	.043	.707	.465	.121	.068
Severity	.215	.039	.239	.145	.676	.305	.957	.361	.058	.105	.290
Frequency	.073	.044	.636	.241	.290	.466	.496	.090	.118	.028	.117

5   Conclusion

Cyber harassment is a growing topic of research due to the rapid rate of the technology advancement society is currently experiencing. However, research concerning minority groups such as LGBTQIA+ and the cyber harassment that those groups incur is severely lacking. The overall aim of this study is to highlight that cyber harassment in minority groups is a topic of importance worthy of more academic research.

The study's results show that majority of the LGBTQIA+ group have been cyber-harassed. The most prevalent type of cyber harassment seems to be the outing of individual, and the platform most preferred by offenders seems to be text-based (SMS WhatsApp etc.). The cyber harassment seems to vary in frequency, duration and severity, with some significant correlations to certain effects experienced, such as depression.

The findings regarding accessibility, ease of spread and lack of fear of offender penalization align with previous literature in that those factors are enablers of cyber-harassment. The study also identified the various coping mechanisms that LGBTQIA+ individuals tend to adopt to deal with cyber-victimization. Further research should be conducted to find rates of effectiveness on remedy and prevention.

The most worrying finding of this research was the severity of the effect of harassment. We found to be significant effects from some types of harassment (denigration, exclusion and cyber-stalking), and harassment duration, as well as frequency. These resulted in statistically significant levels of depression, substance abuse, self-harm and suicide contemplation. This highlights the importance of this research and motivates strongly for further research to in this space as well as the importance of regulating or monitoring social platforms.

6   Limitations and Further Research

The major limitation with this study is response bias (respondents who have been harassed are more likely to respond to the survey) and the sampling approach. The majority of the participants were mostly university students as this sample was the most easily accessible. This may mean that the results may not be as general to the wider public as students represent a distinct age and educational group, and are perhaps more homogenous than the rest of the LGBTQIA+ population.

Further research needs to focus on further validation of this study's findings, how effective coping strategies provided by online platforms are in the remedy and prevention of cyber harassment, and harassment experiences in less liberal environments than South Africa. A longitudinal study with a control group could also yield critical insights.

References

1. Anon: Internet: Statistics and Market Data about the Internet (2017). https://www.statista.com/markets/424/internet/
2. Aricak, T., et al.: Cyberbullying among Turkish adolescents. Cyber-Psychol. Behav. **11**(3), 253–261 (2008)
3. Dietrich, H.: Victimology: an emphasis on the lifestyle-exposure theory and the victim precipitation theory as it applies to violent crime, s.l.: s.n (2008)
4. Devji, Z.Z.: Forging paths for the African queer: is there an "African" mechanism for realizing LGBTIQ rights? J. Afr. Law **60**(3), 343–363 (2016)
5. GottheilN, F., Dubow, E.F.: Tripartite beliefs models of bully and victim behavior. Bully. Behav.: Curr. Issues Res. Intervent. **2**, 25–47 (2001)
6. Gunawardena, C.N.: Social presence theory and implications for interaction and collaborative learning in computer conferences. Int. J. Educ. Telecommun. **1**(2/3), 147–166 (1995)
7. Inglehart, R., Welzel, C.: Modernization, Cultural Change, and Democracy: The Human Development Sequence. Cambridge University Press, Cambridge and New York (2005)
8. Jackson, C.: Your students love social media. Teach. Tolerance Issue **39**, 38–41 (2011)
9. Kuzma, J.: Empirical study of cyber harassment amount social networks. Int. J. Technol. Hum. Interact. **9**(2), 53–65 (2013)
10. LaMorte, W.W.: Behavioral change models: social norms theory. Boston University School of Public Health, s.l. (2016)
11. Locke, A., Lawthom, R., Lyons, A.: Social media platforms as complex and contradictory spaces for feminisms: visibility, opportunity, power, resistance and activism. Feminism Psychol. **29**(1), 3–10 (2018)
12. Madero, A.: Lifestyle Exposure Theory of Victimisation. Wiley-Blackwell, Hoboken (2018)
13. Mishna, F., Khoury-Kassabri, M., Gadalla, T., Daciuk, J.: Risk factors for involvement in cyber bullying: victims, bullies and bully-victims. Child. Youth Serv. Rev. **32**, 63–70 (2012)
14. Mitchell, Y., Nel, J.A.: The hate and bias crimes monitoring form project. The Hate Crimes Working Group, Johannesburg (2018)
15. OUT: New LGBTI hate crime reporting platform launched (2018). http://www.out.org.za/index.php/what-s-hot/news/558-new-lgbti-hate-crime-reporting-platform-launched
16. Sabella, R.A., Patchin, J.W., Hinduja, S.: Cyberbullying myths and realities. Comput. Hum. Behav. **29**, 1703–2711 (2013)

17. Sandfort, T.G., Reddy, V.: African same-sex sexualities and gender-diversity: an introduction. Cult. Health Sex. **15**(1), 1–6 (2013)
18. Saunders, M., Lewis, P., Thornhill, A.: The purpose of your research. In: Research Methods for Business Students, 5 edn., pp. 139–140. Pearson Education, Harlow (2009)
19. Slonje, R., Smith, P.K., Frisen, A.: Processes of cyberbullying, and feelings of remorse by bullies: a pilot study. Eur. J. Dev. Psychol. **9**, 244–259 (2012)
20. Swearer, S.M., Hymel, S.: Understanding the psychology of bullying: moving toward a social-ecological diathesis-stress model. Am. Psychol. **70**(4), 344–353 (2015)
21. Tokunaga, R.S.: Following you home from school: a critical review and synthesis of research on cyberbullying victimization. Comput. Hum. Behav. **26**(3), 277–287 (2010)
22. Willard, N.E.: Cyberbullying and Cyberthreats: Responding to the Challenge of Online Social Aggression, Threats, and Distress. Research Press (2007)

Online Identity Theft on Consumer Purchase Intention: A Mediating Role of Online Security and Privacy Concern

Abdul Bashiru Jibril$^{(\boxtimes)}$ ⓘ, Michael Adu Kwarteng ⓘ,
Fortune Nwaiwu ⓘ, Christina Appiah-Nimo ⓘ, Michal Pilik ⓘ,
and Miloslava Chovancova ⓘ

Faculty of Management and Economics, Tomas Bata University in Zlin,
Mostni 5139, 76001 Zlin, Czech Republic
{Jibril,Kwarteng,Nwaiwu,Appiah-Nimo,Pilik,
Chovancova}@utb.cz

Abstract. This study measures the influence of fear of financial loss (FOFL), fear of reputational damage (FORD), with the mediating effect of online security and privacy concern (OSPCON) towards online purchase intentions in an emerging economy's context. Data was conveniently collected from University students of four of the public higher institutions in Ghana. Out of the 201 questionnaires distributed, 179 were eligible for analysis. A Quantitative methodological approach was adopted which relied on the Partial Least Square approach to Structural Equation Modelling (PLS-SEM) for the statistical analysis. Seemingly, FOFL and FORD constructs were not seen to be a significant direct predictor of online purchase intention. However, the mediating effect of OSPCON for both FOFL and FORD towards online purchase intention in the Ghanaian context was found to be significant, hence the mediated-hypotheses were supported. Nonetheless, we have highlighted the need for additional and further research taking a cue from the study's limitations. The study contributes to our knowledge of how online identity theft practices lead to the unwillingness of online customers to embark on online transactions in an emerging economy, given the rampant outburst of online transactions in the developed world. The originality of this study is in the fact that it focuses on an emerging economy, which is under-researched.

Keywords: Online identity theft · Purchase intentions · Security and privacy concern · Emerging economy · Ghana

1 Introduction

The saturation of society by new technologies results in increasing levels of adoption and use in daily life activities, this brings with it unprecedented opportunities as well as threats and risks. Information and communication technologies and other related digital technologies especially digital platforms have brought along with them a new dimension to how society is evolving, especially in relation to how people interact and transact business. They have in their own unique way also introduced new challenges

© IFIP International Federation for Information Processing 2020
Published by Springer Nature Switzerland AG 2020
M. Hattingh et al. (Eds.): I3E 2020, LNCS 12067, pp. 147–158, 2020.
https://doi.org/10.1007/978-3-030-45002-1_13

and concerns for users. Some of the challenges and concerns pertaining to the protection of the privacy and sensitive information of users of these technologies. Identity theft is a major example of such challenges faced by users of these technologies, as Cavoukian (2013) noted, identity theft is the fastest-growing form of consumer fraud in North America. The problem of identity theft is not peculiar to North America alone, several authors have reported a growing incidence of this problem around the world (Kahn and Liñares-Zegarra 2016; Reyns 2013; Williams 2016). The issue of identity theft has become ubiquitous especially as a result of the migration of a lot of activities associated with human social and economic activities to online platforms.

This migration of a significant amount of human social and economic activities to online platforms has led to the evolution of the nature and characteristics of identity theft to be in line with the sociotechnical changes currently being experienced by society. Consequently, the regimes of digital safety and security as informed by the threat of online identity theft that has become prevalent globally should not be merely viewed as a political reaction to the risks brought about by the proliferation of digital in society. Rather, online identity theft further constitutes an active threat and factor that influences consumers' purchase intentions especially in developing economies where proactive measures of protection are not particularly up to the standards obtainable in more advanced economies. Thus, where the incipient digital society is collectively re-imagined, negotiated, and created.

Therefore, online identity theft is an issue of major concern for online retailers of goods and services in these developing economy markets where the state of an emerging digital society and the sociotechnical relationships of checks and balances required to govern its emergence are in a constant state of transition (Haddad and Binder 2019). Though the work by Jordan et al. (2018) replicated some constructs used in this present study to measure the impact of fear of identity theft, perceived risk in online purchase intentions; their work was not narrowed to measure the mediating role of online security and privacy concern that becomes the focal lens of this study. Moreover, their research was neither specific to young students in public higher institutions or to the more definite of an emerging economy's context considered in this paper. We further argue that given the varied and complex reasons manifesting in low levels of eCommerce transactions in the developing world, such as low level of internet penetrations, high levels of income poverty, a high rate of illiteracy, and infrastructural challenges that manifest in logistical inefficiencies even have a repelling effect on purchase intentions. Based on these insights, the current study aims at addressing the prognosis of online identity theft on consumer purchase intentions from a developing economy's perspective by (1) Evaluating the predictive influence of identity theft (FOFL and FORD) towards online transactions (2) Establishing the mediating role of online security and privacy concern (OSPCON) towards online purchase intentions/transactions. Specifically, two research questions emerged:

RQI: What impact does online identity theft have on online transactions from university students in a developing country (Ghana)?

RQ2: What influence does the mediating effect of OSPCON have on online transactions from university students in a developing economy (Ghana)?

The rest of the study is structured as follows: Related works on online identity theft are briefly highlighted. Next, the theoretical foundations of the present study are discussed. Then, the conceptual framework of the study as well as the hypotheses are stated. Methodology and the results are presented. Finally, the study's implication to theory and practice are discussed.

2   Related Works on Online Identity Theft

According to Jordan et al. (2018), a major consequence of the emergence of the internet has been the rise in cybercrime which has accompanied its increasing use as a medium for transacting commercial activities through electronic means. Cybercrime manifests itself invariants that span across a broad range of criminal activities that leverage the electronic exchange of information of users. One of the most pervasive being the incidence of online identity theft which has led to victims suffering significant losses and harm which often leaves them traumatized both emotionally and financially. By applying widely available Internet tools, malicious actors trick unsuspecting computer users into divulging personal data, which is then exploited for illicit purposes, thereby causing mistrust of online payment and banking services (Venkatesh and Goyal 2010) These malicious individuals often apply techniques such as "phishing" and "pharming" as means of tricking their target victims, this is largely facilitated by the fact that because of the nature of the internet and other electronically mediated interactions, face-to-face contact between interacting parties does not exist or is reduced to the barest minimum. The potential for fraud continues to remain a major obstacle in the evolution and proliferation of e-commerce and online-based financial transactions (Furnell 2010; Wang and Huang 2011).

While it is acknowledged that there is no standard definition of identity theft whether it is online or offline (Smith 2007; Wang and Huang 2011), for the purpose of this study, it is imperative to examine some definitions identified in literature for the purpose of establishing conceptual clarity that would serve as a guide that would facilitate the achievement of the research objectives. According to Reyns (2013), identity theft is the terminology used in describing the fraudulent use of an individual's personal information for criminal purposes and without the owner's consent. More specifically, Jordan et al. (2018) define online identity theft as an act of online fraud and crimes that involve the duplication of digital information or the high-jacking of online accounts for the purposes of committing identity fraud against individuals or businesses. Also, Cornelius (2016) defines online identity theft as the illicit use of another person's identifying facts for the perpetration of economic fraud or for masquerading another person's identity on the internet.

Online identity theft is prevalent in developed societies as a result of the high levels of internet and mobile penetration in their societies. However, as the levels of internet and mobile penetration continues to rise in developing economies, there is also a corresponding increase in the incidence of online identity theft. Vijaya Geeta (2011, p. 237) discusses online identity theft from a developing economy perspective by accessing the impact of phishing attacks which has gained prominence as one of the common techniques frequently employed by criminal elements. He comments that phishing attacks have risen in countries like India, which as of 2009 accounted for 15% of all malicious activity in the Asia-Pacific/Japan (APJ) region, increasing from 10% in 2008. He also comments that "for specific categories of measurement in the APJ region, India increased rank in malicious code, spam zombies and phishing hosts from 2008. This made India being the third highest country of spam origin globally."

Ebem et al. (2017, p. 2) reveal that "despite the giant strides and achievements of internet banking, the Nigerian financial sector is currently battling with the twin evils of identity theft and financial frauds, just like other advanced economies of the world". Also, Ladan (2014, p. 17) conducted research which reviewed recent developments in cyberlaw responses to cybercrime and cybersecurity in Nigeria and the economic community of West African States (ECOWAS), from the findings of his research, he established that "online identity theft which includes the act of capturing another person's credentials and/or personal information via the Internet with the intent to fraudulently reuse it for criminal purposes is now one of the main threats to further deployment of e-government and e-business services in Nigeria and across the West African sub-region". Hence, these observations make it imperative to understand the phenomenon of online identity theft from the perspective of developing economies, especially in relation to its impact on consumer purchase intentions.

However, for the sake of argument, and also towards the nature and rationale of this study, we will be limiting the investigation to the mechanism of online security and privacy concern as a risky component of influence in online identity theft in a developing context. In framing our arguments, we have been inspired by the scale of the validated construct of Fear of reputational damage and Fear of financial loss by Hille et al. (2015).

2.1 Conceptual Model Development and Research Hypotheses

2.1.1 The Relationship Between Fear of Financial Loss, Online Security and Privacy Concern, and Online Customer Purchase Intention

According to Gurung and Raja (2016), concerns about privacy protection is one of the primary obstacles for consumers to participate in electronic eCommerce transactions that require them to divulge personal information, such as their date of birth, social security number, personal phone number, and credit card information, etc. This makes the protection of consumers' privacy as an important factor for the success of e-commerce businesses. This view is also supported by Martín et al. (2011) who in their research focused on online shoppers in Portugal, explored the effect of trust on perceived benefits of online purchase, by looking at how security and privacy considerations of the online shoppers in Portugal influenced their trust levels and confidence to use the system. They found a causal relationship between users' perceptions of risk and their decision to trust the system, which ultimately influenced their purchase intentions along with the perceived benefits of using the system. Hence, based on evidence in order to extend the scope of understanding based on scientific evidence, the following hypothesis is proposed as a basis to investigate the causal relationship between fear of financial loss and online customers' purchase intentions, this will be done by looking at the mediating effects (if any) of online security vis-à-vis privacy concerns

H1: Fear of financial loss will predict online customers' purchase intentions via the mediating effect of online security and privacy concern.

H3: Fear of financial loss directly affects online customers' purchase intention.

2.1.2   The Relationship Between Fear of Reputational Damage, Online Security and Privacy Concern, and Online Purchase Intention

As consumer patronage via online shopping medium continues to increase, there are still doubts and restraining factors that impact on the consumers' behavioral intentions and willingness to use such systems. Some of these factors bother on issues such as the fear of reputational damage that is connected to online security and privacy concerns held by consumers. As part of scientific inquiry that aims to investigate the relationships between fear of reputational damage and issues such perceived risk associated the intentions to embark on online transactions from the consumers' perspective, results from the research conducted by Jordan et al. (2018) showed that there is a positive correlation in the relationship between fear of financial losses, fear of reputational damage, perceived risk, and the relation between the constructs of perceived risk and online purchase intention was negative. Their research was conducted within the context of understanding the impact of fear of identity theft and perceived risk on the Online Purchase Intention of consumers. This is in tandem with the works by other researchers who have investigated related issues Gurung and Raja (2016) and that of Jordan et al. (2018). Consequently, this research further aims to investigate specifically, how the fear of reputational damage influences online consumers' purchase intentions with online security and privacy concerns as mediating effects. Hence, the relevant hypothesis is proposed as follows

H2: Fear of reputation damage will predict online customers 'purchase intentions via the mediating effect of online security and privacy concern

H4: Fear of reputational damage directly affects online customers' purchase intention.

To conclude, we deduced a conceptual model, as well as the summary of research constructs and their measurement items from the literature, are given below in Fig. 1 and Table 1 respectively.

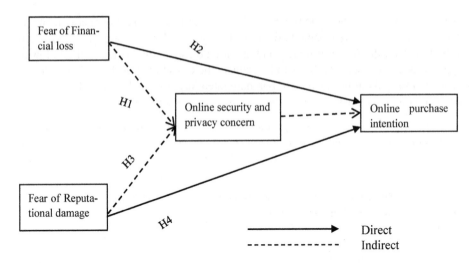

Fig. 1. Conceptual model

3   Methodology

Data was conveniently collected from University students of four of the public higher institutions in Ghana. Out of the 201 questionnaires distributed, 189 were eligible for analysis. Survey respondents were pre-qualified to ensure that their knowledge of online buying or shopping, as well as its accompanying online theft and cybercrime instances, was adequate to answer the survey questions. Data collection was undertaken in the months between June to September 2019. On average, the questionnaire took 10 min to fill. As earlier stated, the respondent positions comprised: University students in some selected public higher institutions in Ghana (University of Cape Coast (UCC), University of Ghana (UG), Kwame Nkrumah University of Science and Technology (KNUST), and the University for development studies (UDS)) and more particularly undergraduate students who frequently visit the Internet - daily and/or weekly activity. This was made possible as a result of getting a fair representation of university students across the length and breadth in Ghana. We must emphasize that all the selected universities are dispersed in all the three belts in Ghana, thus the Northern, Southern, and Middle belt of Ghana.

Partial least squares (PLS) path modeling was used to simultaneously estimate both the measurement and structural components of the model. Furthermore, our work is consistent with most of the views expressed in Podskaoff et al. (2003) regarding the minimization of common method variance.

3.1   Constructs Measurement

In line with previous studies, this study adapted constructs from existing studies. The measures for FOLF, FORD were based on the works of Hille et al. (2015); Doherty et al. (2006), while the measure of OSPCON was mostly culled from the works of Tan et al. (2010). Hille et al. (2015) and Ajzen (1991). Finally, the measure of OPI was sourced from; Fishbein and Ajzen (1975); Duan et al. 2019 and Hille et al. (2015). Readers should also note that measurement items were anchored on a six-point scale with 1 - being completely agreed and 6 - completely disagree.

4   Results

4.1   Model Fit Tests

Assessing measurement models is the initial step in performing any PLS-SEM. This stage confirms that indicator variables (unobserved) are actually measuring constructs (observed variables) they ought to do. Therefore, we assessed our measurement model using convergent validity, and reliability following the suggestion of Hair et al. (2014). Consistent with recent investigations, and also acknowledging the initial step in evaluating PLS-SEM results as earlier suggested, the measurement model must be first assessed, using the indicator loadings (see Hair et al. 2017). With this in mind, loadings of approximately 0.708 are deemed fit since they best explain more than 50% of the indicator variance, hence providing an acceptable threshold for item reliability. Going by this rule of thumb, all items associated with our indicator reliability exhibited more than 50% of the indicator cross-loadings which suggest the level of associations (items correlation) to their respective construct (see Table 1).

For internal consistency reliability, both Cronbach alpha (CA) and the composite reliability (CR) were used as a metric in the assessment. With a minimum threshold and a rule of thumb recording 0.5 and 0.6 respectively (see Bagozzi and Yi 1988). Therefore, both CA and CR exceeded the baseline recording as follows for all the latent constructs as 0.92, 0.93 respectively for FOFL, 0.86, 0.91 respectively for FORD, 0.84, 0.91 respectively for OPI and 0.89, 0.93 respectively for OSPCON. For convergent validity, the Average Variance Extracted (AVE) was used to measure the extent to which the constructs congregate in order to explain the variance of all items on each construct (Hair et al. 2019). However, the minimum acceptable AVE is 0.50 or more, thus an indication of 50% or more on how the variance of items makes up with the specified construct. Reflecting on this threshold, all AVE for our latent constructs exceeded the minimum acceptable baseline (see Table 1) for more details.

Table 1. Item loadings

Items	Construct			
	FOFL	FORD	OPI	OSPCON
FOFL1	0.745003			
FOFL2	0.740739			
FOFL3	0.756215			
FOFL4	0.870122			
FOFL5	0.832757			
FOFL6	0.858748			
FOFL7	0.902154			

AVE = 0.668216
CR = 0.933411
CA = 0.917131

FORD1		0.869112		
FORD2		0.828146		
FORD3		0.830033		
FORD4		0.834515		

AVE = 0.706638
CR = 0.905937
CA = 0.862968

OPI1			0.769416	
OPI2			0.91521	
OPI3			0.905006	

AVE = 0.749549
CR = 0.899249
CA = 0.841929

OSPCON1				0.918411
OSPCON2				0.919658
OSPCON3				0.858576

AVE = 0.808801
CR = 0.926888
CA = 0.884311

Note: AVE = Average variance extracted, CR = Composite reliability, CA = Cronbach's Alpha
Sources: Authors' estimation from SmartPLS

4.2　Test of Structural Model: A Mediation Analysis

Following the validity of the measurement model, assessment of the structural model is necessary since it justifies the model's ability to predict the endogenous variables or dependent variables. Therefore, the assessment of the structural model follows a procedure which took inspiration from (Hair et al. 2017) in order to advance issues in partial least squares structural equation modeling. To proceed, it is important to remind readers that the focal point of this study was to measure the mediation of OSPCON on

FOFL and FORD towards OPI consequently the direct effect of OSPCON on the former. To accomplish this, we examined two direct relations, namely, *H2 and H4* whiles the remaining hypothesized scenarios were centered on the observation of mediated relationship (i.e. *H1 and H3*). Going by our empirical estimates, our findings from the direct relationships revealed that FOFL has a positive coefficient but a weak predictor of OPI. However, the bootstrapping t-test (with t* > 1.96 as significant level), but our estimate indicated an insignificant direct relationship ($\beta = 0.099$, $t = 0.649$) between FOFL and OPI which therefore does not offer empirical support for H2 (See Table 2 for more details). With respect to *H4*, our estimate also suggested that FORD though positive and weak predictor of OPI, but also insignificant ($\beta = 0.165$, $t = 0.665$) indicating that H4 was not supported. With the mediated observations, it can be seen from Table 2 that OSPCON as a mediator to both FOFL and FORD towards OPI are all supported (*H1 and H3*), thus, statistically recording as follows: FOFL -> OSPCON -> OPI = ($\beta = 0.418$, $t^* = 4.594$) and FORD -> OSPCON -> OPI = ($\beta = 0.392$, $t^* = 3.740$) as shown from Table 2 below.

Table 2. Direct and indirect effect on online identity theft.

Direct and indirect effect (Hypothesis)	Path coefficient (β)	T-test (Bootstrapping)	Decision
(H2) FOFL -> OPI	0.099	0.649	Not supported
(H4) FORD -> OPI (H4)	0.165	0.665	Not supported
(H1) FOFL -> OSPCON -> OPI	0.418	4.594*	Supported
(H3) FORD -> OSPCON-> OPI	0.392	3.740*	Supported

t* > 1.96 equal p-value < 0.05 significant level
(Readers should note that the significance testing has been executed using the bootstrapping procedure)
Sources: Authors' estimation from SmartPLS

5   Discussions

Research Question One:
This question, addresses whether there is a direct relationship amongst FOFL, FORD, and OPI in an event of online identity theft towards online transactions amongst university students in a developing country (Ghana)? With the general consensus of online identity theft in an emerging country, this study does shed more light, by considering the scenario in an emerging economy. Hence, the present findings are inconsistent with the study of Mitchison et al. (2004) that stated that personal and financial data can have a dire lasting financial consequence for victims and does incur a negative financial credit rating for such victims. Disputing the claims by Mitchison and co, the present study does elucidate the tendency that FOFL will predict or affect the customers' decision to engage in online transactions in an emerging economy. Again, with the research works of Jordan et al, (2018) regarding FOFL and FORD relative to the OPI, their study turned out to have positive relationships even though their work was not situated in a developing context. Adding to this debate is the findings that emanated from the multiple

research works of Hille et al. (2015) stating that FOFL has a stronger magnitude of effect on OPI than FORD whiles our present study refutes this claim by reporting that the two constructs have no positive or direct relations with OPI. Alternatively, in their findings from study 3 of the same research works of Hille et al. (2015), it was established that FORD does not play a significant major role in affecting OPI.

Research Question Two:

Research Question two addresses whether there is an influence on the mediating role of OPSCON towards online transactions amongst university students in a developing economy (Ghana) context. Concerning H1a as earlier stated, the authors propose that the positive or direct link between FOFL and OPI will be mediated by OPSCON, our research estimate, however, establishes support for H1a (See Table 2). This finding, though largely studied under different contexts in literature, mirrors with previous research works in the risk concerning online buying behaviour (see Hong and Cha 2013; Miyazaki and Fernandez 2001; Chuang and Fan 2011). With this said, we opine that more research works in the emerging context is required to be performed to address the issue of security and privacy concerns as a conduit of online purchase intentions; reflecting on the notion of online identity theft circumstances.

5.1 Limitations and Future Research

While the present study adds to the existing body of knowledge in the perceived risk associated with online transactions by examining the given model between the online customers considering an emerging economy, several limitations are present that remain to be addressed and creates an avenue for future research. First, the sample has 189 respondents. Adding to this limitation is the fact that, the study was conducted using a student population and so makes it difficult to generalize beyond the target population.

Although the sample is well enough, this sample is somewhat below the recommendations of the pioneer scholars well versed with the application of the structural equation model (Hair et al. 2017). Future research should consider augmenting the sample size for the given model. The second limitation of the study is geared towards the failure to address the question of potential experience of the respondents. Future works should include a construct to measure the experience from online identity theft from the developing or emerging economy's perspective.

5.2 Concluding Observations

The aim of the study was to develop and test a theoretical framework bent on eliciting the notion of online identity theft on consumer purchase intention via the mediating role of online security and privacy concern; within a sub-Saharan African context (Ghana). Like the emerging concept of online buying behavior in developing context, the study explores the relationships of both direct and indirect effect of FOFL and FORD towards OPI whiles OSPCON are mediated towards the former. While the study finds no support for 2 direct links with 2 support of the mediated variable, this study highlights the differences between online identity theft on one hand and its associated online intentions on the other hand. While this study is able to predict customers' in an emerging economies fear of online identity theft towards their zeal to embark on online transactions, specifically using three major constructs i.e. FOFL, FORD, and OSPCON. In sum, this study provides a strong reference point to continue to broaden the literature in the developing economy so far as online transactions are concerned, arguing that the internet is not leaving in extinction any time soon.

Acknowledgment. This work was supported by the Internal Grant Agency of FaME through TBU in Zlín No. IGA/FaME/2019/008; IGA/FaME/2020/002 and further by the financial support of research project NPU I no. MSMT-7778/2019 RVO - Digital Transformation and its Impact on Customer Behaviour and Business Processes in Traditional and Online markets.

References

Ajzen, I.: The theory of planned behavior. Organ. Behav. Hum. Decis. Process. **50**(2), 179–211 (1991)

Bagozzi, R.P., Yi, Y.: On the evaluation of structural equation models. J. Acad. Mark. Sci. **16**(1), 74–94 (1988). https://doi.org/10.1007/BF02723327

Cavoukian, A.: *Privacy by Design* and the Promise of SmartData. In: Harvey, I., Cavoukian, A., Tomko, G., Borrett, D., Kwan, H., Hatzinakos, D. (eds.) SmartData, pp. 1–9. Springer, New York (2013). https://doi.org/10.1007/978-1-4614-6409-9_1

Chuang, H.M., Fan, C.J.: The mediating role of trust in the relationship between e-retailer quality and customer intention of online shopping. Afr. J. Bus. Manag. **5**(22), 9522–9529 (2011)

Cornelius, D.R.: Online identity theft victimization: an assessment of victims and non-victims level of cyber security knowledge. ProQuest Dissertations and Theses, Colorado Technical University, Ann Arbor (2016). https://search.proquest.com/docview/1870624251?accountid=15518

Doherty, N.F., Ellis-Chadwick, F., Allred, C.R., Smith, S.M., Swinyard, W.R.: E-shopping lovers and fearful conservatives: a market segmentation analysis. Int. J. Retail Distrib. Manag. **34**(4/5), 308–333 (2006). https://doi.org/10.1108/09590550610660251

Duan, Y., Edwards, J.S., Dwivedi, Y.K.: Artificial intelligence for decision making in the era of Big Data–evolution, challenges and research agenda. Int. J. Inf. Manag. **48**, 63–71 (2019)

Ebem, D.U., Onyeagba, J.C., Ugwuonah, G.E.: Internet banking: identity theft and solutions - the Nigerian perspective. J. Internet Bank. Commer. **22**(2), 1–15 (2017). https://search.proquest.com/docview/1949087351?accountid=15518

Hair Jr., J.F., Sarstedt, M., Hopkins, L., Kuppelwieser, V.G.: Partial least squares structural equation modeling (PLS-SEM). An emerging tool in business research. Eur. Bus. Rev. **26**(2), 106–121 (2014)

Fishbein, M., Ajzen, I.: Belief, Attitude, Intention, and Behavior: An Introduction to Theory and Research. Addison-Wesley, Reading (1981, 1975)

Furnell, S.M.: Online identity: giving it all away? Inf. Secur. Tech. Rep. (2010). https://doi.org/10.1016/j.istr.2010.09.002

Gurung, A., Raja, M.K.: Online privacy and security concerns of consumers. Inf. Comput. Secur. **24**(4), 348–371 (2016)

Haddad, C., Binder, C.: Governing through cybersecurity: national policy strategies, globalized (in-)security and sociotechnical visions of the digital society. Österreichische Zeitschrift Für Soziologie **44**(1), 115–134 (2019). https://doi.org/10.1007/s11614-019-00350-7

Hair Jr., J.F., Sarstedt, M., Ringle, C.M., Gudergan, S.P.: Advanced Issues in Partial Least Squares Structural Equation Modeling. Sage Publications, Thousand Oaks (2017)

Hair Jr., J.F., Risher, J.J., Sarstedt, M., Ringle, C.M.: When to use and how to report the results of PLS-SEM. Eur. Bus. Rev. **31**(1), 2–24 (2019)

Hille, P., Walsh, G., Cleveland, M.: Consumer fear of online identity theft: Scale development and validation. J. Interact. Mark. **30**, 1–19 (2015)

Hong, I.B., Cha, H.S.: The mediating role of consumer trust in an online merchant in predicting purchase intention. Int. J. Inf. Manage. **33**(6), 927–939 (2013)

Jordan, G., Leskovar, R., Marič, M.: Impact of Fear of Identity Theft and Perceived Risk on Online Purchase Intention. Organizacija **51**(2), 146–155 (2018). https://doi.org/10.2478/orga-2018-0007

Kahn, C.M., Liñares-Zegarra, J.M.: Identity theft and consumer payment choice: does security really matter? J. Financ. Serv. Res. **50**, 121–159 (2016). https://doi.org/10.1007/s10693-015-0218-x

Ladan, M.T.: Review of recent developments in cyberlaw responses to cybercrime and cybersecurity in Nigeria and the Economic Community of West African States (ECOWAS). Law Technology **47**(4), 14–84 (2014). https://search.proquest.com/docview/1656056536?accountid=15518

Martín, S.S., Camarero, C., José, R.S.: Does involvement matter in online shopping satisfaction and trust? Psychol. Mark. **28**(2), 145–167 (2011)

Mitchison, N., et al.: Identity theft: a discussion paper. European Commission Joint Research Center, March 2004. https://www.prime-project.eu/community/furtherreading/studies/IDTheftFIN.pdf

Miyazaki, A.D., Fernandez, A.: Consumer perceptions of privacy and security risks for online shopping. J. Consum. Aff. **35**(1), 27–44 (2001)

Podsakoff, P.M., MacKenzie, S.B., Lee, J.Y., Podsakoff, N.P.: Common method biases in behavioral research: a critical review of the literature and recommended remedies. J. Appl. Psychol. **88**(5), 879 (2003)

Reyns, B.W.: Online routines and identity theft victimization: further expanding routine activity theory beyond direct-contact offenses. J. Res. Crime Delinq. (2013). https://doi.org/10.1177/0022427811425539

Smith, R.: Cybercrime and society. Aust. N. Z. J. Criminol. (2007). https://doi.org/10.1375/acri.40.3.360

Tan, K.S., Chong, S.C., Loh, P.L., Lin, B.: An evaluation of e-banking and m-banking adoption factors and preference in Malaysia: a case study. Int. J. Mob. Commun. **8**(5), 507–527 (2010)

Venkatesh, V., Goyal, S.: Expectation disconfirmation and technology adoption: polynomial modeling and response surface analysis. MIS Q. **34**, 281–303 (2010)

Vijaya Geeta, D.: Online identity theft – an Indian perspective. J. Financ. Crime **18**(3), 235–246 (2011). https://doi.org/10.1108/13590791111147451

Wang, B.S.K., Huang, W.: The evolutional view of the types of identity thefts and online frauds in the era of the internet. Internet J. Criminol. (2011)

Williams, M.L.: Guardians upon high: an application of routine activities theory to online identity theft in Europe at the country and individual level. Br. J. Criminol. (2016). https://doi.org/10.1093/bjc/azv011

On the Ethics of Using Publicly-Available Data

Antony K. Cooper[1,2](✉) ⓘ and Serena Coetzee[2] ⓘ

[1] Smart Places, CSIR, PO Box 395, Pretoria 0001, South Africa
acooper@csir.co.za
[2] Department of Geography, Geoinformatics and Meteorology,
University of Pretoria, Private Bag X20, Hatfield 0028, South Africa
serena.coetzee@up.ac.za

Abstract. Publicly-available mobile data can be used to derive fine grain commuting and travel patterns. These types of data include geocoded or geo-tagged discrete units of communication: messages, posts, tweets, status updates, check-ins, images and the like on a variety of social networking services. Clearly, there are ethical issues concerning the use of such data, particularly the invasion of privacy. A review of the literature has been done to explore these issues.

Keywords: Privacy · Surveillance · Mobile data · Social networking service

1 Introduction

The more one knows about people and their condition(s), actions, needs, preferences, beliefs and the like, the better one can provide services to them – if one is in a purely benevolent, altruistic, caring and diligent society. However, there are problems or ethical issues with such data, and with capturing, the processes for capturing, and using the data. Even then, interpretation of the data might be invalid.

As a concept, *publicly-available data* usually refers to data found readily (such as on the Internet) and accessed (downloaded) easily and for free. Many of these data sets are created and distributed by public organisations. Publicly-available data includes open data (freely usable, reusable and redistributable without restrictions), data available on request, public-domain data (without copyright), copyrighted data, commercially-sold data and data with limited availability (eg: for a limited time or for only specified uses). Clearly, any data could fall into more than one of these types.

This paper draws on PhD research and a project that investigated using publicly-available mobile data to derive commuting and travel patterns. Clearly, there are ethical issues over using such data, particularly invading privacy. We review and analyse the literature to explore the ethics of using publicly-available data. We do not attempt to pick a framework of normative ethics on using such data. Rather, we explore some of the issues, focusing on surveillance-type data and hence on privacy.

1.1 Characteristics of Publicly Available Data

The following are some characteristics of publicly-available data.

© IFIP International Federation for Information Processing 2020
Published by Springer Nature Switzerland AG 2020
M. Hattingh et al. (Eds.): I3E 2020, LNCS 12067, pp. 159–171, 2020.
https://doi.org/10.1007/978-3-030-45002-1_14

- **Surrogates:** digital data are not the real world, but merely represent the real world, and often because of costs, availability, laws and so on, the data actually recorded are merely a surrogate (or proxy or approximation) for the phenomena in the real world that are meant to be measured or assessed.
- **Big data:** it is easy to capture vast quantities of data, but often difficult to extract meaning or to forewarn from the overwhelming data. Even worse, some assume the sheer volume provides greater objectivity, neutrality and accuracy, but "*data are always the result of conscious, subjective decisions on the part of researchers, and are the result of inherently social processes*" [1]. The perceived authority or effectiveness is lost by being overwhelmed by all the automatically-collected data, by mistaking omniscience for omnipotence or intelligence: "*the more you know about the secret lives of others, the less powerful you turn out to be!*" [2].
- **False precision:** digital geographical coordinates are often given to some arbitrary precision based on a data storage decision (eg: single vs double precision), rather than the accuracy of the recording method, giving incorrect perceptions of coordinate accuracy. For example, a point geocoded from a toponym (eg: Tshwane) could have a precision of a second (about 30 m), though the toponym encompasses many square kilometres. False precision also applies to other types of data.
- **Quality:** many factors can inhibit the quality of data, but these are often not well understood by the end users.
- **Metadata:** documenting data, their quality and characteristics are essential for being able to use the data meaningfully, but metadata is often not well understood by the end users and is often not provided adequately.

1.2   Potential Ethical Issues with Publicly-Available Data

Whatever the nature of the data, the following are some issues (which have ethical aspects) with the creation, distribution and use of publicly-available data.

- **Privacy:** there are moral and legal concerns over the invasion of the privacy (or **surveillance**) of individuals, groups and organisations, and these are the main focus of this paper.
- **Bias:** because of the above and subjectivity in deciding what attributes to collect and how, any data set is invariably a biased representation of the population. While this can be ameliorated through other data, local knowledge and insights, and careful statistical analysis, it is of particular concern when those using the data are blissfully unaware of the bias. Bias also occurs in training sets for models, such as in machine learning. Error is ubiquitous [3].
- **Liability:** this could be for incorrect data, which then compromises someone's rights, endangers safety and security, wastes money and other resources, and so on.
- **Right to exploit content:** on the other hand, for some (such as entertainers and artists) it is important to be able to exploit their content publicly which might be inhibited by corporations controlling the content – analogous to censorship.
- **Censorship:** this can be disguised and rationalized as prudent selection, due to the limited budget of a public library, to suppress hate speech, to maintaining literary excellence, to ensure balance and/or to meet the audience's requirements [4, 5].

Invading privacy (or surveillance), censorship and liability are often used as excuses for one another. For example, content could be denied or restricted (censored) to "protect" privacy or because of "concern" over liability. Further, claims over content ownership are used to censor content or restrict use, frustrating creators: Toya Delazy released her album online as her record label was limiting stock availability [6].

On the other hand, privacy could be compromised over "concerns" over liability, such as when a company monitors staff emails. The issues are not well understood either, such as when "poor" data (eg: low resolution remotely-sensed imagery) is considered to be censored data, because it covers in inadequate detail, an area of interest to a conspiracy theorist, or the like. However, *"privacy and security do not have to contradict each other; indeed, secure online interactions, enabled by a secure online identity, is a precondition for full internet freedom"* [7].

These issues also apply to private or restricted data, as inappropriate surveillance or data exploitation can be done within limited or closed groups.

2 Ethics

Ethics concerns the nature of ultimate value and the standards by which human actions can be judged right or wrong. Ethical judgement is influenced by the values of a person or group: their convictions of what is good or desirable [8]. Values are determined by different factors, including culture, religion, social and economic status, personal experiences, age, gender and profession. Data are often shared globally and the ethics of using such data is subject to significantly diverse value systems. **Normative ethics** aims at establishing the norms or standards for appropriate conduct and applied ethics is how these are used to deal with practical moral problems. There are three major approaches in normative ethics, which in practice, are often mixed:

1. **Virtue ethics** emphasises virtues or moral character as a way of assessing or justifying each and every action or non-action.
2. **Consequentialism** emphasises the consequences of actions, which can be interpreted as the end justifies the means; and
3. **Deontological ethics** emphasises duties or rules, which can be reduced to a check list of what to do in different situations [8, 9].

Deontological ethics is perhaps the easiest to adhere to in practice, because in each situation, one can look up what is the appropriate thing to do. Essentially, legislation is a form of deontological ethics. However, problems with deontological ethics are:

- Someone can use them without having any moral understanding of exactly what they are doing (or not doing) and the implications thereof;
- If there is no obviously applicable rule in a particular situation, the person has no meta-framework or set of values to use to decide on the best course of action;
- Reciprocity can be difficult as the values or rules one person uses for determining how to behave towards another might be incompatible with those used by the second person, causing conflicting understanding of the actions and reactions; and

- Without a meta-framework, people will tend towards the softest option and/or try to push the boundaries of what is acceptable [8, 9].

Virtue ethics focuses on the moral character and the need to educate and develop such a moral character. Considering what a 'virtuous person' would do can guide ethical decision-making [8]. There are various forms of consequentialism, such as utilitarianism (good conduct has consequences that achieve the greatest good to the greatest number of people) and situational ethics (considers the context in which conduct takes place and the consequences within this context).

Artificial intelligence and other sophisticated tools can be used to identify ethical and unethical behaviour, such as on social media, and assess the veracity of news stories and images [10]. Such tools can also be used unethically and to create and disseminate fake news. One needs to consider how these tools function and their outputs, to embed robust ethical analysis and decision making in the tools [11].

When conducting research that collects private data, one obtains *informed consent* to invading someone's privacy and publishing the research results, as part of a research ethics process. What constitutes informed consent is in itself an interesting problem in ethics, due to language, literacy, education, coercion, rewards, etc.

A problem with informed consent is that the research subject needs to remember what they have agreed to and when. Unfortunately, this is not always the case, as we found in a project tracking participants to and from an event [9, 12]. If the user has to opt-in to the tracking, there is likely to be a high loss rate. If the user has to opt-out, they might forget to stop the tracking. Such issues of informed consent apply to private data obtained for government, commercial and other purposes, which are often obtained without a formal ethical review and might have the *informed* part buried in fine print and the *consent* part implicit rather than explicit.

3   Privacy and Protecting Privacy

"The right to life has come to mean the right to enjoy life, – the right to be let alone; the right to liberty secures the exercise of extensive civil privileges" [13]. Their primary concern was over making private details public: *"each crop of unseemly gossip, thus harvested, becomes the seed of more, and, in direct proportion to its circulation, results in the lowering of social standards and of morality"* [13]. Further, *"it is also immaterial that the intrusion was in aid of law enforcement"* [14].

Perhaps the antithesis of data democratization and freedom of information is making too much available, compromising the privacy of individuals especially, but also of organisations. Privacy is complex to define, being perceived differently by different cultures and treated differently in legislation. Privacy is perceived as being about protecting people's personal information, but it also includes territorial (or location) privacy, physical (or bodily or health) privacy and privacy of communications. Privacy is not the same as confidentiality or secrecy, though they can overlap [15].

Many sacrifice their privacy voluntarily, especially when using social media, but they could be doing so through ignorance, deception, coercion or peer-pressure. Unfortunately, social media sites are notorious for changing privacy settings (sometimes through "errors") and/or for making them complex. Even when personal data are secured in a private area, they could still be exposed through changes in legislation, decisions by courts (eg: search warrants) and company buy-outs.

Many governments have introduced legislation to protect privacy to varying extents. Perhaps the best known and most significant because of its wide applicability is the European General Data Protection Regulation (GDPR), which came into effect on 25 May 2018 [16]. The principles of the GDPR are lawfulness, fairness and transparency; purpose limitation; data minimisation; accuracy; storage limitation; integrity and confidentiality; and accountability. The South African equivalent to the GDPR is the Protection of Personal Information Act (POPI) [17].

4   Invasion of Privacy

"Privacy is mostly an illusion. A useful illusion, no question about it, one that allows us to live without being paralyzed by self-consciousness. The illusion of privacy gives us room to be fully human, sharing intimacies and risking mistake" [18].

4.1   Covert Surveillance

Covert surveillance is possibly what many consider surveillance to be: monitoring behaviour and communications surreptitiously, for detecting, investigating and monitoring threats (criminal, terrorist, social unrest, etc), influencing and controlling society, and, hopefully, protecting citizens. For example, "brain fingerprinting" is claimed to detect the presence or absence of information in someone's brain, using electroencephalography (EEG) [19], though there are concerns over the studies [20].

4.2   Trans-Jurisdiction Surveillance

One feature of the designed-in robustness of a packet-switching network such as the Internet, is one cannot guarantee the routing of individual data packets. Even with a high-speed, high-bandwidth Internet connection directly between two countries, parts of the connection might be routed through other countries – which might capture and/or study the data traffic *en route* [21]. Such trans-jurisdiction surveillance might be accidental; though those doing the surveillance should realise it happens. For example, Internet traffic to and from the United Nations in New York is presumably routed through the USA and hence likely to be recorded by the NSA. It appears that Internet traffic can be misdirected deliberately and surreptitiously, particularly across national boundaries, to inspect and/or modify the transmitted data [22].

Another example concerns virtual private networks (VPNs). They are used to ensure that anyone intercepting the (often encrypted) traffic cannot read what is being transmitted (or perhaps even where the source and destination are), but the traffic gets routed through servers, which lends itself to surveillance by the server owners.

Another form of trans-jurisdiction surveillance is remote sensing, with an early use of LANDSAT satellites being to monitor wheat crops in the Soviet Union [23].

4.3   Overt Surveillance

Not all surveillance is covert, with overt forms including those visible and well identified (such as CCTV surveillance cameras in public, or disclaimers of a call being recorded) or to which one agrees explicitly (such as the small print for using a web site). However, in some jurisdictions, such supposed agreements might be unenforceable, being excessively long or changed arbitrarily and without notice [24].

Further, it is easy to forget one's actions are being observed, even when giving explicit consent [9, 12]. Clearly, this leads to complacency and the risk of becoming accustomed to the surveillance society. It is also easier to accept surveillance when under the influence of someone one trusts, such as parents recommending their children enable mobile phone location disclosure services [25].

4.4   Overloaded Surveillance

Apparently, the American NSA "*intercepts and stores nearly two billion separate e-mails, phone calls, and other communications every day*", making the system too complex to determine if it actually works [26]. Rather than wisdom, the sheer volume creates information entropy – so information becomes noise as it "*is routinely distorted, buried in noise, or otherwise impossible to interpret*" [26].

Consequently, such agencies probably create their own filter bubbles, due to, not in spite of, the sheer volumes they harvest. Much of the content (facts, opinions, allegations, imagery, comments, conversations, etc) will be contradictory, so the selection, rating and analysis will be biased by preconceived notions and desire to "*simply want to believe something that feels right*" [26]. It is easy to be so enamoured with sophisticated and expensive technology the basics get forgotten, with tragic consequences, such as the Boston Marathon bombing [27] and Navy Yard shootings [28].

Being able to conduct surveillance over the Internet, or use it to interfere with the rights of others, or conduct information warfare over the Internet are all quite different from being able to control the Internet! The genie is out of the bottle and cannot be replaced. The Internet was designed to be robust (distributed, with data sent in small packets) and self-healing if any node broke [29]. As the Internet pioneer John Gilmore put it, "*the Net interprets censorship as damage and routes around it*" [30].

4.5   Becoming Accustomed to the *Surveillance Society*

It is easy to forget one is being observed. This can result in acting carelessly whilst being observed and/or accepting the lack of privacy by becoming used to it, or even by expecting it. Americans have been accustomed to limits on their privacy for many years [18], realizing Bentham's idea of the Panopticon [31]. The *Panopticon* is a circular building with an *inspection house* in the middle from which a custodian could observe secretly the inmates (around the perimeter) who could not communicate with anyone. Foucault [32] invoked the Panopticon concept[1] as a metaphor for the tendency of modern "disciplinary" societies to observe and attempt to "normalise" their citizens.

---

[1] Though Brunon-Ernst [33] suggests that Foucault distorted Bentham's philosophy.

"The panopticon induces a sense of permanent visibility that ensures the functioning of power" [34]. Unsurprisingly, this can lead to limited, or even curtailed, political and personal freedoms, and the loss of self-reliance [35]. Dobson and Fisher [36] took Foucault's metaphor further, identifying three "post-panoptic" models:

1. *Bentham's original concept*, which they consider to be the one Foucault used;
2. *Panopticism II*, in the form of the "Big Brother" type of surveillance of [37]; and
3. *Panopticism III*, technology tracking humans and their activities, such as cell-phone tracking [9, 12, 38], GNSS receivers, RFID[2] and geo-fences[3]. Crucially, the technology for Panopticism III is relatively cheap, effective and widely available to anyone, and not just well-resourced national security agencies.

The 1844 British postal espionage crisis concerned the Post Office opening letters at the behest of a foreign power. As the Law Magazine observed, *"the post-office must not only be CHEAP AND RAPID, but SECURE AND INVIOLABLE"* [39]. However, even though widely known and causing a 'paroxysm of national anger', it did not impact on the popularity of the Penny Post, which increased rapidly thereafter [39]. *"Snowden's revelations will have demonstrated that in practice, the web-surfing, texting and emailing public are indifferent to the risks they run to their privacy"* [39]. Similarly, Lanier [40] was concerned 2013 would be the year of *digital passivity*, when the cool gadgets (such as tablets running only applications approved by a central commercial authority) made us accept the commercial and government *surveillance economy*. Carr [35] fears privacy could be perceived as an outdated and unimportant concept inhibiting efficient transactions, such as socializing or shopping.

4.6 Mutual Surveillance

The psychological and social effects of prevalent surveillance result in people being so intimidated by authority and/or so used to surveillance they conduct self-policing and can be forced or encouraged to spy on one another, extending easily, cheaply and significantly the surveillance reach of the authority, be it a government, the military, a corporation or any other type of organisation [32, 41].

4.7 Making Data Already in the Public Domain More Visible

A common claim is that it is fine to put data online that are already in the public domain but otherwise difficult to access, such as documents and photographs in archives. However, that allows data matching. Such online content can also be accessed readily by anyone without revealing their interests, for example, using Google Street View to examine a neighbourhood, be it to find security weaknesses for targeting burglaries, stalking a resident, or mere curiosity. Similarly, much personal data are published, often unwittingly, in online genealogies.

---

[2] Radio frequency identification, small passive or active transponders.

[3] Virtual or conceptual geographical perimeter or barrier.

This could apply to archives themselves, though they have established procedures (file plans) for what can be archived, how, where, when, why and by whom. Archiving is complicated by legal issues such as copyright and technical issues such as accessing the deep Web, volatile communities, broken links and dynamic content [42].

Some assume naïvely that content made publicly available on the Web can be expunged permanently at a whim. The European Court of Justice decided that anyone has *"the right to be forgotten"* and can require search engines to remove pages from search results for specified terms [43], going against the advice of its own Advocate General [44][4]. This has obviously been used by the unscrupulous to hide their activities. Such pages are not deleted; they are just removed from searches.

As a result, legitimate reporting by respectable organisations such as the BBC gets proscribed, contravening the public interest [45, 46]. Essentially, this defames that article's author by declaring their work illegitimate. The search engine's operator has to decide what is a valid removal request, but that is inappropriate [47, 48].

Some applications use ephemeral data to (hopefully) protect privacy, that is, content deleted permanently after a specified time. Examples are SnapChat for photographs and Silent Circle for two-way transmissions of voice, email, video, etc. However, there is doubt that ephemerality can be enforced securely [49].

Web scraping or harvesting takes content from Web sites. Collecting can be targeted and pre-arranged, such as harvesting metadata and data from members of a collaborative system, for instance data providers in a spatial data infrastructure (SDI). Collecting can use well-behaved bots (as search engines do for indexing the Web), or simulated human access. This raises issues of copyright, such as the "Google Defense" case concerning thumbnails of images [50].

A search engine obviously does some form of Web scraping to locate the content first, before being able to provide the rapid search responses users expect. To return results as quickly as they do, search engines are not always accurate (particularly the results count) and there is much of the Web they cannot access [51].

4.8   Combining and Processing Available Data

It requires much skill, intelligence and persistence to link together analogue data from diverse sources to find common threads, as good detectives do [52, 53]. Now, it is far easier to combine data from different sources using pattern recognition, artificial intelligence or other sophisticated tools (data matching, behavioural tracking, text analysing, data mining, linkage analysis, statistical analysis, spatial analysis and machine translation), exploiting fast hardware and huge and persistent digital data bases.

Most 'big data' analysis is not done to invade privacy, but to examine questions otherwise unexplorable, to understand human, physical and environmental behaviours in different contexts, and (hopefully) benefit society [54]. Unfortunately, an individual can be identified uniquely with very few data points, even coarse ones, such as with

---

[4] The Court issues only one judgement and no dissenting opinions, and all deliberations are secret. As we pointed out to the Court's press office, this encourages bad law by forcing judges to support the majority opinion and protects incompetent judges from public scrutiny.

cellular telephone use [55], power consumption of a mobile device [56] or renting public bicycles [57]. Personal traits can be gleaned from the digital footprints people leave on social media, which some exploit for trust and resilience modelling [58]. There are also services available for a fee to track a mobile telephone [59]. Hence, *"there is no such thing as anonymous online tracking"* [60].

4.9   Opting in vs Opting Out

To varying extents in different jurisdictions, one has limited control over how much of one's personal information is known, retained by others and/or shared. Sharing one's information (*opting in*) can provide access to services, opportunities or prizes[5], such as loyalty programmes (sharing personal and behavioural data for discounts or loyalty points), subscriptions to paid content, exposing one's resumé to potential (and hopefully desirable) employers, security services such as vehicle tracking, research collaboration or even friendships. Further, for some the *right of publicity* [61] is key for their profession and income, through exploiting their names, photographs, likenesses, recordings and the like – but only if they have consented and are remunerated appropriately. In many jurisdictions, one nominally can *opt out* of divulging one's private information, but even that explicit declaration gets ignored [62].

User-generated geographical data are known as *volunteered geographical information* (VGI). Some object to the term because data so collected might not be *volunteered*, but rather contributed, collected or harvested irrespective of whether the subject opted in, opted out, was even aware they were contributing their personal details, or had forgotten they were doing so. Harvey [62] suggests differentiating between volunteered (VGI) and contributed (CGI) geographical (or locational) information. Further, *truth in labelling* in the metadata following pragmatic ethics would explain the provenance of the information, allowing assessment of its *fitness for use* and if the quality of the data has been compromised by lax standards or even malfeasance [62].

4.10   Assuming One Has Nothing to Hide

For anyone who lived through Apartheid (or communism, fascism, etc), it should be obvious that everyone has something to hide from a repressive government. Even in a reasonably open and stable democracy such as the USA, an innocent person has the right to remain silent [63], and keep their matters private. *"The skeptics no doubt have noticed that governments are made up of people and that people are prone to misuse information when driven by greed or curiosity or a will to power"* [18].

Examples of ripostes to those justifying surveillance are: show me your credit card details; show me yours first; none of your business; and those with nothing to hide don't have a life [64]. The person wanting to protect their privacy does not have to justify their position: the person wanting to invade someone's privacy needs to justify it first [64]. The metadata of one's communications can also reveal personality traits,

---

[5] Which is why there are so many competitions out there, because they are a cheap way to harvest personal data that are up to date.

religion, politics, habits, movements, condition, relationship issues, etc [65]. It is not only keeping 'facts' about oneself private, but also the assumptions made about us from the available data [66]. Further, there is the problem of identity theft.

4.11   Legal Complexities

Human beings need space where they are guaranteed to be free from surveillance or interference by anyone, such as to establish and preserve intimate human relationships and develop intellectual faculties through reading, private conversation or writing privately [67]. It is very difficult to grow intellectually if one cannot experiment with ideas without fear of surveillance and resulting misinterpretation. *"Experience should teach us to be most on our guard to protect liberty when the government's purposes are beneficent. Men born to freedom are naturally alert to repel invasion of their liberty by evil-minded rulers. The greatest dangers to liberty lurk in insidious encroachment by men of zeal, well-meaning but without understanding"* [14].

5   Conclusions and Discussion

This paper presents a review and analysis of the literature on the ethics of using publicly-available data, particularly concerning privacy. It presents the characteristics of publicly-available data and explores potential ethical issues, such as surveillance, becoming accustomed to the surveillance society, increasing access to data, combining and processing data and assuming one has nothing to hide. There is clearly much research that still needs to be done on these issues, particularly given the different perspectives on vales and ethics due to culture, religion, politics, experiences, age, gender, social status and so on.

This research comes out of the CSIR's Mobile Data Platform for Urban Mobility (MDP) work package of the Spatial Urban Dynamics 2014/2015 project and the PhD research [68] of the first author. We would like to thank Quintin van Heerden, Peter Schmitz and Derrick Kourie for their contributions to developing this research.

References

1. Shelton, T., Poorthuis, A., Zook, M.: Social media and the city: rethinking urban socio-spatial inequality using user-generated geographic information. Landscape Urban Plan. **142**, 198–211 (2015)
2. Engelhardt, T.: The NSA mistakes omniscience for omnipotence. The Nation, 12 November 2013
3. Ioannidis, J.: Anticipating consequences of sharing raw data and code and of awarding badges for sharing. J. Clin. Epidemiol. **70**, 258–260 (2016). https://doi.org/10.1016/j.jclinepi.2015.04.015
4. Asheim, L.: Selection and censorship: a reappraisal. Wilson Libr. Bull. (R) **28**(1), 180–184 (1953)
5. Asheim, L.: Not censorship but selection. Wilson Libr. Bull. **58**(3), 63–67 (1983)
6. Channel24: A frustrated Toya Delazy leaks her own album online, 14 May 2015

7. Ilves, T.H.: Keynote Address by President Toomas Hendrik Ilves at Panel Discussion "A Secure and Free Internet", the UN Dag Hammarskjöld Library Auditorium. Permanent Representation of Estonia to the UN, 29 September 2013

8. Kretzschmar, L., et al.: Ethics for Accountants and Auditors, 3rd edn. Oxford University Press, Cape Town (2013)

9. Cooper, A.K., Ittmann, H.W., Stylianides, T., Schmitz, P.M.U.: Ethical issues in tracking cellphones at an event. OMEGA **37**(6), 1063–1072 (2009)

10. Vidgen, R., Hindle, G., Randolph, I.: Exploring the ethical implications of business analytics with a business ethics canvas. Eur. J. Oper. Res. **281**, 491–501 (2020)

11. Yavary, A., Sajedi, H., Saniee Abadeh, M.: Information verification in social networks based on user feedback and news agencies. Soc. Netw. Anal. Min. **10**, 2 (2020). https://doi.org/10.1007/s13278-019-0616-4

12. Cooper, A.K., Schmitz, P.M.U., Krygsman, S.C.: Tracking cellular telephones to build transport models. In: South African Transportation Conference (SATC), Pretoria, 16–19 August 2010

13. Warren, S.D., Brandeis, L.D.: The right to privacy. Harvard Law Rev. **4**(5), 193–220 (1890)

14. Brandeis, L.D.: Olmstead v. United States/Opinion of the Court, 277 U.S. 438, United States Supreme Court, dissenting opinion, 4 June 1928

15. OAIC: What is privacy? Office of the Australian Information Commissioner (OAIC) (2015). http://www.privacy.gov.au/aboutprivacy/what

16. European Parliament: Regulation (EU) 2016/679 of the European Parliament and of the Council of 27 April 2016 on the protection of natural persons with regard to the processing of personal data and on the free movement of such data, and repealing Directive 95/46/EC (General Data Protection Regulation). OJ L 119, 4.5.2016, p. 1, 23 May 2018

17. South Africa: Protection of Personal Information Act (Act No 4 of 2013) (2013)

18. Von Drehle, D.: The surveillance society: secrets are so 20th century now that we have the ability to collect and store billions of pieces of data forever. TIME, 1 August 2013

19. Farwell, L., Richardson, D.C., Richardson, G.M.: Brain fingerprinting field studies comparing p300-mermer and p300 brainwave responses in the detection of concealed information. Cogn. Neurodyn. **7**(4), 263–299 (2013)

20. Meijer, E.H., Ben-Shakhar, G., Verschuere, B., Donchin, E.: A comment on Farwell (2012): brain fingerprinting: a comprehensive tutorial review of detection of concealed information with event-related brain potentials. Cogn. Neurodyn. **7**(2), 155–158 (2013)

21. Holputch, A.: Brazil's controversial plan to extricate the internet from US control. The Guardian, 20 September 2013

22. Cowie, J.: The new threat: targeted internet traffic misdirection. Renesys Blog. http://www.renesys.com/2013/11/mitm-internet-hijacking/. Accessed 19 Nov 2013

23. Erickson, J.D.: The LACIE experiment in satellite aided monitoring of global crop production. In: Woodwell, G.M. (ed.) The Role of Terrestrial Vegetation in the Global Carbon Cycle: Measurement by Remote Sensing. Wiley, Hoboken (1984)

24. Hudson, A.: Is small print in online contracts enforceable? BBC News: Technology, 5 June 2013

25. Jiow, H.J., Lin, J.: The influence of parental factors on children's receptiveness towards mobile phone location disclosure services. First Monday **18**(1) (2013) https://doi.org/10.5210/fm.v18i1.4284

26. Schweller, R.L.: The age of entropy: why the new world order won't be orderly. Foreign Aff. (2014). https://www.foreignaffairs.com/articles/united-states/2014-06-16/age-entropy

27. Investors.com: So Why Didn't NSA Catch The Tsarnaev Brothers? Investor's Business Daily, Inc., 13 June 2013

28. Leonnig, C., O'Keefe, E.: Contractor would not have hired shooter if past brushes with law were known. Wash. Post (2013)
29. Ananthaswamy, A.: Welcome to the age of the splinternet. N. Sci. **211**(2821), 42–45 (2011)
30. Elmer-Dewitt, P.: First nation in cyberspace. TIME Int. **142**(49), 62–64 (1993)
31. Bentham, J.: Panopticon; or the Inspection-House: Containing the Idea of a New Principle of Construction Applicable to Any Sort of Establishment, ... Letters of Bentham (1787). Transcription and HTML by Cartome, 16 June 2001, from Bentham, Jeremy The Panopticon Writings. Ed. Miran Bozovic (London: Verso, 1995). p. 29–95
32. Foucault, M.: 'Panopticism' from 'discipline & punish: the birth of the prison'. Race/Ethn.: Multi. Glob. Contexts **2**(1), 1–12 (2008). English Translation by Alan Sheridan, 1977 (New York: Pantheon). Originally published in French in 1975 as Surveiller et Punir (Paris: Editions Gallimard)
33. Brunon-Ernst, A.: Introduction. In: Beyond Foucault: New Perspectives on Bentham's Panopticon. Ashgate Publishing, Ltd. (2012)
34. SparkNotes Editors: Sparknote on discipline and punish. SparkNotes LLC (nd). http://www.sparknotes.com/philosophy/disciplinepunish/
35. Carr, N.: Tracking is an assault on liberty, with real dangers. Wall Street J. **7** (2010). https://www.wsj.com/articles/SB10001424052748703748904575411682714389888
36. Dobson, J.E., Fisher, P.F.: Geoslavery. IEEE Technol. Soc. Mag. **22**, 47–52 (2003)
37. Orwell, G.: Nineteen eighty-four. eBook No 0100021, Project Gutenberg of Australia (1949). http://gutenberg.net.au/ebooks01/0100021.txt
38. Schmitz, P.M.U., Cooper, A.K.: Using cellular telephones to track participants' movements to and from an event. In: South African Transportation Conference (SATC), Pretoria, 11–14 July 2011
39. Vincent, D.: Surveillance, privacy and history. History and Policy. http://www.historyandpolicy.org/papers/policy-paper-151.htm. Accessed Oct 2013
40. Lanier, J.: Digital Passivity. The New York Times, 27 November 2013
41. Foucault, M.: The subject and power. Crit. Inq. **8**(4), 777–795 (1982)
42. Stirling, P., Chevallier, P. and Illien, G.: Web archives for researchers: representations, expectations and potential uses. D-Lib, **18**(3/4) (2012). https://doi.org/10.1045/march2012-stirling
43. Court of Justice of the European Union: Judgement of the Court (Grand Chamber) in Case C-131/12, Google Spain SL, Google Inc v Agencia Española de Protección de Datos (AEPD), Mario Costeja González. InfoCuria, 13 May 2014
44. Court of Justice of the European Union: Advocate General's Opinion in Case C-131/12, Google Spain SL, Google Inc. v Agencia Española de Protección de Datos, Mario Costeja González. PRESS RELEASE No 77/13. InfoCuria, 25 June 2013
45. Lane, E.: Google removes 12 BBC News links in 'right to be forgotten'. BBC News: Technology, 19 August 2014. http://www.bbc.com/news/technology-28851366
46. Peston, R.: Why has Google cast me into oblivion? BBC News: Business. http://www.bbc.com/news/business-28130581. 2 July 2014
47. Scott, M.: Google reinstates some links in Europe. The New York Times, 4 July 2014
48. Zittrain, J.: Is the EU compelling Google to become about me? The Future of the Internet. http://blogs.law.harvard.edu/futureoftheinternet/2014/05/13/is-the-eu-compelling-google-to-become-about-me/. Accessed 13 May 2014
49. Shein, E.: Ephemeral data. Commun. ACM **56**(9), 20–22 (2013)
50. US Court of Appeals for the Ninth Circuit: Perfect 10, Inc v Amazon.com, Inc and A9.com Inc and Google Inc. Case F.3d, US Court of Appeals for the Ninth Circuit (2007)
51. Alexander, R.: Are search engine result figures accurate? BBC News Magazine. http://www.bbc.co.uk/news/magazine-17068044. Accessed 20 Feb 2012

52. Cooper, A.K., Byleveld, P., Schmitz, P.M.U.: Using GIS to reconcile crime scenes with those indicated by serial criminals. In: 5th Annual International Crime Mapping Research Conference, Dallas, Texas, USA, 1–4 Dec 2001
53. Schmitz, P.M.U., Cooper, A.K., Byleveld, P., Rossmo, D.K.: Using GIS and digital aerial photography to assist in the conviction of a serial killer. In: 4th Annual International Crime Mapping Research Conference, San Diego, California, USA, 9–12 December 2000
54. Gutmann, M.P., Stern, P.C. (eds.): Putting People on the Map: Protecting Confidentiality with Linked Social-Spatial Data. National Academies Press (2007). ISBN 978-0-309-10414-2
55. De Montjoye, Y.-A., Hidalgo, C.A., Verleysen, M., Blondel, V.D.: Unique in the crowd: the privacy bounds of human mobility. Sci. Rep. **3**(1376), 1–5 (2013)
56. Michalevsky, Y., Boneh, D., Schulman, A., Nakibly, G.: PowerSpy: location tracking using mobile device power analysis. arXiv:1502.03182v1 (2015)
57. Siddle, J.: I know where you were last summer: London's public bike data is telling everyone where you've been. The Variable Tree. http://vartree.blogspot.co.uk/2014/04/i-know-where-you-were-last-summer. 10 Apr 2014
58. Zhou, M.X., Wang, F., Zimmerman, T., Yang, H., Haber, E., Gou, L.: Computational discovery of personal traits from social multimedia. In: 2013 IEEE International Conference on Multimedia and Expo Workshops (ICMEW), San Jose, CA, 15–19 July 2013, pp. 1–6 (2013). https://doi.org/10.1109/icmew.2013.6618398
59. Timberg, C.: For sale: systems that can secretly track where cellphone users go around the globe. Wash. Post (2014)
60. Narayanan, A.: There is no such thing as anonymous online tracking. The Center for Internet and Society at Stanford Law School, 28 July 2011. http://cyberlaw.stanford.edu/node/6701
61. Nimmer, M.B.: The right of publicity. Law Contemp. Prob. **19**(2), 203–223 (1954)
62. Harvey, F.: To volunteer or to contribute locational information? Towards truth in labeling for crowdsourced geographic information. In: Sui, D.Z., Elwood, S., Goodchild, M.F. (eds.) Crowdsourcing Geographic Knowledge, pp. 31–42. Springer, Heidelberg (2013). https://doi.org/10.1007/978-94-007-4587-2_3
63. Supreme Court of the United States: Ohio v Matthew Reiner, No. 532, U.S., 19 March 2001
64. Solove, D.J.: 'I've got nothing to hide' and other misunderstandings of privacy. San Diego Law Rev. **44** (2007). http://papers.ssrn.com/sol3/papers.cfm?abstract_id=998565
65. Big Brother Watch: Briefing note: Why communications data (metadata) matter. What are communications data? Big BrotherWatch, London, United Kingdom, July 2014. https://www.bigbrotherwatch.org.uk/wp-content/uploads/2014/07/Communications-Data-Briefing.pdf
66. Collins, K.: You have more to hide in your data trail than you think. Wired UK, 19 August 2014
67. Phillipson, G.: Q&A: the right to privacy. BBC Religion & Ethics, 14 June 2013
68. Cooper, A.K.: An exposition of the nature of volunteered geographical information and its suitability for integration into spatial data infrastructures. PhD thesis, University of Pretoria, South Africa, July 2016. http://hdl.handle.net/2263/57515

Social Media

Introducing the Media Use Behaviour Conceptual Framework

Douglas A. Parry(✉) and Daniel B. le Roux

Information Science, Stellenbosch University, Stellenbosch, South Africa
{dougaparry,dbleroux}@sun.ac.za

Abstract. In an increasingly digitally connected world researchers have sought to understand behaviour associated with digital communications media. We argue that a more consistent conceptualisation of media use behaviour and its etiological foundations is a necessary basis for research in this regard to progress. To this end, through the adoption of an affordances approach, we propose the *Media Use Behaviour Conceptual Framework* to describe the reciprocal relations between users (described in relation to personal characteristics and cognitive factors), the situations (consisting of social, physical, and technological dimensions) in which they use media, their media use behaviour, and the outcomes (both realised and expected) of this behaviour. This framework seeks to integrate the behaviourist and cognitivist approaches to action and, additionally, acknowledges the socially constructed and deterministic role of media in action. It is argued that such a framework will provide a useful basis upon which researchers can consider various individual differences in observed media use behaviours and associated outcomes and, importantly, understand why particular media use behaviours occur.

Keywords: Media use · Conceptual framework · Behaviour · Affordances

1 Introduction

Despite growing public concern and academic attention, there remains little scientific consensus on the existence, nature, and mechanisms for the effects of digital media use on psychological well-being. Mirroring the growth of social media and the widespread use of mobile computing devices, over the preceding decade, a surge of studies have sought to quantify media use and assess possible adverse associations with a variety of well-being indicators. Across this research base effects are inconsistent, generally inconclusive and, as Orben and Przybylski [22, p. 682] note, often small. While measurement artefacts present in retrospective self-report scales [6], questionable research practices [23,26], or indeed particularly nuanced relations between media use and well-being may account for disparate outcomes, the manner in which researchers conceptualise media use behaviour and its etiological foundations merits consideration as an important contributing factor to the outcomes observed.

© IFIP International Federation for Information Processing 2020
Published by Springer Nature Switzerland AG 2020
M. Hattingh et al. (Eds.): I3E 2020, LNCS 12067, pp. 175–186, 2020.
https://doi.org/10.1007/978-3-030-45002-1_15

In this paper, driven by three motivations, we present a conceptual framework for media use behaviour. First, due to cycles of technological advancement the media we use have diversified rapidly and, as a result, the notion of *media use* has become increasingly complex. Second, extending from this complexity and the *centrality* of media in our lives today is the need to make sense of the agency of media use in all aspects of our lives, including, in particular, well-being. A third motivation for presenting the *Media Use Behaviour Conceptual Framework* acknowledges studies indicating that different types of media use are associated with a variety of effects, and, importantly, that such effects can differ across individual and situational factors [22]. A conceptual framework for media use behaviour will aid researchers in identifying specific drivers for particular media use behaviours. To follow, a description of the conceptual framework is provided, with a detailed explanation of its constituent components thereafter.

2   A Conceptual Framework for Understanding Media Use Behaviour

This framework, presented in Fig. 1, adopts an affordances perspective to describing interactions between individuals and the communications artefacts or *media* they use. Through affordances, building on an integration of behaviourist and cognitivist perspectives on behaviour, a situated conception of media use is proposed. Artefacts, consisting of both physical (hardware) and virtual (software) dimensions present various affordances which, drawing on the subjective and situational characteristics of the user, can be enacted in a variety of ways to enable particular uses and actions that, through both realised and expected outcomes, contribute to subsequent use-instances. Such a perspective enables a *dualistic* understanding of media use behaviour which simultaneously acknowledges the agency of technology as well as the subjective-situational dimensions of action. A medium—for instance a mobile phone—through its affordances provides a number of action possibilities for the user which, dependent on the social and physical nature of their present situation, their personal and cognitive characteristics, and previous experiences of use, can be enacted in a variety of ways. While the user has agency, this agency is constrained by the finite possibilities of action offered by the medium and the situations in which use occurs.

From a behaviourist perspective two models, both building on social learning theory, provide an initial basis for the framework. The *SOBC model*, proposed by Davis and Luthans [4], extending earlier theories (e.g., antecedent-behaviour-consequence), postulates that aspects of an environmental situation (S) influence the internal states of an organism (O; in this case a person), which then trigger associated behavioural responses (B) and consequences (C). Building on a similar basis, emphasising the role of cognition in behaviour, the *Social Cognitive Theory* (SCT), [1, p. 24] proposes that behaviour occurs from the reciprocal interaction between personal (cognitive, affective, and biological), environmental, and behavioural factors. Environmental factors refer to aspects external to

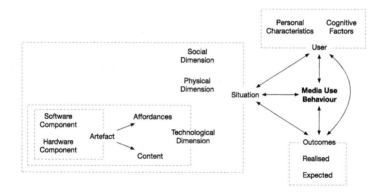

Fig. 1. Media use Behaviour Conceptual Framework

the individual which influence the ability to perform an action, behavioural factors describe the consequences resulting from an action, and personal factors relate to an individual's self-efficacy towards the behaviour. While these models recognise the mediating role of cognition, little attention is afforded to the reciprocal manner in which various executive functions and cognitive frames relate to behaviour. To provide a more holistic conception of media use behaviour, we argue that, from the perspective of situated action, affordances provide a conceptual bridge, enabling the aforementioned behaviourist models to be augmented with ideas from cognitivism (e.g., executive functions, cognitive schemas) and considerations of relevant technological factors. For each dimension of the framework, acknowledging the limited and subjective nature of the selections, we have identified appropriate conceptual theories as explanatory lenses.

3   An Affordances Perspective

The concept of *affordances*, first used by Gibson [9] to describe relations between an organism and its environment, is frequently adopted to describe the properties of an artefact—either perceived or actual—framing how it can be used. Norman [21] proposes that, through 'perceived affordances', artefacts can be designed to encourage or determine particular uses. Extending this, Gaver [7, p. 80] proposes that affordances can be both perceptible and hidden—they can be inferred—and are, as a result, 'properties of the world defined with respect to people's interaction with it'. In this way, affordances do not just apply to individual actions but, perhaps more importantly, to social interaction and the associated social conventions or *cultures* surrounding their enactment [8, p. 114]. While Gaver [8] avoids casting overly deterministic aspersions about the role *technological affordances* play in directing action, in proposing that the material (or perceptual) qualities of various communicative artefacts are, at least partly, responsible for associated actions and sociality, the foundation for the related concepts of *social* and *communicative affordances* is established. The notion of social affordances concerns the ways in which 'technology affords social practice' [13], while communicative affordances refers to the 'possibilities for action that emerge from [. . .] given technological forms' [14, p. 30]. In emphasising action *possibilities* this definition draws together Gibson [9]'s relational conception with the more functional conceptions of Norman and Gaver. Affordances, accordingly, enable the consideration of media use as both socially constructed and technologically deterministic [14]. Actions are enabled (and constrained) not only by the technological features and affordances of an artefact but also the subjective and situational circumstances of the user. Affordances, consequently, present a useful perspective to consider the reciprocal interactions between individuals, situations, media, media use behaviour, and behavioural outcomes.

4   User Factors

The framework distinguishes between two user factors. Cognitive factors describe the internal mental processes of the user, while personal characteristics refer to various traits (e.g., gender, age, personality), states (e.g., sleep, intoxication, anxiety, stress), and motivations (e.g., goals, intentions, needs). We argue that the uses of, and outcomes associated with, media are, partly, dependent on individual differences for these factors.

4.1   Cognitive Factors

Action, from a cognitivist perspective, occurs through internal mental processes contingent on the operation of various executive functions (e.g., working memory, inhibitory control, cognitive flexibility) [20]. Instead of the relatively simple stimulus-response relationships advanced by behaviourists, an individual is seen to play an important mediating role in these relationships. For cognitivists, an individual's internal mental processes (attention, memory, perception) are deemed to be central to behaviour. An information processing metaphor captures this notion: information is perceived, is processed by various executive functions and, depending on the stimulus and prevailing goals, behavioural responses are issued.

This information processing metaphor reflects the notion of *action-oriented perception* –sensory input is a function of an individual's active exploration of the world which, importantly, is framed in relation to various *anticipatory schemas* – clusters of related information, knowledge, or memories [20]. Stimuli are processed into schemas or cognitive frameworks of objects or events—mental frames produced through experience and knowledge. Schemas, consequently, represent recurrent patterns of embodied experience and pre-perceptual biases developed through previous interaction experiences. Acting on the basis of a schema entails the expectation of certain consequences, borne through experience. Johnson [17, p. 14] proposed the notion of *embodied schemas*, arguing that meaning, and the formation of meaning, stems from "patterns of embodied experience and preconceptual structures of our sensibility (i.e., our mode of perception, or orienting ourselves, and of interacting with other objects, events, or persons)". As we interact with the world, and the objects within it, conceptions of meaning are formed and captured in schemas. Consequently, cognition is embodied. Johnson [17, p. 14] further contends that, not only are schemas shaped by the artefacts we interact with but, in addition, "shared cultural modes of experience [...] help to determine the nature of our meaningful, coherent, understanding of our world". These shared cultural modes shape, and are themselves shaped by, the artifacts we use. In considering the materiality of media, the cognitive processes that direct thought and action take on a new meaning and are, themselves, dependent on various social and physical practices [17].

4.2 Personal Characteristics

At any point an individual's behaviour is influenced by various dispositional characteristics or *traits* and more momentary *states*. Traits, represent stable and enduring user characteristics (e.g., personality, ethnicity, cultural background, behavioural preferences). A state, in contrast, is a temporary way of being or condition (e.g., negative affect, intoxication, sleep deprivation). Importantly, while many states only manifest momentarily (i.e, in the short-term), others (e.g., mindfulness or self-control) can function as both a trait or a state and, in many cases, occur through the interaction between longer term dispositions and present situations or cognitions (e.g., self-control) [2]. Commonly referred to as *individual differences*, researchers frequently consider the role that various traits (physical, mental, and socially constructed) play in associations between situations, users, behaviour, and effects. Frequently analysed as moderators, such personal characteristics are seen to lead to different behavioural outcomes given the same technological affordances, depending on the individual user's assortment of traits and, in many cases, reporting of various states.

In addition to their traits and present states, users approach media use with a variety of intentions, goals, and motivations. The affordances provided by different media offer users the opportunity to gratify these needs. Uses and gratifications are, accordingly, simultaneously a function of user needs and of media affordances. The *Uses and Gratifications Theory* (UGT), frequently used in conjunction with the SCT, seeks to explain media use in terms of a medium's capacity to gratify a set of user needs [24]. Three assumptions are fundamental to this approach: (i) behaviour is goal-directed; (ii) users are aware of their needs; and (iii) users actively seek to gratify these needs through media use. Additionally, two distinct gratifications are advanced—process gratifications (obtained by using the media) and content gratifications (obtained from the informational content acquired through media use). Rubin [24, p. 167] considers behaviour to be largely goal-directed, arguing that "people typically choose to participate and select media [...] from an array of communication alternatives in response to their expectations and desires" which "emanate from, and are constrained by, personal traits, social context, and interaction". As noted, in addition to the needs of a user, media use behaviour is, in part, prescribed by the affordances made available by the medium. Consequently, Sundar and Limperos [29, p. 511] argue that, while some gratifications are driven more by user needs, others are driven more by the action possibilities of the medium.

5   Situational Factors

Actions do not occur in a vacuum solely extending from various schemata or motivations, nor are they mere reflexive outcomes of stimulus-response relationships with technological affordances. Rather, as in the *situated action* approach, along with personal characteristics and cognitions, actions are influenced by the material and social circumstances of the actor [28]. Extending Gibson [9]'s relational conception of affordances, this perspective holds that inherent qualities in the environment permit or constrain action. Importantly, while Gibson [9] advocated for a direct relationship between perception and action, this approach postulates that, rather than an unmediated process, *situational affordances* are mediated by individual mental models or schemata for action—thought and action are situated in physical and social contexts [11]. Cognition is situated. This conception aligns with the affordances perspective adopted. Situational affordances do not determine action but, rather, should be considered as preconditions for action, affecting the likelihood that a particular action will occur.

While, theoretically, it is straightforward to propose that action is situated, practically, researchers have struggled to settle on a widely adopted definition for what constitutes a situation. Zhang and Zhang [32, p. 1885] argue that this is due to the ontological understanding of situation as fundamentally diverse and the ethnomethodological stance that denies any a priori classifications of situational factors. Goffman [10] considers situations to be settings defined by interpersonal relationships and communication. Commenting on this Meyrowitz [19] suggests that this understanding of physical space and social situation needs to be reconsidered to account for the ability of digital media to extend communication across situations previously held to be distinct. Moreso than ever before, due to increases in the networked mobility and accessibility of mobile communications devices, social interaction occurs simultaneously through physically co-located and digitally mediated exchanges. Moreover, these developments in portability increase the number and diversity of situations in which media are used. Integrating ethnographic observations of media use in various physical locations with research considering the setting of use to be constructed by the technological artefact itself Ito and Okabe [15] proposed the concept of *technosocial situations* to account for the technological, social, and physical dimensions of a situation. Just as Gaver [8] avoids framing technological affordances as principle determinants of action, Ito and Okabe [15] are careful to acknowledge the continued importance of the physical and social dimensions of a situation, along with the importance of various cognitions, as enablers of action.

Situation, then, can be understood through three dimensions: the *physical environment*, the *technological environment*, and the *social environment*. The physical environment refers to the material properties of the setting in which media use occurs. While some media are used in relatively static locations (e.g., desktop computers) others are used in a large number of diverse locations (e.g., mobile phones, laptops). Different physical locations (e.g., university lectures, private bedrooms, public restaurants, open offices) present various factors which either enable or constrain particular actions. Chief among such factors are the social relationships and norms embedded within a physical location. Through various social conventions, norms, and expectations the social environment supports particular media uses, while restricting others. In specifying acceptable behaviour in a given situation, norms motivate action through promising social sanctions for counternormative conduct. Importantly, social boundaries and conventions simultaneously shape media use and are, themselves, shaped by media use [15]. Conversations on mobile phones, for instance, follow generally accepted conversational cues but are now accompanied by an expectation of continuous, uninterrupted availability. The technological dimension refers to the artefacts available in a given situation. Such artefacts determine the nature of the technological affordances available for the user to enact. Situational dimensions can, reciprocally, interact with various user, behavioural, and outcome-related factors. For instance, needs, which in turn drive various gratifications, differ from situation to situation but, as Zhang and Zhang [32] argue, situations are, themselves, influenced by various psychological needs. Similarly, an expected outcome of a particular form of media use behaviour may differ between situations.

5.1 Artefacts

Today, popular devices such as laptops, tablets, and smartphones provide an array of communication modes to users. In this context, two dimensions of the technological artefact merit consideration—hardware and software. Together, these dimensions determine the affordances available to a user. Hardware refers to the material, physical component of any communications artefact or medium, while software refers to the virtual component of a medium represented by the encoding of information through various programming languages and frameworks and, as perceived by the user, typically forms the graphical user interface through which interactions occur. Importantly, while differences exist, from a user's perspective, the same software can be used or accessed in the form of programs, applications, or web-services, across multiple distinct hardware forms (e.g., *Facebook* can be accessed on mobile phones, tablets, laptops, as a standalone mobile application, or through a web browser). The communications artefact or medium is constituted by the combination of various hardware and software characteristics. Together, this determines the nature of the affordances available to be enacted. Additionally, while media convergence increasingly implies that distinctions are difficult to make [16], the hardware and, in particular, the software components of an artefact influence the nature of content interacted with. In addition to the individual affordances of any one medium, Helles [12] argues that, owing to the increasing convergence of media, it is also necessary to account for *intermediality*. Referring to the interconnectedness of modern communications media, intermediality accepts that, further to the individual affordances of a particular medium, actual use frequently involves the combination and interrelation of multiple distinct media [16], across both hardware and software components.

Through the combination of various hardware, software, and inter-media relations, communications *media* present a variety of unique characteristics that, it is argued, interact with other situational dimensions, user characteristics, and outcomes, to facilitate various forms of media use behaviour. These include, but are not limited to, *accessibility, flexibility,* and *centrality.*

Extending from advances in processing power, mobility, energy storage, and information transmission, access to media, across a variety of locations and situations, is now possible. Many modern popular communications devices are designed to be portable, with batteries and wireless network connections enabling use that is untethered from physical connections to electrical power or networks. This enables the same artefact to be used across multiple distinct situations. Media are always available, always accessible, ubiquitous. Stiegler [27] proposes that the ability of users to receive and transmit information across time and space dislocates experiences from spatial and temporal contexts. Mediated interactions are reduced to a 'real-time present'. Castells [3, p. 491], accordingly, notes how media engender experiences of 'timeless time' in which both simultaneity and timelessness characterise interactions and instances of media use.

Modern communications media are highly flexible, adaptable and, given intermediality, integrated across devices, applications, and modalities. Rather than more linear modes of interaction, as in more traditional notions of mass media communication, mediated communication no longer consists of active senders and passive receivers. Rather, all *users* actively engage in the transmission, reception and modification of information in a manner which draws upon their existing identities, contexts and capacities. Users are free to use media in a variety of ways and for a variety of purposes, many of which were not conceived by the original producers. Considering the prominence of the World Wide Web, built on the hypertextual architecture of the Internet, as a *hypermedium* of communication and the manner in which modern operating systems allow the ad-hoc navigation between various programs and applications, it is argued that users are afforded a great deal of flexibility in how they can use various media. In addition to user flexibility, many media are in constant flux, with continuous release cycles prompting rapid changes in appearances and features.

Advancements in the accessibility and adaptability of media, coupled with continued developments in software capabilities and increases in the variety and richness of content made available, have enabled considerable improvements in the extent to which digital communications media can gratify a wide range of needs. Media are motivationally relevant and, consequently, *central* to how people work, socialise, communicate, and interact with the world around them [31]. It is argued that media are central to individuals lived-experiences to such an extent that distinctions between physical interactions and mediated interactions have become increasingly blurred. In addition to various technological affordances, the *content* interacted with through a medium is central to this.

Traditionally, media use and effects have been studied in relation to the modality of communication—the medium itself—and not the content or the message, to use McLuhan [18]'s aphorism. Valkenburg et al. [30, p. 322], however, argue that, content properties cannot be ignored when seeking to understand media use behaviour and effects. Media content is typically understood to refer to the subject matter communicated by the medium (e.g., sports, news, gossip, advice, entertainment), while content properties refer to various qualities of the content (e.g., violence, aggression, outrage). Given the complexity and possible range of content-types and properties, no comprehensive theory relating media content to use behaviour, and associated effects has been produced [30]. The UGT, discussed previously, does, however, provide a useful lens to understand possible associations between media content and subsequent media use behaviour. Rubin [24, p. 167] argues that "communication behavior, including the selection and use of the [sic] media, is goal-directed, purposive, and motivated". Users actively seek out and engage with media content that gratifies their needs, desires, or goals. Traditionally, the UGT has been used to predict television viewing levels in relation to various gratifications (e.g., entertainment, information seeking) and associated content forms [25]. More recently, this approach has been used to predict specific media use behaviours in relation to categories of content accessible through various social networking services: informational, entertainment, remunerative, and relational [5]. According to the UGT, different patterns of gratifications, driven by different needs, satisfied by different media content and affordances, contribute to different behavioural outcomes. Mediated content, consequently, influences media use and, as a consequence, should not be ignored when seeking to understand various forms of media use behaviour.

6   Behavioural Outcomes

Media use is, typically, purposive and driven, in part, by users' needs, desires, and goals [24]. In the SCT, it is proposed that the consequences resulting from an action, in this case media use, reciprocally influence subsequent considerations of whether to perform the same action. Consequently, in the context of media use behaviour, previously *realised* outcomes are important drivers of subsequent media use, through *expectations* of similar outcomes. This draws on the UGT. Outcomes associated with interacting with media content, in the aid of gratifying associated needs, firstly, reinforce these needs and, secondly, drive users to gratify them again through similar media use behaviour. There is an expectancy that, if the same action is performed, a similar outcome will be experienced. Moreover, behavioural outcomes are key to the formation of cognitive schemas and are, as such, central to embodied cognition and the subsequent framing of action as mediated by the individual [17]. Acting on the basis of a schema entails the expectation of particular consequences, borne through experience of previous media use instances. While various effects on psycho-social well-being have been investigated [23], and are, largely inconclusive, here it is proposed, at least, media use is driven by expectations of effects associated with use. Such effects are, however, more closely linked with the gratification of various needs, and possible affective responses. In addition to expectations, media use behaviour, and associated outcomes, through shared patterns of enactment, shape the social, cultural, and situational norms around media use. As in the SCT, behaviour producing outcomes deemed socially normative are encouraged, while behaviour producing outcomes considered to be counternormative is discouraged.

7   Discussion and Conclusions

In this paper we proposed a conceptual framework for understanding media use behaviour in relation to technological artefacts, their affordances and content, a user's subjective and situational circumstances, the enactment culture emerging from repeated patterns of use, and the potential outcomes of use itself. This framework does not presume to describe all factors potentially precipitating communicative action with media. Rather, it serves to guide researchers in identifying and describing the factors needed to understand a particular instance of media use behaviour and the potential effects this behaviour may enable. In particular, the framework seeks to demonstrate the complex multi-causality that is present in the formation, enactment, and potential consequences of media use behaviour. There is, accordingly, a need to move past simple conceptions of 'screen-time' and consider media use as a complex, nuanced behaviour [22,23].

Table 1. Example application of the Media Use Behaviour Conceptual Framework.

	Factor	Example
Artefact	Hardware	Which computing device is being used? (E.g., smartphones, laptop computers, tablets)
	Software	Which platforms are being used? (E.g., WhatsApp, Snapchat)
	Affordances	How is the platform used? (E.g., reading/sending messages, updating profile/status)
	Content	What is the thematic nature of the messages sent/received? (E.g., gossip, schoolwork)
Situation	Physical	Where is the user located? (E.g., home, school, public space)
	Social	Who is with the user? (E.g., friends, family, peers)
User	Personal	What are the personal traits/states of the media user? (E.g., age, gender, personality, ethnicity, stress)
	Cognitive	What is the nature of the cognitive schemas held the media user? (E.g., frames of reference, perceived social norms)
Outcomes	Expected	Which outcomes were expected before/during media use? (E.g., positive feedback, mood optimisation)
	Realised	Which outcomes actualised? (E.g., positive self-esteem)

As we argue with this framework, the etiological foundations of media use behaviour are, arguably, particularly complex, reciprocal, multi-causal and, specifically, highly contextual on individual and situational differences. This would suggest that, similarly, any effects of media use behaviour would share such characteristics and, as a consequence, require similarly nuanced conceptions, operationalisations, and empirical models for their assessment. It is envisaged that the framework may present as a useful tool for researchers seeking to understand why a particular form of media use behaviour occurs. This is especially the case for studies using qualitative data, where such a framework can, potentially, guide the identification and classification of various behavioural drivers. For example, when analysing an individual adolescent's participation in group-based instant messaging among a circle of friends, the framework draws the researchers' attention to the following factors depicted Table 1.

Notwithstanding the value of the framework, its theoretical basis, and the subsequent conceptual discussion presented in this paper, it is acknowledged that, as a high-level conceptual description, there exist a number of limitations to the media use behaviour conceptual framework. Specifically, as a conceptual framework, no direct empirical claims to causality are proposed, described, or assessed. Additionally, the framework is presented at an abstract level. Researchers adopting the framework to consider any specific form of media use behaviour and potentially associated effects would need to draw on other research to identify the relevant operationalisations for each of the framework's components.

References

1. Bandura, A.: Social Foundations of Thought and Action: A Social Cognitive Theory. Prentice-Hall Series in Social Learning Theory. Prentice-Hall, Upper Saddle River (1986)
2. Baumeister, R.F., Schmeichel, B., Vohs, K.: Self-regulation and the executive function: the self as controlling agent. In: Kruglanski, A., Higgins, E. (eds.) Social Psychology: Handbook of Basic Principles, Chap. 22, 2nd edn, pp. 516–539. The Guilford Press, New York City (2007)
3. Castells, M.: The Rise of the Network Society: The Information Age: Economy, Society, and Culture. Wiley, New York City (2011)
4. Davis, T.R., Luthans, F.: A social learning approach to organizational behavior. Acad. Manag. Rev. **5**(2), 281–290 (1980)
5. Dolan, R., Conduit, J., Fahy, J., Goodman, S.: Social media engagement behaviour: a uses and gratifications perspective. J. Strat. Mark. **24**(3–4), 261–277 (2016)
6. Ellis, D.A.: Are smartphones really that bad? Improving the psychological measurement of technology-related behaviors. Comput. Hum. Behav. **97**, 60–66 (2019)
7. Gaver, W.W.: Technology affordances. In: Proceedings of the SIGCHI Conference on Human Factors in Computing Systems, pp. 79–84. ACM (1991)
8. Gaver, W.W.: Situating action II: affordances for interaction: the social is material for design. Ecol. Psychol. **8**(2), 111–129 (1996)
9. Gibson, J.J.: The Ecological Approach to Visual Perception. Houghton, Mifflin and Company, Boston (1979)

186   D. A. Parry and D. B. le Roux

10. Goffman, E.: Behavior in Public Places; Notes on the Social Organization of Gatherings. Free Press, New York (1963)
11. Greeno, J.G.: A perspective on thinking. Am. Psychol. Assoc. **44**, 134–141 (1989)
12. Helles, R.: Mobile communication and intermediality. Mob. Media Commun. **1**(1), 14–19 (2013)
13. Hsieh, Y.: Online social networking skills: the social affordances approach to digital inequality. First Monday **17**(4) (2012)
14. Hutchby, I.: Conversation and Technology: From the Telephone to the Internet. Wiley, Hoboken (2013)
15. Ito, M., Okabe, D.: Technosocial situations: emergent structurings of mobile Email use. Pers. Portable Pedestr. Mob. Phones Jpn. Life **20**(6), 257–273 (2005)
16. Jensen, K.B.: Intermediality. In: The International Encyclopedia of Communication (2008)
17. Johnson, M.: The Body in the Mind: The Bodily Basis of Meaning, Imagination, and Reason. University of Chicago Press, Chicago (2013)
18. McLuhan, M.: Understanding Media: The Extensions of Man. MIT Press, Boston (1964)
19. Meyrowitz, J.: No Sense of Place: The Impact of Electronic Media on Social Behavior. Oxford University Press, Oxford (1986)
20. Neisser, U.: Cognitive Psychology. Century Psychology Series. Appleton-Century-Crofts, Detroit (1967)
21. Norman, D.A.: The Design of Everyday Things. Basic Books, New York City (1988)
22. Orben, A., Przybylski, A.K.: Screens, teens, and psychological well-being: evidence from three time-use-diary studies. Psychol. Sci. **30**(5), 682–696 (2019)
23. Orben, A., Przybylski, A.K.: The association between adolescent well-being and digital technology use. Nat. Hum. Behav. **3**(2), 173–182 (2019)
24. Rubin, A.M.: Uses-and-gratifications perspective on media effects. In: Bryant, J., Oliver, M. (eds.) Media Effects: Advances in Theory and Research, pp. 165–184. Taylor & Francis, New York (2009)
25. Rubin, A.M.: Television uses and gratifications: the interactions of viewing patterns and motivations. J. Broadcast. Electron. Media **27**(1), 37–51 (1983)
26. Simmons, J.P., Nelson, L.D., Simonsohn, U.: False-positive psychology: undisclosed flexibility in data collection and analysis allows presenting anything as significant. Psychol. Sci. **22**(11), 1359–1366 (2011)
27. Stiegler, B.: Technics and Time: Disorientation. Stanford University Press, San Jose (1998)
28. Suchman, L.A.: Plans and Situated Actions: The Problem of Human-Machine Communication. Learning in Doing: Social, Cognitive and Computational Perspectives. Cambridge University Press, Cambridge (1987)
29. Sundar, S., Limperos, A.: Uses and grats 2.0: new gratifications for new media. J. Broadcast. Electron. Media **57**(4), 504–525 (2013)
30. Valkenburg, P.M., Peter, J., Walther, J.B.: Media effects: theory and research. Annu. Rev. Psychol. **67**, 315–338 (2016)
31. Vorderer, P., Krömer, N., Schneider, F.M.: Permanently online - permanently connected: explorations into university students' use of social media and mobile smart devices. Comput. Hum. Behav. **63**, 694–703 (2016)
32. Zhang, W., Zhang, L.: Explicating multitasking with computers: gratifications and situations. Comput. Hum. Behav. **28**(5), 1883–1891 (2012)

The Town Square in Your Pocket: Exploring Four Metaphors of Social Media

Daniel B. le Roux$^{(\boxtimes)}$ ⓘ and Douglas A. Parry ⓘ

Information Science, Stellenbosch University, Stellenbosch, South Africa
{dbleroux,dougaparry}@sun.ac.za

Abstract. In this paper we explore the use of four metaphors as a means to illuminate particular dimensions of social media logic—the norms, strategies, and economics underpinning its dynamics. Our objective is to utilise metaphor to instigate critical reflection about the nature of social media use behaviour and the role of habitual social media use in our experiences of reality. The first metaphor, social media as a town square, draws attention to the centrality of social media platforms in their users' lives, fear of missing out, augmented reality and digital dualism. Through the second metaphor, social media as a beauty pageant, we explore self-presentation or image crafting, social comparison and self-evaluation. The third metaphor, social media as a parliament, emphasises the role of social media platforms as spaces for online deliberation and we consider social media capital, homophily and polarisation as themes. Finally, we explore anonymity, deindividuation and deceptive self-presentation through our fourth metaphor, social media as a masquerade ball. We argue that social media scholars can use these and other metaphors to enhance communication of their research findings. Additionally, we believe that social media metaphors can be powerful pedagogical and communication tools, particularly when working with students for whom high levels of social media use is the norm.

Keywords: Social media · Metaphor · Town square · Beauty pageant · Parliament · Masquerade ball

1 Introduction

It would be difficult to overstate the rapidity of the increase in agency that social media platforms have had in our sensemaking of the world. On a superficial level this agency is reflected in both the number of users on social media platforms and in the amount of time users spend on these platforms. However, the true impact of these technologies is perhaps most apparent in the way high levels of social media use have become enmeshed in our daily routines and, by extension, our ongoing experiences of reality. Obvious testament of the centrality that social media now occupy in our lives is the important role platforms like Facebook played in recent elections/referendums in the US and UK.

© IFIP International Federation for Information Processing 2020
Published by Springer Nature Switzerland AG 2020
M. Hattingh et al. (Eds.): I3E 2020, LNCS 12067, pp. 187–198, 2020.
https://doi.org/10.1007/978-3-030-45002-1_16

A consequence of the habituation of social media use is that we run the risk of becoming desensitised to its role in shaping our subjective and social realities. In this paper we turn to *metaphor* as a means to counter this desensitisation and obtain a degree of objectivity about the underlying logic of social media use. As a linguistic and conceptual tool, metaphor has served, across the ages, as a powerful instigator of critical thinking in multiple domains [15]. Its value was emphasised by Aristotle who described its command as the mark of genius [15] and, in recent times, a substantial body of theoretical work and psychological studies directed at the process of metaphor comprehension has emerged [15, p. 641]. Franke [9], accordingly, argues that, in recent decades, the "fortunes of metaphor have revived and flourished in tandem with those of rhetoric as a whole". Central to this revival is a renewed appreciation of the important role of metaphor in human cognition.

Our primary objective in this paper is to utilise metaphor to instigate and facilitate critical reflection about *social media logic*—"the norms, strategies, mechanisms, and economics underpinning its dynamics" [6]. In principle, this is akin to the objective of Morgan [23] whose oft-cited book, *Images of Organisation*, has achieved broad recognition for its analysis of various metaphors of organisation to "explore and develop the art of understanding organisational life" [23, p. 4]. Our objective, similarly, is to explore and develop understanding of *social media life* through the analysis of specific metaphors of social media. We aim to achieve this by mapping selected properties from a set of selected source domains to properties of particular aspects of social media logic to produce creative and rich descriptions of this logic. These descriptions, we propose, offer a vantage point from which critical reflection and analyses may be performed.

We propose and briefly analyse four metaphors of social media. Importantly, we do not undertake systematic analyses of metaphors as they appear in some form of qualitative data source. Such analyses answer questions concerning the discourse about and social construction of a phenomenon by a particular collective, and "metaphors or metaphorical ideas are framed as mediators or artefacts at the social cultural level of discourse and cognition" which influence mind and behaviour [16, p. 206]. Our approach, rather, is to utilise particular source domains in an attempt to clarify complex ideas about social media logic. In doing so we hope to harness the ability of metaphors to create complexities which promote reflection leading to additional questioning and the clarification of concepts [34]. Ricoeur [30] argues that "metaphorical meaning does not merely consist of a semantic clash but of the new predicative meaning which emerges from the collapse of the literal meaning". It is our aim to, through exploration of this new predictive meaning, advance insight into social media logic.

2 Defining Metaphor

In accordance with Shen [33] we define a metaphor as "a selective mapping of properties between two (conceptual) domains, the source and the target". When we say that *social media is like a party*, we selectively map properties of

a *source or vehicle* (a party) to a *target or tenor* (social media) [15, p. 644].
The metaphor operates on the basis of preexisting similarities between source
and target, enabling the mapping of systematic correspondences between the
source and target domains. This mapping, Lakoff [20] notes, permits us to reason
about the target phenomenon by drawing on our knowledge and experience of the
source domain. He argues, on this basis, that metaphors are not merely a matter
of language, but that the ontological and epistemic mapping across domains is a
matter of thought and reason. Metaphors have long been appreciated for playing
a pedagogical role in science, helping to "sell new ideas by providing vivid or
concrete relations and ways of representing those ideas" which, in turn, "sheds
light on new features of an important phenomenon" [16, p. 199].

It is important to recognise and acknowledge the selective nature of source-
target mapping when applying metaphor. When proposing a metaphor, only a
specific subset of source properties are mapped to the target—those that represent *likeness* between source and target. For example, parties involve social
interaction and this property is mappable to social media. However, parties also
take place at a particular place and time, properties that are not mappable to
the target. Morgan [23], accordingly, argues that a metaphor, like any theory, is
a partial, abstract truth rather than an absolute. A consequence of this principle
is that a single target phenomenon can be described through the use multiple,
different source domains, and *vice versa*. Additionally, in our analysis, we also
consider differences or *non-likeness* between our proposed source domains and
social media. It is our view that the recognition of both likeness and difference
advances critical thinking about the target (i.e., social media logic).

Lastly, before commencing our analyses, it is worth briefly describing the
process followed to identify the source domains we selected. Beyond this paper
our primary area of interest concerns social media use patterns and, in particular,
the effects of social media use for mental well-being. In discussions, seminars
and lectures we have often found ourselves utilising metaphors informally to
describe particular dimensions of social media logic. A growing appreciation of
the communicative and pedagogical value of these metaphors encouraged us to
develop a list of source domains that we have found to resonate with students
and/or other audiences. The four metaphors we describe here were selected from
that list and were chosen due to their emphases on different themes or discourses
that are prominent in contemporary research on social media.

3   Metaphors

3.1   Social Media as a Town Square

The notion that social media platforms are like physical spaces is implicit in much
of our informal language about it. When someone states that they are *on Twitter*
or that they *left Instagram*, the metaphor is invoked. The primary purpose of
the *Town Square* metaphor, accordingly, is to frame social media as somewhere
one can go, be and leave, and as a location or setting where events can occur. We
use as source domain the notion of a village town square, a central place where

events of importance occur and which serves as a meeting point characterised by continuous social interactions. The town square, typically located in or close to the centre of the village, is easily and always accessible, mirroring the ubiquitous and pervasive nature of social media. Of course, in reality, the events that are mediated through social media occur across time space, but the medium, through its collation of content into streams, pages, groups etc., centralises the digital traces of dispersed events into a single online *place*. When combined in this way, the disparate digital cues become perceived as a new whole, which, in turn, gives new meaning to its parts. The event, which took place in some real location at a particular time, now exists as a digital cue (e.g., video of the event) on the platform which serves as its new location. We explore two themes through this metaphor. The first concerns the perceived pressure to be on social media and the perception that one misses out on gratifying experiences when one isn't. The second concerns the tension between digital dualism and augmented reality.

As social media platforms increasingly became central *meeting hubs* on the world wide web (i.e., town squares), they gained prominence as places where one *must be*. This is well reflected in the rapid growth of platform user communities before 2010 – in 2009 Facebook was growing by a staggering five million users every week [14]. This trend solidified the belief, particularly among first-world adolescent populations, that having a social media profile is an essential dimension of one's social life [25]. The broad adoption of this belief can be ascribed to an iterative relationship between, firstly, the advancement and diversification of the affordances of social media platforms, and secondly, their increasing primacy in the dynamics of real (offline) social networks. The effect was the transformation of social media from a little known cafe mainly frequented by students to the *town square*. This transformation strengthened the perception that one *had to be there*, firstly, because everyone else is there and, secondly, to engage in the important and gratifying experiences it offers.

Extending from this belief is the view that *missing out* on events occurring on social media is undesirable, raising anxiety about this possibility among users. Much like being away from the town square and the exciting or gratifying experiences it offers, being offline is equated to not being physically present at important events. Scholars have explored this theme under the banner of FoMo or fear of missing out, defined as "pervasive apprehension that others might be having rewarding experiences from which one is absent" [28]. As can be expected, experiences of FoMo are associated with increased social media use [2,28], creating a positive feedback loop which solidifies the belief that *life happens* in the town square. More recently, Reinecke et al. [29] use the term "online vigilance" to describe "users' permanent cognitive orientation towards online content and communication as well as their disposition to exploit these options constantly".

An important feature of likening social media to a physical location is that it draws attention to the distinction between digital dualism and augmented reality. Digital dualists argue that "the digital world is virtual and the physical world real", while the notion of augmented reality suggests that the digital and physical become increasingly meshed through our permanently online, permanently connected lives [17]. The ubiquity of mobile computing devices implies that we always have *the town square in our pockets*, enabling us to switch from uneventful experiences on the edge of town (i.e., being offline) to exciting and rewarding social media experiences. We can continuously *be* in two or more places *at once*. By framing social media as a physical location, the metaphor forces us to critically consider this meshing of multiple realities and its effects for identity and well-being. The argument that such switching involves the augmentation of physical reality implies that cues from the physical and digital realities are continuously related to each other and, for the individual, meshed into a single reality. It is conceivable that this premise may hold in some media use scenarios, but it is equally conceivable that there are many in which it may not.

Extending from the notion of rapid switching between physical and digital cues, the metaphor of the town square also draws attention to communication and information load, and the manner in which users' attentional resources are vied for. The volume of sensory cues experienced when moving through a bustling town square requires continuous filtering of environmental stimuli and selection of attentional targets. Within the context of social media business models, the phrase "attention economy" [22] is often used to emphasise the primacy of controlling users' attentional allocation in achieving growth. This has cultivated interest in the science of persuasive design techniques focused on increasing both the frequency and duration of social media use, the principles of which are effectively applied on social media platforms. Much like those moving through the town square are confronted with attention seeking traders and artists, social media platforms employ various techniques in an attempt to manipulate users' attentional allocation decisions. The increase in time spent on social media platforms indicates that these techniques have been particularly effective, prompting researchers to investigate the nature and consequences of *problematic social media use*, and debate the possibility of *social media addiction* [1].

3.2 Social Media as a Beauty Pageant

Our second metaphor likens social media to a beauty pageant. Through this metaphor we draw attention to two distinct roles which social media users continuously play. The first role is that of participant and concerns the manner in which social media affordances enable the presentation of the self. The second role is that of judge (or audience member) and concerns the manner in which social media platforms facilitate and encourage both social comparison and self-evaluation. We use the metaphor to emphasise how the creation and maintenance of a social media profile can be viewed as a form of "social comparison and interpersonal feedback-seeking" [24]. While these behaviours are considered a normal dimension of identity development, we argue that the ubiquity, pervasiveness and affordances of social media platforms have, firstly, increased their frequency of and, secondly, changed their nature.

Participants in beauty pageants compete against each other on the basis of physical appearance, self-presentation and, more recently, other personal traits. Users of social media platforms, in a comparable way, present themselves to an audience (e.g., their connections). These presentations include, on a basic level, the creation and maintenance of a profile, but the affordances of social media platforms enable users to *compete* using "several techniques to optimise their self-presentation and promote desired relationships", including carefully edited messages and selected images, highlighting positive attributes, presenting an ideal self, deep self-disclosure, and association with certain people or material objects [4, p. 117]. The beauty pageant metaphor prompts us to consider these actions as carefully planned attempts to impress other users who are perceived to be continually judging their network. Moreover, it makes explicit the existence of a competitive dimension in social media use, emphasising, by extension, the notion that there are winners and losers. These ideas have received ample attention from scholars investigating the subjective and social underpinnings of *self presentation* or *image crafting* by social media users. Narcissism has, for instance, been associated with higher levels of social activity on social media platforms and the creation of more self-promoting content [3]. Halpern et al. [13] found that the online sharing of flattering images of oneself creates the perception, for the sharer, of an online ideal persona that diverges from real-life self-perception.

In addition to enabling social media users to compete in the pageant by presenting themselves, platform affordances enable and encourage users to judge each other. Features such as *liking*, *retweeting* and *commenting* are used by *judges* to provide *contestants* with feedback. Importantly, platforms present this feedback to contestants in quantitative form enabling comparison with other contestants, thereby determining ranking among them. In a qualitative study by Fox and Moreland [8, p. 172], interviewees highlight this competitive dimension by comparing the process of *getting friends on Facebook* to an *arms race*.

The beauty pageant metaphor also draws attention to the manner in which cycles of presentation and judgement shape social networks. The network, through these feedback loops, continually determines standards and norms which, in turn, influence users' future behaviours. Second, these standards are determined by the particular properties of the network in which the contestants participate. For example, the judging criteria applied among members of a teenage gaming community would be different from those applied among a group of middle-aged golfing friends. Third, building upon the first two, an individual's degree of social (media) capital, by extension, may differ substantially across the various networks he or she *competes* in.

An important implication of continuously competing is that it cultivates self-judgement. For example, Fox and Moreland [8, p. 172] report that "participants in romantic contexts, wherein they would use Facebook's affordances of persistent history and connectivity to self-compare with a romantic interest's potential or former mates". Importantly, self-judgement is not limited to quantitative indicators (e.g., numbers of followers, friends, likes etc.), but also involves qualitative comparison of experiences, achievements, property etc. In order to *beat their competitors*, social media users seek ways to enhance their profiles by sharing content that emphasises their own achievements or experiences. The metaphor brings to the fore the degree to which this *crafting* of an image can become a false representation of the actual lived experience of an individual, created for the purpose of *winning* the pageant.

While acknowledging the potential benefits for self-esteem of positive feed-back from *judges*, a growing body of studies have emphasised the role of social comparison and self-judgement in explaining findings which associate social media use with negative well-being outcomes [19].

3.3   Social Media as a Parliament

Our third metaphor adopts the notion of a *parliament* as source domain. Parliaments, as government institutions, generally perform a number of functions relating to the governance of democratic countries by representing the electorate. These functions may include, amongst others, making laws, overseeing the executive and representing the interests, views and grievances of citizens. Parliaments are typically constituted by elected members, and their activities are managed, at various levels, by political leaders, parliamentary officials, presiding officers and committee chairs. Political deliberation or debate is a key feature of parliaments. Winetrobe [35, p. 1], accordingly, describes them as "forums where strong, very public, and often adversarial political debates take place, reflecting the party competition of the wider political system".

We argue that social media platforms, like parliaments, provide a context which enables *deliberation* among members of their user communities. Deliberation involves the "interchange of rational critical arguments among a group of individuals, triggered by a common or public problem" [12]. Importantly, our interest in the source domain is not the content of deliberation (i.e., political debate), but rather the nature of the context in which deliberation occurs, the mechanisms (and affordances) by which it is guided, and the manner in which it impacts network structures. The metaphor, accordingly, is as relevant to political debate on social media platforms as it is to deliberation about sports teams, stock markets, or the duties of the local neighbourhood watch.

The affordances of social media platforms enable users to organise themselves into smaller networks based on commonalities (e.g., shared interests, place of residence, occupation etc.). These *sub-committees* do not, per definition, involve exclusive access to members. For example, on a platform like Twitter, one can consider deliberation around particular *hashtags* as a *sub-committee*. All Twitter users can, from the *public gallery*, view the deliberation activities without (necessarily) taking an active role. Much like the sub-committees of parliaments, these smaller networks deliberate aspects specific to their commonality. Additionally, the affordances of some platforms enable communities to assign roles (e.g., administrators, moderators etc.) to specific members who, like those managing parliamentarian processes, have particular rights and privileges that enable them to perform managerial or administrative activities during deliberation among members. Importantly, just as not all members of parliament are considered equal in terms of political capital, there exists asymmetry in influence among social media users due to a wide variety of factors [22].

de Zúñiga et al. [36] argue that the processes of obtaining and using social capital on social media differs in nature from those relating to social capital in face-to-face settings. They argue that "social media has changed the structure and nature of social connection, and therefore that they may alter the distribution and nature of social capital embedded in those social relationships" [36, p. 45]. In this regard the metaphor draws our attention to the processes of deliberation within social media communities, and the interplay between deliberation, user behaviour and community structures. On many social media platforms users, like parliamentarians, do not address a particular target but rather the community as a whole. Community members are then free to respond to the content, creating a *thread* of deliberation. In addition to *liking* or *retweeting* the statement presented, affordances enable engagement through responses, counter-arguments or supportive comments. These forms of feedback enable the community to gauge the degree of support for particular viewpoints and determine the alignment between their personal views and those of other members. On this basis factions or alliances emerge which, in turn, drive the disintegration of existing, and formation of new networks.

A theme which has received ample attention from scholars is the role of *homophily*, "the tendency to favour interaction with like-minded people" [10], in network formation on social media platforms. The product, when this tendency is enacted, is the formation of *echo chambers*—communities in which users are only exposed to ideas aligning with their own. Gayo-Avello [10] argues that while social media users have "a certain degree of exposure to cross-cutting ideas (even to users who are clearly partisans) and can interact with users who have opposing ideas", they mostly avoid such discussions. Additionally, his research suggests that when users encounter arguments that are in conflict with their views, they do not propagate them within their networks. This theme has primarily been explored in the context of political polarisation where a key concern is the manner in which online deliberation reinforces preexisting views by perpetuating a confirmation bias [5]. However, contrary findings have also been reported. For example, Semaan et al. [32] found that some social media users purposefully seek diverse information and discussants and that such interactions often lead to alterations of personal views. This form of use aligns, in many ways, with the ethos of parliamentary deliberation.

3.4   Social Media as a Masquerade Ball

Our final metaphor likens social media to a *masquerade ball*. We envision a masquerade ball as a social event where attendees obscure, to a lesser or greater degree, their true identities by wearing a mask or costume. Social interaction, accordingly, occurs under conditions of some degree of anonymity. The dynamics of behaviour and interaction are influenced by this property, creating an element of excitement and novelty to the event. This excitement can be attributed to liberation from the constraints associated with the presentation and maintenance of a single, true identity. Scott and Orlikowski [31, p. 5] argue that "anonymity is related to freedom from identification, secrecy and lack of distinction".

We propose that, like the *masks* or *constumes* worn to masquerade balls, social media affordances enable users to obscure their identities to achieve some degree of freedom from the constraints associated with the maintenance of a socially acceptable personal identity. This freedom affords users the opportunity to pursue interests or engage in behaviour online which may, for various reasons, be inaccessible to or incongruent with their true identity. Research has shown that anonymity impacts the behaviour on social media in various ways [12] and that some social media platforms (e.g., *Reddit* and *4/chan/*) leverage anonymity, "as a design choice", to influence online interaction and norms [21, p. 3857]. Importantly, the metaphor (as we intend it) is not concerned with *fake accounts* or *bots* which we consider to be a separate domain of interest.

Anonymity encourages *deindividuation*, allowing people to be less self aware, engage less in self-evaluation and be less "concerned about social comparison and evaluation" [27, p. 138]. As a result, behaviour becomes "socially deregu-lated" [12, p. 2]. Findings suggest that such deregulation is associated less polite interaction. Halpern and Gibbs [12], for example, found that messages posted on YouTube, which is generally more anonymous, were more impolite than mes-sages in the "more identifiable Facebook medium". They argue that this occurs "due to the greater level of information access to users' broader social networks" on Facebook. Additionally, anonymity has been associated with higher levels of self-disclosure on social media [21]. Pavalanathan [26, p. 315], for example, investigates the role of anonymity in the use of online fora concerning mental health, arguing that users "withhold their actual identities allowing themselves to engage in more candid self-disclosure than is possible in offline settings, or through their identified online personas".

While *image crafting*, as a dimension of the *beauty pageant* metaphor, draws attention to how users emphasise or highlight aspects of their identities, the masquerade ball draws our attention to the manner in which image crafting also involves obscuring of identity aspects. In this way the two metaphors describe how the same outcome (i.e., desired self-presentation) can be achieved through different strategies (i.e., accentuating vs obscuring). The masks worn at mas-querade balls may not fully obscure the person, but be carefully chosen to hide particular physical features. We argue, accordingly, that social media users care-fully utilise affordances, like masks, to find an optimal balance between disclosure and anonymity based on their goals and the nature of the social media space. Guadagno et al. [11] use the phrase "deceptive self-presentation" to describe such behaviour and argue that "it increases as a function of the pressure to engage in self-presentation" [11, p. 642]. Alternatively, users may wish to dis-close personal information but avoid identifiability. For example, users of online dating platforms may, due to the stigma traditionally associated with the prac-tice [7], obscure information making them identifiable, but disclose aspects like physical appearance to attract attention to their profiles. It is our view that these and other forms of *masquerading* have become salient features of social media logic, with broad adoption serving to obscure their novelty and signifi-cance. The metaphor brings them to the fore and invites critical reflection about their enactment and effects.

4   Discussion

In this paper we explored four metaphors of social media with the aim of elucidating particular dimensions of social media logic—the norms, strategies, and economics underpinning its dynamics. It is our view that the four metaphors presented here provide an initial indication of the potential value of utilising metaphor in the analysis and communication of social media logic. We foresee two specific contexts where this value can be realised.

The first is teaching and, in particular, teaching to *digital natives* for whom chronic social media use is the norm. For such individuals the dynamics of behaviour and network formation on social media may be so embedded in their understanding of social interaction in general that they may altogether disregard the agency of the technical affordances of social media platforms in their behaviour. Metaphors of non-mediated social spaces will enable educators to draw students' attention to the role of these affordances in shaping mediated socialisation patterns and the extent to which they determine behavioural norms on social media platforms.

The second context where these metaphors can be of value is the communication of scientific findings to non-scientific stakeholder groups. For example, therapists or psychologists can utilise the *beauty pageant* metaphor to help their clients to make sense of the role social media use may play in processes of self-esteem updating. School teachers and parents can use the *town square* metaphor to encourage adolescents to critically reflect about their attention allocation habits and the impacts chronic media multitasking on academic and other performance.

Importantly, while the four metaphors presented here may provide a useful starting point, they are obviously limited in scope and only cover a small subset of social media phenomena that have been investigated. For example, one may argue that none of our metaphors adequately addresses underlying business models of social media platforms, and how these models drive, firstly, the development of affordances and, secondly, user behaviour. Other prominent themes which are not explicitly addressed include cyberbullying, marketing through influencers and compulsive or problematic social media use. To address these and other themes, future work in this area can consider metaphors in relation to the seven functional blocks of social media as proposed by Kietzmann et al. [18].

References

1. Andreassen, C.S.: Online social network site addiction: a comprehensive review. Curr. Addict. Rep. **2**(2), 175–184 (2015). https://doi.org/10.1007/s40429-015-0056-9
2. Beyens, I., Frison, E., Eggermont, S.: "I don't want to miss a thing": adolescents' fear of missing out and its relationship to adolescents' social needs, facebook use, and facebook related stress. Comput. Hum. Behav. **64**, 1–8 (2016)
3. Buffardi, L.E., Campbell, W.K.: Narcissism and social networking web sites. Pers. Soc. Psychol. Bull. **34**(10), 1303–1314 (2008)

4. Chou, H.T.G., Edge, N.: "They are happier and having better lives than I am": the impact of using facebook on perceptions of others' lives. Cyberpsychology Behav. Soc. Netw. **15**(2), 117–121 (2012)
5. Davis, R.: The Web of Politics: The Internet's Impact on the American Political System. Oxford University Press, Oxford (1999)
6. van Dijck, J., Poell, T.: Understanding social media logic. Media Commun. **1**(1), 2–14 (2013)
7. Finkel, E.J., Eastwick, P.W., Karney, B.R., Reis, H.T., Sprecher, S.: Online dating. Psychol. Sci. Public Interest **13**(1), 3–66 (2012)
8. Fox, J., Moreland, J.J.: The dark side of social networking sites: an exploration of the relational and psychological stressors associated with Facebook use and affordances. Comput. Hum. Behav. **45**, 168–176 (2015)
9. Franke, W.: Metaphor and the making of sense: the contemporary metaphor renaissance. Philos. Rhetor. **33**(2), 137–153 (2000)
10. Gayo-Avello, D.: Social media, democracy, and democratization. IEEE Multimed. **22**(2), 10–16 (2015)
11. Guadagno, R.E., Okdie, B.M., Kruse, S.A.: Dating deception: gender, online dating, and exaggerated self-presentation. Comput. Hum. Behav. **28**(2), 642–647 (2012)
12. Halpern, D., Gibbs, J.: Social media as a catalyst for online deliberation? Exploring the affordances of Facebook and YouTube for political expression. Comput. Hum. Behav. **29**(3), 1159–1168 (2013)
13. Halpern, D., Katz, J.E., Carril, C.: The online ideal persona vs. the jealousy effect: two explanations of why selfies are associated with lower-quality romantic relationships. Telemat. Inform. **34**(1), 114–123 (2017)
14. Hempel, J.: How Facebook is taking over our lives. Fortune **159**(4), 48–56 (2009)
15. Holyoak, K.J., Stamenković, D.: Metaphor comprehension: a critical review of theories and evidence. Psychol. Bull. **144**(6), 641–671 (2018)
16. Hung, D.W.L.: Metaphorical ideas as mediating artifacts for the social construction of knowledge: implications from the writings of Dewey and Vygotsky. Int. J. Instr. Media **29**, 197+ (2002)
17. Jurgenson, N.: Digital dualism versus augmented reality. The Society Pages (2011)
18. Kietzmann, J.H., Hermkens, K., McCarthy, I.P., Silvestre, B.S.: Social media? Get serious! Understanding the functional building blocks of social media. Bus. Horiz. **54**(3), 241–251 (2011)
19. Krause, H.V., Baum, K., Baumann, A., Krasnova, H.: Unifying the detrimental and beneficial effects of social network site use on self-esteem: a systematic literature review. Media Psychol. 1–38 (2019)
20. Lakoff, G.: A figure of thought. Metaphor. Symb. Act. **1**(3), 215–225 (1986)
21. Ma, X., Hancock, J., Naaman, M.: Anonymity, intimacy and self-disclosure in social media. In: Proceedings of the 2016 CHI Conference on Human Factors in Computing Systems - CHI 2016, pp. 3857–3869 (2016)
22. Marwick, A.E.: Instafame: luxury selfies in the attention economy. Public Cult. **27**(1(75)), 137–160 (2015)
23. Morgan, G.: Images of Organization. Sage Publications, London (2006)
24. Nesi, J., Prinstein, M.J.: Using social media for social comparison and feedback-seeking: gender and popularity moderate associations with depressive symptoms. J. Abnorm. Child Psychol. **43**(8), 1427–1438 (2015). https://doi.org/10.1007/s10802-015-0020-0

25. Parry, D.A., le Roux, D.B.: Off-task media use in lectures: towards a theory of determinants. In: Kabanda, S., Suleman, H., Gruner, S. (eds.) SACLA 2018. CCIS, vol. 963, pp. 49–64. Springer, Cham (2019). https://doi.org/10.1007/978-3-030-05813-5_4

26. Pavalanathan, U.: Identity management and mental health discourse in social media identity in online communities. In: International World Wide Web Conference Committee (IW3C2), vol. 18, no. 22, pp. 315–321 (2015)

27. Polder-Verkiel, S.E.: Online responsibility: bad samaritanism and the influence of internet mediation. Sci. Eng. Ethics 18(1), 117–141 (2012). https://doi.org/10.1007/s11948-010-9253-z

28. Przybylski, A.K., Murayama, K., Dehaan, C.R., Gladwell, V.: Motivational, emotional, and behavioral correlates of fear of missing out. Comput. Hum. Behav. 29(4), 1841–1848 (2013)

29. Reinecke, L., et al.: Permanently online and permanently connected: development and validation of the online vigilance scale. PloS One 13(10) (2018)

30. Ricoeur, P.: The metaphorical process as cognition, imagination, and feeling. Crit. Inq. 5(1), 143–159 (1978)

31. Scott, S.V., Orlikowski, W.J.: Entanglements in practice: performing anonymity through social media. MIS Q. 38(3), 873–893 (2014)

32. Semaan, B., Robertson, S.P., Douglas, S., Maruyama, M.: Social media supporting political deliberation across multiple public spheres: towards depolarization. In: Proceedings of the ACM Conference on Computer Supported Cooperative Work, CSCW, pp. 1409–1421 (2014)

33. Shen, Y.: Principles of metaphor interpretation and the notion of 'domain': a proposal for a hybrid model. J. Pragmat. 31(12), 1631–1653 (1999)

34. Van Engen, R.B.: Metaphor: a multifaceted literary device used by Morgan and Weick to describe organizations. Emerg. Leadersh. Journeys 1(1), 39–51 (2008)

35. Winetrobe, B.K.: Political but not partisan: marketing parliaments and their members. J. Legis. Stud. 9(1), 1–13 (2003)

36. de Zúñiga, H.G., Barnidge, M., Scherman, A.: Social media social capital, offline social capital, and citizenship: exploring asymmetrical social capital effects. Polit. Commun. 34(1), 44–68 (2017)

How Can Critical Thinking Be Used to Assess the Credibility of Online Information?

Albie van Zyl(iD), Marita Turpin$^{(\boxtimes)}$(iD), and Machdel Matthee(iD)

Department of Informatics, University of Pretoria, Pretoria 0001, South Africa
marita.turpin@up.ac.za

Abstract. The prevalence of unverified information on the internet and the associated potential adverse effect on society led to the development of a number of models and theories to assess the credibility of online information. Existing research consists of two diverse approaches: the first consists of checklist approaches or normative guidelines on how to assess the information whereas the second provides descriptive models and theories of how users actually go about when assessing credibility. The above mentioned approaches consider aspects related to the presentation and content of the information. However, the reasoning in the content is not a concern that is covered in these approaches. Critical thinking is considered an increasingly important 21st century work place skill. This paper investigates the potential value of using critical thinking in assessing the credibility of online information. The paper commences with an overview of existing approaches for assessing the credibility of online information. It then argues that the presence of a well-developed argument in online information to be an indication of credibility. Critical thinking also helps to evaluate the credibility of evidence. These thinking skills can be developed through training. It is shown how a group of first year Information Systems students were able to more critically engage with the content of online news after a course on critical thinking. This paper contributes to the literature on the assessment of the credibility of online information.

Keywords: Credibility assessment · Critical thinking · Information literacy

1 Introduction

The internet has become indispensable as a source of information and news. Given the vast amount of information available as well as the large numbers of information sites, it has become increasingly difficult to judge the credibility of online information [1]. Metzger argues that in the past, traditional publishing houses used to act as gatekeepers of the information published. There was a cost barrier to printing and the print process allowed for quality control. In the digital age, anyone can be an author of online content. Digital information and content can be published anonymously, and easily plagiarized and altered [1, 2]. Online news platforms are in a continual race against time to be the first to publish online, and in the process they sacrifice quality control. In the process, the gatekeeping function of evaluating the credibility of online information has shifted to the individual users.

© IFIP International Federation for Information Processing 2020
Published by Springer Nature Switzerland AG 2020
M. Hattingh et al. (Eds.): I3E 2020, LNCS 12067, pp. 199–210, 2020.
https://doi.org/10.1007/978-3-030-45002-1_17

To date, scholars in information literacy have developed checklists to assist users in assessing the credibility of online information, as well as various theories and models to describe how users evaluate information in practice [2–5]. These models highlight aspects such as the influence of the subjectivity of the user in evaluating content, the process of evaluation as well as the cognitive heuristics that users typically apply during evaluation. The models also recognize that in the era of social computing and social media, evaluation has a strong social component [6].

In an overview of studies on the assessment of the credibility of online information, it was found that neither the established normative guidelines for evaluating credibility, nor the descriptive models for evaluating credibility consider the quality of reasoning and argumentation contained in the information that is evaluated. That is strange, since critical thinking is generally regarded as an important information literacy skill, and in addition it is viewed as an important 21st century workplace skill [7, 8].

In this paper, we present a case for the use of critical thinking as a means to assess the quality and credibility of online content. We suggest how critical thinking could be used to enhance current credibility assessment practices. The known processes have in common with critical thinking the fact that they are all concerned with the credibility of evidence that is presented to substantiate the findings of an online article. Whereas credibility models mainly focus on presentation and content, critical thinking extends the evaluation of content by evaluating the quality of the argument presented. Admittedly, many fake (and other) news stories contain limited if any arguments to evaluate. While the absence of an argument is not enough to discredit an online article, its presence can be used as a quality indicator. The presence of a weak argument will reduce the perceived credibility of the claim or finding of an article, while a strong argument will enhance its credibility.

This paper commences with a short overview of existing guidelines and descriptive models for evaluating the credibility of online information. The common themes among these models are summarized. Next, the paper introduces the building blocks of critical thinking and proceeds to indicate how critical thinking is used for argument evaluation. A means to assess the credibility of online information is proposed that uses critical thinking in a way that recognizes and builds on previous work related to credibility assessment.

2   Existing Research on Assessing the Credibility of Online Information

Credibility refers to the believability of information [4]. Credibility is regarded to be subjective: it is not an objective attribute of an information source, but the subjective perception of believability by the information receiver [4, 9]. As such, two different information receivers can have different assessments of the credibility of the same piece of information.

Research on assessing the credibility of online information can be categorized into research on normative guidelines (in other words, what should people be looking at when they assess credibility) and research related to descriptive models or theories (how people are assessing credibility in practice).

2.1 A Checklist for Information Credibility Assessment

The normative approach to the assessment of information credibility is promoted by the proponents of digital literacy, who aim to assist internet users in developing the skills required for evaluating online information. Their assumption is that online information can be evaluated in the same manner as information found elsewhere [1]. A checklist approach is usually followed, where the list covers the following five components: accuracy, authority, objectivity, currency, and coverage or scope [1]. Accuracy refers to the degree that the content is free from errors and whether the information can be verified elsewhere. It is an indication of the reliability of the information on the website. Authority refers to the author of the website, and whether the website provides contact details of the author and the organisation. It is also concerned with whether the website is recommended or endorsed by a trusted source. Objectivity considers whether the content is opinion or fact, and whether there is commercial interest, indicated for example by a sponsored link. Currency refers to the frequency of updates, and whether the date is visible. Coverage refers to the depth and comprehensiveness of the information [1]. In a checklist approach, a user is given a list of questions of things to look out for. For example, in terms of currency, the user has to look for evidence of when the page was last updated.

In a series of studies conducted by Metzger and her colleagues [1], it was found that even when supplied with a checklist, users rarely used it as intended. Currency, comprehensiveness and objectivity were checked occasionally, whilst checking an author's credentials, was the least preferred by users. This correlates with findings by Eysenbach and Köhler [10] who indicate that the users in their study, did not search for the sources behind their website information, or how the information was compiled. This lack of thoroughness is ascribed to the users' lack of willingness to expend cognitive effort [6]. The apparent attempt by users to minimise cognitive effort has given rise to studies on how users apply cognitive heuristics as well as other means to assess credibility more quickly and with less effort. This research led to the development of a number of descriptive models and theories on how users assess credibility in practice.

2.2 Descriptive Models and Theories Related to Information Credibility Assessment

The Use of Cognitive Heuristics. A number of studies indicate that internet users avoid laborious methods of information evaluation, and that they prefer to use more superficial cues, such as using the look and feel of a website as a proxy for credibility rather than analyzing the content [5, 6, 11]. When evaluating credibility, people tend to apply cognitive heuristics, which are mental short cuts or rules of thumb. Based on their previous experience people respond to cues and act on these subconsciously, without the need to spend mental effort [6, 12, 13]. Five heuristics are identified that users commonly apply to decide on the credibility of online content [6]. The *reputation* heuristic is applied when users recognize the source of the information as one they believe to be reputable, possibly because of brand familiarity or authority. The *endorsement* heuristic means that a source is believed to be credible if other people believe so too; either people they know or people that have given it a good rating. The *consistency* heuristic means that if similar information about something appears on multiple websites, the information is deemed to be credible. The *expectancy violation heuristic* is a strong negative heuristic. Information that is contrary to the user's own beliefs is not deemed to be credible. Lastly, when using the *persuasive intent heuristic*, users assess whether there is an attempt to persuade them or sell something to them. In this case, the information is perceived to be not credible because there is a perceived ulterior motive or an attempt to manipulate the user.

The Prominence-Interpretation Theory. The Prominence-Interpretation theory comprises two interlinked components that describe what happens when a user assesses the credibility of a website [14]. First, a user notices something (prominence), and then they interpret what they see (interpretation). If one of the two components are missing, there is no credibility assessment. A user will notice existing and new elements of a website and interpret the elements for credibility in an iterative fashion until being satisfied that a credibility assessment can be made. Conversely, the user may stop when they reach a constraint, such as running out of time [14]. A visual representation of the Prominence-Interpretation theory is provided in Fig. 1.

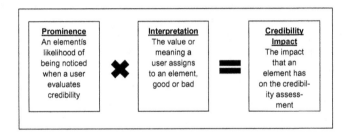

Fig. 1. Prominence-interpretation theory [14]

Prominence refers to the likelihood that certain elements will be noticed or perceived by the user. The user must first notice the element, to form a judgement of the credibility of the information. If the user does not notice the element, it does not play a role. Five factors are identified that influence prominence, namely: Involvement, topic, task, experience and individual differences. The most dominant influence is user involvement, referring to the user's motivation and ability to engage with content. Topic refers to the type of website the user visits. The task is the reason why the user is visiting the websites. Experience refers to the experience of the user, in relation to the subject or topic of the website. Individual differences refer to the user's learning style, literacy level or the user's need for cognition. When a user's involvement is high, and the user's experience is of expert status, the user will cognitively notice more elements [14].

Interpretation refers to the user's judgement of the element under review. For example, a broken link on a website will be interpreted as bad and lead to a lower credibility assessment of the website. Interpretation of elements is affected by a user's assumptions, skills, knowledge and context.

Consolidation. When comparing the research on the use of heuristics [6] with the Prominence-Interpretation theory [14], one can see that the use of heuristics fits well into the "interpretation" component of Prominence-Interpretation theory.

A Web Credibility Framework. Fogg's web credibility framework [15] contains the categories of *operator, content* and *design*. *Operator* refers to the source of the website, the person who runs and maintains the website. A user makes a credibility judgement based on the person or organisation operating the website. *Content* refers to what the site provides in terms of content and functionality. Of importance is the currency, accuracy and relevance of the content and the endorsements of a respected outside organisation. *Design* refers to the structure and layout of the website. Design has four elements namely information design (structure of the information), technical design (function of the site on a technical level, and search function), aesthetic design (looks, feel and professionality of the design) and interaction design (user experience, user interaction and navigation) [15].

The web credibility framework was extended by Choi and Stvilia [3] who divided each of the three categories (operator, content and design) into the two dimensions of trustworthiness and expertise, thereby forming what is called the Measures of Web Credibility Assessment Framework.

Consolidation. When consolidating the web credibility framework [15] and its extension [3] with the work on credibility assessment presented in the prior sections, one can say that the web credibility frameworks contribute to *prominence* as well as the *interpretation*. The web design contributes to the *prominence* or noticeability of the information. Further, the level of professionality of the design can be *interpreted* by means of a heuristic such as the reputation heuristic. The website operator and content, when noticed, get *interpreted* by means of evaluation heuristics. Hence, the work presented in 2.2.1 – 2.2.3 can be reconciled into different aspects of online information that, when noticed, get interpreted by means of heuristics.

Iterative Models on the Evaluation of Online Information. According to the Prominence-Interpretation theory [14] the interpretation of information occurs in an iterative fashion until a credibility assessment can be made. Two other models also recognize the iterative nature of credibility assessment. These are the cognitive authority model [2] and Wathen and Burkell's model [16].

With the cognitive authority model, the information seeker iteratively assesses the authority and credibility of online content by considering the author, document, institution and affiliations [2]. These are integrated into a credibility judgement. The model is similar to the checklist [1], but proposes that users employ the technology available to them to make the judgement. Like the checklist, the cognitive authority model is normative.

Wathen and Burkell [16] also propose an iterative way of assessment. According to their research users first do a *surface* credibility check based on the appearance and presentation of the website. Secondly, the user will look for *message* credibility by assessing the source and the content of the message. Lastly, the *content* itself is evaluated. During this final stage, sense-making of the content occurs, depending on factors such as the user's previous level of knowledge on the topic. If, at any stage, the user becomes aware of a reason to doubt the credibility of the information, the iterative process is stopped. Wathen and Burkell's model [16] is normative but also incorporates descriptive research on information evaluation.

2.3   A Synthesised Summary of Existing Work on the Credibility Assessment Process

To synthesise the joint findings from previous work on credibility assessment of online information:

- Credibility cues need to be noticed before they are processed [14].
- The evaluation process is iterative and moves from surface level checks (such as look and feel of a website) through to engagement with the content [14, 16].
- From the onset of the evaluation process, cognitive or judgmental heuristics are applied to assess credibility. This is especially true during the interpretation phase, when a user evaluates the content itself [1, 4–6]. Judgmental heuristics are used in order to reduce cognitive effort as the user is inundated with information.
- The evaluation process takes part in a social context and some of the evaluation cues are socially generated, such as number of website visitors, user recommendations or social rankings [6].

In the section that follows, the principles of critical thinking will be introduced. This is in order to assess how critical thinking might be used to evaluate online content in the light of what is already known about credibility evaluation.

3   Critical Thinking

The Foundation of Critical Thinking considers critical thinking as "that mode of thinking - about any subject, content, or problem - in which the thinker improves the quality of his or her thinking by skillfully analyzing, assessing, and reconstructing it" [17]. Some authors consider it an indispensable skill in problem solving. Halpern suggests a taxonomy of critical thinking skills covering a broad range of skills as (1) verbal reasoning skills, (2) argument analysis skills, (3) skills in thinking as hypothesis testing, (4) dealing with likelihood and uncertainties and (5) decision making and problem solving skills [18]. The aspect of critical thinking of interest in this paper, relates to the analysis of arguments. A useful definition for critical thinking is therefore the one suggested by Tiruneh and his co-authors [19]: critical thinking is the ability to analyse and evaluate arguments according to their soundness and credibility, respond to arguments and reach conclusions through deduction from given information [19]. Booth et al. [20], basing their work on ideas of Toulmin et al. [21], consider a basic argument to consist of a claim (or conclusion), backed by reasons which is supported by evidence. An argument is stronger if it acknowledges and responds to other views and if necessary, shows how a reason is relevant to a claim by drawing on a general principle (which is referred to as a warrant).

The following argument, adopted from [20: 112] illustrates these components: "TV violence can have harmful psychological effects on children" (CLAIM), "because their constant exposure to violent images makes them unable to distinguish fantasy from reality" (REASON). "Smith (1997) found that children ages 5–7 who watched more than 3 h of violent television a day were 25% more likely to say that what they saw on television was 'really happening'" (EVIDENCE). "Of course, some children who watch more violent entertainment might already be attracted to violence" (ACKNOWL-EDGEMENT). "But Jones (1999) found that children with no predisposition to violence were as attracted to violent images as those with a violent history" (RESPONSE).

Booth and his co-authors [20: 114] use the following argument to illustrate the use of a warrant in an argument: "We are facing significantly higher health care costs in Europe and North America (CLAIM) because global warming is moving the line of extended hard freezes steadily northward." (REASON). In this case the relevance of the reason to the claim should be stated by a general principle: "When an area has fewer hard freezes, it must pay more to combat new diseases carried by subtropical insects no longer killed by those freezes" (WARRANT).

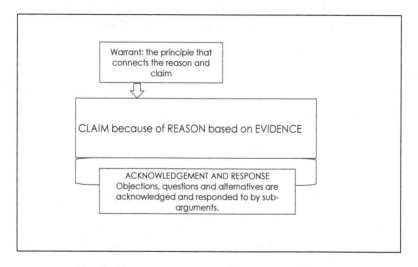

Fig. 2. The core components of an argument [20: 116]

Of course, good arguments need more than one reason in support of conclusions and complex arguments contains sub-arguments. However the main components remain the same. Figure 2 summarizes the main components of a basic argument.

Critical thinking entails the identification of the core components in an argument (analysis) in order to judge its credibility, quality and to formulate a response to it. According to Butterworth and Thwaites [7], a good quality argument is one where the reasons are true or justified and where the conclusion follows from the reasons. By using these criteria in the evaluation of arguments, classical fallacies such as the *post hoc fallacy* or *circular reasoning* can be identified. In addition, the evaluation of an argument entails asking questions and finding counter examples. A good quality argument will pre-empt objections or counter examples and respond to it. Butterworth and Thwaites [7] consider a credible argument as one which is plausible/believable (acknowledging that some highly improbable claims can be true), and having a trusted source. The credibility is enhanced if the claim is corroborated by different sources with different kinds of evidence.

3.1   The Use of Critical Thinking in the Context of Existing Credibility Assessment Models

It is suggested that critical thinking is included in the credibility assessment process, as follows. With reference to the Prominence-Interpretation theory [14], critical thinking can be applied during the interpretation phase. It can be used to assess the quality of evidence as well as evaluate the argument itself. It will only be used during a later stage in the iterative process of credibility assessment, possibly in the third phase of Wathen an Burkell's iterative model [16].

4   Discussion: Potential Challenges to Using Critical Thinking to Assess the Credibility of Online Information

When considering the use of critical thinking to evaluate the credibility of online information, some challenges are apparent.

First, as indicated earlier, it is known that users, who are flooded with information, are applying as a coping mechanism the use of judgmental heuristics to reduce cognitive effort. Therefore, they prefer to use cues that will give them immediate reason to believe or not believe the information presented to them. Argument evaluation is an exercise that requires cognitive effort, especially when a complex claim is presented. Therefore, users will not go to the effort of thoroughly evaluating an argument if they can help it, unless there is high motivation to do so, for example when university level students are looking for material to support the arguments in their essays.

A second challenge to the use of critical thinking in this context is that online news or other online content does not always contain an argument. A piece of news on social media may just consist of evidence. In that case, critical thinking would require the evaluation of the credibility of the evidence.

A third possible challenge is that in an effort to mislead, the author of fake news may present a credible looking argument on the basis of fake evidence that cannot readily be verified. Hence, while good argumentation is often associated with good quality content, this may not always be the case. However, the cognitive effort of trying to second-guess the veracity of a well presented argument is so high that this is not a feasible task in everyday credibility assessment situations.

4.1   Addressing the Challenges

The above mentioned challenges could be addressed as follows.

The challenge of the cognitive effort of critical thinking may be improved by means of training. As motivated earlier in the paper, critical thinking forms part of information literacy and is an important 21st century user skill. Training and regular exercise in argument evaluation will make it become an easier habit, so that it can be more easily applied. A number of universities have compulsory first year information literacy courses, and this is where critical thinking can be introduced. The authors are involved in the teaching of critical thinking and problem solving to IS first year students. A study with a pre- and post- assessment exercise to determine the effect of the course, was done during the first half of 2019. A total of 154 students participated in the pre-assessment evaluation and 166 students in the post-assessment evaluation. The objective of the course was not to train students to identify fake news but to analyse and evaluate arguments and to cultivate a critical attitude towards reading and interpreting texts.

Findings from a Course on Critical Thinking. *Pre-assessment:* During the pre-assessment, students were asked several questions to test their critical thinking skills and one question to determine the credibility of a piece of information found online. The information presented to them [22] was part of fake news and presented an argument against the use of prison inmates to provide laughter in CBS sitcoms. In the pre-assessment only 16% of students could identify it as fake news. Students who identified it as fake news, applied most of the cognitive heuristics listed in Sect. 2.2. For example, a few students knew that The Onion is a website known for its satire articles (reputation heuristics). A handful of students applied the expectancy violation heuristics (*"It just doesn't make sense to me honestly"; "In today's day and age, such practice would never be accepted seeing as people get offended by even the most futile things"; "In today's age, laughter can be produced on computers or a group of laughs taken once and then played back whenever the producers feel"*). Consistency heuristics were also used (*"This is my first time hearing about it"*). Quite a number of students pointed out the lack of credible evidence.

Post-assessment: In the post-assessment questions were asked to assess critical thinking skills in general and the last question focused on fake news. Two different pieces of information were provided, one fake news and the other not (see Table 1).

Table 1. Article 1 and Article 2

	Title	Main idea	Source
Article 1 (fake)	Psychologists warn parents, don't allow your children to watch Peppa Pig	Argument that watching Peppa Pig can lead to copying the bad behavior of Peppa Pig (envious, arrogant, proud, disrespectful etc.)	Adapted from Healthy Fit website [23]
Article 2 (real)	Sheep registered as pupils in bid to save classes at French Alps primary school	A report of French parents registering sheep as pupils to increase pupil numbers since "National education is only about numbers"	SkyNews [24]

Both articles contained far-fetched claims. Article 1 [23] is an argument containing unsubstantiated claims, sweeping statements and emotional language. Article 2 [24] was sourced from a 'strange but true' SkyNews site. Article 2 is a report based on claims backed by credible evidence. Students were asked to determine which one is fake news and to provide an argument for their choice. The results are given in Table 2.

Table 2. Responses on question to identify articles as fake news

Question options	Response
Article 1 only is an example of fake news	36%
Article 2 only is an example of fake news	36%
Both articles are examples of fake news	20%
Neither of the articles are fake news	8%

Article 1. Students who correctly identified Article 1 as fake news (56% of students), typically mentioned the relative obscurity of the website and the absence of names of experts (*"there is said that experts were used in the article but none of the so called "experts" names or institutions were called to show the research"*). In other words, they applied the reputation heuristic. The following student applied the expectancy violation heuristic to (incorrectly) identify Article 1 as real news: (*"Article 1 can be seen as real news because the facts are not absurd"*). What was clearly noticeable was that in their assessment, most students used the critical thinking skills taught during the semester: they pointed out that the claims are not supported by evidence (*"they state that there are parents who burned?? the film but no numbers are provided it could be 2 out of 1000 but nothing is stated to prove this reason"*). They further mentioned the subjective nature of the article (*"The use of adjectives such as "arrogant", "disrespectful", "envious" makes the article sound extremely biased"*) as well as harsh language (*"The article is also very opinionated and the language used is quite harsh"*). They also think the reasoning to be faulty (*"And the argument is unstructured − "the "reasoning" doesn't lead up to a suitable conclusion."*)

Article 2. Students who incorrectly identified Article 2 as fake news (56% of students) in general used the expectancy violation heuristic. They could not imagine sheep to be school pupils. (*"Although article 2 comes from a reliable source the facts are absurd. [However] Article 1 can be seen as real news because the facts are not absurd"*).

Discussion. Article 1 is an argument whereas Article 2 a report. This explains why students were able to use critical thinking skills to evaluate article 1. In article 2, where no clear argument was present, critical thinking could only be applied to evaluate the evidence. Students found the evidence to be specific and traceable which contributed to its credibility. Only 36% of students were able to classify both articles correctly. However, the fact that only 8% said that neither articles were fake news, was encouraging, compared to the pre-assessment result where 84% of students were not able to recognize the supplied article as fake news. The post-assessment results indicate that most students had developed a critical attitude towards the supplied texts.

Recommendations on Combining Critical Thinking and Cognitive Heuristics. The use of critical thinking skills in identifying fake news can be complemented by applying the *consistency* heuristic [6] to seek for other online sources that carry similar evidence.

Lastly, since the assessment of credibility of online information has been found to be a socially interactive activity [6], the *endorsement* heuristic could be used to inquire on a social platform whether information is credible. For example, a hoax website can be visited to see if the information has been exposed by other users as a hoax.

5   Conclusion

This paper considered the work that has been done to date on the assessment of the credibility of online information. A concise overview was presented of some of the major contributions in this domain. These contributions were synthesized into a list of common attributes that represent the key characteristics of credibility assessment models. Following this, the elements of critical thinking was introduced. Suggestions were made as to how critical thinking could be used for credibility assessment. The challenges related to the use of critical thinking in practice were also considered, and suggestions were made to overcome these challenges. The outcomes of the effect of the teaching of critical thinking skills on IS students' ability to identify fake news, were discussed. Preliminary findings show that where fake news are presented as arguments, students use their skills of analysis and evaluation of arguments to identify fake news. Where fake news are reports, students look for quality evidence.

This paper contributes to the literature on the assessment of the credibility of online information. It argues that, and suggests how, the important 21st century skill of critical thinking can be applied to assess the credibility of online information. In doing so, this paper makes a contribution in terms of the responsible design, implementation and use of current day information and communications technology.

References

1. Metzger, M.J.: Making sense of credibility on the Web: models for evaluating online information and recommendations for future research. J. Am. Soc. Inf. Sci. Technol. **58**, 2078–2091 (2007)
2. Fritch, J.W., Cromwell, R.L.: Evaluating Internet resources: identity, affiliation, and cognitive authority in a networked world. J. Am. Soc. Inform. Sci. Technol. **52**, 499–507 (2001)
3. Choi, W., Stvilia, B.: Web credibility assessment: conceptualization, operationalization, variability, and models. J. Am. Soc. Inf. Sci. Technol. **66**, 2399–2414 (2015)
4. Metzger, M.J., Flanagin, A.J.: Psychological approaches to credibility assessment online. In: The Handbook of the Psychology of Communication Technology, vol. 32, pp. 445–466 (2015)
5. Sundar, S.S.: The MAIN model: a heuristic approach to understanding technology effects on credibility. In: Digital Media, Youth, and Credibility, vol. 73100 (2008)
6. Metzger, M.J., Flanagin, A.J., Medders, R.B.: Social and heuristic approaches to credibility evaluation online. J. Commun. **60**, 413–439 (2010)
7. Butterworth, J., Thwaites, G.: Thinking Skills: Critical Thinking and Problem Solving. Cambridge University Press, Cambridge (2013)
8. WEF: The World Economic Forum Future of Jobs Report 2018. WEF (2018)

9. Tseng, S., Fogg, B.: Credibility and computing technology. Commun. ACM **42**, 39–44 (1999)

10. Eysenbach, G., Köhler, C.: How do consumers search for and appraise health information on the world wide web? Qualitative study using focus groups, usability tests, and in-depth interviews. BMJ **324**, 573–577 (2002)

11. Fogg, B.J., Soohoo, C., Danielson, D.R., Marable, L., Stanford, J., Tauber, E.R.: How do users evaluate the credibility of Web sites?: A study with over 2,500 participants. In: Proceedings of the 2003 Conference on Designing for User Experiences, pp. 1–15. ACM, (Year)

12. Kreitner, R., Kinicki, A., Buelens, M.: Organizational behaviour. McGraw Hill, London (2002)

13. Simon, H.A.: Rational decision making in business organizations. Am. Econ. Rev. **69**, 493–513 (1979)

14. Fogg, B.J.: Prominence-interpretation theory: explaining how people assess credibility online. In: CHI 2003 extended abstracts on human factors in computing systems, pp. 722–723. Citeseer (2003)

15. Fogg, B.J.: Persuasive technology: using computers to change what we think and do. Ubiquity **2002**, 5 (2002)

16. Wathen, C.N., Burkell, J.: Believe it or not: factors influencing credibility on the Web. J. Am. Soc. Inf. Sci. Technol. **53**, 134–144 (2002)

17. The Foundation of Critical Thinking. https://www.criticalthinking.org/pages/our-conception-of-critical-thinking/411

18. Halpern, D.F.: Teaching critical thinking for transfer across domains: disposition, skills, structure training, and metacognitive monitoring. Am. Psychol. **53**, 449 (1998)

19. Tiruneh, D.T., Verburgh, A., Elen, J.: Effectiveness of critical thinking instruction in higher education: a systematic review of intervention studies. High. Educ. Stud. **4**, 1–17 (2014)

20. Booth, W.C., Colomb, G.G., Williams, J.M., Bizup, J., Fitzgerald, W.T.: The Craft of Research. University of Chicago Press, Chicago (2008)

21. Toulmin, S., Rieke, R., Janik, A.: An Introduction to Reasoning. Macmillan Publishing Co., Inc., Nova York (1979)

22. G/O Media Inc. https://entertainment.theonion.com/cbs-sitcoms-under-fire-for-using-prison-laughter-1833206200

23. Theme WordPress Par MH Themes. http://healthynfit.org/do-not-let-your-children-watch-peppa-pig-psychologists-warn-parents/

24. Sky UK. https://news.sky.com/story/sheep-registered-as-pupils-in-bid-to-save-classes-at-french-alps-primary-school-11714338

An Analysis of Problematic Media Use and Technology Use Addiction Scales – What Are They Actually Assessing?

Adrian Abendroth[2], Douglas A. Parry[3(✉)], Daniel B. le Roux[3], and Jana Gundlach[1,2]

[1] Weizenbaum Institute for the Networked Society,
Hardenbergstraße 32, 10623 Berlin, Germany
[2] Faculty of Economic and Social Sciences, Chair of Business Informatics,
esp. Social Media and Data Science, University of Potsdam,
Karl-Marx-Straße 67, 14482 Potsdam, Germany
{abendroth,janagundlach}@uni-potsdam.de
[3] Stellenbosch University, Stellenbosch, South Africa
{dougaparry,dbleroux}@sun.ac.za

Abstract. Increasingly, research attention is being afforded to various forms of problematic media use. Despite ongoing conceptual, theoretical, and empirical debates, a large number of retrospective self-report scales have been produced to ostensibly measure various classes of such behaviour. These scales are typically based on a variety of theoretical and diagnostic frameworks. Given current conceptual ambiguities, building on previous studies, we evaluated the dimensional structure of 50 scales targeting the assessment of supposedly problematic behaviours in relation to four technologies: Internet, smartphones, video games, and social network sites. We find that two dimensions ('compulsive use' and 'negative outcomes') account for over 50% of all scale-items analysed. With a median of five dimensions, on average, scales have considered fewer dimensions than various proposed diagnostic criteria and models. No relationships were found between the number of items in a scale and the number of dimensions, or the technology category and the dimensional structure. The findings indicate, firstly, that a majority of scales place an inordinate emphasis on some dimensions over others and, secondly, that despite differences in the items presented, at a dimensional level, there exists a high degree of similarity between scales. These findings highlight shortcomings in existing scales and underscore the need to develop more sophisticated conceptions and empirical tools to understand possible problematic interactions with various digital technologies.

Keywords: Technology addiction · Problematic media use · Self report scales · Systematic review

The original version of this chapter was revised: the missing acknowledgment has been added. The correction to this chapter is available at https://doi.org/10.1007/978-3-030-45002-1_40

© IFIP International Federation for Information Processing 2020, corrected publication 2021
Published by Springer Nature Switzerland AG 2020
M. Hattingh et al. (Eds.): I3E 2020, LNCS 12067, pp. 211–222, 2020.
https://doi.org/10.1007/978-3-030-45002-1_18

1   Introduction

Despite recent recognition of *gaming disorders* in the latest edition of the *World Health Organisation*'s *International Classification of Diseases* (ICD-11) diagnostic system, there remains much debate about the veracity and theoretical basis for a variety of supposed pathological forms of media use behaviour [9,12,13,17]. Described in relation to a range of technologies (e.g., games, smartphones, the Internet) such behaviours are typically framed as problematic and, in some cases, addictive [8,21]. Examples include: Internet gaming disorder, problematic media use, Internet addiction, and technology use addiction among many other labels. Despite the widespread adoption of various umbrella terms, some researchers have criticised the use of these labels, arguing that, in many cases, the behaviours and outcomes referred to are often particularly heterogeneous, influenced by a variety of personal characteristics, and potentially driven by distinct etiological mechanisms [13,15]. For the purposes of this paper, acknowledging the ambiguity, the term problematic media use will be adopted to refer, broadly, to various forms of pathological or addictive engagements with digital technologies.

Nomenclature aside, the notion of problematic media use is further beset by a variety of theoretical and empirical challenges. At a theoretical level, for many proposed technology-related addictions, a conceptual consensus has yet to be reached [9,13,17]. Furthermore, many competing theoretical frameworks have been proposed for the same supposed construct. Laconi et al. [15], for instance, note that Internet addiction is considered by some to be an impulse control disorder and, for others, a behavioural addiction, or even a combination of the two. Additionally, further contributing to the conceptual quagmire, studies have shown a number of comorbid psychopathologies (e.g., depression, attention-deficit hyperactivity disorder, or anxiety disorders) with various forms of problematic media use [14]. Finally, there exist criticisms that many definitions are pathologising everyday behaviour [10,11]. This is especially the case for gaming-related behaviours where researchers have struggled to differentiate between higher levels of engagement and truly problematic use [13].

In an early definition for technology-related addictions, Griffiths [7, p. 15] noted linkages with substance addictions and defined technological addiction as a class of behavioural addiction that involves some form of human-machine interaction. Subsequently, in considering the clinical diagnostic criteria of substance addiction, Griffiths [8] proposed a 'components' model of addiction consisting of six dimensions: salience, mood modification, tolerance, withdrawal symptoms, conflict, and relapse. He argues that such components are not only key for substance-related addictions but, from the perspective of a biopsychosocial framework of the individual, are also present in behavioural addictions.

Empirically, the assessment of problematic media use is hindered by unresolved theoretical and etiological foundations, as well as general challenges in assessing media use [6]. Adopting a tendency present in much of modern Social Psychology [4], researchers have relied on retrospective self-report questionnaires (or scales) to assess individuals' propensities for various behaviours, disorders, or other related outcomes. This has seen the proliferation of an inordinate number of scales designed to assess various forms of problematic media use, many of which target the same or substantially overlapping constructs (e.g., the Smartphone Addiction Scale, the Smartphone Application-Based Addiction Scale, and the Problematic Mobile Phone Use Questionnaire). Owing to the scale-development processes typically followed, such measures are normally reliable. Ellis et al. [6, p. 1], however, argue that, in general, 'less emphasis has been placed on establishing validity' when it comes to the assessment of problematic media use.

While weak correlations have been shown for a number of scales for both smartphone use in general and addiction in particular, and more objective assessments of media use [6], this does not necessarily imply that scales purporting to assess problematic behaviours are invalid or spurious – use is only one component of the behavioural and mental patterns targeted. Nevertheless, in a review of 45 tools designed to assess Internet addiction, Laconi et al. [15] found that only 26 had been evaluated for their psychometric properties. Additionally, supporting assertions that, for many scales, construct validity is low, outcomes of factor analyses differed substantially between studies for a number of instruments [15]. This lack of validation and conceptual clarity is problematic for both the interpretation of findings produced on the basis of these scales, as well as their usefulness as diagnostic screening tools in clinical settings.

Many scales are based on criteria for substance dependencies described in the *Diagnostic and statistical manual of mental disorders* (DSM-IV-TR) published by the *American Psychiatric Association* [2], or the component model described by Griffiths [8]. Adopting a grounded approach, Lortie and Guitton [16] examined the dimensional structure of 14 Internet addiction scales published between 1993 and 2011. All scale-items were pooled into seven categories on the basis of their conceptual similarity: compulsive use, negative outcomes, salience, withdrawal symptoms, mood regulation, escapism, and social comfort. For scales targeting Internet addiction, this analysis found that 'compulsive use' and 'negative outcomes' were the two most prominent dimensions assessed, followed by 'salience'. To compare their findings to existing norms Lortie and Guitton [16] considered how their seven dimensions related to the diagnostic criteria for substance dependence in the DSM-IV-TR [2] and ICD-10 [20]. With the exception of 'social comfort' the authors mapped each of their dimensions to the relevant diagnostic criteria, providing motivations for each assignment (a description of the dimensions is provided in Table 1).

1.1   The Present Study

Acknowledging the theoretical and empirical challenges in this domain, and the large number of sometimes overlapping measurement tools, the objective of the present study is to systematically review the dimensional structure of retrospective self-report scales used to assess problematic media use. In particular, the study aims to analyse the dimensional structure of the items presented in these scales in relation to prominent diagnostic criteria for substance dependence, models of behavioural addiction, and previous research in this regard, for four technologies frequently considered in the literature: the Internet, smartphones, video games, and social network sites (SNSs). Such a study will, firstly, aid in identifying shortcomings in existing scales, secondly, contribute a degree of conceptual clarity, thirdly, extend previous research focusing on only a single form of technology and, fourthly, provide a clearer foundation for improved assessment tools. To this end, building on the guidelines provided by Webster and Watson [18], a systematic review methodology was adopted to identify, collect, extract, and analyse a sample of such assessment tools.

2   Methodology

To systematically review scales supposedly assessing various forms of problematic media use we specified inclusion criteria and, subsequently, implemented a bibliographic database search strategy. Next, a set of a priori dimensions were specified and, in a series of iterative coding rounds, applied to each item presented in all relevant scales extracted from the included studies.

2.1   Inclusion Criteria

Research reports were included in the review if they (i) described the development of a self-report scale for the assessment of problematic use of at least one of the four technologies considered; (ii) were not merely a validation or language translation of an existing scale; (iii) were published in a peer-reviewed outlet; and (iv) were published between January 2007 and August 2018 (the time of data collection), with the exception of scales concerning Internet related addictions. For such scales an earlier start date of 1996 was selected due to the earlier development of relevant scales [21]. For the remainder, 2007 was selected as a cutoff due to the rise of smartphones and popular SNSs from this period [19].

2.2   Search Strategy

To locate a sample of eligible scales a systematic search of nine bibliographic databases was conducted over a three-week period in August 2018: *GoogleScholar, ScienceDirect, PubMed, EmeraldInsight, Wiley, SpringerLink, ACM, iEEE,* and *JSTOR.* To query these databases a search string was developed and, as required, tailored for each database. The following three clauses, each separated by an OR operator, were designed to target various keyword combinations:

- `(consequence* OR impact OR effect OR symptom*) AND`
  `(addiction OR habit* OR obsession OR problem* OR`
  `('problematic use')) AND VARIABLE`
- `(consequence* OR impact OR effect OR symptom*) AND`
  `(addiction OR habit* OR obsession OR problem* OR`
  `('problematic use')) AND (scale OR test OR inventory OR`
  `questionnaire) AND VARIABLE`

- (development OR creating) AND (consequence* OR impact OR
  effect OR symptom*) AND (addiction OR habit* OR obsession OR
  problem* OR ('problematic use')) AND (scale OR test OR
  inventory OR questionnaire) AND VARIABLE

For each of the four technology categories considered, the VARIABLE component in the three primary clauses was replaced with one of the following clauses:

- internet OR web OR www OR online
- smartphone OR cellphone OR 'cell-phone' OR phone OR mobile
- (social OR online) AND (network* OR social) AND (site* OR
  network* OR activity) OR sns OR 'social network sites' OR
  'online social networks'
- (online OR web OR internet OR www OR video) AND (play* OR
  gam*)

2.3   Data Extraction, Management, and Analysis Procedures

The bibliographic information and full-text records of each result were downloaded and stored in reference management software for subsequent extraction and analysis. All duplicated results were noted and removed, after which, titles and abstracts were reviewed against the inclusion criteria. For all eligible studies, the relevant scale-items were extracted to be coded. Noting the alignment between the seven dimensions provided by Lortie and Guitton [16] and the diagnostic criteria described in the ICD-10 [20] and DSM-IV-TR [2], as well as the component model described by Griffiths [8], these seven dimensions were generalised to refer more broadly to all media and used as deductive, a priori categories for the analysis. Table 1 provides a summary of the dimensions used. The description provided represents a synthesis of Lortie and Guitton [16]'s definitions, as well as their mapping of the dimensions to the diagnostic criteria in the ICD-10 [20] and DSM-IV-TR [2], the descriptions provided in the component model [8], and the updated criteria in the DSM-V [3]. Coding took place in three rounds and was performed by three independent coders. When a match was not possible, new dimensions were proposed. The process is described in Sect. 3.2.

3   Analysis and Results

We first describe the results of the systematic search procedure before outlining the process of mapping the extracted scale-items to relevant dimensions. Thereafter, we describe the dimensional structure of the included scales.

3.1   Search Results

The systematic search produced 4698 results. After removing duplicates ($n = 1676$), the remaining records ($n = 3022$) were examined for inclusion and ineligible records ($n = 2908$) were removed. After reviewing the full-texts of the

Table 1. A priori dimensions built on Lortie and Guitton [16]'s seven dimensions, with augmented descriptions.

Dimension	Description
Compulsive use	Tolerance and the inability to control, reduce, or stop the behavior
Negative outcomes	Deleterious consequences of the activity
Salience	The activity becomes the most important activity for an individual and they are cognitively preoccupied with it
Withdrawal symptoms	Unpleasant feeling states and/or physical effects which occur when the particular activity is discontinued or reduced
Mood regulation	The medium is used to regulate mood due to resulting subjective experiences
Escapism	The medium is used to escape from other problems or activities
Social comfort	A preference for social interaction through the medium

remaining reports ($n = 114$), 58 contained scales which met the inclusion criteria. During extraction eight scales were removed due to either missing or incomplete information, or because the scale described was a language translation of an existing scale. For scales with missing information, if available, supplementary material were reviewed and, if the necessary information was still missing, the original authors were contacted. This left a final sample of 50 scales. The inclusion process is summarised in Fig. 1, with a list of the included scales available in the online supplementary materials hosted on the Open Science Framework.[1]

The 50 scales included in the analysis were assigned to one of four categories –smartphones ($n = 20$; 40%), Internet ($n = 14$; 28%), video games ($n = 12$; 24%), SNSs ($n = 4$; 8%) – on the basis of their titles and original descriptions. From the 50 scales, 971 items were extracted, with the shortest scale consisting of six items, the largest 52 items, and a mean of 19.42 (SD $= 8.91$) items per scale. Given the discrepancy in the number of scales included for each technology, as well as the differences in scale length, there was a substantial difference in the number of items considered for each technology: Internet (316; 32.54%), smartphone (408; 42.02%), video games (197; 20.20%), and SNSs (50; 5.15%).

3.2   Mapping of Scale Items to Dimensions

Each of the 971 items were mapped to one of the a priori dimensions. If the mapping from item to dimension was unclear, the descriptions in the DSM-V and Griffiths [8] 'Component' Model were considered as guides. During the initial

---

[1] https://osf.io/84mve/?view_only=1ddad05f3fe84ebe8d3920be8a4467d6.

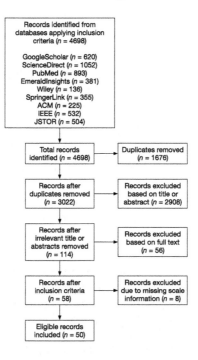

Fig. 1. Flowchart for inclusion.

round of coding, with the three independent coders in agreement for 828 of 971 items (85.27%), a strong level of agreement was achieved (Cohen's $\kappa = 0.813$).

During three iterative rounds of review new codes were developed to account for items not captured by the seven a priori dimensions. These dimensions and their descriptions are provided in Table 2. With the exception of *cognitive absorption*, these dimensions were primarily tangential to problematic media use. Agarwal and Karahanna [1, p. 655] define cognitive absorption to involve: (i) temporal resolution in which passage of time is not registered; (ii) total immersion in the activity where other basic needs are ignored; (iii) intensified pleasure in doing the activity; (iv) the user's perception of being responsible for the interaction; and (v) curiosity that responds to sensory and cognitive sensitivities. Following the development of these dimensions, items were re-categorised and moved to newly specified dimensions if deemed appropriate by all three coders.

3.3 The Dimensional Structure of the Scales

Table 3 provides a summary of the dimensional structure of the scales for each of the four technologies considered. Columns 2–5 present the number of items for a given dimension for each technology category, with the proportion of items in each category mapped to a given dimension represented in parentheses. The 'total' column represents the total for a given dimension across all technologies,

Table 2. Additional a posteriori dimensions

Dimension	Description
Future use intention	Perceptions of future use
Utility loss	Perceptions of the degree to which a technology's absence would impact the ability to function
Use description	Only descriptive of various forms of media use
Cognitive absorption	A "state of deep involvement with software" [1, p. 655]
Irrelevant	Irrelevant to problematic, pathological, or addictive media use

while the final column represents the mean proportion for each dimension across the four technnologies. A majority of the items ($n = 921$, 94.85%) were mapped to the seven dimensions proposed by Lortie and Guitton [16], with the remaining 50 items mapped to new categories proposed. The three most used dimensions were compulsive use (n = 287), followed by negative outcomes ($n = 279$) and withdrawal symptoms (n = 126). Together, compulsive use and negative outcomes account for 58.29% of all items analysed. Of Lortie and Guitton [16]'s dimensions, social comfort appeared the least. Despite this, across the technologies considered, escapism demonstrated the lowest mean proportion of the a priori dimensions at $M = 4.25$ ($SD = 4.36$). Figure 2 depicts the distribution of the dimensions across the four technologies considered.

Table 3. Summary of the dimensional structure for each technology category.

Dimension	INT n (%)	SMP n (%)	SNS n (%)	GAM n (%)	Total n	Proportion M (SD)
Compulsive use	91 (28.80)	123 (30.15)	9 (18.00)	64 (32.49)	287	27.36 (6.42)
Negative outcomes	85 (26.90)	130 (31.86)	12 (24.00)	52 (26.40)	279	27.29 (3.30)
Withdrawal symptoms	28 (8.86)	69 (16.91)	9 (18.00)	20 (10.15)	126	13.48 (4.64)
Salience	42 (13.29)	26 (6.37)	3 (6.00)	25 (12.69)	96	9.59 (3.94)
Mood regulation	20 (6.33)	22 (5.39)	7 (14.00)	8 (4.06)	57	7.45 (4.47)
Escapism	25 (7.91)	4 (0.98)	0 (0.00)	16 (8.12)	45	4.25 (4.36)
Social comfort	16 (5.07)	15 (3.68)	6 (12.00)	0 (0.00)	37	5.19 (5.05)
Cognitive absorption	2 (0.63)	5 (1.23)	3 (6.00)	6 (3.05)	16	2.73 (2.41)
Use description	7 (2.22)	0 (0.00)	1 (2.00)	5 (2.54)	13	1.69 (1.15)
Utility loss	0 (0.00)	13 (3.19)	0 (0.00)	0 (0.00)	13	0.80 (1.60)
Irrelevant	0 (0.00)	0 (0.00)	0 (0.00)	1 (0.51)	1	0.13 (0.26)
Future use intention	0 (0.00)	1 (0.25)	0 (0.00)	0 (0.00)	1	0.06 (0.13)
Total per area n (%)	316 (100)	408 (100)	50 (100)	197 (100)	971	

Note: INT = the Internet, SMP = smartphones, SNSs = social networking sites, and GAM = video games.

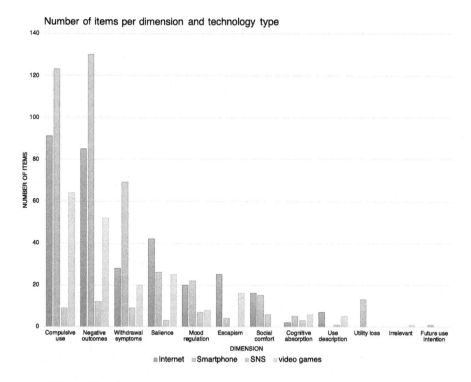

Fig. 2. Number and distribution of dimensions across technology types

Across all 50 scales, a mean of 5.48 ($SD = 1.36$) dimensions were considered per scale (Median = 5). No statistically significant correlation between the number of items and the number of dimensions assessed was found ($r = 0.48$, $p = 0.63$). No single dimension was used in all scales considered. Two dimensions (compulsive use and negative outcomes) appeared in 49 of the 50 scales. Both dimensions did not appear in any of the items in the *Mobile Phone Addiction Craving Scale* (MPACS) [5] – all items in this scale were mapped to withdrawal symptoms. Following these two dimensions, 47 and 42 scales included items assessing withdrawal symptoms and salience, respectively. In contrast, the three remaining a priori dimensions –escapism, mood regulation, and social comfort– were only included in 28, 26, and 11 scales respectively. Of the newly created categories, only cognitive absorption appeared with any frequency, being used in nine different scales (through 16 items). A Chi-square test of independence was calculated comparing the proportional frequency of each of the dimensions for each technology category. Owing to the relatively small number of observations for SNSs, this analysis was only conducted for the three remaining technology categories (the Internet, smartphones, and video gaming). The analysis revealed no statistically significant interaction between the technology category and the proportional distribution of dimensions ($\chi^2(22) = 29.82$, $p = 0.123$).

4   Discussion

Despite a growing amount of research into various forms of media behaviour and the effects thereof, there remains much uncertainty and debate about the existence and possible nature of many proposed pathological technology-interactions. Given the conceptual ambiguity and disputed existence of many frequently cited phenomena—Internet gaming disorder, Internet addiction for instance—there exists a need for more sophisticated and nuanced understandings of the theoretical and etiological nature of these 'disorders'. In particular, it is necessary to understand the factors distinguishing various proposed disorders, or whether they are merely manifestations of other underlying factors, pathologies, or individual characteristics. This study found that, for just four technologies, there exist at least 50 unique assessment scales, many of which substantially overlap. We question the need for such a large number of scales.

To guide our analysis we used Lortie and Guitton [16]'s seven dimensions, augmented with the component model and recent diagnostic criteria for substance dependence, as a priori categories. Five additional categories were produced in three rounds of iterative coding. With the exception of cognitive absorption, these new dimensions were primarily descriptive and labeled items assessing peripheral, and sometimes irrelevant, aspects of media use. Given Agarwal and Karahanna [1]'s definition of cognitive absorption, while conceptual overlaps exist with elements of salience and mood-regulation, this dimension potentially provides a further feature differentiating behavioural addictions involving technology from other more general notions of behavioural addiction.

Across all 50 scales two dimensions –compulsive use and negative outcomes– were found to account for over 50% of all items. Moreover, with the exception of SNSs, where 'withdrawal symptoms' was similarly frequent, these dimensions accounted for a majority of items presented. For all technology categories, while the absolute number of items and the specific questions posed differed, the overall dimensional structure was found to be particularly comparable. The prominence of compulsive use and negative outcomes supports Lortie and Guitton [16] who found a similar outcome when analysing 14 scales produced prior to 2012 only targeting Internet-related addiction. For compulsive use, a possible explanation, in both cases, rests on the inclusion of tolerance, considered by some to be a separate dimension, in its description. Nevertheless, given the imbalance in dimensions considered, future studies need to consider, firstly, how representative these scales are of the supposed dimensions of technology-related behavioural addictions and, secondly, whether under-representation of particular dimensions is a valid concern. Furthermore, researchers intending to use an existing scale should, in addition to considering the scale description, account for the dimensional structure of items when determining the fit between a scale and their research questions.

The present study should be considered as only a single point of reference for further research into the assessment of pathological interactions with digital technology. Despite the systematic approach adopted, there are, nonetheless, a number of limitations which bare acknowledgement. First, while the search string was designed to enable the collection of a comprehensive sample, there remains the possibility that relevant scales could have been inadvertently omitted. Furthermore, while four distinct technology categories were used, it is acknowledged that, in many cases it is not possible to distinguish between them. For instance, many uses of a smartphone involve engagement with the Internet or various SNSs. This is especially the case for scales targeting Internet-related behaviours. While an imperfect solution, scales were allocated to a category on the basis of their titles and original descriptions. Finally, while the a priori dimensions used were based on related previous research [16], it is acknowledged that, although general characteristics of behavioural addictions are likely to exist [8], dimensions pertinent to one domain might not be well-suited to other domains (e.g., Internet vs. gaming-related behaviour). Similarly, in using Lortie and Guitton [16]'s dimensions the 'tolerance' dimension from the component model [8] was not included as an explicit dimension itself. Rather, as with Lortie and Guitton [16], it was considered to be an element of 'compulsive use'.

5   Conclusion

Building on previous analyses [16] focusing on only a single technology, this study aimed to systematically review the dimensional nature of self-report scales used to assess various forms of problematic media use in relation to prominent models and diagnostic criteria for substance dependence and behavioural addiction [8,16] for four technologies: Internet, smartphones, video games and SNSs. Lortie and Guitton [16, p. 108] note that the dimensional structure of an assessment questionnaire is inherently linked to the researchers' conception of the phenomenon of interest. Consequently, the findings of the study provide a lens through which to interpret current conceptions of purportedly pathological interactions with technology. Overwhelmingly, a majority of scale-items concern compulsive use, negative outcomes associated with use and, to a lesser extent, withdrawal symptoms. Therefore, whether intentional or not, these dimensions are seen by researchers to be central to various conceptions of problematic use. Building on this study, efforts should be made to establish conceptual clarity about what constitutes problematic or addictive technology interactions and, on this basis, curb the development of novel scales, consolidate existing items, and conduct more extensive validations of current scales. Only with more sophisticated and theoretically-sound measurement tools will we be able to produce the empirical evidence necessary for truly understanding the existence and possible nature of problematic engagements with various digital technologies.

Acknowledgements. This work has partially been funded by the Federal Ministry of Education and Research of Germany (BMBF) under grant no. 16DII116 ("Deutsches Internet-Institut").

References

1. Agarwal, R., Karahanna, E.: Time flies when you're having fun: cognitive absorption and beliefs about information technology usage. MIS Q. **24**, 665–694 (2000)

2. American Psychiatric Association: Diagnostic and Statistical Manual of Mental Disorders, 4th edn. American Psychiatric Association, Washington, DC (2000). Text rev. edn

3. American Psychiatric Association: Diagnostic and Statistical Manual of Mental Disorders (DSM-5). American Psychiatric Publisher, Philadelphia (2013)

4. Baumeister, R.F., Vohs, K.D., Funder, D.C.: Psychology as the science of self-reports and finger movements: whatever happened to actual behavior? Perspect. Psychol. Sci. **2**(4), 396–403 (2007)

5. De-Sola, J., Talledo, H., Rubio, G., de Fonseca, F.R.: Development of a mobile phone addiction craving scale and its validation in a Spanish adult population. Front. Psychiatry **8**, 90 (2017)

6. Ellis, D.A., Davidson, B.I., Shaw, H., Geyer, K.: Do smartphone usage scales predict behavior? Int. J. Hum.-Comput. Stud. **130**, 86–92 (2019)

7. Griffiths, M.: Technological addictions. In: Clinical Psychology Forum, pp. 14–14. Division of Clinical Psychology of the British Psychological Society (1995)

8. Griffiths, M.: A 'components' model of addiction within a biopsychosocial framework. J. Subst. Use **10**(4), 191–197 (2005)

9. Griffiths, M.D., et al.: Working towards an international consensus on criteria for assessing internet gaming disorder: a critical commentary on Petry et al. (2014). Addiction **111**(1), 167–175 (2016)

10. Kardefelt-Winther, D.: Meeting the unique challenges of assessing internet gaming disorder. Addiction **109**(9), 1568–1570 (2014)

11. Kardefelt-Winther, D.: A critical account of DSM-5 criteria for internet gaming disorder. Addict. Res. Theory **23**(2), 93–98 (2015)

12. Kuss, D., Griffiths, M., Karila, L., Billieux, J.: Internet addiction: a systematic review of epidemiological research for the last decade. Curr. Pharm. Des. **20**(25), 4026–4052 (2014)

13. Kuss, D.J., Griffiths, M.D., Pontes, H.M.: Chaos and confusion in DSM-5 diagnosis of internet gaming disorder: issues, concerns, and recommendations for clarity in the field. J. Behav. Addict. **6**(2), 103–109 (2017)

14. Kuss, D.J., Lopez-Fernandez, O.: Internet addiction and problematic internet use: a systematic review of clinical research. World J. Psychiatry **6**(1), 143 (2016)

15. Laconi, S., Rodgers, R.F., Chabrol, H.: The measurement of internet addiction: a critical review of existing scales and their psychometric properties. Comput. Hum. Behav. **41**, 190–202 (2014)

16. Lortie, C.L., Guitton, M.J.: Internet addiction assessment tools: dimensional structure and methodological status. Addiction **108**(7), 1207–1216 (2013)

17. Petry, N.M., et al.: An international consensus for assessing internet gaming disorder using the new DSM-5 approach. Addiction **109**(9), 1399–1406 (2014)

18. Webster, J., Watson, R.T.: Analyzing the past to prepare for the future: writing a literature review. MIS Q. **26**, 22–23 (2002)

19. West, J., Mace, M.: Browsing as the killer app: explaining the rapid success of Apple's iPhone. Telecommun. Policy **34**(5–6), 270–286 (2010)

20. World Health Organization: The ICD-10 Classification of Mental and Behavioural Disorders: Clinical Descriptions and Diagnostic Guidelines. World Health Organization, Geneva (1992)

21. Young, K.S.: Psychology of computer use: XL. Addictive use of the internet: a case that breaks the stereotype. Psychol. Rep. **79**(3), 899–902 (1996)

A Systematic Review on Fake News Themes Reported in Literature

Marlie Celliers[(✉)] and Marie Hattingh

Department of Informatics, University of Pretoria, Pretoria, South Africa
marliecelliers22@gmail.com, marie.hattingh@up.ac.za

Abstract. In this systematic literature review, a study of the factors involved in the spreading of fake news, have been provided. In this review, the root causes of the spreading of fake news are identified to reduce the encouraging of such false information. To combat the spreading of fake news on social media, the reasons behind the spreading of fake news must first be identified. Therefore, this literature review takes an early initiative to identify the possible reasons behind the spreading of fake news. The purpose of this literature review is to identify why individuals tend to share false information and to possibly help in detecting fake news before it spreads.

Keywords: Fake news · Misinformation · Social media · Systematic review

1 Introduction

The increase in use of social media exposes users to misleading information, satire and fake advertisements [3]. Fake news or misinformation is defined as fabricated information presented as the truth [6]. It is the publication of known false information and sharing it amongst individuals [7]. It is the intentional publishing of misleading information and can be verified as false through fact-checking [2]. Social media platforms allow individuals to fast share information with only a click of a single share button [4]. In previous studies the effect of the spreading and exposure to misleading information have been investigated [6]. Some studies determined that everyone has problems with identifying fake news, not just users of a certain age, gender or education [11]. The literacy and education of fake news is essential in the combating of the spreading of false information [8].

This review identify and discuss the factors involved in the sharing and spreading of fake news. The outcome of this review should be to equip users with the abilities to detect and recognise misinformation and also to cultivate a desire to stop the spreading of false information [5].

M. Hattingh et al. (Eds.): I3E 2020, LNCS 12067, pp. 223–234, 2020.
https://doi.org/10.1007/978-3-030-45002-1_19

2 Literature Background

2.1 The Impact of Fake News

The internet is mainly driven by advertising [13]. Websites with sensational headlines are very popular, which leads to advertising companies capitalising on the high traffic to the site [13]. It was subsequently discovered that the creators of fake news websites and information could make money through automated advertising that rewards high traffic to their websites [13]. The question remains how misinformation would then influence the public. The spreading of misinformation can cause confusion and unnecessary stress among the public [10]. Fake news that is purposely created to mislead and to cause harm to the public is referred to as digital disinformation [17]. Disinformation has the potential to cause issues, within minutes, for millions of people [10]. Disinformation has been known to disrupt election processes, create unease, disputes and hostility among the public [17].

2.2 Fake News and Social Media

These days, the internet have become a vital part of our daily lives [2]. Traditional methods of acquiring information have nearly vanished to pave the way for social media platforms [2]. It was reported in 2017 that Facebook was the largest social media platform, hosting more 1.9 million users world-wide [18]. The role of Facebook in the spreading of fake news possibly has the biggest impact from all the social media platforms [14]. It was reported that 44% of worldwide users get their news from Facebook [14]. 23% of Facebook users have indicated that they have shared false information, either knowingly or not [19]. The spreading of fake news is fuelled by social media platforms and it is happening at an alarming pace [14].

3 Research Method

In this systematic literature review, a qualitative methodology was followed. A thematic approach was implemented to determine the factors and sub-factors that contribute to the sharing and spreading of fake news. The study employed the following search terms: ("Fake News" (NEAR/2) "Social Media") AND (defin* OR Factors OR Tools) ("Misinformation" (NEAR/2) "Social Media") AND (defin* OR Factors OR Tools).

In this literature review, only published journal articles between 2016 and 2019 were considered. This review is not be specific to certain sectors i.e. the health sector or the tourism sector but rather consider on all elements that contribute to individuals sharing false information.

Studies that are not in English have been excluded in this review. Only studies that are related to the research question have been taken into account. This article does not discuss the detection of fake news but rather the reasons behind the spreading of fake news.

The analysis consisted of four phases: identification phase; screening phase; eligibility phase and inclusion phase. When conducting this literature review, the selection of articles were based on three main criteria: firstly, to search for and select articles containing the search terms identified above; secondly, selection based on the title and abstract of the article and finally selection based on the content of the article.

In the identification phase of this literature review, Science Direct and Emerald Insight were selected to perform the literature review. Science Direct offered a total of 177 journal articles matching the search terms. Emerald Insight generated 121 journal articles that matched the search terms. Continuing with the identification phase, the various articles were then combined and the duplicates were removed. In the screening phase of the source selection, all the article titles were carefully screened and a few articles were excluded as unconvincing. The eligibility of the abstract in the remaining articles were consulted and some articles were excluded based on the possible content of the article. The rest of the articles were further thoroughly examined to determine if they were valuable and valid to this research paper. Upon further evaluation, these final remaining articles were further studied to make a final source selection.

4   Analysis of Findings

In this paper, possible reasons for and factors contributing to the sharing and spreading of false information are discussed. The reasons are categorized under various factors highlighted in the journal articles used to answer the research question. These factors include: social factors, cognitive factors, political factors, financial factors and malicious factors.

While conducting the literature review, 22 articles highlighted the social factors; 13 articles discussed the role that cognitive factors have in contributing to the sharing and spreading of fake news; 13 articles highlighted the role of political factors; nine articles discussed how financial gain could convince a social media users to spread false information and 13 articles debated malicious factors and the effect that malicious factors have on the sharing and spreading of false information.

Figure 1 gives a breakdown of all 38 articles containing references to all the sub-categories listed above. It was clearly evident that the two single sub-categories of social comparison and hate propaganda were the most debated. With the sub-factor, knowledge and education, closely behind. A high percentage of the articles, 34.2% (13 of 38), refer to the effects of social comparison on the spreading of false information; followed by 26.3% (10 of 38) of the articles referencing hate propaganda. Knowledge and education was measured at 23.6% (9 of 38).

Furthermore, it was concluded that the majority of the 38 articles highlighted a combination of the social factors i.e. conformity and peer influence, social comparison and satire and humorous fakes, which measures at 60.5% (23 of 38). Where the combination of the cognitive factors e.g. knowledge and education and ignorance measured at 39.4% (15 of 38). Political factors and sub-factors e.g. political clickbaits and political bots/cyborgs, were discussed in 34.2% (13 of 38) of the articles. In addition, financial factors e.g. advertising and financial clickbaits were referenced in 23.6% (9 of 38) of the journal articles. And lastly, malicious factors e.g. malicious bots and cyborgs, hate propaganda and malicious clickbaits measured at 34.2% (13 of 38).

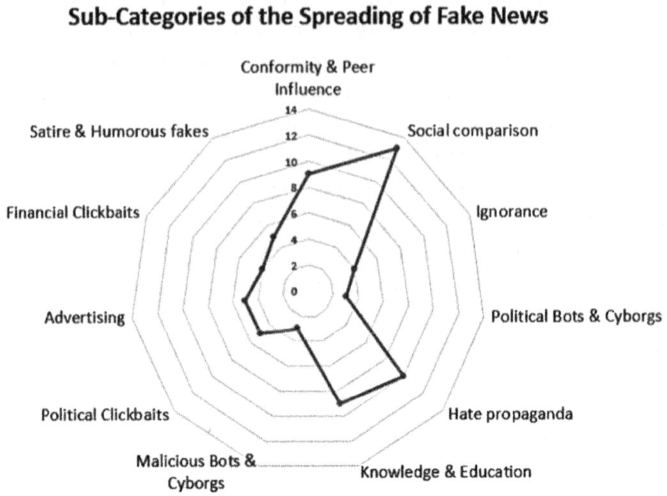

Fig. 1. Articles discussing the sub-categories of the spreading of fake news

5 Discussion

5.1 Social Factors

Fake news stories are being promoted on social media platforms to deceive the public for ideological gain [20]. In various articles it was stated that social media users are more likely to seek information from people who are more like-minded or congruent with their own opinions and attitudes [21, 22].

Conformity and Peer Influence. It is the need of an individual to match his or her behaviour to a specific social group [9]. The desire that social media users have to enhance themselves on social media platforms could blur the lines between real information and false information [12]. Consequently, social media users will share information to gain social approval and to build their image [12]. Recent studies have shown that certain false information can be strengthened if it belongs to the individuals in the same social environment [23]. The real power lies with those certain individuals who are more vocal or influential [24]. The need for social media users to endorse information or a message can be driven by the perception the social media user has about the messenger [25]. These messengers or *"influencers"* can be anyone ranging from celebrities to companies [24].

Studies show that messages on social media platforms, like Twitter, gain amplification because the message or information is associated with certain users or influencers [25]. Information exchanging depends on the ratings or the influential users associated with the information [23]. Social media users' influence among peers enhance the impact and spreading of all types of information [25]. These social media influencers have the ability to rapidly spread information to numerous social media users [26]. The level of influence these influencers have, can amplify the impact of the information [27].

The lack of related information in online communities could lead to individuals sharing the information based on the opinions and behaviours of others [23]. Some studies show that social media users will seek out or share information that reaffirms their beliefs or attitudes [18].

Social Comparison. The whole driving force of the social media sphere is to post and share information [1]. Social comparison can be defined as certain members within the same social environment who share the same beliefs and opinions [12]. When they are unable to evaluate certain information on their own, they adapt to compare themselves to other members, within the same environment, with the same beliefs and opinions [12]. The nature of social media allows social media users to spread information in real-time [28]. Social media users generate interactions on social media platforms to gain "*followers*" and to get "*likes*" which lead to an increasing amount of fake news web-sites and accounts [10]. One of the biggest problems faced in the fake news dilemma, is that social media users' newsfeed on social media platforms, like Facebook, will generally be populated with the user's likes and beliefs, providing a breeding ground for users with like-minded beliefs to spread false information among each other [16]. Social media users like to pursue information from other members in their social media environment whose beliefs and opinions are most compatible with their own [21].

Social media algorithms designed to make suggestions or filter information based on the social media users' preferences [29]. The "*like*" button on social media platforms, e.g. Facebook, becomes a measuring tool for the quality of information, which could make social media users more willing to share the information if the information has received multiple likes [30]. Social media users' belief in certain information depends on the number of postings or "*re-Tweets*" by other social media users who are involved in their social media sphere [23]. One article mentioned that the false news spreading process can be related to the patterns of the distribution of news among social media users [31]. The more a certain piece of information is shared and passed along the more power it gains [6].

This "*endorsing*" behaviour results in the spreading of misleading information [25]. It is also known as the "*herding*" behaviour and is common among social media where individuals review and comment on certain items [23]. It is also referred to as the "*bandwagon effect*" where individuals blindly concentrate on certain information based on perceived trends [32]. The only thing that matters is that the information falls in line with what the social media user wants to hear and believe [16]. Many studies also refer to it as the "*filter bubble effect*" where social media users use social media platforms to suggest or convince other social media users of their cause [33]. Communities form as a result of these filter bubbles where social media users cut themselves off from any other individual that might not share the same beliefs or opinions [33]. It was found that social media users tend to read news or information that are ideologically similar to their own ideologies [29].

Satire and Humorous Fakes. Some of the content on social media are designed to amuse users and are made to deceive people into thinking that it is real news [2]. Satire is referred to as criticising or mocking ideas or opinions of people in an entertaining or comical way [7, 29]. These satire articles consist of jokes or forms of sarcasm that can be written by everyday social media users [10]. Most satire articles are designed to mislead and instruct certain individuals [13]. Some social media users will be convinced that it is true information and will thus share the information [2].

5.2   Cognitive Factors

The study of cognition is the ability of an individual to make sense of certain topics or information by executing a process of reasoning and understanding [34]. It is the ability of an individual to understand thought and execute valid reasoning and understanding of concept [34]. With an increasing amount of information being shared across social media platforms it can be challenging for social media users to determine which of the information is closest to the original source [22]. The issue of individuals not having the ability to distinguish between real and fake news have been raised in many articles [10]. Users of social media tend to not investigate the information they are reading or sharing [2]. This can therefore lead to the rapid sharing and spreading of any unchecked information across social media platforms [2].

Knowledge and Education. An important aspect of surfing social media is the ability of the social media users to distinguish between what is real and what is fake [10]. The trustworthiness of a certain article is based on how successful the exchange of the articles are [12]. The more successful the exchange, the more likely social media users will share the information [12]. Social media users make supposedly reasonable justifications to determine the authenticity of the information provided [35].

People creating fake news websites and writing false information exploit the non-intellectual characteristics of some people [13]. For social media users to determine if the information they received is true or false, expert judgement of content is needed [1].

In a recent study, it was found that many social media users judge the credibility of certain information based on detail and presentation, rather than the source [11]. Some individuals determine the trustworthiness of information provided to them through social media on how much detail and content it contains [11].

It is believed that people are unable to construe information when the information given to them, are conflicting with their existing knowledge base [34]. Most social media users lack the related information to make a thorough evaluation of the particular news source [23]. For many years, companies and people have been creating fake news articles to capitalize on the non-intellectual characteristics of certain individuals [13].

Ignorance. A driving force of the spreading of false information is that social media users undiscerningly forward false information [5] A reason for the spreading of false information in many cases are inattentive individuals who do not realise that some websites mimic real websites [2]. These false websites are designed to look like the real website but in essence only contain false information. Social media users tend to share information containing a provocative headline, without investigating the facts and sources [16]. The absence of fact-checking by social media users on social media platforms, increases the spreading of false information [2]. Social media users tend to share information without verifying the source or the reliability of the content [2]. Information found on social media platforms, like Twitter, are sometimes not even read before they are being spread among users, without any investigation into the source of the information [16]. As mentioned earlier in Sect. 5.1, the bandwagon effect causes individuals to share information without making valued judgement [32].

5.3   Political Factors

The spreading of false political information have increased due to the emergence of streamline media environments [22]. There has been a considerable amount of research done on the influence of fake news on the political environment [14, 18]. By creating false political statements, voters can be convinced or persuaded to change their opinions [3]. Critics reported that in the national election in the UK (regarding the nation's withdrawal out of the EU) and the 2016 presidential election in the US, a number of false information was shared on social media platforms that have influenced the outcome of the results [8, 22]. Social media platforms, like Facebook, came under fire in the 2016 US presidential election, when fake news stories from unchecked sources were spread among many users [10]. The spreading of such fake news have the sole purpose of changing the public's opinion [8, 29].

Various techniques can be used to change the public's opinion. These techniques include repeatedly retweeting or sharing messages often with the use of bots or cyborgs [15]. It also includes misleading hyperlinks that lures the social media user to more false information [15].

Political Clickbaits. Clickbaits are defined as sources that provide information but use misleading and sensational headiness to attract individuals [16]. In the 2016 US presidential elections it was apparent that clickbaits were used to shape peoples' opinions [4]. In a recent study it was found that 43% (13 of 30) false news stories were shared on social media platforms, like Twitter, with links to non-credible news websites [22].

Webpages are purposely created to resemble real webpages for political gain [3]. News sources with URLs similar to the real website URL have been known to spread political fake news pieces, which could influence the opinion of the public [10].

Political Bots/Cyborgs. A social media users' content online is managed by algorithms to reflect his or her prior choices [22]. Algorithms designed to fabricate reports are one of the main causes of the spreading of false information [33]. In recent years, the rapid growth of fake news have led to the belief that cyborgs and bots are used to increase the spreading of misinformation on social media [22]. In the 2016 US election social bots were used to lead social media users to fake news websites to influence their opinions on the candidates [3]. Hundreds of bots were created in the 2016 US presidential elections to lure people to websites with false information [3] These social bots can spread information through social media platforms and participate in online social communities [3].

5.4   Financial Factors

One of the biggest problems with fake news is that it allows the writers to receive monetary incentives [13]. Misleading information and stories are promoted on social media platforms to deceive social media users for financial gain [20, 29].

One of the main goals of fake news accounts are to generate traffic to their specific website [10]. Articles with attractive headlines lure social media users to share false information thousands of times [2]. Many companies use social media as a platform to advertise their products or to promote their products [26].

Advertising. People earn money through clicks and views [36]. The more times the link is clicked the more advertising money is generated [16]. Every click corresponds to advertising revenue for the content creator [16]. The more traffic companies or social media users get to their fake news page, the more profit through advertising can be earned [10]. The only way to prevent financial gain for the content creator is inaction [16]. Most advertising companies are more interested in how many social media users will be exposed to their product rather than the possible false information displayed on the page where their advertisement is displayed [13]. Websites today are not restricted on the content displayed to the public, as long as they attract users [13]. This explains how false information is monetized, providing monetary value for writers to display sensational false information [13].

Financial Clickbaits. Clickbaits are used to lure individuals to other websites or articles for financial gain [2]. One of the main reasons for falsifying information is to earn money through clicks and views [36]. Writers focus on sensational headlines rather than truthful information [13]. Appeal rather than truthfulness drives information [5]. These attractive headlines deceive individuals into sharing certain false information [2].

Clickbaits are purposely implemented to misguide or redirect social media users to increase the views and web traffic of certain websites for online advertising earnings [4]. Social media users end up spending only a short time on these websites [4]. Clickbaits have been indicated as one of the main reasons behind the spreading of false information [2].

5.5   Malicious Factors

Studies debating the trustworthiness of information and veracity analytics of online content have increased recently due to the rise in fake news stories [37]. Social media has become a useful way for individuals to share information and opinions about various topics [3]. Unfortunately, many users share information with malicious intent [3]. Malicious users, also referred to as "trolls", often engage in online communication to manipulate other social media users and to spread rumours [37].

Malicious websites are specifically created for the spreading of fake news [2]. Malicious entities use false information to disrupt daily activities like the health–sector environment, the stock markets or even the opinions people have on certain products [3]. Some online fake news stories are purposely designed to target victims [3]. Websites, like Reddit, have been known as platforms where users can get exposed to bullying [38]. Some individuals have been known to use the social media platform to cause confusion and fear among others [39].

Malicious Bots/Cyborgs. Malicious users, with the help of bots, target absent-minded individuals who do not check the article facts or source before sharing it on social media [2]. These AI powered bots are designed to mimic human behaviour and characteristics, and are used to corrupt online conversations with unwanted and misleading advertisements [38]. In recent studies it was found that social bots are being created to distribute malware and slander to damage an individual's beliefs and trust [3].

Hate Propaganda. Many argue that the sharing of false information fuel vindictive behaviour among social media users [12]. Some fake news websites or pages are specifically designed to harm a certain user's reputation [5, 10]. Social media influencers influence users' emotional and health outcomes [12]. Fake news creators specifically target users with false information [3]. This false information is specifically designed to deceive and manipulate social media users [21]. Fake news stories like this, intend to mislead the public and generate false beliefs [21]. In some cases, hackers have been known to send out fake requests to social media users to gain access to their personal information [39]. The spreading of hoax has also become a problem on social media. The goal of hoaxes is to manipulate the opinion of the public and to maximize public attention [35]. Social spammers have also become more popular over the last few years with the goal to launch different kinds of attacks on social media users, for example spreading viruses or phishing [2]. Fake reviews have also been known to disrupt the online community through writing reviews that typically aim to direct people away from a certain product or person [2]. Another method used by various malicious users, is to purchase fake followers to spread harmful malware more swiftly [26].

Malicious Clickbaits. It was reported on in a previous article that employees in a certain company clicked on a link, disguised as important information, where they provide sensitive and important information to perpetrators [4]. Malicious users intending to spread malware and phishing hide behind a fake account to further increase their activities [26]. Clickbaits in some cases are designed to disrupt interactions or to lure individuals into arguing in disturbed online interactions or communications [37]. These clickbaits have also been known to include malicious code as part of the webpage [4]. This will cause the social media users to download malware onto their device once they select the link [4].

6 Conclusion

Various articles were used to identify and study the factors and reasons involved in the sharing and spreading of misinformation on social media. Upon retrieving multiple reasons for the spreading of false information, they were categorized into main factors and sub-factors. These factors included social factors, cognitive factors, political factors, financial factors and malicious factors. Considering the rapidly expanding social media environment, it was found that especially social factors have a very significant influence in the sharing of fake news on social media platforms. Its sub-factors of conformity and peer-influence; social comparison and satire and humorous fakes have great influence when deciding to share false information. Secondly, it was concluded that malicious factors like hate propaganda also fuel the sharing of false information with the possibility to financially gain or to do harm.

In addition, it was concluded from this review that knowledge and education plays a very important role in the sharing of false information, where social media users sometimes lack the logic, reasoning and understanding of certain information. It was also evident that social media users may sometimes be ignorant and indifferent when sharing and spreading information. Fact-checking resources are available but the existence thereof is fairly unknown and therefore often unused. Hopefully better knowledge and education will encourage a desire among social media users to be more aware of possible unchecked information and the sources of information and to stop the forwarding of false information. A better understanding of the motives behind the sharing of false information can potentially prepare social media users to be more vigilant when sharing information on social media. The goal of this literature review was only to identify the factors that drive the spreading of fake news on social media platforms and did not fully address the dilemma of combatting the sharing and spreading of false information.

While this literature review sheds light on the motivations behind the spreading of false information, it does not highlight the ways in which one can detect false information. This proposes further suggestions for follow-up research or literature studies using these factors in an attempt to detect and limit or possibly eradicate the spreading of false information across social media platforms. Despite the limitations of this literature review, it helps to educate and provide insightful knowledge to social media users who share information across social media platforms.

References

1. Obelitz Søe, S.: Algorithmic detection of misinformation and disinformation: Gricean perspectives. J. Doc. **72**(2), 309 (2018)
2. Bondielli, A., Marcelloni, F.: A survey on fake news and rumour detection techniques. Inf. Sci. **497**, 38–55 (2019)
3. Zhang, X., Ghorbani, A.A.: An overview of online fake news: characterization, detection, and discussion. Inf. Process. Manag. **57**(2), 102025 (2019)
4. Aldwairi, M., Alwahedi, A.: Detecting fake news in social media networks. Proc. Comput. Sci. **141**, 215–222 (2018)
5. Chen, X., Sin, S.-C.J., Theng, Y.-L., Lee, C.S.: Why students share misinformation on social media: motivation, gender, and study-level differences. J. Acad. Librariansh. **41**(5), 583–592 (2015)
6. Shin, J., Jian, L., Driscoll, K., Bar, F.: The diffusion of misinformation on social media: Temporal pattern, message, and source. Comput. Hum. Behav. **83**, 278–287 (2018)
7. Gravanis, G., Vakali, A., Diamantaras, K., Karadais, P.: Behind the cues: a benchmarking study for fake news detection. Expert Syst. Appl. **128**, 201–213 (2019)
8. Kanoh, H.: Why do people believe in fake news over the Internet? An understanding from the perspective of existence of the habit of eating and drinking. Proc. Comput. Sci. **126**, 1704–1709 (2018)

9. Colliander, J.: 'This is fake news': Investigating the role of conformity to other users' views when commenting on and spreading disinformation in social media. Comput. Hum. Behav. **97**, 202–215 (2019)
10. Figueira, Á., Oliveira, L.: The current state of fake news: challenges and opportunities. Proc. Comput. Sci. **121**, 817–825 (2017)
11. Atodiresei, C.-S., Tănăselea, A., Iftene, A.: Identifying fake news and fake users on Twitter. Proc. Comput. Sci. **126**, 451–461 (2018)
12. Talwar, S., Dhir, A., Kaur, P., Zafar, N., Alrasheedy, M.: Why do people share fake news? Associations between the dark side of social media use and fake news sharing behavior. J. Retail. Consum. Serv. **51**, 72–82 (2019)
13. Burkhardt, J.M.: History of fake news. Libr. Technol. Rep. **53**(8), 5–9 (2017)
14. Anderson, K.E.: Getting acquainted with social networks and apps: combating fake news on social media. Libr. Hi Tech News **35**(3), 1–6 (2018)
15. Al-Rawi, A., Groshek, J., Zhang, L.: What the fake? Assessing the extent of networked political spamming and bots in the propagation of #fakenews on Twitter. Online Inf. Rev. **43**(1), 53–71 (2019)
16. Rochlin, N.: Fake news: belief in post-truth. Libr. Hi Tech **35**(3), 386–392 (2017)
17. IEC South Africa: Real411. Keeping it real in digital media. Disinformation Destroys Democracy (2019)
18. Lor, P.J.: Democracy, information, and libraries in a time of post-truth discourse. Libr. Manag. **39**(5), 307–321 (2018)
19. Yu, F., Liu, Q., Wu, S., Wang, L., Tan, T.: Attention-based convolutional approach for misinformation identification from massive and noisy microblog posts. Comput. Secur. **83**, 106–121 (2019)
20. Jang, S.M., Kim, J.K.: Third person effects of fake news: fake news regulation and media literacy interventions. Comput. Hum. Behav. **80**, 295–302 (2018)
21. Buschman, J.: Good news, bad news, and fake news: going beyond political literacy to democracy and libraries. J. Docum. **75**(1), 213–228 (2019)
22. Jang, S.M., et al.: A computational approach for examining the roots and spreading patterns of fake news: evolution tree analysis. Comput. Hum. Behav. **84**, 103–113 (2018)
23. Wang, Q., Yang, X., Xi, W.: Effects of group arguments on rumor belief and transmission in online communities: an information cascade and group polarization perspective. Inf. Manag. **55**(4), 441–449 (2018)
24. Lewandowsky, S., Ecker, U.K.H., Cook, J.: Beyond misinformation: understanding and coping with the 'Post-Truth' era. J. Appl. Res. Mem. Cogn. **6**(4), 353–369 (2017)
25. Vijaykumar, S., Nowak, G., Himelboim, I., Jin, Y.: Virtual Zika transmission after the first U.S. case: who said what and how it spread on Twitter. Am. J. Infect. Control **46**(5), 549–557 (2018)
26. Jang, B., Jeong, S., Kim, C.: Distance-based customer detection in fake follower markets. Inf. Syst. **81**, 104–116 (2019)
27. Borges-Tiago, M.T., Tiago, F., Cosme, C.: 'Exploring users' motivations to participate in viral communication on social media. J. Bus. Res. **101**, 574–582 (2018)
28. Alzanin, S.M., Azmi, A.M.: Detecting rumors in social media: a survey. Proc. Comput. Sci. **142**, 294–300 (2018)
29. Rayess, M.E., Chebl, C., Mhanna, J., Hage, R.-M.: Fake news judgement: the case of undergraduate students at Notre Dame University-Louaize, Lebanon. Ref. Serv. Rev. **46**(1), 146–149 (2018)
30. Wessel, M., Thies, F., Benlian, A.: The emergence and effects of fake social information: evidence from crowdfunding. Decis. Supp. Syst. **90**, 75–85 (2016)

31. Ishida, Y., Kuraya, S.: Fake news and its credibility evaluation by dynamic relational networks: a bottom up approach. Proc. Comput. Sci. **126**, 2228–2237 (2018)

32. Lee, S., Ha, T., Lee, D., Kim, J.H.: Understanding the majority opinion formation process in online environments: an exploratory approach to Facebook. Inf. Process. Manag. **54**(6), 1115–1128 (2018)

33. Seargeant, P., Tagg, C.: Social media and the future of open debate: a user-oriented approach to Facebook's filter bubble conundrum. Discourse Context Media **27**, 41–48 (2019)

34. De keersmaecker, J., Roets, A.: 'Fake news': incorrect, but hard to correct. The role of cognitive ability on the impact of false information on social impressions. Intelligence **65**, 107–110 (2017)

35. Park, K., Rim, H.: Social media hoaxes, political ideology, and the role of issue confidence. Telematics Inform. **36**, 1–11 (2019)

36. Weidner, K., Beuk, F., Bal, A.: Fake news and the willingness to share: a schemer schema and confirmatory bias perspective. J. Prod. Brand Manag. (2019). https://doi.org/10.1108/JPBM-12-2018-2155

37. Mihaylov, T., Mihaylova, T., Nakov, P., Màrquez, L., Georgiev, G.D., Koychev, I.K.: The dark side of news community forums: opinion manipulation trolls. Internet Res. **28**(5), 1292–1312 (2018)

38. Baccarella, C.V., Wagner, T.F., Kietzmann, J.H., McCarthy, I.P.: Social media? It's serious! Understanding the dark side of social media. Eur. Manag. J. **36**(4), 431–438 (2018)

39. Zhang, Z., Gupta, B.B.: Social media security and trustworthiness: overview and new direction. Future Gener. Comput. Syst. **86**, 914–925 (2018)

The Use of Critical Thinking to Identify Fake News: A Systematic Literature Review

Paul Machete and Marita Turpin$^{(\boxtimes)}$ (iD)

Department of Informatics, University of Pretoria, Pretoria 0001, South Africa
marita.turpin@up.ac.za

Abstract. With the large amount of news currently being published online, the ability to evaluate the credibility of online news has become essential. While there are many studies involving fake news and tools on how to detect it, there is a limited amount of work that focuses on the use of information literacy to assist people to critically access online information and news. Critical thinking, as a form of information literacy, provides a means to critically engage with online content, for example by looking for evidence to support claims and by evaluating the plausibility of arguments. The purpose of this study is to investigate the current state of knowledge on the use of critical thinking to identify fake news. A systematic literature review (SLR) has been performed to identify previous studies on evaluating the credibility of news, and in particular to see what has been done in terms of the use of critical thinking to evaluate online news. During the SLR's sifting process, 22 relevant studies were identified. Although some of these studies referred to information literacy, only three explicitly dealt with critical thinking as a means to identify fake news. The studies on critical thinking noted critical thinking as an essential skill for identifying fake news. The recommendation of these studies was that information literacy be included in academic institutions, specifically to encourage critical thinking.

Keywords: Critical thinking · Fake news · Information literacy · Systematic literature review

1 Introduction

The information age has brought a significant increase in available sources of information; this is in line with the unparalleled increase in internet availability and connection, in addition to the accessibility of technological devices [1]. People no longer rely on television and print media alone for obtaining news, but increasingly make use of social media and news apps. The variety of information sources that we have today has contributed to the spread of alternative facts [1]. With over 1.8 billion active users per month in 2016 [2], Facebook accounted for 20% of total traffic to reliable websites and up to 50% of all the traffic to fake news sites [3]. Twitter comes second to Facebook, with over 400 million active users per month [2]. Posts on social media platforms such as Facebook and Twitter spread rapidly due to how they attempt to grab

© IFIP International Federation for Information Processing 2020
Published by Springer Nature Switzerland AG 2020
M. Hattingh et al. (Eds.): I3E 2020, LNCS 12067, pp. 235–246, 2020.
https://doi.org/10.1007/978-3-030-45002-1_20

the readers' attention as quickly as possible, with little substantive information provided, and thus create a breeding ground for the dissemination of fake news [4].

While social media is a convenient way of accessing news and staying connected to friends and family, it is not easy to distinguish real news from fake news on social media [5]. Social media continues to contribute to the increasing distribution of user-generated information; this includes hoaxes, false claims, fabricated news and conspiracy theories, with primary sources being social media platforms such as Facebook and Twitter [6]. This means that any person who is in possession of a device, which can connect to the internet, is potentially a consumer or distributor of fake news. While social media platforms and search engines do not encourage people to believe the information being circulated, they are complicit in people's propensity to believe the information they come across on these platforms, without determining their validity [6]. The spread of fake news can cause a multitude of damages to the subject; varying from reputational damage of an individual, to having an effect on the perceived value of a company [7].

The purpose of this study is to investigate the use of critical thinking methods to detect news stories that are untrue or otherwise help to develop a critical attitude to online news. This work was performed by means of a systematic literature review (SLR). The paper is presented as follows. The next section provides background information on fake news, its importance in the day-to-day lives of social media users and how information literacy and critical thinking can be used to identify fake news. Thereafter, the SLR research approach is discussed. Following this, the findings of the review are reported, first in terms of descriptive statistics and the in terms of a thematic analysis of the identified studies. The paper ends with the Conclusion and recommendations.

2 Background: Fake News, Information Literacy and Critical Thinking

This section discusses the history of fake news, the fake news that we know today and the role of information literacy can be used to help with the identification of fake news. It also provides a brief definition of critical thinking.

2.1 The History of Fake News

Although fake news has received increased attention recently, the term has been used by scholars for many years [4]. Fake news emerged from the tradition of yellow journalism of the 1890s, which can be described as a reliance on the familiar aspects of sensationalism—crime news, scandal and gossip, divorces and sex, and stress upon the reporting of disasters, sports sensationalism as well as possibly satirical news [5]. The emergence of online news in the early 2000s raised concerns, among them being that people who share similar ideologies may form "echo chambers" where they can filter out alternative ideas [2]. This emergence came about as news media transformed from one that was dominated by newspapers printed by authentic and trusted journalists to one where online news from an untrusted source is believed by many [5]. The term later grew to describe "satirical news shows", "parody news shows" or "fake-news comedy shows" where a television show, or segment on a television show was dedicated to political satire [4]. Some of these include popular television shows such as *The Daily Show* (now with Trevor Noah), *Saturday Night Live*'s "The Weekend Update" segment, and other similar shows such as *Last Week Tonight* with John Oliver and *The Colbert Report* with Stephen Colbert [4]. News stories in these shows were labelled "fake" not because of their content, but for parodying network news for the use of sarcasm, and using comedy as a tool to engage real public issues [4]. The term "Fake News" further became prominent during the course of the 2016 US presidential elections, as members of the opposing parties would post incorrect news headlines in order to sway the decision of voters [6].

2.2 Fake News Today

The term fake news has a more literal meaning today [4]. The Macquarie Dictionary named fake news the word of the year for 2016 [8]. In this dictionary, fake news is described it as a word that captures a fascinating evolution in the creation of deceiving content, also allowing people to believe what they see fit. There are many definitions for the phrase, however, a concise description of the term can be found in Paskin [4] who states that certain news articles originating from either social media or mainstream (online or offline) platforms, that are not factual, but are presented as such and are not satirical, are considered fake news. In some instances, editorials, reports, and exposés may be knowingly disseminating information with intent to deceive for the purposes of monetary or political benefit [4].

A distinction amongst three types of fake news can be made on a conceptual level, namely: serious fabrications, hoaxes and satire [3]. Serious fabrications are explained as news items written on false information, including celebrity gossip. Hoaxes refer to false information provided via social media, aiming to be syndicated by traditional news platforms. Lastly, satire refers to the use of humour in the news to imitate real news, but through irony and absurdity. Some examples of famous satirical news platforms in circulation in the modern day are *The Onion* and *The Beaverton*, when contrasted with real news publishers such as *The New York Times* [3].

Although there are many studies involving fake news and tools on how to detect it, there is a limited amount of academic work that focuses on the need to encourage information literacy so that people are able to critically access the information they have been presented, in order to make better informed decisions [9].

Stein-Smith [5] urges that information/media literacy has become a more critical skill since the appearance of the notion of fake news has become public conversation. Information literacy is no longer a nice-to-have proficiency but a requirement for interpreting news headlines and participation in public discussions. It is essential for academic institutions of higher learning to present information literacy courses that will empower students and staff members with the prerequisite tools to identify, select, understand and use trustworthy information [1]. Outside of its academic uses, information literacy is also a lifelong skill with multiple applications in everyday life [5]. The choices people make in their lives, and opinions they form need to be informed by the appropriate interpretation of correct, opportune, and significant information [5].

2.3   Critical Thinking

Critical thinking covers a broad range of skills that includes the following: verbal reasoning skills; argument analysis; thinking as hypothesis testing; dealing with likelihood and uncertainties; and decision making and problem solving skills [10]. For the purpose of this study, where we are concerned with the evaluation of the credibility of online news, the following definition will be used: critical thinking is "the ability to analyse and evaluate arguments according to their soundness and credibility, respond to arguments and reach conclusions through deduction from given information" [11]. In this study, we want to investigate how the skills mentioned by [11] can be used as part of information literacy, to better identify fake news.

The next section presents the research approach that was followed to perform the SLR.

3   Research Method

This section addresses the research question, the search terms that were applied to a database in relation to the research question, as well as the search criteria used on the search results. The following research question was addressed in this SLR:

- *What is the role of critical thinking in identifying fake news, according to previous studies?*

The research question was identified in accordance to the research topic. The intention of the research question is to determine if the identified studies in this review provide insights into the use of critical thinking to evaluate the credibility of online news and in particular to identify fake news.

Delimitations. In the construction of this SLR, the following definitions of fake news and other related terms have been excluded, following the suggestion of [2]:

- Unintentional reporting mistakes;
- Rumours that do not originate from a particular news article;
- Conspiracy theories;
- Satire that is unlikely to be misconstrued as factual;
- False statements by politicians; and
- Reports that are slanted or misleading, but not outright false.

Search Terms. The database tool used to extract sources to conduct the SLR was Google Scholar (https://scholar.google.com). The process for extracting the sources involved executing the search string on Google Scholar and the retrieval of the articles and their meta-data into a tool called Mendeley, which was used for reference management.

The search string used to retrieve the sources was defined below:

("critical think*" OR "critically (NEAR/2) reason*" OR "critical (NEAR/2) thought*" OR "critical (NEAR/2) judge*" AND "fake news" AND (identify* OR analyse* OR find* OR describe* OR review).

To construct the search criteria, the following factors have been taken into consideration: the research topic guided the search string, as the key words were used to create the base search criteria. The second step was to construct the search string according to the search engine requirements on Google Scholar.

Selection Criteria. The selection criteria outlined the rules applied in the SLR to identify sources, narrow down the search criteria and focus the study on a specific topic. The inclusion and exclusion criteria are outlined in Table 1 to show which filters were applied to remove irrelevant sources.

Table 1. Inclusion and exclusion criteria for paper selection

Inclusion criteria	Exclusion criteria
Publications related to alternative facts, fake news and fabrications	Publications related to alternative facts, fake news and fabrications
Academic journals published in information technology and related fields	Academic journals published in information technology and related fields
Academic journals should outline critical thinking, techniques of how to identify fake news or reviewing fake news using critical thinking	Academic journals should outline critical thinking, techniques of how to identify fake news or reviewing fake news using critical thinking
Academic journals should include an abstract	Academic journals should include an abstract
	Publications related to alternative facts, fake news and fabrications

Source Selection. The search criteria were applied on the online database and 91 papers were retrieved. The criteria in Table 1 were used on the search results in order to narrow down the results to appropriate papers only.

PRISMA Flowchart. The selection criteria included four stages of filtering and this is depicted in Fig. 1. In then Identification stage, the 91 search results from Google Scholar were returned and 3 sources were derived from the sources already identified from the search results, making a total of 94 available sources. In the screening stage, no duplicates were identified. After a thorough screening of the search results, which included looking at the availability of the article (free to use), 39 in total records were available – to which 55 articles were excluded. Of the 39 articles, nine were excluded based on their titles and abstract being irrelevant to the topic in the eligibility stage. A final list of 22 articles was included as part of this SLR. As preparation for the data analysis, a data extraction table was made that classified each article according to the following: article author; article title; theme (a short summary of the article); year; country; and type of publication. The data extraction table assisted in the analysis of findings as presented in the next section.

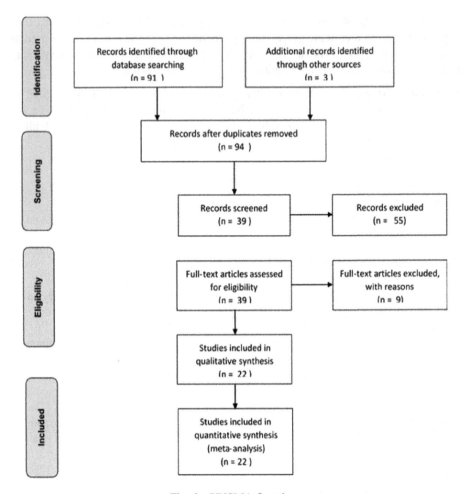

Fig. 1. PRISMA flowchart

4 Analysis of Findings

4.1 Descriptive Statistics

Due to the limited number of relevant studies, the information search did not have a specified start date. Articles were included up to 31 August 2019. The majority of the papers found were published in 2017 (8 papers) and 2018 (9 papers). This is in line with the term "fake news" being announced the word of the year in the 2016 [8].

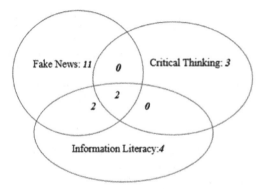

Fig. 2. Venn diagram depicting the overlap of articles by main focus

The selected papers were classified into themes. Figure 2 is a Venn diagram that represents the overlap of articles by themes across the review. Articles that fall under the "fake news" theme had the highest number of occurrences, with 11 in total. Three articles focused mainly on "Critical Thinking", and "Information Literacy" was the main focus of four articles. Two articles combined all three topics of critical thinking, information literacy, and fake news.

An analysis of the number of articles published per country indicate that the US had a dominating amount of articles published on this topic, a total of 17 articles - this represents 74% of the selected articles in this review. The remaining countries where articles were published are Australia, Germany, Ireland, Lebanon, Saudi Arabia, and Sweden - with each having one article published.

In terms of publication type, 15 of the articles were journal articles, four were reports, one was a thesis, one was a magazine article and one, a web page.

4.2 Discussion of Themes

The following emerged from a thematic analysis of the articles.

Fake News

Fake News and Accountability. With the influence that social media has on the drive of fake news [2], who then becomes responsible for the dissemination and intake of fake news by the general population? The immediate assumption is that in the digital age, social media platforms like Facebook and Twitter should be able to curate information, or do some form of fact-checking when posts are uploaded onto their platforms [12], but that leans closely to infringing on freedom of speech. While different authors agree that there need to be measures in place for the minimisation of fake news being spread [12, 13], where that accountability lies differs between the authors. Metaxas and Mustafaraj [13] aimed to develop algorithms or plug-ins that can assist in trust and postulated that consumers should be able to identify misinformation, thus making an informed decision on whether to share that information or not. Lazer et al. [12] on the other hand, believe the onus should be on the platform owners to put restrictions on the kind of data distributed. Considering that the work by Metaxas and Mustafaraj [13] was done seven years ago, one can conclude that the use of fact-checking algorithms/plug-ins has not been successful in curbing the propulsion of fake news.

Fake News and Student Research. There were a total of four articles that had a focus on student research in relation to fake news. Harris, Paskin and Stein-Smith [4, 5, 14] all agree that students do not have the ability to discern between real and fake news. A Stanford History Education Group study reveals that students are not geared up for distinguishing real from fake news [4]. Most students are able to perform a simple Google search for information; however, they are unable to identify the author of an online source, or if the information is misleading [14]. Furthermore, students are not aware of the benefits of learning information literacy in school in equipping them with the skills required to accurately identify fake news [5]. At the Metropolitan Campus of Fairleigh Dickson University, librarians have undertaken the role of providing training on information literacy skills for identifying fake news [5].

Fake News and Social Media. A number of authors [6, 15] are in agreement that social media, the leading source of news, is the biggest driving force for fake news. It provides substantial advantage to broadcast manipulated information. It is an open platform of unfiltered editors and open to contributions from all. According to Nielsen and Graves as well as Janetzko, [6, 15], people are unable to identify fake news correctly. They are likely to associate fake news with low quality journalism than false information designed to mislead. Two articles, [15] and [6] discussed the role of critical thinking when interacting on social media. Social media presents information to us that has been filtered according to what we already consume, thereby making it a challenge for consumers to think critically. The study by Nielsen and Graves [6] confirm that students' failure to verify incorrect online sources requires urgent attention as this could indicate that students are a simple target for presenting manipulated information.

Fake News That Drive Politics. Two studies mention the effect of social and the spread of fake news, and how it may have propelled Donald Trump to win the US election in 2016 [2, 16]. Also, [8] and [2] mention how a story on the Pope supporting Trump in his presidential campaign, was widely shared (more than a million times) on Facebook in 2016. These articles also point out how in the information age, fact-checking has become relatively easy, but people are more likely to trust their intuition on news stories they consume, rather than checking the reliability of a story. The use of paid trolls and Russian bots to populate social media feeds with misinformation in an effort to swing the US presidential election in Donald Trump's favour, is highlighted [16]. The creation of fake news, with the use of alarmist headlines ("click bait"), generates huge traffic into the original websites, which drives up advertising revenue [2]. This means content creators are compelled to create fake news, to drive ad revenue on their websites - even though they may not be believe in the fake news themselves [2].

Information Literacy. Information literacy is when a person has access to information, and thus can process the parts they need, and create ways in which to best use the information [1]. Teaching students the importance of information literacy skills is key, not only for identifying fake news but also for navigating life aspects that require managing and scrutinising information, as discussed by [1, 17], and [9]. Courtney [17] highlights how journalism students, above students from other disciplines, may need to have some form of information literacy incorporated into their syllabi to increase their awareness of fake news stories, creating a narrative of being objective and reliable news creators. Courtney assessed different universities that teach journalism and media-related studies, and established that students generally lack awareness on how useful library services are in offering services related to information literacy. Courtney [17] and Rose-Wiles [9] discuss how the use of library resources should be normalised to students. With millennials and generation Z having social media as their first point of contact, Rose-Wiles [9] urges universities, colleges and other academic research institutes to promote the use of more library resources than those from the internet, to encourage students to lean on reliable sources. Overall, this may prove difficult, therefore Rose-Wiles [9] proposes that by teaching information literacy skills and critical thinking, students can use these skills to apply in any situation or information source.

Referred to as "truth decay", people have reached a point where they no longer need to agree with facts [18]. Due to political polarisation, the general public hold the opinion of being part of an oppressed group of people, and therefore will believe a political leader who appeals to that narrative [18]. There needs to be tangible action put into driving civil engagement, to encourage people to think critically, analyse information and not believe everything they read.

Critical Thinking. Only three of the articles had critical thinking as a main theme. Bronstein et al. [19] discuss how certain dogmatic and religious beliefs create a tendency in individuals to belief any information given, without them having a need to interrogate the information further and then deciding ion its veracity. The article further elaborates how these individuals are also more likely to engage in conspiracy theories, and tend to rationalise absurd events. Bronstein et al.'s [19] study conclude that dogmatism and religious fundamentalism highly correlate with a belief in fake news. Their study [19] suggests the use of interventions that aim to increase open-minded thinking, and also increase analytical thinking as a way to help religious, curb belief in fake news. Howlett [20] describes critical thinking as evidence-based practice, which is taking the theories of the skills and concepts of critical thinking and converting those for use in everyday applications. Jackson [21] explains how the internet purposely prides itself in being a platform for "unreviewed content", due to the idea that people may not see said content again, therefore it needs to be attention-grabbing for this moment, and not necessarily accurate. Jackson [21] expands that social media affected critical thinking in how it changed the view on published information, what is now seen as old forms of information media. This then presents a challenge to critical thinking in that a large portion of information found on the internet is not only unreliable, it may also be false. Jackson [21] posits that one of the biggest dangers to critical thinking may be that people have a sense of perceived power for being able to find the others they seek with a simple web search. People are no longer interested in evaluation the credibility of the information they receive and share, and thus leading to the propagation of fake news [21].

5   Discussion of Findings

The aggregated data in this review has provided insight into how fake news is perceived, the level of attention it is receiving and the shortcomings of people when identifying fake news. Since the increase in awareness of fake news in 2016, there has been an increase in academic focus on the subject, with most of the articles published between 2017 and 2018. Fifty percent of the articles released focused on the subject of fake news, with 18% reflecting on information literacy, and only 13% on critical thinking.

The thematic discussion grouped and synthesised the articles in this review according to the main themes of fake news, information literacy and critical thinking. The *Fake news and accountability* discussion raised the question of who becomes accountable for the spreading of fake news between social media and the user. The articles presented a conclusion that fact-checking algorithms are not successful in reducing the dissemination of fake news. The discussion also included a focus on *fake news and student research*, whereby a Stanford History Education Group study revealed that students are not well educated in thinking critically and identifying real from fake news [4]. The *Fake news and social media* discussion provided insight on social media is the leading source of news as well as a contributor to fake news. It provides a challenge for consumers who are not able to think critically about online news, or have basic information literacy skills that can aid in identifying fake news. *Fake news that drive politics* highlighted fake news' role in politics, particularly the 2016 US presidential elections and the influence it had on the voters [22].

Information literacy related publications highlighted the need for educating the public on being able to identify fake news, as well as the benefits of having information literacy as a life skill [1, 9, 17]. It was shown that students are often misinformed about the potential benefits of library services. The authors suggested that university libraries should become more recognised and involved as role-players in providing and assisting with information literacy skills.

The articles that focused on critical thinking pointed out two areas where a lack of critical thinking prevented readers from discerning between accurate and false information. In the one case, it was shown that people's confidence in their ability to find information online gave made them overly confident about the accuracy of that information [21]. In the other case, it was shown that dogmatism and religious fundamentalism, which led people to believe certain fake news, were associated with a lack of critical thinking and a questioning mind-set [21].

The articles that focused on information literacy and critical thinking were in agreement on the value of promoting and teaching these skills, in particular to the university students who were often the subjects of the studies performed.

6   Conclusion

This review identified 22 articles that were synthesised and used as evidence to determine the role of critical thinking in identifying fake news. The articles were classified according to year of publication, country of publication, type of publication and theme. Based on the descriptive statistics, fake news has been a growing trend in recent years, predominantly in the US since the presidential election in 2016. The research presented in most of the articles was aimed at the assessment of students' ability to identify fake news. The various studies were consistent in their findings of research subjects' lack of ability to distinguish between true and fake news.

Information literacy emerged as a new theme from the studies, with Rose-Wiles [9] advising academic institutions to teach information literacy and encourage students to think critically when accessing online news. The potential role of university libraries to assist in not only teaching information literacy, but also assisting student to evaluate the credibility of online information, was highlighted. The three articles that explicitly dealt with critical thinking, all found critical thinking to be lacking among their research subjects. They further indicated how this lack of critical thinking could be linked to people's inability to identify fake news.

This review has pointed out people's general inability to identify fake news. It highlighted the importance of information literacy as well as critical thinking, as essential skills to evaluate the credibility of online information.

The limitations in this review include the use of students as the main participants in most of the research - this would indicate a need to shift the academic focus towards having the general public as participants. This is imperative because anyone who possesses a mobile device is potentially a contributor or distributor of fake news.

For future research, it is suggested that the value of the formal teaching of information literacy at universities be further investigated, as a means to assist students in assessing the credibility of online news. Given the very limited number of studies on the role of critical thinking to identify fake news, this is also an important area for further research.

References

1. Taala, W., Franco Jr., F.B., Teresa, P.H.S.: Library literacy program: library as battleground for fighting fakenews. Open Access Libr. J. **6**, e5296 (2019)
2. Allcott, H., Gentzkow, M.: Social media and fake news in the 2016 election. J. Econ. Perspect. **31**(2), 211–236 (2017)
3. Pérez-Rosas, V., Kleinberg, B., Lefevre, A., Mihalcea, R.: Automatic detection of fake news, arXiv preprint arXiv:1708.07104 (2017)
4. Paskin, D.: Real or fake news: who knows? J. Soc. Media Soc. **7**(2), 252–273 (2018)
5. Stein-Smith, K.: Librarians, information literacy, and fake news. Strateg. Libr. **37**, 1–4 (2017)
6. Nielsen, R.K., Graves, L.: News you don't believe": audience perspectives on fake news. Reuters Institute for the Study of Journalism (2017). https://reutersinstitute.politics.ox.ac.uk/ourresearch/news-you-dont-believe-audience-perspectives-fake-news
7. Vosoughi, S., Roy, D., Aral, S.: The spread of true and false news online. Science **359**(6380), 1146–1151 (2018)
8. Hunt, E.: Fake news' named word of the year by Macquarie Dictionary. The Guardian (2017). https://www.theguardian.com/australia-news/2017/jan/25/fake-news-named-word-of-the-year-by-macquarie-dictionary
9. Rose-Wiles, L.M.: Reflections on fake news, librarians, and undergraduate research. Ref. User Serv. Q. **57**(3), 200–204 (2018)

10. Halpern, D.F.: Teaching critical thinking for transfer across domains: disposition, skills, structure training, and metacognitive monitoring. Am. Psychol. **53**(4), 449 (1998)
11. Tiruneh, D.T., Verburgh, A., Elen, J.: Effectiveness of critical thinking instruction in higher education: a systematic review of intervention studies. High. Educ. Stud. **4**(1), 1–17 (2014)
12. Lazer, D.M., et al.: The science of fake news. Science **359**(6380), 1094–1096 (2018)
13. Metaxas, P.T., Mustafaraj, E.: Trails of trustworthiness in real-time streams (extended summary) (2012)
14. Harris, F.J.: CIPA/Internet filtering. In: The International Encyclopedia of Media Literacy, pp. 1–11 (2019)
15. Janetzko, D.: Social bots and fake news as (not) seen from the viewpoint of digital education frameworks. MedienPädagogik: Zeitschrift für Theorie und Praxis der Medienbildung, pp. 61–80 (2017)
16. Bodine-Baron, E., Helmus, T.C., Radin, A., Treyger, E.: Countering Russian Social Media Influence. RAND Corporation, Santa Monica (2018)
17. Courtney, I.: In an era of fake news, information literacy has a role to play in journalism education in Ireland. Dublin Business School (2017)
18. O'Brien, S., Rich, M.D., Fukuyama, F.: The Perils of Truth Decay: Q&A with Three RAND Leaders (2018). https://www.rand.org/blog/rand-review/2018/02/the-perils-of-truth-decay-qa-with-three-rand-leaders.html. Accessed 17 Nov 2019
19. Bronstein, M.V., Pennycook, G., Bear, A., Rand, D.G., Cannon, T.D.: Belief in fake news is associated with delusionality, dogmatism, religious fundamentalism, and reduced analytic thinking. J. Appl. Res. Mem. Cogn. **8**(1), 108–117 (2019)
20. Howlett, B.: What evidence-based practice is and why it matters. In: Evidence-Based Practice for Health Professionals: An Interprofessional Approach, pp. 5–30 (2014)
21. Jackson, S.: How a Critical Thinker Uses the Web, Windsor Studies in Argumentation (2019)
22. Koulolias, V., Jonathan, G.M., Fernandez, M., Sotirchos, D.: Combating Misinformation: An ecosystem in co-creation. OECD Publishing (2018)

A Conceptual Model of the Challenges of Social Media Big Data for Citizen e-Participation: A Systematic Review

Khulekani Yakobi[1](✉) ⓘ, Brenda Scholtz[1] ⓘ,
and Benjamin vom Berg[2] ⓘ

[1] Nelson Mandela University, Port Elizabeth, South Africa
khulekaniy4@gmail.com, brenda.scholtz@mandela.ac.za
[2] University of Applied Science, Bremerhaven, Germany
benjamin.wagnervomberg@hs-bremerhaven.de

Abstract. The emergence of Citizen Relationship Management (CzRM) for government plays a central role in developing citizen relationships and e-participation. As such, the South African government has shown its commitment towards citizenry and the provision of effective service delivery. Social Media Analytics (SMA) has emerged as a potential new solution to support decision-making for service delivery in CzRM. It is believed that the demand for SMA adoption will increasingly rise. However, the reality of social media Big Data comes with the challenges of analysing it in a way that brings Big Value. The purpose of this paper is to identify the challenges of social media Big Data Analytics (BDA) and to incorporate these in a conceptual model that can be used by governments to support the e-participation of citizens. The model was developed through a systematic literature review (SLR). The findings revealed that data challenges relate to designing an optimal architecture for analysing data that caters for both historic data and real-time data at the same time. The paper highlight that process challenges relate to all the activities in the data lifecycle such as data acquisition and warehousing; data mining and cleaning; data aggregation and integration; analysis and modelling; and data interpretation. The paper also identifies six types of data management challenges: privacy, security, data governance, data and information sharing, cost/operational expenditures, and data ownership.

Keywords: Citizen Relationship Management · Data lifecycle · Big Data · Big Data Analytics · e-Participation · Social Media Analytics

1 Introduction

Social Media Analytics (SMA) can provide a decision-making framework that can influence the quality of social media Big Data for citizen e-participation; however, this attempt will need well-defined tools and guidelines for the usage thereof [1]. SMA has also the potential to use advanced techniques to analyse patterns in social media data to enable informed and insightful decision-making for Citizen Relationship Management (CzRM) [2, 3]. CzRM is the growing effort of governments around the world to strive

M. Hattingh et al. (Eds.): I3E 2020, LNCS 12067, pp. 247–259, 2020.
https://doi.org/10.1007/978-3-030-45002-1_21

to respond rapidly to their citizens by fostering a closer relationship with them, thereby creating more efficient service delivery and e-participation. e-Participation often empowers citizens through social media to act in bottom-up decision-making processes. Information and Communication Technology (ICT) has led to the rise of e-participation, whereby governments adopt digital tools to promote citizen involvement in what is referred to as "CzRM" [4]. Recently, [5] argued that the potential of Big Data for digital tools is often not met since it presents a data set that is so large or complex that it is difficult to process and manage this data using traditional data processing and management applications. The effective and efficient storage and retrieval of vast amounts of structured as well as unstructured data, referred to as Big Data, remains a challenge [6].

The many advantages of social media for government have been highlighted in several studies [7–10]. Some of these advantages are improved service delivery, improved decision-making, transparency, an improved organisation image and more inclusive policy processes. However, [11, 12] report that governments lack valid and reliable measures for determining and analysing the effects of social media. Without these measures they remain unable to align their social media initiatives with organisational strategies and ultimately create business value. Several studies [13–15] indicate that the use of social media and ICTs in a government context increases collaboration amongst stakeholders, enabling feedback and promoting citizen e-participation.

Whilst there are a few studies of social media adoption in Africa that show evidence of developing countries joining the social media race [16], there are very few studies reporting on social media Big Data, BDA or SMA in these countries. The most popular social media platforms used in Africa were found to be Twitter and Facebook [17]. Twitter was mostly used for political election campaigns, political movements, strategies for African tourism on cultural heritage, and topic models, while Facebook was mostly used for political revolutions, communication and health delivery.

The main problem identified in this paper is that existing models are more focused on SMA and Big Data Analytics (BDA) in general [18–21] and are not specific to social media BDA (i.e. SMA) for citizen e-participation. They also do not consider the data value chain or the challenges for addressing service delivery and citizen e-participation with social media. There is also a lack of related research in Africa. This gap was addressed by conducting a systematic literature review (SLR) in order to design a conceptual model. The structure of the paper is as follows: Sect. 2 provides an overview of the research question and method adopted in the research. Section 3 reports on review findings: the data lifecycle and SMA challenges. Section 4 reports on discussions and implications for research in Africa. Section 5 concludes the paper and provides an agenda for future possible research.

2 Research Question and Method

The research reported on in this paper adopted the SLR approach to answering research questions as proposed by [22]. The SLR will contribute by means of identifying, evaluating and interpreting all available research relevant to the main research question for this study: *"What are the challenges of social media Big Data for addressing the e-participation of citizens?*". The SLR adopted followed the five steps proposed by [23] as shown in Fig. 1. They are: framing questions for a review; identifying relevant work; assessing the quality of studies; summarising the evidence; and interpreting the findings.

2.1 Framing Questions for a Review

The problems that were addressed by the review were specified in the form of clear, unambiguous and structured questions before beginning the review work.

2.2 Identifying Relevant Work

The search for studies was extensive and multiple sources (both computerised and printed) were searched using keywords including "*BDA, social media, SMA*". A total of 87 papers were used in this research, however, a total of 54 papers were sampled and selected for more detailed analysis. The study selection criteria flowed directly from the review question. Papers older than seven years were excluded as SMA is a nascent phenomenon in the field of Information Systems.

2.3 Assessing the Quality of Studies

In Step 3, the 54 selected studies from Step 2 were subjected to a more refined quality assessment by use of general critical appraisal guides and design-based quality checklists. These assessments were used for exploring heterogeneity and informing decisions regarding suitability of meta-analysis (Step 4).

2.4 Summarising the Evidence

Data synthesis consists of tabulation of study characteristics. Therefore, two tables were compiled to achieve this synthesis.

2.5 Interpreting the Findings

The findings were interpreted and exploration for heterogeneity helped the research determine whether the overall summary can be trusted, and, where necessary, the effects observed in high-quality studies were used for generating inferences. Any recommendations were graded by reference to the strengths and weaknesses of the evidence.

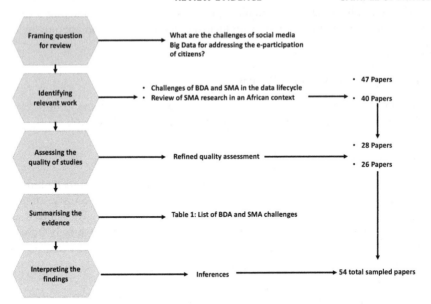

Fig. 1. Adoption of the five comprehensive steps of SLR (Authors' own source)

3   Review Findings: Data Lifecycle and SMA Challenges

A study conducted by [24] argues that all data available in the form of Big Data are not useful for analysis or decision-making. For this reason, the challenges of Big Data, with a focus on social media data, were reviewed in the SLR as these challenges might also influence the quality of social media Big Data, which can influence the adoption and success of SMA. These challenges have not yet been adequately addressed [25–28]. The number of studies [29, 30] that have reported challenges of Big Data, do not consider associated challenges related to techniques for data analysis and those related to SMA and BDA. There are limited studies that focus on SMA for government and e-participation. A recent study of Big Data challenges proposed by [28] provided useful insight into the research problem and classified the challenges according to three categories of the data lifecycle. The categories are: Data; Process and Management. The findings of the SLR for this study was classified according to the same three categories and the summary is shown in Table 1. The conceptual model of SMA challenges in the data lifecycle is then illustrated in Fig. 2.

Table 1. Challenges of BDA and SMA in the data lifecycle

Challenge	Context	Source
Data challenges		
Designing an analytics architecture to cater for 7 Vs with legacy databases	Big Data	[31]
Process challenges		
Lack of reliable data sources for data collection	Big Data	[32, 33]
Lack of value to service delivery due to unreliable alignment between social media initiatives and government strategies	Service Delivery to citizens; e-participation; Social media; Government	[14]
Lack of fault tolerance techniques	SMA	[34, 35]
Visualisation of data	Big Data	[35, 36]
Management challenges		
Data privacy, security and control issues due to heterogeneous data and data sources	Big Data	[37]
The lack of Big Data management presents difficulties for government to sort this data on privacy levels and to apply security according to these levels	Big Data; Government	[6, 33]
The lack of Big Data infrastructure has compromised the security, privacy & confidentiality of data through unintended, unauthorised access or inappropriate access by privileged users	Big Data	[38–43]
The lack of data management tools and techniques result in a negative impact on the decision making process of government	Government; Decision making	[28, 44]
The lack of Big Data governance causes low levels of accessibility for SMA	SMA	[35]
The lack of data ownership results in the quick spread of incorrect or false information	Big Data	[40]
Operational costs & budget allocations	Decision making	[45]
A lack of skills for SMA & related tools presents difficulties for government to interpret data	SMA	[46]

3.1 Data Challenges

Relate to the seven characteristics of the data itself (e.g. volume, velocity, variety, variability, veracity, visualisation and value) [30]; called the 7 'V's of Big Data. These characteristics make the data an unfit candidate to currently employed and tested database architectures [31]. As such, the challenges include capturing, analysis, storage, searching, sharing, visualisation, data transfer and privacy violations, which have been characterised as contributing factors to the 7 'V's [32]. Data challenges relate to designing an optimal architecture for analysing data that caters for both historic data and real-time data at the same time [31, 35]. Legacy database architectures are insufficient.

3.2   Process Challenges

Are related to the series of "how" techniques, which include: how to capture data, how to integrate data, how to transform data, how to select the right model for analysis and how to provide the results [28]. The heterogeneity, scale, timeliness, complexity, and privacy problems with Big Data hamper the progress at all phases of the process that can create value from data [32]. Regardless of where Big Data is generated from and shared to, the lack of analysis techniques results in huge challenges of not capitalising on crucial data which might bring *"Big Value"* for government [24, 28, 29, 47]. Process challenges relate to all the activities in the data lifecycle such as data acquisition and warehousing; data mining and cleaning; data aggregation and integration; analysis and modelling; and data interpretation. These challenges can therefore be further classified into the phases of the data value chain proposed by [48].

Data acquisition scenarios involves high-volume, high-velocity, high-variety, but low-value data, which makes it important to have adaptable and time-efficient gathering, filtering, and cleaning algorithms that ensure that only the high-value fragments of the data are actually processed by data warehouse analyses [49]. A study conducted by [24] suggest that in order to handle the challenges there is a need to know various computational complexities, information security, and computational methods in order to analyse Big Data. The lack of fault tolerance techniques results in unpredicted failures and compromises data analysis [34, 35].

Organisations are struggling to create business value from social media initiatives since they lack valid and reliable measures for SMA and therefore cannot align these initiatives with organisational strategies [14]. The lack of information on who social media users are, and how they decide what to post online, can contribute to difficulties in confidently interpreting the content of social media posts [46]. Visualisation is needed for intelligence, but this is a challenge since tools lack capacity due to large data sets and the continuous evolving nature of the data. It is presently difficult to recognise interesting patterns and correlations from social media data. The increasing size and number of datasets due to technological advancements in data collection introduces problems of complexity, transparency, integrity and interpretation [50].

3.3   Management Challenges

Relate to the tools and techniques needed for effective data management and for obtaining valuable information from voluminous and multifaceted data, which supports decision-making in an organisation [44]. Big Data consists of a large amount of complex data; therefore, it is very difficult for an organization to sort this data on privacy levels and apply security according to these levels [51]. "Big Data is not just about volume and from various sources; it is about its other characteristics such as size, speed of data, structure and quality and new-generation analytic technologies that help organisations get more value from their information assets" [52].

The six types of data management challenges proposed by [28] are: (1) Privacy; (2) Security; (3) Data governance; (4) Data and information sharing; (5) Cost/operational expenditures; and (6) Data ownership. However, our model incorporates privacy within security as done in [41]. Data and information sharing and ownership were grouped together due to the close relationship between these concepts. The resulting model therefore has four types of data management challenges.

Privacy and Security – According to [37], data security and privacy issues can be potentially exasperated by the volume, variety, and wide area deployment of the system infrastructure to support Big Data applications. Social networks are all around us and their popularity is vast. People share a lot of personal information in these networks without any concern for what the organisation behind these networks will do with their data, resulting in a huge threat to our personal privacy [40, 41, 43]. It is not an easy task to address this problem. One suggestion is for new redefined legislation to increase the protection of data privacy. Other have proposed a technique that can be used to increase the control that users have over their own data in social networks, whilst others have recommended distorting the data by adding noise.

According to [38], there is always a possibility of occurrence of security violations by unintended, unauthorised access or inappropriate access by privileged users. As such, securing data from security breaches should be top priority for organisations. IT infrastructure security was particularly highlighted by [41] and [39] as security challenges. IT infrastructure security can be of a major concern since Big Data is a new technology and it may not be understood well by all companies or governments [39, 41]. Integrity and reactive security were emphasised by [42] as challenges related to Big Data. Integrity is the maintenance of the consistency, trustworthiness and accuracy of data and is one of the three dimensions of security (along with confidentiality and availability).

Data Governance – Governments desire data management and information quality, which forms part of data governance [28]. Data governance can be defined as "the processes, policies, standards, organisation and technology required to manage and ensure the availability, accessibility, quality, consistency, auditability and data security in organisations or institutions" [53]. According to [54], "adopting data governance is advantageous, because it is a service based on standardised, repeatable processes and is designed to enable the transparency of data-related processes and cost reduction. It is also useful, because it refers to rules, policies, standards; decision rights; account-abilities and methods of enforcement".

Data and Information Sharing and Ownership – The rising increase of social media has resulted in a new, dynamic form of interpersonal communication globally [55]. It provides users with constant and continuous information sharing, a platform for connecting and collaborating with others and for conveying their thoughts across the world through various mediums; for example, social networking (Facebook), micro-blogging (Twitter, Tumblr), image sharing (Imgur, Flickr) and video hosting and sharing (YouTube, Dailymotion, Vimeo). However, where organisations store large scale datasets, it is an overwhelming task to share and integrate key information across the organisation or between different organisations [28]. The need to share data and information should be balanced and controlled to ensure maximum effect, as this will allow organisations to establish close connections and harmonisation with other stakeholders.

Cost/Operational Expenditures – Decision makers find it difficult to decide on budget and cost allocation for handling, managing, and analysing Big Data [1].

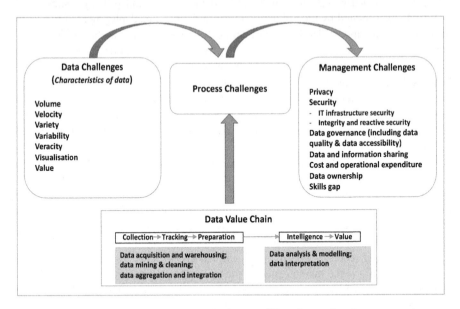

Fig. 2. Model of SMA challenges in the data lifecycle (Authors' own source)

4   Discussions and Implications for Research in Africa

In the SLR, only two papers [40, 43] related to challenges in Big Data in Africa. The search was therefore extended to include a review of studies that reported on Big Data or SMA activities occurring in Africa. From this review only 40 papers were identified and only 26 were deemed relevant for a more detailed analysis. A summary of these papers is provided in Appendix A. From this review it is evident that there is a paucity of research related to Big Data and SMA in Africa. This section reflects on these studies in light of the challenges and findings identified in the previous sections.

The study of [56] report that the use of social media by anti- and pro-government groups has been widely publicised, and some suggest that social media was afforded too much credit in the political changes and reforms that occurred in places such as Tunisia, Egypt, Libya, and the ongoing conflict in Syria. The impact of online social media on the voting behavior of the Tunisian voters in the 2014 elections was investigated by [57]. The findings unveiled the debate about the political uses of social networks and their effect on the voting behavior of the Tunisian voters.

A study conducted on Nigeria's general election of 2015 [16] revealed social media as the major influencer and that SMA can contribute in predicting trends that may influence developing economies. On the other hand, the substantial benefits from Big Data and analytics that were reaped by the mobile phone industry in Nigeria [58] revealed that proper correlations of social media data can help to reveal more complete and deeper insight of customer needs, thus enriching the operators with more revenue.

A qualitative study done by [40] highlighted the impact of social media as a communication tool, its efficacy and the paradigm change it has brought to the communication process in Namibia. The findings showed that social media challenges were the quick spread of incorrect information as well as compromised security for Internet users. A study showing the role of social media in South Africa explored social media contributions on communication and interaction between health practitioners and patients; this type of ever-growing, social media subscriber–based platform can be of significant use in improving healthcare delivery to society [59]. The study also proposed a framework to guide integration of social media with healthcare Big Data through which service delivery to patients can be improved. The model contributed to healthcare workers' awareness on how social media can possibly be used to improve the services that they provide to the needy. Another study of healthcare Big Data in Morocco [43] also highlighted the privacy challenges in healthcare, mainly related to methods used to ensure the privacy of patient data such as diagnosed diseases, doctor's appointments with patients and prescribed medication.

Furthermore, [60] explored how different features, extracted from social media data, impact the performance of different classifiers of social media in South Africa. The findings revealed that the researchers were able to build models that can classify posts using text features as well as a mixture of text features.

A study showing the role of social media and its impact on the 2011 Egyptian revolution was conducted by [61]. This revolution has often been termed the "Facebook Revolution" or "Twitter Revolution". There are many ambiguities as to the extent to which social media affected these movements. An investigation conducted by [62] aimed to shed some light on the broad characteristics of tweets about African cultural heritage. The findings identified possible implications and strategies for tourism stakeholders in their use of social media in general and Twitter in particular. It was found that tourism stakeholders could use text analysis of publicly available tweet messages to improve tourism. Social media interactions on the financial performance of commercial banks in Kenya was found to offer a platform for marketing and sales of products, development of new product brands and access to real-time customer feedback thereby supporting an enhanced understanding of the needs of their customers [63].

5   Conclusions and Future Work

This paper reports on the initial, exploratory phase of a larger, ongoing research project. The aim of the paper was to identify the challenges of social media Big Data and SMA and to propose a model that can provide guidance to practitioners and researchers. If these challenges are addressed, the success of SMA projects can be improved, particularly in government. This classification has three categories, based on the data life cycle, namely: (1) Data; (2) Process; and (3) Management. The challenges of social media Big Data for supporting the context of citizens' e-participation, service delivery and decision making were identified (Table 1). An important contribution of the paper is the extension of the data challenge category to the full data value chain, so as to reach the potential Big Value of Big Data (see Fig. 2). The paper also made a contribution to research conducted in Africa.

In Africa there is great potential for using SMA to support decision making and e-participation of citizens. However, many challenges need to be overcome. By addressing the challenges of Big Data and SMA identified in this study (Table 1 and Fig. 2), governments can improve decision making, e-participation and ultimately service delivery to citizens. There is a dire need for additional research on the challenges and future research directions regarding analysing social media Big Data. The novelty of this paper lies in the design and use of a conceptual model for social media Big Data to inform the e-participation of citizens and decision making of management in government. Improved decision-making can assist in a smart city strategy for governments. The study limitation is that it has no empirical evaluation in a practical context as it is based on secondary data from existing literature studies. Future work will include the evaluation of the proposed model.

References

1. Jukic, T., Merlak, M.: The use of social networking sites in public administration: the case of Slovenia. Electron. J. E-Gov. 15(1), 2 (2017)
2. Gunawong, P.: Open government and social media: a focus on transparency. Soc. Sci. Comput. Rev. 33(5), 587–598 (2015)
3. Kimutai, G.K., Aluvi, P.A.: Good governance and service delivery: a study of citizen participation in Kisumu County. Univers. J. Manag. 6(2), 59–69 (2018). https://doi.org/10.13189/ujm.2018.060203
4. Zheng, Y., Schachter, H.L.: The impact of administrator willingness on website e-participation: some evidence from municipalities. Public Perform. Manag. Rev. 41(1), 1–21 (2018)
5. Bhadani, A.K., Jothimani, D.: Big data: challenges, opportunities, and realities. In: Effective BD Management and Opportunities for Implementation, pp. 1–24. IGI Global (2016)
6. Mehta, B.B., Rao, U.P.: Privacy preserving unstructured big data analytics: issues and challenges. Procedia Comput. Sci. 78, 120–124 (2016)
7. Bekmamedova, N., Shanks, G.: Social media analytics and business value: a theoretical framework and case study. In: 2014 47th Hawaii International Conference on System Sciences (HICSS), pp. 3728–3737. IEEE (2014)
8. Hussain, A., Vatrapu, R.: Social data analytics tool (SODATO). In: Tremblay, M.C., VanderMeer, D., Rothenberger, M., Gupta, A., Yoon, V. (eds.) DESRIST 2014. LNCS, vol. 8463, pp. 368–372. Springer, Cham (2014). https://doi.org/10.1007/978-3-319-06701-8_27
9. Grubmüller, V., Götsch, K., Krieger, B.: Social media analytics for future oriented policy making. Eur. J. Futures Res. 1(1), 20 (2013)
10. Corrêa, A.S., Paula, E.C.D., Correa, P.L.P., Silva, F.S.C.D.: Transparency and open government data: a wide national assessment of data openness in Brazilian local governments. Transform. Gov.: People Process Policy 11(1), 58–78 (2017)
11. Landon-Murray, M.: Social media and US intelligence agencies: just trending or a real tool to engage and educate? J. Strateg. Secur. 8(3), 67–79 (2015)
12. Verma, R.K., Kumar, S., Ilavarasan, P.V.: Government portals, social media platforms and citizen engagement in India: some insights. Procedia Comput. Sci. 122, 842–849 (2017)

13. Singh, V., Srivastava, I., Johri, V.: Big data and the opportunities and challenges for government agencies. Int. J. Comput. Sci. Inf. Technol. **5**(4), 5821–5824 (2014)
14. Risius, M., Beck, R.: Effectiveness of corporate social media activities in increasing relational outcomes. Inf. Manag. **52**(7), 824–839 (2015)
15. Zeng, D., Chen, H., Lusch, R., Li, S.H.: Social media analytics and intelligence. IEEE Intell. Syst. **25**(6), 13–16 (2010)
16. Udanor, C., Aneke, S., Ogbuokiri, B.O.: Determining social media impact on the politics of developing countries using social network analytics. Program **50**(4), 481–507 (2016)
17. Whillans, A.V., Chen, F.S.: Facebook undermines the social belonging of first year students. Personality Individ. Differ. **133**, 13–16 (2018)
18. Lu, Y., et al.: Integrating predictive analytics and social media. In: 2014 IEEE Conference on Visual Analytics Science and Technology (VAST), pp. 193–202. IEEE (2014)
19. Elgendy, N., Elragal, A.: Big data analytics in support of the decision-making process. Procedia Comput. Sci. **100**, 1071–1084 (2016)
20. Stieglitz, S., Dang-Xuan, L.: Social media and political communication: a social media analytics framework. Soc. Netw. Anal. Min. **3**(4), 1277–1291 (2013). https://doi.org/10.1007/s13278-012-0079-3
21. Islam, O., Alfakeeh, A., Nadeem, F.: A framework for effective big data analytics for decision support systems. Int. J. Comput. Netw. Appl. (IJCNA) **4**(5), 129–137 (2017). https://doi.org/10.22247/ijcna/2017/49227
22. Higgins, J.P., Thompson, S.G., Deeks, J.J., Altman, D.G.: Measuring inconsistency in meta-analyses. BMJ **327**(7414), 557–560 (2003)
23. Khan, K.S., Kunz, R., Kleijnen, J., Antes, G.: Five steps to conducting a systematic review. J. R. Soc. Med. **96**(3), 118–121 (2003)
24. Acharjya, D.P., Ahmed, K.: A survey on big data analytics: challenges, open research issues and tools. Int. J. Adv. Comput. Sci. Appl. **7**(2), 511–518 (2016)
25. Adrian, C., Abdullah, R., Atan, R., Jusoh, Y.Y.: Conceptual model development of big data analytics implementation assessment effect on decision-making. Technology **23**, 24 (2018)
26. Gupta, M., George, J.F.: Toward the development of a big data analytics capability. Inf. Manag. **53**(8), 1049–1064 (2016)
27. Lee, I.: Big data: dimensions, evolution, impacts, and challenges. Bus. Horiz. **60**(3), 293–303 (2017)
28. Sivarajah, U., Kamal, M.M., Irani, Z., Weerakkody, V.: Critical analysis of BD challenges and analytical methods. J. Bus. Res. **70**, 263–286 (2017)
29. Fan, J., Han, F., Liu, H.: Challenges of big data analysis. Natl. Sci. Rev. **1**(2), 293–314 (2014)
30. Rajaraman, V.: Big data analytics. Resonance **21**(8), 695–716 (2016)
31. Uddin, M.F., Gupta, N.: Seven V's of big data understanding big data to extract value. In: Proceedings of the 2014 Zone 1 Conference of the American Society for Engineering Education, pp. 1–5. IEEE (2014)
32. Anuradha, J.: A brief introduction on big data 5Vs characteristics and Hadoop technology. Procedia Comput. Sci. **48**, 319–324 (2015)
33. Khan, N., et al.: Big data: survey, technologies, opportunities, and challenges. Sci. World J. **2014**, 18 (2014)
34. Ganesh, A., Sandhya, M., Shankar, S.: A study on fault tolerance methods in cloud computing. In: 2014 IEEE International Advance Computing Conference (IACC), pp. 844–849. IEEE (2014)
35. Mishra, S., Dhote, V., Prajapati, G.S., Shukla, J.P.: Challenges in big data application: a review. Int. J. Comput. Appl. **121**(19) (2015)

36. Ali, A., Qadir, J., ur Rasool, R., Sathiaseelan, A., Zwitter, A., Crowcroft, J.: Big data for development: applications and techniques. Big Data Anal. **1**(1), 2 (2016)

37. Moura, J., Serrão, C.: Security and privacy issues of big data. In: Handbook of Research on Trends and Future Directions in Big Data and Web Intelligence, pp. 20–52. IGI Global (2015)

38. Jaseena, K.U., David, J.M.: Issues, challenges, and solutions: big data mining. Comput. Sci. Inf. Technol. (CS & IT) **4**, 131–140 (2014)

39. Kanchi, S., Sandilya, S., Ramkrishna, S., Manjrekar, S., Vhadgar, A.: Challenges and solutions in big data management–an overview. In: 2015 3rd International Conference on Future Internet of Things and Cloud, pp. 418–426. IEEE (2015)

40. Matali, M.: An investigation of the impact of social media as an effective communication tool in Namibia: a case study of the Affirmative repositioning Movement (ARM). Doctoral dissertation, University of Namibia (2017)

41. Moreno, J., Serrano, M.A., Fernández-Medina, E.: Main issues in big data security. Future Internet **8**(3), 44 (2016)

42. Sari, A., Karay, M.: Reactive data security approach and review of data security techniques in wireless networks. Int. J. Commun. Netw. Syst. Sci. **8**(13), 567 (2015)

43. Mounia, B., Habiba, C.: Big data privacy in healthcare Moroccan context. Procedia Comput. Sci. **63**, 575–580 (2015)

44. Bagga, S., Sharma, A.: Big data and its challenges: a review. In: 2018 4th International Conference on Computing Sciences (ICCS), pp. 183–187. IEEE (2018)

45. Baraka, Z.: Opportunities to manage big data efficiently and effectively. Doctoral dissertation, Dublin Business School (2014)

46. Lopez, B.E., Magliocca, N.R., Crooks, A.T.: Challenges and opportunities of social media data for socio-environmental systems research. Land **8**, 107 (2019). https://doi.org/10.3390/land8070107

47. Khatana, P., Soni, Y.: Big data techniques: today and tomorrow. Int. J. Res. Eng. Sci. Manag. **1**(11), 282–284 (2018)

48. Abadi, M., et al.: TensorFlow: large-scale machine learning on heterogeneous distributed systems. arXiv preprint arXiv:1603.04467 (2016)

49. Lyko, K., Nitzschke, M., Ngonga Ngomo, A.-C.: Big data acquisition. In: Cavanillas, J.M., Curry, E., Wahlster, W. (eds.) New Horizons for a Data-Driven Economy, pp. 39–61. Springer, Cham (2016). https://doi.org/10.1007/978-3-319-21569-3_4

50. Specht, A., et al.: Data management challenges in analysis and synthesis in the ecosystem sciences. Sci. Total Environ. **534**, 144–158 (2015)

51. Ularu, E.G., Puican, F.C., Apostu, A., Velicanu, M.: Perspectives on big data and big data analytics. Database Syst. J. **3**(4), 3–14 (2012)

52. Saleh, S.H., Ismail, R., Ibrahim, Z., Hussin, N.: Issues, challenges and solutions of big data in information management: an overview. Int. J. Acad. Res. Bus. Soc. Sci. **8**(12) (2018)

53. Putro, B.L., Surendro, K., Herbert: Leadership and culture of data governance for the achievement of higher education goals (case study: Indonesia University of Education). In: AIP Conference Proceedings, vol. 1708, no. 1, p. 050002. AIP Publishing (2016)

54. Koltay, T.: Data governance, data literacy and the management of data quality. IFLA J. **42**(4), 303–312 (2016)

55. Curry, E.: The big data value chain: definitions, concepts, and theoretical approaches. In: Cavanillas, J.M., Curry, E., Wahlster, W. (eds.) New Horizons for a Data-Driven Economy, pp. 29–37. Springer, Cham (2016). https://doi.org/10.1007/978-3-319-21569-3_3

56. Biswas, M., Sipes, C.: Social media in Syria's uprising and post-revolution Libya: an analysis of activists' and Blogger's online engagement. Arab Media Soc. **19**, 1–21 (2014)

57. Kavanaugh, A., Sheetz, S.D., Skandrani, H., Tedesco, J.C., Sun, Y., Fox, E.A.: The use and impact of social media during the 2011 Tunisian revolution. In: Proceedings of the 17th International Digital Government Research Conference on Digital Government Research, pp. 20–30. ACM (2016)
58. Nwanga, M.E., Onwuka, E.N., Aibinu, A.M., Ubadike, O.C.: Impact of big data analytics to Nigerian mobile phone industry. In: 2015 International Conference on Industrial Engineering and Operations Management (IEOM), pp. 1–6. IEEE (2015)
59. Mgudlwa, S., Iyamu, T.: Integration of social media with healthcare big data for improved service delivery. S. Afr. J. Inf. Manag. **20**(1), 1–8 (2018)
60. Marivate, V., Moiloa, P.: Catching crime: detection of public safety incidents using social media. In: 2016 Pattern Recognition Association of South Africa and Robotics and Mechatronics International Conference (PRASA-RobMech), pp. 1–5. IEEE (2016)
61. Chebib, N.K., Sohail, R.M.: The reasons social media contributed to the 2011 Egyptian revolution. Int. J. Bus. Res. Manag. (IJBRM) **2**(3), 139–162 (2011)
62. Alemneh, D.G., Rorissa, A., Assefa, S.: Harnessing social media for promoting tourism in Africa: an exploratory analysis of tweets. In: IConference 2016 Proceedings (2016)
63. Njeri, M.W.: Effect of social media interactions on financial performance of commercial banks in Kenya. M.Sc. project, University of Nairobi, Kenya (2014)

Knowledge and Knowledge Management

Knowledge Transfer in Science Education: The Case for Usability-Based Knowledge Visualization Guidelines

Olakumbi A. Fadiran[✉], Judy van Biljon, and Marthie A. Schoeman

School of Computing, University of South Africa, Pretoria, South Africa
olakumbi@gmail.com, {vbiljja,schoema}@unisa.ac.za

Abstract. There is growing evidence that visualization aids knowledge transfer. However, the cases where learners have been actively involved as co-creators of knowledge visualization aids are limited. Furthermore, employing knowledge visualization for teaching and learning in high-school science have been proposed but empirical evidence of the effect on knowledge transfer is limited. The purpose of this study is to report on the knowledge transfer effect of applying usability-based knowledge visualization guidelines. A design-based research methodology guided by pragmatism was applied. The data capturing methods include a questionnaire-based survey, interviews and observations. The results suggest that the use of knowledge visualization can support knowledge transfer and the students' learning experience in secondary school education, but more research is required to confirm this. The contribution of this paper is to add to the emerging discourse on the use of knowledge visualization for teaching and learning, and to report on how knowledge visualization guidelines can be used in practice.

Keywords: Knowledge visualization · Usability-based knowledge visualization guidelines · Knowledge transfer

1 Introduction

Digital technology is widely used for educational purposes. In this scenario a salient duty of a teacher is to assist in the transfer of knowledge to students in a meaningful and understandable manner [1]. To aid this role, teachers use their proficiency to choose and use teaching materials such as lecture notes, textbooks, multimedia tools etc. [2], while learners are expected to engage with these study materials. Teachers often employ specific strategies to create and transfer knowledge, and one such technique is visualization [3, 4]. Visualization involves the use of images to transfer data, information or knowledge [5, 6]. These are often created by teachers, educational, learning and instructional designers for teaching and learning [7], with minimal or negligible contribution from learners. According to Bada [8], it benefits learners to be co-creators of their learning experience. Actively involving students in knowledge visualization (KV) is one way of compelling them to engage with learning material and to achieve knowledge transfer (KT). In addition, producing KV allows learners to demonstrate their knowledge acquisition. The problem is a lack of knowledge

M. Hattingh et al. (Eds.): I3E 2020, LNCS 12067, pp. 263–273, 2020.
https://doi.org/10.1007/978-3-030-45002-1_22

visualization guidelines and standards in the extant literature, this hampers evidence-based implementation of knowledge visualization initiatives.

This paper is an extension of the work done by Fadiran, van Biljon and Schoeman [9], which focused on evaluating the usefulness of usability-based knowledge visualization guidelines for high school science learners to create, illustrate and internalise the new knowledge that they are expected to become proficient in. For this paper, the investigation focuses on *learners' experience of KT* while applying the usability-based knowledge visualization guidelines in creating images to demonstrate their knowledge acquisition, as well as the *effect on the images created by learners* when they apply the usability-based knowledge visualization guidelines. To investigate learners' experience of KT via the use of usability-based knowledge visualization guidelines, a group of science learners in high school were asked to create visual diagrams to illustrate the rocket launch phase. Usability-based knowledge visualization guidelines was introduced to learners after which the initial images created by learners were revised to meet these guidelines. The exercise aims to investigate the impact of each guideline on the images created by the learners when using the guidelines to improve their knowledge representation to demonstrate their knowledge acquisition and transfer. The remainder of the paper gives an overview on: what KV entails; KT; how Human Computer Interaction (HCI) usability guidelines was used to inform KV principles, culminating in the usability-based knowledge visualization guidelines artefacts developed for this study; and the effect of usability-based knowledge visualization guidelines on images produced by learners as well as learners experience of KT through KV.

2   Literature Review

Visualization is defined as the technique of changing measurable data into visual images in a manner that unveils their patterns and relations [5, 10]. The subsequent sections describe KV, KT and usability-based knowledge visualization guidelines in relation to this study.

2.1   What Is Knowledge Visualization?

Knowledge visualization consists of exploring the use of visual representations in the form of graphs, diagrams, drawings, sonographs etc. to enhance knowledge creation and transfer between at least two people [11, 12]. Eppler views KV as the use of graphics to create, integrate and administer knowledge [13]. Van Biljon and Renaud noted that the primary aim of KV is *knowledge transfer* in contrast to information visualization which aims to support *pattern identification* [7]. In summary, KV entails the creation of knowledge, using available visual resources in a manner that is understandable and communicable to other people.

2.2   Knowledge Transfer

The term 'knowledge transfer' according to [14] "involves both the sharing of knowledge by the knowledge source and the acquisition and application of knowledge by the recipient". KT can be defined as the transmission of knowledge from one place, person or ownership to another [15].

According to [16], teachers can impart information and knowledge to learners in the process of teaching and learning. However, for learners to internalise the information they need to rebuild the knowledge. KV is an approach to assist in the process of rebuilding knowledge. In addition, teachers can use KV to transfer easily understandable visual metaphors since the brain can process images more easily than text [17].

2.3   Usability-Based Knowledge Visualization Guidelines

A systematic literature review (SLR) was used to extract design principles from the field of information and knowledge visualization from literature, as well as HCI usability guidelines. The SLR was chosen as a replicable, open, impartial and comprehensive protocol [18, 19]. The mapping of KV principles onto HCI usability guidelines is explained in Fadiran et al. [9]. That mapping is the theoretical basis of the usability-based knowledge visualization guidelines developed for this study. The guidelines relevant to this study are: Abstract (or compress) the knowledge, Easy to understand, Know your data, Clarity, Use natural representations, Legend, Use of colours, Avoid decorations, Relationship between concepts clearly shown, Simplicity and Clear boundaries.

3   Research Methodology

A design-based research (DBR) methodology was employed in this study with pragmatism as the philosophy. DBR was selected as it: relates with circumstances in the real world [20, 21]; and incorporates the application of data triangulation which enhances the reliability and internal validity of findings [22]. A research group comprising a teacher and science learners in high school was set up and organized to collect information about the impact of usability-based knowledge visualization guidelines to support KT. The approach promoted the interaction of teachers and learners and allowed us to obtain qualitative and quantitative information from the participants.

3.1   Procedure

Twenty-one representative participants (18 learners, 1 educator and 1 usability tester) took part in the research. Participants were selected based on convenience sampling. The learners (12 males) were high school science students attending schools in the Gauteng province (private and public). This ensured that a cross-section of participants has been chosen as advocated by [23]. A standard introduction and explanation of the purpose of the research was delineated to participants at the beginning of the session. The phases of a rocket launch were taught, and learners were requested to provide a diagrammatic representation of the topic. Learners created their first image after which they were introduced to usability-based knowledge visualization guidelines. The learners created a second image by applying these guidelines to the initial image.

The link between HCI usability guidelines and knowledge visualization can be summarized as follows, for more detail please see Fadiran et al. [9].

1. Abstract: Extracting essential components and their relationships from a body of knowledge [24, 25] distinguish relevant information [26, 27].
2. Present overview and details on demand: This ease navigation and support the search task [28].
3. Consistency: Using the same specific graphic design element to indicate a specific concept or relationship in a visualization and combining distinct concepts and ideas adheres to standards [26, 27].
4. Easy to understand: Presenting the visualization in a simple comprehensive manner requires no prior knowledge of the content [29, 30].
5. Know your data: Comprehending and exploring the data domain while being aware of previous and related work [27] allows the designer to create meaningful and appropriate images [30, 31].
6. Clarity: Clarifying goals, objectives and outcomes [26] and the use of defined symbols avoid ambiguity [32, 33].
7. Know your audience: User-centred design, understanding the audience's needs, abilities, interests, and expectations [27] are fundamental concepts in HCI.
8. Use natural representations: Associating the visualization with the real world allows a recognition-based approach to interpreting images [34, 35].
9. Legend: A supplementary object that offers detailed explanations of the symbols provides multiple views of the data [36].
10. Use of colours: Colour can differentiate relationships, beautify, group, map and classify images [24, 31, 37]
11. Avoid decorations: Avoid the use of unrelated elements [32, 34].
12. Relationship between concepts clearly shown: Use links to demonstrate relationships between concepts [33, 38].
13. Motivate audience: Present the knowledge in an engaging manner [26].
14. Simplicity: Minimize the number of concepts on each level of visualization to 7 ± 2 objects [33].
15. Dual coding: The use of text and graphics to explain the same construct [39] allows processing of information with both textual and visual representation [40].
16. Clear boundaries: Navigate and embed knowledge within a domain [41].

After the introduction to the visualization guidelines some learners edited their initial image while others resolved to creating a new image. The two images each learner created were then compared and evaluated to determine the effect of the guidelines on knowledge acquisition and transfer. Quantitative and qualitative analysis was conducted to: compare the two images produced by each learner to demonstrate their knowledge acquisition; evaluate learners' marks for the respective images produced to demonstrate their knowledge acquisition before and after a brief on using usability-based knowledge visualization guideline; and document their experience of using KV to demonstrate their knowledge acquisition.

4   Results and Findings

Previous research proposed a set of validated KV guidelines towards the theory and practice of using KV in teaching and learning [9]. Effective KT from teachers to learners influence learners' performance and satisfaction [2]. Figure 1 shows the difference in the marks of learners before and after the brief on usability-based knowledge visualization guidelines. The marks for the visualization created after the brief is consistently higher which suggests a positive influence on KT. However, we acknowledge that there are other contributing factors and the limitation of the sample size. Therefore, we can only conclude that the results merit further investigation. Table 1 shows the post survey reaction of learners to the use of KV in teaching and learning. A large percentage of the learners think the use of KV influenced their knowledge acquisition and transfer.

4.1   Analysis

From Fig. 1, it can be observed that the average marks of learners increased from 52% to 56% following the brief on usability-based knowledge visualization guidelines.

Notably, the study content was not revisited before the second visualization was created. Learners who did not feel a need to modify their images show a minimum percentage difference of 0% in marks while the maximum was 12% for a learner who took advantage of the usability-based knowledge visualization guidelines to modify the initial image produced.

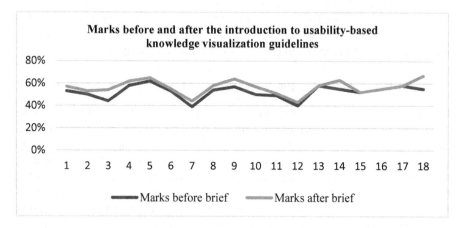

Fig. 1. Learners' marks before and after the brief on usability-based knowledge visualization guidelines

Table 1 depicts learners' post survey reaction to the use of KV in teaching and learning. All learners indicated that they had used images before to represent school work in form of sketches, graphs, charts, tables and pictures while 61% agreed that implementing the usability-based knowledge visualization guidelines influenced their final diagram. Furthermore, 83% stated that they will consider the usability-based knowledge visualization guidelines to exhibit knowledge transfer to others. Finally, 94% of the learners believe the use of KV influenced their knowledge acquisition.

Table 1. Post survey reaction of learners to the use of knowledge visualization

Response	Have you ever used images to represent your school work?	Did the use of KV guidelines had any effect on your final diagram?	Will you consider using the KV as a means of exhibiting knowledge transfer to others?	Do you think the use of KV had any effect on your knowledge acquisition?
Yes	100%	61%	83%	94%
No	–	39%	17%	6%

Some of the explanations given by learners are shown below:

– *Effect of KV on the final diagram includes:* Images produced are clearer and simpler, useful in abstraction, improves image quality.
– *Effect of KV on knowledge acquisition includes:* Easier studying, learning new knowledge, easier to understand new topics, promotes memorability, simplifies learning, clarity.

Images produced by learners before and after the introduction to KV guidelines were compared and the observations are described in the next section. The analysis was carried out on the KV guidelines presented in Sect. 3.1. The subsequent sections show observations made on samples of some of the learners' visualizations before and after introducing the learners to usability-based knowledge visualization guidelines.

4.2 Guidelines with Major Effect on the Final Diagram

The guidelines 'Know your data, Clarity, Easy to understand, Use of colours, Clear boundaries, Legend and Relationship between concepts clearly shown' had a noticeable effect on learners' final visualizations. Figure 2 is a sample of how a learner incorporated some of these guidelines into his/her final diagram. In the new image produced, the learner added a title added to the visualization (Easy to understand) as well as a description of the symbols used (Legend). No learners included a legend in their initial visualization. However, the brief prompted half of them to add a legend, solving their need to give a meaningful explanation of the symbols used and thereby aiding other usability-based knowledge visualization guidelines. The clarity of the boundaries may be dependent on the context of the topic being visualised i.e. it is less relevant for visualizations in the same domain.

The 'Easy to understand' guideline had a high level of compliance which was influenced by the compliancy of other guidelines, suggesting inter-guideline dependencies. Although the 'Use of colours' guideline had a noticeable increase in compliance after the brief on usability-based knowledge visualization guidelines, a number of participants were cautious in their application of this principle to avoid compromising other principles such as 'Avoid decorations'. For others, it was a quick resolve to implement the 'Clear boundaries' principle.

Before introduction of knowledge visualization guidelines	After introduction of knowledge visualization guidelines

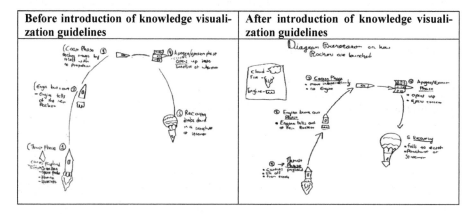

Fig. 2. Sample of learners' visualization before and after usability-based knowledge visualization guidelines brief

4.3   Guidelines with Little Effect on Final Diagrams

The guidelines 'Abstract knowledge, Avoid decorations and Simplicity' had negligible visible influence on learners' final diagram. Figure 3 is another sample of images produced by a learner with the brief on usability-based knowledge visualization guidelines having little effect on the final image produced.

Before introduction of knowledge visualization guidelines	After introduction of knowledge visualization guidelines

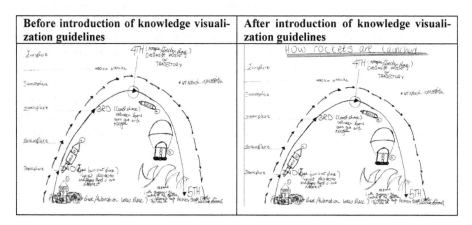

Fig. 3. Sample of learners' visualization before and after usability-based knowledge visualization guidelines brief

From observation, the 'Avoid decorations' principle did not make a significant difference in the final images created by learners, especially after a legend clarified symbols used. The visualizations produced by most learners was void of symbols not related to the content of the study. Also, the 'Abstract knowledge' and 'Simplicity' principles appeared to have little impact on the final images created by learners. In both cases, this could be due to time constraints which caused learners to include only the most important constructs visualised in their simplest form. These principles could become more prominent when visualizations have been created over a period.

Before introduction of knowledge visualization guidelines	After introduction of knowledge visualization guidelines

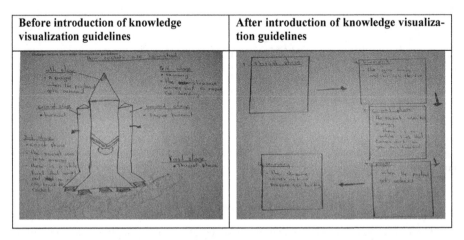

Fig. 4. Sample of learners' visualizations before and after the introduction of the guidelines

4.4   Guideline with Reduced Compliance (Use of Natural Representation)

Learners in the research group had personal preferences in using visualization to represent knowledge. Some learners believed an artistically inclined individual is better suited to exploring the concept of visualization with the majority of the learners agreeing that they are willing to use images to represent and transfer knowledge. In addition, some learners were concerned that their representation of the real world may violate another principle i.e. the *Avoid decorations* principle.

A designer's background can influence their use of natural representation. Figure 4 shows a learner producing a new visualization void of images. The initial incorporated the guideline 'Use of natural representation' while the latter implemented 'Avoid decorations'.

5   Challenges and Limitations

The challenges and limitations encountered during this study includes: factors that may have influenced learners' conformity to usability-based knowledge visualization guidelines i.e. disorientation, information and cognitive overload, time constraint; the risk of possible distortion of reality through misinterpretations; the diversity in learners literacy skills and learning styles; inadequate automatization support in the process of creating KV; and number of participants.

6   Summary and Future Work

This paper contributes to the discourse on how usability-based knowledge visualization guidelines could provide support in improving knowledge acquisition and transfer amongst high school science learners. Learners experienced the use of KV in their knowledge acquisition and transfer as positive. The findings indicate that most of the guidelines considered in this study provided various degrees of impact on the images produced by learners, showing evidence of the effect of the guidelines on knowledge transfer. This correlates with findings from literature indicating that KV can be used to: improve learning abilities; improve communication and interaction around cognitive processes; and improve learners' attitude towards learning [7, 38, 42, 43].

Future work would be to repeat the research with a larger number of participants and in other school subjects in order to refine KV guidelines and to study the effect of using the guidelines to achieve and enhance knowledge transfer. In addition, the differences in how learners of previous generations and the Net Generation approaches visualization and use it for teaching and learning needs to be investigated.

Acknowledgement. This paper is based on the research supported by the South African Research Chairs Initiative of the Department of Science and Technology and National Research Foundation of South Africa (Grant No. 98564).

References

1. Stürmer, K., Könings, K.D., Seidel, T.: Declarative knowledge and professional vision in teacher education: effect of courses in teaching and learning. Br. J. Educ. Psychol. **83**(3), 467–483 (2013)
2. Ahmad, K.B., Ahmad, M., Rejab, M.: The influence of knowledge visualization on externalizing tacit knowledge. In: Proceeding of the International Conference on Advanced Science Engineering and Information Technology, pp. 124–128 (2011)
3. Strakhovich, E.: Ontological engineering in education: tools for knowledge transfer and knowledge assessment. In: International Conference on Advanced Learning Technologies, pp. 714–715 (2014)
4. Wang, P., Wu, P., Wang, J., Chi, H., Wang, X.: A critical review of the use of virtual reality in construction engineering education and training. Int. J. Environ. Res. Public Health Rev. **15**(6), 1204 (2018)

5. Manovich, L.: What is visualization? J. Initiat. Digit. Humanit. Media Cult. **2**(1), 1–32 (2010)
6. Ursyn, A.: Knowledge Visualization as a Teaching Tool. Visual Approaches to Cognitive Education With Technology Integration, pp. 1–23. IGI Global, Hershey (2018)
7. van Biljon, J., Renaud, K.: Facilitating knowledge visualisation as communication and knowledge transfer mechanism in postgraduate learning. In: Brown, T.H., van der Merwe, H.J. (eds.) mLearn 2015. CCIS, vol. 560, pp. 156–171. Springer, Cham (2015). https://doi.org/10.1007/978-3-319-25684-9_12
8. Bada, S.O.: Constructivism learning theory: a paradigm for teaching and learning. J. Res. Method Education. **5**(6), 66–70 (2015). https://doi.org/10.9790/7388-05616670
9. Fadiran, O.A., van Biljon, J., Schoeman, M.A.: How can visualization principles be used to support knowledge transfer in teaching and learning? In: 2018 Conference on Information Communications Technology and Society, ICTAS 2018 – Proceedings, pp. 1–6 (2018)
10. Munzner, T.: Visualization. In: Shirley, P., et al. (eds.) Fundamentals of Graphics, ch. 27, 3rd edn., pp. 675–707 (2009)
11. Yusoff, Z., Katmon, S.A., Ahmad, M.N., Miswan, S.H.M.: Visual representation: enhancing students's learning engagement through knowledge visualization. In: International Conference on Informatics and Creative Multimedia, pp. 242–247 (2013)
12. Chaolong, J., Hanning, W., Lili, W.: Research on visualization of multi-dimensional real-time traffic data stream based on cloud computing. Procedia Eng. **137**, 709–718 (2016)
13. Eppler, M.J.: What is an effective knowledge visualization? Insights from a review of seminal concepts. In: Proceedings of the International Conference on Information Visualization, pp. 3–12 (2011)
14. Wang, S., Noe, R.A.: Knowledge sharing: a review and directions for future research. Hum. Resour. Manag. Rev. **20**(2), 115–131 (2010)
15. Sarala, R.M., Junni, P., Cooper, C.L., Tarba, S.Y.: A sociocultural perspective on knowledge transfer in mergers and acquisitions. J. Manag. **42**(5), 1230–1249 (2016)
16. Zhong, D., Zhang, J.: Knowledge visualization-an approach of knowledge transfer and restructuring in education. In: International Forum on Information Technology and Applications, IFITA 2009, vol. 3, pp. 716–719 (2009)
17. Eppler, M.J., Burkhard, R.A.: Visual representations in knowledge management: framework and cases. J. Knowl. Manag. **11**(4), 112–122 (2007)
18. Oates, B.J., Edwards, H.M., Wainwright, D.W.: A model-driven method for the systematic literature review of qualitative empirical research. In: ICIS 2012 Proceedings, China, pp. 1–18 (2012)
19. Xiao, Y., Watson, M.: Guidance on conducting a systematic literature review. J. Plann. Educ. Res. **39**(1), 93–112 (2019)
20. Bakker, A., van Eerde, D.: An introduction to design-based research with an example from statistics education. In: Bikner-Ahsbahs, A., Knipping, C., Presmeg, N. (eds.) Approaches to Qualitative Research in Mathematics Education. Advances in Mathematics Education, pp. 429–466. Springer, Dordrecht (2015). https://doi.org/10.1007/978-94-017-9181-6_16
21. Anderson, T., Shattuck, J.: Design-based research: a decade of progress in education research? Educ. Res. Rev. **41**(1), 16–25 (2016)
22. Stemberger, T., Cenci, M.: Design-based research in an educational research context. J. Contemp. Educ. Stud./Sodobna Pedagogika **65**(1), 62–75 (2014)
23. Krueger, R.A., Casey, M.A.: Participants in a focus group. In: Focus Groups: A Practical Guide for Applied Research, pp. 63–84 (2009). https://www.sagepub.com/sites/default/files/upm-binaries/24056_Chapter4.pdf
24. Scarpato, N., Maria, P., Pazienza, T.: Knowledge-based visualization systems. University of Rome Tor Vergata (2012)

25. Kumar, S.: A review of recent trends and issues in visualization. Int. J. Comput. Sci. Eng. (IJCSE) **8**(3), 41–54 (2016)
26. Ssemugabi, S., De Villiers, R.: Effectiveness of heuristic evaluation in usability evaluation of e-learning applications in higher educ. S. Afr. Comput. J. **45**(45), 26–39 (2010)
27. Ferreira, D.J.: Human computer interaction teaching method to encourage creativity. In: The Seventh International Conference on Software Engineering Advances (ICSEA), pp. 472–478 (2012)
28. Burigat, S., Chittaro, L.: On the effectiveness of overview + detail visualization on mobile devices. IEEE Trans. Visual Comput. Graphics **17**(2), 1–18 (2013)
29. Zhou, Y., Yin, L., Wang, L.: A research for the classification of knowledge visualization. In: International Conference on Electrical and Control Engineering, pp. 6235–6238 (2011)
30. Figueiras, A.: How to tell stories using visualization. In: 8th International Conference on Information Visualization, pp. 18–26 (2014)
31. Ware, C.: Information Visualization: Perception for Design, 3rd edn. Elsevier, Amsterdam (2012)
32. Bresciani, S., Eppler, M.J.: The pitfalls of visual representations. SAGE Open **5**(4), 1–14 (2015). http://journals.sagepub.com/doi/10.1177/2158244015611451
33. Gavrilova, T., Leshcheva, I., Strakhovich, E.: Gestalt principles of creating learning business ontologies for knowledge codification. Knowl. Manag. Res. Pract. **13**(4), 418–428 (2015)
34. Haroz, S., Kosara, R., Franconeri, S.L.: ISOTYPE visualization – working memory, performance, and engagement with pictographs. In: Proceedings of the 33rd Annual ACM Conference on Human Factors in Computing Systems - CHI 2015, pp. 1191–1200 (2015). http://dl.acm.org/citation.cfm?id=2702123.2702275
35. Borkin, M.A., et al.: Beyond memorability: visualization recognition and recall. IEEE Trans. Visual Comput. Graphics **22**(1), 519–528 (2016)
36. Hall, A., Virrantaus, K.: Visualizing the workings of agent-based models: diagrams as a tool for communication and knowledge acquisition. Comput. Environ. Urban Syst. **58**, 1–11 (2016)
37. Zhi, Q., Su, M.: Enhance collaborative learning by visualizing process of knowledge building with padlet. In: International Conference of Educational Innovation through Technology (EITT), vol. 1, pp. 221–225 (2015). http://ieeexplore.ieee.org/document/7446182/
38. Wang, M., Peng, J., Cheng, B., Zhou, H., Liu, J.: Knowledge visualization for self-regulated learning. Educ. Technol. Soc. **14**(3), 28–42 (2011)
39. Marchese, F.T., Banissi, E.: Knowledge Visualization Currents: From Text to Art to Culture. Springer, London (2012). https://doi.org/10.1007/978-1-4471-4303-1
40. Bresciani, S., Ge, J., Niu, Y.: The effect of visual mapping on attitude toward organizational strategy: scale development and application in Europe and China. In: International Conference on Communication, Media, Technology and Design, vol. 2, pp. 275–283 (2014)
41. Diakopoulos, N., Kivran-Swaine, F., Naaman, M.: Playable data: characterizing the design space of game-y infographics. In: Proceedings of the 2011 Annual Conference on Human Factors in Computing Systems, pp. 1717–1726 (2011)
42. Bertschi, S., et al.: What is knowledge visualization? Perspectives on an emerging discipline. In: Proceedings of the International Conference on Information Visualization, pp. 329–336 (2011)
43. Sun, N., Li, K., Zhu, X.: Action research on visualization learning of mathematical concepts under personalized education idea: take learning of geometrical concepts of elementary math for example. In: Cheung, S.K.S., Kwok, L., Shang, J., Wang, A., Kwan, R. (eds.) ICBL 2016. LNCS, vol. 9757, pp. 348–359. Springer, Cham (2016). https://doi.org/10.1007/978-3-319-41165-1_31

A Knowledge Asset Management Implementation Framework for Information Systems Outsourcing Projects

Hanlie Smuts[(⊠)] and George Maramba

Department of Informatics, University of Pretoria, Pretoria, South Africa
hanlie.smuts@up.ac.za, georgemaramba@gmail.com

Abstract. Organisations are increasingly outsourcing information systems (IS) to external service providers. These IS outsourcing decisions are driven by multiple organisational factors such as outsource vendor expertise and knowledge, process performance improvement due to better IS, and enabling the organisation's ability to focus on its core capabilities. In order to harnass such vendor knowledge to achieve business outcomes, the importance of a shared knowledge asset base, between the client organisation and outsource vendor, is emphasised. However, outcomes from IS outsourcing remain poor despite consideration of experience and research. Therefore, the aim of this study is to design and propose a knowledge asset management implementation framework that may be applied in IS outsourcing projects. The proposed framework was evaluated by an experienced programme director and its applicability was tested against a large scale IS outsourcing project. The purpose of such a framework is to enable organisations to manage and institutionalise knowledge assets that are created during the IS outsourcing project and to ensure that the organisation may gain the benefit from such knowledge assets as an outcome of the IS outsourcing arrangement.

Keywords: Knowledge asset management · Information systems outsourcing · Knowledge management · Framework · Knowledge asset management implementation

1 Introduction

Information systems (IS) outsourcing, where an organisation contracts external service providers to effectively deliver IS-enabled business processes, application services and/or infrastructure solutions for business outcomes, is regarded as an important business strategy [1]. Recently, as experience and knowledge have deepened, outsourcing as a business phenomenon has been positioned as an opportunity to be applied to IS activities in line with an organisation's overall sourcing strategy [2]. Several reasons are cited by organisations for adopting IS outsourcing, such as; ensuring a high level of productivity, and to offer maximum quality to their customers [3].

The importance of knowledge management (KM) and a shared knowledge base between the client organisation and outsource vendor, are highlighted as a basis for organisational performance gains [4]. In order to realise these performance gains, an environment for client organisation and outsource vendor knowledge integration must

© IFIP International Federation for Information Processing 2020
Published by Springer Nature Switzerland AG 2020
M. Hattingh et al. (Eds.): I3E 2020, LNCS 12067, pp. 274–286, 2020.
https://doi.org/10.1007/978-3-030-45002-1_23

be created through common language and frequent interaction, consequently fostering knowledge transfer and ultimately, knowledge asset management [5, 6]. Knowledge asset management is a commonly stated objective for organisations, although difficult to achieve, as knowledge creation is rewarded rather than knowledge reuse [7].

However, outcomes from IS outsourcing continue to remain poor despite consideration of experience and research [8, 9]. Recent studies suggest that one of the reasons for this lack of improvement is due to the complex nature of outsourcing agreements as they shift from being a mere cost cutting exercise to one which holds significant strategic and social importance to the organisation [9, 10]. Furthermore, knowledge asset management is considered most valuable in the knowledge-driven economy, although the focus on tasks of knowledge asset understanding and management, have not been prioritised compared to their physical counterparts [11]. While scholars highlight the significance of knowledge asset management in addressing IS outsourcing complexity, little research has been conducted on how organisations manage knowledge assets and knowledge reuse in IS outsourcing circumstances [7, 12, 13]. Therefore, the research question that this paper aims to address is: *"What are the components of a knowledge asset management implementation framework for managing knowledge assets in IS outsourcing projects?"*. By addressing this question, organisations are able to reference an approach to the management of knowledge assets during IS outsourcing projects, ensuring that institutional knowledge is not lost during outsourcing and that new knowledge that is created through the partnership, is captured and managed.

In Sect. 2 we present the background to the study followed by the research approach in Sect. 3. Section 4 details the data analysis and findings, while Sect. 5 concludes the paper.

2 Background

The management of knowledge in the context of IS outsourcing, is a comprehensive course of action that requires focus and commitment throughout an organisation in order to achieve the desired results [13, 14]. The outcome of this organisational focus and commitment, is an important factor for IS outsourcing arrangements, seeing as the aim is to increase the collective knowledge of each other's knowledge domain [5, 15]. Technology-specific knowledge, such as the IS services provided, flows from the organisation to the outsource supplier, and business-specific knowledge about processes and procedures flows from the supplier to the organisation. The purpose of this knowledge transfer is to increase the knowledge shared by the organisation and the outsource vendor [5, 16]. Knowledge sharing and management in the context of IS outsourcing is not a stand-alone practice; it should be integrated into all aspects of the outsourcing arrangement [5, 15, 17]. The inseparability of IS from the internal production service in the client organisation implies that even in situations of absolute outsourcing, a minimum set of capabilities are retained in-house by the client organisation [18].

In the next sections we consider IS outsourcing, KM, and highlight the role of knowledge asset management in order to manage knowledge in an IS outsourcing arrangement.

2.1   IS Outsourcing as a Business Phenomenon

IS outsourcing refers to the contractual agreement between the client organisation and an outsource vendor for the transfer of assets and/or the development and implementation of IS within an agreed time period and a specified cost [9, 18]. The transfer of assets view of IS outsourcing is also applicable to subcontracting in IS [19]. Once the outsource vendor has been selected and prior to embarking on transition, several elements should be considered to further guide the outsourcing arrangement process such as a transition planning, communication strategy planning, transfer conditions identification and resource mobilisation [20].

IS outsourcing initiatives consist of many tasks that have to be executed in an interrelated manner [9]. These interdependent steps must enable an organisation to obtain the correct information in order to be able to select the right services for the right reasons, consequently maximising business leverage in the outsourcing arrangement [20, 21]. Several outsourcing lifecycle models exist each consisting of numerous steps. Examples of such interrelated project steps include; the IS outsourcing programme lifecycle consisting of the request for proposal and vendor selection, contracts and negotiations, setup and logistics, programme execution, implementation and testing, and programme completion stages [22]. The three phase IS outsourcing building block approach consists of the architect, engage and govern stages [20]. Alborz et al. [23] defined 3 stages: (1) pre-contract stage (scoping and evaluation), (2) contract stage (negotiation) and (3) post-contract stage. Outsourcing strategy and due diligence operationalise the *pre-contract* stage and contract development the *contract* stage. The *post-contract* stage is operationalised through governance, performance management, contract management, working relationship management and knowledge management.

Such an IS outsourcing project lifecycle guides an organisation in realising the full value that outsourcing can provide to become an informed purchaser, to plan and design the commercial arrangement, to carefully select the best value for money supplier and to put in the appropriate management skills and effort [20, 24]. Outsourcing should give an organisation a strategic advantage and involves judgements about quantitative and qualitative factors [19]. If it fails to deliver these advantages then an outsourcing arrangement should not be considered [22].

In the next section, we present an overview of the KM and knowledge asset management.

2.2   IS Outsourcing and Knowledge Asset Management in Context

The importance of a shared knowledge base between the client organisation and outsource vendor is highlighted as a basis for performance gains, as it creates sensitivity to the organisational environment of the other party and encompasses goals, constraints, interpretations and behaviour [4, 13]. Such an environment for knowledge integration is created through a common language and frequent interaction, consequently fostering knowledge transfer and adding value [5, 6]. Such knowledge asset value add constitutes what is known by the organisation and employees resulting in a potential long lasting, open-ended value. The organisational knowledge asset value may be derived in two ways: firstly, the degree to which knowledge assets may be abstracted and gen-eralised, and secondly, the extent to which a knowledge asset may be codified [25].

As the same knowledge is used to solve multiple problems, it is recognised that the same IS capability can transform different organisations in different ways [13]. Out-source vendors benefit fully from their knowledge resources as they reuse the same knowledge in different contexts for different customers. Similarly, IS organisations have to design adequate knowledge transfer strategies to build expertise so that new problems can be addressed by reusing the same knowledge [26]. However, the fact that an organisation relies on an outsource vendor does not mean that it should ignore the importance of an ongoing knowledge management programme specifically related to knowledge transfer [6, 27]. Knowledge transfer has come to the fore in response to the increasing size, complexity and scope of organisations, as well as the increasing capabilities of modern IS to support knowledge-orientated activities [13, 28].

Organisations discover the effective deployment of IS management and derive business value from it through experiential learning and hands-on experience. Chal-lenges are not always appreciated unless they are experienced, as the understanding of the value of an IS innovation tends to materialise in an evolutionary manner. Organ-isations choosing to outsource may unintentionally fragment this knowledge by missing critical learning opportunities, with a resulting loss of ensuing business gains. This necessitates constant assessment of the impact of IS outsourcing decisions on the protection and enhancement of an organisation's knowledge base [6, 27].

Before we present the proposed knowledge asset management implementation (KAMI) framework, we present an overview of the research methodology followed for this research paper.

3   Research Approach

The overall objective of this paper was to define a KAMI framework for managing knowledge in IS outsourcing projects. The purpose of such a framework is to assist organisations with the management of knowledge in IS outsourcing projects. In order to achieve this outcome, we followed a design-based approach [29]. Design based research is a "systematic but flexible methodology aimed to improve educational practices through iterative analysis, design, development, and implementation, based on collab-oration among researchers and practitioners in real-world settings, and leading to contextually-sensitive design principles and theories" [31:6]. Design based research produces both theories and practical interventions as its outcomes [31] and encompasses five basic characteristics [30]. The first characteristic is *pragmatic*, referring to the research focus on solving current real-world problems through the design of interven-tions. The *grounded* characteristic points to the fact that the research is grounded in both theory and the real-world context, while *interactive, iterative* and *flexible* refer to the nature of the research process. *Integrative* highlights that researchers integrate a variety of research methods and approaches from both qualitative and quantitative research paradigms, depending on the needs of the research. The final characteristic, *contextual*, emphasises that research outcomes are connected with both the design process through which results are generated and the setting where the research is conducted.

With these characteristics guiding our research, we built upon prior literature about IS outsourcing and knowledge asset management in order to create a KAMI framework (pragmatic nature of our research). Our research approach was of a qualitative nature and the context of our research was IS and organisations. We approached our research on both theory and a real-world context (grounded) by considering existing knowledge management implementation frameworks and gaps identified. Thereafter, we designed our proposed KAMI framework through an iterative process by considering and finally, we evaluated the proposed KAMI framework with a real-world case in order to establish its practical application.

Multiple knowledge management system implementation frameworks focusing on operations exist, however, none of the frameworks specifically encompass knowledge asset management across all phases of an IS outsourcing project. Table 1 summarises the frameworks; in each instance listing the focus of the framework, the steps included in the framework and the reference.

Table 1. Overview of knowledge management system frameworks

Focus of framework	Steps	Source
KMS development	Sense making; envisioning; designing; exploring	[32]
KMS process implementation	Acquisition; storage; sharing; retention; application	[33]
KMS process implementation	Creation; acquisition; storing and retrieving; sharing and distribution; transformation; use	[34]
KMS life cycle	Create; organise; store; share; evaluate	[35]
KMS cycle model	Identify; create; store; share; use; learn; improve	[25]
KMS management implementation framework	Acquisition; evaluation; storage and retrieval; utilisation and creation; application; management	[36]
KMS implementation activities	Create; organise; store; share; evaluate	[37]
KMS implementation	Identify; create; store; share; use	[38]
KMS implementation approach	Initialisation; domain mapping; profiles and policies identification; implementation and personalisation; validation	[39]
KMS implementation approach	Draft; planning; analysis; design; development; implementation; control	[40]
KMS implementation factors model	Strategise; implement; organise	[41]
KMS implementation framework and methodology	Strategise; evaluate; develop; validate; implement	[42]

By mapping the KAMI activities in Table 1 to the stages of IS outsourcing presented in Sect. 2.2, a proposed KAMI framework for IS outsourcing projects is derived and depicted in Fig. 1. Cognisance is taken of the unique attributes of the IS outsourcing life-cycle stages and arrows indicate the flow of the diagram. The *pre-contract stage* [23] of an IS outsourcing project is operationalised through considering the outsourcing strategy where an organisation reflects on the reason and scope for outsourcing, followed by a due diligence evaluating the commercial potential of the outsourcing project. As the organisation is still considering the viability of the IS outsourcing project, the knowledge asset management activities only centre around high level *strategic activities* such as agreeing on the associated principles and governance for managing knowledge assets during the IS outsourcing project and the identification of the accountable organisational structure, as well as the organisational sponsor. The scope of which knowledge assets will be impacted, which knowledge assets will be required for the project and what new knowledge assets will be created during the IS outsourcing project, must also be considered during this strategising activity.

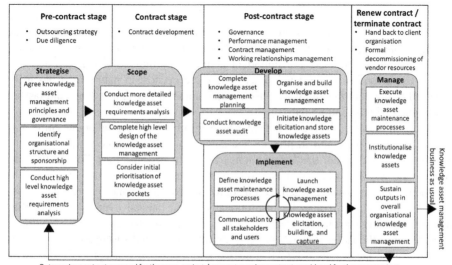

Fig. 1. KAMI Framework for IS Outsourcing Projects

Once the organisation approves that the IS outsourcing project should continue, the project proceeds to the *contract stage* [23]. During this stage the organisation appoints the outsource vendor, normally through a procurement process, and negotiate all aspects of the IS outsourcing contract with the chosen outsource vendor. As it is fairly certain that the IS outsourcing project will proceed, but the contract is just not signed yet, the knowledge asset management activities now move to the *scope phase*. During the scope phase a more detailed knowledge asset requirements analysis must be concluded now that the scope of the IS outsourcing agreement is clear. The identification of knowledge assets impacted will also advise prioritisation as the IS outsourcing project proceeds and with this scope in mind, a high level design of the knowledge asset management system can also be concluded. The scoping of knowledge asset management activities may kick off towards the end of the pre-contract stage, especially once the organisation has completed the due diligence as this activity informs the scope of the knowledge assets impacted. Towards the end of the contract stage, the initial activities of the knowledge asset management implementation development phase may be initiated to ensure that the KAMI is prepared to kick off shortly after the outsourcing contract is signed. If the time between the signing of the contract and the means to capture knowledge assets is too long, knowledge assets may be jeopardised and even lost. These initial activities include the completion of the KAMI planning, as well as the initiation of a knowledge asset audit relevant to the scope of the IS outsourcing agreement.

Once the organisation and the chosen outsource vendor signed the IS outsourcing agreement, the *post-contract stage* is initiated, [23] focusing on the active management of the outsourcing agreement, the working relationships management and the performance management of the vendor. These activities take place within the agreed contract governance framework. From a KAMI perspective, focus is now on the organisation, building and storing knowledge assets. Knowledge elicitation during this phase is key as the elicitation process may include outsource vendor resources. The definition and implementation of knowledge asset management processes and the training of all stakeholders are important activities during the KAMI *development phase*. The activities in the development phase are cyclical in nature as it has to be managed throughout the entire IS outsourcing contract management stage and last for the duration of the contract term.

Once the IS outsourcing contract reached its termination date, the organisation may choose to extend the contract, procure and appoint a new outsource vendor or ensure that the outsource vendor hands operations over to the organisations. For the first two options, the KAMI process will kick off again as the new extended scope has to be considered. In the instance where an outsource vendor must hand over to the organisation, the KAMI must also be institutionalised and handed over to the identified sponsors and organisational structures. This will ensure that the knowledge assets created during the IS outsourcing project, are maintained and sustained.

We applied the proposed KAMI framework in a proof of concept evaluation in an actual IS outsourcing project. The application and subsequent findings of the KAMI framework are discussed in the next section.

4   Application of the KAMI Framework

In order to do a proof of concept evaluation of the KAMI framework, we applied the KAMI framework to a real world IS outsourcing project from an organisation operating in the Information Communication Technology (ICT) sector in South Africa (SA). The organisation utilises an IS multi-sourcing approach as a strategy with a significant number of IS projects and IS operational functions that are outsourced. The specific IS outsourcing project used for the proof of concept evaluation was for the replacement of a large scale legacy system that was outsourced to two vendors, necessitating the appointment of a systems integrator. The scope of work outsourced included business process modelling, high level solution design and architecture, an implementation programme work plan and a data migration strategy. A programme director, an experienced, independent consultant, appointed by the organisation to work with both outsource vendors, systems integrator, as well as the organisation's IS outsourcing project team members, applied the proposed KAMI framework to the project in order to establish its applicability to a real-world situation. We believed that such an experienced programme director overseeing a complex IS outsourcing agreement will be in a position to provide valuable insight into the practical application of the proposed KAMI framework. As the IS outsourcing project was in progress already i.e. in the post-contract phase, the programme director mapped the proposed KAMI framework to the project and could, in addition to providing feedback, also share lessons learnt in terms of the early stages of the IS outsourcing project.

The programme director provided comments based on each stage of the IS outsourcing project and related KAMI framework activities. For the *strategise phase* as part of the *pre-contract stage*, the programme director indicated that by considering an overview of the knowledge asset management principles as well as high level scope, presents great advantages. Market knowledge, knowledge of the strategic objectives informing the IS outsourcing and knowledge about the operational benefits that will be derived from the outsourcing, are important. A key enabler identified by the programme director pointed to the outsource vendor knowledge of the client organisation. Such knowledge ensures that engagement takes place at the correct organisational level, that the external skills from the outsource vendor complement existing skill sets and that emphasis is placed on the up-skilling of the client organisation in terms of managing an outsource partner. As knowledge exchange in the pre-contract phase of IS outsourcing deals with the structure of the agreement, negotiation position knowledge and negotiation skills are key. In terms of requirements analysis at this stage of the project, identification and documentation of organizational intellectual property, knowledge of different outsource models, quantification of the business case for outsourcing and multiple benchmarks and performance measure identification present major knowledge exchanges. These particular knowledge exchanges are considered as part of the high level knowledge asset requirements analysis.

In terms of the *scope* phase of the framework, the programme director highlighted knowledge exchange in terms of how the knowledge audit methodology procedure step attracted significant input. These included a knowledge repository of the client organisation business processes, knowledge of service level agreements, project planning, support constructs, scope of outsourcing, resource mobilization time and the definition of a model to retain key knowledge and skill in the organisation. Due diligence, live demonstrations and presentations, research and intelligence re outsource vendors and the knowledge embedded in a lessons learnt repository, informed the initiative scoping procedure. The knowledge audit and initiative scoping steps were relevant in the handover between the post-contract and contract phases. Prioritisation focuses on the understanding of the key objectives of knowledge transfer into measurable services and products in order to inform vendor selection. Technology solution assessment in the *contract* phase pointed to the assessment of a solution benchmarking repository and an outcomes based assessment of the usability of the perceived end product.

The programme director highlighted that the *post-contract* stage included multiple knowledge exchanges in terms of planning. These include knowledge of joint execution key drivers and processes, contract management, escalation paths and the planning of the work contribution of the outsourcing arrangement with appropriate stakeholders.

A key step in the *development* phase is the knowledge elicitation procedure where knowledge is exchanged through integration sessions, knowledge sharing sessions and a culture of knowledge sharing is fostered. During the building procedure, traceability of knowledge elements, agreed way of work, organisational monitoring capabilities and joint delivery presented opportunities for knowledge exchange. The planning and knowledge elicitation procedures are positioned within the hand over between the contract and post-contract stages. The *implement* phase includes key knowledge exchange identified and points to conducting formal knowledge transfer workshops of learning that has taken place during the project in order to create a lessons learnt knowledge base. As this procedure is in the post-contract phase, formal knowledge transfer mechanisms from outsource vendor to client organisation must be facilitated and sufficient planning for hand over time must be allocated. With a strong focus on maintenance and support, knowledge transfer regarding the monitoring of the service level agreement, housekeeping and general operational tasks, and decommissioning of vendor resources must be enabled. A knowledge repository with all relevant solution information, decisions made during the project and risks identified and mitigated, including proper security controls, must be created. Here well-defined quantifiable business benefits linked to well defined and measureable business processes, facilitation of proof of concept and demonstrations of the solution, as well as the creation of a common knowledge repository between the client organisation and outsource vendor as part of the outsourcing arrangement, are important knowledge exchanges. The programme director highlighted the utilisation of joint documentation responsibilities between the client organisation and outsource vendor. The KAMI activities in the implement phase of the KAMI framework are cyclical in nature and has to be managed throughout the entire period of IS outsourcing contract execution.

Finally, in the *contract ended/terminated stage*, the programme director emphasised knowledge maintenance procedures in two important areas. Firstly, the institutionalisation of appropriately transparent knowledge transfer channels, where client organisation stakeholders are kept up to date on the processes used, including the rationale for vendor selection and subsequent contract terms. Secondly, the facilitation of focus group meetings where all key stakeholders are mandated to attend and participate with access to a central document repository to ensure transparency to all participants in the process. He also identified the unique contribution of communication and change management and indicated that it should not be limited to the final phase only. He stressed the value of having communication and change management at initiation of the outsourcing project through to the close out of the project.

In addition, the senior programme director commented on the advantages of the KAMI framework based on his experience with large scale IS outsourcing programmes and also made KAMI framework improvement suggestions. Firstly, he reflected on the cyclical nature of the KAMI framework as he experienced that knowledge assets are often lost when an IS outsourcing contract is terminated or ends. The cycles indicated in the KAMI framework ensures that the organisation considers to capture these knowledge assets before the outsource vendor exists. The programme director reflected on the management of 3 knowledge flows namely, new knowledge created by the joint IS outsourcing team, organisation-to-vendor knowledge exchange, and vendor-to-organisation knowledge exchange. He believed that although it was implied in the

KAMI framework, it will add value to make it explicit, especially as different mechanisms may be applied in order to manage these different knowledge flows. The programme director highlighted that he believes two distinct sets of knowledge assets must be managed: firstly, the knowledge assets created by the IS outsourcing project related to the business rationale for using outsourcing, e.g. the implementation of a new software solution. Secondly, he indicated that knowledge assets are also utilised in the management of the IS outsourcing agreement, e.g. the project documentation, outsourcing process knowledge, negotiation guidelines, contract management knowledge etc. He mentioned that he believes it will add great value of the KAMI framework guided both of these knowledge asset sets. By including the second knowledge asset set, namely the IS outsourcing project assets, it will enable the commercial team to negotiate and include key knowledge asset management principles in the commercial agreement with the outsource vendor. The programme director stressed that the fact that a contract which includes knowledge asset management clauses, will assist in enforcing the vendor to share knowledge as some contract payments may be linked to the delivery of knowledge sharing. Lastly, he suggested that the inclusion of an agreement on a knowledge taxonomy related to the project within the context of the bigger organisation should form part of the *strategise* phase of KAMI. This will be important for the institutionalisation of the knowledge assets created during the IS outsourcing project and when the assets have to be integrated into the organisational knowledge context.

5   Conclusion

The implementation of knowledge management at an organisational level is a key enabler for managing the knowledge assets in the organisation during the implementation of an IS outsourcing arrangement. In order to assist organisations embarking on IS outsourcing to pro-actively manage their knowledge assets during the IS outsourcing project, the aim of this study was to develop a KAMI framework. The KAMI framework was designed based on the analysis of multiple KM frameworks and then evaluated by an experienced senior programme director. The objective with this proof of concept evaluation was to establish whether the KAMI framework was applicable to IS outsourcing projects where multiple knowledge exchanges take place, namely; organisation-to-vendor knowledge exchange, vendor-to-organisation knowledge exchange and new knowledge that was created by the IS outsourcing implementation project. The proof of concept evaluation was done through an interview with the senior programme director and the data regarding knowledge exchange in an IS outsourcing project that he managed, was analysed and reported in the context of the KAMI framework. The data included comments regarding each of the stages of the IS outsourcing lifecycle.

It was established that due to the iterative nature of the KAMI framework, the activities were well suited to be applied in the context of an IS outsourcing project. The KAMI framework captured the knowledge asset management activities well and the proposed activities aligned well to the execution of the IS outsourcing stages. The programme director made suggestions for the improvement of the proposed KAMI framework and this may be included in future research. Furthermore, the revised KAMI framework may be applied in an actual IS outsourcing project to test the applicability of the framework in a real-world IS outsourcing project scenario. In addition, a comparative study may be conducted between the KAMI framework and the ISO standard for knowledge management systems (ISO 30401:2018).

References

1. Piotrowicz, W., Kedziora, D.: Outsourcing of information technology and business processes in Poland: motivations and environmental factors. Manag. Glob. Transit. **16**(4), 307–333 (2018)
2. Jeong, J., et al.: Enhancing the application and measurement of relationship quality in future IT outsourcing studies. In: 26th European Conference on Information Systems (ECIS2018), Portsmouth, UK (2018)
3. Norina, P., Camelia, M.: Outsourcing management: outsourcing services worldwide and in Romania. Econ. Sci. Ser. **XVIII**(1), 376–381 (2018)
4. Cruz, N.M., Perez, V.M., Cantero, C.T.: The influence of employee motivation on knowledge transfer. J. Knowl. Manag. **13**(6), 478–490 (2009)
5. Blumenberg, S., Wagner, H., Beimborn, D.: Knowledge transfer processes in IT outsourcing relationships and their impact on shared knowledge and outsourcing performance. Int. J. Inf. Manage. **29**, 342–352 (2009)
6. Beyah, G., Gallivan, M.: Knowledge management as a framework for understanding public sector outsourcing. In: 34th International Conference on System Sciences. IEEE, Hawaii (2001)
7. Davenport, T.H.: Process management for knowledge work. In: vom Brocke, J., Rosemann, M. (eds.) Handbook on Business Process Management 1. IHIS, pp. 17–35. Springer, Heidelberg (2015). https://doi.org/10.1007/978-3-642-45100-3_2
8. St. John, J., Guynes, C.S., Vedder, R.: The client–vendor offshore relationship: success factors. Inf. Syst. Manag. **31**(2), 120–125 (2014)
9. Nurye, S.A., Molla, A., Desta, T.A.: Factors influencing knowledge transfer in onshore information systems outsourcing in Ethiopia. Afr. J. Inf. Syst. **11**(4), 279–298 (2019)
10. Roy, S., Sivakumar, K.: Global outsourcing relationships and innovation: a conceptual framework and research propositions. J. Prod. Innov. Manag. **29**(4), 513–530 (2012)
11. Smuts, H., et al.: Knowledge asset management pertinent to information systems outsourcing. Adv. Intell. Syst. Comput. **353**, 43–55 (2015)
12. Teo, T.: Knowledge management in client-vendor partnerships. Int. J. Inf. Manag. **2012**(32), 451–458 (2012)
13. Vishwakarma, H.R., Tripathy, B.K., Kothari, D.P.: An architectural design for knowledge asset management system. In: Muttoo, S.K. (ed.) System and Architecture. AISC, vol. 732, pp. 329–338. Springer, Singapore (2018). https://doi.org/10.1007/978-981-10-8533-8_31
14. Archer-Brown, C., Kietzmann, J.: Strategic knowledge management and enterprise social media. J. Knowl. Manag. **22**(6), 1288–1309 (2018)
15. Aydin, M.N., Bakker, M.E.: Analyzing IT maintenance outsourcing decision from a knowledge management perspective. Inf. Syst. Front. **10**, 293–305 (2008)
16. Bandyopadhyay, S., Pathak, P.: Knowledge sharing and cooperation in outsourcing projects: a game theory analysis. Decis. Support Syst. **43**, 349–358 (2007)
17. Balaji, S., Ahuja, M.K.: Critical team-level success factors of offshore outsourced projects: a knowledge integration perspective. In: Proceedings of the 38th Hawaii International Conference on System Sciences. IEEE, Hawaii (2005)

18. Miozza, M., Grimshaw, D.: Modularity and innovation in knowledge-intensive business services: IT outsourcing in Germany and the UK. Res. Policy **34**, 1419–1439 (2005)
19. Akomode, O.J., Lees, B., Irgens, C.: Constructing customised models and providing information for IT outsourcing decisions. Logist. Inf. Manag. **11**(2), 114–127 (1998)
20. Cullen, S., Willcocks, L.: Intelligent IT outsourcing: eight building blocks to success. In: Remenyi, D. (ed.) Computer Weekly Professional Series, p. 224. Butterworth-Heinemann, Oxford (2003)
21. Gartner: Marketplace realities in strategic outsourcing, R-17-7896, pp. 1–22. Gartner Inc. (2002a). Editor
22. Sood, R.: IT, Software and Services: Outsourcing & Offshoring, p. 178. AiAiYo Books, Austin (2005)
23. Alborz, S., Seddon, P., Scheepers, R.: A model for studying IT outsourcing relationships. In: 7th Pacific Asia Conference on Information Systems, Adelaide, South Australia (2003)
24. Gellings, C.: Outsourcing relationships: the contract as IT governance tool. In: Proceedings of the 40th Hawaii International Conference on System Sciences. IEEE, Hawaii (2007)
25. Evans, M., Dalkir, K., Bidian, C.: A holistic view of the knowledge life cycle: the knowledge management cycle (KMC) model. Electron. J. Knowl. Manag. **12**(2), 85–97 (2014)
26. Mohamed, M.D., et al.: information systems outsourcing drivers and service delivery of commercial banks in Kenya. Int. J. Bus. Manag. Res. **3**(1), 10–14 (2019)
27. Smuts, H., et al.: Framework for managing shared knowledge in an information systems outsourcing context. Int. J. Knowl. Manag. (IJKM) **13**(4), 1–30 (2017)
28. Niederman, F.: International business and MIS approaches to multinational organisational research: the cases of knowledge transfer and IT workforce outsourcing. J. Int. Manag. **11**, 187–200 (2005)
29. Sandoval, W.A., Bell, P.: Design-based research methods for studying learning in context: introduction. Educ. Psychol. **39**(4), 199–201 (2004)
30. Wang, F., Hannafin, M.J.: Design-based research and technology-enhanced learning environments. Educ. Tech. Res. Dev. **53**(4), 5–23 (2005)
31. Edelson, D.C.: Design research: what we learn when we engage in design. J. Learn. Sci. **11**(1), 105–121 (2002)
32. Moteleb, A.A., Woodman, M., Critten, P.: Towards a practical guide for developing knowledge management systems in small organizations. In: 10th European Conference on Knowledge Management, Vicenza, Italy (2009)
33. Badimo, K.H., Buckley, S.: Improving knowledge management practices in the South African healthcare system. Int. Sch. Sci. Res. Innov. **8**(11), 3449–3455 (2014)
34. Bolisani, E., Bratianu, C.: The emergence of knowledge management. Emergent Knowledge Strategies. KMOL, vol. 4, pp. 23–47. Springer, Cham (2018). https://doi.org/10.1007/978-3-319-60657-6_2
35. Evans, M., Ali, N.: Bridging knowledge management life cycle theory and practice. In: International Conference on Intellectual Capital, Knowledge Management and Organisational Learning ICICKM 2013–Conference Proceedings (2013)
36. Karemente, K., et al.: Knowledge management frameworks: a review of conceptual foundations and a KMF for IT-based organizations. Strengthening the Role of ICT in Development, p. 35 (2009)
37. Meher, D.P., Mahajan, N.: Study of knowledge management frameworks (2013)
38. Mostert, F., Snyman, I.: Analysis of the South African surrogate for a TMRP-6 anti-tank mine. In: 23th International Symposium on Ballistics (2007)

39. Amine, M.M., Ahmed-Nacer, M.: An agile methodology for implementing knowledge management systems: a case study in component-based software engineering. Int. J. Softw. Eng. Appl. **5**(4), 159–170 (2011)
40. Orenga-Roglá, S., Chalmeta, R.: Methodology for the implementation of knowledge management systems 2.0. A case study in an oil and gas company. Bus. Inf. Syst. Eng. **61**(2), 195–213 (2017)
41. Butler, T., Heavin, C., O'Donovan, F.: A theoretical model and framework for understanding knowledge management system implementation. In: Clarke, S. (ed.) Evolutionary Concepts in End User Productivity and Performance: Applications for Organizational Progress, Information Science Reference, pp. 204–225, Hershey, New York (2009)
42. Smuts, H., et al.: A framework and methodology for knowledge management system implementation. In: Proceedings of the Annual Research Conference of the South African Institute of Computer Scientists and Information Technologists. ACM, Vanderbijlpark, Emfuleni, South Africa (2009)

A Conceptual Knowledge Visualisation Framework for Transfer of Knowledge: An Organisational Context

Hanlie Smuts[(⊠)] and Iddo-Imri Scholtz

Department of Informatics, University of Pretoria, Pretoria, South Africa
hanlie.smuts@up.ac.za, iddo.imri@gmail.com

Abstract. Revolutionary advances in science and technology enables organisations to apply and optimise a world of visual and experiential learning in order to enhance the skills and knowledge of their employees. Furthermore, the volume and complexity of knowledge and information are such that unless a reporting structure is overlaid upon it, it may remain meaningless. Knowledge visualisation uses graphical representations to convey organisational knowledge, enabling employees to share and recall relevant knowledge. However, in order to assist organisations to create and transfer knowledge more effectively through knowledge visualisation, the aim of this study is to provide a conceptual knowledge visualisation framework for the transfer of knowledge for organisations. A conceptual knowledge visualisation framework was designed through a systematic literature review process where 15 organisational knowledge visualisation elements were identified. The 15 elements were grouped and presented in a 4-layered, embedded conceptual framework that organisations may apply to their knowledge visualisation efforts. By using such a framework, organisations may optimise learning and improve knowledge and skills of its employees.

Keywords: Knowledge visualisation framework · Knowledge transfer · Organisational knowledge · Knowledge sharing · Knowledge management

1 Introduction

The world is seeing revolutionary advances in science and technology, labelled the 4th Industrial Revolution or Industry 4.0 [1]. With the evolution of digital technologies, many opportunities are realised through the application of the digital technologies [2, 3]. Some of these include cyber-physical systems where control and monitoring are done by computer-based algorithms e.g. autonomous vehicles, the internet of things creating a connected world e.g. enabling smart cities, cloud computing providing on-demand availability of data storage and computing power and cognitive computing e.g. artificial intelligence [4, 5]. The ability of organisations to apply and optimise Industry 4.0 technologies require digital citizens to have the knowledge and skills to effectively use and apply these digital technologies [6]. Both from a commercial perspective, as well as a knowledge and skill outlook, digital technologies enable two options: firstly, they provide multiple options for an organisation to embrace digital transformation and

© IFIP International Federation for Information Processing 2020
Published by Springer Nature Switzerland AG 2020
M. Hattingh et al. (Eds.): I3E 2020, LNCS 12067, pp. 287–298, 2020.
https://doi.org/10.1007/978-3-030-45002-1_24

secondly, they enable a world of visual and experiential learning in order to enhance skills and knowledge [6, 7].

Whether an organisation addresses smart offerings for customers or digital skills for employees, the transfer and creation of knowledge may be achieved more effectively through knowledge visualisation [7]. Therefore, the aim of this research is to understand the key considerations for organisations aiming to utilise knowledge visualisation in an organisational context. Therefore, the research question that this paper aims to address is: *"What are the elements of a knowledge visualisation framework in an organisational context?* By addressing this question and applying such a framework, organisations are able to utilise digital technologies to visualise organisational knowledge in an attempt to optimise learning and improve knowledge and skills.

In Sect. 2 we present the background to the study followed by the research approach in Sect. 3. Section 4 details the data analysis and findings, while Sect. 5 concludes the paper.

2 Background

In an organisational context, blended training is defined by the proportions of face-to-face versus online training material, including media-rich elements [6, 7]. The requirement is to scale blended learning and to design learning experiences that take full advantage of digital platforms and digital technologies, an attribute of industry 4.0 [1, 8]. The transfer of knowledge is a core process in knowledge management in organisations and making knowledge visible so that it can be better accessed, discussed, valued and managed is a key objective [9, 10]. Over and above the mere conveyance of facts, knowledge visualisation aims to transfer insights, experiences, attitudes, values, expectations, perspectives, opinions and predictions [8]. Knowledge visualisation enables employees to re-construct, remember and apply insights gained through knowledge visualisation [9, 10].

In the next sections we consider knowledge visualisation as a phenomenon and organisational context of knowledge visualisation.

2.1 Knowledge Visualisation as a Phenomenon

Visualisation, from a scientific perspective, is an advanced field that is comprised of a resource base of accepted methods and meticulous processes which includes guidelines to assist with the development of data and information visualisations [9–11]. Knowledge visualisation on the other hand is not as mature [12, 13] and therefore, lacks a generic set of guidelines [10, 14]. An interconnected field and predecessor of knowledge visualisation is information visualisation and both these fields are utilising our natural abilities to successfully process visual representations. Although both these fields make use of our natural visual abilities, the way of utilising these abilities differ in both fields: Information visualisation intends to examine a large amount of abstract data to obtain new perceptions or to make the data more approachable. Knowledge visualisation, on the other hand, intends to enhance the transfer and creation of knowledge amongst people by providing a richer approach to communicate what they know. While information visualisation assists in improving the retrieval, access and presentation of information from large data sets, knowledge visualisation is mainly concerned with increasing knowledge-intensive communication amongst people [15].

The seminal work of Eppler and Burkhard [15] first coined the term knowledge visualisation and defined it as "the use of visual representations to improve the creation and transfer of knowledge between at least two people" [15: 3]. Based on this definition, Renaud and van Biljon [10] extended the definition as "the use of graphical means to communicate experiences, insights and potentially complex knowledge. Such means should be flexible enough to accommodate changing insights, and facilitate conversations. Such representations facilitate and expedite the creation and transfer of knowledge between people by improving and promoting knowledge processing and comprehension" [10: 3]. The aim of knowledge visualisation is to use visualisation to promote effective and efficient transfer of knowledge from one person to another [12, 13, 16]. Proper implementation of knowledge visualisation has the potential to utilise key strengths of the human cognitive processing system to improve communication and the transfer and sharing of knowledge [15, 17].

We discuss knowledge visualisation in an organisational context in more detail in the next section.

2.2   The Organisational Context of Knowledge Visualisation

The role of organisational learning includes the development of cross-boundary knowledge and requires new approaches to knowledge generation and transmission as employees are required to apply knowledge in- and outside of work structures [18, 19].

Data essentially consists of structured recordings of transactions and events and is presented without context [20]. *Information* is data with relevance and purpose added, while knowledge comes with insights, framed experiences, intuition, judgement and values and encompasses the scope of understanding and skills that are created by people through cognitive processes [20]. *Knowledge* can be categorised as either being *explicit* (has been articulated) or *implicit* (less tangible, deeply embedded knowledge) [21]. *Tacit knowledge*, as a dimension of implicit knowledge, is personal and context-specific, and therefore hard to communicate and formalise [21]. In order to act on information, a person should internalise the information and achieve this by progressing through knowledge conversion processes namely socialisation, externalisation, combination and internalisation [21]. *Socialisation* ensures that knowledge is acquired, after which externalisation enables students to express their tacit knowledge (mental models and know-how). *Combination* is the process of integrating concepts, while *internalisation* is closely related to learning-by-doing, or experiential learning [21]. This process of knowledge application ensures that knowledge is advanced through practice, guidance, imitation and observation [19].

Knowledge visualisation in the context of organisations may therefore be described as the use of visual representations to improve the creation and transfer of knowledge, using available visual resources to create, integrate and administer knowledge [22].

In the next section we present an overview of our research approach.

3   Research Approach

The overall objective of this paper was to define a knowledge visualisation framework as a tool for knowledge sharing and – recall in organisations. The purpose of such a framework is to guide organisations from two perspectives: firstly, with the visualisation of knowledge in order to improve the transfer and sharing of knowledge, and secondly, to leverage the strength of human visual processing capabilities [23].

In order to achieve the aim of this paper, a systematic literature review (SLR) was conducted [24–26]. The purpose of and contributions associated with a SLR may vary, yet the approach offers the benefit of the development of conceptual frameworks to reconcile and extend past research [27]. According to Tranfield, Denyer and Smart [28], the SLR process comprises of 3 consecutive stages: (1) planning the review, (2) conducting the review and (3) reporting and dissemination. *Planning the review* includes the identification of the review requirement, the preparation of the review proposal and the development of the review proposal. *Conducting the review* consists of the selection of studies, the study quality assessment, data extraction and data synthesis. *Reporting and dissemination* encompass the reporting of findings, recommendations and consideration of applicability for practice [28].

The first stage, *planning*, was guided by the aim of the research study, namely, to propose a knowledge visualisation framework for an organisational context. The keywords "organisation" AND "knowledge visualisation" (with accommodating the United States English "z") were used to find relevant studies in specific scientific databases, peer-reviewed publications such as journal papers, conference proceedings, books, case studies, book chapters, and technical reports identified for the SLR process. The initial search produced a list of 456 papers. The research studies were screened by applying specific criteria to exclude papers such as studies not associated with the research questions, non-English studies, and opinion-based papers. Duplicate studies retrieved were also removed. During the second stage of the SLR, conducting the review, the selected papers were analysed in detail. Knowledge visualisation elements were extracted as shown in Table 1 - summarising the knowledge visualisation framework elements, a short description of the element and the reference where the element was extracted from.

Fifteen knowledge visualisation elements were identified through the systematic review pertaining to an organisational context and where the target audience of the knowledge visualisation specifically points to employees. Two elements specifically pointed to the target audience of the knowledge visualisation namely, need and engagement. *Audience need* indicates key considerations relevant to the target audience such as an individual or a team, while *audience engagement* points to the audience-knowledge visualisation interaction with specific reference to how the knowledge visualisation enhance and facilitate learning engagement through interaction and experience. The focus of *graphical excellence* is on usability of the visualisation and ensuring that irrelevant items or decoration do not distract the target audience from the content of the topic. *Essence* refers to the identification and utilisation of the essentials, as well as their relationships, from a body of knowledge identified for visualisation, while *accessibility* indicates the relationship the target audience holds with the knowledge subject area, namely ensure that the level of abstraction is aligned to the target audience's prior knowledge of the particular knowledge subject area. The minimisation of the number of concepts in each level of knowledge visualisation points to the *simplicity* element, and *intelligibility* focuses on the objective that the knowledge visualisation should not carry ambiguity and that it is easy to understand. *Uniformity* of visual elements such as colour, symbols, shapes, etc. should be the same for the same kinds of information.

Table 1. Overview of the knowledge visualisation framework elements from the literature

Knowledge visualisation element	Description	Source
Audience need	Consider for whom the visualisation is intended e.g. an individual, a class, a group, a community, etc. and ensure that the intended audience need is met	[16, 29, 30]
Audience engagement	Enhance and facilitate learning engagement through interaction and experience	[16, 22]
Graphical excellence	Focus on usability of the visualisation and avoid irrelevant elements that may distract the audience from the content of the topic	[22, 31, 32]
Essence	Identify and utilise the essentials and their relationships from a body of knowledge	[16, 33, 34]
Accessibility	Ensure that the level of abstraction is aligned to the audience's prior knowledge of the knowledge subject area	[31, 35]
Simplicity	Minimize the number of concepts in each level of visualisation	[36, 37]
Intelligibility	Ensure that the visualisation does not carry ambiguity and is easy to understand	[29, 38]
Uniformity	Use of visual elements such as colour, symbols, shapes, etc. should be the same for the same kinds of information	[34, 39]
Context	Present the overview and detail. Overview gives context information of a field, while detail gives more information about a part of the overview. The boundaries around elements and the connections to other elements should be clear	[16, 30, 32, 40]
Cohesion	Clearly show the relationship between knowledge concepts and how it works together	[18, 35, 38, 40]
Explanatory power	Visualisation must have explanatory power and not merely descriptive value. The knowledge visualisation requirement must be considered in this instance i.e. is it for recall, sharing new insights or elaborating existing knowledge	[16, 20, 32]

(*continued*)

Table 1. (*continued*)

Knowledge visualisation element	Description	Source
Familiarity association	Utilisation of recognisable and familiar visual images associated with real-world experiences, ensure that visualisation elements are recognised rather than recalled	[22, 39]
Legend	Provides the information required for clarifying and explaining the knowledge visualisation meaning and interpretation	[36, 41–43]
Knowledge transfer cognitive process	Process of transferring knowledge from one part of the organisation to another by organising, creating, capturing or distributing knowledge and ensuring its availability for future users	[16, 18, 20, 44]
Visual integrity	The knowledge visualisation should not distort the underlying knowledge or create a false impression or interpretation of that knowledge	[30–32, 38]

Context is about presenting both the detail required for the knowledge visualisation, as well as the overview of where the detailed portion fits in. Context in an organisation highlights the combination of internal and external factors relevant to the organisation that may impact its products, services, business models, operating model, etc. *Cohesion* is the principle of working together and in the context of knowledge visualisation, it implies that the relationship among knowledge concepts, must be shown clearly. The *explanatory power* element ensures that knowledge visualisation has both explanatory and descriptive value. Descriptive value gives details and describes the knowledge that the target audience needs to understand, while explanatory value gives the reasons for it. In the organisational context, its application is closely related to whether knowledge recall is required, whether new insights are shared or whether existing knowledge is elaborated upon. By *associating* knowledge visualisation with *familiar* real world images, the target audience is enabled to recognise and interpret visuals rather than to have to remember and recall meaning. The *legend* element provides the information needed for the knowledge visualisation to make sense and assists in explaining meaning and interpretation. The process of transferring knowledge from one part of the organisation to another by organising, creating, capturing or distributing knowledge and ensuring it is available for future users, depicts the *knowledge transfer cognitive process* elements. The last element, *visual integrity*, points to the principle that the knowledge visualisation should have uncompromising adherence to underlying knowledge and should not create a false impression or interpretation of that knowledge.

The purpose of the 15 knowledge visualisation elements that were extracted is to guide organisations on how to approach their knowledge visualisations in order to improve the transfer and sharing of knowledge in the organisation. In the next section we discuss the conceptual framework for knowledge visualisation in an organisation, in more detail.

4 Conceptual Knowledge Visualisation Frameworks for Organisations

The aim of this paper is to define a knowledge visualisation framework as a tool for organisations in support of improved knowledge transfer, -sharing and -management. In terms of the final stage of the SLR, reporting and dissemination, the list of 15 elements identified, were considered, as well as its contribution at different levels in an organisational context.

According to Jabareen [45: 58], "conceptual frameworks aim to help us understand phenomena rather than to predict them". By applying the conceptual framework analysis [45] and considering the unique features and constructs of the elements defined in Table 1, we identified 4 impact levels in the organisation as depicted in Table 2: target audience, design elements, design principles and organisational purpose.

Table 2. Organisational impact of 15 knowledge visualisation elements identified

Knowledge visualisation element	Organisational impact level	Knowledge visualisation element	Organisational impact level
Audience need	Target audience	Context	Target audience
Audience engagement	Target audience	Cohesion	Design principle
Graphical excellence	Design element	Explanatory power	Design principle
Essence	Organisational purpose	Familiarity association	Design principle
Accessibility	Target audience	Legend	Design element
Simplicity	Design principle	Knowledge transfer cognitive process	Organisational purpose
Intelligibility	Design principle	Visual integrity	Design element
Uniformity	Design principle		

The main driver of knowledge visualisation is the *organisational purpose* i.e. the reason why the knowledge visualisation is done or created. Purpose talks to the required scope within the organisational body of knowledge that must be visualised with the aim to achieve transferring and sharing knowledge, as well as communicating ideas and insights. *Design principles* depicts the key considerations when designing the knowledge visualisation aligned to the purpose, and aims to establish a good design that is simple to understand, cohesive and explanatory in nature. Employees must be able to easily associate the knowledge visualisation with the organisational purpose and the objective of what needs to be achieved with the knowledge transfer. *Design elements* is another impact level and includes graphical excellence, legend and visual integrity. These are typical elements that relates to the interface with employees and in particular the usability of the knowledge visualisation interface.

The *target audience* impact level includes knowledge visualisation elements related to the target audience in the organisation, namely the employees. Elements impacting the employees in the organisation includes the need of different employees e.g. individuals, functional teams, project teams, etc. Knowledge visualisation must address the need from the particular employee or employee group it is intended for. Related to audience need, is audience engagement as the interaction with the visualised knowledge should enhance and facilitate learning engagement or the employee or employee group. Context and accessibility are also elements that impact the employees engaging with the knowledge visualisation as organisational boundaries and the particular scenario that must be visualised, is a key consideration. Accessibility is a key enabler as this element needs to ensure that an employee can place the knowledge visualisation subject area in context and interpret it within the organisational context.

However, the 4 impact levels of the 15 knowledge visualisation elements identified is not standalone and are interrelated. By bearing Table 2 in mind and considering the interrelated nature of the impact levels, an embedded and layered knowledge visualisation framework for organisations may be defined and is depicted in Fig. 1. Figure 1 illustrates 4 layers with organisational purpose as the inner most layer, followed by design principles, design elements and ultimately target audience. For each layer, the particular elements relevant to that layer are shown. Organisational purpose at the core, impacts greatly on the focus of the knowledge visualisation and each layer contribute further to guide or clarify what is required for the organisation.

An example of such knowledge visualisation application relates to software requirements elicitation in an organisation. The required elicitation process in an organisation is acknowledged as one of the most crucial, knowledge-intensive processes and is built on the knowledge of the stakeholders. During requirement elicitation, each stakeholder communicates their requirements in a distinctive way which could lead to ambiguous and vague understandings translated into the capturing of inaccurate requirements. The involved stakeholders have a diverse knowledge background that requires collaboration in order to reach an agreement on the elicited requirements for an Information Systems development project.

In order to deal with the potential requirements elicitation challenges encountered, attention needs to be given to the identification and assessment of knowledge involving the identification and assessment of required knowledge benefits. By utilising the proposed framework for knowledge visualisation in an organisational context (Fig. 1) as a guide, insights, experiences, point of views, values, assumptions, outlook, beliefs and prognosis may be transferred in such a manner that empowers an employee to rebuild, recall and implement these insights accurately. Therefore, knowledge visualisation could serve as a viable option to address the challenges encountered in requirements elicitation.

By applying the conceptual framework presented in Fig. 1, organisations are guided towards relevant and fit-for-purpose knowledge visualisations, aligned to real world scenarios and adding value within the context of the particular organisation.

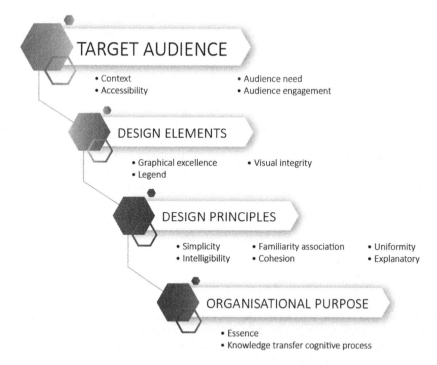

Fig. 1. Framework for knowledge visualisation in an organisational context

5   Conclusion

Organisations have the opportunity to leverage digital technologies for the visualisation of organisational knowledge with the aim to empower employees with knowledge sharing and –recall. In addition, the volume and complexity of knowledge and information amplified by big data management and data-driven decision-making requirements, requires structure to ensure that it is meaningful. The emerging field of knowledge visualisation uses graphical representations to convey complex insights, experiences, methods, etc. enabling the employee engaging with the knowledge visualisation to reconstruct and remember the relevant knowledge. In order to assist organisations in creating fit for purpose knowledge visualisations, the aim of this study was to extract, design and propose a conceptual knowledge visualisation framework.

The proposed knowledge visualisation framework was derived through a SLR process by extracting 15 relevant elements for knowledge visualisation in an organisational context and by considering the organisational impact level of each element identified. The four, layered and embedded impact levels form the basis for the conceptual knowledge visualisation framework that organisations may reference when utilising knowledge visualisation.

In terms of future research opportunity, the conceptual knowledge visualisation framework presented in this study may be tested in a real-world scenario in an organisation and the application of the framework measured. Through such application, additional, relevant knowledge visualisation elements may be identified and the proposed framework enriched.

References

1. Tabarés, R.: Harnessing the power of Digital Social Platforms to shake up makers and manufacturing entrepreneurs towards a European Open Manufacturing ecosystem. Res. Innov. Action (2016)
2. Ganju, K.K., Pavlou, P.A., Banker, R.D.: Does information and communication technology lead to the wellbeing of nations? A country-level empirical investigation. MIS Q. **40**(2), 417–430 (2016)
3. Rocha, L., et al.: Cloud management tools for sustainable SMEs. Procedia CIRP **40**, 220–224 (2016)
4. Pfohl, H., Yahsi, B., Kurnaz, T.: The impact of Industry 4.0 on supply chain. In: Kersten, W., Blecker, T., Ringle, C. (eds.) Innovations and Strategies for Logistics and Supply Chains, pp. 31–58 (2015)
5. Martinez, F.: Process excellence the key for digitalisation. Bus. Process Manag. J. **25**(7), 1716–1733 (2019)
6. Khairuddin, S.M., Omar, F.I., Ahmad, N.: Digital inclusion domain in entrepreneurship: a preliminary analysis. Adv. Sci. Lett. **2018**(24), 2721–2724 (2018)
7. O'Connor, B.: Digital Transformation A Framework for ICT Literacy, in A Report of the International ICT Literacy Panel (2007)
8. Prifti, L.: Professional Qualification in "Industrie 4.0": Building a Competency Model and Competency-Based Curriculum. Faculty Informatics, p. 258. Technischen Universität München (2019)
9. Kelleher, C., Wagener, T.: Short communication: ten guidelines for effective data visualization in scientific publications. Environ. Model Softw. **26**(6), 822–827 (2011)
10. Renaud, K., van Biljon, J.: Charting the path towards effective knowledge visualisations. In: Proceedings of the South African Institute of Computer Scientists and Information Technologists SAICSIT 2017. ACM Press, Thaba 'Nchu (2017)
11. Elmqvist, N., Fekete, J.D.: Hierarchical aggregation for information visualization: overview, techniques, and design guidelines. IEEE Trans. Vis. Comput. Graph. **16**(3), 439–454 (2010)
12. Cañas, A.J., et al.: Concept maps: integrating knowledge and information visualization. In: Tergan, S.-O., Keller, T. (eds.) Knowledge and Information Visualization. LNCS, vol. 3426, pp. 205–219. Springer, Heidelberg (2005). https://doi.org/10.1007/11510154_11
13. Eppler, M.J.: What is an effective knowledge visualization? Insights from a review of seminal concepts. In: 15th International Conference on Information Visualisation (2011). https://doi.org/10.1109/iv.2011.13
14. Meyer, R.: Knowledge Visualization in Trends in Information Visualization, pp. 23–30. University of Munich, Munich (2010)
15. Eppler, M.J., Burkhard, R.: Knowledge visualization: towards a new discipline and its fields of application. Lugano, Università della Svizzera italiana, Faculty of Communication Sciences, Institute for Corporate Communication (2004)
16. Burkhard, R.A.: Towards a framework and a model for knowledge visualization: synergies between information and knowledge visualization. In: Tergan, S.-O., Keller, T. (eds.) Knowledge and Information Visualization. LNCS, vol. 3426, pp. 238–255. Springer, Heidelberg (2005). https://doi.org/10.1007/11510154_13

17. Keller, T., Tergan, S.-O.: Visualizing knowledge and information: an introduction. In: Tergan, S.-O., Keller, T. (eds.) Knowledge and Information Visualization. LNCS, vol. 3426, pp. 1–23. Springer, Heidelberg (2005). https://doi.org/10.1007/11510154_1
18. Štorga, M., Mostashari, A., Stankovic, T.: Visualisation of the organisation knowledge structure evolution. J. Knowl. Manag. 17(5), 724–740 (2014)
19. Smuts, H., Hattingh, M.J.: Towards a knowledge conversion model enabling programme design in higher education for shaping industry-ready graduates. In: Kabanda, S., Suleman, H., Gruner, S. (eds.) SACLA 2018. CCIS, vol. 963, pp. 124–139. Springer, Cham (2019). https://doi.org/10.1007/978-3-030-05813-5_9
20. Boehnert, J.: Knowledge visualization in environmental communication, in relating systems thinking and design (RSD5). In: Jones, P. (ed.) 2016 Symposium, Ontario College of Art and Design, Ontario, Canada (2016)
21. Nonaka, I., Toyama, R., Konno, N.: SECI, Ba and leadership: a unified model of dynamic knowledge creation. Long Range Plann. 33, 5–34 (2000)
22. Eppler, M., Burkhard, R.: Visual representations in knowledge management: framework and cases. J. Knowl. Manag. 11(4), 112–122 (2007)
23. Renaud, K., van Biljon, J.: A framework to maximise the communicative power of knowledge visualisations. In: Conference of the South African Institute of Computer Scientists and Information Technologists 2019 (SAICSIT 2019). ACM, New York (2019)
24. Rouhani, B.D., et al.: A systematic literature review on enterprise architecture implementation methodologies. Inf. Softw. Technol. 62, 1–20 (2015)
25. Aromataris, E., Pearson, A.: The systematic review: an overview. AJN Am. J. Nurs. 114, 53–58 (2014)
26. Hart, C.: Doing a Literature Review: Releasing the Social Science Research Imagination. SAGE Publications, London (2018)
27. Palmatier, R.W., Houston, M.B., Hulland, J.: Review articles: purpose, process, and structure. J. Acad. Market. Sci. 46(1), 1–5 (2018)
28. Tranfield, D., Denyer, D., Smart, P.: Towards a methodology for developing evidence-informed management knowledge by means of systematic review. Br. J. Manag. 14, 207–222 (2003)
29. Lanfranchi, V., et al.: A semantic knowledge management framework for informal communication exchanges. In: 10th International Semantic Web Conference (ISWC 2011), Bonn, Germany (2011)
30. Marchese, F.T., Bannisi, E.: Knowledge Visualization Currents: From Text to Art to Culture. Springer, New York (2013). https://doi.org/10.1007/978-1-4471-4303-1
31. Mazumdar, S., Varga, A., Lanfranchi, V., Petrelli, D., Ciravegna, F.: A knowledge dashboard for manufacturing industries. In: García-Castro, R., Fensel, D., Antoniou, G. (eds.) ESWC 2011. LNCS, vol. 7117, pp. 112–124. Springer, Heidelberg (2012). https://doi.org/10.1007/978-3-642-25953-1_10
32. Figueiras, A.: How to tell stories using visualization: strategies towards Narrative Visualization. Faculdade de Ciências Sociais e Humanas and the Universidade NOVA de Lisboa: Lisbon (2014)
33. Joel-Edgar, S., Gopsill, J.: Understanding user requirements in context: a case study of developing a visualisation tool to map skills in an engineering organisation. In: International Conference on Information Management and Processing (ICIMP). IEEE, London (2018)
34. Fadiran, O., Van Biljon, J., Schoeman, M.: How can visualisation principles be used to support knowledge transfer in teaching and learning? In: Proceedings of the 2018 Conference on Information Communications Technology and Society (ICTAS 2018). IEEE, Durban (2018)

35. Seppänen, H., Virrantaus, K.: Shared situational awareness and information quality in disaster management. Saf. Sci. **77**, 112–122 (2015)
36. Jiawei, H., Bailey, A., Sutcliffe, A.: Visualisation design knowledge reuse. In: Eighth International Conference on Information Visualisation. IEEE, London (2004)
37. Yaacob, S., et al.: Giving the boss the big picture: demonstrating convergence visualization design principles using business intelligence and analytical tools. J. Fundam. Appl. Sci. **10** (5S), 1328–1337 (2018)
38. Olshannikova, E., et al.: Visualizing Big Data with augmented and virtual reality: challenges and research agenda. J. Big Data **2**(1), 1–27 (2015)
39. Grainger, S., Mao, F., Buytaert, W.: Environmental data visualisation for nonscientific contexts: literature review and design framework. Environ. Model Softw. **85**, 299–318 (2016)
40. Succar, B., et al.: A proposed framework to investigate building information modelling through knowledge elicitation and visual models. In: Conference of the Australasian Universities Building Education Association, Melbourne (2007)
41. Heer, J., Shneiderman, B., Park, C.: A taxonomy of tools that support the fluent and flexible use of visualizations. Interact. Dyn. Vis. Anal. **10**, 1–26 (2012)
42. Candello, H., Fernandes Cavalcante, V., Braz, A., De Paula, R.A.: A validation study of a visual analytics tool with end users. In: Marcus, A. (ed.) DUXU 2014. LNCS, vol. 8520, pp. 381–391. Springer, Cham (2014). https://doi.org/10.1007/978-3-319-07638-6_37
43. Shamim, A., Balakrishnan, V., Tahir, M.: Evaluation of opinion visualization techniques. Inf. Vis. **14**(4), 339–358 (2015)
44. Vande Wiele, P., Ribiere, V.: Using knowledge visualisation techniques to support the development of curriculum for employability: exploring the capability tree representation. Int. J. Knowl. Learn. **9**(1/2), 43–62 (2014)
45. Jabareen, Y.: Building a conceptual framework: philosophy, definitions, and procedure. Int. J. Qual. Methods **8**(4), 49–62 (2009)

ICT and Gender Equality and Development

Can Technology Be Leveraged for Bridging the Rural-Urban Divide?

Anuragini Shirish[1]([⊠]) [iD], Shirish C. Srivastava[2] [iD],
and G. Shainesh[3] [iD]

[1] LITEM, Univ Evry, IMT-BS, Université Paris-Saclay, 91025 Evry, France
anuragini.shirish@imt-bs.eu
[2] HEC Paris, Paris, France
[3] IIM Bangalore, Bengaluru, India

Abstract. Inequalities exist and persist in society in different forms and are often areas of prime concern for governments and policy makers around the globe. One such inequality that plagues societies is the rural-urban divide. Several social entrepreneurs are attempting to leverage technology to bridge this divide. In our research-in-progress paper, we describe the case of an Indian company, which is leveraging technology to create knowledge-based jobs for the rural Indian population. The approach adopted by the company in initiating and sustaining such an effort was an inside-out approach in contrast to the usual approach of focusing only on the internal resources within the company. Specifically, our research aims at abstracting the process mechanisms that enabled such an initiative. The unearthed mechanisms would inform future research on the modalities for orchestrating such an initiative. The findings would also help practitioners, especially social entrepreneurs, to think of innovative business models that would create value not only for the company but also for society as a whole. The delineated learnings would also help enthused social entrepreneurs to transplant such initiatives to other regions of the world.

Keywords: Rural-urban divide · Reverse innovation · ICT for development · Business model innovation

1 Introduction

Global wealth has risen to a new high of 361 trillion US Dollars in 2019 but unfortunately, only a very small group at the top has captured most of the increase. The top 1% of the world's population accounts for nearly 45% of the total wealth, while the bottom 50% owns only 1% of the total wealth [5]. Such stark inequalities exist and persist in the society in different forms (e.g. regional, racial and gender) and are often areas of prime concern for governments and policy makers around the globe. For example, the recent yellow vests protests (Gilets Jaunes) in France or the farmer protests in India are attributable to the growing discontentment due to the rural-urban divide [2, 3]. While governments are primarily responsible for reducing these inequalities are primarily viewed as governmental tasks, several grassroots social entrepreneurs, especially in developing countries are implementing innovative local solutions to bridge these gaps

© IFIP International Federation for Information Processing 2020
Published by Springer Nature Switzerland AG 2020
M. Hattingh et al. (Eds.): I3E 2020, LNCS 12067, pp. 301–306, 2020.
https://doi.org/10.1007/978-3-030-45002-1_25

[11]. Such innovative bridging solutions often involve extensive use of Information and Communication Technologies (ICTs) [16]. However, the modalities and mechanisms through which these solutions are orchestrated are highly contextualized and need to be examined [1, 9]. Deep theoretical abstractions emerging from an understanding of these inequality-bridging mechanisms can greatly benefit other inequality-ridden contexts and regions through the process of reverse innovation [7].

Grounding our work in social resource-based view (SRBV) and the literature on reverse innovation and information systems, we examine an impactful social entrepreneurship initiative in a developing country context, with a view to transplant the learnings to the required pockets in other developing and developed economies [6, 7, 12, 14, 17]. We believe that such an effort will be useful in developing impactful theories for reducing the inequalities within countries. In our study, we focus on bridging the urban-rural divide, as it is one of the areas that the governments of most countries around the world are concerned. In specific, we focus on a grassroots social entrepreneurship initiative (rather than focusing on government-sponsored initiatives) aimed at reducing the rural-urban inequalities. Our study is set in the Indian context, which serves as a fertile ground for many social entrepreneurship initiatives. As aforementioned, our focus will be on how the learnings/theoretical abstractions from this initiative could be translated to benefit other parts of the world.

The two research questions that we intend to examine in our study are:-

1. How are social entrepreneurship initiatives in developing countries conceptualized and executed to bridge the rural-urban divide?
2. What are the key enablers that facilitate delivery of such ICT-enabled bridging solutions in the context of developing countries?

2   Research Context

To better appreciate the research setting and the problem proposed to be examined in our study, it would be necessary to understand the rural-urban divide in the Indian context. According to the 2011 Census Report, 83.3% of India's population lives in rural areas. However, most economic and service benefits are accrued by the urban centers. For example, in the health care sector nearly 75% of medical dispensaries, 60% of the hospitals and 80% of doctors are located in urban areas. Similarly, there are limited regular employment opportunities in rural areas leading to a large-scale migration to the urban centers creating undue pressure on the limited resources in Indian cities. According to the 2017 National Economic Survey, 8 to 9 million people migrate for work opportunities within India annually, which is severely affecting the quality of life in urban centers. Some studies have projected that by 2050, more than half of India will be living in urban areas, which will further accentuate the issues related to the quality of life in urban centers.

3   Background Literature

We ground our research in the social resource-based view (SRBV). So far literature has mainly used the resource based view (RBV) or natural resource based view (NRBV) approach to understand how companies can achieve economic performance or environmental performance as a competitive advantage by using their own internal resources and by deploying internal capabilities [8]. Recent work by Tate and Bals [18] uses social entrepreneurship literature and extends the RBV and NRBV logic, which is primarily based on instrumental parameters of economic performance, to that of social performance. In summary, SRBV integrates social capabilities with Triple Bottom Line (TBL) sustainability outcomes related to social, economic and environmental impacts.

Tate and Bals [18], through inductive case studies, conceptualized several social strategic capabilities, social driving forces and key resources that contribute to shared TBL value creation. An SRBV allows us to study social capabilities, allows us to examine complex stakeholders embedded in different domains such as those with economic, environmental, and/or social stakes. The theory also offers the possibility to link social capabilities and shared TBL value creation. Thus, SRBV allows us to study the social capabilities of grassroot social entrepreneurs acting as the micro-foundations for bringing about societal change. However, the propositions of SRBV have not yet been tested empirically, and the process view on how the resource and capabilities integration takes place, needs further examination. Because embedded innovation and social innovations are influenced by ambiguities and uncertainties in the external environment, exploring TBL value creation by social entrepreneurs is highly complex. Research that demonstrates how social capabilities are orchestrated by hybrid organizations such as grassroots social entrepreneurs using SRBV for alleviating social issues at the Bottom of the Pyramid (BoP) will be a valuable contribution to academic literature as well as practice [8, 18].

We believe that actions taken at various stages of an entrepreneurship project in general and a resource-constrained social entrepreneurship project in particular are based on the ability of the entrepreneur to leverage the internal resources within the company and garner resources from outside the company (based on the emergent need) as shown by SRBV. This resource orchestration exercise is a dynamic one that continuously evolves as the project unfolds. Our aim is to understand this evolutionary process with a view to perhaps replicate it in other contexts.

4   Method

This research aims at theory building by adopting a social resource-based view (SBRV) perspective. We intend to use a qualitative case-based methodology and a process view to analyze data from an Indian company (VillageTechServ[1]) (VTS) to understand the social resource-based actions that the company undertook to fulfil their objective of creating jobs for the rural Indian population. We will also examine how these patterns

---

[1] Name camouflaged – VillageTechServ (VTS for short).

evolve over time [see 4, 13, 15]. Consistent with the case study approach, we will provide an overview of some of the streams of research that will contribute to our theory building, namely, literature on social resource-based view and the role of ICT for bridging societal inequalities. Finally, we intend to situate each of our findings within the literature to contextualize the emergent theoretical concepts before arriving at our theoretical and practical implications.

Our study utilizes a mix of primary and secondary data to analyze the research problem. We have already conducted 42 interviews and have attended several presentations given by the senior management team of the VTS. Many of the key respondents were interviewed multiple times to clarify new facts as they emerged during the data collection process. We took detailed notes during all interviews. We also had email exchanges with officials for an in-depth understanding of the underlying processes, mechanisms, and interactions associated with their implementation process.

We also visited the VTS work centers at different locations in India and took detailed observational notes during the site visits, which will form part of the data for our analysis. For secondary data, we went through the organizations' activity reports, websites, published articles, internal reports, and video clips. We are using a process view to analyze the data, aimed at unearthing the patterns of their resource-based actions to understand how their implementation unfolded [4, 10].

5   Preliminary Findings and Expected Implications

India, traditionally has been one of the world's major IT-services provider hub. However, these IT service centers are primarily located in big cities such as Bangalore, New Delhi, Hyderabad and Chennai. VTS was initiated in 2008 on the premise of creating knowledge-based jobs for rural Indian population. The founder of VTS had the idea of sourcing some of the knowledge work from the villages with a view to provide the rural population with steady incomes through meaningful employment. The mission of VTS is a social one—to enskill, employ, empower and engage the rural youth. Their objective is to provide sustainable employment to 100,000 rural youth by opening business process outsourcing (BPO) centers in each of the 500 rural districts of India. They particularly want to create shared value in TBL, i.e. on the economic front, the social front and the environmental front. They are a hybrid organization that focuses on integrating their resources and capabilities for creating shared values through impact souring, training, rural employment, family saving, social engagement and conserving environmental ecosystems of the local rural districts. As of 2019, they have 16 Business Process Outsourcing (BPO) rural centers in north, south, east, west and central India. 65% of their clients are from the telecom sector and the remainder 35% comprise diverse sectors related to logistics and retail. VTS is perhaps the world's largest and relatively oldest (10 years) rural IT services company offering sustainable direct and indirect social value to its stakeholders since its inception.

Although setting a village IT service center may appear to be a straightforward process, it is not a simple exercise. Many of the taken for granted resources in the urban centers are unavailable in rural areas. The two primary contextual constraints, which made this venture extremely difficult, were (1) the rural areas did not have efficient

Internet connectivity and regular power supply, and (2) there was an absence of sufficiently trained employable workers for knowledge based IT service jobs in rural areas. To tackle these challenges, VTS took upon itself to arrange for the required infrastructure as well as to develop the required manpower skills for making the IT-enabled service centers operational. Apart from socially driven motivations, the founders of VTS were confident that the trained employees would be permanent assets for the company because the jobs (or rather opportunities) had moved to their villages so there would be less attrition. Job turnover or attrition is one of the major challenges faced by the IT services sector in India (with attrition rates in some cities touching a high of 25%). In addition to having near zero attrition rates, the cost of wages are also much lesser in rural centers simply because the living costs in rural areas are significantly lesser than in cities.

Some measurable social value impacts created by VTS include, providing direct employment for 5280 rural youth (in 2018). Out of these 90% were internally trained after employment. 40% of employment was provided for the female youth. 5% of these beneficiary are persons with disabilities. The average family income increased by 65% from the current income level due to jobs at VTS. At the societal level the rate of migration from rural area to cities in search of jobs have reduced to 55% in the villages where the initiative has been undertaken. A positive spinoff that the research team discovered in its initial interviews is that some of the villages that were initially selected by VTS for starting IT service centers now have permanent schools and the income levels in these villages have risen, leading to better quality of life for many people living in those villages. The journey of VTS has been one of trial and error. In fact, following the philosophy of reverse innovation, VTS has set up a centre in San Jose, California to create employment opportunities to the underprivileged and disadvantaged youth.

Thus far, we see empirical evidence for propositions of the emergent theory on SRBV. VTS is an example of how TBL values are generated by grassroots social entrepreneurs who know how to use their social capabilities such as social innovative model, mission driven approach and stakeholder management for bridging opportunity divide in the society. Social values that are generated by this initiative include providing access to food, access to decent livelihood, access to education, access to secure income, access to meaningful employment, access to equality and access to involve in community engagement. In our research, we seek to unravel these theoretical mechanisms which can perhaps be replicated by other aspiring social entrepreneurs. This allows us to understand how social entrepreneurship initiatives in developing countries can be conceptualized and executed to bridge the rural-urban divide. Our study hopes to unearth specific key enablers for facilitating the delivery of ICT-enabled bridging solutions in the context of developing countries.

References

1. Bamberger, P.: Beyond contextualization: using context theories to narrow the macro-micro gap in management research. Acad. Manage. J. **51**(5), 839–846 (2008). https://doi.org/10.5465/amj.2008.34789630

2. Bera, S.: Farmers' protests brings urban rural divide to the fore. https://www.livemint.com/Politics/HS3QyD9dGUfCjXfThTZUHL/Farmers-protests-brings-urban-rural-divide-to-the-fore.html. Accessed 28 Oct 2019

3. Bruneau, I., Mischi, N., Renahy, J.: Rural France in Revolt. https://jacobinmag.com/2019/03/gilets-jaunes-rural-dispossession-macron. Accessed 28 Oct 2019

4. Chakraborty, S., Sarker, S., Sarker, S.: An exploration into the process requirements elicitation: a grounded approach. J. Assoc. Inf. Syst. 11(4), 212–249 (2010). https://doi.org/10.17705/1jais.00225

5. Suisse, C.: Global Wealth Report 2019, Credit Suisse Research Institute. https://www.credit-suisse.com/about-us/en/reports-research/global-wealth-report.html. Accessed 28 Oct 2019

6. Govindarajan, V., Trimble, C.: Reverse Innovation: Create Far From Home, Win Everywhere. Harvard Business Review Press, Cambridge (2012). https://doi.org/10.1108/sajgbr-03-2013-0023

7. Govindarajan, V., Ramamurti, R.: Reverse innovation, emerging markets, and global strategy. Global Strategy J. 1(3–4), 191–205 (2011). https://doi.org/10.1002/gsj.23

8. Hart, S.L., Dowell, G.: A natural-resource-based view of the firm: fifteen years after. J. Manage. 37(5), 1464–1479 (2010). https://doi.org/10.1177/0149206310390219

9. Johns, G.: The essential impact of context on organizational behavior. Acad. Manage. Rev. 31(2), 386–408 (2006). https://doi.org/10.5465/amr.2006.20208687

10. Lyytinen, K., Newman, M.: Explaining information system change: a punctuated socio-technical change model. Eur. J. Inf. Syst. 17(6), 589–613 (2008). https://doi.org/10.1057/ejis.2008.50

11. Mair, J., Marti, I., Canly, K.: Institutional voids as spaces of opportunity. Eur. Bus. Forum 31, 34–39 (2007). https://doi.org/10.1016/j.jbusvent.2008.04.006

12. Saebi, T., Foss, N.J., Linder, S.: Social entrepreneurship research: past achievements and future promises. J. Manag. 45(1), 70–95 (2019). https://doi.org/10.1177/0149206318793196

13. Sarker, S., Sarker, S., Sahaym, A., Bjorn-Andersen, N.: Exploring value cocreation in relationships between an ERP vendor and its partners: a revelatory case study. MIS Q. 36(1), 317–338 (2012). https://doi.org/10.2307/41410419

14. Sen, A.K.: Development as capability expansion. J. Dev. Plan. 19, 41–58 (1989). https://doi.org/10.1007/978-1-349-21136-4_3

15. Silva, L., Hirschheim, R.: Fighting against windmills: strategic information systems and organizational deep structures. MIS Q. 31(2), 327–354 (2007). https://doi.org/10.2307/25148794

16. Srivastava, S.C., Mithas, S., Jha, B.: What is your global innovation strategy? IT Prof. 15(6), 2–6 (2013). https://doi.org/10.1109/mitp.2013.102

17. Srivastava, S.C., Shainesh, G.: Bridging the service divide through digitally enabled service innovations: evidence from Indian healthcare service providers. MIS Q. 39(1), 245–267 (2015). https://doi.org/10.25300/misq/2015/39.1.11

18. Tate, W.L., Bals, L.: Achieving shared triple bottom line (TBL) value creation: toward a social resource-based view (SRBV) of the firm. J. Bus. Ethics 152(3), 803–826 (2016). https://doi.org/10.1007/s10551-016-3344-y

Exploring the Determinants of Internet Usage in Nigeria: A Micro-spatial Approach

Kayode Odusanya[1]([⊠]) [iD] and Morakinyo Adetutu[2]

[1] School of Business and Economics, Loughborough University,
Loughborough, UK
k.odusanya@lboro.ac.uk
[2] Centre for Sustainable Development, Warwick University, Coventry, UK

Abstract. The dearth of Information Communication Technology (ICT) infrastructure in the Sub-Saharan Africa region underscores the argument that the spread of broadband infrastructure can foster internet adoption in the region. Consequently, the aim of this paper is to present results on the determinants of internet adoption in a sub-Saharan African country. Drawing on a dataset of households in Nigeria, this study presents findings on the demographic, socio-economic and infrastructure factors that predict internet usage in Nigeria. The novelty of our analysis stems from a unique dataset constructed by matching geo-referenced information from an inventory of network equipment to a nationally representative street-level survey of over 20,000 Nigerians, by far one of the largest technology adoption surveys in sub-Saharan Africa to date within the information systems literature. The results are discussed and concluding remarks highlighting next steps are made.

Keywords: Internet usage · Broadband · Socio-economic determinants · Technology diffusion · Micro-spatial approach

1 Introduction

Internet access is perhaps one of the most significant indicators of human and socio-economic development. It fosters productivity and innovation (Avgerou 2008; Paunov and Rollo 2016), social interactions (Liang and Guo 2015) and reduces communication and search costs (Beard et al. 2012). Yet, there is a digital divide in the level of internet access among developing countries, especially those in sub-Saharan Africa (SSA) compared to the rest of the world. Within SSA, the lack of internet access is a recognized barrier to the adoption of information communication technologies (ICTs) (Afolayan et al. 2015). This argument seems to be supported by regional broadband statistics, as shown in Fig. 1 where SSA is portrayed to have the lowest levels of internet penetration and wireless broadband infrastructure per capita, relative to other regions of the world. While previous studies have shed light on the regional variation in internet adoption by focusing on the determinants of internet penetration in the context of the "digital divide" (e.g. Oyelaran-Oyeyinka and Lal 2005; Chinn and Fairlie 2010), these studies often employ infrastructure measures/proxies (such as fixed telephone lines per sq. km, main telephone lines per capita, etc.,) thereby overlooking the peculiar

© IFIP International Federation for Information Processing 2020
Published by Springer Nature Switzerland AG 2020
M. Hattingh et al. (Eds.): I3E 2020, LNCS 12067, pp. 307–318, 2020.
https://doi.org/10.1007/978-3-030-45002-1_26

nature of broadband infrastructure in the SSA region. More specifically, we note that internet use across the SSA region is undertaken mainly via wireless broadband access, rather than fixed-line broadband. Thus, in this paper, we draw on a unique dataset that combines geo-referenced (longitude and latitude) information on 3G and 4G wireless network equipment to examine factors that predict of internet usage in Nigeria – a sub-Saharan country. Consequently, this study offers two potential contributions to the literature.

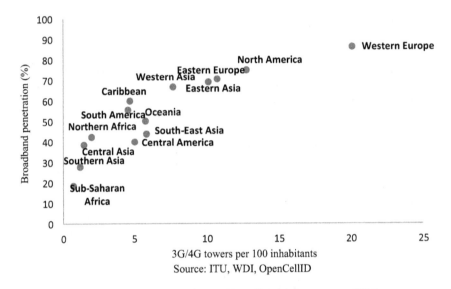

Fig. 1. Internet penetration and broadband infrastructure, 2017

First, unlike previous studies, we demonstrate a measure of broadband infrastructure is micro-spatial in nature, i.e., it is based on the density or concentration of 3G and 4G equipment around each household's dwelling over specified spatial domains. To achieve this, we match street-level information from the technology survey to the Global Positioning System (GPS) coordinates of 3G and 4G cell towers. This micro-spatial approach renders more nuanced and invaluable insights on whether/how spatial proximity or access to wireless internet connection shapes adoption decisions at the local level. Afterall, without connectivity, it is practically impossible to adopt/use broadband services. Furthermore, this spatial approach also embodies the reality that signal quality, a key determinant of actual usage behaviour, is shaped by the physical proximity of users to broadband connections (Neto et al. 2005; DeStefano et al. 2018). Hence, in addition to treating the spatial diffusion of wireless network infrastructure as an appropriate measure of broadband infrastructure, it is also a quality-weighted indicator that enriches our analysis.

Second, our focus on Nigeria provides a plausible and timely case study of the effect of broadband infrastructure diffusion on internet usage in SSA and the broader developing country context. Given that it accounts for the largest proportion (18%) of the entire SSA region's 1.03 billion population (World Development Indicators, 2018), we would argue that Nigeria is the most representative country of the SSA region. Furthermore, ITU estimates indicate that more than 90% of the youth population in developed countries use the internet compared to 30% in less developed regions of the world. Considering that the proportion of Nigeria's population below 40 years is projected to reach 81% by 2030, broadband penetration is likely to have a significant role in shaping Nigeria's participation in an increasingly digitalized future economy. Finally, despite growing to become Africa's largest economy and one of the major emerging economies in the world, Nigeria epitomizes the co-existing low levels of internet penetration and ICT infrastructure deficit (The Economist 2016). The remainder of this paper is organized as follows. In Sect. 2, we undertake a critical review of related literature on internet adoption and ICT infrastructure. This is followed by the model specification and the methods section. In Sect. 5, we discuss the results and conclude in Sect. 6 highlighting next steps and expected contributions of our study to the information systems literature and policy.

2 Related Literature

The literature on internet adoption and penetration is large. Consequently, due to space constraints, the goal of this review is not to present an extensive discussion of existing literature. Rather, we highlight a gap in the use of proxy measures in accounting for technology adoption. A more comprehensive review can be found in Cardona et al. (2013).

A dominant strand in the literature pertains to cross-country studies aimed at evaluating the determinants of internet usage and penetration in the context of the digital divide in developing countries. One of such studies is Dasgupta et al. (2005) who investigated the determinants of internet intensity (internet subscriptions per telephone mainline) for a cross country sample of 44 OECD and developed countries. Similarly, Chinn and Fairlie (2007) provide an analysis of internet penetration using a larger sample of based on panel data for 161 countries over the 1999–2001 period. They control for a range of macro-level determinants on telecoms prices, per capita income, education, age structure, urbanization, regulatory environment, etc. Although this study also controls for ICT infrastructure, their reliance on telephone density may not be applicable to the African context. Other internet diffusion/penetration studies use large cross-country samples from developing regions of the world (e.g. Chinn and Fairlie 2010). A few studies however focus on internet penetration for more specific sub-groups/regions of the world such as OECD (Lin and Wu 2013), The Americas (Galperin and Ruzzier 2013), APEC (Liu and San 2006), Africa (Oyelaran-Oyeyinka and Lal 2005) and Asia (Feng 2015). Greenstein and Spiller (1995) investigate the impact of telecommunication infrastructure (measured by the amount of fiber-optic cables employed by local exchange telephone companies) on economic growth in the U.S. Roller and Waverman (2001) investigate the linkages between broadband investment and economic growth across 21 OECD countries and 14 developing countries during 1970 to 1990. More recent studies have focused specifically on the impact of broadband infrastructure. For instance, Czernich et al. (2011) investigated the effect of broadband infrastructure on the economic growth for a panel of OECD countries over the period 1996-2007. However, they model this relationship by analyzing how broadband infrastructure (proxied by broadband penetration) shifts the growth parameter of technological progress within a macroeconomic production function setting. Tranos (2012) explored the causal effect of broadband infrastructure (internet backbone capacity) on the economic development across European city regions over the period 2001–2006 with ICT infrastructure found to stimulate economic development.

Three important observation can be gleaned from the above literature review. First, the cross-country studies tend to focus on the digital divide, attempting to explain internet adoption and penetration based on changes in economic, social, demographic and regulatory/institutional factors. Even when these studies attempt to account for the role of telecoms infrastructure, they do so by using variables such as personal computers per 100 people, main telephone lines per 100 people, customers' equipment (e.g. telephone set, facsimile machine), etc. Second, studies based on microdata tend to focus on developed country contexts, while also relying on infrastructure proxies that are analogous to the cross-country studies. Moreover, the developing country studies are not free from this problem too. Third, even studies that focus mainly on the effect of ICT infrastructure on economic measures and internet adoption also employ similar ICT infrastructure measures such as investments in telephone/broadband cables.

In comparison to the cited studies, we take a different approach by employing a true measure of internet infrastructure that is based on the prevalence of wireless network equipment (i.e. towers and radios). We then explore the effect of wireless network access on internet adoption at the individual level, based on physical proximity to broadband connection. Research has shown that variations in technology adoption are shaped by heterogeneity in geographical network access, such that the physical proximity to broadband connection or infrastructure can be expected to shape adoption decisions at the local level. For instance, it is well established that urban areas benefit from higher concentration of ICT infrastructure, which may enable social learning and adoption of ICT technologies (Liu and San 2006). Hence, unless this type of analysis is undertaken, these disparities in network access may be inadvertently explained away as differences across individual income or demographic characteristics.

This paper is also related to a small and evolving body of studies that exploit spatial data towards analyzing the diffusion of telecommunications technologies. Our review shows that research conducted by Buys et al. (2009) and Hodler and Raschky (2017) come close to the line of inquiry pursued in this study. However, they differ significantly from this study in two crucial ways. Firstly, both studies conduct country-level spatial analysis while we adopt a micro-level spatial approach. Secondly, while the former investigates the determinants of mobile operators' spatial location of network sites across Sub-Saharan Africa, the latter explores the role of ethnic politics in shaping the spatial diffusion of mobile phone infrastructure in Africa. As far as we know, the closest relative to this study is DeStefano et al. (2018) where the authors investigated how the arrival of ADSL broadband technology influenced the IT-productivity gap among UK firms. Comparatively, this study is therefore the first to explore the individual-level influence of broadband infrastructure on internet adoption using a micro-spatial approach, especially in a developing country context.

3 Model Specification

This study uses a probit model to examine the determinants of internet usage in Nigeria. Probit models are used when the dependent variable is dichotomous. We employ a set of explanatory variables in our model, namely: demographic factors include age, gender, marital status and religious affiliation; socio-economic factors such as expenditure, education, whether they are employed or not and a location variable indicating whether respondents live in rural or urban areas. Finally, we also include a micro-spatial infrastructure representing the number of internet infrastructure within a radius of where they live (i.e. towers) and the average tariff per megabyte of data used (tariff). Both towers and tariffs represent our infrastructure variables included in our model. Thus, our model is represented by the equation: Internet Use = f (age, gender, income and education, marital status, religious affiliation, towers, tariffs, urban).

We expect monthly expenditures (our proxy for income) to affect broadband adoption/usage positively. The probability of this adoption decision is also likely to rise for more educated individuals. However, the need for possessing an internet subscription, however, may fall for older and unemployed respondents. In terms of age, one could argue that, whereas younger individuals may have lower income, they tend to demonstrate a greater degree of technological affinity (Hübler and Hartje 2016). We add a gender variable as an additional characteristic, given that the preferences and decisions of men are more dominant than the preferences of their spouse(s) in patriarchal societies (Bulte et al. 2016). Similar considerations can be extended to the marital status of an individual on the adoption of internet technologies. Finally, technology adoption decisions are often shaped by religious reasons, as some religious beliefs may restrict the adoption of conventional technological products (Fungáčová, et al. 2017). Hence, we control for the religious beliefs of each sampled individual.

To examine the effect of broadband infrastructure on internet adoption, used a measure that captures individual-level access to wireless broadband network. Hence, we employ a microspatial variable that captures the prevalence of wireless network infrastructure at the individual level. We calculate this variable using information from our two data sources in four steps. First, inspired by Hodler and Raschky (2017), we extract and map the 3G and 4G cell tower locations from OpenCellID (see Fig. B in the appendix section). Secondly, we extract and map the street-level dwelling locations from the survey data. Thirdly, to use both data for our purpose, we link them by overlaying the towers map with the dwelling location map. Finally, we compute a micro-spatial infrastructure variable as the total number of cell towers within 5-km radius of everyone. This 5-km specification is premised on the fact that network coverage in SSA is mainly based on base stations that can provide service up to a 5–10-km radius (Aker and Mbiti 2010, p. 209). We achieve this using the Stata '*spmap*'[1] command.

---

[1] See https://www.stata.com/support/faqs/graphics/spmap-and-maps/ for resources on the spmap command.

4 Method

4.1 Data Collection

To investigate the effect of wireless connectivity on internet usage, we rely on a unique nationally representative market survey of Nigeria carried out by Africa's largest mobile operator, MTN[2] during April–July 2018. The MTN survey, which covers 730 localities (i.e., villages or towns), is by far and away one of the largest and most comprehensive technology surveys in sub-Saharan Africa to date. The data was collected via the use of paper questionnaire distributed to respondents in all 36 states of the country. Figure A in the appendix section plots the centroid GPS coordinates of surveyed areas at the municipality level. The wide geographical spread of the survey areas confirms the nationally representative nature of the survey. A total number of 21,844 observations were obtained for the final analysis. Our second data resource is the OpenCellID database which contains information on the micro-spatial independent variable (towers). The database contains raw information on the geo-location (longitude and latitude) of around seven million unique cell sites across the world (Hodler and Raschky 2017). One key benefit of the OpenCellID database is the possibility to identify the technology (radio) type for each telecommunications tower (i.e. GSM, UMTS, LTE, etc.). This allowed us to identify the two wireless network classes: "UMTS" (third-generation technology, 3G) and the more advanced "LTE" (fourth-generation technology, 4G) types. Specifically, we identified a total of 13246 unique tower locations from the OpenCellID data consisting of 11470 3G and 1776 4G sites. These sites are geo-coded at the GPS (longitude and latitude) - level (see Fig. B in the appendix).

4.2 Measures

Our main dependent variable is represented by a broadband usage variable for the use of broadband services. To construct this indicator variable, we convert survey responses on broadband subscription using the question: "Which of the following telecommunication services[3] do you use nowadays?". We then calculate the dependent indicator variable as a dummy that takes the value "1" if "Data service (Accessing internet)" was selected in response to the question. Otherwise, a dummy value of "0" was assigned to the observation. Table 1 provides the summary statistics of the variables employed in this study. The internet adoption rate within our dataset is 12%, falling firmly within the same ballpark as the 13.7% and 15.2% broadband penetration rates reported by Business Monitor International (BMI 2018) and the ITU, respectively. The summary statistics in Table 1 also indicate that there are on average 28 wireless network towers within 5 km of each respondent's street. However, the standard

---

[2] https://www.mtn.com/ MTN is the market leader in the Nigerian telecoms industry, accounting for 40% market share. See statutory regulatory data at https://www.ncc.gov.ng/stakeholder/statistics-reports/industry-overview.

[3] The listed service options include "Voice services", "Data service (Accessing internet)" and "Digital/2G services".

deviation of 40 towers within the 5 km radius suggests a reasonable spread or dispersion of the cell tower variable.

Table 1. Summary statistics of variables employed

Variable	Mean	Standard deviation
Internet adoption	0.119	0.324
Internet infrastructure	28.075	40.016
Expenditure[a]	55055.25	79552.62
Tariffs	0.627	0.088
Age	43.974	18.394
Education	13.314	4.978
Male	0.561	0.496
Married	0.624	0.484
Unemployed	0.118	0.323
Christian	0.619	0.486

Note: Internet infrastructure: 3G/4G towers within 5 km of respondent; Expenditure: sum of expenditures on food, rent, fuel, clothing & healthcare; Age: age of the individual in years; Education: no of years of formal education; Male: Dummy = 1 if individual's gender is male; Married: Dummy = 1 if individual is married; Unemployed: Dummy = 1 if individual is unemployed; Christian: Dummy = 1 if individual's religion is Christianity; Tariffs: average tariff per megabyte (MB) of data use. Number of individuals: 21844
[a]Expenditure is in Nigerian Naira (1 Nigerian Naira = £0.0022 – as at 14 November 2019)

5   Results

Table 2 presents the marginal effects from baseline probit estimations. In column 1, we start by measuring the network infrastructure effects on broadband adoption: probability of adopting internet services, without any control variables or locality effects. Due to the cross-sectional nature of our data, we interpret these results as associations. It is clear from the results in columns (1) that a strong positive correlation exists between the concentration of broadband infrastructure around each individual and internet adoption. This coefficient is significant at the 1% level. From column 2 to 10, we add the control variables one by one, but the infrastructure coefficient remains statistically significant at the 1% level, albeit the magnitude of the coefficient drops. In column 11, we include locality effects to draw inference only from the variation in individual adoption decisions. Besides employing controls and locality effects, we use heteroskedasticity-robust standard errors clustered at the locality level that allow the data to be independent across localities by restricting the error terms to be correlated for individuals within the same areas on account of omitted regional characteristics.

Table 2. Results of probit model for the determinants of Internet usage in Nigeria

Der var: Prob (internet)	(1)	(2)	(3)	(4)	(5)	(6)	(7)	(8)	(9)	(10)	(11)
towers	0.0205***	0.0194***	0.0193***	0.0197***	0.0191***	0.0171***	0.0168***	0.0171***	0.0149***	0.0146***	0.0121***
	[0.0015]	[0.0014]	[0.0014]	[0.0014]	[0.0014]	[0.0015]	[0.0015]	[0.0014]	[0.0018]	[0.0017]	[0.0018]
expenditure		0.0108***	0.0117***	0.0116***	0.0116***	0.0102***	0.0096***	0.0097***	0.0098***	0.0095***	0.0074***
		[0.0010]	[0.0010]	[0.0011]	[0.0010]	[0.0010]	[0.0010]	[0.0010]	[0.0010]	[0.0010]	[0.0010]
tariffs			−0.0003***	−0.0004***	−0.0004***	−0.0003***	−0.0003***	−0.0003***	−0.0003***	−0.0003***	−0.0002***
			[0.0001]	[0.0001]	[0.0001]	[00001]	[0.0001]	[0.0001]	[0.0001]	[0.0001]	[0.0001]
age				−0.1424***	−0.1130***	−0.1005***	−0.1030***	−0.1111***	−0.1114***	−0.1108***	−0.1147***
				[0.0066]	[0.0068]	[0.0070]	[0.0069]	[0.0071]	[0.0071]	[0.0042]	[0.0061]
married					−0.0443***	−0.0442***	−0.0417***	−0.0341***	−0.0337***	−0.0346***	−0.0217***
					[0.0052]	[0.0052]	[0.0051]	[0.0052]	[0.0052]	[0.0052]	[0.0046]
education						0.0473***	0.0454***	0.0405***	0.0398***	0.0384***	0.0323***
						[0.0169]	[0.0164]	[0.0143]	[0.0139]	[0.0136]	[0.0107]
christian							0.0172***	0.0255***	0.0261***	0.0246***	0.0179***
							[0.0065]	[0.0066]	[0.0066]	[0.0065]	[0.0050]
male								0.0515***	0.0518***	0.0495***	0.0463***
								[0.0047]	[0.0047]	[0.0047]	[0.0036]
urban									0.0199**	0.0195**	0.0268***
									[0.0087]	[0.0087]	[0.0078]
unemployed										−0.0475***	−0.0416***
										[0.0091]	[0.0070]
constant	−1.7096***	−2.2363***	−2.2851***	0.5212***	0.0935	−0.6895**	−0.6581**	−0.6434**	−0.6363**	−0.5643	−0.2237
	[0.0478]	[0.0648]	[0.0644]	[0.1380]	[0.1422]	[0.3018]	[0.2961]	[0.2671]	[0.2649]	[0.2623]	[0.2308]
Pseudo R-squared	0.0326	0.0512	0.0522	0.0889	0.0944	0.1127	0.1135	0.1222	0.1232	0.1251	–
Regional effects	No	No	No	No	No	No	No	No	No	No	Yes
Number of localities	730	730	730	730	730	730	730	730	730	730	730
Number of observations	21844	21844	21844	21844	21844	21844	21844	21844	21844	21844	21844

Notes: This table reports the marginal effect values from linear probability (random effects) models for predicting the effects of wireless network infrastructure on internet adoption. Standard errors clustered at the locality-level are in parentheses. ***, **, and * denote significance at the 1%, 5%, and 10% level, respectively.

As seen in Column 11, the infrastructure coefficient retains its statistical significance but drops further. Specifically, infrastructure coefficient of 0.012 suggests that a unit increase in the number of cell towers within 5 km of a respondent increases the probability of internet adoption by 1.2%, which corresponds to an increase in the likelihood of adoption from around 12% to around 13.2% in an average respondent. Also, in the full specification in column 11, the coefficients on the control variables are consistent with intuition and they are all statistically significant at the 1%-level. For instance, older and unemployed respondents are less likely to adopt broadband services, whereas higher income earners, more educated individuals and urban dwellers are more likely to adopt the internet. For religion, being a Christian increases the probability of adoption. The positive coefficient on the male gender variable is consistent with the patriarchal nature of the Nigerian society, which indicates that the men are more likely to adopt internet services, perhaps reflecting the stronger socio-economic power of the male gender. Interestingly, in terms of the magnitude of the coefficients, we find age and gender to have the greatest effect on broadband adoption, with both coefficients indicating 11% and 5% positive impact on the probability of adoption, respectively. The age coefficient lends weight to our opening arguments on the implications of broadband adoption for the participation of the large projected youth population of Nigeria in an increasingly digitalized global economy in the future. For all the specifications in Table 2, the results also show that individuals in areas with a higher concentration of network infrastructure are more likely to adopt and use broadband services.

6 Concluding Remarks and Next Steps

This paper presents first-stage results showing factors that influence internet adoption in Nigeria. Using geo-referenced information of an inventory of broadband network infrastructure, we employ a more appropriate micro-spatial measure of internet infrastructure based on 3G/4G network equipment at the local level alongside a range of explanatory variables to explain internet adoption in Nigeria. In general, the results obtained are economically important, and they can help explain the adoption patterns of broadband services particularly when network infrastructure effects are likely to play an important role in driving internet penetration. For instance, in many regions across developing countries, network coverage is usually the first modern technology of any kind (Aker and Mbiti 2010). Hence, we would argue that the failure to control for this network infrastructure effect in the study of broadband adoption across developing countries could well result in significant omitted variable bias. Furthermore, the network infrastructure effect may also explain the nuances embodied in the varied adoption of broadband services across different regions, given that the quality of service (QoS) and user experience may well depend on the diffusion and reliability of the underlying network infrastructure.

Although the first-stage results presented in this paper revealed preliminary drivers of internet adoption, they also provide interesting avenues for further study which we aim to explore in subsequent analysis of the dataset. In the first place, the significant urban variable shows that there are likely to be regional differences with regards to the factors that influence internet adoption in Nigeria. Given that Nigeria has one of the largest rural population in Africa (World Bank 2018), we expect that further analysis testing the relationships in this study across rural and urban dwellers, will contribute significantly to the policy debate on bridging the urban-rural internet divide in Nigeria. Further, having microeconomic information that is representative of the national population of the type used in this research, permits clear visualization of the digital divide as an additional form of inequality that can hinder access to other internet-reliant technologies. For instance, the telecommunications sector in Nigeria is currently undergoing several policy changes, one of which is the granting of mobile money licenses to mobile network operators. Therefore, it is earmarked that further analysis with our data will explore diffusion constraints for other technologies covered in the survey data and how usage patterns might vary in different parts of the country. We hope that the results of these avenues of research will provide new insights that contribute to both policy and research.

Acknowledgements. The authors also gratefully acknowledge the support of Africa's leading mobile operator MTN, for providing the market survey and operator data employed in this study. Special thanks to the staff of the Business Intelligence and Research Departments. We also like to thank participants at various seminars and workshops for their helpful comments. The usual disclaimer applies.

Appendix Section

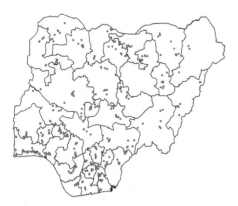 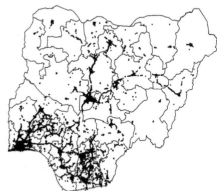

Fig. A. Nigerian map showing surveyed areas   **Fig. B.** Tower sites in Nigeria (source: OpenCellID data)

References

Afolayan, A., Plant, E., White, G.R., Jones, P., Beynon-Davies, P.: Information technology usage in SMEs in a developing economy. Strategic Change **24**(5), 483–498 (2015)

Aker, J.C., Mbiti, I.M.: Mobile phones and economic development in Africa. J. Econ. Perspect. **24**(3), 207–232 (2010)

Avgerou, C.: Information systems in developing countries: a critical research review. J. Inf. Technol. **23**(3), 133–146 (2008)

Beard, T.R., Ford, G.S., Saba, R.P., Seals Jr., R.A.: Internet use and job search. Telecommun. Policy **36**(4), 260–273 (2012)

Business Monitor International (BMI): Nigeria Telecommunications Report, Q2 (2018). http://www.bmiresearch.com. Accessed 27 Dec 2018

Bulte, E., Lensink, R., Vu, N.: Gender training and female empowerment: experimental evidence from Vietnam. Econ. Lett. **145**, 117–119 (2016)

Buys, P., Dasgupta, S., Thomas, T.S., Wheeler, D.: Determinants of a digital divide in Sub-Saharan Africa: a spatial econometric analysis of cell phone coverage. World Dev. **37**(9), 1494–1505 (2009)

Cardona, M., Kretschmer, T., Strobel, T.: ICT and productivity: conclusions from the empirical literature. Inf. Econ. Policy **25**(3), 109–125 (2013)

Chinn, M.D., Fairlie, R.W.: The determinants of the global digital divide: a cross-country analysis of computer and internet penetration. Oxford Econ. Pap. **59**(1), 16–44 (2007)

Chinn, M.D., Fairlie, R.W.: ICT use in the developing world: an analysis of differences in computer and internet penetration. Rev. Int. Econ. **18**(1), 153–167 (2010)

Czernich, N., Falck, O., Kretschmer, T., Woessmann, L.: Broadband infrastructure and economic growth. Econ. J. **121**(552), 505–532 (2011)

Dasgupta, S., Lall, S., Wheeler, D.: Policy reform, economic growth and the digital divide. Oxford Dev. Stud. **33**(2), 229–243 (2005)

DeStefano, T., Kneller, R., Timmis, J.: Broadband infrastructure, ICT use and firm performance: evidence for UK firms. J. Econ. Behav. Organ. **155**, 110–139 (2018)

Feng, G.C.L.: Determinants of internet diffusion: a focus on China. Technol. Forecast. Soc. Change **100**, 176–185 (2015)

Fungáčová, Z., Hasan, I., Weill, L.: Trust in banks. J. Econ. Behav. Organ. **157**, 452–476 (2017)

Galperin, H., Ruzzier, C.A.: Price elasticity of demand for broadband: evidence from Latin America and the Caribbean. Telecommun. Policy **37**(6–7), 429–438 (2013)

Greenstein, S.M., Spiller, P.T.: Modern telecommunications infrastructure and economic activity: an empirical investigation. Ind. Corporate Change **4**(4), 647–665 (1995)

Hodler, R., Raschky, P.A.: Ethnic politics and the diffusion of mobile technology in Africa. Econ. Lett. **159**, 78–81 (2017)

Hübler, M., Hartje, R.: Are smartphones smart for economic development? Econ. Lett. **141**, 130–133 (2016)

Liang, P., Guo, S.: Social interaction, internet access and stock market participation—an empirical study in China. J. Comp. Econ. **43**(4), 883–901 (2015)

Lin, M.S., Wu, F.S.: Identifying the determinants of broadband adoption by diffusion stage in OECD countries. Telecommun. Policy **37**(4–5), 241–251 (2013)

Liu, M.C., San, G.: Social learning and digital divides: a case study of internet technology diffusion. Kyklos **59**(2), 307–321 (2006)

Neto, I., Niang, C., Ampah, M.: Fostering pro-competitive regional connectivity in Sub-Saharan Africa. Global ICT Department, The World Bank, Washington, DC (2005)

Oyelaran-Oyeyinka, B., Lal, K.: Internet diffusion in sub-Saharan Africa: a cross-country analysis. Telecommun. Policy **29**(7), 507–527 (2005)

Paunov, C., Rollo, V.: Has the Internet fostered inclusive innovation in the developing world? World Dev. **78**, 587–609 (2016)

Roller, L.H., Waverman, L.: Telecommunications infrastructure and economic development: a simultaneous approach. Am. Econ. Rev. **91**(4), 909–923 (2001)

The Economist: Building a digital Nigeria, Economist Intelligence Unit (2016)

Tranos, E.: The causal effect of the internet infrastructure on the economic development of European city regions. Spatial Econ. Anal. **7**(3), 319–337 (2012)

World Bank: Rural population – Nigeria (2018). https://data.worldbank.org/indicator/SP.RUR. TOTL?locations=NG. Accessed 22 Oct 2019

Enablers and Barriers for Mobile Commerce and Banking Services Among the Elderly in Developing Countries: A Systematic Review

Nkosikhona Theoren Msweli$^{(\boxtimes)}$ ⓘ and Tendani Mawela ⓘ

Department of Informatics, University of Pretoria, Pretoria 0002, South Africa
nkosikhona.msweli@gmail.com, tendani.mawela@up.ac.za

Abstract. The rollout of mobile banking has taken over the traditional banking space in both developed and developing countries. Banking institutions are continuously seeking innovative digital solutions to stay ahead of competitors and be the first preference to consumers. Scholars have also shown some interest in investigating mobile commerce and banking implementation and adoption. However, research studies focusing on the elderly and mobile banking are scant. This paper seeks to understand the current state of knowledge regarding the enablers and barriers of mobile banking and commerce among the elderly by providing a systematic review of the existing literature on the phenomenon.

The literature review showed that there is minimal research to date that has been conducted on this topic of interest. Consequently, issues of investigating enablers and barriers of mobile banking among the elderly have been fairly neglected. The main barriers noted in the literature include: security concerns, trust and privacy, a lack of personalization and limited technical knowledge of the elderly. Significant enablers that may be considered are: perceived ease of use of mobile banking applications, perceived value, convenience and consumer attitudes. Future directions for research and practice on mobile banking for the elderly are suggested.

Keywords: Elderly · Mobile commerce · Mobile banking · M-banking · Cellphone banking · Developing countries

1 Introduction

The growth in the proliferation of smartphones and implementation of fast wireless network connections such as 4G and now 5G, means that the mobile market can have a variety of offerings such as mobile banking worldwide without any space or time limitations. Mobile commerce and as such mobile banking removes spatial and temporal limitations, enabling customers to conduct ubiquitous payments [1] and to shop globally. The driver behind mobile electronic offerings such as mobile banking and commerce was to enable the suppliers to reach a wider audience at an affordable and convenient level, while increasing their revenue at the same time. The elderly population, in particular, may gain powerful assistance through having mobile applications and m-commerce on hand for their daily requirements [2].

© IFIP International Federation for Information Processing 2020
Published by Springer Nature Switzerland AG 2020
M. Hattingh et al. (Eds.): I3E 2020, LNCS 12067, pp. 319–330, 2020.
https://doi.org/10.1007/978-3-030-45002-1_27

The banking industry is among the early adopters of these mobile technological innovations [3]. However, the use of m-banking is still lower than anticipated, especially among the elderly population group. The youth are reported to be leading in technology usage whereas the elderly are reportedly lagging. It is important that various customer groups are afforded an equal opportunity to benefit from online public and private services [4] especially in the digital era. Research has reported the exclusion of the elderly in as far as the deployment of Information and Communication Technology (ICT) [4, 5]. Unfortunately, the case of the elderly's digital inclusion seems to receive little attention. Digital barriers can be a factor behind the exclusion of the elderly [6]. The digital inclusion of the elderly could positively impact on the social and economic welfare for this segment of the population subsequently improving their quality of life [7]. It is worth mentioning that the current elderly people are not digital natives. Thus, if the users have a limited understanding or familiarity of any given technology, it is likely that they will not use the products offered through that technology [8].

The elderly represent a significant business opportunity for online marketers [9], and it may be a missed opportunity if the elderly's needs are not catered for in the technology rollout. Technology continuously changes and the elderly lack educational opportunities to keep up with it [10]. Some authors indicate that it is not always clear whether the elderly will participate actively on the online and mobile commerce solutions [7]. Iyer and Eastman [9] found that most of the elderly have used the internet before, but the study further revealed that only 35% used the internet for m-commerce.

The objective of this research study was to understand how mobile banking and commerce has been investigated in the context of the elderly in developing countries in order to identify existing enablers and barriers. The research question driving the study was: *What are the enablers and barriers for mobile commerce and banking among the elderly in developing countries?*

The remainder of the paper is structured as follows: The next section contains the background and motivating information about the elderly, mobile banking and developing countries. Then the research methodology which details how papers were identified, selected and analysed. Finally, the discussion of findings, conclusions and recommendations are presented.

2 Background and Motivation

2.1 Mobile Commerce and Banking

There is no agreed upon definition that has been put forward to define mobile banking in the extant literature. Nonetheless, Shaikh and Karjaluoto [11] argue that accessing banking or financial services from a laptop should not be considered m-banking, since the user interface is similar to that of desktop PCs. According to Touchaie and Hashim [12], m-banking is the act of conducting monetary transactions in a mobile environment, using mobile or wireless network and mobile devices such as smartphones and tablets. Mobile payments are considered a subset of mobile banking. Houghton [13] considered paying for your car fuel or parkade tickets through vending machine via smartphone's credits as a payment method to be an example of m-commerce. Some authors refer to it as cellphone banking. Mlitwa and Tshetsha [14] described it as a convenient banking channel to manage finances using a mobile phone. According to Al-jabri and Sohail [15], mobile banking services allow customers to take full advantage of the latest technology which enables them to: check account details; view a mini-statement; transfer funds; pay credit cards and loan installments and place remittances to beneficiaries in local banks or abroad, to highlight a few.

Mobile banking technology offers a variety of possible products and services that banks can avail to consumers [16]. Among other services, M-banking systems offer a variety of financial features such as micropayments to merchants, bill-payments to utilities, person to person (P2P) transfers, business to business (B2B) transfers, business to person (B2P) transfers and long-distance remittances [17]. Khan, Varshney and Qadeer [18] suggested that it is mobile commerce (m-commerce), they continued to define it as buying and selling of goods and services using wireless technology. Khan, Varshney and Qadeer further identified mobile banking as one of the products and services available in the mobile commerce (m-commerce). Thus, mobile financial services fall under this umbrella such as mobile personal banking and payments [19]. Mobile banking is currently available via SMS technology and WAP-enabled mobile phones [20, 21]. The capability to use banking and other m-commerce applications with such a small device effectively with good interaction is a critical success factors of mobile buying and selling [22]. Mobility is often a challenge for a number of elderly individuals. Thus mobile shopping and banking can be beneficial to this cohort who would then essentially not have to leave their homes or comfort to perform financial transactions [1].

Mobile banking seems to offer several possibilities to either increase revenues or reduce costs [16], however the usage rate remains low [20], except in developed countries where it is heavily adopted [21]. For South Africa and other developing countries, mobile banking serves as a vital interface between consumers and the banks by permitting money transfer, saving and investment opportunities [23]. Mobile banking is further described as a contributor towards financial inclusion for such countries with a tele-density of 70% [24]. The provision of mobile banking is increasing but awareness of the service by banking consumers and the convenience that it entails requires more effort on the part of banking services providers [25].

M-banking dates back to the late 1990s where it was first launched in Germany [11]. Primary research on mobile banking was conducted in the early 2000s [25]. The adoption of mobile banking and related services in developing economies has been studied [19] over the past years in countries such as: South Africa (MTN money, Wizzit), Kenya (mPESA), India (Eko) and in continents such as Asia (SmartMoney and G-Cash) [26–30]. However, studies about the elderly behaviour on mobile banking and commerce are rare [2, 31], a few studies have examined ease of use and extrinsic and intrinsic motivations for the elderly's usage of mobile applications [32]. Convenience and efficiency are top mobile banking benefits [26] cited in the literature.

2.2 The Elderly Population

Most scholars define the elderly as individuals aged 50 and above [12, 33]. Applying policies and regulations from different countries, this definition is argued. Similarly, in natural science or clinical psychology various issues are considered. In addition, the needs of the elderly are linked to the age-related changes that they face [34]. Mallenius, Rossi and Tuunainen [35] argue that, ageing differs with individuals, while there are energetic and sharp elderly aged over 80, there are 60-year-old people, who struggle with their daily routine.

People are living longer than at any other time recorded in history [36]. The elderly population globally is growing dramatically [33, 37]. In this digital economy the elderly's needs and concerns as technology users differ from other groups due to natural changes associated with aging [38]. Considering the available medicines and technologies, many of today's elderly people desire an active retirement and prefer learning new skills [9] that they can use in this digital era. Furthermore, the elderly are using digital technologies for work and entertainment [38].

In the commercial market, to understand the elderly consumer behavior, it is important to understand who elderly people are [12] and their attitudes and behavior towards technology [36]. It is worth mentioning that the relationship with technology might be different for older adults compared to young people, since the elderly did not grow up with technology and currently have less contact with these innovations [39]. However, the literature reports that in China the elderly had positive attitudes and beliefs concerning information technology [36].

Technology has been reported to have an ability to simplify the lives of elderly individuals. In the view of Jayachandran [40], the elderly have developed a technophobia which may prompt them to stay away from any technology. Although the elderly group may believe in traditional resources, having digital skills to easily access available digital technologies may allow people to engage with and participate in almost every level of public life, from social networking to e-Government [41]. The elderly can have a hard time assimilating digital technologies like mobile banking. As such it is important that mobile service providers consider how to support the elderly integrate into modern societies [4].

2.3   Developing Countries

Mobile commerce has presented several benefits to many individuals and organisations in developing countries [42]. However, mobile banking in developing countries is still constrained, with only few individuals who can access it, due to strict banking regulations and a high number of unbanked individuals [43–45]. Developing countries, heavily dominated by low-income individuals [30], are faced with a variety of challenges and limitations such as access to quality health services and education, and they are lagging in technology implementation. Such countries with a high rate of unbanked citizens, have relied on low-cost banking solutions such as MPesa [26] to accommodate the unbanked citizens.

Previous research on developing countries has indicated that financial literacy is an important factor for effective financial decision making which in turn influences citizens' financial behavior [46]. In many cases, individuals with low financial literacy will ignore banking applications and the benefits they may bring. Examining issues such as trust, may increase the use of mobile technologies in developing countries [47]. Considering the disadvantaged background, change in political structures for these countries does not culminate in economic power or wealth [23]. Also, poverty is evident in such countries and the digital technologies and other (ICT) infrastructure are still under development [13]. Thus, low-cost banking may benefit citizens in these countries. Some researchers have indicated that mobile technology can reduce the effect of poverty [47]. However, it is unclear if people in low-income countries will adopt mobile banking technology [26], since the appetite for banking services in these countries is not high. According to Thakur [50], Dass and Pal [48], as well as Sharma [49], the demand for m-banking can be improved by increasing the demand for banking and financial services through increased awareness about various available products.

3   Research Method

The study adopted a systematic literature review (SLR) approach which provides a transparent research process to study patterns and evidence from prior research studies [50]. The approach used is based on the guidelines proposed by [51]. The procedure undertaken was as follows: Define search terms; Select sources (digital libraries) on which to perform the search; Application of search terms on sources; and Selection of primary studies by application of inclusion and exclusion criteria on search results.

The aim of a SLR is to identify all research studies, those that are published and unpublished that address a specific question [50]. Like any other research approach, the SLR has benefits and limitations. The major advantage of this method is that it provides information about the effects of some phenomenon across different environments, and also maintaining the ability to establish whether the study is robust and transferable [51]. Even though the SLR approach requires more effort compared to other approaches [51], it matched the requirement of the study which was to understand what is known in the scholarly literature about the barriers and enablers for the elderly regarding mobile commerce and banking. The approach adopted in this study, looked at the published papers in the last 10 years (2009–2019), focusing on the association between mobile banking, m-commerce and the elderly in developing countries. The following search terms and combinations were used in this systematic review: (Mobile banking OR m-banking OR mbanking OR Mobile commerce OR Mcommerce OR m-commerce) AND (Elderly OR Senior citizen OR Seniors OR Older adults OR Older people) AND (Developing Countries). The electronic libraries did not yield much data on the phenomena of interest. Mobile banking is still emerging in several countries [33], thus few studies were returned, and most did not contain the search text. The articles that did not contain the search text were omitted immediately. Due to a minimal number of relevant research studies returned, it was decided that research articles should not be limited only to developing countries but rather focus on elderly and mobile banking and m-commerce in general.

To minimize bias in a review, inclusion and exclusion selection criteria needs to be clearly defined [50]. It happens in some cases that the selected studies are irrelevant to the research question and objectives. Having selection criteria eliminate such issues. Publications that met any of the following criteria were selected as primary studies: A research study that primarily focuses on mobile banking or m-commerce and the elderly; A research study that focuses on mobile payments and the elderly, and Studies published in English between year 2009 and 2019, the intention was to focus on research development in the past 10 years. Publications that met any of the following criteria were excluded from the review: Mobile banking or mobile commerce studies that do not focus on the elderly; Studies published before 2009; and Studies not published in English.

Figure 1 highlights the process followed to select the papers. The studies were reviewed to extract the drivers and barriers towards mobile banking and commerce. The search resulted in 11 relevant publications, of which four were published in different journals and some published as part of conference proceedings and student dissertations. Based on the search results, only four of these research studies were conducted in the developing countries. The majority of the papers investigated adoption using a quantitative approach. The searches were conducted on ACM Digital Library, IEEE Xplore Digital Library, Science Direct, ISI Web of Knowledge and Google Scholar. Due to scarcity of research papers focusing on this context, the search was extended to the top eight IS Journals as identified by the Association for Information Systems (AIS). After reviewing the eight IS journals, there were no new articles identified which were relevant to the subject.

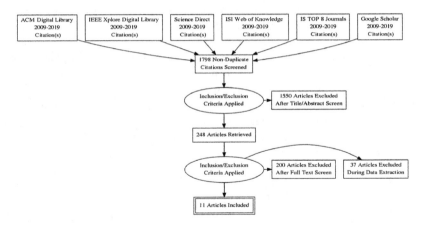

Fig. 1. Articles included in the review

4   Discussion of the Findings

Previous studies have reported a lack of interest in this subject area, similarly this study discovered limited literature to examine and extract enablers and barriers for mobile commerce. The research studies included in this review investigated enablers and barriers for mobile commerce and banking among elderly. Most of the studies focus on the factors influencing the use of mobile financial services. It is noted that such technology trends are new, and most elderly consumers still need to be educated or trained on these technologies [52]. Barriers are existing which negatively impact acceptance, adoption and use of mobile commerce among the elderly. Among other things, security and trust are major concerns for this group of individuals [2]. Financial institutions must instill trust to reach this audience, despite the existing perceptions of distrust in this sector [47].

Jayachandran [40] studied senior citizens aged 50-plus, to ascertain the type of banking they preferred and reason for their preference. The study was conducted in Kerala, a state located in one of the developing countries in India. The survey method was used in the study, with a sample of 400 banking customers chosen through convenience sampling. The study found that the seniors preferred branch banking since it offers personalized interaction and dealings. This indicated that most elderly have not adopted mobile banking due to lack of personalization or customizing mobile financial applications accommodating their special needs.

Ayaratne, Ryan and Cripps [53] investigated the factors that affect the adoption of M-banking by using a combined Technology Acceptance Model (TAM)-Unified Theory of Acceptance and Use of Technology (UTAUT) framework. Data was collected from 70 elderly people in Australia. Australia is one of the high-income countries. The study was selected due to limited literature available. The results revealed that performance expectancy, facilitating conditions and, perceived ease of use were significant factors that determined the use of mobile banking. Based on the results, the banking application needs to be clear, understandable, user-friendly, and not require a lot of mental effort to learn. The author further noted that the elderly did not find the banking app trustworthy. Due to smaller sample, the study cannot be generalized across the population.

Touchaie and Hashim [12] revealed that there was a negative effect of dispositional resistance to change (DRTC) on mobile banking adoption among elderly. This means there is high resistance to change around this population segment. The data was collected using the survey method in Kuala Lumpur from elderly aged over 50. The participants were non-users of mobile banking. A sample of 384 was obtained and Partial Least Squares Structural Equation Modelling (PLS-SEM) was used to analyze the data. It can be recorded that resistance to change is a barrier towards adoption of mobile banking. Marketing strategies used by online services providers such as m-banking were not appropriate to attract the market segment that is unwilling to use services such as senior market. Thus, understanding factors that negatively impact the adoption of m-banking by a particular market segment may help to develop strategies which assist to overcome the barriers in their adoption.

Choudrie et al. [33] conducted a systematic review of studies on mobile banking, and older adults and on older adults and smartphones. The aim of the paper was to understand and explain the factors that influence the adoption, use and diffusion of mobile banking among older adults. The study found that there are few studies of older adults' relationships with mobile banking and smartphones. The results further revealed that the innovativeness of device and a product or service such as mobile banking needs to be compatible with individuals' lifestyles and also offer support service by way of its novelty. The author noted that, by offering support, the consumer perceived difficulties and complexities are often reduced or eliminated, consequently promoting trust while reducing risks. Focusing on trust, the study also introduced a conceptual framework which can be used for future studies. Lian and Yen [2] studied drivers and barriers affecting older consumers' intention to shop online. The study used UTAUT and innovation resistance theory. By comparing younger consumers with their older counterparts, and considering gender, the findings indicate that the major factors driving older adults toward online shopping are performance expectation and social influence which is the same with younger consumers. Their study revealed the following barriers: value, risk, and tradition which is different from younger users.

4.1 Identified Key Enablers

Use of technology is not an instant act, especially for non-digital natives. Prior experience with technology may lead to positive acceptance of new digital technologies. Ayaratne, Ryan and Cripps [53] showed that individuals who were familiar with other technology were likely to perceive M-banking as easy to use and useful to their lives, and also confirmed this positive factor by finding user-friendliness as the driver of mobile banking adoption. Organisations need to understand that, to leverage the available opportunities, it is important to tap into the right kind of consumer behavior and attitude [1]. Mobile opportunities should be usable and accessible hence, it is vital that mobile applications are suitable for all types of consumers [4]. Usefulness and attitude are direct factors influencing consumer satisfaction leading to the adoption of mobile technologies [54].

4.2 Identified Key Barriers

Even though there are a number of benefits reported on mobile banking and commerce, the barriers from internal and external environment do exist preventing the innovation from reaching its potential. Trust was a commonly cited barrier in the literature. Consumers have different views and attitude regarding mobile technologies which generate a number of issues when it comes to acceptance and adoption. In general factors such as a lack of trust of technology and a lack of technology readiness act as barriers to the adoption of mobile financial services [48]. The digital divide and digital literacy are two areas that also caught the attention of the researchers when considering the elderly as digital immigrants [41]. For instance, operating a small user interface of a mobile device may be difficult for the elderly. Also a mobile application with a complicated menu may be difficult for the elderly to remember [12]. While studies prove that elderly customers who have access to electronic services and products are ready for electronic banking and commerce [3], the opposite is reported for mobile commercial products and services. Among barriers, the elderly reported professionally written instructions for operating devices which they did not understand and also the absence of a person who can teach them as key constraints. Additionally, fear is another reason for not using digital technologies. The elderly are afraid of being lost in smartphone or tablet and that they will not be able to login or sign out of the application [41]. Performing online payment is another issue for the elderly attempting to shop online, many consumers preferred cash on delivery due to trust and security issues [2] and privacy [55].

5 Conclusion and Recommendations

The findings of this study revealed that the elderly group certainly have unique requirements that need to be communicated to mobile commerce providers and designers in order to cater for this growing segment. Mobile banking is still in the emerging stage in various parts of the world, thus future research should focus on building the body of knowledge around this context. There is a need to conduct research studies that adopt data collection methods that probe for answers, which can deliver rich primary data from the elderly. Additionally, the study found that there is a gap in research focusing on the elderly and mobile banking and commerce, which confirmed the findings of [33]. In the light of this, the opportunity for further studies is identified particularly from the perspective of developing countries. Future research should address this gap by focusing on how the elderly needs can be met in this digital era focusing on digital or technology needs.

M-banking and M-commerce are thriving in the global market based on the research studies and published reports on financial markets. The growing numbers of elderly people globally signifies that there is an opportunity to market directly to this group or develop products customized for this segment. However, to customize services for this segment group, enablers and barriers need to be understood, hence the need for research studies in this area of interest. Even though there are barriers, it can be argued that, with time, the elderly will become more interested in mobile commerce and banking to enhance their quality of life. Banks need to communicate to their consumers the measures they will employ to address the elderly issues and concerns being raised [55]. Thus, ICT practitioners and researchers need to propose age-specific design guidelines for mobile devices and mobile applications [34]. Furthermore, in-house training and usage guidance would prove to be useful to this vulnerable group [40].

References

1. Motwani, B.: Prediction of intention of senior professionals to prefer mobile banking. FIIB Bus. Rev. **5**(4), 51–64 (2016)
2. Lian, J., Yen, D.C.: Computers in human behavior online shopping drivers and barriers for older adults: age and gender differences. Comput. Hum. Behav. **37**, 133–143 (2014)
3. Diako, B., Lubbe, S., Klopper, R.: The degree of readiness of South African senior citizens for electronic banking: an exploratory investigation. Altern. J. **5**, 255–287 (2012)
4. Ekberg, S.: A study of how Swedish agencies are working with eService accessibility for elderly people (2015)
5. Hur, M.H.: Empowering the elderly population through ICT-based activities: an empirical study of older adults in Korea. Inf. Technol. People **29**(2), 318–333 (2015)
6. Ordonez, T.N., Yassuda, S., Cachioni, M.: Elderly online: effects of a digital inclusion program in cognitive performance. Arch. Gerontol. Geriatr. **53**(2), 216–219 (2011)
7. Ramón-Jerónimo, M.A., Peral-Peral, B., Arenas-Gaitán, J.: Elderly persons and internet use. Soc. Sci. Comput. Rev. **31**(4), 389–403 (2013)
8. Boontarig, W., Chutimaskul, W., Chongsuphajaisiddhi, V., Papasratorn, B.: Factors influencing the Thai elderly intention to use smartphone for e-health services. In: 2012 IEEE Symposium on Humanities, Science and Engineering Research, pp. 479–483 (2012)

9. Iyer, R., Eastman, J.K.: The elderly and their attitudes toward the internet: the impact on internet use, purchase, and comparison shopping. J. Mark. Theory Pract. **14**(1), 57–67 (2014)

10. Pikna, J., Fellnerova, N., Kozubik, M.: Information technology and seniors. In: CBU International Conference on Innovations in Science and Education, pp. 702–708 (2018)

11. Shaikh, A.A., Karjaluoto, H.: Mobile banking adoption: a literature review. Telemat. Inf. **32** (1), 129–142 (2015)

12. Touchaie, S.A., Hashim, N.H.: The influence of dispositional resistance to change on seniors' mobile banking adoption in Malaysia. J. Soft Comput. Decis. Support Syst. **5**(6), 1–12 (2018)

13. Alfahl, H., Houghton, L., Sanzogni, L.: Mobile commerce adoption in Saudi organizations: a qualitative study. Int. J. Enterp. Inf. Syst. **13**(4), 31–57 (2017)

14. Mlitwa, N., Tshetsha, N.: Adoption of cell-phone banking among low-income communities in rural areas of South Africa. iBusiness **4**, 362–370 (2012)

15. Al-jabri, I.M., Sohail, M.S.: Mobile banking adoption: application of diffusion of innovation theory. J. Electron. Commer. Res. **13**(4), 379–391 (2012)

16. Ha, K., Canedoli, A., Baur, A.W., Bick, M.: Mobile banking — insights on its increasing relevance and most common drivers of adoption. Electron. Mark. **22**(4), 217–227 (2012)

17. Chitungo, S.K., Munongo, S.: Extending the technology acceptance model to mobile banking adoption in rural Zimbabwe. J. Bus. Adm. Educ. **3**(1), 51–79 (2013)

18. Khan, D., Varshney, P., Qadeer, M.A.: E-commerce: from shopping carts to credit cards. In: 2011 IEEE 3rd International Conference on Communication Software and Networks, pp. 81–85 (2011)

19. Agwu, E.M., Carter, A.: Mobile phone banking in Nigeria: benefits, problems and prospects. Int. J. Bus. Commer. **3**(6), 50–70 (2014)

20. Laukkanen, T., Lauronen, J.: Consumer value creation in mobile banking services. Int. J. Mob. Commun. **3**(4), 325–338 (2005)

21. Sripalawat, J., Thongmak, M., Ngramyarn, A.: M-banking in metropolitan Bangkok and a comparison with other countries. J. Comput. Inf. Syst. **51**(3), 67–76 (2015)

22. Hussain, A., Abubakar, H.I., Hashim, N.B.: Evaluating mobile banking application: usability dimensions and measurements. In: Proceedings of the 6th international Conference on Information Technology and Multimedia, no. 1, pp. 138–142 (2014)

23. Chigada, J.M., Hirschfelder, B.: Mobile banking in South Africa: a review and directions for future research. SA J. Inf. Manag. **19**(1), 1–9 (2017)

24. Behl, A., Singh, M., Venkatesh, V.G.: Enablers and barriers of mobile banking opportunities in rural India: a strategic analysis. Int. J. Bus. Excell. **10**(2), 209–239 (2016)

25. Al-jabri, I.M.: The intention to use mobile banking: further evidence from Saudi Arabia. South African J. Bus. Manag. **46**(1), 23–34 (2015)

26. Ismail, T., Masinge, K.: Mobile banking: innovation for the poor. African J. Sci. Technol. Innov. Dev. **4**(3), 98–127 (2012)

27. Borg, F., Persson, M.: Assessing Factors Influencing the Diffusion of Mobile Banking in South Africa - A case study on the company Wizzit Carried (2010)

28. Ayo, C.K., Adewoye, J.O., Oni, A.A.: Framework for mobile money implementation in Nigeria. J. African Res. Bus. Technol. **2011**(1), 1–8 (2011)

29. Firdhous, M.F.M., Karunaratne, P.M.: An ICT enhanced life quality for the elderly in developing countries: analysis study applied to Sri Lanka. J. Health Inform. Dev. Ctries. **5**, 47–59 (2011)

30. Medhi, I., Ratan, A., Toyama, K.: Mobile-banking adoption and usage by low-literate, low-income users in the developing world. In: Aykin, N. (ed.) IDGD 2009. LNCS, vol. 5623, pp. 485–494. Springer, Heidelberg (2009). https://doi.org/10.1007/978-3-642-02767-3_54

31. Zhang, F., Soto, C.G.: Older adults on electronic commerce: a literature review. Int. J. Bus. Adm. **9**(3), 10–17 (2018)
32. Kim, M.J.: Does knowledge matter to seniors' usage of mobile devices? Focusing on motivation and attachment. Int. J. Contemp. Hosp. Manag. **28**(8), 1702–1727 (2016)
33. Choudrie, J., Junior, C.O., McKenna, B., Richter, S.: Understanding and conceptualising the adoption, use and diffusion of mobile banking in older adults: a research agenda and conceptual framework. J. Bus. Res. **88**, 449–465 (2018)
34. Almao, E.C., Golpayegani, F.: Are mobile apps usable and accessible for senior citizens in smart cities? In: Zhou, J., Salvendy, G. (eds.) HCII 2019. LNCS, vol. 11592, pp. 357–375. Springer, Cham (2019). https://doi.org/10.1007/978-3-030-22012-9_26
35. Mallenius, S., Rossi, M., Tuunainen, V.K.: Factors affecting the adoption and use of mobile devices and services by elderly people – results from a pilot study. 6th Annu. Glob. Mobil. Roundtable **31**, 12 (2007)
36. Chen, A.N., Downey, J.P., Mcgaughey, R.E., Jin, K.: Seniors and information technology in China. Int. J. Hum. Comput. Interact. **32**(2), 132–142 (2016)
37. Gatsou, C., Politis, A., Zevgolis, D.: Seniors' experiences with online banking. In: 2017 Federated Conference on Computer Science and Information Systems, vol. 11, pp. 623–627 (2017)
38. Ganor, N., Te'eni, D.: Designing interfaces for older users: effects of icon detail and semantic distance. AIS Trans. Hum.-Comput. Interact. **8**(1), 22–38 (2016)
39. Seifert, A.: Mobile seniors: mobile use of the internet using smartphones or tablets by Swiss people over 65 years. Gerontechnology **1**(1), 56–62 (2015)
40. Jayachandran, A.: E-banking or branch banking? Preference of senior citizens in Kerala. IUP J. Bank Manag. **18**(2), 19–29 (2019)
41. Švecová, M., Odlerová, E.: Smartphone and mobile application usage among seniors in Slovakia. Eur. J. Sci. Theol. **14**(6), 125–133 (2018)
42. Cullen, M., Kabanda, S.K.: The role of demographic and motivational factors on mobile commerce usage activities in South Africa. South African J. Inf. Manag. **20**(1), 1–8 (2016)
43. Medhi, I., Gautama, S.N.N., Toyama, K.: A comparison of mobile money-transfer UIs for non-literate and semi-literate users. In: Proceedings of the SIGCHI Conference on Human Factors in Computing Systems, pp. 1741–1750 (2009)
44. Deb, M., Agrawal, A.: Factors impacting the adoption of m-banking: understanding brand India's potential for financial inclusion. J. Asia Bus. Stud. **11**(1), 22–40 (2017)
45. Thakur, S.: The impact of information technology advancement in Indian banking sector. Int. J. Eng. Technol. Sci. Res. **5**(1), 833–841 (2018)
46. Oseifuah, E.K.: Financial literacy and youth entrepreneurship in South Africa. African J. Econ. Manag. Stud. **1**(2), 164–182 (2010)
47. Benamati, J.S., Serva, M.A.: Trust and distrust in online banking: their role in developing countries. Inf. Technol. Dev. **13**(2), 161–175 (2007)
48. Dass, R., Pal, S.: Exploring the factors affecting the adoption of mobile financial services among the rural under-banked. In: European Conference on Information Systems (ECIS), p. 246 (2011)
49. Sharma, S.K., Govindaluri, S.M., Al-Muharrami, S., Tarhini, A.: A multi-analytical model for mobile banking adoption: a developing country perspective. Rev. Int. Bus. Strateg. **27**(1), 133–148 (2017)
50. Nightingale, A.: A guide to systematic literature reviews. Surgery **27**(9), 381–384 (2009)
51. Kitchenham, B.: Procedures for Performing Systematic Reviews, UK (2004)
52. Albashrawi, M., Motiwalla, L.: Understanding mobile banking usage: an integrative perspective. In: Proceedings of the 2017 ACM SIGMIS Conference on Computers and People Research, pp. 63–70 (2017)

53. Ayaratne, M.G.S.D.N., Ryan, M., Cripps, H.: Mobile banking adoption by senior citizens in Perth. In: The Proceedings of 2nd Business Doctoral and Emerging Scholars Conference, p. 105 (2017)

54. Kargin, B., Basoglu, N., Daim, T.: Adoption factors of mobile services. Int. J. Inf. Syst. Serv. Sect. **1**(1), 15–34 (2009)

55. Malaquias, R.F., Hwang, Y.: An empirical study on trust in mobile banking: a developing country perspective. Comput. Hum. Behav. **54**, 453–461 (2016)

A Methodology for Addressing the Second-Level Digital Divide
A Practical Experience

Susana Muñoz Hernández[ID], Clara Benac Earle[(✉)][ID], and Lars-Åke Fredlund[ID]

Universidad Politécnica de Madrid, Madrid, Spain
{susana,cbenac,lfredlund}@fi.upm.es
http://www.techpeople.care

Abstract. In this article we describe a methodology, and its evaluation, for achieving technical competence through digital literacy training
using self-learning training material. The key component is self-learning
in the sense that the targeted population learns digital operational skills
without the need of a teacher. This is achieved through the adaptation
of the training material to the trained group. As training groups are
diverse, e.g., including both populations in developing and developed
countries, and varying in age aspects, gender, languages, literacy levels
and technological literacy levels, materials and the speed which training
takes place has to be adapted to take into account these differences. The
methodology involves use of training videos, and use a dual screen approach where training material is shown on one screen and training takes
place on a second screen (computer). The approach has been evaluated in
both developing countries and developed countries, with training groups
of different capabilities and backgrounds (in Kenya, El Salvador, Spain,
France and The Netherlands), with promising results.

Keywords: Digital literacy training · Localisation · Individual
training · e-learning · Digital skills acquisition

1 Introduction

Since the 1990s, the digital divide [14] has been defined as the inequalities
in access to and use of Information and Communication Technologies (ICTs),
mostly the Internet [3]. Initially, the study of the digital divide observed the
distinction between those who had access to the internet and those who had
not. This is called the first-level digital device. Regarding the first-level digital
divide, there is a clear divide among developed countries, where the majority of
the population has internet access, to less developed countries where, although
the internet access is constantly growing, there are still large parts of the population that do not have easy access to the internet.

Supported by the "e-Health inclusion through ICT training" project funded by EIT-
Health.

M. Hattingh et al. (Eds.): I3E 2020, LNCS 12067, pp. 331–337, 2020.
https://doi.org/10.1007/978-3-030-45002-1_28

Later, the second-level digital divide mostly focuses on digital skills [5]. Researchers on digital skills distinguish between technical competence or operational skills, i. e., skills like using a mouse or a keyboard, information literacy, which is "the ability to recognise when information can solve a problem or fill a need and to effectively employ information resources". Additionally, Scheerder et al. [12], distinguished "information navigation skills" (the ability to find, select, and evaluate sources of information on the Internet), "social skills" (the ability to use online communication and interactions to understand and exchange meaning and acquire social capital) and "creative skills" (needed to create different types of content and to publish or share this with others on the Internet).

The second-level digital divide, in particular, operational skills, is an important social issue both in developing countries an in developed countries. In developing countries, young people need to have certain skills (for example, effective use of text editors and spreadsheets) in order to get a better job. In developed countries, society is clearly becoming more digital, providing many new digital services, some for very basic services like to get a doctor appointment, at a fast pace. Unfortunately, the most vulnerable people are often left behind. Many seniors, migrants and minorities are suffering social exclusion due to their lack of digital literacy, Thus, large segments of the population lacks the necessary skills to interact effectively with such digitalized services

To address the second-level digital divide, in particular, operational skills, the usual approach to train the population, both in developing and developed countries, involves face-to-face training with teachers, since the usual training material (MOOCS, etc.) is not suitable for those without the most basic digital skills. However, often such face-to-face training activities has limited effectiveness. The typical training in groups has many problems: logistics (participants with different time availability) and pedagogical (participants with different learning speed) problems, and teachers are sometimes ill-equipped to deal with individuals not only experiencing digital illiteracy but also experiencing low literacy in general. Of course, there are many qualified teachers but, in general, scaling such face-to-face training activities to be able to train big sectors of a population is very costly in terms of the human resources needed; in general it is simply not a sustainable activity. In addition when the trainees are located in rural or remote areas the human resources needed (teachers) may not be available in sufficient quantities. In developing countries typically both problems occur, i.e., too high training costs, and limited availability of qualified teachers.

To address these issues, we have developed a methodology that relies on self-learning, i. e., training without the need of teachers [6,13]. Given such a methodology, we formulate the following research question – *can the methodology be applied with success both in developing and developed countries?* To answer this research question, we have conducted a series of training activities in both developing countries, e.g., Kenya and El Salvador, and developed countries such as Spain, France and The Netherlands.

The rest of the paper is organised as follows: in Sect. 2 a summary of the characteristics of the methodology is presented. Next, Sect. 3 describes the evaluation of the methodology in the aforementioned countries, and Sect. 4 summarises the results, discusses the work, and presents plans for the future.

2   Methodology

In this section, we summarise the key ingredients of our methodology which is in essence based on e-learning and self-learning concepts [8–10], and which does not require trained teachers to assist trainees.

No teachers: The methodology does not require a trained teacher to assist trainees. In the practical studies we have conducted (see Sect. 3) assuring that the practical necessities for conducting the literacy training (e.g., availability of working computers, access to literacy training material) are met is the responsibility of a local training *coordinator*, who does not need to be familiar with the literacy training material.

Use of a two-screen approach: The methodology follows a learning-by-doing approach where the trainee is presented with two screens: (i) one, typically a tablet, where the training material, a number of videos, is shown and (ii) a second one, typically a desktop computer, used by the trainee to practice the practical exercises shown in the first screen. The benefits of using dual screens has been studied in a number of works, e.g., [4, 7].

Adapting training material to the trained group: When training diverse populations the training material used should be localised, e.g., in general with respect to languages utilised, with respect to literacy levels, etc. In general such a localisation (e.g., in the website domain [11]) process typically consists of a translation to a language and a cultural adaptation. In our methodology, both the language used for instructions, and the video speed, is adapted to the trained groups: (i) *Language adaptation*: normally the videos are in the native language of the trainees. However, in the case of migrants, they may choose to either receive instructions in their native language or in the language of the country they currently reside; (ii) *Age adaptation*: for instance, the speed of the videos is slower for elderly people than for younger people; (iii) *Literacy adaptation*: for instance, the language in the video is "simpler" for people with low literacy than for other with higher levels of literacy; (iv) *Gender adaptation*, for instance, we use inclusive language; (v) *Technology literacy adaptation*: for many trainees the use of our training setup comprising tablets and desktop computers can be their first contact with such technological equipment; we have extensive experiences with adapting training material with regards to such concerns.

As an example, in the training of young women in Kenya with reduced school experience, the videos played rapidly, but the language used was simplified, and adapted to their gender, and level of technological literacy.

Use of specially developed software training applications: We have developed a number of new software training applications to ensure that the interactions with the training application is intuitive, providing a controlled environment specifically adapted to users without digital background.

3   Evaluation

In this section we summarise the studies (Fig. 1) that have been used for evaluation: Lamu (Kenya), Tecoluca (El Salvador), and a study in the context of a EIT-Health project with sessions in Spain, France and The Netherlands.

Fig. 1. Digital literacy training in Lamu, Kenya (left), and Madrid region, Spain (right)

3.1   The Lamu Study

A report on a first experience (from 2011) applying this methodology in Lamu at the northeast of Kenya is given in [13]. The Digital Opportunities project [2] dealt with the digital literacy of a target group of young people who wanted to improve their chances of getting a job by acquiring some basic computing skills such as using word processors, web browsing, working with spreadsheets, etc. Interestingly, they had already attended local private IT courses teaching e.g. basic word processor tools skills, and had even received a diploma. However, in these courses, the students would typically just observe the teacher demonstrating an application, without the students getting a chance to experiment themselves.

Evaluation. Most of the students had previous training in the subject matter but when their skill level was evaluated through a practical exam before the start of the course, it was found to be poor. In total 86 students attended our training, and passed a final exam which evaluated that their skills were at a satisfactory level. Of these 86 students, 39 answered a questionnaire after the course, regarding what skill level (from 0 to 10) in the subject matter that they then perceived themselves to possess *before* the course, as well as *after* the course. The results was an average perceived skill level of 2.5 before the course, and 8.5 after having taken the course. That is, the students considered that the course had greatly improved their operational skills.

3.2   The Tecoluca Study

Another training experience using our methodology took place in Tecoluca, El Salvador, during 2016–2017. The goal of the PALDICA project was the digital training of adults, with a particular focus towards the digital service needs and interests of adult farmers, in particular, acquiring basic operational skills (for instance, how to use the mouse and the keyboard), basic use of a word processor and basic email and internet browsing. The training was to take place at centers funded by an international cooperation agency.

Evaluation. In this project, the training material was developed (localised) and first used in a pilot project where the coordinators of the centers were trained, before they were due to assist the target population in their training. This prior training activity had not been planned, and indeed was not strictly needed from the point-of-view of the training methodology. However, in practice it was deemed necessary to ensure that the training coordinators were sufficiently motivated to assist in future training activities. 7 coordinators took part in this pilot projects, and two of them filled in a written questionnaire stating that the training had greatly improved their operational skills. Unfortunately, at that moment the funding of the centers where the training was to have taken place ceased, and the centers were closed. The more large-scale training of adult farmers that we had planned for could not take place. On the positive side, we gained new insights from developing further, and localising, the training material, and moreover we came to appreciate the financial difficulties of conducting such training activities.

3.3   The EIT-Health Study

Recently, we have continued the development of the training methodology and platform, and its evaluation, in the context of a European project oriented to the digital inclusion of European seniors and migrants, "e-Health inclusion through ICT training" (eHi-ICTT) funded by EIT-health [1], which ended on December 31st, 2019. The project focused specifically on helping its target audience (senior people including migrants) to be able to access e-health services. The partners in the project were: (i) SERMAS, the public health service of the Madrid region. (ii) E-seniors, a French association which provides ICT classes to seniors. (iii) Leyden academy, a knowledge institute in the Netherlands, which conducts scientific research on various topics focused upon vitality and ageing; (iv) Universidad Politécnica de Madrid (the university of the article authors).

Evaluation. The project had the following main activities: (i) definition of training contents, including the collaborative process with project participants to obtain the agreed upon training program for each collective; (ii) development of the audiovisual material; (iii) conducting training session to evaluate the success of the approach. The results were measured as follows. First, a pre-questionnaire was created to measure the operational skills owned by the target population before taking the course. Secondly, a post-questionnaire was designed to measure the acquisition of the same skills after taking the course. In Madrid, a group of 42 Arab migrants and 28 seniors attended the training; in Pairs 26 seniors; and 28 Arab migrants in The Netherlands. We are still analysing the detailed results, but the informal feedback we have received has been very positive, with several participants for instance telling us that they were able for the first time to make an appointment with a doctor using an online system. A detailed analysis showing to what extent the goals of the project has been met, through measuring the outcome of the training sessions (e.g., to what extent trainees can successfully use medical digital systems), will be presented in a future article.

4   Conclusions and Future Work

In this paper, we have presented the key characteristics of our self learning based methodology to address the second-level digital divide with regards to operational skills. The approach works with specially developed software training applications, and uses a two-screen approach. The methodology has been applied in a number of training events in Kenya, El Salvador, and Europe. In all locations students reported an improvement in their operational skills due to the training. Based on these findings, we are now working on reducing the amount of work needed to adapt the overall methodology to different contexts, e.g., to account for differences in language, gender, literacy, etc.

We believe that our methodology holds great promise, and future plans include demonstrating its potential for training on a significantly larger scale. Moreover, we are eager to cooperate with other institutions that share the ambition of reducing the second-level digital divide.

References

1. https://www.eithealth.eu/
2. Digopps, digital opportunities project. https://digopps.wixsite.com/digitaloppor tunities
3. Castells, M.: The Internet Galaxy: Reflections on the Internet, Business, and Society. Oxford University Press on Demand, Oxford (2002)
4. Colvin, J., Tobler, N., Anderson, J.: Productivity and multi-screen computer displays. Rocky Mt. Commun. Rev. **2**, 31–53 (2004)
5. Hargittai, E.: Second-level digital divide: differences in people's online skills. First Monday **7**(4) (2002)
6. Hernandez, S.M.: Looking for sustainable software for education in developing countries. In: 2014 IEEE Global Engineering Education Conference, EDUCON 2014, Istanbul, Turkey, 3–5 April 2014, pp. 1108–1111. IEEE (2014)
7. Hsu, J.-M., Chang, T.-W., Yu, P.-T.: Learning effectiveness and cognitive loads in instructional materials of programming language on single and dual screens. Turk. Online J. Educ. Technol. **11**, 156–166 (2012)
8. Mayer, R.E.: Cognitive Theory of Multimedia Learning. Cambridge Handbooks in Psychology, pp. 31–48. Cambridge University Press, Cambridge (2005)
9. Mitra, S., Khas, H.: Minimally invasive education for mass computer literacy. CSI Commun. **32**, 1216 (1999)
10. Mohammadyari, S., Singh, H.: Understanding the effect of e-learning on individual performance: the role of digital literacy. Comput. Educ. **82**, 11–25 (2015)

11. Pym, A.: Website localizations. In: Malmkjær, K., Windle, K. (eds.) The Oxford Handbook of Translation Studies. Oxford University Press, Oxford (2011, 2013)
12. Scheerder, A.J., van Deursen, A., van Dijk, J.: Determinants of internet skills, uses and outcomes. A systematic review of the second- and third-level digital divide. Telem. Inf. **34**(8), 1607–1624 (2017)
13. Silvestre, M., Munoz, S., Rubio, M.A.: A successful entrepreneurship formula for solving computer illiteracy. In: IEEE Global Humanitarian Technology Conference, GHTC 2014, USA, October 2014. IEEE (2014)
14. Srinuan, C., Bohlin, E.: Understanding the digital divide: a literature survey and ways forward. In: Innovative ICT Applications - Emerging Regulatory, Economic and Policy Issues 52191, International Telecommunications Society (ITS) (2011)

Investigating Aid Effectiveness in Developing Countries: The Case of Nepal

Yashoda Karki[1](✉) and Ilias O. Pappas[1,2] (iD)

[1] University of Agder, Kristiansand, Norway
{yashoda.karki,ilias.pappas}@uia.no
[2] Norwegian University of Science and Technology, 7491 Trondheim, Norway

Abstract. Foreign aid serves as an important source of capital for any developing or under-developed country. It is very important to see how the recipient country can utilize this aid in the economic upliftment of the nation. Taking a case of Nepalese economy, this paper investigates the effectiveness of foreign aid in developing countries. The result from Johansen's cointegration test reveals that foreign aid independently is not adequate for the economic growth. Increased capital and technological infrastructures, improved skills on human capital, on the other hand, significantly changes the result for the positive aid impact on growth in the long run. Therefore, we can conclude that a good policy environment helps increase the aid effectiveness. However, the prevailing trade policy in the country is negatively affecting the aid effectiveness due to the extremely increased trade deficit. In the short-run, there is a negative impact of aid on growth.

Keywords: Foreign aid · Economic growth · Cointegration · Error correction model · Developing countries · Nepal

JEL Classification: C01 · F35 · O47

1 Introduction

Initially, foreign aid has been the most important source of external finance for developing countries to meet the basic human needs, infrastructure development in accordance with nation building. Aid was channeled through capital transfers and investment projects to overcome the capital shortage which hindered development in many nations. Several growth-oriented aid programs were initiated including poverty reduction, military development, educational upliftment, etc. [1]. The lack of countries' internal savings is one of the motivations for foreign aid donors to take part in the assistance. Over time, the focus of such aid has been changed to the macroeconomic stabilization, structural adjustment and debt reduction, political and economic transition, poverty reduction and social infrastructure. Past few decades, the donors started to put more emphasis on performance-based aid allocation, focusing on the global health, governance and security [2] and sustainable development goals. For the creation and development of sustainable and prosperous societies, all the actors in the society play an equally important role [3]. Foreign aid helping each sector of the societal development is an important factor for the attainment of sustainability and therefore the aid effectiveness has become a widespread topic of discussion.

The main objective of this paper is to analyze how effective foreign aid is to contribute on the recipient country's economic growth. We investigate the aid effectiveness taking a case of Nepalese economy. Being one of the least developed countries in the world, Nepal is highly dependent on foreign aid. The country has been deploying foreign aid both as aid for budget support and non-budgetary aid for over six decades. However, the Ministry of Finance reports show that the share of foreign aid on the government's total budget has been declining by the improved mobilization of domestic resources which shows that the country is transforming into a self-reliant economy.

There is evidence that foreign aid has negative impact on growth or the country's economic growth [4, 5]. However, donors continue to disburse aid. One of the reasons for such disbursement could be that the real aim of granting aid to the recipient might not be to increase growth in many instances. "Part of aid is disbursed to alleviate human disasters in the wake of natural catastrophes. Other parts might directly be granted to increase consumption of the poor in recipient countries" The strategic interests of the donor have always been relevant in giving foreign aid [6]. The aid effectiveness study covering the period of 1983–2002 for Nepal has found that foreign aid has a positive and statistically significant effect on per capita real GDP in the long run but a negative impact in the short run. The aid effectiveness is increased in the presence of good policy environment [7]. Another recent contribution on the aid-growth literature for Nepal covers the period until 2008 which finds the similar results on aid effectiveness [8].

The study for aid effectiveness in Bangladesh shows marginal effect of aid on GDP growth [9]. "Foreign grants mostly finance non-productive civil expenditures, but foreign loans generally finance public investment projects and human capital building programs, which eventually lead to higher output growth" [9]. Several cross-country panel estimations have found the evidence of positive aid effectiveness [10, 11]. Foreign aid, however, depends on the aid apparatus. The adaptability of foreign aid, availability, and know-how of the latest technology is something that needs to be considered for aid to be effective in future [5]. The next section of the paper discusses the data and methodology used in the study followed by model specification and selection of policy variables. The rest of the paper consists empirical results, their implication and discussions with some concluding remarks.

2 Methodology

The annual time series data for Nepal from 1983 to 2013 have been used in this study. All the data are downloaded from publicly available online databases (World Bank; WDI, FRED, OECD; IDS and Ministry of Finance, Nepal). Since many time series data follow non-stationarity nature, in most of the cases, the regression result obtained from such series are spurious and are not good enough to use in economic and financial decision making. However, with cointegration, there is no problem of spurious regressions and the result obtained are adequate despite of their non-stationarity nature. We have used Johansen's maximum likelihood estimation [12] and error correction model (ECM), suggested by [13] originally stated and proved by [14], to identify the long-run and short-run relationship among the variables.

3 Model Specification and Policy Indicators

Based on the neo-classical production function, we estimate the following model:

$$\ln RGDPP_t = \theta_1 + \theta_2 \ln GCFR_t + \theta_3 \ln AR_t + \theta_4 \ln EDU_t + \theta_5 \ln MONR_t + \theta_6 \ln BDR_t + \theta_7 \ln TR_t + u_t$$

$$(1)$$

where, ln is the natural logarithm, RGDPP is the per capita real GDP, GCFR is the gross capital formation as a percentage of GDP, AR is aid/GDP ratio, EDU is secondary level school enrollment. the policy variables MONR is broad money supply (M2) to GDP ratio, BDR is budget deficit as a percentage of GDP and TR is trade as a percentage of GDP. Similarly, θ_i is the parameters that explain the elasticity of dependent variable related to independent variables, u_t is the random error, ln represents natural logarithm, and the subscript t represents time.

The data we are using has relatively a shorter time period, therefore, we have a smaller number of observations. To avoid degree of freedom problem, we have only taken two policy variables at a time in conducting Johansen's cointegration test in the following section.

4 Empirical Results

To conduct cointegration, it is a prerequisite that all the series to be included in the model must be integrated of same order. For example, if a non-stationary series becomes stationary after differentiating the series once, then the series is said to be integrated of order 1 or I(1). Similarly, if the series is stationary itself then it is I(0). Therefore, it is necessary to test for stationarity of the series to check if the series are integrated of same order or not.

Table 1. Phillip-Perron unit root test results

Variables	Constant only		Constant and time trend	
	Level	1st difference	Level	1st difference
lnRGDPP	−0.364	−7.177***	−3.419	−7.139 ***
lnAR	−1.687	−6.344***	−2.347	−6.387***
lnTR	−1.553	−4.044***	−1.299	−4.131**
lnMONR	0.558	−5.387***	−3.240	−5.387***
lnEDU	−0.814	−3.700**	−2.131	−3.634**
lnGCFR	−0.535	−6.630***	−2.182	−6.575 ***
lnBDR	−1.078	−4.589***	−2.724	−4.394***

Note: (***, ** significant at 1%, 5%)

We have followed the Phillips-Perron (PP) test [15], which provides more robust estimates despite the series having serial correlation or any structural breaks. The results from PP test in (Table 1) show that all variables show stationarity either at 5% or 1% significance level. While, all the variables are integrated of order 1, i.e., I(1), our variables are ready to test for cointegration.

5   Johansen's Cointegration and Error Correction Model

Johansen's likelihood ratio test has been performed to check if there exists any cointegrating relationship between the variables. First, only per capita real GDP and aid variable have been taken to see how the foreign aid would impact on the economic growth. The trace statistics suggest that there is one cointegrating vector, meaning that, there exists a long-run relationship between foreign aid and per capita real GDP (). The long-run coefficient for aid on tells us that there exists a significant negative impact of aid on per capita real GDP. This indicated that foreign aid independently, is not adequate for economic growth. The positive and significant error correction term implies an explosive model with no long-run convergence of any disequilibrium.

For the developing countries like Nepal, foreign aid is playing an important role to meet the shortfall in revenue as it is found to be used as a source of revenue in the government budget. This somehow relaxes the government budget constraint. Aid, nonetheless, should not be used only to meet the non-development expenditures. Aid has a stronger positive impact on non-development expenditures than on development expenditures of Nepal [16]. Here we can get an idea that a greater portion of aid could have been used in non-development expenditures which typically do not help in the economic growth of a nation. According to the OECD data, we see that the percentage of grants on foreign aid to Nepal is more than the percentage of loans. Foreign grants mostly finance non-productive public expenditures while loans are used in public investment projects [9] therefore foreign loans can raise GDP, but grants don't. Therefore, foreign aid being highly used in public expenditures than in developmental activities, we can conclude that foreign aid does not help in economic growth.

Introduction of control variables in the model remarkably changes the result. The impact of aid on per capita real GDP is significantly positive in the long-run while taking the variable for capital and school enrolment in our existing model. This implies that, with the higher level of capital formation in-lined with enhanced technology and improved skills on human capital, foreign aid helps significantly to increase per capita real GDP in long-run. As shown in the second half of (Table 2) the significant negative error correction term indicates that any long-run disequilibrium is corrected within the current year at the adjustment speed of 2.8%. In the short-run, aid has a negative and significant coefficient which signifies that there is a negative impact of aid on per capita real GDP in the short run.

Table 2. Johansen's Likelihood ratio test estimates and long run normalized coefficients

H_0	H_1	Eigenvalues	(λ_{trace})	Critical value	(λ_{max})	Critical value
VAR = 4		Variables: lnRGDPP and lnAR				
r = 0	r = 1	0.40471	15.8798	15.41	14.005**	14.07
r ≤ 1	r = 2	0.06708	1.8746**	3.76	1.875	3.76
VAR = 4		Variables lnRGDPP, lnAR, lnGCFR and lnEDU				
r = 0	r = 1	0.77986	69.6279	47.21	40.864	27.07
r ≤ 1	r = 2	0.51679	28.7638***	29.68	19.637***	20.97
VAR = 2		Variables lnRGDPP, lnAR, lnGCFR, lnEDU, lnTR and lnMONR				
r = 0	r = 1	0.82570	125.8335	94.15	50.663	39.37
r ≤ 1	r = 2	0.67143	75.1704***	68.52	32.277***	33.46
r ≤ 2	r = 3	0.51848	42.8931**	47.21	21.194	27.07
VAR = 2		Variables lnRGDPP, lnAR, lnGCFR, lnEDU, lnTR and lnBDR				
r = 0	r = 1	0.74513	97.8680	94.15	39.643	39.37
r ≤ 1	r = 2	0.50497	58.2246**	68.52	20.391**	33.46
VAR = 2		Variables lnRGDPP, lnAR, lnGCFR, lnEDU, lnMONR and lnBDR				
r = 0	r = 1	0.70885	106.9048	94.15	35.783***	39.37
r ≤ 1	r = 2	0.63974	71.1215***	68.52	29.607	33.46
lnRGDPP		1.000	1.000			
lnAR		0.862***	−0.930***	0.014	0.579***	−0.083***
lnGCFR			−1.280**	0.122***	0.221	0.073**
lnEDU			−1.367***	−0.234***	−1.143***	−0.168***
lnTR				0.013	0.250***	
lnMONR				−0.537***		−0.522***
lnBDR					−0.351***	0.087**
ECT		0.041**	−0.028***	−0.096	0.032	−0.166
ΔlnRGDPP$_{t-1}$		−0.531**	−0.541***	−0.122	−0.159	−0.152
ΔlnAR$_{t-1}$		−0.040**	0.017	−0.035***	−0.045	−.045***
ΔlnGCFR$_{t-1}$			0.009	0.057**	0.050	0.046
ΔlnEDU$_{t-1}$			−0.017	−0.022	−0.017	−0.034
Δ lnTR$_{t-1}$				−0.042	−0.041	
Δ lnMONR$_{t-1}$				0.089		0.066
Δ lnBDR$_{t-1}$					−.016	−0.018
Serial correlation		(0.815)	(0.903)	(0.473)	(0.850)	(0.811)
Jarque-Bera test for normality		2.124 (0.713)	12.773 (0.119)	7.736 (0.805)	10.880 (0.539)	7.851 (0.796)

Note: (***, ** significant at 1%, 5% respectively)

The negative effect of aid in per capita real GDP is due to the less absorptive capacity of the country. The aid allocation may not be completed promptly because of the involvement of too many agencies which might lead to role mismatch and lack of coordination among them. Due to a poor bureaucracy, the development budget of the country is being frozen. In such circumstances, it is obvious that aid receipts are not being utilized immediately. The longer time taken to utilize the disbursed aid is also because of the aid conditionalities.

Considering the policy variables, the results from first two estimates having trade component in the model support the evidence that there is significantly negative impact of aid on per capita real GDP in the long run. One possible situation that trade leads to negative aid impact on economic growth is when the economy is facing a higher trade deficit. The Ministry of Finance data from Nepal exhibits that Nepal is having trade deficit in an increasing trend over the past two decades. The combination of policy variables money supply and budget deficit in the model, however, provides the evidence in favour of positive long-run impact of aid on per capita real GDP. On the other hand, all three different combinations of the policy variables in the model suggests that there is significant negative aid effect in the short run.

The serial correlation and normality do not seem to be a problem in all the models we have tested. The VECM diagnostic tests presented in the last section of (Table 2) explains that there is no autocorrelation in the variables and the random errors follow a normal distribution for all the equations in our model. This indicates that the variables used in the models explain the relationship very well in all cases.

6 Conclusion

Foreign aid serves as an important source of fund for developing and under-developed countries. There have been countless arguments over the period on whether aid has been utilized effectively for the economic upliftment and growth of the recipient countries [7, 8]. Taking a case of Nepal, we have been analyzed the effectiveness of aid in the economic growth of developing countries. The results show that foreign aid independently is not adequate for economic growth. The higher level of capital formation in-lined with enhanced technology and improved skills on human capital significantly increases the aid effectiveness. Aid effectiveness increases when the macroeconomic indicators show an improvement resulting in an enhanced economic situation. There is a negative impact of aid on per capita real GDP in the short run which is because of ineffective aid monitoring, problems related to aid management and aid conditionalities.

The country's monetary policy and fiscal policy, measured in the form of broad money supply and government budget status, are supportive on positive aid effectiveness. However, the prevailing trade policy is negatively affecting the aid effectiveness due to high trade deficit. Current status of trade in the economy is impeding foreign aid to be utilized in the targeted sector. The policy should be reviewed so that the size of ever-increasing trade deficit reduces. Similarly, foreign aid should be monitored strictly in order that its goal is fulfilled. A sudden increase in remittance, resulting in a culture of dependency, also fuels up the trade deficit which directly or indirectly reduces aid effectiveness. However, further investigation should be carried out to draw a conclusion on how remittance affects the effectiveness of foreign aid. Although one of the main objectives of this study was to research on the latest economic activities, it was not possible to cover the recent years because of the lack of data. This restricted the outcome of the paper as we were not able to see the most recent impact of aid on the growth.

References

1. Paul, E.: A survey of the theoretical economic literature on foreign aid. Asian-Pac. Econ. Lit. **20**, 1–17 (2006)
2. Akramov, K.T.: Foreign Aid Allocation, Governance, and Economic Growth. University of Pennsylvania Press, Philadelphia (2012)
3. Pappas, I.O., Mikalef, P., Giannakos, M.N., Krogstie, J., Lekakos, G.: Big data and business analytics ecosystems: paving the way towards digital transformation and sustainable societies. Inf. Syst. e-Bus. Manag. **16**(3), 479–491 (2018). https://doi.org/10.1007/s10257-018-0377-z
4. el Hamid Ali, H.A.: Foreign aid and economic growth in Egypt: a cointegration analysis. Int. J. Econ. Finan. Issues **3**, 743–751 (2013)
5. Rajan, R.G., Subramanian, A.: Aid and growth: what does the cross-country evidence really show? Rev. Econ. Stat. **90**, 643–665 (2008)
6. Bandyopadhyay, S., Vermann, E.K.: Donor motives for foreign aid. Federal Res. Bank St. Louis Rev. **95**, 327–336 (2013)
7. Bhattarai, B.P.: Foreign aid and growth in Nepal: an empirical analysis. J. Dev. Areas **42**, 283–302 (2009)
8. Sharma, K., Bhattarai, B.: Aid, policy, and growth: the case of Nepal. J. Econ. Issues **47**, 895–910 (2013)
9. Quazi, R.M.: Effects of foreign aid on GDP growh and fiscal behavior: an econometric case study of Bangladesh. J. Dev. Areas **38**, 95–117 (2005)
10. Moolio, P., Kong, S.: Foreign aid and economic growth: panel cointegration analysis for Cambodia, Lao PDR, Myanmar, and Vietnam. Athens J. Bus. Econ. **2**, 417–428 (2016)
11. Qayyum, U., Haider, A.: Foreign aid, external debt and economic growth nexus in low-income countries: the role of institutional quality. Pak. Dev. Rev. **51**, 97–115 (2012)
12. Johansen, S., Juselius, K.: Maximum likelihood estimation and inference on cointegration—with applications to the demand for money. Oxford Bull. Econ. Stat. **52**, 169–210 (1990)
13. Engle, R.F., Granger, C.W.: Co-integration and error correction: representation, estimation, and testing. Econ. J. Econ. Soc. **55**, 251–276 (1987)
14. Granger, C.W., Weiss, A.A.: Time series analysis of error-correction models. In: Studies in Econometrics, Time Series, and Multivariate Statistics, pp. 255–278. Elsevier (1983)
15. Phillips, P.C., Perron, P.: Testing for a unit root in time series regression. Biometrika **75**, 335–346 (1988)
16. Bhattarai, B.P.: Foreign aid and government's fiscal behaviour in Nepal: an empirical analysis. Econ. Anal. Policy **37**, 41–60 (2007)

The Influence of Culture on Women's IT Career Choices

Andre P. Calitz$^{(\boxtimes)}$ ⓘ, Margaret Cullen ⓘ, and Dudu Fani ⓘ

Department of Computing Sciences,
Nelson Mandela University, Port Elizabeth, South Africa
{Andre.Calitz,Margaret.Cullen,
Duduetsang.Fani}@Mandela.ac.za

Abstract. Skilled Information Technology (IT) professionals are essential to support businesses and the economy. Businesses increasingly require more qualified IT professionals, be they male or female. In South Africa, the number of women professionals participating in the IT industry is less than 20%. A number of factors influence women's IT career choices, such as previous programming exposure, parents, teachers and role models. Research suggests that there are gender differences in preferences and beliefs that may affect career choices, including cultural influences. The role of culture in women's IT career decisions has not been extensively explored in South Africa. The aim of this exploratory study was to determine if the factor, Culture influences women's IT career choices in South Africa. An on-line survey was conducted amongst women IT professionals in South Africa to determine the factors that influenced their IT career choices. The data from the survey were analysed using Exploratory Factor Analysis. The results, specifically relating to the factor *Culture,* are reported in this paper. The findings indicate that the factor Culture plays an important role when women make IT career choices as well as when females decide to remain in an IT career. The study found that culture does play a significant role in IT career decisions for different ethnic groups in South Africa. The findings suggest that efforts must be made to educate young women in computational thinking and expose them to the many career opportunities available for women in the IT industry.

Keywords: Women in IT · Culture · IT career choices

1 Introduction

The IT industry has been a vital component in modern business evolution and has enabled sustained business operational success. Skilled IT professionals are an essential component for business success, however businesses are experiencing an IT skills shortage. The European Commission estimated that there will be approximately 500,000 vacant positions in all sectors of the economy for IT specialists by 2020 [15].

Worldwide, females are a large pool of participants in the workforce, with over half the global workforce being female [30]. However, in the IT industry there is a notable gender imbalance with fewer females participating in the workforce with a lesser number involved in technical leadership positions [12, 19, 28]. The OECD [28] report

© IFIP International Federation for Information Processing 2020
Published by Springer Nature Switzerland AG 2020
M. Hattingh et al. (Eds.): I3E 2020, LNCS 12067, pp. 345–357, 2020.
https://doi.org/10.1007/978-3-030-45002-1_30

indicates that men are four times more likely than women to become IT specialists. In South Africa, the number of women professionals participating in the IT industry is less than 20% [26].

A number of factors influence young persons' career decisions. Sources of information and the impact of relatives, teachers and IT role-models have been highlighted as important career choice influencers [24]. A young person's intrinsic and extrinsic motivation, previous exposure to technology and specific programming, all strongly correlated with the decision to pursue a career in IT [3, 9].

Culture can also influence peoples' career decisions [16]. Culture is defined as the arts, customs and habits that characterise a certain society or nation. Culture includes the way the people in a society dress, the customs they practice in their marriages, the languages they speak, as well as their family lives, their work patterns, religious ceremonies and leisure pursuits [20]. Zimmermann [34] further describes culture as the beliefs, values and material objects that constitute a people's way of life. Culture is the characteristics and knowledge of a particular group of people encompassing language, religion, cuisine, social habits, music and arts [34]. Cultural factors that influence career choice include but are not limited to religion, personal relations, family responsibilities and attitudes towards networking [16].

The aim of this exploratory study is to determine the influence of culture on career decisions made by women working in the IT sector. This paper provides preliminary insights into the role of culture in career decisions by women working in the IT industry. The results highlight the importance of culture and the traditional roles bestowed on women. The layout of the paper is as follows: the research problem, research question and the *Women in IT* survey are discussed in Sect. 2. Literature on culture and the influence of culture on career decisions for women are discussed in Sect. 3. The Women in IT survey results are presented in Sect. 4. Conclusions and recommendations, relevant to young women wanting to choose a career in IT and future work are presented in Sect. 5.

2 Literature Review

The field of IT is one of the most evolving fields requiring expert skills. According to CareerJunction [8], IT is one of South Africa's top five employment sectors. Software Development is named as the most sought-after skill in the job market having grown by 12% from month to month during 2019. In addition, InformationWeek states that fast-growing jobs are emerging in the tech space with many relating to artificial intelligence and machine learning [10]. CareerJunction [8] advertised 2872 IT jobs in South Africa and the IT jobs most in demand are software development and programming. South Africa is a developing country where IT skills are in high demand. These IT skills are not met by Higher Education Institutions' IT graduate numbers [14, 22].

In examining the contrasts of the genders participating in IT leadership positions, Rogers [30] noted that the number of women professionals involved in high ranking professional IT jobs was significantly lower compared to their male counterparts. Less than 15% of females are in leadership positions in the IT industry [26]. During the year 2014, technology companies that are IT industry drivers disclosed their staff demographics. Companies such as Google, revealed that only 17% of their IT staff were female, while Apple and Facebook had 20% and 15% respectively [5].

Careers in the field of Science, Technology, Engineering and Mathematics (STEM) have historically experienced low levels of representation from females [11, 24]. Study fields such as Medicine [11, 30] have achieved successes in recruiting more females to the profession than in the past, due to their early career education, focused training methods and research strategies that are designed to attract female participants to the profession. IT on the other hand, continues to lag behind and is experiencing the opposite, with decreasing numbers of women participants compared to earlier decades [23].

Career choices are made by young people during their early secondary school career [27]. This is a similar assertion made by Armstrong and Riemenschneider [4] who examined an earlier model by scholar Ahuja [2], which noted that the choice of a career in IT is made years before the individual starts working. The high school era is a critical time where young people are guided by their family, teachers, career counsellors and role models most influential to them, to choose school subjects that later direct them to future fields of study and careers.

Teachers who act as career counsellors have been noted to have a strong influence on the career choices of their scholars, however this advice has resulted in furthering the gender imbalance in IT. Adya and Kaiser [1] discovered that teachers were more likely to encourage girls towards traditionally female careers such as pre-primary teaching, nursing and secretarial work and males towards technical careers [24]. This is due to their own limited perspectives, societal biases with partial information of the profession of IT and other career options. Cultural factors also influence career choice and include but are not limited to religion, personal relations, frame of reference and attitudes towards networking among others [16].

2.1 Women in IT

Although women outnumber men in terms of enrolment in higher learning institutions, when it comes to technology-based degrees, men dominate. The number of women obtaining degrees in computer and information systems continues to decrease while the number of women in law school, medical school and other STEM fields gradually increases [21]. The major influences that Jung et al. [21] identified were the influence of marketing, media portrayal of women in technology, role models, social encouragement and education impact.

Factors influencing the career choices of scholars according to Snyman [32] are self-efficacy, outcome expectations, goal representations, interest and sources of advice, financial expectations and the gender gap. The gender gap particularly identifies factors that influence women. Seeing women working in the technical field and female IT role models also influences girls when deciding on their careers [32]. It is important for children to have access to and use computers at home and in schools [21]. Parental support is another influential factor on whether women choose a technology related major. Researchers have highlighted the important role of parents, specifically the role the father plays in the children's career choices [9, 31].

High performance in school in problem solving subjects like mathematics is linked to increased self-confidence. Women who opt for a successful career in IT have been noted to be those who experimented with technology and viewed themselves early in life as capable. By choosing this career path, women often want to engage with their skills, grow through promotional opportunities and have the ability to reach top management levels. Women who have opted for IT find the salaries, future status and lifestyle attractive features of a career in IT [31]. Women with STEM degrees were noted to earn more than their peers who opted for other degrees and had projected job growth of 17% compared to 9.8% of those in non-STEM degrees [7].

Great lengths have been taken by society and families to attract and encourage young high school scholars of all genders to enter professional careers due to increased status for the family [5, 33]. The careers include doctors, accountants and lawyers. However IT, whilst misunderstood as a profession by society and families at large, is seen and respected as a smart profession often reserved for technical males [9, 25].

The lack of prominent female IT role models influences societal views on the profession. Culturally, females have not been socialised to view the field of IT as an important field of study. Pretorius and De Villiers [29] revealed that 66% of females in South Africa view the field of IT as cold with great emphasis on functional, abstract, procedural and task-oriented characteristics. They associate IT as mainly concerned with programming and building hardware.

Male dominance and the results of one-sided involvement in the IT field can be seen in the entertainment industry of gaming where technology has been used to develop recreational games. These games largely cater for the male population thus possibly reducing the potential profits that could be earned from involving female participants. Games are not being used as a tool to raise interest in technology in females [1]. The use of video games was noted by Main and Schimpf [23] as a contributing factor to computer biases. Access to games arouses technical interest, improves skills, such as design and rotational abilities and thus serves as an entry to the IT field and is a promoter of interest as it develops skills such as graphic design in participants.

2.2   Culture and Societal Attitudes Regarding Family

Females are often noted to have strong societal ties to family units, religion and cultural activities and thus participation in a career often hinges on the support from these communities and the ability to continue with the associated activities with these groups [23, 29]. Du Bow [13] outlined that even though high achieving females outnumber males in the mathematics field, the under-representation of women in IT reflects social, cultural and family thinking [31]. While women live in modern times, the traditional family structure has not changed. Women continue to be the primary care givers of families. Pretorius and De Villiers [29] observed that women battle to balance a demanding IT job while still being heavily involved at home.

Family influence is the reason for the high volume of females participating in the IT field in Mauritius, as the family and national culture encourage females to view IT as a potentially viable career [29]. Over 53% of Computer Science enrolments in Mauritius in 2011 were women. This is a similar situation in the Indian society, where the family structure supports the idea of women actively choosing the IT field as a career of choice. In societies such as India and the Soviet Union, women participate in IT careers in higher numbers when compared to men [17].

In South Africa, this reality is different as women view themselves according to traditional society's expectations, which emphasise women as homemakers before being viewed as career women. Adya and Kaiser [1] concurred that females who opt for IT have been noted to come from families where the parents are highly educated. The influence of parents with degrees allows the family structure to choose non-traditional careers where success is highly valued.

3 Research Design

Women are under-represented in the South African IT industry with only 17% of women pursuing careers in the IT sector [14]. A higher percentage of males graduate with IT qualifications from universities and colleges than women [14]. Scholars making career choices are influenced by parents, role models, society and the educational system. It has been shown that culture does play a role in the career choices women make worldwide [16]. The research problem addressed in this study is that many young South African women (female scholars) do not consider a career in IT, possibly as a result of cultural influences. The research question addressed in this study is: *Does the factor Culture influence women IT professionals' IT career choices?*

A questionnaire was compiled from a combination of similar questionnaires used in previous gender based studies and from literature [13, 29]. An anonymous survey was conducted and the questionnaire included both closed and open-ended questions. The questionnaire was divided into two sections consisting of demographic information and items relating to the independent factors. A five-point Likert rating scale (1 = Strongly disagree to 5 = Strongly agree) was used to gather information from respondents regarding the factors that led them to choose a career in IT and to stay in the IT profession.

The Institute of Information Technology Professionals South Africa (IITPSA) represents IT professionals in South Africa. IITPSA has over 10000 members including over 1700 female members. The request to participate in the study was sent to the female members. In addition, the questionnaire was sent to the Computer Science and Information Systems Alumni of three S.A. universities. The questionnaire was captured using the Nelson Mandela University on-line survey tool, QuestionPro. The data were statistically analysed using Statistica. The following hypotheses relating to culture were tested in this study:

- HO_1: Culture and societal attitudes regarding an IT career exert no influence on females opting for a career in IT.
- HA_1: Culture and societal attitudes regarding an IT career positively influence females on opting for a career in IT.
- HO_2: Culture and societal attitudes regarding IT career exert no influence on females remaining in the field of IT.

- HA$_2$: Culture and societal attitudes regarding IT career positively influence females remaining in the field of IT.

A conceptual model was designed to test the various factors that contribute to participation levels. The independent variable was *culture* and the two dependant variables were *Females opting for an IT career* and *Females remaining in an IT career*. The model to test the factor *Culture* is demonstrated in Fig. 1.

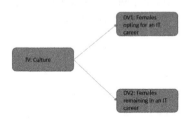

Fig. 1. Proposed conceptual model

The items for the factor Culture were obtained from a literature study [13, 16, 29]. The items relating to the independent factor *Culture* were as follows:

- An IT career is respected in my community;
- In my culture, IT is not seen as a career for women;
- In my culture, people have a clear understanding of IT;
- In my culture, people have a clear understanding of IT careers;
- In my community, people are familiar with IT careers;
- In my culture, having a large family is important; and
- In my culture, a woman is expected to have a family and children.

The two dependent factors with 12 items were:

(1) Females opting for an IT career; and
(2) Females remaining in an IT career.

3.1 Theory of Reasoned Action

Decisions to choose and persist in a career or to change careers, are made from adolescence to middle age and are influenced by a number of factors. These factors may be internal to the individual, such as interests or skills, or external, such as influences by families, the economy, or even certain policies [18]. An important theory that relates to career choices is the theory of reasoned action (TRA) by Azjen and Fishbein [6], which states that an individual's behavioural intention is influenced by his/her own attitude and the social subjective norms prevalent in their environment. This theory is derived from the expectancy theory, which indicates that motivation for career decision is the result of the individual's belief in future possible outcomes. The theory of reasoned action stresses that an individual's behaviour can be examined and predicted through the examination of their underlying basic motivation. Thus, voluntary decisions of women, such as career choices can be predicted based on their respective attitude and the influence of those in their social circle and in this case culture [18].

4 Women in IT Culture Survey Results

The survey was completed by 93 respondents after three calls for participation. The marital status of the female respondents (Fig. 2) indicated that out of 90 responses, 9% (n = 8) were divorced, 10% (n = 9) living together, 51% (n = 46) were married, 29% (n = 26) were single and one widowed. The respondents indicated that 44% (n = 40) did not have any children, 49% (n = 44) had one to two children, while 7% (n = 6) had three or more. The Age responses (Fig. 3) showed that 29% (n = 26) were twenty one to twenty nine years old, 33% (n = 29) were thirty to thirty nine years old, 24% (n = 21) were forty to forty nine years old, 15% (n = 13) were fifty to fifty-nine years old. There was no one older than sixty. The majority of the women were White 55% (n = 49), followed by Africans 26% (n = 23), and the rest are 11% (n = 10) Coloured, 6% (n = 5) Indian and 2% (n = 2) did not discloses their ethnicity (Fig. 4).

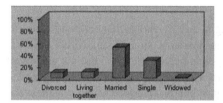

Fig. 2. Marital status

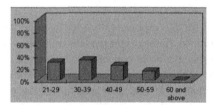

Fig. 3. Age

Fig. 4. Ethnicity

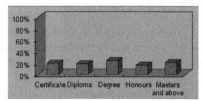

Fig. 5. Highest IT qualification

The highest IT qualification indicated (Fig. 5) by respondents were that 20% (n = 17) had Certificates, 19% (n = 16) had Diplomas, 24% (n = 21) had Degrees, 16% (n = 14) had Honours degrees and 21% (n = 18) had a Masters degree or above. Twenty percent (n = 18) had zero to two years of IT work experience, 8% (n = 7) had three to four years experience, 26% (n = 23) had five to nine years experience, 21% (n = 19) had ten to nineteen years experience, 25% (n = 22) had more that 20 years experience. Twenty nine percent (n = 26) indicated that they had role models when they started their career.

The five point Likert scale responses to the items below are reported by combining the results for Strongly Disagree/Disagree, as well as for Agree/Strongly agree.

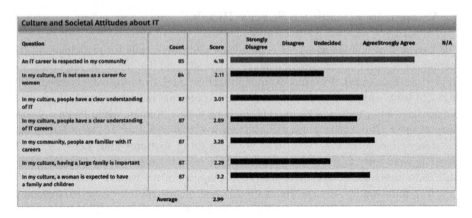

Fig. 6. Culture and societal attitudes about IT

Mixed responses were received pertaining to culture and societal attitudes about IT (Fig. 6). Eighty eight percent (n = 60) of the respondents agreed that *a career in IT was respected in the community*. In contrast, sixty-nine percent (n = 47) did not agree with the statement that *culturally IT was not seen as a career for women*, thus implying that *culturally IT was seen as a career for women*. A mixed response to the statement that *people in their respective cultures had a clear understanding of IT* was made with 41% (n = 29) disagreeing, 36% agreeing while 23% were neutral regarding the statement. Fifty one percent (n = 36) disagreed that people in their *cultures had a clear understanding of IT careers*, 50% (n = 35) agreed that *their community was familiar with careers in IT*. When it came to *societal and cultural perception of females*, 71% (n = 50) disagreed that *in their cultures having a large family was important* and 58% (n = 41) agreed that *in their culture a woman is expected to have a family and children*. These findings are supported by the EFA results presented below.

The Cronbach alpha for the items for the factor Culture was 0.88 (n = 90) indicating 'excellent reliability'. The correlations were statistically significant at 0.05 level for n ranging from 71 to 55 if $|r| \geq$ rcrit ranging from .234 to .266 and practically significant if $|r| \geq$ .300. In Table 1, the null hypothesis was accepted (HO$_1$) indicating that Culture and societal attitudes regarding an IT career exert *no influence* on females opting for a career in IT. The alternative hypothesis was accepted indicating that Culture and societal attitudes regarding IT career *positively influence* females remaining in the field of IT.

Table 1. Correlations

	Hypotheses	Pearson correlations	Correlation strength	Accepted or rejected
HO$_1$	'Culture and societal attitudes regarding an IT career' exert no influence on females opting for a career in IT	0.094	Low positive	Accepted
HA$_2$	'Culture and societal attitudes regarding IT career' positively influence females remaining in the field of IT	0.427	Large positive	Accepted

The Exploratory Factor Analysis (EFA) for the factor *Culture* indicated that one item had to be deleted and three items reversed (Table 2). The six remaining items explained 70% of the total variance for this factor.

Table 2. EFA remaining items for the factor: culture

Culture and Societal Attitudes about IT	
Cul.04 In my culture, people have a clear understanding of IT careers	.936
Cul.03 In my culture, people have a clear understanding of IT	.913
Cul.05 In my community, people are familiar with IT careers	.839
Cul.01 An IT career is respected in my community	.580
Cul.07* In my culture, a woman is expected to have a family and children*REVERSED In my culture, a woman is not expected to have a family and children	.826
Cul.06* In my culture, having a large family is important *REVERSED In my culture, having a large family is not important	.770
Cul.02* In my culture, IT is not seen as a career for women*REVERSED In my culture, IT is seen as a career for women	.670
Minimum loading deemed significant = .649; Percentage of Total Variance Explained = 70.0%	

The t-test conducted with two categories and one-way ANOVA for the demographic variables with three or more categories indicated no statistical difference between Culture and the demographic variables marital status, age and number of children for different groups. The demographic variable Ethnicity, however indicated a statistical difference (p = 0.004) between the groups African/Coloured/Indian and White, with a medium practical statistical difference (Cohen's d = 0.73) for the factor Culture (Table 3).

Table 3. Ethnicity t-test

Culture	African/Coloured/Indian	34	3.11	0.91	-0.66	-3.02	66	.004	0.73
	White	34	3.77	0.90					Medium

The demographic variable Highest Qualification, further indicated a statistical difference (p = 0.046) between the highest qualifications *Diploma/Degree* and *Honours/Masters and above* with a medium practical statistical difference (Cohen's d = 0.51) for the factor Culture (Table 4). No statistical differences were recorded for the demographical variables *IT Work experience* and *Role models*.

Table 4. Highest IT qualification t-test

Culture	Diploma/Degree	30	3.66	0.87	0.46	2.03	62	.046	0.51
	Honours/Masters and above	34	3.19	0.95					Medium

5   Conclusions and Future Research

The theory of reasoned action indicates that voluntary decisions of women such as career choices can be predicted based on their respective attitude and the influence of those in their social circle and in this case, culture [18]. In formative years, the influence of others is important, specifically the father [9, 31]. A young person's preferences may be influenced by the perceptions of those in their culture. This study contributes to the TRA theory as the subjective norms, included in the TRA model, which reflect the perception of how others think an individual should behave [6] are evident in this study's findings.

Societal gender stereotypes and social norms regarding careers and specifically IT, limit the number of females attracted to and staying in the IT profession [28]. Women, in general are less informed about the content of the work in IT, however they are informed about the inequalities in the field [19, 23]. The findings of this study indicate that although IT is noted as not being understood in the community (41%, n = 29), it is seen as a respectable profession in society (88%, n = 60). The Pearson correlation analysis confirmed that *Culture and societal attitudes regarding an IT career* exert no influence on females opting for a career in IT and that *Culture and societal attitudes regarding IT career* positively influence females remaining in the field of IT.

An important finding in this study (Table 3) indicates that for the two ethnic groupings, *African/Coloured/Indian* and *White*, the respondents perceived the influence of culture on an IT career choice statistically differently. Thus, the ethnic groups of African, Coloured and Indian women working in the IT industry perceive that culture does play a statistical significant role in women's IT career choices. These findings support Gathungu and Mwangi [16] that culture does influence women's career choice. Additionally, a statistical difference (Table 4) was also observed between the *undergraduate* vs the *post-graduate* degree groups regarding their perceptions on the role of culture in women's IT career choices.

This exploratory study has provided the foundation for evaluating Woman in IT career choices in South Africa and the influence of the factor *Culture* on the career choices and remaining in the IT industry. Future research will investigate the role of culture in women's IT career choices in more detail, by obtaining a larger sample size and evaluating the views of men as well. The study will be extended internationally and compare the South African results with other countries.

References

1. Adya, M., Kaiser, K.: Early determinants of women in the IT work-force: a model of girl's career choices. Inf. Technol. People **18**(3), 230–259 (2005). https://doi.org/10.1108/09593840510615860
2. Ahuja, M.K.: Women in the information technology profession: a literature review, synthesis and research agenda. Eur. J. Inf. Syst. **11**, 20–34 (2002). https://doi.org/10.1057/palgrave.ejis.3000417
3. Aivaloglou, E., Hermans, F.: Early programming education and career orientation: the effects of gender, self-efficacy, motivation and stereotypes. In: SIGCSE 2019, Minneapolis, MN, USA, 27 February–2 March 2019 (2019). https://doi.org/10.1145/3287324.3287358
4. Armstrong, D.J., Riemenschneider, C.K.: The barriers facing women in the information technology profession: an exploratory investigation of Ahuja's model. In: SIGSIM-CPR 2014, Singapore, 29–31 May 2014, pp. 85–96 (2014). https://doi.org/10.1145/2599990.2600006
5. Appianing, J., Van Eck, R.: Gender differences in college students' perceptions of technology-related jobs in computer science. Int. J. Gend. Sci. Technol. **7**(1), 28–56 (2015)
6. Azjen, I., Fishbein, M.: Understanding Attitudes and Predicting Social Behaviour. Prentice Hall, New Jersey (1980)
7. Boedeker, P., Capraro, M., Capraro, R., Nite, S.: Women in STEM: the impact of STEM PBL implementation on performance, attrition and course choice of women. In: 2015 IEEE Frontiers in Education Conference (FIE), El Paso, TX, USA, 21–24 October 2015 (2015). https://doi.org/10.1109/fie.2015.7344178
8. CareerJunction: South Africa's Most In-Demand Skills (Executive Summary) (2019). http://cj-marketing.s3.amazonaws.com/CJI_Executive_Summary.pdf
9. Collain, M., Trytten, D.: "You don't have to be a white male that was learning how to program since he was five:" computer use and interest from childhood to a computing degree. In: 50th ACM Technical Symposium on Computer Science Education (SIGCSE 2019), Minneapolis, MN, USA, 27 February–2 March 2019 (2019). https://doi.org/10.1145/3287324.3287383
10. Davis, J.: 6 Top Emerging Technology Jobs for 2019. InformationWeek (2019). https://www.informationweek.com/strategic-cio/team-building-and-staffing/6-top-emerging-technology-jobs-for-2019/d/d-id/1333522
11. Diekman, A., Brown, E., Johnston, A., Clark, E.: Seeking congruity between goals and roles: a new look at why women opt out of science, technology engineering and mathematics careers. Assoc. Psychol. Sci. **21**(8), 1051–1057 (2010)

12. Drury, M.: Women technology leaders: gender issues in higher education information technology. NASPA J. About Women High. Educ. **4**(1), 96–123 (2011)
13. Du Bow, W.: Attracting and retaining women in computing. IEEE Comput. Soc. **14**, 90–93 (2014)
14. Esterhuyse, A., Calitz, A.P., Cullen, M.: Post-graduate CS and IS students' career awareness. In: SACLA 2019 Conference, Drakensberg, South Africa, 15–17 July 2019 (2019)
15. European Commission: Digital Skills & Jobs (2019). https://ec.europa.eu/digital-single-market/en/policies/digital-skills
16. Gathungu, J.M., Mwangi, P.W.: Entrepreneurial intention, culture, gender and new venture creation: critical review. Int. J. Bus. Soc. Res. (IJBSR) **4**(2), 112–132 (2014). https://doi.org/10.18533/ijbsr.v4i2.402
17. Gharibyan, H., Gunsaulus, S.: Gender gap in computer science does not exist in one former soviet republic: results of a study. In: Proceedings of 11th SIGCSE Conference on Innovation and Technology in Computer Science Education, vol. 1, pp. 222–226 (2006)
18. Govender, I., Khumalo, S.: Reasoned action analysis theory as a vehicle to explore female students intention to major in information systems. J. Commun. **5**(1), 35–44 (2014)
19. Hyrynsalmi, S.M.: The underrepresentation of women in the software industry: thoughts from career-changing women. In: Proceedings of the 2nd International Workshop on Gender Equality in Software Engineering, Montreal, Quebec, Canada (2019). https://doi.org/10.1109/ge.2019.00008
20. Itulua-Abumere, F.: Sociological concepts of culture and identity, pp. 1–5 (2014). www.Flourishabumere.com
21. Jung, L., Clark, U., Patterson, L., Pence, T.: Closing the gender gap in the technology major. Inf. Syst. Educ. J. **15**(1), 26–41 (2017)
22. Kirlidog, M., van der Vyer, C., Zeeman, M., Coetzee, W.: Unfulfilled need: reasons for insufficient ICT skills in South Africa. Inf. Dev. **34**(1), 5–19 (2018). https://doi.org/10.1177/0266666916671984
23. Main, J., Schimpf, C.: The underrepresentation of women in computing fields: a synthetic of literature using a life course perspective. IEEE Trans. Educ. **60**, 1–10 (2017). https://doi.org/10.1109/TE.2017.2704060
24. Mbilini, S.N., le Roux, D.B., Parry, D.A.: Does automation influence career decisions among South African students? In: SAICSIT 2019 Conference, Skukuza, South Africa, 17–18 September 2019 (2019). doi.org/10.1145/3351108.3351137
25. McKinney, V., Wilson, D., Brooks, N., O'Leary-Kelly, A., Hardgrave, B.: Women and men in the IT profession. Commun. ACM **51**(2), 81–84 (2008). https://doi.org/10.1145/1314215.1314229
26. Muro, C., Gabriel, M.: Women engagement in ICT professions in Tanzania: exploring challenges and opportunities. Int. J. Comput. Inf. Technol. **5**(5), 443–447 (2016)
27. Njoki, M.M., Wabwoba, F., Micheni, E.J.: ICT definition implication on ICT career choice and exclusion among women. Inf. Technol. Comput. Sci. **5**, 62–71 (2016)
28. OECD: Bridging the Digital Gender Divide (2018). http://www.oecd.org/internet/bridging-the-digital-gender-divide.pdf
29. Pretorius, H., De Villiers, C.A.: South African perspective of the international discourse about women in information technology. In: SAICSIT 2010 Conference, Bela, South Africa, 11–13 October 2010, pp. 265–274 (2010). https://doi.org/10.1145/1899503.1899533
30. Rogers, V.L.N.: Women in IT: the endangered gender. In: Proceeding of the 2015 ACM Annual Conference on SIGUCCS, pp. 95–98 (2015). https://doi.org/10.1145/2815546.2815558
31. Sharif, N., Ahmed, N., Sarwar, S.: Factors influencing career choices. IBT J. Bus. Stud. **15**(1), 33–45 (2019)

32. Snyman, M.: South African scholar ICT career choice model. Unpublished Honours study. Department of Computing Sciences, Nelson Mandela University, South Africa (2012)
33. Vitores, A., Gil-Juarez, A.: The trouble with 'women in computing': a critical examination of the deployment of research on the gender gap in computer science. J. Gend. Stud. **25**(6), 666–680 (2016). https://doi.org/10.1080/09589236.2015.1087309
34. Zimmermann, K.: What is culture? Live Science (2017). https://www.livescience.Com/21478-what-is-culture-definition-of-culture.html

Exploring Digital Competence Requirements for Junior Financial Analysts in the UK Banking Industry

Matthias Murawski[✉], Mahdieh Darvish, Charlotte Marie Prinz, and Markus Bick

ESCP Business School Berlin, Berlin, Germany
{mmurawski,mdarvish,mbick}@escpeurope.eu,
charlotte_marie.prinz@edu.escpeurope.eu

Abstract. Although young adults familiar with digital technology join the workforce and bring in more advanced digital competences, the demand for digital competences in many industries increases even faster. In this study, we place the focus on the banking industry in the United Kingdom and aim for exploring those digital competences that are required for junior financial analysts. For this purpose, we apply a qualitative research approach which consists of two steps. First, we analyze job advertisements and code the identified competences by using the DigComp 2.0 framework. Second, we conduct interviews to validate and discuss our findings from the previous step. Our analysis reveals that the most important required competence categories are information and data literacy, followed by digital content creation. This paper contributes to the research field of digital competences and provides relevant insights for, amongst others, applicants, HR professionals, and training and education providers.

Keywords: Banking industry · Digital competences · DigComp 2.0 framework · Financial analysts · Interviews · Job advertisements · Qualitative analysis

1 Introduction

Today's young adults are raised in an environment in which they are surrounded by technology, and they consequently possess different digital competences compared to people from older generations [1]. Thus, entry-level workers bring new competences into the workforce [2]. At the same time, work becomes more digital: computer technology substitutes workers in performing routine tasks that can be described with programmed rules, while also complementing workers in executing non-routine tasks demanding flexibility, creativity, generalized problem-solving capabilities and complex communications [3].

While the level of digital competences increases in the workforce, the demand for digital competences seems to grow even faster [4, 5]. According to Newhouse, society is currently facing a period in which technological capabilities accelerate so swiftly that talent and knowledge cannot keep up, which consequently leads to a digital competence gap [6].

© IFIP International Federation for Information Processing 2020
Published by Springer Nature Switzerland AG 2020
M. Hattingh et al. (Eds.): I3E 2020, LNCS 12067, pp. 358–369, 2020.
https://doi.org/10.1007/978-3-030-45002-1_31

The financial industry has been, and still is, in the center of innovation concerning information systems and technologies [7]. Information technology (IT) investments in the financial sector are among the highest due to the enormous profit potentials within the industry as well as the economic incentives for substituting expensive human labor by cheaper computers [8]. Furthermore, digital strategies are part of banks' core strategic decision making and hiring the right people to work within a more digital environment is of central importance [9]. Consequently, the financial sector has also been one of the first sectors to experience challenges with acquiring people possessing the right digital competences as well as managing the digital competences of the existing workforce. A Capgemini survey from 2017 shows that 62% of the banks see the digital talent gap widening, which is the highest rate among all other industries analyzed (e.g. automotive, retail, consumer products, telecom) [10]. However, considering the specificities of the technological applications in the banking industry, the question remains what type of digital competences are needed and required in this field. Scholars in the information systems discipline have been researching the required digital competences for specific occupational groups for a long time. For instance, recent studies have already addressed digital competences of communicators or data professionals [5, 11]. Other studies emphasize the general need for further research on this topic [4].

In this context, we focus on the occupation *financial analyst* which has not been investigated in other academic studies, yet. More detailed, we consider *junior* financial analyst which we define as financial analysts with less than three years of job experience (including graduates). This selection is based on two assumptions formulated in the work of Rynes et al. [12]. First, applicants for entry-level or junior positions have less concrete "proof" of their ability to work on the job. It can thus be assumed that the digital competence requirements are stated more clearly and precisely in job descriptions (which build the basis for our analysis, see Sect. 3) while experienced hires have to show their competencies through work samples. Second, graduate hires are a long-term investment for companies, as their productivity levels are significantly lower in the beginning than more experienced hires. It can therefore be assumed that companies not only require the competences for these entry-level positions that are relevant for their current responsibilities, but they also look at the suitability of candidates for further career steps. Looking at entry level position thus also gives insights into medium- and long-term competence requirements.

Following similar research [e.g. 5], we limit our study to a specific geographic region – in our case the United Kingdom (UK). The UK shows a high level of technology-related jobs, especially in the financial sector, along with an increasing demand for digital competences. Thus, the research question (RQ) of this paper is:

RQ: Which digital competences are required for junior financial analysts in the UK banking industry?

The paper is structured as follows. A review of the existing literature in connection to the research question provides information on the definition of digital competence and the theoretical background of the topic in Sect. 2. Our research design is laid out in Sect. 3. Subsequently, the findings of the data analyses are presented and discussed (Sect. 4), before the paper ends with some concluding remarks in Sect. 5.

2 Literature Review

We started our literature review with the objective to elaborate the current state of research on digital competences. Thus, the term "digital competence*" was searched for in business and information system online databases such as EBSCO, JSTOR, WILEY, Springer and ScienceDirect, which led to only a few results, mostly related to educational purposes and limited to a specific geographical region defining and measuring digital competences specifically in connection to the local culture. By adding terms such as "financial analyst", the searches led to no (peer-reviewed) results. Consequently, the scope was extended to non-peer-reviewed publications, e.g., reports by consultancies such as Deloitte and McKinsey & Company addressing digital competences in the finance sector.

2.1 Definition of Digital Competences and the DigComp 2.0 Framework

The term digital competence is still relatively recent. Instead of a definable construct, it can be understood as a boundary concept applicable to various contexts but always related to skills and practices required to use new technologies in a meaningful way [13]. The idea of understanding and being able to operate technologies is however concomitant with their invention and use in the workplace and society. For example, Calvani et al. [14] suggest a definition of digital competence involving the flexibility to explore new technologies and the ability to select and evaluate data critically to solve problems and gain knowledge. Ferrari [15] applies the KSA framework of competence to define digital competences as a set of required knowledge, skills and attitudes to use information and communication technology (ICT) and digital media to perform tasks such as information management and communication. Furthermore, most definitions include content creating and sharing, building knowledge effectively and being critical as well as reflective when using IT for work, leisure and communication [16, 17].

Aside from its definition, another important question is how to measure digital competences. For this purpose, an updated digital competence framework (the so-called *DigComp 2.0 framework*) was developed and published by the European Commission, consisting of five key categories and 21 subcategories defining digital competences from an institutional perspective [18].

In this paper, we will rely our analysis on the DigComp 2.0 framework as presented in Table 1. It is one of the most recent, well-known and up-to-date frameworks covering a wide range of competence areas and has been the basis of many studies in different disciplines such as education and healthcare [19–21]. It is also a very appropriate framework as it covers a wide range of competence areas and accordingly is rather exhaustive. Another advantage of using the DigComp 2.0 framework is that it allows comparability between both different occupations and studies conducted at different points of time.

Table 1. DigComp 2.0 framework [18]

Categories	Subcategories
1. Information and data literacy	1. Browsing, searching and filtering data, information and digital content 2. Evaluating data, information and digital content 3. Managing data, information and digital content
2. Communication and collaboration	4. Interacting through digital technologies 5. Sharing through digital technologies 6. Engaging in citizenship through digital technologies 7. Engaging in citizenship through digital technologies 8. Netiquette 9. Managing digital identity
3. Digital content creation	10. Developing digital content 11. Integrating and re-elaborating digital content 12. Copyright and licenses 13. Programming
4. Safety	14. Protecting devices 15. Protecting personal data and privacy 16. Protecting health and well-being 17. Protecting the environment
5. Problem solving	18. Solving technical problems 19. Identifying needs and technological responses 20. Creatively using digital technologies 21. Identifying digital competence gaps

2.2 Digital Competences of Financial Analysts

Due to novelty and specification of the topic there are hardly any studies addressing digital competences required for financial analysts in the banking industry. Existing ones are mainly not of academic (i.e., double-blind, peer-reviewed) nature, such as consultancy reports.

For example. McKinsey & Company analyze the shift in competence requirements in banking and insurance, among other sectors, in a discussion-paper [22]. Considering the banking industry, a growth in technological skills, especially in data analytics, is identified. As a result, the need for a workforce with advanced technology skills will grow. In this context, recent studies show that there is a shortage of supply of professionals who are able to deal with data appropriately [5].

A Deloitte survey shows that finance leaders of the future will have to gain new competences to frame the function in a technology-driven environment [8]. In addition, the Deloitte study elaborates that many CFOs see a substantial shift in the tasks of the finance workforce toward analysis, prediction, and decision support.

3   Research Design

The first part of our study aims at addressing the research question through a qualitative content analysis of online job advertisements. The results of this analysis are subsequently checked for validity through expert interviews in the second empirical part of our study. These interviews were also conducted to gain insights into possible explanations behind the primary findings of the content analysis.

3.1   Analysis of Job Advertisements

3.1.1   Data Collection

Similar to other studies that aimed for identifying required competences, we used job advertisements as the source of data to gain insights into the competence requirements for financial analysts [5, 23]. 50 job advertisements were taken from currently open junior positions in the UK job market in January 2019.

The data was collected from indeed.co.uk, a widely used online job portal in the UK and one of the biggest job search engines in the world. The choice of search term resulted from research and tests of related terms. The search term *financial analyst* provided the most relevant results regarding the research question. However, when searching for *financial analyst*, many related positions appeared as well, which were relevant for the scope of the research. Thus, the job portal was searched for the term *of financial analyst* and related positions as follows: *risk analyst, global markets sales & trading analyst, quantitative analyst, business analyst, risk analyst, debt analyst, corporate broking analyst, IT business analyst, credit analyst, treasury analyst, enterprise risk analyst and financial planning analyst.*

Job advertisements were briefly screened for relevant content before considering in the sample. The screening criteria included were:

- Job advertisement is for entry-level or junior positions. Meaning, the position is aimed at recent graduates or professionals with less than 3 years of work experience.
- The creator of the job advertisement is a bank or similar financial institution and not a company outside of the financial sector.
- The job title is related to financial analyst positions (as mentioned above).

3.1.2   Data Analysis

The data was analyzed with QCAmap [24] for conducting a qualitative content analysis as proposed by Mayring [25]. The coding unit was set to phrase or clause and multiple categorizations were allowed within the system. In the coding guideline all subcategories of the DigComp 2.0 framework were entered including their definition and anchor samples as a reference.

A trial coding was undergone leading to a revision of the coding scheme. We had to rethink the meaning of some of the subcategories as they were sometimes difficult to distinguish from each other. The use of software tools such as Microsoft Office for example was difficult to clearly match to one of the subcategories as it used for various purposes. Therefore, we revised the anchor samples in a way that more quantitative tasks such as the use of Excel belonged to *information and data literacy* whereas more creative tasks such as the use of PowerPoint were matched to *digital content creation*. We also decided to allow for multiple categorization of content in the QCAmap tool in case a word or phrase represented more than one subcategory.

Subsequently, the data set was coded and recoded completely leading to the analysis results. In case subcategories occurred more than once in a job advertisement they were coded multiple times. This allowed us to gain insights into the relative importance of digital competences within a job advertisement. This assumes that digital competences that are named frequently than others within a job advertisement have higher relevance to the publishing company. After finishing the coding on the QCA-map tool online, an Excel spreadsheet, containing the frequency counts of the sub-categories was prepared for further analysis. One main differentiation was made between looking at the frequencies across all subcategories and looking at the five overarching digital competence categories only.

3.2   Additional Interviews

In addition to the analysis of the job advertisements (see Sect. 3.1), four expert interviews have been conducted to validate and discuss our findings. In order to guide the respondents through the research's findings while keeping an open discussion possible, the interviews were conducted as semi-structured interviews, and were audiotaped [26]. The conversations were transcribed for later review and analysis. To conduct the interviews, an interview protocol according to Creswell and Creswell was prepared [27].

The first respondent (R1) was a Merger & Acquisition (M&A) financial analyst from an American investment bank in London. He has worked in his job for eight months in addition to previous summer analyst roles in various investment banks. The second interviewee (R2) was a M&A financial analyst for Corporate Finance International (CFI) where he has been working for a little over six months. He previously held a summer analyst positions at Citibank from which he could additionally derive some insights during the interviews. The third interview (R3) was conducted with a structured finance analyst at the Royal Bank of Scotland (RBS) since September 2018. Considering his position was not in M&A, he had some differing opinions and explanations for the findings of the research, while still corroborating arguments made by the first two interviewees. The fourth and last interview (R4) was conducted with a director at an American investment bank in the UK. As director, he has a mainly managerial function, which includes making hiring decisions.

The main findings and selected quotes out of the four interviews are presented and discussed in Sect. 4.2.

4 Findings and Discussion

4.1 Job Advertisements

The five categories of the DigComp 2.0 framework are used to illustrate "the big picture" of the digital competence requirements named in the job advertisements, whereas the 21 subcategories are used to understand them in more detail.

Table 2 depicts both the frequency counts and the share of each competence category within the data set of the 50 job advertisements.

Table 2. Frequency counts per digital competence categories

Category	Frequency counts	Frequency
Information and data literacy	278	54%
Digital content creation	113	22%
Communication and collaboration	69	13%
Problem solving	52	10%
Safety	3	1%

Category 1 (*information and data literacy*) is the most important category and requirement for entry-level positions in the UK banking industry in terms of frequency (278). As the name "analyst" already reveals, being able to understand and interpret information and data is a significant aspect of analysts' responsibilities. Category 3 (*digital content creation*) follows as second strongest category and requirements with a share of nearly one fourth and a frequency count of 113. Category 2 (*communication and collaboration*) only represents 13% of all requirements in the data set with a total of 69 frequency counts. It is therefore the third most frequent subcategory in the data set. Accordingly, next to working with data and creating digital content, it is important that financial analysts can communicate and collaborate with others to create and distribute their analysis. Although being the third most frequent category it remains surprising that this category plays a relatively small role in the digital competence requirements. One potential explanation could be that the job of analysts is very individualistic and thus more based on individual performance and competences rather than the ability to work with others. Investigating this issue is part of the interview study (see Sect. 3.2).

Combined, *information and data literacy*, *digital content creation* and *communication and collaboration* represent 89% of all competence requirements in the data set. After this initial analysis it can be assumed that these three digital competences are the *digital core competences* of a junior financial analyst in the UK banking industry.

Figure 1 contains the frequencies of the 21 subcategories of the DigComp 2.0 framework. The undoubtedly most required competence with a total of 163 frequency counts is subcategory 2 (*evaluating data, information and digital content*), indicating the importance of understanding and analyzing data for the work of analysts. It is followed by subcategory 3 (*managing data, information and digital content*) with 95 frequency counts. Subcategory 3 was, within the job advertisements, often related to managing client data as well as the volume of data available in relation to investments. Subcategory 10 (*developing digital content*) is the extension of the data analysis and management into reports and presentations for other stakeholders and was mentioned a total of 54 times within the data set. These top three competences are often combined with the skill of using specific software programs such as Microsoft Excel, Word and/or PowerPoint. With a frequency count of 40, subcategory 11 (*integrating and re-elaborating digital content*) represents the fourth most frequent subcategory.

Frequencies of DigComp 2.0 Subcategories in the Job Descriptions

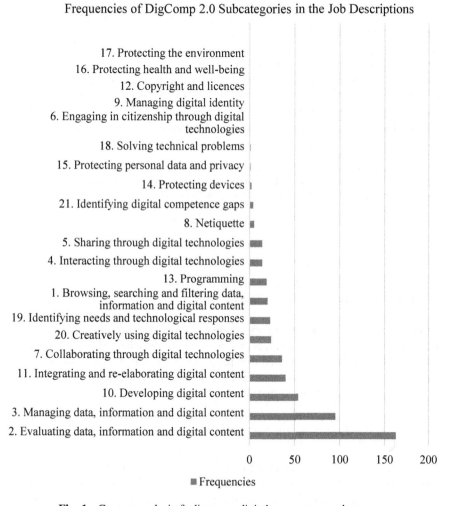

Fig. 1. Content analysis findings per digital competence subcategory

4.2   Interviews

The interview findings are matched to the categories and subcategories as in 4.1 and ranked according to the relevance they played in the interviews.

Information and Data Literacy. When confronted with category 1 (*information and data literacy*), there was consensus among all interviewees that this category was by far the most important one for a job as junior financial analysts.

> *"Analysts have to be extremely well versed in terms of information and data literacy. I would definitely put it as number one."* (R1)
> *"So, it [work at Citi Bank] was financial analysis [...], making research online, working on databases and keeping them up to date."* (R2)

Communication and Collaboration. When moving on to *category 2* (*communication and collaboration*), respondents agreed on some aspects while refuting others. During the job advertisement analysis, it was surprising to see that *communication and collaboration* was mentioned so little in the job descriptions (see Sect. 4.1), as it is often mentioned to be a key competence when working in a digital environment. This view was also shared by some respondents.

> *"Communication and collaboration are extremely important. [...] Communication is huge, I think, and I am quite surprised why they do not mention this is the job description, but it is definitely a big part of what we do as financial analysts."* (R1)
> *"So, you are on the trading floor with other hundreds of people around you; there is a lot of face to face; there are a lot of face to face meetings."* (R4)

The interviewees further mentioned that communication competences might be taken for granted and are thus not specifically asked for in the job advertisements.

> *"People are expected to be already good at this."* (R2)
> *"I guess it is important but taken for granted."* (R3)

Digital Content Creation. Category *3* (*digital content creation*), was seen as less important than *category 1* and *category 2* by most respondents. Although information and analysis must be integrated and prepared for presentation, other competences in *category 3* were evaluated as irrelevant or outside of the scope of junior financial analysts. One respondent stated that:

> *"Digital content creation - I think we are not as advanced as we should in that regard. Because we still use PowerPoint. We definitely do not do any programming or any crazy work in terms of graphics."* (R1)

In conclusions, digital content creation played a less important role for financial analysts than *data and information literacy*, and *communication and collaboration*. One factor that plays into the low relevance of this factor for the respondents is the support of special departments in the creation of documents. A further interesting insight, when discussing this category, were the arguments made in relation to *programming*. It became apparent that *programming* is highly relevant in financial analyst positions on the trading floor, while being irrelevant in financial analyst role in advisory functions.

Problem Solving. Looking at digital competence category 5 (*problem solving*), this was seen by all respondents as something that is the competence of a separate IT department and therefore not relevant for them most of the time.

> "*Problem Solving, that is IT. I mean, to give you a very simple example: When my Excel crashed, I don't even think about it twice, I just call the help desk. Let alone if I need to have an extra RAM for speed or extra flash desk or whatever. So, everything in terms of technology and problem solving is handled by the back office, by the IT guys.*" (R1)

Safety. When discussing category 4 (*safety*) with respondents, it became apparent that digital safety, in some of its aspects, was a discussed and relevant issue in their workplace, but something that was handled by other teams and departments.

> "*In terms of safety we have a huge safety and compliance division that just focuses on that stuff. And then goes on protecting devices, protecting personal data.*" (R1)

The overall learnings from discussing this category with the interview partners was that, although there is awareness about safety topics, they are not of central importance to financial analysts and digital competence in this category might be covered by specialized departments.

4.3   Summary and Discussion of Findings

As the name of the job position "analyst" entails, it was to be expected that *information and data literacy* was the most important competence for junior financial analysts. Within the *digital content creation* category, *programming* was an interesting competence to investigate within the general discussion of digital competences. The low frequency counts of the content analysis were a little surprising. However, it became apparent during the interviews that *programming* is a competence needed in some divisions of a bank, while irrelevant in others.

Furthermore, there were opposing results for the competence of *communication and collaboration*. The content analysis of the job advertisements revealed not a high importance of this competence (13% of all frequency counts), while interviewees emphasized the relevance of *communication and collaboration* at the workplace. It is important to emphasize that *communication and collaboration* must be understood here in a digital context. Financial analysts from around the world can simultaneously edit data and documents through modern software and ERP systems which is essential in today's banking industry.

In relation to our research question, we could show that for junior financial analyst positions in the UK banking industry *data and information literacy, communication and collaboration*, as well as *digital content creation* are the most required digital competences. *Safety* and *problem solving* on the other hand are nearly irrelevant categories.

5   Conclusion

Undoubtedly, digital technology significantly impacts the way firms are operated, managed and how they sell their products and/or services, thus influencing their employment patterns [28]. Therefore, it is important that research on digital competences continuously contributes to the right equipment of the labor market with the right knowledge, skills and attitudes. With the study at hand, we contribute to a better understanding of job requirements for junior financial analysts. This is not only relevant for graduates, applicants and junior analysts themselves, but also for HR professionals in the banking industry. Other contributors of our study are training and education providers, who are asked to adjust their offerings following the required competencies in the market.

As every research study, also our paper has limitations that could serve as the basis for future research. One of the major limitations of our study is the snapshot data analysis that lacks the investigation of historical developments or potential future requirements. An obvious research recommendation is therefore to conduct longitudinal studies in order to observe the data over several points of time.

Furthermore, in our study the numbers of both analyzed job advertisements and interviews are relatively small. Thus, an avenue for further research is replicating our study using extended data pools. Future research might also benefit from the presented analysis approach by applying it to other contexts such as different occupations.

We interpret our study as a first step of a larger project. Identifying required competences is the beginning while developing a more comprehensive competence model could be the next step. This, however, requires further research efforts as described in the previous paragraphs. Finally, the long-term objective could be to empirically test the relation of individual competence levels and, for example, job performance.

References

1. Palfrey, J.G., Gasser, U.: Born digital: understanding the first generation of digital natives. ReadHowYouWant.com (2011)
2. Colbert, A., Yee, N., George, G.: The Digital Workforce and the Workplace of the Future. Academy of Management, Briarcliff Manor (2016)
3. Autor, D.H., Levy, F., Murnane, R.J.: The skill content of recent technological change: an empirical exploration. Q. J. Econ. **118**, 1279–1333 (2003)
4. Murawski, M., Bick, M.: Digital competences of the workforce – a research topic? Bus. Process. Manag. J. **23**, 721–734 (2017)
5. Murawski, M., Bick, M.: Demanded and imparted big data competences: towards an integrative analysis. In: Proceedings of the 25th European Conference on Information Systems (ECIS), Guimarães, Portugal, 5–10 June 2017, pp. 1375–1390 (2017)
6. Newhouse, B.: Closing the digital competence gap. Train. Ind. Mag. **May/June**, 40–42 (2017)
7. Gomber, P., Kauffman, R.J., Parker, C., Weber, B.W.: On the fintech revolution: interpreting the forces of innovation, disruption, and transformation in financial services. J. Manag. Inf. Syst. **35**, 220–265 (2018)

8. Deloitte Insights: Global CIO Survey. Deloitte Insights (2017)
9. Black, L.K., Khetan, S., Akwafo, E., Halmrast, N., Harris, C., Oppenheimer, A.: Digital innovation, generational shifts, and the transformation of financial services. Chicago Fed Letter (2018)
10. Buvat, J., Crummenerl, C., Slatter, M., Puttur, R.K., Pasquet, L., van As, J.: The digital talent gap. Are companies doing enough. Capgemini Research Institute and LinkedIn (2017)
11. Shahlaei, C., Rangraz, M., Stenmark, D.: Transformation of competence - the effects of digitalization on communicators' work. In: Proceedings of the 25th European Conference on Information Systems (ECIS), Guimarães, Portugal, pp. 195–209 (2017)
12. Rynes, S.L., Orlitzky, M.O., Bretz Jr., R.D.: Experienced hiring versus college recruiting: practices and emerging trends. Pers. Psychol. **50**, 309–339 (1997)
13. Ilomäki, L., Paavola, S., Lakkala, M., Kantosalo, A.: Digital competence – an emergent boundary concept for policy and educational research. Educ. Inf. Technol. **21**, 655–679 (2016)
14. Calvani, A., Cartelli, A., Fini, A., Ranieri, M.: Models and instruments for assessing digital competence at school. J. E-Learning Knowl. Soc. **4**, 183–193 (2008)
15. Ferrari, A.: Digital Competence in Practice: An Analysis of Frameworks. Publication Office of the EU, Joint Research Centre, Luxembourg (2012)
16. European Parliament and Council of the European Union: Recommendation of the European Parliament and of the Council of 18th December 2006 on key competences for lifelong learning. Official Journal of the European Union, pp. 10–18 (2006)
17. Ala-Mutka, K.: Mapping Digital Competence: Towards a Conceptual Understanding. Institute for Prospective Technological Studies, Sevilla (2011)
18. Vuorikari, R., Punie, Y., Gomez, S.C., van den Brande, G.: DigComp 2.0: the digital competence framework for citizens. Update phase 1: the conceptual reference model. European Union, Joint Research Centre (2016)
19. Siiman, L.A., et al.: An instrument for measuring students' perceived digital competence according to the DIGCOMP framework. In: Zaphiris, P., Ioannou, A. (eds.) LCT 2016. LNCS, vol. 9753, pp. 233–244. Springer, Cham (2016). https://doi.org/10.1007/978-3-319-39483-1_22
20. Balula, A. (ed.): The use of DigComp in teaching and learning strategies: a roadmap towards inclusion. ACM (2016)
21. Evangelinos, G., Holley, D.: A qualitative exploration of the EU digital competence (DIGCOMP) framework: a case study within healthcare education. In: Vincenti, G., Bucciero, A., Vaz de Carvalho, C. (eds.) eLEOT 2014. LNICST, vol. 138, pp. 85–92. Springer, Cham (2014). https://doi.org/10.1007/978-3-319-13293-8_11
22. Berruti, F., Ross, E., Weinberg, A.: The Transformative Power of Automation in Banking. McKinsey & Co., New York (2017)
23. Debortoli, S., Müller, O., Vom Brocke, J.: Comparing business intelligence and big data skills. Bus. Inf. Syst. Eng. **6**, 289–300 (2014)
24. QCAMap Software. https://www.qcamap.org/
25. Mayring, P.: Qualitative content analysis: theoretical foundation, basic procedures and software solution. https://www.ssoar.info/ssoar/handle/document/39517
26. Misoch, S.: Qualitative Interviews. De Gruyter Oldenbourg, Berlin, Boston (2019)
27. Creswell, J.W., Creswell, D.W.: Research Design: Qualitative, Quantitative, and Mixed Methods Approaches. Sage Publications, London (2018)
28. Makridakis, S.: The forthcoming artificial intelligence (AI) revolution: its impact on society and firms. Futures **90**, 46–60 (2017)

Conceptualizations of E-recruitment: A Literature Review and Analysis

Mike Abia[1(✉)] and Irwin Brown[2(✉)]

[1] Department of Computer Science, Namibia University
of Science and Technology, 13 Jackson Kaujeua Street, Windhoek, Namibia
abiamike@gmail.com
[2] Department of Information Systems, University of Cape Town, Rondebosch,
Cape Town 7701, South Africa
Irwin.Brown@uct.ac.za

Abstract. There is diversity in understanding of electronic recruitment (e-recruitment) which results in confusion on the meaning and use of the term. The purpose of this paper is to bring conceptual clarity by investigating the alternative conceptualizations of e-recruitment in academic literature. Using Grounded Theory Methodology (GTM) techniques we analyzed literature to reveal five alternative conceptualizations; these being: (1) E-recruitment as a Technology Tool, (2) E-recruitment as a System, (3) E-recruitment as a Process, (4) E-recruitment as a Service, and (5) E-recruitment as a Proxy. The conceptualizations map to the scope of the definition and utilization of e-recruitment. Identifying conceptualizations of e-recruitment sets a platform for further research. Further research may include determining the relationships between the conceptualizations and determining conceptualizations in different settings among many other possible research focus topics.

Keywords: E-recruitment · Conceptualization · Literature review · Grounded Theory Methodology

1 Introduction

E-recruitment has many labels that include; internet recruitment, online recruitment, web-recruitment and many others. Unlike traditional recruitment, e-recruitment makes use of information technology to handle the recruitment processes. Breaugh et al. [1] defined a recruitment model that presents the recruitment process at a macro level with the following activities: Setting recruitment objectives, developing a strategy, performing the recruitment activity and obtaining and evaluating recruitment results. Recruiters compete with each other for candidates (jobseekers suitable for available jobs), while jobseekers compete for jobs; which drives both groups to adopt information technologies at accelerated rates in order to take the strain out of some of the recruitment activities [2–7]. *"For most job seekers, the Internet is where the action is"*

© IFIP International Federation for Information Processing 2020
Published by Springer Nature Switzerland AG 2020
M. Hattingh et al. (Eds.): I3E 2020, LNCS 12067, pp. 370–379, 2020.
https://doi.org/10.1007/978-3-030-45002-1_32

[3, p. 140]. Thus, to get candidates, recruiters need to move swiftly to locate and hire, which may require use of a multitude of information technologies in the process [8, p. 130].

There is evidence in research papers that academic disciplines and stakeholders have varied definitions of e-recruitment. The variety of definitions of e-recruitment is expected because it is part of e-HRM (electronic Human Resource Management) that has in itself different definitions depending on the context [6, p. 26], [9, p. 98]. Studies based on these definitions tend to reveal overlapping and contradictory results due to the overlaps or differences in definitions [9, p. 100]. The differences in definitions, aside from being problematic, is evidence of the variety in conceptualization of e-recruitment. Thus to find a standard definition of e-recruitment, conceptualizations of e-recruitment need to be known. To our knowledge, no research paper in e-recruitment has focused on conceptualization of e-recruitment, however there are studies in other areas of information systems (IS) that have focused on conceptualization [10–19]. Most view conceptualization as the formulation of a view about the nature of a phenomenon. The research questions to be answered are:

1. *What conceptualizations of e-recruitment exist in literature?*
2. *How can the conceptualizations be described and explained?*

2 Methodology for Reviewing Literature

Because of the large number of research papers on e-recruitment we aimed at selecting papers for review that would embrace the full variety of conceptualizations of e-recruitment. Also, we wanted a flexible review methodology that would allow for selection and analysis of papers simultaneously, as the conceptualizations emerged, rather than a sequential review methodology that required all research papers to be selected beforehand. Such flexibility is provided for by applying grounded theory methodology (GTM) as a suitable review methodology [20]. GTM techniques used in this study included open coding to identify concepts, constant comparative analysis to refine and differentiate conceptualizations, and theoretical sampling to identify further relevant literature [21, 22].

Figure 1 is a flowchart depicting how the literature was processed from search until conceptualizations of e-recruitment were identified, saturated and completed.

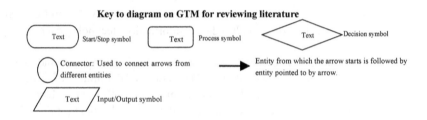

Key to diagram on GTM for reviewing literature

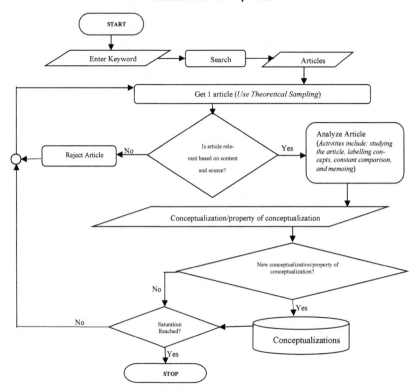

Fig. 1. GTM for reviewing literature

2.1   Searching for Articles

We used the web search engine Google Scholar to search electronically for the articles. We fed keywords synonymic with the word e-recruitment into the searching tool. These are: e-recruiting, e-HRM, e-Human Resource Management, electronic HRM, electronic Human Resource Management, e-recruiting, e-recruitment, internet recruiting, internet recruitment, online recruiting, online recruitment, recruiting online, recruiting on the internet, recruiting on the web, recruitment online, web-based recruiting, web-based recruitment, web recruiting, web recruitment [20].

After an initial search on Google Scholar and filtering of articles for relevancy based on paper titles and abstracts we had 445 journal articles and conference papers published in the period 1998 to 2019 in approximately 145 sources. The search process provided a set of many articles, but it did not qualify all of them as useful for the review. The selection process had to take place to sample useful and relevant articles for the review.

2.2 Theoretical Sampling of Articles

Ideally all papers on e-recruitment needed to be included in the review. Alternatively, papers included in the analysis had to be a representative sample of all papers in e-recruitment that were relevant for the developing conceptualizations. However with the vast amount of research in e-recruitment and the huge number of articles from our search and filtering it would be difficult or time consuming to include all relevant e-recruitment research articles for the review. The alternative of having a representative sample was viable and using GTM's theoretical sampling [21] was feasible for the objectives of this research to be met.

An initial article to be analyzed was picked from the population of 445 articles. Picking of subsequent articles for inclusion in the sample was informed by the emerging conceptualizations. Theoretical sampling was performed until all the conceptualizations got saturated and completed. Glaser [22] defines saturation as a state where new data does not bring new properties to the concepts. In an effort to attain completeness a check was done to make sure all conceptualizations were included. Theoretical sampling ended when saturation and completeness was achieved. This is the point at which the number of research articles involved in identifying conceptualizations in e-recruitment were counted. In the end 26 research articles were relevant for identifying and explaining conceptualizations of e-recruitment.

2.3 Analyzing Articles

Analysis of the articles that let conceptualizations of e-recruitment emerge (see Fig. 1) required that constant comparison be applied by comparing codes to codes and concepts to concepts to find and note their relationships and further develop the labelled conceptualizations [21, 22]. The emerging conceptualizations served as a framework for further selection of articles and using systematic deduction from the emerging conceptualization possibilities and probabilities were determined to guide the next cycle of article selection. Memos were created to note the emergent ideas. Memoed ideas also served to direct which article to sample next.

Every sampled article was investigated for its perspective on the essence of e-recruitment or the most essential or most vital part that embodied the conceptualization of e-recruitment. Indicators in the article brought forth the conceptualizations. The moment of departure from the analysis to getting another article for analysis came only after the article was fully analyzed. The resulting conceptualizations are detailed in the next section.

3   Conceptualizations of E-recruitment

Five conceptualizations of e-recruitment emerged from extent literature, namely: e-recruitment as a technology tool, e-recruitment as a system, e-recruitment as a process, e-recruitment as a service and e-recruitment as a proxy. Although many of the articles had a mixture of conceptualizations, one or two stood out in each article and for each conceptualization Table 1 gives example research articles. After the presentation in Table 1 each of the conceptualizations is described and explained in sub-sections that follow.

Table 1. Conceptualizations of E-recruitment

Conceptualization of e-Recruitment (*Label Created in this Study*)	Description	Articles
1. E-recruitment as a Technology Tool	E-recruitment is viewed in some studies as a technology tool	[23]
2. E-recruitment as a System	E-recruitment is a group of independent but interrelated elements comprising a unified whole. These elements include technology, society, organizations, etc.	[23–29]
3. E-recruitment as a Process	E-recruitment is a set of systematic well-coordinated activities. The activities are done by information technology or traditionally	[25, 29–37]
4. E-recruitment as a Service a. E-recruitment as a Repository b. E-recruitment as a Medium c. E-recruitment as a Program (E-recruitment as an Implemented Algorithm)	E-recruitment is a service to recruitment. It cannot be entrusted to do all that is needed for successful recruitment, therefore it only provides certain functionalities a. E-recruitment provides storage facilities for recruitment data b. E-recruitment is a communications conduit between stakeholders in recruitment c. E-recruitment is a set of precise rules for solving a problem	[7, 38, 39] a. [33, 37, 40] b. [31, 41–44] c. [23, 25, 35]
5. E-recruitment as a Proxy	E-recruitment acts on behalf of organizational and societal entities	[35, 45, 46]

3.1   E-recruitment as a Technology Tool

E-recruitment as a technology tool is a conceptualization of e-recruitment as a technical artefact [19]. This means is demonstrated by Faliagka et al. [23] who presented a tool to automate the ranking of applicants in recruitment.

3.2   E-recruitment as a System

Studies that view e-recruitment as a system conceptually divide e-recruitment into independent but interrelated elements, at the core of which is information technology, society, organizations, etc. The system view allows each component to receive input from the other elements and produce input for other components [25]. The system view of e-recruitment assigns all automating functions to the IT artefact of the system while organizational recruitment experts evaluate the outcome [24]. While some stakeholders view e-recruitment as a system, others view it as a process.

3.3   E-recruitment as a Process

Instead of focusing on entities, the process view of e-recruitment focuses on e-recruitment activities [37]. There is no attempt to set boundaries between the IT artefact, society and organization, but activities are clearly identified and can be performed by either the IT artefact or by human actors. Examples include e-recruitment being seen as data collection activity using an online system [33]. However recruitment activities can be performed by human actors too [37]. With the process view of e-recruitment the end goal is the execution of all the recruitment activities.

3.4   E-recruitment as a Service

The view exists that e-recruitment is a service to recruiters and job-seekers. Many e-recruitment platforms are independent of the organizations or societies they serve. Sub-views of e-recruitment as a service include: e-recruitment as a repository, e-recruitment as a medium, and e-recruitment as a program.

E-recruitment as a repository. Some studies portrayed e-recruitment as a repository for data about jobs, recruiters and employers [40]. In another study online forms were filled in by jobseekers and the data provided on the forms was stored for recruiters and other stakeholders to retrieve [33]. While the view of e-recruitment as a repository is usually held when e-recruitment is newly adopted, other services follow suit.

E-recruitment as a medium is another view held, e.g. Bartram [41] portrays e-recruitment as a facilitator of communication between jobseekers and organizations. Traditional media like newspaper [42] are sometimes found inconvenient thus e-recruitment takes their place. Some organizations employ e-recruiters who form part of e-recruitment and serve to link the IT artefact and other elements in recruitment. Although e-recruitment as a medium improves communication speed it also comes with a downside, e.g. information overload [37].

E-recruitment as a program is a view that associates e-recruitment with calculations and logical interpretation and processing of data. One study included, as an algorithmic module, a Pre-screening Management System to automatically assess the extent of match between an applicant's qualification and job requirements [25]. Such module or similar modules are found in many e-recruitment systems given the high volumes of applications associated with e-recruitment. Therefore, many studies espouse the view that e-recruitment serves to provide a convenient matching program.

3.5   E-Recruitment as a Proxy

Orlikowski and Iacono [19] reveal the pervasiveness of the proxy view of the IT artefact in IS literature. E-recruitment may act to present the image of the company, culture of the company, etc. Braddy et al. [45] examined the effects of website content features on people's perceptions of organizational culture. Their study implies that e-recruitment, especially the IT artefact (website) acts on behalf of some corporate image management entity in the organization. Some studies focused on website content [45], while others focused on website characteristics [46].

4   Contribution and Implications of Conceptualizations of E-recruitment

Conceptualizations of e-recruitment contribute to understanding of e-recruitment and have implications for both practice and research as discussed in this section.

4.1   Contribution of the Research

This study mapped the scope of the definition of e-recruitment by explaining the diversity in understanding. This mapping was done by identifying five conceptualizations of e-recruitment and labelling them as: E-recruitment as a Technology Tool, E-recruitment as a System, E-recruitment as a Process, E-recruitment as a Service and E-recruitment as a Proxy. Taking note of conceptualizations provides practitioners with a tool to enhance productivity while allowing researchers to have more focus in their research.

4.2   Implications of Conceptualizations of E-recruitment

The implications of conceptualizations of e-recruitment stem from being able to attach a label to the said stakeholders' conceptualizations and put it to their trade or scholarly pursuits. Labelling conceptualizations provides a pathway to standardization of e-recruitment. The benefits of such standardization include having common understanding of concepts, and ease of communication. While these are overarching implications, some implications are specific to practice or research.

Implications for Practice. Labelled and well defined conceptualizations of e-recruitment sets bounds on what practitioners should expect in their practice and strive towards when they adopt a particular conceptualization. Well defined conceptualizations as ones in this study provide alternative conceptualization options that practitioners can adopt depending on their needs. Practitioners can always adopt a conceptualization that best reflects their situation. As there are implications for practice, there are implications for research as well.

Implications for Research. Through this identification, description and explanation of conceptualizations of e-recruitment, there are a number of conceptualizations to consider. Therefore, focus on a specific conceptualization or focus on specific conceptualizations is possible. Such focus allows the researcher to delimit research.

5   Conclusion and Further Research

5.1   Conclusion

The study highlighted the problem of diversity in understanding of e-recruitment that goes without explicit attention in literature and proposed that identifying and labelling the varied conceptualizations of e-recruitment can be part of better articulation of the diversity. Using GTM, literature on e-recruitment was reviewed and conceptualizations of e-recruitment were identified. Taking note of conceptualizations provides practitioners with a tool to enhance productivity while allowing researchers to have more focus in their research. In addition this study provides insight into directions for potential further study.

5.2   Further Research

While this research contributes to understanding of e-recruitment, further research related to it can respond to several issues which are not addressed herein. Understanding of relationships between conceptualizations helps to avoid conceptual chaos. Therefore, further research aimed at relating the conceptualizations is essential. Conceptualizations of e-recruitment may be compared to conceptualizations of other forms of e-phenomena, and hence to the development of more general understanding of IS and the IT artefact.

References

1. Breaugh, J.A., Macan, T.H., Grambow, D.M.: Employee recruitment: current knowledge and directions for future research. Int. Rev. Ind. Organ. Psychol. **23**, 45–82 (2008)
2. Borstorff, P.C., Marker, M.B., Bennett, D.S.: Online recruitment: attitudes and behaviors of job seekers. J. Strateg. E-Commer. **5**(1/2), 1 (2007)
3. Cappelli, P.: Making the most of on-line recruiting. Harv. Bus. Rev. **79**(3), 139–146 (2001)
4. Cober, R.T., Brown, D.J., Levy, P.E.: Form, content, and function: an evaluative methodology for corporate employment web sites. Hum. Resour. Manage. **43**(2–3), 201–218 (2004)
5. Pfieffelmann, B., Wagner, S.H., Libkuman, T.: Recruiting on corporate web sites: perceptions of fit and attraction. Int. J. Sel. Assess. **18**(1), 40–47 (2010)
6. Simón, C., Esteves, J.: The limits of institutional isomorphism in the design of e-recruitment websites: a comparative analysis of the USA and Spain. Int. J. Hum. Resour. Manag. **27**(1), 23–44 (2016)
7. Smyth, B., Bradley, K., Rafter, R.: Personalization techniques for online recruitment services. Commun. ACM **45**(5), 39–40 (2002)
8. Koong, K.S., Liu, L.C., Williams, D.L.: An identification of internet job board attributes. Hum. Syst. Manag. **21**(2), 129–135 (2002)
9. Bondarouk, T., Parry, E., Furtmueller, E.: Electronic HRM: four decades of research on adoption and consequences. Int. J. Hum. Resour. Manag. **28**(1), 98–131 (2017)

10. Doherty, N.F., Coombs, C.R., Loan-Clarke, J.: A re-conceptualization of the interpretive flexibility of information technologies: redressing the balance between the social and the technical. Eur. J. Inf. Syst. **15**(6), 569–582 (2006). https://doi.org/10.1057/palgrave.ejis. 3000653

11. Pinsonneault, A., Heppel, N.: Anonymity in group support systems research: a new conceptualization, measure, and contingency framework. J. Manag. Inf. Syst. **14**(3), 89–108 (1997). https://doi.org/10.1080/07421222.1997.11518176

12. Sun, J., Teng, J.T.C.: Information systems use: construct conceptualization and scale development. Comput. Hum. Behav. **28**(5), 1564–1574 (2012). https://doi.org/10.1016/j. chb.2012.03.016

13. Hong, W., Thong, J.Y.L.: Internet privacy concerns: an integrated conceptualization and four empirical studies. MIS Q. **37**(1), 275–298 (2013)

14. George, J.F.: The conceptualization and development of organizational decision support systems. J. Manag. Inf. Syst. **8**(3), 109–125 (1991)

15. Wang, Y.-S., Liao, Y.-W.: The conceptualization and measurement of m-commerce user satisfaction. Comput. Hum. Behav. **23**(1), 381–398 (2007). https://doi.org/10.1016/j.chb. 2004.10.017

16. Tilly, R., Posegga, O., Fischbach, K., Schoder, D.: Towards a conceptualization of data and information quality in social information systems. Bus. Inf. Syst. Eng. **59**(1), 3–21 (2017). https://doi.org/10.1007/s12599-016-0459-8

17. Jasperson, J., Carter, P.E., Zmud, R.: A comprehensive conceptualization of post-adoptive behaviors associated with information technology enabled work systems. MIS Q. **29**(3), 525 (2005). https://doi.org/10.2307/25148694

18. Barki, H., Titah, R., Boffo, C.: Information system use—related activity: an expanded behavioral conceptualization of individual-level information system use. Inf. Syst. Res. **18** (2), 173–192 (2007)

19. Orlikowski, W.J., Iacono, C.S.: Research commentary: desperately seeking the 'IT' in IT research—a call to theorizing the IT artifact. Inf. Syst. Res. **12**(2), 121–134 (2001)

20. Wolfswinkel, J., Furtmueller, E., Wilderom, C.: Using grounded theory as a method for rigorously reviewing literature. Eur. J. Inf. Syst. **22**(1), 45–55 (2013)

21. Glaser, B.G.: Advances in the Methodology of Grounded Theory: Theoretical Sensitivity. Sociology Press, California (1978)

22. Glaser, B.G.: Doing Grounded Theory: Issues and Discussions. Sociology Press, California (1998)

23. Faliagka, E., Tsakalidis, A., Tzimas, G.: An integrated e-recruitment system for automated personality mining and applicant ranking. Internet Res. Bradf. **22**(5), 551–568 (2012)

24. Chiwara, J.R., Chinyamurindi, W.T., Mjoli, T.Q.: Factors that influence the use of the internet for job-seeking purposes amongst a sample of final-year students in the Eastern Cape Province of South Africa. SA J. Hum. Resour. Manag. **15**(1), 1–9 (2017)

25. Lee, I.: An architecture for a next-generation holistic e-recruiting system. Commun. ACM **50** (7), 81–85 (2007)

26. Yoon Kin Tong, D.: A study of e-recruitment technology adoption in Malaysia. Ind. Manag. Data Syst. **109**(2), 281–300 (2009)

27. Braddy, P., Thompson, L.F., Wuensch, K., Grossnickle, W.: Internet recruiting: the effects of web page design features. Soc. Sci. Comput. Rev. **21**(3), 374–385 (2003)

28. Pavon, F., Brown, I.: Factors influencing the adoption of the world wide web for job-seeking in South Africa. South Afr. J. Inf. Manag. **12**(1), 1–9 (2010)

29. Lee, I.: Modeling the benefit of e-recruiting process integration. Decis. Support Syst. **51**(1), 230–239 (2011)

30. Ehrhart, K.H., Mayer, D.M., Ziegert, J.C.: Web-based recruitment in the millennial generation: work-life balance, website usability, and organizational attraction. Eur. J. Work Organ. Psychol. **21**(6), 850–874 (2012)
31. Feldman, D.C., Klaas, B.S.: Internet job hunting: a field study of applicant experiences with on-line recruiting. Hum. Resour. Manag. **41**(2), 175–192 (2002)
32. Parry, E., Tyson, S.: An analysis of the use and success of online recruitment methods in the UK. Hum. Resour. Manag. J. **18**(3), 257–274 (2008)
33. García-Izquierdo, A.L., Aguinis, H., Ramos-Villagrasa, P.J.: Science–practice gap in e-recruitment. Int. J. Sel. Assess. **18**(4), 432–438 (2010)
34. Kashi, K., Zheng, C.: Extending technology acceptance model to the e-recruitment context in Iran. Int. J. Sel. Assess. **21**(1), 121–129 (2013)
35. Jansen, B.J., Jansen, K.J., Spink, A.: Using the web to look for work: implications for online job seeking and recruiting. Internet Res. **15**(1), 49–66 (2005)
36. Smith, A.D., Rupp, W.T.: Managerial challenges of e-recruiting: extending the life cycle of new economy employees. Online Inf. Rev. **28**(1), 61–74 (2004)
37. Llorens, J.J.: A model of public sector e-recruitment adoption in a time of hyper technological change. Rev. Public Pers. Adm. **31**(4), 410–423 (2011)
38. Koch, T., Gerber, C., de Klerk, J.J.: The impact of social media on recruitment: are you LinkedIn? SA J. Hum. Resour. Manag. **16**(2), 1–14 (2018)
39. Vidros, S., Kolias, C., Kambourakis, G.: Online recruitment services: another playground for fraudsters. Comput. Fraud Secur. **2016**(3), 8–13 (2016)
40. Wang, B., Guo, X.: Online recruitment information as an indicator to appraise enterprise performance. Online Inf. Rev. Bradf. **36**(6), 903–918 (2012)
41. Bartram, D.: Internet recruitment and selection: kissing frogs to find princes. Int. J. Sel. Assess. **8**(4), 261–274 (2000)
42. Selden, S., Orenstein, J.: Government e-recruiting web sites: the influence of e-recruitment content and usability on recruiting and hiring outcomes in US state governments. Int. J. Sel. Assess. **19**(1), 31–40 (2011)
43. Sylva, H., Mol, S.T.: E-recruitment: a study into applicant perceptions of an online application system. Int. J. Sel. Assess. **17**(3), 311–323 (2009)
44. Van Hoye, G., Lievens, F.: Investigating web-based recruitment sources: employee testimonials vs word-of-mouse. Int. J. Sel. Assess. **15**(4), 372–382 (2007)
45. Braddy, P., Meade, A., Michael, J., Fleenor, J.: Internet recruiting: effects of website content features on viewers' perceptions of organizational culture. Int. J. Sel. Assess. **17**(1), 19–34 (2009)
46. Walker, H.J., Feild, H.S., Giles, W.F., Bernerth, J.B., Short, J.C.: So what do you think of the organization? A contextual priming explanation for recruitment web site characteristics as antecedents of job seekers' organizational image perceptions. Organ. Behav. Hum. Decis. Process. **114**(2), 165–178 (2011)

Alumni Reflections on Gender Equality in the ICT Context

Eija Koskivaara[1](✉) 🆔 and Brita Somerkoski[2] 🆔

[1] Turku School of Economics, University of Turku (Turun yliopisto),
20014 Turku, Finland
eija.koskivaara@utu.fi
[2] Department of Teacher Education, University of Turku (Turun yliopisto),
20014 Turku, Finland

Abstract. This study aims to bridge the digital gender divide in information and communication technology (ICT) education and field by reflecting the alumni opinions on gender equality in the ICT context. The study aims to raise the awareness of gender equality issues through the work-life reflections. This is done to understand better the gender equality issue, and to give proposals to promoting equality also for the faculty members who teach ICT related subjects in the university. The data for the study was collected from 131 (n = 131) ICT alumni that represent 25 nationalities. Results reveal that men with 77% share dominate the closest supervisor positions and 14% of the previous ICT students in the university have felt some kind of gender-based discrimination in their work. The data-driven content analysis was used to analyze the data. In the analysis we found five main categories behind the gender-based discrimination: society, organizational; individual action; hard facts and zero. We argue, that society, organizational, and individual action proposals illustrate the digital transformation process.

Keywords: Information technology · Digital gender divide · Equality

1 Introduction

Nelson Mandela [1] said: "Education is the most powerful weapon which we can use – which we can use in order to prepare our youth for their role as leaders of tomorrow." One success story of the power of education comes from Finland, where free education and equal access to education is a constitutional right [2] and where 15 year old students have performed very well in the OECD Programme for International Student Assessments (PISA) [3].

Today, another powerful weapon to change the world is digital transformation or digitalization. The digital transformation may be categorized into three dimensions: the use of new digital technologies; the change of organizational processes or the creation of new business models; and influencing all aspects of human life [4]. The digital transformation has changed the phenomenon of the digital divide from a situation of access to acquiring sufficient skills to use information and communication technology (ICT) effectively [5, 6]. Based on the latest OECD report [7], digitalization, ICT and

M. Hattingh et al. (Eds.): I3E 2020, LNCS 12067, pp. 380–386, 2020.
https://doi.org/10.1007/978-3-030-45002-1_33

technical skills development are seen as key components for human well-being and social development. Nevertheless, a gender gap in the access, use, and ownership of digital transformation is still present in G20 economies [7]. This gap is defined as the digital gender divide. Based on the findings of OECD, the digitalization and fighting the digital gender divide offers opportunities, enhances women empowerment and holds promises for enhanced productivity growth. The digital gender divide is well recognized at the work-life balance: Women and girls with poor digital literacy skills will struggle to find jobs as technology advances and this is an urgent global problem [8]. It is argued that girls are less confident in their maths, science and IT abilities, often due to or fueled by societal and parental biases, and parents' expectations about the future of their teenagers by leading girls' lower engagement in science and ICTs [9]. The effective promotion of women´s digital adoption from the government, from the private sector and the civil society is proposed as one solution [10]. However, this is not enough. Also educational elements in fighting against the digital gender divide are needed. It is essential to understand the work-life reflections to be able to develop education. This paper aims to research the perceptions and reflections on gender equality in the context of ICT.

Since 1979, it has been possible to study Information System Science (ISS) as a major subject at the Turku School of Economics (TSE) in the University of Turku. During these 40 years there has been 580 graduates of which 36% are women. The percentage of female graduates has been slightly diminishing; from the 1980s 48%, 1990s 33%, after that stayed at that level for the next two decades - 34% for the 2000 and 36% for the 2010s [11]. Unfortunately, this finding supports the northern gender-equality paradox in STEM (science, technology, engineering, mathematics) education: Based on that idea the more equal the society, the fewer women are doing the STEM education [12].

The concept of co-creation and acting together with work-life is proposed to be one solution for developing ICT education [13]. In the universities, alumni surveys are frequently used to get feedback about employability and employment. ISS subject/institute has been running alumni surveys regularly to get feedback on the ICT knowledge and skill requirements of the employers. Therefore, one purpose to carry out an alumni survey is to support the employability of graduates by improving the curriculum of the university according to the industry requirements. The latest alumni survey was carried out in the spring 2019 and it included equality related questions. In this case study, we are analyzing these alumni responses and proposals against inequality. The research question of this study is: What are the alumni experiences and perceptions towards equality in work in the context of ICT? Furthermore, we are interested in what proposals alumni will give to change the situation in the ICT context.

2 Data Collection and Analysis

The data for the study was collected with the alumni questionnaire (AQ). It was originally established to tighten the relationship with the ICT alumni, to enhance the work-life connections with the studies and to engage the alumni with the faculty activities such as guest lecturers, visits and practical training opportunities. The faculty has been involved with a Horizon 2020 project concerning gender equality issues in the context of ICT. Based on this activity we added some gender equality questions to the AQ.

The current AQ was pilot-tested with the faculty members and researchers. The questionnaire was designed is such a way that privacy issues and the European GDPR regulations were taken into account. We collected and analyzed the answers anonymously. The final AQ has 40 questions and we sent the questionnaire to 381 alumnus whose email is in a voluntary database of the alumnus. 91 emails were not responding. The online survey was distributed also via the social media channels of international alumni network.

Altogether 131 (n = 131) alumni representing 25 nationalities replied, of these 28% were women. In this study, we analyzed two quantitative questions for background purposes. These questions were about the gender of the closest supervisor (131 responses) and whether responders have felt any gender-based discrimination in their work (131 responses).

For the qualitative data of equality in work (51 open responses 37% women), we used the content-based thematic analysis with three iterations by reading the texts many times. The meaning units (hits) were collected in a matrix and encoded. The meaning units were labeled based on text content. Content analysis and the matrix were used to provide replicable and valid inferences about gender equality. To secure reliability, two researchers were analyzing the hits and categorizing them. After many overlaps, typical for this kind of research design, the content was organized under themes with lower and upper categories. Based on the text analysis we formulated 16 sub-categories, which were grouped into five super-categories and further conceptualized to theory with three main categories.

3   Results

The quantitative gender bias fact is that men dominate as their closest supervisor with 77%. Table 1 shows the overall gender distribution of the closest supervisors.

Table 1.   Gender of closest supervisor.

Gender	N	Percent
Men	101	77,1
Women	24	18,32
Other	2	1,53
I do not want to say, or I do not know	4	3,05

14% of alumnus have felt some kind of gender-based discrimination in their work (Table 2). The answers were based on their last five year working experience. About seven percent think that the promotion or higher salary was given to the other less qualified gender. Eight people mentioned the following reasons when we asked a description of the unfair situations. The reasons are related to age, management, gender, and country:

- "Based on age, I've been treated as too young not based on my experience and skills." (R97)
- "Age discrimination" (R30)
- "Actually I think few people should have deserved a promotion, but were not give one." (R31)
- "More like Nepotism" (R37)
- "I never experienced any gender-based discrimination in Finland. Currently I work in a big global company in the other country and here I sometimes feel that my men colleagues threat me like their secretary." (R116)
- "One firm did not grant a loan and I felt very strongly it would have been granted if I were a man. Seriously." (R114)
- "Men are always preferred for the most interesting work, while women are mostly used for their organizational skills" (R129)

Table 2. Gender-based discrimination at work.

	N	Percent
No kind of gender-based discrimination in their work	111	84,73
Yes, some kind of gender-based discrimination in their work	14	10,69
Somebody, other gender than me got the work although I was more qualified	5	3,82
Somebody, other gender than me got the promotion or salary prize although I was more qualified	4	3,05
I was treated unfairly for another reason. How? Describe the situation shortly	8	6,11
I do not want to say	2	1,53

We asked our alumni "If you feel that the equality in the IT/IS field/education could be better, do you have any proposal on how to change the situation?" 51 alumni responded (f = 51) to the question that equality in the IT/IS field/education could be better. We asked the respondents to give proposals on how to change the situation.

In the thematic content analysis, we made the following iterations:

- 1st iteration (analyzing text meanings): 16 categories (no opinion, zero, general awareness, raising awareness, content development, work-life connections, identity support, social competence, age, national identity, the state of art/more women)
- 2nd iteration (grouped into super-categories): 5 categories (zero, awareness-raising, education and work-life connection development, soft skills, hard facts)
- 3rd iteration (conceptualizing categories to theory): 3 main categories (0-category, digital transformation-category with three dimensions: individual, organizational and societal dimension, hard facts-category)

Conceptualized categories and their hits:

- Zero-category: no problem, no opinion: 21 hits

- Digital transformation-category: societal awareness (10 hits), organizational (education) development (12 hits), individual development (7 hits): 29 hits
- Hard facts-category: age (4), nationality (3), more women (5): 12 hits

To better understand the issue we provide some examples of the responses. Firstly, the respondents suggested that companies should provide general awareness of the work tasks and especially whether the work is suitable for both genders. "Stats regarding the recruiting processes be open in a way that it's possible to recognize companies who avoid hiring women that are in a certain age (Man 9)". Also, some of the respondents pointed out that all the students should get more education on programming "More focus on specialization skills so that students know how a real business works to manage their IT (Woman 22)." Secondly, there should be enough connections to work-life and hands-on training. "More practical education (Woman 2)." Some respondents answered that the students need more teaching of social skills and support for professional identity. "More project management skills and tools; Purchasing negotiation skills; Emotional IQ skills (understanding others); Influencing people; Presentation and performing skills (Man 24)."

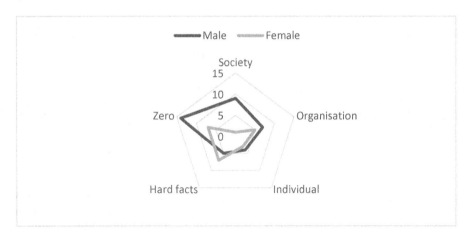

Fig. 1. Differences between male and female proposals for changing the inequality in the ICT education and field.

In Fig. 1, we are illustrating the inequality proposals and the levels between men and women. Men dominate the proposals 14 > 7 that there are no actions needed to change the inequality situation. An example of men's proposal: "I guess this means equality between male and female? I believe that women selecting career within IT/IS, have excellent opportunities to be successful. Now gender equality is such a topic that all companies take this issue seriously. The biggest challenge is to increase the amount of female workers in IT/IS clusters. That is growing all the time, the challenge is to communicate women, what kind of career opportunities there are, and maybe to help them to understand that IS/IT positions are not necessarily very technology focused (which I believe is one main barrier to women) (Man 42)." But at the same time, men also dominate society based actions 9 > 1 to be taken to change the situation. Individual action proposals are more or less at the same level. An example of woman proposal: "I think it would be important to support the development of professional identity of all the students, but perhaps women need to be focused particularly, at least as long as there is a lack of role models for women. You could ask all the students how confident they are as ISS professionals, and how their confidence could be further enhanced, and make gender analysis of the results, too (Woman 12)."

Altogether, men gave 21 proposals and women nine proposals related to digital transformation and gender inequality. As men dominates the number of the proposals it is also interesting to see the shape of the figure. Women seem to be more sensitive to identify the hard facts such as gender, age and nationality (7 > 5) than men.

4   Discussion

To be able to develop and better understand the ICT education we researched the work-life reflections of the ICT alumni. All the results are based on the responses for the alumni survey (n = 131).

It seems that men dominate the closest supervisor status - only 19% of the respondents had women supervisors. Most of the respondents did not experience any kind of discrimination in their work yet 14% did. The most common form of discrimination was gender-based, but also nationality and age-based forms of discrimination were reported.

However, alumni seem to be ready to change the situation and they gave several proposals for changing the situation in the future. The development proposals could be categories based on the current definition of digital transformation, i.e. some proposals were society level whereas others where either organizational or individual level. The respondents stated that we should approach the inequality questions to change the same procedures at the workplaces, such as making the recruiting more transparent and providing support in the identity building. In the context of education, the respondents stated that the students should get teaching in both the technical and social skills. Based on this paper and the alumni survey results our university should still continue the activities that connect the work-life and the university as this was seen as a good way for fighting inequalities.

Our alumni research reveals that our graduates have both faced and recognized gender inequality in the work-life and they are willing to change it. These findings are important as high equality and free education in the society do not guarantee gender equality in the ICT field. Digitalization is the most powerful weapon which we can use to change the world and to create a new kind of future. No society, nowhere in the world, does afford to create the digital future under the gender bias, which today is an undesirable situation globally.

To summarise, with this study we are:

1. Illuminating the extent of male domination in the ICT workforce
2. Calling for recruitment to be transparent
3. Calling for support in identity building and
4. Highlighting the need for students to attain both technical and social skills.

References

1. Nelson Mandela speech at the Madison Park High School in Roxbury, Boston, 23 June 1990, 9.21/14.47. https://www.youtube.com/watch?v=b66c6OkMZGw
2. Dickinson, K.: How does Finland's top-ranking education system work? (2019). https://bigthink.com/politics-current-affairs/how-finlands-education-system-works
3. PISA: What is PISA? (2019). http://www.oecd.org/pisa/
4. Reis, J., Amorim, M., Melão, N., Matos, P.: Digital transformation: a literature review and guidelines for future research. In: Rocha, Á., Adeli, H., Reis, L.P., Costanzo, S. (eds.) WorldCIST 2018. AISC, vol. 745, pp. 411–421. Springer, Cham (2018). https://doi.org/10.1007/978-3-319-77703-0_41
5. Becking, S.K., Grady, M.L.: Contemporary Issues in Educational Leadership, 1:5 (2019). http://digitalcommons.unl.edu/ciel/. https://doi.org/10.32873/unl.dc.ciel.1011. ISSN 2472-9744
6. Van Deursen, A., van Dijk, J.: Toward a multifaceted model of internet access for understanding digital divides: an empirical investigation. Inf. Soc. **3**, 379–391 (2015)
7. OECD: Bridging the digital gender divide (2018). http://www.oecd.org/internet/bridging-the-digital-gender-divide.pdf
8. Taylor, L.: As technology advances, women are left behind in digital divide, Reuters, Big Story 10 (2018). https://www.reuters.com/article/us-britain-women-digital/as-technology-advances-women-are-left-behind-in-digital-divide-idUSKBN1K02NT
9. OECD: The ABC of Gender Equality in Education: Aptitude, Behaviour, Confidence, PISA. OECD Publishing (2015). http://dx.doi.org/10.1787/9789264229945-en
10. Mariscal, J., Mayne, G., Aneja, U., Sorgner, A.: Bridging the gender digital gap. Econ. Open-Access Open-Assess. E-J. **13**(2019-9), 1–12 (2019). https://doi.org/10.5018/economics-ejournal.ja.2019-9
11. Koskivaara, E.: Finnish paradox of IS graduates. In: Proceedings of 25th American Conference of Information Systems (2019). ISBN 978-0-9966831-8-0
12. Stoet, G., Geary, D.C.: The gender-equality paradox in science, technology, engineering, and mathematics education. Psychol. Sci. **29**(4), 581–593 (2018)
13. Aho, A.M., Sinclair, J.: Co-creation workshops for work life oriented ICT education. In: Uden, L., Liberona, D., Sanchez, G., Rodríguez-González, S. (eds.) LTEC 2019. CCIS, vol. 1011, pp. 302–312. Springer, Cham (2019). https://doi.org/10.1007/978-3-030-20798-4_26

Information Systems for Governance

An Ordinance-Tweet Mining App to Disseminate Urban Policy Knowledge for Smart Governance

Christina Varghese[1], Aparna S. Varde[1,3(✉)], and Xu Du[2,3]

[1] Department of Computer Science,
Montclair State University, Montclair, NJ, USA
{varghesec1, vardea}@montclair.edu
[2] Department of Earth and Environmental Science,
Montclair State University, Montclair, NJ, USA
dux3@montclair.edu
[3] Environmental Science and Management PhD Program,
Montclair State University, Montclair, NJ, USA

Abstract. This paper focuses on how populations by the use of technology, more specifically an app, can comprehend the enactment of ordinances (local laws) in an urban area along with their public reactions expressed as tweets. Furthermore, they can understand how well the area is developing and enhancing as a Smart City. The main goal of this research is to develop an Ordinance-Tweet Mining App that disseminates the results of analyzing ordinances and tweets about them, especially related to Smart City Characteristics such as Smart Environment, Smart Mobility etc. This app would be beneficial to various users such as environmental scientists, policy makers, city committees as well as the common public in becoming more aware of legislative bodies, and possibly contributing in different aspects to make the urban area improve as a Smart City. This work fits the realm of Smart Governance due to transparency via public involvement.

Keywords: App development · Human Computer Interaction (HCI) · Legislative information · Opinion mining · Twitter data · Smart cities · Urban policy

1 Introduction

The paradigm of Smart Governance leverages transparency through public inclusion. This is gaining impetus with Smart Cities [1, 2]. It is thus important to disseminate knowledge on urban policy to the public. Ordinances (local laws) are often publicly available, e.g. [3], yet many residents view them as impervious due to complex legalese. Thus, ordinances need mining to discover knowledge that a wide spectrum of users can comprehend. A related aspect is public opinion on social media. It is important to gauge public reactions on issues related to ordinances by opinion mining. The results of mining ordinances and their public reactions need dissemination to be easily accessible and understandable. This is the focus of our overall research [4, 5].

© IFIP International Federation for Information Processing 2020
Published by Springer Nature Switzerland AG 2020
M. Hattingh et al. (Eds.): I3E 2020, LNCS 12067, pp. 389–401, 2020.
https://doi.org/10.1007/978-3-030-45002-1_34

We address ordinances from publicly available sites, and reactions to them expressed on Twitter. We conduct mining on these to discover knowledge on how well the ordinances enhance the given area into a Smart City, and to what extent the public is satisfied with the ordinances.

We conduct such ordinance and tweet mining, guided by commonsense knowledge (CSK) [6] to capture subtle human reasoning. We use CSK sources, along with the well-known word2vec [7] for ordinance-tweet mapping, and with sentiment polarity classification for mining. Based on this, we develop an Ordinance-Tweet Mining App, to disseminate the analysis. In this paper, we describe the app development using principles from HCI (Human Computer Interaction), e.g. [8, 9]. We explain the mining of ordinances and tweets leading to useful legislative information disseminated by the app. This app provides QA (Question Answering) on interesting issues in urban policy. It is user-friendly, including interactive graphs and FAQs (Frequently Asked Questions) that facilitate comprehension by the public and experts. Targeted users, including the common public and domain experts in environmental management evaluate this app. In this paper, we focus on disseminating the results of mining NYC ordinances available on its public legislative council website [3]. We collect tweets from NYC through location-based data available on Twitter. We consider NYC since it is the financial capital of the USA, one of the major metropolitan cities in the world and a leading Smart City (see Fig. 1) [3, 10]. As per world rankings, NYC is among the top 25 smart cities worldwide [11]. This is a good achievement. Yet there is scope for enhancement. We address this in the mining of ordinances and tweets, and in the corresponding app.

We present the development and experimentation of our Ordinance-Tweet Mining App herewith. To the best of our knowledge, ours is the first app disseminating the outcomes of ordinance-tweet mining, leveraging HCI. This app contributes to Smart Governance by making information on urban policy ubiquitous and comprehensible.

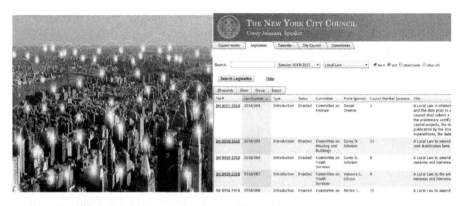

Fig. 1. NYC (New York City) as a prominent smart city [left] and NYC council website [right]

2   Overview of Ordinance and Tweet Mining

In our earlier works, we propose methods for mining of ordinances from websites [4, 12] and furthermore, the mining of public opinions about them expressed on Twitter [5, 13, 14]. We use these methods for ordinance-tweet mining within NYC and conduct evaluation as included in our papers [4, 5, 12–14]. As stated in [5, pp. 1721–1722], "an important focus in our work is to determine to what extent such ordinances contribute to establishing the relevant urban region as a Smart City. Hence, we categorize ordinances based on their pertinent Smart City Characteristics (SCCs). We aim to connect ordinances to relevant tweets by drawing on their semantic relatedness. This is non-trivial, as ordinances and tweets both involve highly intricate and rather heterogeneous natural language, so simple keyword matching does not suffice. We propose a two-step approach for mapping that exploits the transitive nature of the connection between ordinances and tweets considering their relationship with SCCs. Specifically, the transitive property we invoke is that: *if the ordinance relates to a given SCC and any tweet relates to the same SCC, then the ordinance bears a connection to the tweet.* This approach is proposed because classical sources of SCC data e.g., [1, 2] are finite and are restricted to a limited set of identifying features that can be relied upon for mapping. Thus, this transitive approach is more feasible than attempting to directly relate a seemingly infinite number of tweets to ordinances from various websites. As a first step, we discover connections between SCCs and ordinances using classical SCC sources [2] guided by commonsense knowledge (CSK) from web-based repositories [15, 16]. In the second step, we consider the mapping of tweets to SCCs, again drawing on such CSK. This approach then enables us to directly relate ordinances and the tweets to the pertinent aspects of Smart Cities and also sets the stage for sentiment polarity classification" [5, pp. 1721–1722]. Based on this, our mapping algorithm is Algorithm 1, as presented herewith [5].

ALGORITHM 1: ORDINANCE-TWEET–SCC MAPPING
1. **for each** SCC S_i **do:**
2.   build domain KB K_i
3. $A \leftarrow \emptyset$
4. **for each** ordinance O_i **do:**
5.   **for each** SCC S_j **do:**
6. $L_{i,j} \leftarrow \sum_{x \in K_j} C(O_i, x)$
7. $A \leftarrow A \cup \{(O_i, S_j) \mid j = \mathrm{argmax}_j L_{i,j}\}$
8. **for each** tweet T_i **do:**
9.   **for each** SCC S_j **do:**
10. $M_{i,j} \leftarrow \sum_{x \in K_j} C(T_i, x)$
11. $A \leftarrow A \cup \{(T_i, S_j) \mid j = \mathrm{argmax}_j L_{i,j}\}$
12. $\theta \leftarrow \{(O_i, T_k) \mid \exists S_j : (O_i, S_j) \in A \wedge (T_k, S_j) \in A\}$
13. **return** θ

(Source: [5])

As stated in [13, pp. 841–842], "we conduct sentiment analysis to discover knowledge specifically with respect to opinion mining of tweets on ordinances. This is conducted after the mapping of ordinances to tweets. The primary database used for

Sentiment Analysis in this work is SentiWordNet [17]. This is an enhanced version of the CSK source WordNet [15]. It groups words into synonym sets (synsets) annotated by how positive the terms are. Accordingly, words are classified as positive, negative or neutral based on polarity of terms. In SentiWordNet, different meanings exhibited by the same word can have different sentiment scores. For example, the word *estimable* when relating to computation has a neutral score of 0.0, while the same word in the sense of *deserving respect* is assigned a positive score of 0.75. The process we deploy for sentiment analysis of tweets constitutes a semi-supervised learning method using SentiWordNet. Through this, subtle human judgment through commonsense in understanding emotions is embodied in the mining processes with specific reference to context" [13, pp. 841–842]. Accordingly, our algorithm for polarity classification of tweets is Algorithm 2 as presented next [13].

ALGORITHM 2: TWEET POLARITY CLASSIFICATION

1. **for each** tweet t_i **do:**
2.   **if not** (t_1 relevant according to SCC KB):
3.   **continue** (with next tweet)
4.   map t_i to ordinances using Algorithm 1
5. $W_i \leftarrow$ set of words in t_i
6.   **for each** $w \in W_i$ **do:**
7. $s_w \leftarrow$ polarity score of w in SentiWordNet
8. $s_i \leftarrow \sum_{w \in W_i} s_w$
9. **return** final polarity scores s_i for relevant t_i

(Source: [13])

As further stated in [13, pp. 841–842], "based on this algorithm, we classify thousands of tweets that we obtain from Twitter. Note that the selection of relevant tweets and also the mapping of tweets to their respective ordinances is guided by CSK. We construct SCC-based Domain KBs (Domain-Specific Knowledge Bases) [5, 13, 14] derived from WebChild [16] and WordNet [15], to filter out unwanted tweets as a first step, followed by the mapping of tweets to relevant ordinances using SCCs as a next step" [13, pp. 841–842]. We start mapping groups of ordinances to tweets [5, 13], and then connect them with each other at finer levels of granularity [14] by mapping individual ordinances to tweets. This is via ordinance KBs in addition to SCC KBs, incorporating pragmatics and semantics through CSK and domain knowledge respectively [14]. The mining in our work is on ordinances and tweets from NYC, using a public council site [3] and Twitter location-based data. The results of the SCC-based ordinance analysis and tweet polarity classification comprise significant inputs for building the Ordinance-Tweet Mining App. We now describe its design process.

3   Approach for App Design

With the advancement in technology over the years, we are now benefiting from the "The Digital Age" which gave rise to the Internet and various mobile devices. This has digitized many institutions over the past few decades with governments processing applications via e-government websites that help people process their applications faster and avoid long wait periods. Retail stores today have e-commerce websites that help them reach a global audience. This progress has evolved the manner in which we do business on a higher scale. New technologies emerging in AI will help improve urban policies significantly [18], especially with respect to outreach initiatives. Users today often wish to have ubiquitous access to information. This leads to the development of apps. Accordingly, in the realm of e-government, an app for disseminating the results of ordinance-tweet mining is useful.

Based on this background and the overview of our ordinance and tweet mining research, we explain our proposed approach to design an Ordinance-Tweet Mining App. We comprehensively use principles from Human Computer Interaction (HCI) [8, 9, 19, 20] to create a user experience that would be all encompassing for various users. An important concept in HCI is *Fitt's Law* [9, pp. 518–519], i.e., "$T = k \ log_2$ *(D/S + 1.0) where T = time to move the pointer to a target, D = distance between the pointer and the target, S = size of the target, k is a constant of approximately* 200 ms/bit". We incorporate Fitt's Law in our app design. Thus, we design items in the app such that they are big enough to enable users to spot them fast, especially as navigation proceeds further from the opening screen. Yet, these items are small enough to fit on the required screens, and hence users do not need to spend much time while searching.

For the layout of the app, we use another HCI concept, i.e. "mockup designs". Mockups are multiple designs created by interviews with "stakeholders" that give an overview of the blueprint of the app [8]. Stakeholders in HCI terminology are various influential groups such as domain experts who have a thorough knowledge of the field; students/working professionals involved in providing data; and end-users ranging from novice to expert, and casual to frequent [8]. Among the mockups, we select the best designs for the app layout and screens. Other HCI aspects we incorporate are the simplicity and efficiency of the interface [20]. These include navigation, the time spent to find an answer to a question asked by the user, and the analytical graphs displayed. Considering HCI, some principles used in the app adhere to the guidelines of Google's material design [19] to ensure that the app is up to date with the current and latest software, and to warrant that the app runs smoothly without errors or bugs. Another HCI aspect is a "metaphor" [9]. The term metaphor refers to conceptualization of actions, typically for the interface. For example, a shopping cart is an interface metaphor used for checkout in online shopping. We incorporate metaphors in our app for various purposes, e.g. to depict different ordinance departments and smart city characteristics.

Good design of this app entails navigating pages without spending too much time on locating the options that the users need [20]. Based on HCI principles, Fig. 2 illustrates the navigation of the app in an efficient manner to access the given information. For details, please see [21]. This navigation keeps the users engaged and alert. Another important factor is the specific usage to assess the emotions of users while navigating the app and seeing the results. In order to incorporate this, we make sure that the intermediate pages and end-results focus on inclusion and interactive design elements [19].

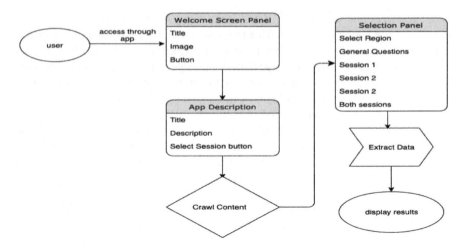

Fig. 2. App navigation flowchart

4 Implementation of the App

For the implementation of the Ordinance-Tweet Mining App, we use Android Studio [22, 23] as the Integrated Development Environment (IDE). Android Studio provides useful features that make the actual programming of app very convenient and efficient. The IDE facilitates development and use for anyone ranging from a beginner to a full-fledged software engineer [24]. Some features of Android Studio are:

- Code Completion
- Creation of Templates
- Instant App Run
- Fast Emulator
- Smart Code Editor
- Kotlin Programming Language Support

Based on these features, we implement the Ordinance-Tweet Mining App deploying Android Studio. Figure 3 illustrates the implementation process using UML for Android Development [23] with a self-explanatory diagram. For a more detailed explanation, please see [21]. Given this implementation, Fig. 4 shows a snapshot of the app layout. The left screen in the figure serves as a landing and welcome page with a call to action button labeled "Get Started". This lets the users know that they can access the app and navigate to the desired location. The center screen gives a brief description of the app. Once the users are ready to select an option, they can click on "Select Ordinance Session". The right screen serves as an action sheet. Action sheets are helpful whenever there are multiple actions [20]. They work well on this screen, since it shows the different options for the region and the sessions that the users can select.

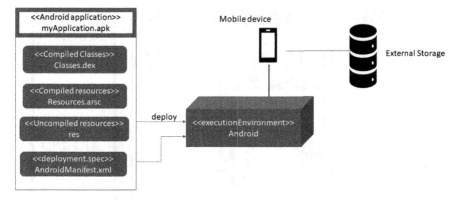

Fig. 3. Implementation process of the app using the Android platform

Figure 5 depicts the screens with FAQs and corresponding results of ordinance mining for the NYC ordinance passing sessions considered [3], i.e. Session 1 (2006–2009) and Session 2 (2010–2103). The leftmost screen includes general questions that users may have for example, "What is a smart city?" "What specific characteristics does a smart city have?" and so on. The other screens depict the outputs from the mining of the specific sessions and the combined results from mining both the sessions.

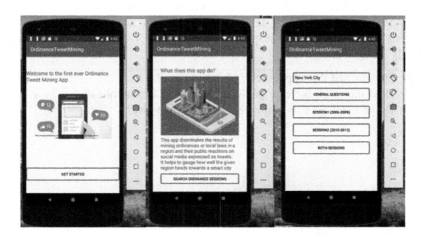

Fig. 4. Layout screens of the Ordinance-Tweet Mining App

Fig. 5. FAQs for various selection categories in the app

5   Experiments and Discussion

In order to evaluate the app, we conduct user surveys [21]. We create survey questions using a Likert Scale format [9]. We summarize the results in Figs. 6, 7 and 8. These encompass the feedback of 34 participants with an assortment of computer and environmental scientists, students, lawyers, policymakers and researchers. The main questions are as follows with responses on a scale of 1–5 [1: Strongly Agree... 5: Strongly Disagree]

- Q1: Do you find this app, quick and easy to use?
- Q2: Does this work increase public awareness of urban policy?
- Q3: Do you feel NYC is getting better as a smart city?

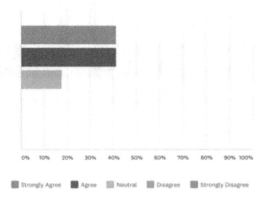

Fig. 6. Responses to Q1: "Do you find the app quick and easy to use?"

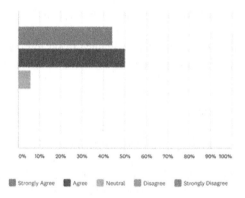

Fig. 7. Responses to Q2: "Does this work increase public awareness of urban policy?"

As seen in these figures, the user survey results indicate favorable responses towards this app. After collecting the data from the surveys, it is evident that the app is feasible for use and makes users more aware of urban policy. Many users feel that NYC is getting better as a smart city while some are neutral. In addition to the Likert scale evaluation, some comments included by the users in the survey are as follows.

- "This can be useful in courses on urban policy"
- "This app looks great – simple and informative is what New Yorkers need. I would have liked to have access to links to the researcher's published work, if available or maybe lists of smart city ordinances as a resource."
- "Very good usage of graphics, makes data easier to understand"
- "Great work you are doing. Well-done"
- "I am interested in understanding the technology behind this product"

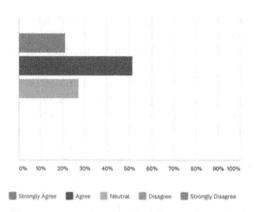

Fig. 8. Responses to Q3: "Do you feel NYC is getting better as a smart city?"

Based on these survey results and the general feedback received from the users we can infer that the work on extracting ordinance data and conducting sentiment analysis through mining of tweets have proven useful by reaching a larger audience and by disseminating information that may not have been readily available to the public earlier. Please note that our research on ordinance-tweet mining as well as the development of this app both constitute pioneering work in the area, to the best of our knowledge. Hence, we do not conduct comparative studies for the mining or the app development.

All this work is in line with the recent concept of greater awareness and more transparency in governance. Some local celebrities have played their part by influencing laws that improve society. Tim Tebow, a quarterback for NY Jets inspired South Carolina legislators to pass the Equal Access to Interscholastic Activities act in May 2012. Also known as the "Tim Tebow Law" [25], this allows homeschooled children to participate in public school extracurricular activities. Candy Lightner founded the "Mothers against Drunk Driving (MADD)" organization to ensure sterner laws against drunk driving [26]. Due to the media attention this organization received with Candy's story, it raised more awareness of driving responsibly. Likewise, our Ordinance-Tweet Mining App, the first of its kind, is likely to play an important role in making the public more aware of legislative policies and take action needed for enhancement. This concept fits the realm of Smart Governance [1, 2], a characteristic of Smart Cities that leverages greater transparency in governing processes via more public involvement.

6 Related Work

Social media users generate massive amounts of information in their daily life. Scientists consider that as valuable data for various studies on urban policy, traffic, energy conservation, climate change, disaster management etc. Social media text mining is therefore a powerful tool to extract useful knowledge.

Gu et al. [27] propose a method to use tweets for gathering road incident information. They build an API (Application Programming Interface) to compare incidents recorded on social media and in traditional databases. This not only validates existing incident information but also finds new incidents, thus supplementing the data in databases. Gandhe et al. [28] conduct sentiment analysis of data from Twitter on political scenarios, urban events etc. As stated in [28, p. 57], the "proposed approach entails a hybrid learning method for classification of tweets based on a Bayesian probabilistic method for sentence level models given partially labeled training data". The advantage is that the approach is semi-supervised, and works even with partly labeled data. Nuortimo [29] studies social media data from multiple platforms to understand public reactions for a system called Case Carbon Capture and Storage, to control carbon dioxide emissions. Results show that the overall reactions are positive. This study indicates that social media mining could be a great tool to measure public awareness and acceptance for topics related to energy and climate. Huang et al. [30] assess disaster analysis of historical and future events. They gather social media, remote sensing and Wikipedia data, performing spatial analysis and social media mining. Their results show that social media mining enhances disaster analysis and provides real-time tracking.

All these works demonstrate the potential of social media mining. Accordingly, if an app disseminates knowledge from such mining for public outreach, it would have broader impacts on sustainability and Smart Cities [1, 2, 11], especially with reference to Smart Governance [2]. It would foster building other related apps. The sharing of data via such apps would benefit pertinent research. Various useful mobile apps for Androids exist in the literature, as described in recent work [31]. Our design and development of the Ordinance-Tweet Mining App contributes to this overall realm.

Various aspects of AI can make an impact on Smart Cities as surveyed in the literature [2, 6, 18, 32–34]. AI can help record car activity, foot traffic, types of shoppers that go to different retailers, their preferences, availability of parking spots etc. These are minor details yet they make big impacts to create efficient solutions [18]. AI can contribute to autonomous and semi-autonomous driving through incorporation of CSK-based techniques for enhanced decision-making [6, 32]. AI can play a role in augmenting object detection for Smart Mobility in Smart Cities with neural models, deep learning, CSK and adversarial datasets [6, 33, 35]. Another major aspect is AI in lighting. NYC has bright lights, which imply significant energy consumption. Thus, if lamppost design occurs with sensors, these can adjust their brightness depending on the amount of traffic within the area. In some cities such as Amsterdam, canal lights dim and brighten based on pedestrian usage [2]. Likewise, AI can contribute to several aspects of Smart Cities [34]. Our work in this paper is a step in this direction, using HCI-based app design and disseminating the results of mining ordinances along with their public reactions. Hence, this paper makes an impact on Smart Governance in Smart Cities.

7   Conclusions

This paper addresses the development of an Ordinance-Tweet Mining App that disseminates knowledge discovered by mining ordinances in a given region and tweets about them, especially relevant to Smart Cities. Through this app, users from various backgrounds can obtain quick and easy access to legislative information. Via the app the public can make better decisions and contributions, e.g. by understanding policies and public reactions, they can participate city council committees, or support their region through financial means and community outreach. In addition, this app can provide decision support to lawmakers by providing ubiquitous information, and can enhance the scope of study for researchers through future issues emerging from the work here. To the best of our knowledge, ours is the first ever Ordinance-Tweet Mining App. While this app focuses on NYC in particular, it can foster the development of similar or related apps for other cities, by reuse of the approaches and data with modification.

Future work includes embedding intricate NLP (Natural Language Processing) along with semantics and pragmatics in order to facilitate direct QA (Question Answering) beyond static FAQs (Frequently Asked Questions) and keywords. This would encompass advances in the field of CSK (Commonsense Knowledge) to fathom the QA text and give enhanced responses in the app based on the mining results. This constitutes part of our ongoing research. In general, our work in this paper makes a broader impact on Smart Governance.

References

1. IEEE Smart Cities: What Makes a City Smart (2020). https://smartcities.ieee.org/
2. TU Wien: European Smart Cities, Technical Report, Vienna University of Technology, Austria, August 2015
3. The New York City Council: Legislative Research Center (2018). http://legistar.council.nyc.gov/
4. Du, X., Liporace, D., Varde, A.: Urban legislation assessment by data analytics with smart city characteristics. In: IEEE UEMCON, pp. 20–25, October 2017
5. Puri, M., Du, X., Varde, A., de Melo, G.: Mapping ordinances and tweets using smart city characteristics to aid opinion mining. In: WWW Companion, pp. 1721–1728, April 2018
6. Tandon, N., Varde, A., de Melo, G.: Commonsense knowledge in machine intelligence. ACM SIGMOD Rec. **46**(4), 49–52 (2017)
7. Mikolov, T., Sutskever, I., Chen, K., Corrado, G., Dean, J.: Distributed representations of words and phrases and their compositionality. In: NIPS, pp. 3111–3119, December 2013
8. Harper, R., Rodden, T., Rogers, Y., Sellen, A.: Being Human: Human-Computer Interaction in the Year 2020. Microsoft Research (2008)
9. Rogers, Y., Sharp, H., Preece, J.: Interaction Design: Beyond Human-Computer Interaction, 4th edn. Wiley, Hoboken (2015). ISBN 978-1-119-02075-2
10. NYC Smart City: Eventa. https://www.eventa.us/events/new-york-ny/nyc-smart-city-trek
11. The EasyPark Group: 2017 Smart Cities Index (2017). https://easyparkgroup.com/smart-cities-index
12. Du, X., Varde, A., Taylor, R.: Mining ordinance data from the web for smart city development. In: DMIN, pp. 84–90. CRSEA Press, July 2017. ISBN 1-60132-453-7
13. Puri, M., Varde, A., Du, X., de Melo, G.: Smart governance through opinion mining of public reactions on ordinances. In: IEEE ICTAI, pp. 838–845, November 2018
14. Puri, M., Varde, A., Dong, B.: Pragmatics and semantics to connect specific local laws with public reactions. In: IEEE Big Data, pp. 5433–5435, December 2019
15. Miller, G.: WordNet: a lexical database for English. Commun. ACM **38**(1), 39–41 (1995)
16. Tandon, N., de Melo, G., Suchanek, F., Weikum, G.: WebChild: harvesting and organizing commonsense knowledge from the web. In: ACM WSDM, pp. 523–532, February 2014
17. Baccianella, S., Esuli, A., Sebastiani, F.: SentiWordNet 3.0: an enhanced lexical resource for sentiment analysis and opinion mining. In: LREC, May 2010
18. Dirican, C.: The impacts of robotics and artificial intelligence on business and economics. Soc. Behav. Sci. **195**, 564–573 (2015)
19. Soni, S.: Google Material Design's Impact on Mobile App Design, February 2019. https://appinventiv.com/blog/mobile-app-designers-guide-on-material-design/
20. So, Y.: Designing for Mobile Apps: Overall Principles, Common Patterns, and Interface Guidelines, May 2012. https://medium.com/blueprint-by-intuit/native-mobile-app-design-overall-principles-and-common-patterns-26edee8ced10
21. Varghese, C., Varde, A.: Disseminating results of mining ordinances and their tweets by Android app development. Technical report, Montclair State University, December 2019
22. Android Developers: The Android Studio. https://developer.android.com/studio
23. Android Application: UML Deployment. https://www.uml-diagrams.org/android-application-uml-deployment-diagram-example.html

24. ADMEC Institute: Top 10 Features of Android, July 2018. https://www.admecindia.co.in/blog/top-10-features-android-studio-developers-not-miss
25. The Week: 7 Celebrities Who Inspired New Laws. Business Insider, September 2012. https://www.businessinsider.com/7-laws-named-for-celebrities-2012-9#tim-tebow-2
26. O'Connell, C.: 15 Ordinary People Who Changed History. Reader's Digest: https://www.rd.com/true-stories/inspiring/inspiring-stories-9-ordinary-people-who-changed-history/
27. Gu, Y., Qian, Z., Chen, F.: From Twitter to detector: real-time traffic incident detection using social media data. Transp. Res. Part C: Emerg. Technol. **67**, 321–342 (2016)
28. Gandhe, K., Varde, A., Du, X.: Sentiment analysis of Twitter data with hybrid learning for recommender applications. In: IEEE UEMCON, pp. 57–63, October 2018
29. Nuortimo, K.: Measuring public acceptance with opinion mining: the case of the energy industry with long-term coal R&D investment projects. J. Intell. Stud. Bus. **8**(2), 6–22 (2018)
30. Huang, Q., Cervone, G., Zhang, G.: A cloud-enabled automatic disaster analysis system of multi-sourced data streams: an example synthesizing social media, remote sensing and Wikipedia data. Comput. Environ. Urban Syst. **66**, 23–37 (2017)
31. Basavaraju, P., Varde, A.: Supervised learning techniques in mobile device apps for Androids. ACM SIGKDD Explor. **18**(2), 18–29 (2016)
32. Persaud, P., Varde, A., Robila, S.: Enhancing autonomous vehicles with commonsense: smart mobility in smart cities. In: IEEE ICTAI, pp. 1008–1012, November 2017
33. Pandey, A., Puri, M., Varde, A.: Object detection with neural models, deep learning and common sense to aid smart mobility. In: IEEE ICTAI, pp. 859–863, November 2018
34. Packt Publishing: Artificial Intelligence for Smart Cities. Becoming Human: AI Magazine. https://becominghuman.ai/artificial-intelligence-for-smart-cities-64e6774808f8
35. Garg, A., Tandon, N., Varde, A.: I am guessing you can't recognize this: generating adversarial images for object detection using spatial commonsense. In: AAA Conference, February 2020

A Multistakeholder-Centric Data Analytics Governance Framework for Medication Adherence and Improvement in Rural Settings

Olawande Daramola[1(✉)] and Peter Nyasulu[2]

[1] Department of Information Technology, Cape Peninsula University
of Technology, Cape Town, South Africa
daramolaj@cput.ac.za
[2] Division of Epidemiology and Biostatistics, Faculty of Medicine and Health
Sciences, Stellenbosch University, Cape Town, South Africa
pnyasulu@sun.ac.za

Abstract. Good medication adherence is directly proportional to good health recovery and general improvement of a patient's health condition. Although many good medication adherence monitoring methods/techniques exist, the level of medication adherence for some chronic diseases by patients in rural settings is still suboptimal. Hence, the need for healthcare organisations to devise viable governance frameworks that will facilitate effective medication adherence monitoring and improved adherence by patients. This paper presents the conceptual overview of a governance framework for medication adherence monitoring and improvement that enables the collaboration of multiple stakeholders and data analytics (MUCODAF) in support of the patient in the treatment journey. The framework allows relevant stakeholders such as Healthcare workers (HCW), family members, and close friends to collaborate in support of a patient through the engagement of critical human factors such as empathy, motivation, encouragement, flexibility, and negotiation. The use cases of the framework, its technical composition, and the implementation plan are discussed in this paper. A concrete example of the application of the governance framework for medication adherence monitoring and improvement for a Tuberculosis patient in the African Country of Lesotho is presented to highlight the plausibility of the framework.

Keywords: Digital healthcare · Medication adherence · Data analytics · Smart wearables · Clinical governance · Data-driven decision making

1 Introduction

Generally, patients have a higher probability of recovery from chronic ailments if they keep to agreed medication schedules as prescribed by medical practitioners [1]. An optimal level of positive adherence behaviour is difficult to attain in low resource settings and rural areas due to many socio-economic problems. So far, several adherence-monitoring technologies such as Direct Observation Therapy (DOT), Video Observation Therapy (VOT), Indirect Monitoring Technology (Patient-facilitated or

© IFIP International Federation for Information Processing 2020
Published by Springer Nature Switzerland AG 2020
M. Hattingh et al. (Eds.): I3E 2020, LNCS 12067, pp. 402–413, 2020.
https://doi.org/10.1007/978-3-030-45002-1_35

Device-facilitated), and Direct Monitoring Technology are being used to monitor adherence [2, 3]. However, these methods have not yielded maximum improvement in treatment outcomes because of the challenges of medication adherence particularly associated with older people, and persons in rural settings [4]. The socio-economic challenges of people in the rural setting ranging from poverty, illiteracy, poor infrastructure, shortage of good medical facilities, and medical experts make it difficult for healthcare organisations to effectively monitor medication adherence of patients in these settings and to motivate them for good adherence behaviour. Generally, existing methods have failed to embrace a multiple stakeholder approach that can encourage the patient towards positive adherence during the treatment journey [3]. There is also a lack of consideration for the dynamics of the everyday life of a patient, which could affect adherence behaviour. A patient is adjudged to have negative adherence behaviour if there is no consistency in the timing, dosage, and frequency of taking medication, or there is an outright disregard for the agreed medication schedule. However, irregular adherence behaviour could be due to challenges of work, home, and other circumstances that obstruct a patient's normal schedule. The existing adherence monitoring methods have failed to include critical human factors such as motivation, encouragement, negotiation, and flexibility that recognise the dynamics of everyday life of a patient into the design of their medication adherence monitoring scheme, which limits their patient-centeredness. These adherence monitoring approaches have not made adherence improvement an integral part of their design in a way that is supportive of the patient. This paper presents the conceptual overview of a governance framework for medication adherence monitoring and improvement that will enable the collaboration of multiple stakeholders and data analytics (MUCODAF) to ensure that good decisions are made by the healthcare organisations when dealing with patients with different observed levels of medication adherence.

Relative to existing adherence monitoring methods, the proposed MUCODAF is conceived to embrace a more patient-centered perspective that makes key human factors such as motivation, encouragement, negotiation, and flexibility an integral part of the medication treatment adherence monitoring process through a multiple stakeholder approach. The composition of the framework is based on the integration of cloud computing, wearable sensors, mobile technology, artificial intelligence (AI), machine learning (ML), and data analytics. The governance framework creates a basis for intelligent and data-driven decision making by allowing relevant messages to be sent to the stakeholders from time to time based on the signals received from the wearable sensor device. Also, the post-analysis report of patients' adherence behaviours can be generated weekly by the healthcare workers (HCW) in healthcare organisations, which will provide a basis to determine the right strategy to deal with individual patients based on their identified adherence behaviours.

The rest of this paper is described as follows. Section 2 provides a review of the literature on medication adherence, while Sect. 3 presents a description of the proposed framework in terms of its core use cases, and its technical composition. In Sect. 4, an example of the application of the proposed framework for tuberculosis (TB) adherence monitoring and improvement is presented. The implementation plan and imperatives for the framework are discussed in Sect. 5, while the paper is concluded in Sect. 6 with a short note.

2 Literature Review

Adherence monitoring approaches can be categorised into direct monitoring methods, and indirect monitoring methods. Direct monitoring methods involve directly observing the patient as the drug is taken or immediately by testing the body fluid of the patient in the laboratory. Indirect monitoring entails the use of technology devices for tracking activities that could signal when a patient has taken the drug or not. Many indirect adherence monitoring methods are device-facilitated by using various technologies [3, 4]. Device-facilitated measuring can be classified into various categories such as sensor-based systems, proximity-based systems, vision-based systems, and fusion-based systems [4]. The sensor-based system can be classified into three subclasses, which are smart pill containers, wearable sensors, and ingestible biosensors. The use of smart pill containers entails the detection of cap opening and bottle pick up to track adherence. Examples of these type of initiatives include Wisepills [5], Memscap [6], GlowCap [3, 7], Evrimed [8], and Amiko [9]. Wearable sensors detect motions related to cap twisting, hand-to-mouth, pouring the pill into the hand, and pill swallowing. Neck-worn sensors [10, 11], and wrist-worn sensors (in the form of smartwatches) [12–14] have been used to track medication adherence.

Also, ingestible biosensors have been used to detect pill ingestion by patients to track medication adherence [15, 16]. Currently, the use of ingestible biosensors has proved to be the most accurate, however, many patients will not find it convenient to ingest a biosensor so that they can be tracked to determine if they have taken their medication or not [3, 15, 17]. Proximity-based systems are non-invasive systems that detect medication presence or absence within the proximity of a reader's antenna by using computer vision technology. Vision-based systems detect medication presence or absence within the scope of the camera, while fusion-based systems try to verify the operation of monitoring the medication-taking activity [4]. All of these methods have been found to perform creditably well in tracking medication adherence with different levels of accuracy, but they are strictly medication adherence monitoring methods. They did not include medication adherence improvement as an integral part of their design as envisioned by our proposed framework in a way that offers support to the patient for improved adherence behaviour.

3 Description of the Proposed Framework

In this section, we present an overview of the affordances of the multistakeholder data analytics framework (MUCODAF) and the technical composition of the framework.

A governance framework for medication adherence and improvement is a system that makes a healthcare organization to be responsible, and accountable for:

- Continuously improving patients' medication adherence behaviours
- Maintaining a high level of medication adherence among patients
- Ensuring good treatment outcomes based on acceptable medication adherence behaviours.

3.1 Affordances of the Multistakeholder Collaborative Data Analytics Framework

The proposed Multistakeholder Collaborative Data Analytics Framework (MUCO-DAF) affords five core use cases that pertain to medication adherence monitoring and improvement. These are described as follows.

Digital Collaboration of Multiple Stakeholders. MUCODAF will enable the exchange of messages between a specific stakeholder (patient supporter) and a patient, and a stakeholder and an HCW via a dedicated mobile app.

Description. Relevant stakeholders that have been enrolled with the consent of the patient to participate in the adherence monitoring process can communicate with a patient directly or share information with the HCW based on their observations on the adherence behaviour of the patient. A dedicated mobile app for adherence monitoring (to be developed) will be installed on a smartphone and other mobile devices for this purpose. The mobile app will enable all stakeholders to send messages to the patient, and the HCW by using four alternative means, which are *app-to-app*, *the app to WhatsApp*, the *app to SMS, and app to email.* A patient supporter that has only a cellphone (not a smartphone) can send an SMS or make a call to the HCW on their observations of the adherence behaviour of the patient. For SMS, this can be sent via a specific code to the mobile app of the HCW. The essence of the specific code is to ensure that such SMS messages are free of charge or at a subsidized rate. Government and other donor agencies could come in to have special arrangements with telecommunication/mobile service providers to support the patients with chronic ailments and in need of critical care in this way. Disease such as Cancer, Tuberculosis, HIV, and Diabetes are prominent in developing countries where this kind of governmental and external support for patients will be useful. A stakeholder (patient supporter) may also prefer to use alternative means of communication such as email that is sent from a desktop or laptop to contact the HCW.

Medication Adherence Monitoring. MUCODAF will enable continuous acquisition of data on specific events that suggest adherent behaviour of the patient through a smartwatch and a mobile device. The information is subsequently stored in a cloud database and also transmitted to relevant stakeholders.

Description. The framework will enable medication adherence monitoring through a coordinated operation that will involve the use of an outdoor, waterproof smartwatch that is worn by the patient. The smartwatch is paired with the smartphone of the patient via Bluetooth Low Energy (BLE) connectivity to ensure that information is sent regularly to a cloud database via Wi-Fi or 2G/3G/4G data transmission. Adherence information is stored locally on the smartphone until a period when the patient has access to WiFi or mobile data when the stored information is transferred into the cloud. Medication adherence tracking with smartwatch will be done by sensing the Near Field Communication (NFC) tag on the drug casing. When the patient opens the drug box, he receives a message asking to confirm if he has taken his drug, if the reply is a yes, the event is recorded as an instance of positive adherence. A timestamped record of the event is stored on his phone for subsequent transfer to the cloud database. From the stored data, a patient supporter who is co-monitoring the adherence of the patient receives a message that the patient has taken his drug for that day. At the end of the week, the patient supporters (stakeholder, HCW, etc.) also get an adherence activity report via the mobile app/email/WhatsApp on the level of adherence of the patient in terms of compliance with the prescribed/agreed medication schedule for that week. Negotiation comes in when a patient requests an adjustment to a previously agreed schedule due to changes in his daily activities which may affect his adherence to an existing schedule. A patient can request adjustment of an existing medication schedule by sending a message to the HCW from the mobile app. Once a negotiated and revised schedule has been approved for the patient, it then becomes the basis for monitoring the patient's adherence by all stakeholders. A cloud-based central coordinating service ensures that information on a patient's adherence is sent through various channels such as SMS, WhatsApp, or email depending on the preferred mode of communication of a patient supporter. The patient supporter will use the available information on the adherence behaviour of a patient to determine how best to support the patient by way of encouragement, advice, or commendation to improve the level of adherence. The patient supporter is also able to contact the HCW when it is deemed necessary.

Data-Driven Decision Making. MUCODAF will facilitate a decision support system for HCW via the Mobile App based on the analysis of medication adherence data. By engaging data analytics services through Machine learning, and intelligent recommendations, the HCW can make informed decisions on the treatment of a patient.

Description. The framework will support various AI-based, and data analytics services such as predictive analytics, descriptive analytics, diagnostic analytics, and prescriptive analytics based on the data that have been acquired over time. These operations will mostly be executed using the backend resources of the framework, but the user will access the results/reports of the analytic services from their mobile apps. By using machine learning and statistical learning algorithms, periodic reports can be generated on a patient's adherence behaviour on a weekly and monthly basis. The report of these analyses will be accessible by HCW via an interface of the adherence monitoring mobile app. It will be possible for an HCW (Doctor, nurse) to obtain reports on adherence of a specific patient, or group of patients or run specific queries based on an issue of interest. Reports on specific patient groups/categories and selected demographics can also be generated from the framework on a monthly, quarterly, bi-annually or yearly basis for decision making at higher levels of healthcare management, and policy formulation.

Personalised Treatment Strategy. MUCODAF will foster decision support for HCW through intelligence recommendations. It will ensure a review of the patient's treatment regimen by HCW.

Description. The intelligent analysis of medication adherence data through various analytics methods will make it possible for the HCW (Doctor, Nurse) to devise the most appropriate way to engage with a patient to ensure a good treatment outcome. This may include scheduling counselling sessions for patients that are found to be non-adherent, and individual follow-up sessions in some cases to ensure improvement in a patient's adherence behaviour. It will also be possible to receive intelligent recommendations as a form of decision support on the course of action to deal with a patient based on the report of the adherence behaviour and the state of his health after clinical examination.

Adherence Behaviour Data Archiving and Curation. MUCODAF will allow automated processing of data in a way that ensures archiving and curation of data into relevant categories and classes for reuse.

Description. The framework will enable data on adherence behaviour that has been collected over time to be categorized and allotted to various classes and clusters. This will aid data retrieval and data reuse particularly for planning and policy formulation by healthcare organizations, and the national government.

The technical composition of the MUCODAF comprising a smartphone, smart-watch, Bluetooth (BLE), and IoT Hub is shown in Fig. 1, while the mapping of the use cases to specific actors in terms of the initiator of an action, the receiver/beneficiaries of such a use case, is shown in Table 1. The BLE ensures that there is a continuous connection between the smartwatch, and the patient's mobile devices as long as both devices are on. The only concern is the need to ensure that the devices are charged regularly. Recent advancement in technology ensures that wearable devices are now able to work for longer periods before it is necessary to recharge their batteries. This explains why an increasing number of medication adherence methods are based on the wearable technologies that use sensors [3, 4].

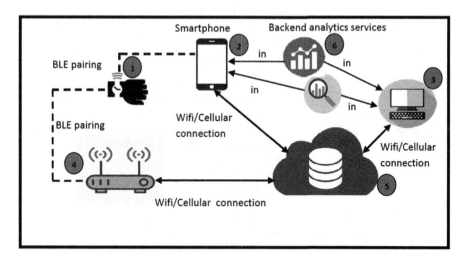

Fig. 1. An overview of the composition of the MUCODAF for improved medication adherence

3.2   Potential for Generalization of the MUCODAF

The selected use cases that are presented are not exhaustive, but those considered as basic to ascertain the plausibility of the proposed MUCODAF framework. It is quite possible that additional valid use cases that pertain to medication adherence and

Table 1. Use case mapping of affordances to specific actors

S/n	Affordance	Description
1	Digital collaboration of multiple stakeholders	**Receiver/Beneficiary** *Patient: motivation, encouragement, negotiation, flexibility* *HCW: timely update on the patient's progress*
2	Medication adherence monitoring	**Initiator** *Patient: initiates action* *Wearable device: smartwatch* *Mobile device: smartphone, cellphone* *Software: cloud-based Adherence monitoring service* **Receiver/Beneficiary** *Stakeholders: HCW, friends, family member(s): timely update on patient's medication adherence*
3	Data-driven decision making	**Initiator** *HCW*: takes decision-based on analysis of gathered data, and observed patterns *Health Sector*: take decisions based on generally observed patterns on adherence behaviour for various patients *Government*: make plans and policies regionally, and nationally **Receiver/Beneficiary** *Patients: improved healthcare* *HCW (Doctors, Nurses, etc.): decision support for improved service delivery* *Health Sector: data for improvement of healthcare services* *Government: data for planning and development* *Society: a healthier society, improved healthcare*
4	Personalised treatment strategy	**Initiator** *HCW: devise person-specific methods and strategies to help a patient based on the observed adherence behaviour* **Receiver/Beneficiary** *Patient: receives the right attention and care that is necessary* *HCW: improved success rate in healthcare*
5	Adherence behaviour data archiving and curation	**Initiator** *MUCODAF*: an automated process of storing relevant data for future use **Receiver/Beneficiary** *Health Sector*: data-driven process improvement in the healthcare sector *Government*: data stored will be used for policy development. Statistics

improvement be can yet be identified in the circumstances of an actual implementation. Therefore, the design of the MUCODAF should be based on a modular architecture that will ensure that additional use cases other than the basic ones highlighted in Sect. 3.1 can be catered for. Thus, with the choice of a modular design, it will be possible to adapt the MUCODAF to suit different contexts on the issue of medication adherence and adherence improvement.

4 Tuberculosis (TB) Medication Adherence with MUCODAF

In this section, we demonstrate by using textual narratives how MUCODAF can be applied to the case of a Tuberculosis (TB) patient under care in need of adherence monitoring. The narrative provided embraces key aspects of the 5 main use cases of MUCODAF.

4.1 Background of the TB Patient in Lesotho

As extracted from [18], Mr. T is a chronic TB patient (age - 45 years old) that works in a major mine in Lesotho. He lives with his wife and four children in a mining community/township that is called Botha Bothe in Lesotho. Mr. T has been enrolled for TB treatment for six months in the local hospital in Botha Bothe and he is expected to take his medication twice a day at 6 h interval. Mr. T has agreed with the healthcare worker that he will take his drug at 7 am every morning and at 1 pm during the lunch break while at work, and maintain the same schedule on non-work days. The medication schedule was agreed with the healthcare worker in the presence of the wife of Mr. T (Mrs. T) and Joe, who is a close friend and associate of Mr. T at work. Mrs. T and Joe have been enrolled as co-monitors and patient supporters to aid Mr. T in the aspect of adherence to the agreed schedule. A challenge with Mr. T is that lunch breaks at work do vary at times depending on the work schedule. For example, there are times when Mr. T and his colleagues need to spend longer periods in the mine, which would require that lunchtime be postponed until a later time.

4.2 Scenario Description of MUCODAF at Work

To apply the MUCODAF, there must be a centralized cloud-based coordination service that runs 24/7. The coordination service should be able to send messages to a patient through a wearable device (smartwatch, smartphone) when it is required, and periodically to all the patient supporters (stakeholders). With this in place, the following scenario can then be realized [18]:

1. The smartwatch device alerts Mr. T 15 min to the time when his drug is due to be taken.
2. At the specified time, the smartwatch starts to make an alarm sound.
3. The smartwatch tracks the medication adherence event by sensing the NFC (Near Field Communication) tag on the drug casing and prompts Mr. T if indeed he has taken his drug.

4. If Mr. T answers in the affirmative, then data consisting of the time when the drug was taken, location, date, and a score that is indicative of a positive adherence behaviour of Mr. T ("Yes" – positive; "No" - negative) is stored in the cloud database. If there is internet connectivity the data is sent directly to the cloud through the local IoT hub. If there is no connectivity, the data is stored temporarily on Mr. T's smartphone, and sent subsequently to the cloud (this is because the patient's smartphone that has been paired with the wearable smartwatch via BLE).

5. A reminder message is sent to Mr. T. via his smartphone and smartwatch every 10 min within 30 min from when he is supposed to have taken his medication to motivate him to take his medication according to the current medication schedule. If a message of positive adherence is not received 45 min after the expected time, then a conclusion of nonadherence is made by the system.

6. A daily report that conveys the adherence behaviour of Mr. T (positive/negative) is sent to Mrs. T, Joe, and HCW. The HCW receives a more detailed report that shows the specific time, date, and place when the drug was taken, and times when medications were missed.

7. Mr. T. is allowed to change the time of his medication (possibly due to work-related, family, emergency, ad hoc events), once a week through the negotiation module of the mobile app. Once a new medication schedule has been selected, this communicated to all stakeholders. The newly negotiated schedule then becomes active from that point forward as the new treatment adherence plan that will be monitored by stakeholders.

8. After a new negotiated treatment plan has been selected by Mr. T., it is then used subsequently by the cloud-based coordination service to send messages to the smartwatch and the smartphone of Mr. T, and other stakeholders.

9. The suite of cloud-based data analytics services that can be accessed from the dedicated mobile app for adherence monitoring is used by the HCW to generate a report on the adherence behaviour of a patient periodically, which could lead to a personalised and differentiated engagement with a TB patient to improve his adherence behaviour.

10. All stakeholders can exchange messages or chat on issues that pertain to the TB patient to which they are affiliated via the mobile app, WhatsApp or email.

5   Implementation Plan for MUCODAF

To ascertain the viability of the MUCODAF, it is essential to demonstrate its application in a real study context. In this section, we discuss the imperatives for the concrete implementation of MUCODAF. This will involve several aspects such as recruitment of participants, selection of the study cites, system development, and training of the participants. These salient aspects are discussed below.

Setting. To assess the plausibility of our proposed approach, a study site called Botha Bothe in Lesotho has been selected. The consent of a local hospital has been secured, while ethical clearance received from the Department of Health in Lesotho, and the two universities that are involved in the research (the university affiliations of the authors of this paper). A cohort study involving a few patients would be undertaken in the first instance (there is a plan to 20–40 patients), which would later be scaled up with more subject when more funding is received. Each of the patients will be provided with a smartwatch, and a smartphone, while a specific patient supporter will also be assisted with appropriate technology devices that would make it possible for them to play their co-monitoring role effectively.

System Development. A mobile app that is dedicated to adherence monitoring shall be provided for the study. The key features of the mobile app will include capability to enable patients, and patient supporters' participant to send messages to the HCW, HCW being able to send messages to relevant persons, HCW receiving intelligent recommendations, and being able to view data analytics results (predictive, prescriptive, diagnostic, descriptive) for decision making. An overview of the key features of the mobile app is shown in Fig. 2.

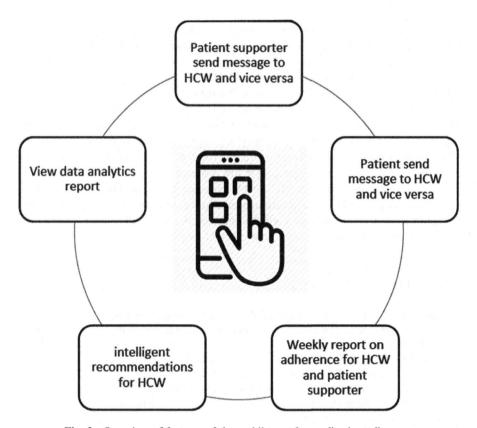

Fig. 2. Overview of features of the mobile app for medication adherence

Training Participants. All participants in the proposed study have to be trained on the use of medication adherence monitoring mobile app, and the smartwatch and smartphone. This is particularly important because the subjects in the study would mostly the less educated persons that not technically savvy. This makes it necessary to conduct orientation and training sessions for them. The training will include all HCWs, patients, and patient supporter that have been selected to participate in the cohort study.

Support of Government and Relevant of Donor Agencies. The conceptualization of the MUCODAF is meant to elicit the support of relevant government agencies and donors who are committed to improved healthcare of the less privileged people. The practicality of MUCODAF for improving medication adherence will require that a patient be supported by providing smartwatches, and smartphones for them. Donor agencies may also need to offer free internet/mobile data packages for a patient and the patient supporters that have been enrolled to co-monitor adherence of a patient at least for the period when the patient is under medication.

6   Conclusion

In this paper, we have presented the concept of a multistakeholder collaborative data analytics framework for improved medication adherence (MUCODAF). In contrast to existing medication adherence monitoring approaches, most of which focus mainly on adherence tracking and measurement, MUCODAF seeks to integrate both medication adherence and adherence improvement of the patient. To achieve this, the notion of multiple stakeholder collaboration that is driven by sensor-based adherence tracking and data analytics was introduced to support the patient in the treatment journey. Although MUCODAF is still at the conceptual stage, the imperatives for its implementation were also discussed, as well as the plausibility of its adoption for medication adherence monitoring and improvement in low resource settings. Our immediate plan is to commence the execution of the MUCODAF based on the research fund that is currently available to us. Thereafter, an evaluation in terms of the usability of the framework from the perspective of the participants will be undertaken, and its effectiveness to monitor medication adherence and endanger improvement medication adherence.

References

1. Alipanah, N., et al.: Adherence interventions and outcomes of tuberculosis treatment: a systematic review and meta-analysis of trials and observational studies. PLoS Med. **15**(7), e1002595 (2018)
2. UNAIDS. UNAIDS Global Report 2016. www.unaids.org/sites/default/files/media_asset/global-AIDS-update-2016_en.pdf. Accessed 29 Feb 2019
3. DiStefano, M., Schmidt, H.: mHealth for tuberculosis treatment adherence: a framework to guide ethical planning, implementation, and evaluation. Glob. Health: Sci. Pract. **4**(2), 211–221 (2016)
4. Aldeer, M., Javanmard, M., Martin, R.: A review of medication adherence monitoring technologies. Appl. Syst. Innov. **1**(2), 14 (2018)
5. Haberer, J., et al.: Real-time adherence monitoring of antiretroviral therapy among HIV-infected adults and children in rural Uganda. AIDS (London, England) **27**(13), 2166–2168 (2013)

6. Byerly, M., et al.: A comparison of electronic monitoring vs. clinician rating of antipsychotic adherence in outpatients with schizophrenia. Psychiatry Res. **133**(2–3), 129–133 (2005)

7. Kalantarian, H., Alshurafa, N., Nemati, E., Le, T., Sarrafzadeh, M.: A smartwatch-based medication adherence system. In: 2015 IEEE 12th International Conference on Wearable and Implantable Body Sensor Networks (BSN), pp. 1–6. IEEE (2015)

8. Sumari-de Boer, M., et al.: Implementation and effectiveness of evriMED with short messages service (SMS) reminders and tailored feedback compared to standard care on adherence to treatment among tuberculosis patients in Kilimanjaro, Tanzania: proposal for a cluster randomized controlled trial. Trials **20**(1), 426 (2019)

9. Braido, F., Paa, F., Ponti, L., Canonica, G.: A new tool for inhalers' use and adherence monitoring: the Amiko® validation trial. Int. J. Eng. Res. Sci. **2**(10), 159–166 (2016)

10. Kalantarian, H., Alshurafa, N., Le, T., Sarrafzadeh, M.: Non-invasive detection of medication adherence using a digital smart necklace. In: Proceedings of the IEEE International Conference on Pervasive Computing and Communication Workshops (PerComWorkshops), St. Louis, MO, USA, 23–27, pp. 348–353 (2015)

11. Kalantarian, H., Alshurafa, N., Sarrafzadeh, M.: A survey of diet monitoring technology. IEEE Pervasive Comput. **16**, 57–65 (2017)

12. Putthaprasat, T., Thanapatay, D., Chinrungrueng, J., Sugino, N.: Medicine intake detection using a wearable wrist device accelerometer. In: Proceedings of the International Conference on Computer Engineering and Technology, Bangi, Malaysia, 4–5 December, vol. 40, pp. 1–5 (2012)

13. Bennett, J., Rokas, O., Chen, L.: Healthcare in the smart home: a study of past, present, and future. Sustainability **9**, 840 (2017)

14. Chen, H., Xue, M., Mei, Z., Bambang Oetomo, S., Chen, W.: A review of wearable sensor systems for monitoring body movements of neonates. Sensors **16**, 2134 (2016)

15. Hafezi, H., Robertson, T.L., Moon, G.D., Au-Yeung, K.Y., Zdeblick, M.J., Savage, G.M.: An ingestible sensor for measuring medication adherence. IEEE Trans. Biomed. Eng. **62**, 99–109 (2015)

16. Kalantar-Zadeh, K., et al.: A human pilot trial of ingestible electronic capsules capable of sensing different gases in the gut. Nat. Electron. **1**, 79–87 (2018)

17. Chai, P., Rosen, R., Boyer, E.: Ingestible biosensors for real-time medical adherence monitoring: MyTMed. In: Proceedings of the Annual Hawaii International Conference on System Sciences, vol. 2016, p. 3416 (2016)

18. Daramola, O., Nysaulu, P.: A digital collaborative framework for improved tuberculosis treatment adherence of patients in rural settings. In: 2019 Open Innovations (OI), pp. 297–303. IEEE (2019)

Experimental Application of Machine Learning on Financial Inclusion Data for Governance in Eswatini

Boluwaji A. Akinnuwesi[✉], Stephen G. Fashoto, Andile S. Metfula, and Adetutu N. Akinnuwesi

Department of Computer Science, University of Eswatini, Kwaluseni, Swaziland
moboluwaji@gmail.com

Abstract. An objectives of good governance is to increase capital base of small scale businesses (SSB) in order to encourage more investments and hence increase employment rate. Embracing good financial inclusion (FI) schemes in a country helps to ensure that entrepreneurs of SSB have access to financial services and hence meet their needs. In this paper we studied FI scheme in Kingdom of Eswatini with the view to establish the extent to which SSB have access to funds in running their businesses such that they could satisfy the target population and meet their desired goals. We got FI dataset for Eswatini for 2018 from Finscope database. Finscope 2018 dataset contains 1385 attributes with 2928 records. This study extracted attributes based on payment channel, registered/unregistered business, usage of commercial banks/insurance/mobile money and source of income for households from the Finscope database. We identified lot of missing data and hence replaced them using Mode method of preprocessing module in WEKA. We split the datasets and carried out cross validation on it. Training data is 80% of the datasets and 20% was used for testing. We carefully classified FI for selected parameters for Hhohho, Manzini, Shiselweni and Lubombo regions of Eswatini using Logistic regression with 80% for training and 10 fold cross-validation. The best 10 fold cross-validation recall rate for Manzini region using support vector machine (SVM) is 69.4% and 63.4% using logistic regression. These results show that veracity of FI dataset is weak and this is due to large number of missing data.

Keywords: Financial inclusion · Machine learning · Governance · Small scale business · Low-income earner

1 Introduction

Business is about producing, selling and buying of goods and services with the view to making money. It is an organized effort(s) of an individual or group of individuals that team up to produce and sell goods and services [1]. The ultimate goal in business is making profit, however some businesses can be for non-profit and hence operate for charitable purposes. Every business organization, small scale, medium scale or large scale, needs valuable FI. Financial inclusion particularly for small scale businesses play very import role when it comes to business governance vis-à-vis meeting the needs of

© IFIP International Federation for Information Processing 2020
Published by Springer Nature Switzerland AG 2020
M. Hattingh et al. (Eds.): I3E 2020, LNCS 12067, pp. 414–425, 2020.
https://doi.org/10.1007/978-3-030-45002-1_36

the target audience and customers [2]. Adequate understanding and proper representation of FI data paves way for good business analytics for proper decision making in business organizations [3].

Financial inclusion is the ability of business entrepreneurs to access financial products and services with the view to satisfy the need of their clients or customers [4]. It has to do with saving, making and receiving payments, transacting, receiving credit, and insurance [5]. It is needed for all business organizations especially the small scale businesses in the developing nations. The inclusion helps the small scaled companies to access credits that could be invested in their businesses. It also helps in saving of cash such that future investments or response to unforeseeable risks can be carried out [6]. Financial inclusion improves the access to insurance products and services which are critical towards addressing vulnerabilities in businesses [7]. Therefore one of the elements of good governance in any country is to have adequate FI schemes for small scale businesses with view to (1) improve production of good and services; (2) increase employment rate and vis-à-vis the standard of living of the people.

The governance of a country relies so much on data aggregated from all private organizations, agencies and government parastatals. Decision making is based on these data [8]. Data grow geometrically in different forms in terms of structure, size, semantics, varieties etc. Therefore this increases the complexity of data and hence use of traditional database management system for data management becomes a challenge. Thus big data technology evolved to help organizations and government collect, organize, represent, process, and analyse data from many sources with the view to reducing cost and time; optimizing the use of resources and developing new products; and making smart decisions [9]. Financial inclusion dataset are big datasets and they are always needed by both private and public sectors. The datasets are diverse in terms of Volume, Velocity, Variety, Variability, Veracity, Visualization, and Value (i.e. 7 V's of Big Data) [10]. Thus, in this paper, we focus on the analysis of the financial inclusion dataset for Eswatini with the view to carefully classify FI data set based on selected parameters for Hhohho, Manzini, Shiselweni and Lubombo regions of Eswatini using Logistic regression (LR) and SVM. Machine learning technique has been identified to be very useful for analysis of government-based data and hence infer relevant hidden facts from them [11].

The paper is organized as follows: Sect. 2 present the general overview of the Kingdom of Eswatini vis-à-vis financial inclusion in the context of Eswatini. Review of related works is presented Sect. 3. Methodology is presented in Sect. 4 while result is presented in Sect. 5. Conclusion is presented in Sect. 6.

2 General Overview of Financial Inclusion in the Kingdom of Eswatini (Formerly Swaziland)

Eswatini is a growing economy and it is a Southern African country with a current population of 1,154,514 which is equivalent to 0.01% of the total world population as of January 10, 2020, based on the United Nations estimates [12]. It is a landlocked country in Southern Africa with total land area of approximately 17,200 Km2 (6,641 sq. miles) [12]. The Gross Domestic Product (GDP) per capital is 3,914.02 US dollars in 2017 and in the long-term, the Swaziland GDP per capita is projected to trend around 3,955.07 USD in 2020, according to World Bank econometric models. The ease of doing business is ranked 112 as at 2017. The country is ranked as middle-income country and is committed to a free market economy and private ownership.

The governments in the African continent have realized the pivotal role that FI plays in combatting poverty and contributing to inclusive economic growth by positively impacting on the low income earners and small scale businesses. Hence reducing income inequality and expanding employment. Recent innovations in financial services for small scale business groups has made governments to know how FI could strengthen the resilience of vulnerable and marginalised populations [13]. Thus a number of countries on the African continent have begun to develop national FI strategies and spearhead key programs and initiatives to improve financial markets.

In the light of the above, the Ministry of Finance in Swaziland in 2017, published the FI strategy for the Government of Swaziland (GoS) [13]. This was based on the critical role that GoS attached for FI. The FI journey for GoS dated back to 2010 in which the government through the Ministry of Finance (MoF) established the Micro Finance Unit (MFU) to implement the International Fund for Agricultural Development (IFAD) supported Rural Finance and Enterprise Development Programme (RFEDP) with the view of facilitating access to financial services for the rural population and the micro and small scale businesses. In 2013, Ministry of Finance of GoS joined the Alliance for Financial Inclusion (AFI), which is a global movement on FI and this helps to impact directly on the welfare of people at microeconomic and household levels. It helps to reduce people's transaction costs and hence enabling them to efficiently manage risks, allocating capital for productive use and supporting the accumulation of wealth over time [13]. There are three dimensions of FI: Access, usage and quality. The comprehensive document of the GoS financial inclusion strategy is well presented in [13]. It is expected that the proposed strategy will lead to increase in reach, depth and quality of FI in Swaziland, and a sustainable financial sector that is able to increase citizen welfare, create economic growth, and hence meet national goals. It also presents the level of readiness of the government of Swaziland about financial inclusiveness. In this light few research works have been reported in the recent time on FI as it affect Swaziland.

The qualitative research reported in [14] was an exploratory study to investigate the competitive advantage and the critical success factors of Swaziland (Eswatini) financial cooperatives. Financial cooperatives are means of providing financial services to low-income earners and hence make them to be in the FI scheme of government. Financial services acquisition journey model in the context of Eswatini was proposed. The model offered an integrated representation whereby financial services are fully extended to low-income earners with the view to access funds and credit facilities and hence guarantees financial inclusiveness for them. Thus financial cooperatives are noted among the distribution channels for credit facilities. This aligns with the interest of United Nations (UN) and International Labour Organization (ILO) towards financial cooperatives as mechanism that should be utilized to promote FI within the low-income earners [15]. However the author in [15] noted the mixed views about the role of savings and credit cooperatives (SACCOs) to facilitate access to financial services for people in Swaziland. Thus it was reported in the research that more knowledge is required about role of SACCOs and development of better scheme for quick access to loan and repayment of loan by their members which are mostly low-income earners.

The authors in [16] considered micro-insurance companies as another distribution channel that could make fund and credit accessible to low-income earners in Swaziland and this further helps to ensure wider coverage for FI. Hence they proposed a framework of micro-insurance distribution and implication based on the data collected in Swaziland. Similarly Mngadi noted in the research reported in [17] the role that microfinance institutions played on entrepreneurship in Swaziland. It was recommended that microfinance institutions should focus more on developmental finance for small scale businesses and low-income earner. In [18] crop insurance was identified as another FI scheme. Though it served as a means of protecting farmers against potential losses and hence minimize risk but it was noted in Swaziland that crop insurance is not well developed and implemented due to shallow knowledge of farmers about the preference for crop insurance. Similar study was carried out by Xolile in [19] focusing on livestock insurance. In [20], investment was also identified as one of the key instruments for equitable income distribution to ensure FI but this is also not well explored in low income countries and fragile environment.

3 Related Works and Deductions

3.1 Related Works

Financial inclusion is a government scheme that is meant to enable citizens to make contribution towards the growth of a country and also make the citizen to make gain from the economic growth [21]. FI is considered as one of the significant indicator of inclusive growth in governance [22]. A number of research works have been done on financial inclusion across the continents. In [23], the authors criticized the unambitious approach that did not include FI as a sustainable goal in 2030 agenda for sustainable development in developing countries. The authors noted that FI was not included as a stand-alone goal among the several sustainable development goals (SDGs). The reasons identified for this are the: instrumentality argument, free market argument, and veil argument. The 2030 agenda was seen as a missed opportunity to focus on finding means to meeting the financial need of the global poor. This implies that in developing economies, the financial bridge between the rich and the poor keep widening as the government fail to extend good governance to the poor through the establishment of a strong financial structure that makes FI to be fully extended to the poor. Similarly in [24] positive influence of mobile micro-insurance on FI in developing countries was investigated and it was established that inclusive financing is more successful in countries that adopt and use mobile micro-insurance compared to countries where such services are not made available to the poor or low-income earners. It is inferred from this study that the use of low-cost mobile channels of micro-insurance would enable low-income earners and small scale businesses to have immediate access to micro-insurance and this contributes to financial inclusiveness. Thus governance should be extended to low-cost or rural communities by erecting good infrastructural facilities and making good policies to support establishment of micro-insurance and low-cost mobile channels in these areas. Ozili in [25] reviewed digital finance (DF) vis-à-vis FI in the context of developing and emerging economies. It was noted that the mesh of DF and FI has lots of benefits to financial services users, DF providers, government and the economy in general. This corroborates with the study reported in [24]. Célerier and Matray in [26] did a study on the effects of FI on wealth accumulation in the context of USA. The authors studied the USA interstate branching deregulation policy between 1994 and 2005 and established that expansion of the bank branches across the states helped to increase access to funds the low-income earners, hence it increase the low-income household FI. These studies presented in [22, 27] looked at empowering women through financial inclusion. The authors noted that most of the Indian women that make up 46% of the India total population are denied opportunities and rights to financial access and this made them to be financially dependent. The authors affirmed that FI is needed for the women in order to pay for micro-insurance and obtain credit from financial institutions. This helps in national development by women improving access to markets and overall empowerment data.

3.2   Deductions from Literature Review

a. We deduce from our review that a number of research works have been carried on financial inclusion with the following set of objectives: (1) Development of framework for FI implementation with view to reduce poverty; (2) Review of factors (e.g. social, political, environmental etc.) that could influence financial inclusiveness; (3) The involvement of adult in banking operations with view to having access to credit facilities; (4) Development of financial structure that make FI fully extended to the poor; (5) Government to focus more on encouraging the establishment of micro-insurance institutions.
b. We further deduced that statistical technique was applied in the data analysis with the view to affirm the financial inclusiveness of households, low-income earners and small scale entrepreneurs.
c. In addition, we found out that despite the wide range of research works done on FI across the continents, few were recorded for the Kingdom of Eswatini and these are mostly doctoral theses and masters dissertations reported in universities outside of Eswatini. These research works are mostly exploratory studies that focus mainly on the behaviour of the people (mostly low income earners and small scale entrepreneurs) towards micro-finance, micro-insurance, financial cooperatives and banks. Some also focused on the saving and investment attitude of low-income earners. None of the works access or make use of FI data set for Eswatini and no computational technique is applied in the course of data analysis.
d. We noted that none of these research works relates FI with governance and neither did the authors make use of intelligent techniques such as machine learning techniques for mining the FI data set with the view to extracting more meaningful information that could impact on the governance of the country as per financial distribution, use and proper management. Also none of the works applied data mining or machine learning technique to process the FI data set with the view to understand the data pattern, ascertain the validity and accuracy of the data set.

In view of the above deduction, we choose in this research to apply machine learning technique for proper pre-processing of FI data set with the aim to clean, validate and classify the data and relate the required attributes of the data set to the governance of the country with regards to financial management (i.e. income distribution through credit facilities and government contribution and use of the income for personal and organizational gains)

4 Methodology

4.1 Dataset Description

The FinScope dataset is made up of 2928 data objects and 1352 attributes. Table 1 presents the description of the dataset and it shows the selected attributes from the FinScope database based on the objective of this study. The FinScope dataset are categorized based on four region (HhoHho, Manzini, Lubombo and Shiselweni). All data object used in this study has numeric attributes as shown in Table 1.

4.2 Data Pre-processing

The data collected was in Microsoft Excel in CSV (comma separated variable) format. After reading the data, the missing data that occurred in the payment channel attributes as displayed in Table 1 was replaced using the Mode method. In the mode method, all the missing attributes value in numeric form is replaced by the most frequent value of the known attribute.

5 Results

5.1 Experimental Results on Logistic Regression and Support Vector Machine

This section provides a comparison of the logistic regression and support vector machine (SVM) in terms of recall, precision and correctly classified instances.

In this experiment, SPSS and WEKA (Waikato environment for knowledge Analysis) were used. SPSS was used to determine the number of missing data in the selected attributes as display in Table 1 and WEKA was employed for the machine learning techniques (logistic regression and SVM) to determine the classification accuracy. The results of the comparison are given in Tables 2, 3, 4 and 5.

From the matrix in Table 2, the correctly classified financial inclusion from the selected parameters for Hhohho region is 269, 337 is incorrectly classified in Manzini, 83 incorrectly classified in Shiselweni and 87 incorrectly classified in Lubombo. The correctly classified financial inclusion from the selected parameters for Manzini region is 563, 104 is incorrectly classified in Hhohho, 87 incorrectly classified in Shiselweni and 134 incorrectly classified in Lubombo. The correctly classified financial inclusion from the selected parameters for Shiselweni region is 137, 80 is incorrectly classified in Hhohho, 250 incorrectly classified in Manzini and 121 incorrectly classified in

Lubombo. The correctly classified financial inclusion from the selected parameters for Lubombo region is 148, 86 is incorrectly classified in Hhohho, 301 incorrectly classified in Manzini and 101 incorrectly classified in Shiselweni.

From the matrix in Table 4, the correctly classified financial inclusion from the selected parameters for Hhohho region is 289, 417 is incorrectly classified in Manzini, 52 incorrectly classified in Shiselweni and 58 incorrectly classified in Lubombo.

Table 1. Description of dataset

Variable name	Data type	Description
C13B_1	Numeric	C13b. Payment channel - Food and drink and other groceries
C13B_2	Numeric	C13b. Payment channel - Water/Electricity, paraffin, gas and other fuel
C13B_3	Numeric	C13b. Payment channel - Education (school fees, university or college fees, uniform, transport, stationery)
C13B_4	Numeric	C13b. Payment channel - Transport expenses (taxi fare, bus fare, train fare, petrol for car)
C13B_5	Numeric	C13b. Payment channel - Bond or home loan, credit card, car financing
C13B_6	Numeric	C13b. Payment channel - Communication, e.g., Airtime, cell phone contract, EPTC telephone line payments, internet payments, data
C13B_7	Numeric	C13b. Payment channel - Medical, health expenses, doctors fees, pharmacy/chemist medicines
C13B_8	Numeric	C13b. Payment channel - Rental payments and rates, levies
C13B_9	Numeric	C13b. Payment channel - Other debt repayments (e.g. clothing store accounts, hire purchase)
C13B_10	Numeric	C13b. Payment channel - Savings, investments and retirement
C13B_11	Numeric	C13b. Payment channel - Insurance and Funeral premium payments (e.g., life insurance, burial society)
C13B_12	Numeric	C13b. Payment channel - Household furnishings, equipment and routine household maintenance
C13B_13	Numeric	C13b. Payment channel - Personal spending e.g. haircuts, gym, lotto, cigarettes, alcohol, clothes
C13B_14	Numeric	C13b. Payment channel - Leisure, entertainment and miscellaneous goods and services
C13B_15	Numeric	C13b. Payment channel - Farming inputs e.g. seeds, feritiliser, equipment, chemical
C13B_16	Numeric	C13b. Payment channel - Business inputs e.g. stock, machinery or equipment
A18	Numeric	A18. Main source of income – for Head of Household
Region	Numeric	Region
E1_1	Numeric	E1. Ever used - Commercial bank
E1_2	Numeric	E1. Ever used - Mobile money operator
E1_3	Numeric	E1. Ever used - Cooperative Society
E1_4	Numeric	E1. Ever used - Insurance provider
E1_5	Numeric	E1. Ever used - Pension fund administrator
E1_6	Numeric	E1. Ever used - Microfinance institution

Table 2. Matrix on cross-validation based on logistic regression

	A = Hhohho	B = Manzini	C = Shiselweni	D = Lubombo
A = Hhohho	269	377	83	87
B = Manzini	104	563	87	134
C = Shiselweni	80	250	137	121
D = Lubombo	86	301	101	148

Table 3. Matrix on cross-validation based on SVM

	A = Hhohho	B = Manzini	C = Shiselweni	D = Lubombo
A = Hhohho	289	417	52	58
B = Manzini	116	616	74	82
C = Shiselweni	98	295	114	81
D = Lubombo	104	361	75	96

Table 4. Recall on logistic and SVM

Region	Logistic	SVM
HhoHho	0.33	0.354
Manzini	0.634	0.694
Shiselweni	0.233	0.194
Lubombo	0.233	0.151

The correctly classified financial inclusion from the selected parameters for Manzini region is 616, 116 is incorrectly classified in Hhohho, 74 incorrectly classified in Shiselweni and 82 incorrectly classified in Lubombo. The correctly classified financial inclusion from the selected parameters for Shiselweni region is 114, 98 is incorrectly classified in Hhohho, 295 incorrectly classified in Manzini and 81 incorrectly classified in Lubombo. The correctly classified financial inclusion from the selected parameters for Lubombo region is 96, 104 is incorrectly classified in Hhohho, 361 incorrectly classified in Manzini and 75 incorrectly classified in Shiselweni.

From the results on Table 5, it is the Manzini region that has a pass mark for the financial inclusion using the logistic regression and the SVM model. The SVM model outperforms the logistic regression model in terms of the recall while the logistic regression model outperforms the SVM model in term of the correctly classified instances as display in Table 5.

Table 5. Precision on logistic and SVM

Region	Logistic	SVM
HhoHho	0.499	0.476
Manzini	0.378	0.365
Shiselweni	0.336	0.362
Lubombo	0.302	0.303

From the results on Table 5, it is the HhoHho region that has the highest precision for the financial inclusion using the logistic regression and the SVM.

Table 6. Classification accuracy

	Logistic regression	SVM
Correctly classified	38.1489	38.0806

From the classification accuracy result show on Table 6 it is discovered that after the pre-processing of the replaced missing data in the financial inclusion dataset of 2018 the result is affected negatively due to large missing data in the original dataset. This is the main reason why the accuracy in the two model considered are below 40%. The classification algorithms will only be able to make an informed decision on the dataset if the accuracy is 80% and above.

5.2   Inferences

The following are our inferences based on the study carried out in this research as far as financial inclusion in the kingdom of Eswatini is concern vis-à-vis governance:

a. Statistically, after the pre-processing, it was discovered that over 80% payment was made by cash while less than 1% was through the bank. On bank usage, it was discovered that only 47.5% has used commercial bank, 66.4% used mobile money, 7.2% used cooperative society, 10% used insurance, 4.9% used pension fund and 0.9% used microfinance. Most households in local communities does not have bank account so government need to come up with a policy to encourage cashless society that will also give room for credit accessibility and use of financial institution.

b. From the classification algorithm in machine learning, the recall result in Table 3 is an indication that the government of Eswatini need to pay more attention to enhance financial inclusion in the these three regions (HhoHho, Shiselweni and Lubombo) with more attention on Lubombo.

c. It was discovered in this study that 66.7% of the household in low-income earning communities make use of mobile money for making payment then the government need to consider mobile money as part of the key indicator for financial inclusion.

d. The government also need to encourage head of household on the importance of business registration since only 3.8% registered their businesses.

e. Research in this area is few in Swaziland and this is attested to by Zikalala in [15] and Kanyangale [16].

f. Low-income earners and small scale entrepreneurs should be encouraged to bank in order to have access to credit facilities with the view to expand FI and thus have all the low-income earners included. Similar recommendation was made in [19].

g. Financial empowerment programmes are recommended to train people in various households on investment vis-à-vis financial management. Such programmes open up the credit opportunities in financial institutions (i.e. Banks, Microfinance, Micro-insurance, Financial cooperatives etc.) and how they can be accessible to low-income earners. This is similar to the recommendations stated in [28, 29].

6   Conclusion

Presently in Africa there is so much interest to promote financial inclusion based on the commitment of so many countries to financial inclusion action plan to reduce poverty and grow their economy [26, 30]. But Africa as a continent is lagging behind other continents in financial inclusion because inclusive development is left out [5, 31]. Our findings in this study show that there is still need to revamp the financial inclusion datasets on the demand-side using machine learning methods for exploring different pre-processing algorithms to eliminate the remaining outliers in the dataset to improve the classification accuracy which is yet to be looked into critically due to lack of data quality. A better classification can only be achieved when there is good quality of data. The Confusion matrix was discussed in this paper using logistic regression and SVM to classify the actual and observations (true positive, true negative, false negative and false positive) from the payment channel, registered/unregistered/licensed business, usage of commercial banks, mobile money, insurance, microfinance, cooperative society and source of income for head of household. The results show that the veracity of the financial inclusion dataset is weak and this is due to the fact that the precision and recall rate is less than 50% and 70% respectively. Therefore, it is expedient to separate the demand-side data from the supply side data from the entire dataset and also to employ different pre-processing approaches or data transformation techniques to improve the quality of the data which will automatically improve the classification accuracy. The misclassification of the features misrepresents the causes underlying financial inclusion due to the precision rate against the recall rate.

References

1. Adam, H.: Business (2019). https://www.investopedia.com/terms/b/business.asp. Accessed 11 Jan 2020
2. Färber, F., Cha, S.K., Primsch, J., Bornhövd, C., Sigg, S., Lehner, W.: SAP HANA database: data management for modern business applications. ACM SIGMOD Rec. 40(4), 45–51 (2012)
3. Choi, T.-M., Chan, H.K., Yue, X.: Recent development in big data analytics for business operations and risk management. IEEE Trans. Cybern. 47(1), 81–92 (2016)

4. Sarma, M., Pais, J.: Financial inclusion and development. J. Int. Dev. **23**(5), 613–628 (2011)
5. Demirguc-Kunt, A., Klapper, L.: Measuring financial inclusion: the Global Findex Database. The World Bank (2012)
6. Atkinson, A., Messy, F.-A.: Promoting financial inclusion through financial education: OECD/INFE evidence, policies and practice. In: OECD Working Papers on Finance, Insurance and Private Pensions, vol. 34, no. 1, pp. 1–55 (2013)
7. Demirgüç-Kunt, A., Klapper, L.: Measuring financial inclusion: explaining variation in use of financial services across and within countries. Brookings Pap. Econ. Act. **2013**(1), 279–340 (2013)
8. Provost, F., Fawcett, T.: Data science and its relationship to big data and data-driven decision making. Big Data **1**(1), 51–59 (2013)
9. SAS: "Big Data: What it is and why it matters," SAS Insight (2019). https://www.sas.com/en_us/insights/big-data/what-is-big-data.html. Accessed 11 Jan 2020
10. Oussous, A., Benjelloun, F.-Z., Lahcen, A.A., Belfkih, S.: Big data technologies: a survey. J. King Saud Univ. Comput. Inf. Sci. **30**(4), 431–448 (2018)
11. Kleinberg, J., Ludwig, J., Mullainathan, S.: A guide to solving social problems with machine learning. Harvard Business Review (2016). http://www.zeshiyang.com/images/Social%20Problems%20with%20Machine%20Learning.pdf. Accessed 10 Jan 2020
12. Worldometer: Eswatini (Swaziland) Population (2020). https://www.worldometers.info/world-population/swaziland-population/. Accessed 11 Jan 2020
13. Ministry-of-Finance: National Financial Inclusion Strategy for Swaziland 2017–2022 (2017). https://www.afi-global.org/sites/default/files/publications/2018-01/Swaziland%20National%20Financial%20Inclusion%20Strategy%202017%20-2022.pdf. Accessed 13 Jan 2020
14. Mashwama, J.: The competitive advantages of and critical success factors for financial cooperatives in Swaziland, Gordon Institute of Business Science, University of Pretoria. M. Sc. dissertation (2014)
15. Zikalala, M.J.: The role of savings and credit cooperatives in promoting access to credit in Swaziland, Agricultural Economics, Faculty of Natural and Agricultural Sciences, University of Pretoria (2016)
16. Kanyangale, M., Lukhele, M.: Pathways to the poor in Swaziland: what is the nature of micro insurance channels and distribution strategy? Afr. J. Bus. Manag. **12**(14), 439–450 (2018)
17. Mngadi, W.P.: The role of microfinance institutions on entrepreneurship development: the case of Swaziland, Law and Management, Wits Business School, Faculty of Commerce, University of the Witwatersrand, Ph.D. thesis (2016)
18. Mbonane, N.D.: An analysis of farmers' preferences for crop insurance: a case of maize farmers in Swaziland, Department of Agricultural Economics, Extension & Rural Development, Faculty of Natural and Agricultural Science, University of Pretoria, M.Sc. dissertation (2018)
19. Mamba, T.X.: The role of contracts in improving access to credit in the smallholder livestock sector of Swaziland, Agricultural Economics, Faculty of Natural and Agricultural Sciences, University of Pretoria, M.Sc. dissertation (2016)
20. Msibi, M.N.: The relationship between monetary attitudes and investment behaviour among teachers in Swaziland. School of Business, University Of Nairobi, M.Sc. dissertation (2017)
21. Kapoor, A.: Financial inclusion and the future of the Indian economy. Futures **56**(1), 35–42 (2014)
22. Subha, S., Unni, A.: Women empowerment and financial inclusion. Heritage **68**(2), 33–38 (2020)
23. Fu, J., Queralt, J., Romano, M.: Financial inclusion and the 2030 agenda for sustainable development: a missed opportunity. Enterp. Devel. Microfinan. **28**(3), 200–211 (2017)

24. Chummun, B.Z.: Mobile microinsurance and financial inclusion: the case of developing African countries, Africa growth Agenda, July/September 2017, vol. 2017, pp. 12–16 (2017)
25. Ozili, P.K.: Impact of digital finance on financial inclusion and stability. Borsa Istanbul Rev. **18**(4), 329–340 (2018)
26. Célerier, C., Matray, A.: Bank-branch supply, financial inclusion, and wealth accumulation. Rev. Finan. Stud. **32**(12), 4767–4809 (2019)
27. Chandradevi, P., Sounderya, P.P., Sudarvizhli, S.: Women empowerment and financial inclusion. Heritage **68**(2), 477–486 (2020)
28. Brixiová, Z., Kangoye, T.: Gender and constraints to entrepreneurship in Africa: new evidence from Swaziland. J. Bus. Ventur. Insights **5**(2), 1–8 (2016)
29. Brixiová, Z., Kangoye, T.: Skills as a barrier to women's start ups: a model with evidence from Eswatini. In: ERSA Working Paper 768, Economic Research Southern Africa (ERSA) (2018). https://www.researchgate.net/profile/Zuzana_Brixiova/publication/329512410_Skill s_as_a_Barrier_to_Women's_Start_Ups_A_Model_with_Evidence_from_Eswatini/links/5c 0ff03d299bf139c752152a/Skills-as-a-Barrier-to-Womens-Start-Ups-A-Model-with-Evidenc e-from-Eswatini.pdf. Accessed 25 Jan 2020
30. Ahamed, M.M., Mallick, S.K.: Is financial inclusion good for bank stability? International evidence. J. Econ. Behav. Organ. **157**(1), 403–427 (2019)
31. Dev, S.M.: Financial inclusion: issues and challenges. Econ. Polit. Wkly **41**(41), 4310–4313 (2006)

User Experience and Usability

How Quickly Can We Predict Users' Ratings on Aesthetic Evaluations of Websites? Employing Machine Learning on Eye-Tracking Data

Ilias O. Pappas[1,2](✉) 📷, Kshitij Sharma[2] 📷, Patrick Mikalef[2] 📷,
and Michail N. Giannakos[2] 📷

[1] University of Agder, 4639 Kristiansand, Norway
ilias.pappas@uia.no, ilpappas@ntnu.no
[2] Norwegian University of Science and Technology, 7491 Trondheim, Norway

Abstract. This study examines how quickly we can predict users' ratings on visual aesthetics in terms of simplicity, diversity, colorfulness, craftsmanship. To predict users' ratings, first we capture gaze behavior while looking at high, neutral, and low visually appealing websites, followed by a survey regarding user perceptions on visual aesthetics towards the same websites. We conduct an experiment with 23 experienced users in online shopping, capture gaze behavior and through employing machine learning we examine how fast we can accurately predict their ratings. The findings show that after 25 s we can predict ratings with an error rate ranging from 9% to 11% depending on which facet of visual aesthetic is examined. Furthermore, within the first 15 s we can have a good and sufficient prediction for simplicity and colorfulness, with error rates 11% and 12% respectively. For diversity and craftsmanship, 20 s are needed to get a good and sufficient prediction similar to the one from 25 s. The findings indicate that we need more than 10 s of viewing time to be able to accurately capture perceptions on visual aesthetics. The study contributes by offering new ways for designing systems that will take into account users' gaze behavior in an unobtrusive manner and will be able inform researchers and designers about their perceptions of visual aesthetics.

Keywords: Eye-tracking · Machine learning · E-commerce · Aesthetics · Design · Artificial Intelligence

1 Introduction

Website and application development have largely focused on good visual design that can support users' interaction with the website and improve their online experience. To this end, previous work has studied several website design characteristics, including their effectiveness and visual appeal [1–4]. Daily, we visit numerous websites or use their applications, and our evaluations are affected by their usability, how they look and feel, as well as their content and service quality [5]. Since website design will influence user experience, designers and the companies they work for strive to offer aesthetically

© IFIP International Federation for Information Processing 2020
Published by Springer Nature Switzerland AG 2020
M. Hattingh et al. (Eds.): I3E 2020, LNCS 12067, pp. 429–440, 2020.
https://doi.org/10.1007/978-3-030-45002-1_37

pleasing websites of high quality. The majority of the studies in the area employ subjective methods (e.g., data collection using questionnaires), while some utilize more objective approaches by collecting physiological data such as fMRI and eye-tracking [6, 7].

The advancement of technology and machine learning techniques allows the implementation of Artificial Intelligence (AI) applications in many fields, including Human Computer Interaction [8] or image aesthetics [9]. Recently, early attempts have been proposed to employ machine learning for assessing aesthetics of websites [10]. Furthermore, previous studies have assessed website aesthetics using eye-tracking techniques to detect areas of interest while looking at a website, mainly by using heatmaps [11–13]. Going beyond heatmaps, eye-tracking techniques can offer deeper insight into users' gaze behavior as they can also capture how one's eyes move during the whole period, including for example speed of eye movement, a change in direction, switching between two spots [14, 15].

Users' first impression is very important when they visit new websites, or they visit re-designed websites. Earlier studies suggest that first impressions are formed very fast when users visit at a website, in the very first seconds [16]. Thus, when taking design decisions different aspects that grab one's attention are more likely to influence their perceptions on visual aesthetics. However, as users become more experienced their perceptions regarding visual aesthetics are likely to evolve as well [15]. Indeed, eye-tracking data show that the more a user fixates on certain elements in a website the more likely it is to find it less appealing [14], which may occur if users start looking into more details as they look at the website. This raises the question if and how fast we can predict users' perceptions on visual aesthetics while they are looking at a website. Thus, we formulate the following research question: *RQ: How fast can we predict users' ratings when judging visual aesthetics in websites in terms of simplicity, diversity, colorfulness, and craftsmanship?*

To address our research question, first we measure how users' look at a website using eye-tracking along with their perceptions on visual aesthetics via a questionnaire. Then, we employ machine learning techniques to predict users' ratings from the gaze behavior and test how fast we can get an accurate prediction with a low error. We conducted an experiment in which users were asked to look at websites and then rate them in terms of simplicity, diversity, colorfulness, craftsmanship. The experiment included websites that ranged from low, neutral, and high visually appealing. We contribute by showing that when examining users' first impressions towards a website more than a few seconds are needed to get an accurate and valuable estimate on their perceptions towards the website's visual appeal. This is a first step towards designing and developing AI applications that will track users' eyes only for a specific amount of time (i.e., the time needed to get an accurate estimate) and inform designers about users' perceptions on visual aesthetics.

The paper is organized as follows. Section 2 presents the background of the study, along with related work on website visual aesthetics. Section 3 presents the details on the experiment, and the methodology that was employed. Section 4 presents the findings, and Sect. 5 provides a discussion along with implications and suggestions for future work.

2 Background and Conceptual Model

2.1 Visual Aesthetics of Websites

Previous studies examining user experience highlight several factors that may influence users' evaluations towards visual aesthetics of websites [1–3, 17]. Capturing such evaluations for websites is highly important for website designers and can be done by examining screen design factors and layout elements which are related with users' perceptions of visual aesthetics [3]. To measure perceptions on visual aesthetics studies commonly use questionnaires which introduce a subjective take on the matter. Visual aesthetics can be divided into two basic types [4]. First, there are classical aesthetics that describe websites that are clear, well organized, and pleasant. Then, there are expressive aesthetics which refer to websites that are creative, colorful, and original.

Additionally, a more precise description of visual aesthetics has been proposed which offers a measure that represents visual aesthetics in a more holistic manner [2]. In detail, this measure includes four dimensions, or facets of visual aesthetics, which are simplicity, diversity, colorfulness, and craftsmanship. Simplicity, part of the classical aesthetics, refers to website design regarding its unity, clarity, orderliness and balance. Next, diversity, part of the expressive aesthetics, refers to a website design having a dynamic, novel, and creative design. For a more holistic representation of visual aesthetics the measure was extended by adding colorfulness and craftsmanship, adopted from Lavie and Tractinsky [4]. The unique effect of colors as well as the skillful and coherent integration of all design dimensions can be evaluated [1, 2]. The present study adopts the four facets of visual aesthetics as they are considered to be more detailed by examining more aspects of aesthetics [2]. This approach enables a better and deeper understanding of perceived visual aesthetics.

2.2 Visual Aesthetics and Eye-Tracking

HCI studies that examine visual aesthetics of e-commerce websites measure users' gaze with different eye tracking techniques [11, 13], offering a better understanding of user behavior when visiting e-commerce websites. Indeed, we can collect data on where exactly the user looks when browsing a website and also how they look at it. The manner we look at an object is related with how we process and think about that object [18]. Our aesthetical preferences can be predicted with the derivatives of the stimulus properties [11, 19, 20]. Furthermore, based on the eye-mind hypothesis [18], what a user looks at indicates their cognitive process. These two notions can be simply described as *"what you perceive is what you see"* and *"what you see is what you process"*. Thus, cognitive load theory has been used to explain gaze behavior and how we process what we see [21], supporting the eye-mind hypothesis [18]. Consequently, what users perceive and what they process is also linked with their gaze.

By being able to capture measurable qualities of an object or a stimulus we can explain users' perceptions on visual aesthetics [22], thus here we employ eye-tracking techniques to examine how specific functions can be used to predict users' ratings on visual appeal. In detail, we use eye-tracking measures and compute their respective features as a proxy for users perceived visual aesthetics, to examine how looking at websites explains perceptions of visual appeal. Previous studies have employed eye-tracking techniques to predict website design characteristics and users' visual attention [11, 13, 21, 23]. Nonetheless, previous studies mainly focus on using heat maps to explain eye behavior, which although is useful to show where the user focused, but it does not provide any information on how his or her eyes moved while looking at the website and interacting with it. Here we combine information from gaze behavior and questionnaires to predict users' ratings and extend previous studies by examining how fast can we get an accurate prediction.

3   Research Methodology

3.1   Context

Building on previous work [11, 12] the homepages of some popular e-commerce sites are used to examine their visual appeal. For this, we use the top-100 popular websites, based on the ranks on Alexa.com (i.e., provider of global traffic estimates in different categories). Fifty e-commerce websites were selected randomly, and 10 HCI experts were asked to evaluate them in terms of visual appeal on a 7-point scale. Amazon websites were removed from the list as Alexa is owned by Amazon to avoid any potential bias. Based on the median score from experts' ratings, nine websites were chosen, creating 3 categories, that is high, neutral and low visually appealing, with 3 websites each. Figure 1 shows examples from each category. A key distinction among the homepages of these websites is the photo-text ration, a main design characteristic in visually appealing websites [2, 11]. Since the first impression of a webpage is formed right away, as soon as one visits it, [16], investigating users' eye-tracking behavior on those very first seconds that they look at a webpage is important and can prove beneficial in explaining how behavior relates to main factors of visual aesthetics and design.

Fig. 1. High, neutral, low appealing e-commerce websites (from left to right)

3.2 Sample and Procedure

Twenty-three users participated in this experiment (10 females, 13 males, average age 27.5 years, SD 7.15 years), with prior experience with e-commerce. Email and social media were used to find participants. We conducted the experiment at a lab space of a large university in Norway with 5 participants at a time.

We gathered information regarding age, gender, and internet experience, while we explained the objective of the study. To calibrate the eye tracker the participant watches a dot that moves to the four corners and center of the screen. The participants were instructed to look at each website for at least ten seconds. Then they were given a questionnaire which used a seven-point scale to capture their appeal ratings regarding the four facets of visual aesthetics. They viewed on average each webpage for about 25 s. Also, they were told not to base their ratings of visual appeal on the content of the page. We did not give them specific tasks because it can influence the way they look at the website and their focus [21], but they were instructed to look at the homepage freely. Participants had not purchased from the e-commerce websites before. Also, they controlled the mouse, allowing them to browse freely and decide on their own when to proceed to the next website.

3.3 Eye-Tracking Device

We used 4 SMI RED 250 and 1 TOBII mobile eye-tracker which look like glasses. They have a sampling rate of 60 Hz, that is considered appropriate in usability studies [24]. The frames of the eye-tracker contain two cameras that record each eye of the participant; and an array of infrared LEDs which are reflected by the cornea. There is a third camera that records the field of view of the participants. Then the software calculates the position of the gaze on the field of view video. Finally, we correct for head movements by employing fiducial markers placed on the computer screen.

3.4 Measurements and Feature Extraction

For the visual aesthetics, we study simplicity, diversity, colorfulness, and craftsmanship [2]. Table 1 shows the actual and theoretical limits (min, max values) for the 4 facets of visual aesthetics. Minimum and maximum values are computed based on the 7-point scale and the fact that some items are reverse coded. Their items are presented in the Appendix.

Table 1. Thresholds for visual aesthetics

Visual aesthetics	Min - Max	Theoretical Min - Max
Simplicity	2, 13	−11, 19
Diversity	−3, 11	−11, 19
Colorfulness	−4, 8	−12, 12
Craftmanship	−5, 8	−12, 12

Eye tracking data offer the mean, variance, minimum, maximum and median of several parameters, such as pupil diameters, fixation details, saccade details, blink details, and event statistics. Table 2 presents an overview of the extracted features along with the respective reference from the literature. In total, we extracted 31 features.

Table 2. Eye-tracking features

Eye-movement parameters	Features extracted	Source
Diameter	Pupil Diameter (mean, median, max, SD)	[25]
Fixation	Fixation duration (mean, median, max, SD)	[26]
	Fixation dispersion (mean, median, max, SD)	[27]
	Skewness of fixation duration histogram	[28]
Saccade	Ratio of forward saccades to total saccades	[29]
	Ratio of global and local saccades with a threshold on sac. vel.	[30]
	Skewness of saccade velocity histogram	[31]
	Saccade velocity (mean, median, max, SD)	[32]
	Saccade amplitude (mean, median, max, SD)	[33]
	Saccade duration (mean, median, max, SD)	[34]
Events	Number of fixations, number of saccades, fixation to saccade ratio	

3.5   Pipeline Formation

In this paper, we present 4 pipelines. Each pipeline has 5 steps. First, we collect the data from 4 different interaction lengths: (1) 25 s, (2) 20 s, (3) 15 s and 10 s. Next, we compute the features given in the Table 1. Once the features are computed, we use a Random Forest regression algorithm to predict the four dependent variables. Next, we compare the prediction for all 4 different interaction lengths to examine how quickly we can get an accurate estimate (Fig. 2).

Data → Pre-processing → Feature Extraction → Prediction using Random Forest Regression

Fig. 2. Pipeline formation

For each pipeline, we kept the data from 10% of the participants for the out of sample testing. We trained the random forest with the data from the remaining 90% participants using a 10-fold cross validation (Fig. 3).

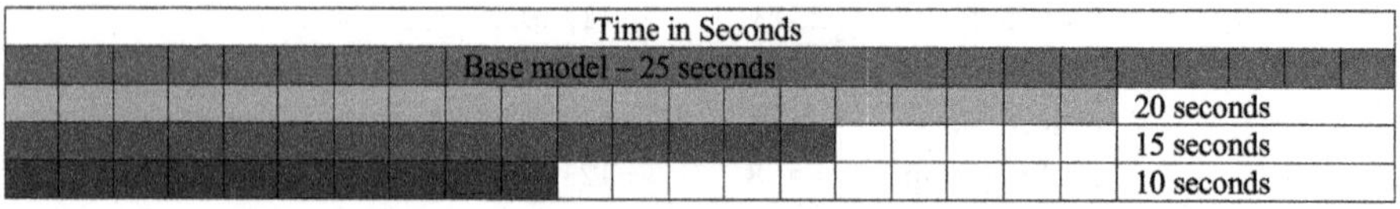

Fig. 3. Data collection for 4 interaction lengths

4 Findings

Table 3 depicts the prediction accuracy, that is the NRMSE (Normalized Root Mean Squared Error) prediction Random Forest regression algorithm by using the selected features (Table 2) for simplicity, diversity, colorfulness, and craftmanship. The NRMSE value should be as low as possible. Tables 3 and 4 show which model can give a good prediction compared to the base model (25 s) and for which model the error rate is significantly different (Table 4) from the base model.

Table 3. Prediction accuracy for the 4 interaction lengths

Duration	Simplicity NRMSE (S.D.)	Diversity NRMSE (S.D.)	Colorfulness NRMSE (S.D.)	Craftmanship NRMSE (S.D.)
25 s (base model)	0.09 (0.02)	0.09 (0.03)	0.10 (0.02)	0.11 (0.03)
20 s	0.10 (0.03)	**0.10 (0.04)**	0.11 (0.05)	**0.13 (0.05)**
15 s	**0.11 (0.05)**	0.12 (0.04)	**0.12 (0.05)**	0.14 (0.04)
10 s	0.16 (0.02)	0.15 (0.03)	0.17 (0.03)	0.16 (0.04)

Note: Normalized Root Mean Squared Error (NRMSE) prediction from Random Forest with the selected features (as presented in Table 2). In bold we show the Error is can be acceptable, compared to the base model, because it is **the one before the error being significantly different (based on T-test presented on Table 4)**

Table 4. Significant differences between the models

Duration	Simplicity	Diversity	Colorfulness	Craftmanship
25 s (base model)	–	–	–	–
20 s	1.24 (0.22)	0.89 (0.37)	0.83 (0.43)	1.53 (0.13)
15 s	1.66 (0.10)	2.67 (0.01)**	1.66 (0.10)	2.68 (.01)**
10 s	11.06 (.001)***	6.32 (0.001)***	8.68 (.001)***	4.47 (.001)***

Note: The difference of the base model with the other shorter in duration models.
*** $p < 0.001$, ** $p < 0.01$

We can observe that in the case of simplicity, the model with 25 s of data has a 9% error while the models with the 20, 15 and 10 s of data have 10%, 11% and 16% errors, respectively. The model with 10 s of data is significantly worse than the model with 25 s of data. Hence, the chosen model is the one with the smallest error that is closest to the base model (model with 25 s of data) and uses the least amount of data. For simplicity the chosen model is the one with 15 s of data.

Next, in the case of diversity, the model with 25 s of data has a 9% error while the models with the 20, 15 and 10 s of data have 10%, 12% and 15% errors. The models with 15 and 10 s of data is significantly worse than the model with 25 s of data. Thus, the chosen model is the one with the smallest error that is closest to the base model (model with 25 s of data) and uses the least amount of data. For diversity the chosen model is the one with 20 s of data.

In the case of colorfulness, the model with 25 s of data has a 9% error while the models with the 20, 15 and 10 s of data have 11%, 12% and 17% errors. The model with 10 s of data is significantly worse than the model with 25 s of data. Similarly, the chosen model is the one with the smallest error that is closest to the base model (model with 25 s of data) and uses the least amount of data. For colorfulness the chosen model is the one with 15 s of data.

Finally, regarding craftsmanship, the model with 25 s of data has a 9% error while the models with the 20, 15 and 10 s of data have 13%, 14% and 16% errors. The models with 15 and 10 s of data are significantly worse than the model with 25 s of data. Similarly, the chosen model is the one with the smallest error that is closest to the base model (model with 25 s of data) and uses the least amount of data. For crafts- manship the chosen model is the one with 20 s of data.

To offer more insight and details on what the NRMSE values show we should point out that they refer to the error on the range that our values get based on their theoretical limits (Table 1). For example, for simplicity the minimum and maximum theoretical limits are -11 and 19, respectively. Thus, the range of simplicity is 30. An 11% error on the range of 30 is basically a 3.3 deviance. Since, simplicity is calculated based on the sum of 5 items (Appendix), it means that per item, the 11% error translates to a 0.66 (i.e., 3.3/5) deviance on the Likert Scale. Thus, the accuracy of our predictions is quite high and can be deviant by approximately half point or less on the Likert scale.

5   Discussion

This study provides evidence on how quickly we can get accurate estimates of users' ratings regarding their perceptions of visual aesthetics measuring and analyzing their gaze behavior. Users perceptions are directly related to what they see, that is a visual stimulus, and the way that the stimulus changes will also influence users' perceptions. This has been described by two basic notions that are "what you perceive is what you see" [19, 20] and "what you see is what you process" [18]. This paper goes one step further from previous studies that predict users' ratings and answers the question on how quickly we can predict these ratings.

The findings show that for simplicity and colorfulness 15 s of gaze data offer a good prediction, similar to the one from 25 s of data. This means that when a user is looking at website, after 15 s they will have formed their first impression of it regarding simplicity and colorfulness and it will not change if they look at the website for up to half a minute. Furthermore, the findings show that 10 s are not sufficient to make a good enough prediction, compared to 25 s, and the error rate goes up to 16% and 17%, for simplicity and colorfulness. Previous studies suggest that our first impression is formed almost immediately [16] and users are instructed to look at websites for about 10 s in similar studies [11]. Similarly, in our study the participants were instructed to look at the websites at least for 10 s, but the findings show that by adding 5 more seconds (i.e., 15 in total) the prediction rate is similar to the prediction from 25 s.

In the case of diversity and craftmanship, the findings show that more data are needed for a good enough prediction. Thus, 20 s give a good prediction as 25 s of viewing. Similarly, to simplicity and colorfulness, 10 s are not enough to get a sufficient prediction as the error rates increase 15% and 16%, being significantly different from those with 25 s of data. We empirically show that in website aesthetic evaluation a user has to look at a website for 15 s or more depending on which facet of visual aesthetics is of interest. The fact that diversity and craftmanship need more time to be predicted (longer interaction lengths) can be explained by the fact that a more diverse website is likely to increase interest and attention of the users [2, 3], making them look for details and spend more time looking at it. Similarly, for craftmanship, users may need to look at the website more carefully, thus need more time, in order to make judgements if a website is well built and of high quality.

This study contributes both theoretically and practically. We contribute to the need of automatizing the process of capturing and explaining users' perceptions towards visual aesthetics. The use of objective data from eye-tracking combined with questionnaires can remove bias and offer more robust results. Drawing on recent discussion in HCI on how machine learning and AI can improve the field [8] as well as to be used to improve image [9] and website aesthetics [10], we offer empirical evidence on how the process of predicting users' preferences can be automated. The findings pave the way to design new systems that will take into account users' gaze behavior in an unobtrusive manner and will be able inform researchers and designers about their perceptions of visual aesthetics. An AI application or an intelligent agent may compute in real time the probability for a user to find a website high or low appealing, which in turn may be used as feedback to improve design. Furthermore, building on previous studies showing that users' gaze is related both with their perceptions and cognitive processing [18, 19], we provide empirical evidence that gaze behavior is linked to perceptions towards the same stimuli.

Managers and websites designers can benefit from our findings and use them to better understand their customers with a focus on their perceptions of visual appeal. As technology evolves, eye-tracking devices are becoming cheaper and accessible to larger audiences. At the same time, machine learning and AI have evolved at a level where we see their applications in our daily lives, and with automated machine learning (AutoML) practitioners can more easily develop such new applications. For example website retailers can use eye tracking or even users' own mobiles phones to evaluate websites [35]. By knowing how quickly we can predict users' ratings, a developer can design an application that will request to track users' eye behavior only for the first 15 or 20 s of using the application. This could serve as a middle ground, where the company will get important data to improve their application and users' data will be recorded at a minimum level, making it more likely for users to accept and share their data. This can be combined with knowledge on gaze behavior, as they can show accurately which parts of a website were more or less important (e.g., high fixation on specific areas or high saccade velocity between two areas) and how that relates to their ratings regarding aesthetics. Thus, if we can predict high ratings on simplicity then we can automatically identify which areas created this perception to the user.

The present study has some limitations. First, we measure visual aesthetics through questionnaires, thus taking a subjective approach [2]. Future studies, may combine subjective and objective methods, such as using screen design factors [1], along with eye-tracking techniques to acquire a deeper understanding of users' judgments of visual appeal. Furthermore, although the sample of the study is relatively small, the low-level data that we capture are able to offer useful insight, allowing us to quantify aesthetic qualities using eye-tracking measures [22]. Finally, to better understand the users and their online experience, complexity theory may be combined with the novel fuzzy-set qualitative comparative analysis (fsQCA) as it can offer deeper understanding of the sample by identifying asymmetric relations inside a dataset [36, 37].

Appendix

Items to measure visual aesthetics

Simplicity
The layout appears too dense (r)
The layout is easy to grasp
Everything goes together on this site
The site appears patchy (r)
The layout appears well structured
Diversity
The layout is pleasantly varied
The layout is inventive
The design appears uninspired (r)
The layout appears dynamic
The design is uninteresting (r)
Colorfulness
The color composition is attractive
The colors do not match (r)
The choice of colors is botched (r)
The colors are appealing
Craftsmanship
The layout appears professionally designed
The layout is not up-to-date (r)
The site is designed with care
The design of the site lacks a concept (r)

References

1. Seckler, M., Opwis, K., Tuch, A.N.: Linking objective design factors with subjective aesthetics: an experimental study on how structure and color of websites affect the facets of users' visual aesthetic perception. Comput. Hum. Behav. **49**, 375–389 (2015)
2. Moshagen, M., Thielsch, M.T.: Facets of visual aesthetics. Int. J. Hum. Comput. Stud. **68**, 689–709 (2010)

3. Tuch, A.N., Bargas-Avila, J.A., Opwis, K.: Symmetry and aesthetics in website design: It's a man's business. Comput. Hum. Behav. **26**, 1831–1837 (2010)

4. Lavie, T., Tractinsky, N.: Assessing dimensions of perceived visual aesthetics of web sites. Int. J. Hum. Comput. Stud. **60**, 269–298 (2004)

5. Hartmann, J., De Angeli, A., Sutcliffe, A.: Framing the user experience: information biases on website quality judgement. In: Proceedings of the SIGCHI Conference on Human Factors in Computing Systems, pp. 855–864. ACM (2008)

6. Reimann, M., Zaichkowsky, J., Neuhaus, C., Bender, T., Weber, B.: Aesthetic package design: a behavioral, neural, and psychological investigation. J. Consum. Psychol. **20**, 431–441 (2010)

7. Bhandari, U., Neben, T., Chang, K., Chua, W.Y.: Effects of interface design factors on affective responses and quality evaluations in mobile applications. Comput. Hum. Behav. **72**, 525–534 (2017)

8. Inkpen, K., Chancellor, S., De Choudhury, M., Veale, M., Baumer, E.P.: Where is the human?: bridging the gap between AI and HCI. In: Extended Abstracts of the 2019 CHI Conference on Human Factors in Computing Systems 2019. ACM (2019)

9. Lu, X., Lin, Z., Jin, H., Yang, J., Wang, J.Z.: Rating image aesthetics using deep learning. IEEE Trans. Multimedia **17**, 2021–2034 (2015)

10. Chen, A., Nah, F.F.-H., Chen, L.: Assessing classical and expressive aesthetics of web pages using machine learning. In: MWAIS 2018 Proceedings, Saint Louis, Missouri, U.S. (2018)

11. Djamasbi, S., Siegel, M., Tullis, T.: Generation Y, web design, and eye tracking. Int. J. Hum Comput Stud. **68**, 307–323 (2010)

12. Djamasbi, S., Siegel, M., Tullis, T., Dai, R.: Efficiency, trust, and visual appeal: usability testing through eye tracking. In: 2010 43rd Hawaii International Conference on System Sciences (HICSS), pp. 1–10. IEEE (2013)

13. Hwang, Y.M., Lee, K.C.: Using an eye-tracking approach to explore gender differences in visual attention and shopping attitudes in an online shopping environment. Int. J. Hum. Comput. Interact. **34**, 1–10 (2017)

14. Pappas, I.O., Sharma, K., Mikalef, P., Giannakos, M.N.: Visual aesthetics of E-commerce websites: an eye-tracking approach. In: Proceedings of the 51st Hawaii International Conference on System Sciences, Big Island, Hawaii (2018)

15. Pappas, I.O., Sharma, K., Mikalef, P., Giannakos, M.N.: A comparison of gaze behavior of experts and novices to explain website visual appeal. In: PACIS, p. 105 (2018)

16. Lindgaard, G., Fernandes, G., Dudek, C., Brown, J.: Attention web designers: you have 50 milliseconds to make a good first impression! Behav. Inf. Technol. **25**, 115–126 (2006)

17. Bhandari, U., Chang, K., Neben, T.: Understanding the impact of perceived visual aesthetics on user evaluations: an emotional perspective. Inf. Manag. **56**, 85–93 (2019)

18. Just, M.A., Carpenter, P.A.: A theory of reading: from eye fixations to comprehension. Psychol. Rev. **87**, 329 (1980)

19. Arnheim, R.: Visual dynamics. Am. Sci. **76**, 585–591 (1988)

20. Livio, M.: The Golden Ratio: The Story of Phi, the World's Most Astonishing Number. Broadway Books (2008)

21. Wang, Q., Yang, S., Liu, M., Cao, Z., Ma, Q.: An eye-tracking study of website complexity from cognitive load perspective. Decis. Support Syst. **62**, 1–10 (2014)

22. Khalighy, S., Green, G., Scheepers, C., Whittet, C.: Quantifying the qualities of aesthetics in product design using eye-tracking technology. Int. J. Ind. Ergon. **49**, 31–43 (2015)

23. Mikalef, P., Sharma, K., Pappas, I.O., Giannakos, M.N.: Online reviews or marketer information? An eye-tracking study on social commerce consumers. In: Kar, A.K., et al. (eds.) I3E 2017. LNCS, vol. 10595, pp. 388–399. Springer, Cham (2017). https://doi.org/10.1007/978-3-319-68557-1_34

24. Poole, A., Ball, L.J.: Eye tracking in HCI and usability research. In: Encyclopedia of Human Computer Interaction, vol. 1, pp. 211–219 (2006)
25. Prieto, L.P., Sharma, K., Kidzinski, Ł., Rodríguez-Triana, M.J., Dillenbourg, P.: Multimodal teaching analytics: automated extraction of orchestration graphs from wearable sensor data. J. Comput. Assist. Learn. **34**, 193–203 (2018)
26. Reichle, E.D., Warren, T., McConnell, K.: Using EZ reader to model the effects of higher level language processing on eye movements during reading. Psychon. Bull. Rev. **16**, 1–21 (2009)
27. Jaarsma, T., Jarodzka, H., Nap, M., van Merrienboer, J.J., Boshuizen, H.P.: Expertise under the microscope: processing histopathological slides. Med. Educ. **48**, 292–300 (2014)
28. Abernethy, B., Russell, D.G.: Expert-novice differences in an applied selective attention task. J. Sport Exerc. Psychol. **9**, 326–345 (1987)
29. Krischer, C., Zangemeister, W.H.: Scanpaths in reading and picture viewing: computer-assisted optimization of display conditions. Comput. Biol. Med. **37**, 947–956 (2007)
30. Zangemeister, W.H., Liman, T.: Foveal versus parafoveal scanpaths of visual imagery in virtual hemianopic subjects. Comput. Biol. Med. **37**, 975–982 (2007)
31. Liao, K., Kumar, A.N., Han, Y.H., Grammer, V.A., Gedeon, B.T., Leigh, R.J.: Comparison of velocity waveforms of eye and head saccades. Ann. New York Acad. Sci. **1039**, 477–479 (2005)
32. Russo, M., et al.: Oculomotor impairment during chronic partial sleep deprivation. Clin. Neurophysiol. **114**, 723–736 (2003)
33. Phillips, M.H., Edelman, J.A.: The dependence of visual scanning performance on search direction and difficulty. Vis. Res. **48**, 2184–2192 (2008)
34. Vuori, T., Olkkonen, M., Pölönen, M., Siren, A., Häkkinen, J.: Can eye movements be quantitatively applied to image quality studies? In: Proceedings of the Third Nordic Conference on Human-Computer Interaction, pp. 335–338. ACM (2004)
35. Zhu, A., Wei, Q., Hu, Y., Zhang, Z., Cheng, S.: MobiET: a new approach to eye tracking for mobile device. In: Proceedings of the 2018 ACM International Joint Conference and 2018 International Symposium on Pervasive and Ubiquitous Computing and Wearable Computers, pp. 862–869. ACM (2018)
36. Pappas, I.O., Giannakos, M.N., Sampson, D.G.: Fuzzy set analysis as a means to understand users of 21st-century learning systems: the case of mobile learning and reflections on learning analytics research. Comput. Hum. Behav. **92**, 646–659 (2019)
37. Pappas, I.O.: User experience in personalized online shopping: a fuzzy-set analysis. Eur. J. Mark. **52**, 1679–1703 (2018)

Designing for Positive Emotional Responses in Users of Interactive Digital Technologies: A Systematic Literature Review

Nabeel Makkan🆔, Jacques Brosens$^{(\boxtimes)}$🆔, and Rendani Kruger🆔

Department of Informatics, University of Pretoria, Pretoria, South Africa
{nabeel.makkan, jacques.brosens,
rendani.kurger}@up.ac.za

Abstract. In this study, 20 papers were reviewed to identify means, methods, techniques, tools or other interventions that practitioners may use to positively influence the affective state of users of digital interactive technologies. A systematic literature review was conducted in order to find such interventions. A literature background covering concepts from the fields of Human-computer interaction, as well as certain concepts from the field of psychology that is relevant to this study is provided. Search criteria were determined and used to identify research papers from various academic resources. Four categories of intervention categories were identified from the papers reviewed, which can be applied to interactive digital technologies by practitioners in order to evoke positive affect on users. These four categories were aesthetics, affective computing, need fulfilment and novel interaction techniques. The identified categories for practitioners were consolidated alongside metadata such as the types of publications of the reviewed papers, the regions the studies were conducted and the growth in the number of studies.

Keywords: User experience · Human-Computer Interaction · Positive affect · Hedonic quality · Delight · Systematic literature review

1 Introduction

Functionality and usability have long been the main considerations taken in to account by practitioners developing interactive digital technologies [1]. However, user experience (UX) design has moved towards a more experiential approach, and no longer focuses on just functionality and usability. Understanding the user that interacts with technology [2] has led to more attention being paid by practitioners to psychological aspects that influence a user's perception of an experience.

There are two attributes of UX that influence the appeal, pleasure and satisfaction in a user, *pragmatic attributes*, i.e. the attributes that fulfil a user's functional and usability needs, and *hedonic attributes*, i.e. those attributes that fulfil a user's psychological needs related to emotion and pleasure [3]. Despite both hedonic and pragmatic qualities having a relation to positive affect, hedonic quality appears to have a stronger relationship to positive affect than the pragmatic quality of a user experience [4].

© IFIP International Federation for Information Processing 2020
Published by Springer Nature Switzerland AG 2020
M. Hattingh et al. (Eds.): I3E 2020, LNCS 12067, pp. 441–451, 2020.
https://doi.org/10.1007/978-3-030-45002-1_38

Given the effect of positive affect and hedonic qualities on the appeal of a technology to a user, the following research question can be raised: *"What practices, techniques or interventions can a practitioner implement to evoke positive affective responses from users of a digital interactive technology?"*. The aim of this review is to evaluate existing research in the discipline of human-computer interaction (HCI) and user experience to identify the different interventions that have been put forward by researchers specifically intended to improve the emotional responses evoked in users of digital interactive technologies. The focus of this review will not be on the functionality or usability *(pragmatic quality)* aspects, but instead on the pleasurable and emotional aspects *(hedonic quality)* of user experiences.

This review firstly describes some of the background knowledge on Human-Computer Interaction, Human-Centered Design, User Experience and the Hedonic/Pragmatic model of UX. The literature background also investigates some concepts from psychology, such as the pleasure-arousal-dominance model [5, 6], and the ten psychological needs [7]. The selection process of articles used for the review is described in Sect. 3 including search terms, sources, as well as the data extraction process. The extracted research was then reviewed to answer the research question.

2   Literature Background

This section describes key concepts that are relevant in this research, such as *Human-Computer Interaction (HCI), Human-centered design (HCD), User Experience (UX)* and *The Hedonic/Pragmatic model*. While the focus of this study is in the context of HCI and UX, answering the research question involved understanding certain concepts or models that relate to a user's emotions from a psychology perspective, and, therefore, this section also describes relevant concepts from the field of psychology.

HCI is a broad term for the study of the interaction between humans and computers [8]. Two key considerations in designing human computer interfaces are functionality and usability [8]. The functionality of a technology is defined by what the technology can do, either actions or services, for the user to achieve goals, while the usability of the system is the degree to which the user can efficiently use a particular function or set of functions provided by the system [9]. The functionality of a technology is only fully realised if it is usable by the intended user of the technology [10], this is an important consideration in the development of systems.

HCD is defined as "an approach to interactive systems development that aims to make systems usable and useful by focusing on the users, their needs and requirements, and by applying human factors/ergonomics, and usability knowledge and techniques" [11]. HCD, originates from *User-Centered Design (UCD)*, is a concept coined by Norman in 1986, and later built on in his book "The Psychology of Everyday Things" [12].

In UCD the user is at the center of the design process [12]. HCD aims to improve the design of technologies/systems by understanding the needs, emotions, abilities and experiences of the intended users [13]. Developing a system that meets the needs of the user through HCD effectively can evoke positive experience from users.

UX is defined as the evaluative feeling experienced by an end user during their interaction with a digital technology [14]. While traditional HCI studies focus more on the usability or utilitarian aspects of user's interaction with a digital technology, UX studies include other, non-utilitarian aspects of these interactions, such as a users' emotions, the meaning and value of the interactions to the user [15].

The hedonic/pragmatic model is a model of UX that recognizes that people perceive their experience of interactive products in two dimensions, *pragmatics* and *hedonics* [16]. *Pragmatics* refers to the product's attributes which provide utility to the user, such as completing a specific task that fulfils a *functional* need of the user [17]. *Hedonics* are the attributes of a product that fulfil the psychological needs of the user, those needs of enjoyment or pleasure, self-expression and even provocation of memories [16].

A model to study hedonics is the Pleasure-Arousal-Dominance (PAD) model by Mehrabian and Russell [5] which suggest that there are three dimensions that represent the affective response of a user to a stimulus: pleasure which is the scale of the pleasantness of the affective response to a stimulus, arousal which represents an individual's degree of excitement, and dominance which is the extent individuals feel as if they are in control [5, 6]. The PAD model has been applied in numerous studies in the field of HCI to measure user intention, behavior and response in various contexts like online gaming [18], online marketplaces [19] and even in UX [20]. Some other models in psychology like the 10 psychological needs by Sheldon, Elliot, Kim and Kasser [7] have also been used in UX to understand human needs that influence their experiences.

In summary, when systems are designed and developed to provide specific functionality to end users, the usability and the experience of those end users should also be considered [10]. Approaches such as HCD involve users throughout the design process, in order to take in to consideration their needs, abilities and emotions [13]. UX design that considers the emotional wellbeing of the user can make a technology more appealing, easier to use and will ultimately improve the effectiveness and usefulness of the end product [2, 4].

3   Research Method

This study followed a systematic literature review (SLR) process [21]. The research question, derived from the title was: *"What practices, techniques or interventions can a practitioner implement to evoke positive affective responses from users of a digital interactive technology?"*.

The IEEE Xplore, Ebscohost, SpringerLink, ACM Digital Library, ScienceDirect, ResearchGate, Google Scholar, Web of Science, Scopus and Semantic Scholar academic databases were used in the SLR process.

The search term used for the SLR to search academic research databases was: ("user experience" **OR** "user (NEAR/2) experience" **OR** UX) **AND** (tool* **OR** Technique* **OR** Method* **OR** Practic* **OR** Intervention **OR** Mean*) **AND** (emotion* **OR** hedoni* **OR** Pleasur* **OR** Delight* **OR** Enjoy* **OR** arous* **OR** Domin* **OR** "positive affect" **OR** affect*).

Once academic sources were extracted from the databases using the search criteria, the sources were filtered based on selection criteria. Sources were included when:

- They were published in English between 1989 and 2019.
- They were peer review academic articles related to HCI and or UX.
- They reported on the effectiveness of a specific practice, technique or method that can be implemented in a digital technology to invoke positive affect or improve hedonic quality.

Articles were excluded from the study if they did not meet the inclusion criteria or if they were duplicates. The SLR process involved (1) using the search terms in each academic database to obtain a preliminary set of articles (2) the removal of duplicate articles (3) the exclusion of articles based on the selection criteria (4) screening and filtering of articles through abstract reviews to determine relevance. Initially 323 articles were identified, 301 were excluded and 20 formed part of the final set of articles used in this study [21].

4   Results

This section contains the findings of this review. The results were analyzed for information such as the types of articles reviewed, the journals the articles were published in, and the geographical spread of the research reviewed. The contents of each article were then analyzed through a thematic analysis to identify the themes and to categorize each article.

4.1   Sources Overview

20 articles were included for review in this study, 16 of the 20 articles were peer-reviewed journal articles, and four were conference proceedings. Four papers (20%) included were published in the International Journal for Human-Computer Interaction, three (15%) in the International Journal of Human-Computer Studies, the rest of the papers were extracted from other journals (1 paper from each individual journal).

Geographically, seven studies included were conducted in Asia, three in China, two in Singapore, one in Japan, and one in South Korea. Seven studies were based in the North American region, five in the USA and two in Canada. Six studies were conducted in Europe, three studies in Germany, and one study each in Finland, France and Italy. There were no studies that included from Africa, South America or the Middle East. There has been an increase in the number of studies released on the subject over the last three decades. Only one of reviewed papers (5%) were published in the period of 1990 to 1999. Four of the papers reviewed (20%) were published in the period of 2000–2010, and 15 papers (75%) were published between 2010 and 2019.

4.2   Findings

The 20 articles were analyzed thematically to categorize them based on the way they suggest designing for positive emotional responses in digital technologies. The identified themes are the specific implementations, practices, or guidelines practitioners can implement in digital interactive technologies to evoke positive affect in users. Many of the papers focused on a specific characteristic, implementation or technique and their influence on the hedonic quality of the user experience or on positive affect invoked on users. They were then grouped together and then categorized into a theme. The identified themes were aesthetics (9 papers), affective computing (6), novel interaction techniques (1 paper) and need fulfillment (4 papers). These themes are depicted in Table 1.

Table 1. Themes and categories used.

Theme	Categories	Articles
Aesthetics	General aesthetics	[22–25]
	Animations and effects	[26–28]
	Color appeal	[29, 30]
Affective computing	Affective language	[31, 32]
	Anthropomorphism	[33–35]
	Conversational interactions	[36]
Novel interaction techniques	Novel interaction techniques	[37]
Need fulfillment	General need fulfilment	[4, 38]
	Need fulfilment through gamified systems	[39, 40]

Aesthetics. From the 20 papers reviewed, 9 studied the influence of aesthetics on UX. These were further categorized under general aesthetics, animations and effects, color appeal.

General Aesthetics. General aesthetics involved studying the influence of aesthetics in general on the affective responses of users, rather than a specific aesthetic quality or implementation. Bhandari et al. [24] performed a study on classical aesthetics (described with the dimensions of symmetry, clarity and cleanliness) and expressive aesthetics (with the dimensions of originality, creativity and special effects), and found that both classical and expressive aesthetics had a significant effect on user emotional states. Classical aesthetics significantly affects the valence (pleasure) dimension of emotions, while expressive aesthetics reflects in the arousal dimension of emotion [24]. Another paper found that beautiful web-pages had a similar effect as pleasant pictures, and ugly web-pages to that of unpleasant pictures [23]. Ugly webpages induced a negative affective state, while pleasant web pages influenced the affective state of the user towards the positive end [23]. A study on the visual complexity of a webpage found that it bears a positive correlation to the arousal and pleasantness experienced by the user [25]. Design aesthetics of an m-commerce site was shown to positively influence the perceived enjoyment by the user, and it was shown that perceived enjoyment is as important to the loyalty of a user as perceived usefulness [22]. Based on these studies it can be said that practitioners can use different general aesthetic characteristics or interventions, such as symmetry, clarity and cleanliness, and expressive aesthetic qualities (creativity, special effects and originality) to evoke a positive affective state in users [24]. Practitioners that implement attractive design aesthetics are more likely to influence the perceived enjoyment of users [22, 23].

Animations and Effects. Articles classified as animations and effects studied the influence of animations and other special effects on the affective responses of users. A website containing both static and animated content is perceived as hedonically superior [28]. A study on the effectiveness of parallax scrolling found that it did not affect the perceived usability, aesthetic or satisfaction of the user experience but did have a significant effect on the perceived "fun" experienced of the participant [26]. Another study on the implementation of parallax effects in an interactive interface found that including such effects on an interface made it more likely to be perceived as "cool" or "vivid" by users [27]. Based on these studies, implementing animations, such as parallax scrolling effects, can allow practitioners to increase the likelihood of inducing positive affect in the users.

Color Appeal. Articles classified under color appeal focused on the relationship between the colors used in an interface and the affective state of users. A study on color appeal of an e-commerce site found that color had a significant link with trust and satisfaction when using an e-commerce platform [30]. The study also tested the effect of different colors on multiple users' (from different cultural backgrounds), and found that certain colors can create an adverse reaction in users [30]. Bonnardel et al. [29] studied the effect of colors on designers and users' cognitive processes. Practitioners should therefore carefully consider the combinations of color that are utilized on their interfaces.

Affective Computing. Six papers reviewed studied the impact of affective computing, which were categorized in to 3 sub-categories, namely affective language, anthropomorphism, and conversational interactions. These papers studied the influence of using emotional, more human-like language or human-like expressions on the affective responses of users.

Affective Language. Affective language refers to the use of language that appeals to the emotion of the reader/listener. The studies in this sub-category focused on the influence of this implementation on the affective responses of users. A paper on the effect of flattery from computers found that both flattery and sincere praise from the computer had a significant effect on the affective response of the user, i.e. users had greater positive affect obtained from the interaction, when compared to generic feedback from the computer [32]. Flattery and sincere praise also improved the user's perception of their own performance, as well as the satisfaction, enjoyment and evaluation of the computer's performance [32]. Another study found that receiving apologetic messages from a computer when something goes wrong made users less likely to experience frustration when compared to non-apologetic or neutral messages [31]. Based on these studies, practitioners could illicit positive affective responses from users through utilising affective language, such as apologetic messages when displaying error messages [31] and providing sincere praise to users through the interface during interactions [32].

Anthropomorphism. Anthropomorphism is described as attributing human-like characteristics or behavior to non-human entities [41]. The articles in this section studied the influence of implementing human-like characteristics to interfaces on the affective responses of the user. Mancini et al. [33] studied the effects of implementing a laughing virtual character in an interface and found that the presence of such character increased their level of activation and puzzlement. Qiu and Benbasat [34] studied the effects of anthropomorphic embodiments in the interfaces of product recommendation agents and found that it can increase the user's perceived enjoyment and trust in the recommendation agent. A study on anthropomorphism in digital voice assistants found that a more human-like interaction between the voice assistant and the user positively influenced the likeability of the digital voice assistant, which in turn also influenced the user's intention to use the assistant again [35]. Based on the above research, practitioners can, therefore, influence the affective responses of users through implementing virtual characters, or other anthropomorphic means/techniques or tools in their interfaces.

Conversational Interactions. A study on conversational agents found that self-disclosure (communicating information about one's self) and reciprocity (adequate responses and continuance of conversation) with the conversational agents significantly influences the perceived enjoyment of the interaction, while interactional enjoyment also influenced the user satisfaction experienced when interacting with the conversational agent [36]. While there is only one study in this sub-category, practitioners could still implement more conversational interactions with users as the study does show that it can significantly influence affective responses.

Need Fulfilment. Four papers studied the effects of need fulfilment. These papers studied the influence of fulfilling user needs on the affective responses of users. These were categorized under general need fulfilment or need fulfilment through gamified systems.

General Need Fulfilment. These papers studied the influence of satisfying the needs as identified by Sheldon et al. [7] on the affective state of the user. Hassenzahl et al. [4] studied the effects of fulfilment of the needs identified by Sheldon and King [42] on the affect and user experience, and found that satisfaction of each need is strongly correlated to positive affect. Hassenzahl et al. [38] studied need fulfilment and positive affect further. Practitioners can evoke positive affective responses in users through fulfilling user needs (such as those identified by Sheldon and King).

Need Fulfilment Through Gamified Systems. The studies in this sub-category look at how gamification can fulfil human needs and as a result influence the affective state of the user positively. Hamari and Koivisto [39] and Suh et al. [40] studied the effects of gamification on user engagement as well as the needs fulfilled by applying gamifying interactions. Gamified systems can fulfil the user needs identified by Sheldon and King [42]. Suh et al. [40] found that gamified elements such as gaining points, levels and badges can positively influence the satisfaction of the user's need to competence and autonomy. Gamified elements can thus be utilized by practitioners to fulfil user needs. Therefore, as was shown by Hassenzahl et al. [4, 38], satisfying these needs can positively influence positive affective responses from users.

Novel Interaction Techniques. One paper, by Dou and Sundar [37], studied the effects of implementing different interaction techniques. Adding swiping gestures to a web interface had a significant effect on the perceived enjoyment of a mobile website [37]. Based on the above study, practitioners that implement interaction techniques such as swiping and clicking can, therefore, influence the perceived enjoyment by the user. While, once again, the findings of this study were not evidenced due to the lack of further research, practitioners may still find benefit in implementing these techniques into their products.

5   Discussion

Aesthetics was the most popular theme covered by the articles reviewed, comprising of nine (9) of the 20 articles reviewed (36%), followed by affective computing, comprising of six (6) of the 20 articles reviewed (30%). Four (4) studies were on the influence of need fulfilment on the affective responses of users. Only one (1) article studied some sort of interaction technique on the affective responses of users.

Based on the above, aesthetic aspects of an interface are more likely to evoke a positive affective response within users, as there is evidence to support the influence of aesthetics qualities, techniques or implementations on the user's affective response [22–30]. Practitioners will likely find that they can evoke affective responses in users through the aesthetics of the interface of a digital technology that they are developing.

Practitioners may also implement affective computing techniques, as there is also evidence to support their influence on the affective responses of users [31–36].

Need fulfilment also influences the affective responses of users, and as such satisfying these needs of users' (such as those identified by Sheldon and King) [4, 38]. Practitioners can evoke affective responses from users through the implementation of techniques such as gamification [39, 40].

Finally, while there is only one study supporting the influence of an interaction technique on the affective responses of users, implementing those techniques may still allow practitioners to evoke positive affect in users. Further studies into interaction techniques and affective responses will benefit practitioners. It is important to note that practitioners do not need to implement every identified means of evoking affective response from users in their technologies, as certain implementations are relevant to specific types of applications. For example, the findings on conversational interaction may only be relevant to those interactive systems that involve users 'conversing' with them, such as digital voice assistants or chatbots. Practitioners should identify the ideal implementations that would best suit the interactive technology that they are developing.

While the number of studies published over the last three decades that were relevant to this study has steadily increased, there were still relatively few papers that were available to review in order to answer the research question of this paper. Certain interventions, while shown to positively influence affective responses, were studied in very few papers, their findings were not verified with other research or similar results. Further studies in this area of research should allow for new knowledge that can be utilized by practitioners of UX.

6   Conclusion

This paper provided a systematic literature review on existing research available in order to identify methods, means, techniques and tools that practitioners can implement into their digital interactive technologies to evoke affective responses from users. 20 articles were obtained through various digital libraries, on which thematic analysis was conducted in order to identify themes that relate to the research question. 16 papers of the papers selected were journal articles and four papers were conference proceedings. In reviewing the selected papers, four overarching themes were identified, aesthetics, affective computing, need fulfilment and novel interaction techniques.

Furthermore, three sub-categories were identified for both the theme of aesthetics and affective computing and two were identified for the theme of need fulfilment. These papers provided studies on the influence of specific techniques, tools, means or methods on the affective responses of the users of digital interactive technologies. This study allows practitioners identify various interventions that UX practitioners can use in their digital interactive technologies to positively influence the affective responses/state of the user. Furthermore, this study identifies the relatively low quantities of studies in the focus area of this research. Further academic research in this area may allow for practitioners to identify more interventions or methods that can be implemented in their products.

References

1. Angeli, A.D., Sutcliffe, A., Hartmann, J.: Interaction, usability and aesthetics: what influences users' preferences? p. 10 (2006)
2. Zimmermann, P.G., Gomez, P., Danuser, B., Schär, S.G.: Extending usability: putting affect into the user-experience, p. 7 (2006)
3. Hassenzahl, M., Platz, A., Burmester, M., Lehner, K.: Hedonic and ergonomic quality aspects determine a software's appeal. In: Proceedings of the SIGCHI Conference on Human Factors in Computing Systems - CHI 2000, pp. 201–208. ACM Press, The Hague (2000). https://doi.org/10.1145/332040.332432
4. Hassenzahl, M., Diefenbach, S., Göritz, A.: Needs, affect, and interactive products – facets of user experience. Interact. Comput. **22**, 353–362 (2010). https://doi.org/10.1016/j.intcom.2010.04.002
5. Mehrabian, A., Russell, J.A.: An Approach to Environmental Psychology. M.I.T. Press, Cambridge (1974)
6. Russell, J.A., Mehrabian, A.: Evidence for a three-factor theory of emotions. J. Res. Pers. **11**, 273–294 (1977). https://doi.org/10.1016/0092-6566(77)90037-X
7. Sheldon, K.M., Elliot, A.J., Kim, Y., Kasser, T.: What is satisfying about satisfying events? Testing 10 candidate psychological needs. J. Pers. Soc. Psychol. **80**, 325–339 (2001)
8. Zhang, P., Carey, J., Te'eni, D.: Human-Computer Interaction: Developing Effective Organizational Information Systems. Wiley, Hoboken (2007)
9. Karray, F., Alemzadeh, M., Abou Saleh, J., Nours Arab, M.: Human-computer interaction: overview on state of the art. Int. J. Smart Sens. Intell. Syst. **1**, 137–159 (2008). https://doi.org/10.21307/ijssis-2017-283

10. Shneiderman, B., Plaisant, C.: Designing the User Interface: Strategies for Effective Human-Computer Interaction, 5th edn. Pearson, New Delhi (2016)
11. International Organization for Standardization: ISO 9241-210:2010 Ergonomics of human-system interaction – Part 210: Human-centred design for interactive systems. International Organization for Standardization (2010)
12. Norman, D.A.: The Design of Everyday Things. Basic Books, New York (1988)
13. Giacomin, J.: What is human centred design? Des. J. **17**, 606–623 (2014). https://doi.org/10.2752/175630614X14056185480186
14. Hassenzahl, M.: User experience (UX): towards an experiential perspective on product quality. In: Proceedings of the 20th International Conference of the Association Francophone d'Interaction Homme-Machine on - IHM 2008, p. 11. ACM Press, Metz (2008). https://doi.org/10.1145/1512714.1512717
15. Law, E.L.-C., Roto, V., Hassenzahl, M., Vermeeren, A.P.O.S., Kort, J.: Understanding, scoping and defining user experience: a survey approach. In: Proceedings of the 27th International Conference on Human Factors in Computing Systems - CHI 2009, p. 719. ACM Press, Boston (2009). https://doi.org/10.1145/1518701.1518813
16. Hassenzahl, M.: The hedonic/pragmatic model of user experience. In: Proceedings Towards a UX Manifesto, Lancaster, UK (2007)
17. Hassenzahl, M.: The thing and I: understanding the relationship between user and product. In: Blythe, M.A., Overbeeke, K., Monk, A.F., Wright, P.C. (eds.) Funology. HCIS, vol. 3, pp. 31–42. Springer, Dordrecht (2003). https://doi.org/10.1007/1-4020-2967-5_4
18. Huang, M., Ali, R., Liao, J.: The effect of user experience in online games on word of mouth: a pleasure-arousal-dominance (PAD) model perspective. Comput. Hum. Behav. **75**, 329–338 (2017). https://doi.org/10.1016/j.chb.2017.05.015
19. Hsieh, J.-K., Hsieh, Y.-C., Chiu, H.-C., Yang, Y.-R.: Customer response to web site atmospherics: task-relevant cues, situational involvement and PAD. J. Interact. Mark. **28**, 225–236 (2014). https://doi.org/10.1016/j.intmar.2014.03.001
20. Bruun, A., Ahm, S.: Mind the gap! Comparing retrospective and concurrent ratings of emotion in user experience evaluation. In: Abascal, J., Barbosa, S., Fetter, M., Gross, T., Palanque, P., Winckler, M. (eds.) INTERACT 2015. LNCS, vol. 9296, pp. 237–254. Springer, Cham (2015). https://doi.org/10.1007/978-3-319-22701-6_17
21. Kitchenham, B.: Procedures for performing systematic reviews, vol. 33 (2004)
22. Cyr, D., Head, M., Ivanov, A.: Design aesthetics leading to m-loyalty in mobile commerce. Inf. Manag. **43**, 950–963 (2006). https://doi.org/10.1016/j.im.2006.08.009
23. Zhou, H., Fu, X.: Understanding, measuring, and designing user experience: the causal relationship between the aesthetic quality of products and user affect. In: Jacko, J.A. (ed.) HCI 2007. LNCS, vol. 4550, pp. 340–349. Springer, Heidelberg (2007). https://doi.org/10.1007/978-3-540-73105-4_38
24. Bhandari, U., Chang, K., Neben, T.: Understanding the impact of perceived visual aesthetics on user evaluations: an emotional perspective. Inf. Manag. **56**, 85–93 (2019). https://doi.org/10.1016/j.im.2018.07.003
25. Deng, P.: Affect in web interfaces: a study of the impacts of web page visual complexity and order. MIS Q. **34**, 711 (2010). https://doi.org/10.2307/25750702
26. Frederick, D., Mohler, J., Vorvoreanu, M., Glotzbach, R.: The effects of parallax scrolling on user experience in web design. J. Usability Stud. **10**, 9 (2015)
27. Wang, R., Sundar, S.S.: How does parallax scrolling influence user experience? A test of TIME (Theory of Interactive Media Effects). Int. J. Hum.-Comput. Interact. **34**, 533–543 (2018). https://doi.org/10.1080/10447318.2017.1373457

28. Lai, Y.-L., Kuan, K.K.Y., Hui, K.-L., Liu, N.: The effects of moving animation on recall, hedonic and utilitarian perceptions, and attitude. IEEE Trans. Eng. Manag. **56**, 468–477 (2009). https://doi.org/10.1109/TEM.2009.2023454

29. Bonnardel, N., Piolat, A., Le Bigot, L.: The impact of colour on website appeal and users' cognitive processes. Displays **32**, 69–80 (2011). https://doi.org/10.1016/j.displa.2010.12.002

30. Cyr, D., Head, M., Larios, H.: Colour appeal in website design within and across cultures: a multi-method evaluation. Int. J. Hum. Comput. Stud. **68**, 1–21 (2010). https://doi.org/10.1016/j.ijhcs.2009.08.005

31. Park, S.J., MacDonald, C.M., Khoo, M.: Do you care if a computer says sorry?: user experience design through affective messages, p. 10 (2012)

32. Fogg, B.J., Nass, C.: Silicon sycophants: the effects of computers that flatter. Int. J. Hum. Comput. Stud. **46**, 551–561 (1997). https://doi.org/10.1006/ijhc.1996.0104

33. Mancini, M., et al.: Implementing and evaluating a laughing virtual character. ACM Trans. Internet Technol. **17**, 1–22 (2017). https://doi.org/10.1145/2998571

34. Qiu, L., Benbasat, I.: Evaluating anthropomorphic product recommendation agents: a social relationship perspective to designing information systems. J. Manag. Inf. Syst. **25**, 145–182 (2009). https://doi.org/10.2753/MIS0742-1222250405

35. Wagner, K., Nimmermann, F., Schramm-Klein, H.: Is it human? The role of anthropomorphism as a driver for the successful acceptance of digital voice assistants, p. 10 (2019)

36. Lee, S., Choi, J.: Enhancing user experience with conversational agent for movie recommendation: effects of self-disclosure and reciprocity. Int. J. Hum. Comput. Stud. **103**, 95–105 (2017). https://doi.org/10.1016/j.ijhcs.2017.02.005

37. Dou, X., Sundar, S.S.: Power of the swipe: why mobile websites should add horizontal swiping to tapping, clicking, and scrolling interaction techniques. Int. J. Hum.-Comput. Interact. **32**, 352–362 (2016). https://doi.org/10.1080/10447318.2016.1147902

38. Hassenzahl, M., Wiklund-Engblom, A., Bengs, A., Hägglund, S., Diefenbach, S.: Experience-oriented and product-oriented evaluation: psychological need fulfillment, positive affect, and product perception. Int. J. Hum.-Comput. Interact. **31**, 530–544 (2015). https://doi.org/10.1080/10447318.2015.1064664

39. Hamari, J., Koivisto, J.: Why do people use gamification services? Int. J. Inf. Manag. **35**, 419–431 (2015). https://doi.org/10.1016/j.ijinfomgt.2015.04.006

40. Suh, A., Wagner, C., Liu, L.: The effects of game dynamics on user engagement in gamified systems. In: 2015 48th Hawaii International Conference on System Sciences, pp. 672–681. IEEE, Waikoloa (2015). https://doi.org/10.1109/HICSS.2015.87

41. Anthropomorphism, n. (1885)

42. Sheldon, K.M., King, L.: Why positive psychology is necessary. Am. Psychol. **56**, 216–217 (2001). https://doi.org/10.1037/0003-066X.56.3.216

A Methodology to Compare the Usability of Information Systems

Rendani Kruger[✉] , Jacques Brosens , and Marie Hattingh

Department of Informatics, University of Pretoria, Pretoria, South Africa
{rendani.kruger, jacques.brosens,
marie.hattingh}@up.ac.za

Abstract. The usability of customer facing software interfaces is a source of competitive advantage for organisations. The usability of systems has also shown to encourage the effective and efficient completion of tasks and in consequence, operations. Furthermore, competitive analysis of the usability of software products has been shown to be a useful tool in the adoption of the user centred design philosophy within organisations. However, low adoption of usability evaluation is prevalent due to a lack of methodologies to support organisations in their endeavours to achieve better usability. Therefore, the purpose of this study is to present a methodology to compare the usability of information systems. By using such a methodology, organisations will be able to gauge the standard of the usability of their information systems, by comparing it to others.

Keywords: Usability · User centred design · Competitive analysis · Benchmarking · Information systems

1 Introduction

The usability of information systems (IS) has been shown to improve the productivity of employees. Furthermore, when customers need to use information systems, bad usability leads to a lack of loyalty, desertion of tasks (such as cart abandonment) and a decrease in satisfaction [1, 2]. Market research suggests that poor usability is the biggest reason why mobile applications are rejected by customers [3]. Sykes and Venkatesh [4] explain that the potential of using enterprise software within organisations is limited because many implementations fail due to a lack of usability testing. They suggest that in addition to testing the usability of customer facing systems, it is important to examine how people use enterprise software systems to do their work and achieve their goals. It is vital that the usability of systems, such as mobile applications and business intelligence systems, remains optimal for organisations to gain and maintain a competitive advantage [5]. For example, a usable system may lead to a reduction in system transaction time, which could have direct cost benefits [6].

Due to the importance of usability, usability evaluations can be used to test how well people use IS and have great potential in improving the usability of systems [7, 8]. Nielsen and Gilutz [9] explains that the main benefits of usability evaluations are: (1) Reduced training cost with relation to the information system, (2) Limited user

© IFIP International Federation for Information Processing 2020
Published by Springer Nature Switzerland AG 2020
M. Hattingh et al. (Eds.): I3E 2020, LNCS 12067, pp. 452–463, 2020.
https://doi.org/10.1007/978-3-030-45002-1_39

investment risk. The user makes less mistakes and completes tasks more effectively when the usability of an information system is optimal, (3) The enhanced performance of users that are completing a task, (4) Enhanced user efficiency and satisfaction, (5) Lower personnel cost for organisations due to computer based tasks being completed more effectively and efficiently by employees, (6) Reduced software development cost and length of the development lifecycle because users are more satisfied with systems, (7) Easier to use online interfaces for enhanced customer interactions, (8) Improved competitive advantage.

One method organisations use to achieve a competitive advantage is through benchmarking. Benchmarking is important because it allows organisations to set standards, measure the effectiveness of operations and processes, and analyse competitive advantage [10]. Organisations often conduct comparative studies to benchmark [11]. Comparative studies may be conducted at the inception, during operations and at the closure of an organisation. Stakeholders in an organisation may have various questions that could be answered through benchmarking. These include why some competing organisations are doing better than others, what the strengths and weaknesses of an organisation are, and why certain organisations may easily mitigate threats and take advantage of opportunities [12–14]. Similar questions could be asked about the organisation's competition and this may enable the organisation posing the questions to gain competitive advantage [12–14].

A typical organisation may compare the current manner of operations to alternative ways in which these operations could be conducted. If the alternative promises to be an improvement and it is feasible to implement the better method of operations, the organisation may do so. This may have a variety of influences on that organisation, including greater profits or business growth [15]. It is challenging for organisations to determine the value they will derive from making a change to an IS or its environment [13]. Thus, a methodology to compare the usability of ISs with the view of obtaining a competitive advantage, may be useful.

A literature search yielded no research regarding methods to compare the usability of information systems within a competitive environment. A/B testing was the closest result. A/B testing, also called split testing or bucket testing, is a method of comparing different versions of an information system to determine the effectiveness of a change or the effectiveness of the operations of a development team [16].

A methodology is a system of methods used in a particular activity. For example, in software development, a general definition of a methodology is: "a recommended series of steps and procedures to be followed during the development of an IS" [17]. The goal of the research presented in this paper was to create a series of methods that practitioners can use to compare the usability of information systems.

Therefore, this paper presents a methodology to compare the usability of two or more corresponding IS (within competitive environments). We used a design-based approach [18] to develop a Comparative Inter-Organisational Usability Evaluation (CIUE) methodology. CIUEs can be used to (1) compare the usability of user interfaces (UIs), (2) work towards the benchmarking of the usability of user interfaces, (3) Create a method to convince stakeholders of IS to invest in the application of User Centred Design (UCD) in systems development, (4) scale the value of an investment made in usability enhancements, (5) encourage the use of usability enhancement mechanisms to gain competitive advantage through user interfaces of IS.

The CIUE is presented by discussing the research context in the next section, followed by a section on the method adopted to create the CIUE, then a section that discusses the results of the method applied and finally the CIUE. Possible future research is presented in the concluding section.

2 Research Context

The main theoretical concepts that form the basis of this research are usability, UCD, usability evaluation and competitive analysis. We begin our contextual discussion by defining these concepts and showing how they relate to each other. We also delve into the lack of adoption of UCD practices by organisations. Since the outcome of this research is a usability evaluation methodology, we provide a critical overview of existing usability evaluation techniques and explain how these informed our CIUE. We further discuss comparative evaluation and benchmarking to substantiate our preference for comparative usability testing above single system evaluations.

2.1 Usability, UCD and Competitive Analysis

Usability relates to the effectiveness, efficiency and satisfaction with which users achieve goals using computer systems [19]. Usability evaluations examine the quality of computer interfaces, particularly regarding how easy they are to use [8]. The improved usability of an IS may reduce the anxiety and fear associated with computer use, improve learnability, could direct users more concisely and may improve the navigation of systems [6].

A user's interaction with an IS is not only bound to that user's interaction with computers as it may include the interaction with human system actors [20]. The term user interface, however, commonly refers to the technological elements through which users interact with computer systems [21].

UCD is a broad term used to describe the design process where the end user has an influence on the design [22]. In UCD, the usability, user environment, user opinions, user characteristics, tasks and workflow of products are key considerations in the design process. What may be an effective design for one group of users may be an ineffective design for a different group [23]. UCD addresses these differing user requirements.

The involvement of users to influence the design of IS increases the number of breakthrough ideas in research and development projects [24]. The formation of concepts and scenarios regarding the adoption of IS, which may otherwise not have been thought of, was also improved when UCD was adopted in a number of projects [24].

Despite its clear benefits for the improvement of the user experience of IS, the adoption of UCD practices in organisations has been limited [25, 26]. This has been attributed to the fact that business potential of an IS and technological requirements are considered before users are attended to [25, 26].

Venturi et al. [27] showed that when competitive analysis is done on the usability of software products it may increase the adoption of UCD. There is a strong emphasis on the usability of information systems when UCD is adopted. Some of the basic UCD principles that relate to usability are [28]:

1. Make it easy to determine which actions are possible for a user at any time.
2. User should easily determine what the current state of task completion is
3. It should be intuitive to follow mappings between intentions and the required actions, between actions and the resulting effect, and between the information that is visible and the system state.

These principles put the user at the center of the design process [28]. UCD is often regarded as a philosophy of IS design as it influences the entire design process.

2.2 Usability Evaluation Techniques

This section presents a summary of the most widely used usability evaluation methods. The discussions to follow informed the development of the CIUE methodology. We look at the advantages and disadvantages of the different methods and consider whether they are appropriate for use in comparative analysis. The main advantages and disadvantages of the various methods to evaluate usability are summarised in Table 1.

Table 1. Advantages and disadvantages of usability evaluation methods

Method of evaluation	Advantages	Disadvantages
Focus group [29–31]	Low cost, quick analysis	Subjective opinion of focus group. Participatory challenges
Heuristic evaluation [30, 32–36]	Low cost and quick	Subjective opinion of usability experts
Remote usability evaluation [37–39]	Low cost	Context is often lost, there is typically no interaction with users
Controlled environment evaluation [39–41]	Objective quantitative data	The environment is not always realistic, i.e. as it would be in the real world

A goal of the methodology is to use objective data, therefore focus groups and heuristic evaluations are not suitable for use in CIUEs. Furthermore, the variable nature of the environment of remote usability evaluation renders remote user evaluation inappropriate for use during CIUEs because it is impossible to account for all the variables in such unknown and vastly different environments.

Controlled environment evaluations are more suited for CIUEs because the variability in data and environment can be controlled. As such, the focus can be placed on the difference between the usability of the different competing computer systems. This can also be optimised by using specialised equipment. This, in turn, increases the value and quality of the comparison. This extensive range of indicators reduces the need for possibly subjective data such as expert recommendations or user opinions.

Benchmarking and comparative evaluations have often been used to identify an entities strengths and weaknesses [42]. Single system evaluations tend to lack data to show how important a system change with be (quantitatively), this can be addressed by CUIEs.

3   Research Method

The study followed a Design Science Research (DSR) approach proposed by Kuechler and Vaishnavi [43]. The study followed five steps as prescribed by the methodology and is outlined in Fig. 1. The first step was the "awareness of the problem" step, this was done from literature analysis and industry requests for CIUEs. The second step was the suggestion step which was done abductively with the use of peer reviewed literature regarding usability and benchmarking. The first version of the CIUE methodology was applied in step three by evaluating and comparing three Mobile communications websites. The CIUE methodology was then refined and evaluated in step 4 through further application in the aviation and medical insurance sectors, and further through expert consultations, both from the organisations involved in the study and from academia.

This paper, however, only reports on the final step of the DSR approach which is the presentation of the artefact – A methodology to conduct CIUEs. The earlier phases were reported on in [44].

4   A Methodology to Conduct CIUEs

The contribution of the research study is a methodology to conduct Comparative Inter-Organisational Usability Evaluations (CIUEs). This section presents the final CIUE methodology in terms of its underlying philosophy, strategies, principles and procedures. The components of the CIUE is depicted in Fig. 2.

4.1   Philosophy

User Centred Design (UCD) is a design process in which the end users influence how an IS is designed [22]. To follow UCD, the user is placed at the centre of the design process [45]. UCD can be regarded as the philosophy that underlies a CIUE.

UCD is about optimising the experience that a user will have when using a product by involving the user in the design process rather than expecting the user to change their behaviour or attitude to accommodate the product [45]. This is done primarily by involving users in the design process. The goal of a CIUE is ultimately to improve the usability of an IS by showing that it is not on the same standard as that of a competing IS, from the user's point of view.

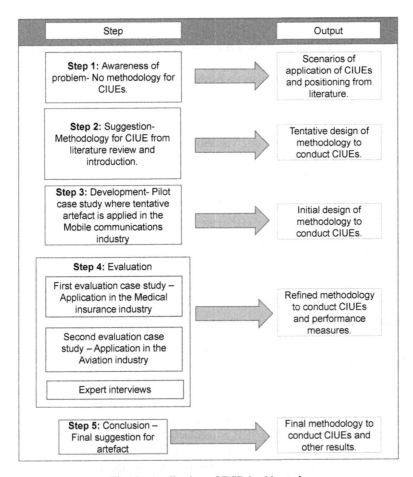

Fig. 1. Application of DSR in this study

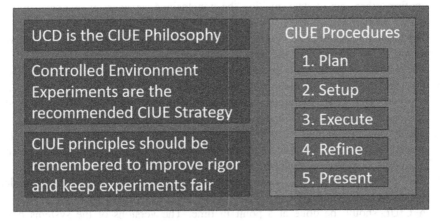

Fig. 2. CIUE components.

4.2   Strategies

A usability evaluation is essentially a research project that has to be designed in a way that will ensure valid results. As in research, the investigator has to make choices with regard to data collection and analysis methods and the type of data that would be suitable for a specific evaluation case. The investigative approach that we recommend for CIUEs is controlled user observation. Controlling the observation requires some form of experimental design. The observation is controlled to minimise the influence of the environment on data collection. Variability in the data should be focused on the differences between the interfaces being compared rather than on contextual factors.

Quantitative or qualitative methods could be used to collect and analyse data that are relevant to the usability of a system interface [46]. A goal of our methodology is objectivity. Collecting data through qualitative methods such as expert recommendations can, for example, be doubted due to their perceived subjective nature [47]. CIUEs therefore follow a quantitative approach in the collection and analysis of the usability data. The epistemological assumption is that an objective reality exists in which the usability of IS can be measured and analysed deductively [46]. The data collected during observation should therefore be suitable for quantitative analysis.

4.3   Principles

In addition to the principles of UCD, we have identified the following principles specific to CIUEs:

1. IS evaluated in a CIUE should not contain any system breaks. A system break will influence the user's interaction with the system and the value of many metrics (e.g. time taken to complete the task) will be meaningless for comparison purposes
2. The environment where the CIUE is conducted should be controlled to minimise contextual or environmental influences on the outcome of the evaluation (e.g. the lighting in the evaluation space should be consistent for the duration of the tests and across all tests)
3. Gather data for as many different metrics as possible. This way one set of data can confirm other sets of data, making the conclusions stronger, or one set can contradict another set, showing that further evidence is required
4. The tasks that the users will perform on the different systems should be similar with regard to the outcome for the user
5. The number of participants should be the same for each system being evaluated
6. The less homogenous the group of participants is, the more participants are required. This is an attempt to minimise the influence that characteristics of the participants have on the comparison
7. The evaluations should be done in the same way for all the participants. The procedure followed, the evaluation environment and the tasks that participants are requested to complete should be the same for all participants and all systems
8. The results of the CIUE should be presented in a manner that is easily understandable and unambiguous
9. A CIUE should be done at a point in time. The versions of the systems being evaluated should not change.

4.4   Procedures

This section discusses the steps and procedures to be followed when conducting a CIUE. The broader steps are planning, setting up the environment, conducting the usability evaluations, exporting data, performing the analysis and presenting results. We elaborate on each step below. Figure 3 provides an overview of the CIUE process.

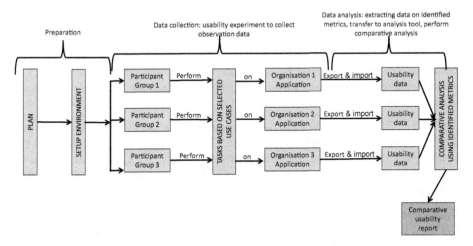

Fig. 3. Overview of the CIUE process

Step 1: Plan the CIUE. The following aspects need to be considered when planning the CIUE:

Timing. If the lifetime of the product is limited, the CIUE may not be useful. Furthermore, if the organisation for which the evaluation is being done, cannot give priority to the CIUE it may not be worthwhile.

Data to be Collected. Depending on the nature of the systems included in the CIUE, the evaluator should identify metrics that will best serve the comparative evaluation. The quality of the data is also important, therefore criteria that will result in the elimination of data should be formulated beforehand (e.g. if eye tracking is used, the required percentage of fixations picked up during the task can be set to 80%, eliminating the data of all users with less than 80% fixations recorded). The cost of data collection and data analysis should also be considered.

The Candidate Organisations. The amount of evaluation resources required for a CIUE increases with the number of organisations, but the CIUE results could be more reliable when more organisations are included. This is due to the performance of a system becomes clearer as the number of systems it is compared to increases. If the data is going to be used to determine benchmarks for the future, the number of organisations should be maximised to increase the reliability of the benchmarks [48].

Recruit Participants for the Study. The number of participants depends on the diversity of the user population of the systems involved. If a group of similar participants are selected, then fewer participants are required. If the user population is diverse, a larger number of participants is required. The advantage of a more diverse group of participants is that the results of the study are valid for a larger part of the total population of possible users. Generally, a sample size of 16 ± 4 is accepted as adequate for usability studies [49]. To make sure all participants have had the same level of exposure to the systems being tested, select people who had not used the systems before. Divide the participants in as many groups as the number of organisations included in the study. These groups have to be equal in size.

Location. The location should be easily accessible for the participants and easy to control in terms of lighting, sounds, smell, available hardware, setup of tools, cleanliness, et cetera.

The Tasks. The tasks should have the same outcome for the user if performed on the different systems. For example, if a participant is going to buy an airline ticket on one of the systems then the same should be done on the rest of the systems involved in the CIUE. The organisation that requested the CIUE should provide input into the task selection.

Data Collection Methods. Make sure the required recording devices are available and working. If specialised methods such as eye tracking will be used, an expert in that method should collect the data. This could influence the cost of a CIUE.

Data Analysis and Reporting. A complete written report should be provided but we recommend that the results are also presented in a face-to-face meeting so that the evaluators can answer questions that arise.

Step 2: Conduct the usability evaluations for each IS. As stated in the section regarding usability evaluation techniques, the controlled lab technique is most suited for CIUEs because the focus can be placed on the comparison. In the case studies we used to develop the methodology to conduct CIUEs, we used an eye tracker to maximise the amount of data collected but the methodology will not be prescriptive regarding this as a CIUE can be done without an eye tracker. Ensure that the data is organised to avoid confusing the results of the CIUE.

Step 3: Extract the data from the recording tools and import the data into the analysis tools. Ensure that the data is strictly organised to avoid mistakes in the results of the CIUE. For example, first create separate spreadsheets for each organisation. Then use a separate spreadsheet to compare all the data. Data should preferably be stored in the cloud and backups should be made to avoid data loss.

Step 4: Perform the analysis of the data by comparing similar metrics. Stick to objective, quantitative analysis. Create graphs that juxtapose the results of the different organisations for easy comparison.

Step 5: Presenting the outcomes. Present the outcomes to the parties that requested the CIUE. This can be done using reports or presentations.

5 Conclusions and Future Research

We developed a methodology to conduct CIUEs and presented the resulting methodology in this article. We used DSR using a multiple-case study and interviews. The distinguishing characteristics of the CIUE methodology are that it should be done in a manner that emphasises the comparison being conducted, and so it was suggested that the CIUE be conducted in a controlled environment. Furthermore, it was found that CIUEs can be useful in selecting IS products based on usability, to work towards the benchmarking of the usability of user interfaces, to scale the value of an investment made in usability enhancements, to encourage the use of usability enhancement mechanisms to gain competitive advantage.

Since UCD is the underlying philosophy of the CIUE methodology, its application may be useful to encourage the adoption of UCD in organisations. CIUE can also aid the development of benchmarks.

During our research, various ways to use CIUEs were identified that may be elaborated in future. Firstly, research can be done into how to conduct a longitudinal CIUEs, where the change in comparison can be measured over time. This would entail comparison of the usability of systems of competing organisations over time to measure, for example, the effectiveness of changes made to improve usability. The application of CIUEs in the selection of software products could also be explored. The development of usability benchmarks using a similar approach as CIUEs may be useful.

References

1. Bilgihan, A.: Gen Y customer loyalty in online shopping: an integrated model of trust, user experience and branding. Comput. Hum. Behav. **61**, 103–113 (2016)
2. Casaló, L.V., Flavián, C., Guinalíu, M.: The role of satisfaction and website usability in developing customer loyalty and positive word-of-mouth in the e-banking services. Int. J. Bank Mark. **26**(6), 399–417 (2008)
3. Hoehle, H., Venkatesh, V.: Mobile application usability: conceptualization and instrument development. MIS Q. **39**(2), 435–472 (2015)
4. Sykes, T.A., Venkatesh, V.: Explaining post-implementation employee system use and job performance: impacts of the content and source of social network ties. MIS Q. **41**(3), 917–936 (2017)
5. Peters, M.D., Wieder, B., Sutton, S.G., Wakefield, J.: Business intelligence systems use in performance measurement capabilities: implications for enhanced competitive advantage. Int. J. Account. Inf. Syst. **21**, 1–17 (2016)
6. Shneiderman, B.: Designing the User Interface: Strategies for Effective Human-Computer Interaction. Pearson Education India, New Delhi (2010)
7. Schneidermeier, T.: Lessons learned in usability consulting. In: Marcus, A. (ed.) DUXU 2015. LNCS, vol. 9186, pp. 247–255. Springer, Cham (2015). https://doi.org/10.1007/978-3-319-20886-2_24
8. Nielsen, J.: Usability 101: introduction to usability (2003)
9. Nielsen, J., Gilutz, S.: Return on investment (ROI) for usability (2013)

10. Doumeingts, G., Browne, J.: Modelling Techniques for Business Process Re-engineering and Benchmarking. Springer, Heidelberg (2016)
11. Glackin, C.: Entrepreneurship: starting and operating a small business, 3e (2013)
12. Cragg, P.B.: Benchmarking information technology practices in small firms. Eur. J. Inf. Syst. **11**(4), 267–282 (2002)
13. Pearlson, K.E., Saunders, C.S.: Strategic management of information systems (2009)
14. Petuskiene, E., Glinskiene, R.: Entrepreneurship as the basic element for the successful employment of benchmarking and business innovations. Eng. Econ. **22**(1), 69–77 (2015)
15. Slack, N.: Operations Strategy. Wiley Online Library (2015)
16. Xu, Y., Chen, N., Fernandez, A., Sinno, O., Bhasin, A.: From infrastructure to culture: A/B testing challenges in large scale social networks. Presented at the Proceedings of the 21st ACM SIGKDD International Conference on Knowledge Discovery and Data Mining, pp. 2227–2236 (2015)
17. Aveson, D., Fitzgerald, G.: Methodologies for developing information systems: a historical perspective. In: Avison, D., Elliot, S., Krogstie, J., Pries-Heje, J. (eds.) The Past and Future of Information Systems: 1976–2006 and Beyond. IIFIP, vol. 214, pp. 27–38. Springer, Boston, MA (2006). https://doi.org/10.1007/978-0-387-34732-5_3
18. Vaishnavi, V.K., Kuechler, W.: Design Science Research Methods and Patterns: Innovating Information and Communication Technology. CRC Press, New York (2015)
19. Bevan, N.: Extending quality in use to provide a framework for usability measurement. In: Kurosu, M. (ed.) HCD 2009. LNCS, vol. 5619, pp. 13–22. Springer, Heidelberg (2009). https://doi.org/10.1007/978-3-642-02806-9_2
20. Stair, R., Reynolds, G.: Principles of Information Systems. Cengage Learning, Boston (2013)
21. Laudon, K.C., Laudon, J.P.: Management information systems 13e (2013)
22. Abras, C., Maloney-Krichmar, D., Preece, J.: User-centered design. In: Bainbridge, W. (ed.) Encyclopedia of Human-Computer Interaction, vol. 37, no. 4, pp. 445–456. Sage Publ., Thousand Oaks (2004)
23. Majchrzak, A., Markus, M.L., Wareham, J.D.: Designing for digital transformation: lessons for information systems research from the study of ICT and societal challenges. Manag. Inf. Syst. Q. **40**(2), 267–277 (2016)
24. Pallot, M., Trousse, B., Senach, B., Scapin, D.: Living lab research landscape: from user centred design and user experience towards user cocreation. Presented at the First European Summer School "Living Labs" (2010)
25. Pretorius, M., Hobbs, J., Fenn, T.: The user experience landscape of South Africa. Presented at the Proceedings of the 2015 Annual Research Conference on South African Institute of Computer Scientists and Information Technologists, p. 32 (2015)
26. Wilkinson, C.R., De Angeli, A.: Applying user centred and participatory design approaches to commercial product development. Des. Stud. **35**(6), 614–631 (2014)
27. Venturi, G., Troost, J., Jokela, T.: People, organizations, and processes: an inquiry into the adoption of user-centered design in industry. Int. J. Hum.-Comput. Interact. **21**(2), 219–238 (2006)
28. Norman, D.A.: Design principles for cognitive artifacts. Res. Eng. Des. **4**(1), 43–50 (1992). https://doi.org/10.1007/BF02032391
29. Krueger, R.A., Casey, M.A.: Focus Groups: A Practical Guide for Applied Research. Sage Publications, Thousand Oaks (2014)
30. Jurca, G., Hellmann, T.D., Maurer, F.: Integrating agile and user-centered design: a systematic mapping and review of evaluation and validation studies of Agile-UX. Presented at the Agile Conference (AGILE), pp. 24–32 (2014)

31. Acocella, I.: The focus groups in social research: advantages and disadvantages. Qual. Quant. **46**(4), 1125–1136 (2012). https://doi.org/10.1007/s11135-011-9600-4
32. Otaiza, R., Rusu, C., Roncagliolo, S.: Evaluating the usability of transactional web sites. Presented at the Advances in Computer-Human Interactions, ACHI 2010, Third International Conference on Advances in Computer-Human Interactions, pp. 32–37 (2010)
33. Nielsen, J.: Usability inspection methods. Presented at the Conference Companion on Human Factors in Computing Systems, pp. 377–378 (1995)
34. Preece, J., Rogers, Y., Sharp, H.: Interaction Design: Beyond Human-Computer Interaction, 4th edn. Wiley, Chichester (2015)
35. Lilholt, P.H., Jensen, M.H., Hejlesen, O.K.: Heuristic evaluation of a telehealth system from the Danish TeleCare North Trial. Int. J. Med. Inf. **84**(5), 319–326 (2015)
36. Nielsen, J., Molich, R.: Heuristic evaluation of user interfaces. Presented at the Proceedings of the SIGCHI Conference on Human Factors in Computing Systems, pp. 249–256 (1990)
37. Alghamdi, A.S., Al-Badi, A., Alroobaea, R., Mayhew, P.: A comparative study of synchronous and asynchronous remote usability testing methods. Int. Rev. Basic Appl. Sci. **1**(3), 61–97 (2013)
38. Hertzum, M.: Usability testing: too early? Too much talking? Too many problems? J. Usability Stud. **11**(3), 83–88 (2016)
39. Bastien, J.C.: Usability testing: a review of some methodological and technical aspects of the method. Int. J. Med. Inf. **79**(4), e18–e23 (2010)
40. Lazar, J., Feng, J.H., Hochheiser, H.: Research Methods in Human-Computer Interaction. Morgan Kaufmann, Burlington (2017)
41. Barnum, C.M.: Usability Testing Essentials: Ready, Set… Test! Elsevier, Amsterdam (2010)
42. Duan, Y., Chen, X., Houthooft, R., Schulman, J., Abbeel, P.: Benchmarking deep reinforcement learning for continuous control. arXiv:160406778 Cs, May 2016
43. Kuechler, B., Vaishnavi, V.: On theory development in design science research: anatomy of a research project. Eur. J. Inf. Syst. **17**(5), 489–504 (2008)
44. Kruger, R.M., Gelderblom, H., Beukes, W.: The value of comparative usability and UX evaluation for e-commerce organisations (2016)
45. Norman, D.A., Draper, S.W.: User centered system design, Hillsdale, NJ, pp. 1–2 (1986)
46. Bryman, A., Bell, E.: Business Research Methods. Oxford University Press, New York (2015)
47. Law, E.L.-C., van Schaik, P.: To measure or not to measure UX: an interview study. Presented at the I-UxSED, pp. 58–63 (2012)
48. Zhu, J.: Quantitative Models for Performance Evaluation and Benchmarking: Data Envelopment Analysis with Spreadsheets, vol. 213. Springer, Cham (2014). https://doi.org/10.1007/978-3-319-06647-9
49. AlRoobaea, R., Mayhew, P.J.: How many participants are really enough for usability studies? Presented at the Science and Information Conference (SAI), pp. 48–56 (2014)

Correction to: Responsible Design, Implementation and Use of Information and Communication Technology

Marié Hattingh⬛, Machdel Matthee⬛, Hanlie Smuts⬛,
Ilias Pappas⬛, Yogesh K. Dwivedi⬛, and Matti Mäntymäki⬛

Correction to:
M. Hattingh et al. (Eds.): *Responsible Design, Implementation*
and Use of Information and Communication Technology,
LNCS 12067, https://doi.org/10.1007/978-3-030-45002-1

The original version of chapter 4 was revised. The acknowledgements section was missing and has been added:
This work has received funding from the European Union's Horizon 2020 research and innovation programme, under the Marie Sklodowska-Curie Grant Agreements No. 751510.

The original version of chapter 18 was revised. The missing acknowledgment has been added.
This work has partially been funded by the Federal Ministry of Education and Research of Germany (BMBF) under grant no. 16DII116 ("Deutsches Internet-Institut").

The updated version of these chapters can be found at
https://doi.org/10.1007/978-3-030-45002-1_4
https://doi.org/10.1007/978-3-030-45002-1_18

Author Index

Printed in the United States
by Baker & Taylor Publisher Services